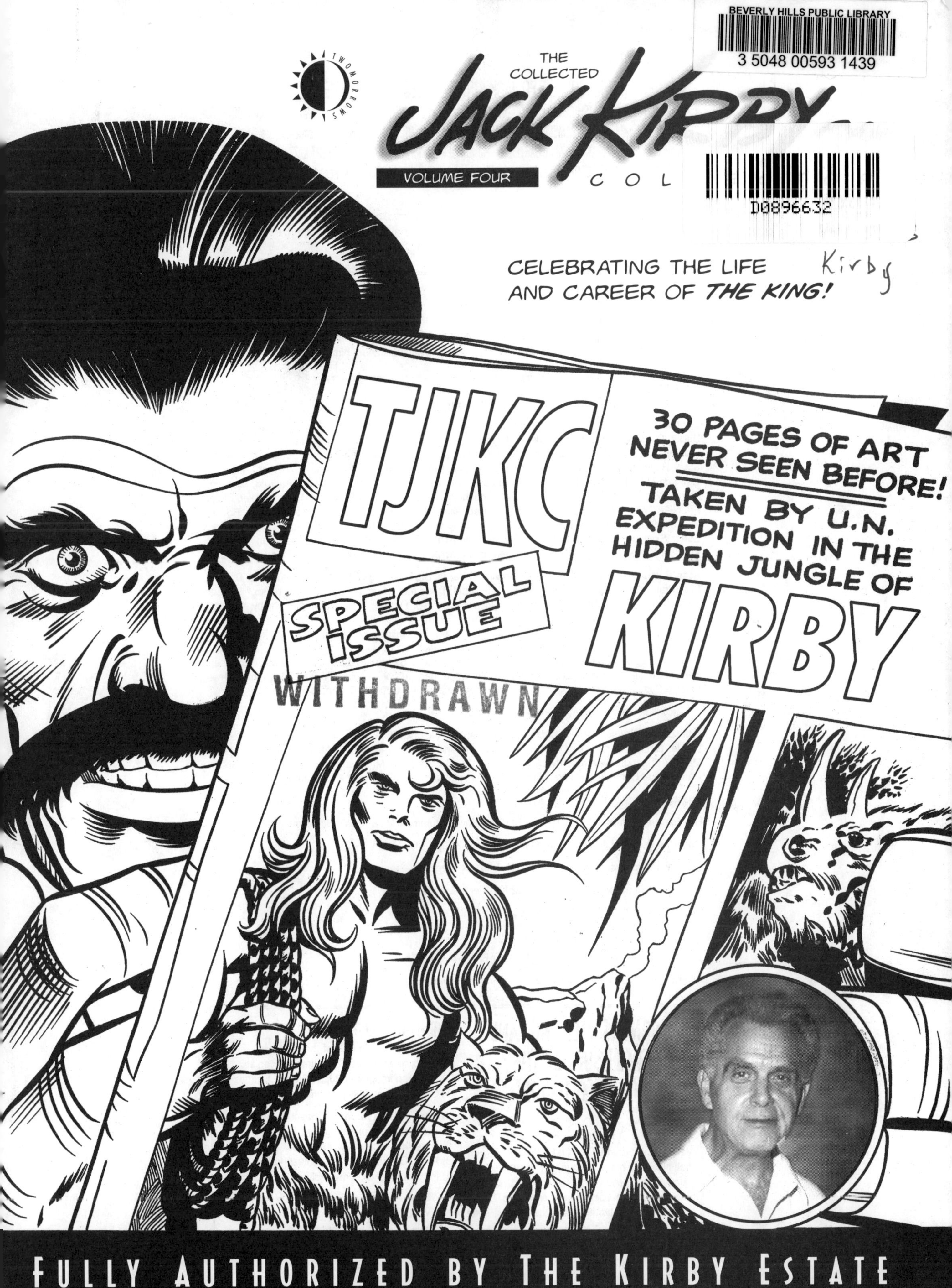
TWOMORROWS
THE COLLECTED
JACK KIRBY
VOLUME FOUR
COL
CELEBRATING THE LIFE
AND CAREER OF *THE KING!*
TJKC
SPECIAL ISSUE
30 PAGES OF ART
NEVER SEEN BEFORE!
TAKEN BY U.N.
EXPEDITION IN THE
HIDDEN JUNGLE OF
KIRBY
FULLY AUTHORIZED BY THE KIRBY ESTATE

THE COLLECTED JACK KIRBY COLLECTOR, VOLUME FOUR

A TWOMORROWS PUBLISHING PRODUCTION IN ASSOCIATION WITH THE KIRBY ESTATE EDITED BY JOHN MORROW
DESIGN & LAYOUT BY JOHN & PAMELA MORROW PROOFREADING BY RICHARD HOWELL COVER COLOR BY TOM ZIUKO
SPECIAL THANKS TO: MARK EVANIER MIKE GARTLAND RAND HOPPE RICHARD HOWELL ROBERT KATZ MIKE THIBODEAUX TOM ZIUKO THE CONTRIBUTORS FROM TJKC #16-19 & OF COURSE THE KIRBY ESTATE FOR THEIR CONTINUING SUPPORT OF OUR EFFORTS

This volume reprints issues #16-19 of *The Jack Kirby Collector,* plus new material

First printing • Printed in Canada

DEDICATED TO:

My delightful daughter Lily. It's a shame you have to grow up in a world without Jack Kirby in it, but your daddy's going to make sure you know all about him.

SUBMIT SOMETHING, AND GET FREE ISSUES OF THE JACK KIRBY COLLECTOR!

The Jack Kirby Collector is a not-for-profit publication, put together with submissions from Jack's fans around the world. We don't pay for submissions, but if we print art or articles you submit, we'll send you a free copy of that issue or extend your subscription by one issue. So get creative, and get writing! And as always, send us copies of your Kirby art!

SUBMISSION GUIDELINES:

Submit artwork in one of these forms:

1) Clear color or black-&-white photocopies.
2) Scanned images - 300ppi IBM or Macintosh.
3) Originals (carefully packed and insured).

Submit articles in one of these forms:

1) Typed or laser printed pages.
2) E-mail to: twomorrow@aol.com
3) An ASCII file, IBM or Macintosh format.
4) Photocopies of previously printed articles OK.

We'll pay return postage and insurance for originals – please write or call first.

Table Of Contents

The Jack Kirby Collector #16

The Jack Kirby Collector #17

The Jack Kirby Collector #18

The Jack Kirby Collector #19

Front cover inks: Steve Rude
Cover color: Tom Ziuko

Alphabetical Index Of New Kirby Art In This Volume

INTRODUCTION

by John Morrow, editor of The Jack Kirby Collector

Well, here we are back again, with a fourth collection of sold out issues of *The Jack Kirby Collector*, the magazine for fans of the King of comics. It's been awhile since we last issued one of these compilations; Volume Three first appeared back in 1999, containing the last of what I thought of as our "low print run" issues. I figured, after *TJKC* #15 (the last issue reprinted in Volume Three), we had more or less reached the majority of the hardcore Kirby fans out there, and were ordering enough extra copies to keep in stock as back issues, thus eliminating the need to ever do another of these books.

Then along came Alex Ross.

You've probably heard or him, and seen his amazing painted images of super-heroes. When he offered (free of charge, I might add) to do a painting based on one of Jack's pencil drawings, how could I resist? His stunning piece graced the cover of *TJKC* #19 (and is on the back cover of this book), and caused quite a hubbub in the comics industry. The issue literally flew off store shelves, getting Kirby's work into the hands of new, younger fans who weren't that familiar with him. #19 sold out quicker than any issue to date, and really helped solidify *TJKC* as more than just a niche item, but a true medium for documenting comics history.

The other issues in this volume (#16-18) quickly sold out as well, as did our first three *Collected* volumes, proving to me two things: 1) that we were achieving our goal of exposing new people to the genius of Jack Kirby, and 2) we weren't printing enough extra copies each issue! So in this, our tenth year of publishing (and the tenth anniversary of Jack's passing), I'm proud to see these issues back in print, as well as or first three *Collected* volumes. It's a great testament to the value of Jack's amazing legacy.

Long live the King!

John Morrow, editor
Raleigh, NC, June 2004

(right) Kirby's uninked pencils from New Gods *#8 (April 1972).*

A MAN AMONGST GODS, A GOD AMONGST MEN

Foreword by TJKC *colorist Tom Ziuko*

Who is Jack Kirby?

From the perspective of the 21st century, looking back through at the 20th, we know that Jack Kirby is without a doubt the single most important and influential creator and artist to have worked in the comic book field. In this uniquely American form of storytelling, with ideas and imagination disseminated on pulp for the masses, Jack Kirby reigned supreme. He created, molded and mastered so many different genres of comics; from super-hero to romance, war and mystery. His artwork and visual style, always evolving, became the virtual template from which super-hero comics in general are forever fashioned. He helped invent, change and perfect the visual vocabulary we use in comics to this very day. His journeys on paper took us from the icy depths of the oceans to the chilling expanse of outer space; from sub-atomic

universes to the horrors of man's inner psyche. He introduced many of us to the worlds of the gods, whether Norse or Greek or cut whole from the fabric of his imagination; his work became infinite and cosmic in scope and execution. Jack Kirby was the foundation upon which all comics that follow him will be built.

Now let us shift our perspective to that of a nine-year-old boy, smack dab in the mid-Sixties, at the height of the Marvel Age of Comics, experiencing that incredible Kirby magic at its crackling zenith. All I knew was that this guy's comics and drawings were the *coolest thing I had ever seen*, and more importantly I wanted to know—*"How does he get his lines so thick and bold?"*

You see, back in those prehistoric days, creator credits in comic books were a fairly new proposition. Oh, you could look at a *Batman* comic, but it would always say "by Bob Kane," yet it was clear that different people had drawn different stories. So over at Marvel, the credits listed the writer, the penciler, the inker and the letterer (but not the colorist). It was obvious to my youthful mind that the penciler had drawn the artwork, so I assumed that the "inks" referred to the printed colors.

Now, when I drew with a pencil, it was a thin, weak and measly line—even if I pressed hard! I wondered how Jack could make the lines of his drawings so dark, so thick and juicy. The blacks practically still looked wet on the paper! I figured he must've used one of those big, soft lead pencils that kindergarten kids are issued when they first learn how to write. The pencil seems to be about an inch in diameter, inevitably painted bright red, with an *enormous* shaft of lead running through the center. That had to be the explanation! (And once you've drawn on paper with one of those things, God forbid you should actually *touch* the paper—the pencil residue would smear all over the place. And your fingers—*my God, look at your fingers!!* Your hands looked like you had either just come up from a coal mine or had given fingerprints with an ink blotter.) I spent quite a while drawing with one of those until I learned that the "inker" goes over the "pencils" with India Ink and a "colorist" colors the finished artwork.

That pesky Kirby Bug (see Collected TJKC Vol. One) *is loose again, in* New Gods #9 *(June 1972).*

Cut to the mid-Eighties. By this time, I'd followed my inspiration and was enjoying a career in comics as, ironically enough, a colorist. I'd worked on a number of projects for DC Comics and the occasional job for their Special Projects office. One of those assignments was a toy company presentation drawn by Kirby; and making an all-too-rare trip to New York City was Jack and his wife Roz. I had the honor of meeting the man himself and actually shook the hand that produced the thousands of images and stories that inspired millions around the world. I related the story of how I had grown up on Jack's artwork and how this inspiration had led to a love of the medium and a career in the comics industry. Roz commented that they had heard the same story, or some slight variation, at least a dozen times that day alone.

So, who is Jack Kirby?

To me, while growing up, Jack Kirby was a better role model and father figure than I ever encountered in my personal life. Through his stories and art he espoused a sense of morality and justice and an outlook on life that you just couldn't help but aspire to. Jack believed in and looked for the best in all of mankind. So here you have this amazing humanitarian spirit who also happens to be incredibly talented. We're so lucky that he shared his overflowing imagination and creativity with all of us... but then, he had so many ideas and stories to tell, maybe he couldn't have contained them even if he tried. His artwork and spirit will live forever in print, in cyberspace, and on into the infinite.

Thanks again, Jack...

...The King Is Dead, Long Live The King!!!

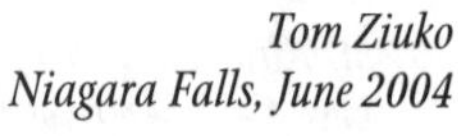

Tom Ziuko
Niagara Falls, June 2004

SOUND--WHAMM!!

Darkseid's Omega Effect takes effect in these pencils from Forever People *#6, page 17 (Dec. 1971) and #7, page 15 (Feb. 1972).*

Mister Miracle *pencils, from issue #5, page 14 (Nov. 1971) and #8, page 25 (May 1972).*

Kirby tackles Superman in two different eras: Jimmy Olsen *#143 (left, Nov. 1971) and* Super Powers *#5 (right, Nov. 1984).*

Examples from two of Jack's early 1970s experimental black-&-white magazines that never got produced: Soul Love *(left, inked by Vince Colletta) and* True Divorce Cases *(right).*

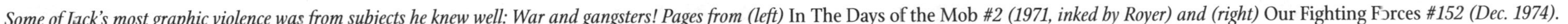

Some of Jack's most graphic violence was from subjects he knew well: War and gangsters! Pages from (left) In The Days of the Mob *#2 (1971, inked by Royer) and (right)* Our Fighting Fɔrces *#152 (Dec. 1974).*

Hard-hitting action in these pencils from OMAC #1 (Sept. 1974) and from the one-shot Manhunter story in First Issue Special #5 (Aug. 1975).

The Dingbats of Danger Street's only appearance was in First Issue Special *#6 (Sept. 1975), but here are pages from two unpublished stories meant for* Dingbats *#2 (inked by Mike Royer) and #3.*

Pencils from Jack's longest-lived 1970s series Kamandi *(#40, page 15, April 1976) and one of his shortest, "Atlas" from* First Issue Special *#1 (page 14, April 1975).*

(left) *Jack's one foray on the series* Richard Dragon, Kung Fu Fighter *(#3, Aug. 1975), and an unknown Kirby animation concept (late 1970s).*

After leaving DC Comics in 1975, Jack jumped to Marvel and tackled Black Panther *(#3, May 1977) and* Captain America's Bicentennial Battles *(1976).*

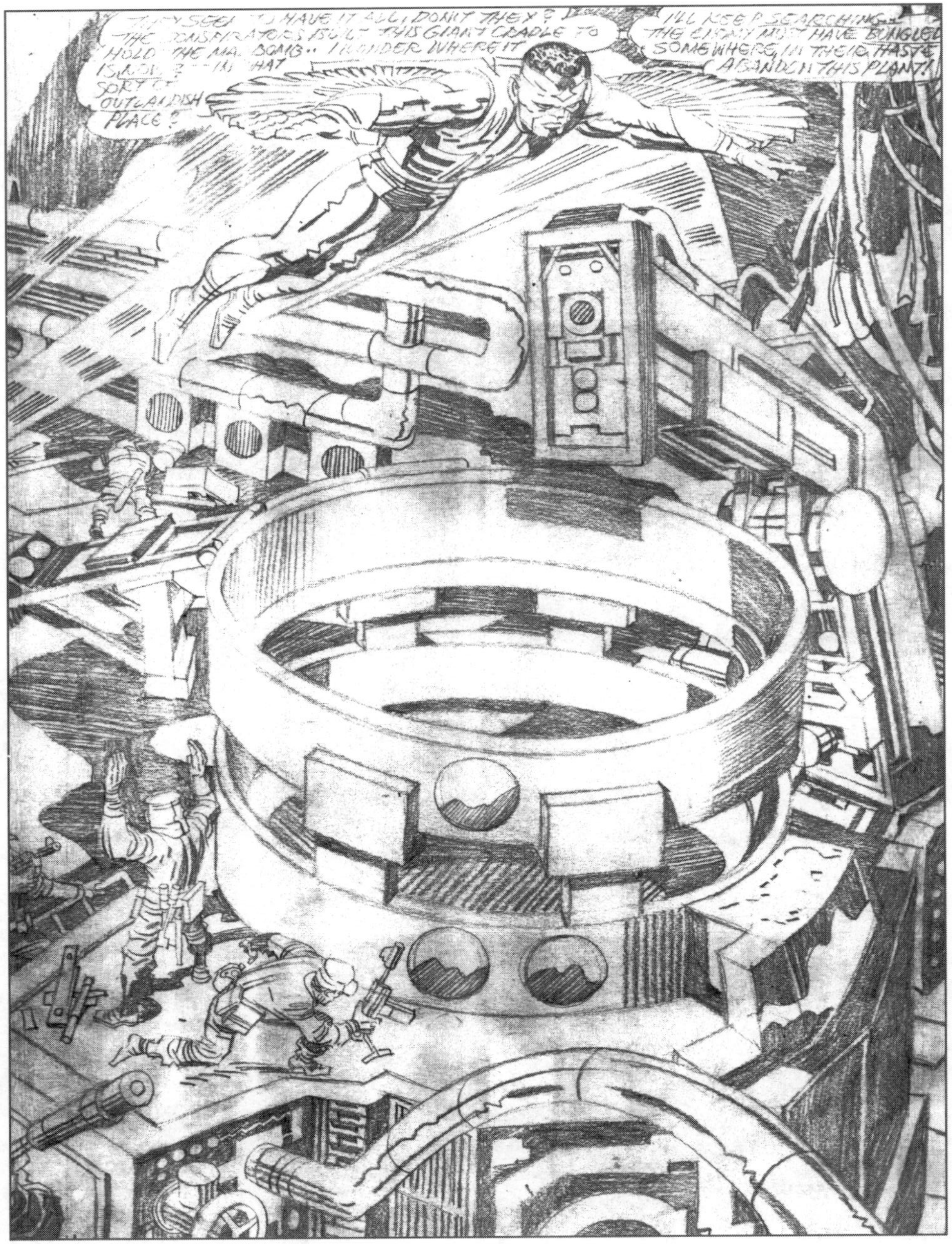

More Marvel pencils, from Captain America #198, page 3 (June 1976) and The Eternals #10, page 14 (April 1977).

It's pre-history, Kirby-style, in these pencils from Devil Dinosaur *#4, page 14 (July 1978), and* 2001: A Space Odyssey *#4, page 4 (March 1977).*

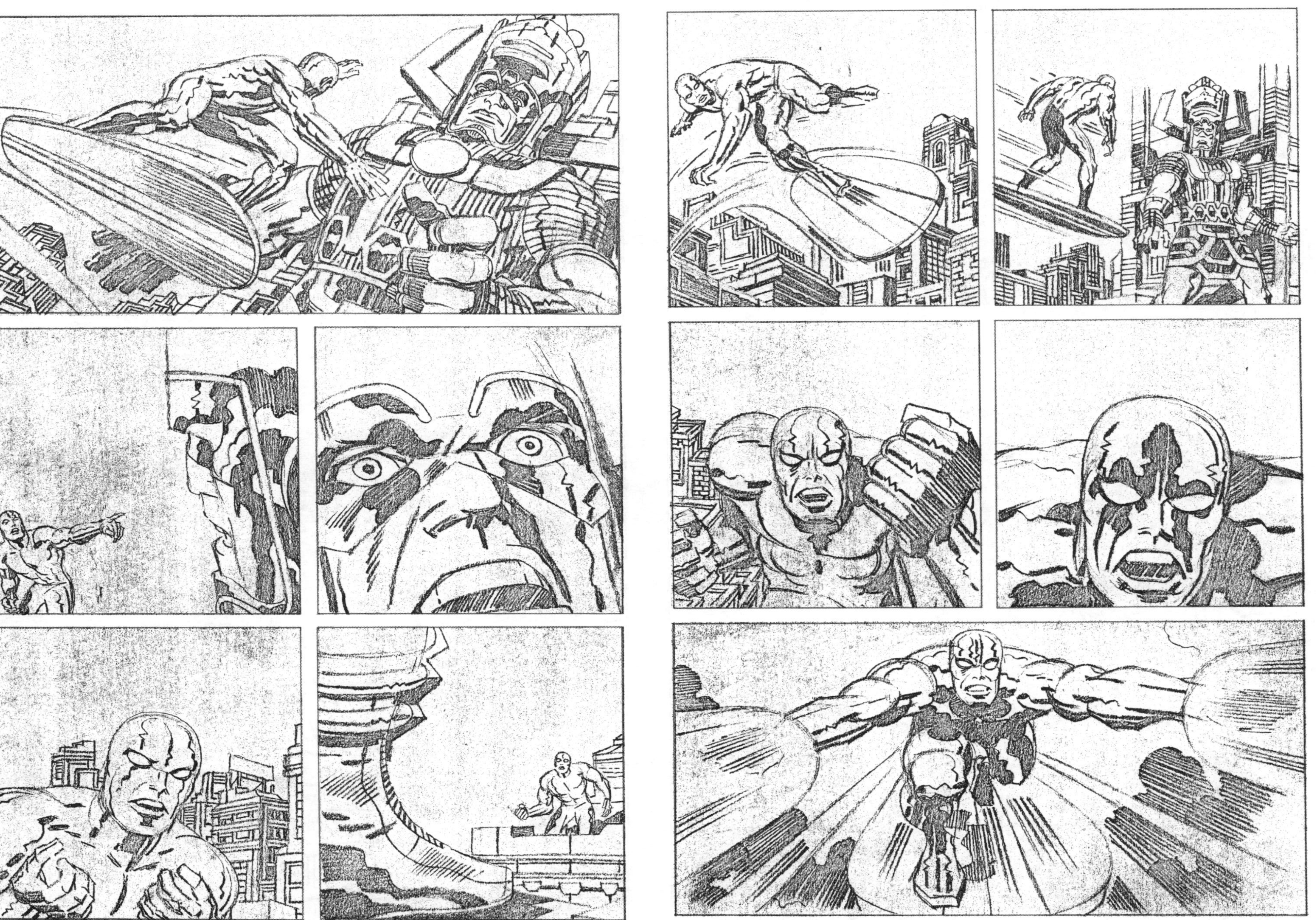

A couple of splendid examples of Jack's work from the Silver Surfer Graphic Novel *(1978).*

Two of the many covers Jack penciled for Marvel in the 1970s: Marvel Triple Action *#29 (May 1976), and Jack's cover for* What If? *#9 (1978)*

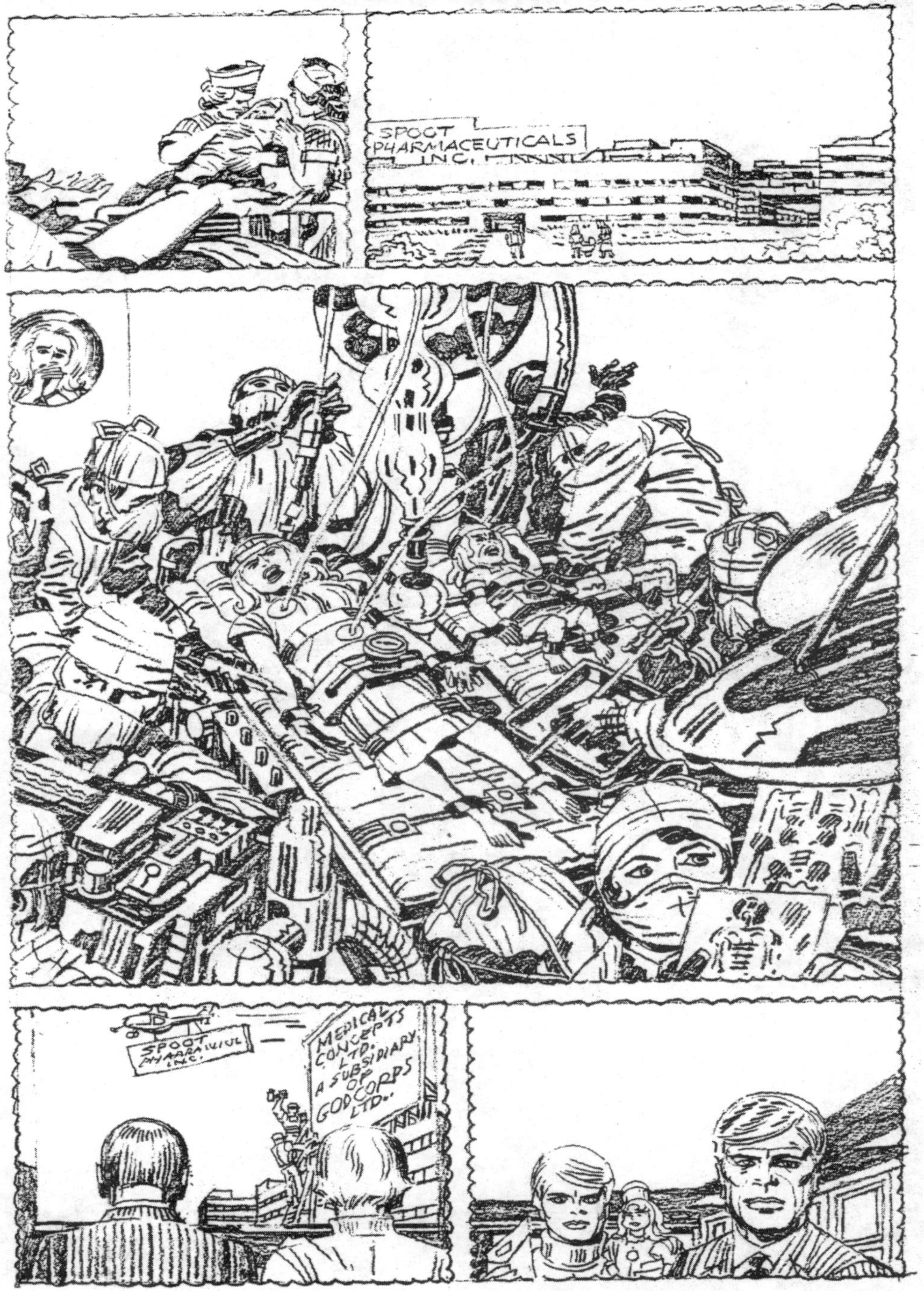

Some of Kirby's final work in comics: Destroyer Duck *#3, page 15 (June 1983), and* Silver Star *#3, page 12 (also June 1983).*

FULLY AUTHORIZED BY THE KIRBY ESTATE

THE JACK KIRBY COLLECTOR

$4.9
In The U

ISSUE #16, JULY 1997

A *52-PAGE* THEME ISSUE FEATURING JACK'S HARD-BOILED *TOUGH GUYS!!*

AN ULTRA-RARE
KIRBY INTERVIEW

INTERVIEW WITH *SIN CITY'S*
RANK MILLER

THE LEGENDARY
WILL EISNER
DISCUSSES KIRBY

AN EXAMINATION OF
IN THE DAYS OF THE MOB

A LOOK AT JACK'S
TOUGH CHILDHOO

SPECIAL FEATU
BULLSEYE, LINK THOR WAR & WEST COMICS, '50S STRIP IDEAS
AND OTHERS

UNPUBLISHED ART
INCLUDING PENCIL PAGES *BEFORE* THEY WERE INKED, AND *MUCH MORE!!*

IT TOOK A *SIMPLE, EVIL, BRUTAL ACT* TO GENERATE THE SPARKS FROM WHICH *A MONSTER SPRANG!!* IT WAS A *FAST-GROWING, VORACIOUS MONSTER!!* -- FRUSTRATED, ANGRY, MURDEROUS, AND *SURPRISED BY SUDDEN POWER!!!!*

THE CRIES OF A *YOUNG GIRL* WERE ITS *BIRTH-PANGS!* SHE HAD BEEN *CRIMINALLY ASSAULTED* AND *THROWN FROM A CAR!* BUT SHE WAS ONLY A PAWN IN THE *LARGER, DEADLIER GAME* -- THAT WOULD BECOME *"MURDER INC.!"*

G'WAN! SQUEAL YER HEAD OFF!!

YOU RAT! YOU DIRTY RAT! YOU WON'T GET AWAY WITH THIS!!

KIRBY/FM

What girl could resist a (slightly modified) offer like this one from Justice Traps The Guilty *#2?*

THE JACK KIRBY COLLECTOR

A custom drawing, circa 1967, that Jack did for his personal bound volume of S&K crime comics.

ISSUE #16 CONTENTS:

Front cover inks: Frank Miller
Back cover inks: Karl Kesel
Cover color: Tom Ziuko

The Jack Kirby Collector, Vol. 4, No. 16, July 1997. Published bi-monthly by and © TwoMorrows Advertising & Design, 1812 Park Drive, Raleigh, NC 27605, USA. 919-833-8092. *John Morrow,* Editor. *Pamela Morrow,* Assistant Editor. Single issues: $4.95 US, $5.40 Canada, $7.40 outside North America. Six-issue subscriptions: $24.00 US, $32.00 Canada and Mexico, $44.00 outside North America. First printing. All characters are © their respective companies. All artwork is © Jack Kirby unless otherwise noted. All editorial matter is © the respective authors. PRINTED IN CANADA.

Kirby's Mean Streets

The Lower East Side of Jacob Kurtzberg, by Jon B. Cooke

"You can take the man out of the city, but you can't take the city out of the man." I don't know who first said that, but it fits when it comes to Jack Kirby. The New York City area he grew up in, the Lower East Side of Manhattan, always has a way of showing up as a setting in his stories. Whether as Suicide Slum of the Guardian, Yancy Street in the *Fantastic Four,* or even Armagetto in *Mister Miracle,* Jack hardly disguises the streets of his youth, giving us a snapshot of a brutal, harsh, even nightmarish place, though sometimes throwing in a wink of nostalgia. And we know that many of his most beloved characters – Scrapper of the Newsboy Legion, Ben Grimm, and Scott Free – are really from those mean streets; they're simply embellished reflections of the pugnacious artist who envisioned them.

Anyone who met the man will tell you what a gracious, giving and kind gentleman Jack Kirby was – but what everyone knows from his work is that he was also angry as hell and tough as pavement, and it was the Lower East Side that made him that way. To know the man, I figured, you've got to understand where he comes from.

So I searched for his old neighborhood. I looked for it in his interviews, on maps, through talks with old buddies, in cultural history books, via cyberspace, and, finally, on the very sidewalks of the big city itself. Overall, I had little to go on. Jack didn't mention specific addresses in interviews, but through his words, and the shared experiences of others who grew up in the real "Suicide Slum," I got a picture I hope isn't too far from the truth.

Home

On August 25, 1917, Jacob Kurtzberg was born to recent Austrian immigrants, Rosemary and Benjamin, into one of the most densely populated places in the world, the Lower East Side – a density of nearly a quarter million people per square mile. His parents came to America along with nearly two million Jews, many escaping persecution and economic hardship in Europe, at a time when the US welcomed immigration to fill industry's need for cheap labor – and most of these new Americans settled, for a time at least, in the Lower East Side.

Jack portrays his youth in "Street Code" from Argosy *Vol. 3, #2.*

Born on Essex Street, Jacob moved with his family a few blocks away into a Suffolk Street tenement house. The average tenement building contained "20 three-room apartments... arranged four to a floor, two in the front and two in the rear. They were reached by an unlighted, ventilated wooden staircase that ran through the center of the building. The largest room (11' x 12' 6") was referred to in plans as the living room or parlor, but residents called it the 'front room.' Behind it came the kitchen and one tiny bedroom. The entire flat, which often contained households of seven or more people, totaled about 325 square feet. Only one room per apartment – the 'front room' – received direct light and ventilation, limited by the tenements that *[hemmed]* it in. The standard bedroom, 8' 6" square, *[was]* completely shut off from both fresh air and natural light..."[1] Rent for their Suffolk Street flat was, according to Kirby, $12 a month.[2]

Poverty was a fact of life. Benjamin Kurtzberg worked in a factory as a tailor. "The immigrants had to make a living," Jack said. "They had to support their families, and they did it on very little, so we had very little..." Everyone who could work, did work to put food on the table; so young Jacob raised what he could, whether by hawking newspapers ("I was terrible at it... and I'd throw 'em away."[2]), or running errands for journalists, to help make ends meet. "The Depression was in full force, and whatever you brought home counted... whatever you brought into the house made it that much easier for *[my mother]* to buy food."[2] (The national crisis truly hit home when Ben became unemployed at a crucial moment in Jacob's life, as Jack was newly enrolled as an art student at the Pratt Institute. Whether his father lost work due to Italian sewing-machine operators – non-unionized and cheap labor – or the highway's access to cheaper production costs in the country is not known, but it was a sobering time.)

The Street

It was the culture of the street that defined the neighborhood, and the boy Kurtzberg had an eyeful. "It wasn't a pleasant place to live; crowded, no place to play ball," Jack said. "You became a toreador at an early age, just dodging the ice wagons."[2] The streets were also filled with pushcarts, itinerant peddlers, and every type of humanity imaginable. Overall the district was diverse, home to a eclectic mix of neighborhoods: The East Village, Chinatown, Little Italy, Astor Place, and Knickerbocker Village, though the area between Delancey Street (true home of the Yancy Street Gang?) and Houston was predominately Jewish. (The area continues the immigrant tradition after recent decades as a Puerto Rican enclave, and today, as a Dominican neighborhood.)

The violence of poverty was everywhere, but not everyone lived in hopeless despair. Kirby-idol and fellow Lower East Side tough guy Jimmy Cagney put it this way: "Though we were poor, we didn't know we were poor. We realized we didn't get three squares on the table every day, and there was no such thing as a good second suit, but we had no objective knowledge that we were poor. We just went from day to day doing the best we could, hoping to get through the really rough periods with a minimum of hunger and want. We simply didn't have time to realize we were poor, although we did realize the desperation of life around us."[4]

The desperation was played out amongst the city kids by scrapping. "Fighting became second nature," Jack said. "I began to like it." Gangs had been a fact of life in New York since the Revolutionary War. A 1900 "East Side Boy" described three kinds of gangs: "The really tough gangs... meet at corners to make trouble." Another kind "hang around a corner to flirt with girls and amuse themselves with people who pass by." And lastly, there's "just a social gang, formed chiefly for the purpose of playing games... especially baseball."[7] "Jakie" Kurtzberg was part of the Suffolk Street Gang. "Each street had its own gang of kids, and we'd fight all the time," Jack said. "We'd cross over the roofs and bombard the Norfolk Street gang with bottles and rocks and mix it up with them."

"Our heroes were great fighters, soldiers or strongarm hoodlums who were top gangsters," a Hard-Knocks alumni, Samuel Goldberg, explained. "Wrongly, we tried to emulate them... we were continually at war between ourselves or with gangs from other districts that were of different races and religions. The Irish gangs came from the East Side Waterfront. They invaded our district with rocks, glass bottles, clubs and all sorts of homemade weapons. Battles would rage in streets, vacant lots, and even in some parks."[5]

The Lower East Side turf belonged to celebrity gangster Charles "Lucky" Luciano, the mastermind behind Murder Inc., a heinous organization Jack recalled in the unpublished *In the Days of the Mob* #2. City homicides peaked as crime gangs reorganized along Lucky's plan. Local son Meyer Lansky saw Prohibition as an opportunity and formed a gang with Benjamin "Bugsy" Siegel, the "Bugs and Meyer

Mob," an association that lasted until Lansky okayed the "hit" on Bugs.

Crime had its allure. "Some of my friends became gangsters," Jack said. "You became a gangster depending upon how fast you wanted a suit. Gangsters weren't the stereotypes you see in the movies. I knew the real ones, and the real ones were out for big money. The average politician was crooked. That was my ambition, to be a crooked politician."[3] Gangsters were a part of history in the district, with one gang, the "Bowery Boys," stretching back to the 1700s. (Jack recalled the moniker of 1890s thug Kid Twist as his subject for the ill-fated *Mob* #2.) But the worst crimes the artist seemed to commit were rooftop fights, monument shop invasions and just general rowdy behavior.

When he wasn't drawing or sneaking time with a pulp magazine, Jakie seemed to be fighting. He fought to defend his fancy-dressed younger brother, David. He fought on fire escapes, rooftops, and on stairways. He was knocked out cold and laid at his mother's door. As tenacious and angry as the city streets were, the code insisted that a good knock-down, drag-out was often the proper thing to do.

"About all this street fighting," Cagney said, "it's important to remember that *[we]* conformed to the well-established neighborhood pattern... We weren't anything more than normal kids reacting to our environment – an environment in which street fighting was an accepted way of life... We had what I suppose could be called colorful young lives."[4]

"My East Side slum training stood me in good stead later in my life," Samuel Goldberg said. "The constant fighting with different gangs toughened me to withstand the blows that life would deal me."[5] Jack would cite his anger as a catalyst. "Yeah, I think anger will save your life. I think anger will give you a drive that will save your life and change it in some manner."[2] And Jacob Kurtzberg's drive was to get out.

A typical tenement scene, circa 1920.

The Escape

"I wanted to break out of the ghetto," Jack said. "It gave me a fierce drive to get out of it. It made me so fearful... that in an immature way, I fantasized a dream world more realistic than the reality around me."[2] He sought out places that could help him hone his drawing ability, going to the renowned Educational Alliance – for one day. "They threw me out for drawing too fast with charcoal," Jack said.[2] But he was accepted into the Boys Brotherhood Republic, a haven (which still exists today) that encouraged his talents and allowed him the peace to enjoy his beloved pursuits: Reading and drawing, pastimes so disdained by his thuggish compatriots on the outside.

"Democracy was practiced here," current BBR director, Ralph Hittman said. "Kids ran the place... it's a miniature city." The organization, located at 290 East 3rd St., was ruled by boys, teaching them a lesson in self-government and democracy. Jakie did cartoons for the weekly (then monthly) newspaper "and eventually he became the editor and grew up."

"It was a great time for me," Jack said. "I made lots of friends."[6] One of those was Hittman, who remembers Jakie as a "quiet guy, who played ball like everyone else, but whose interest was always in drawing and comic strips." The director remembers an activity called "Fighting for Fun," when Jakie boxed a boy named Milt Cherry. "And I think he lost! *(laughter)* Jack looked pugnacious but he really wasn't."

The BBR still honors the talent and success of the artist. "We have his photograph up, his drawings up," Recreational Director Peter Doyle said. "The kids all talk about him... when the kids see the X-Men, or the Avengers and you tell them that the guy who invented them was a BBR kid, it inspires them. A lot of them do paintings based on comic books; it's our main stock in trade." The neighborhood is currently "a very, very violent area," Doyle relates. "In the ten years I've been here, I know quite a few kids who have been shot in the street... I've stepped out and seen bodies covered in sheets."

"Kids don't have an awful lot of role models," Doyle said. "You can talk about Jimmy Cagney, but that was 50 years ago. But Jack is still a role model for these kids because, well, it's comic books. It's great that this guy who was here so long ago is still giving kids hope. Many of these kids really feel that they're going to end up on the street with no future, but when they see that Jack Kirby, the father of Marvel, went to the BBR, it gives them a little more hope. That's why we keep his picture up downstairs."

I tried to find the streets of Jacob Kurtzberg's Lower East Side and found it had mostly dissipated with the immigrants who went onto greater things in the American frontier. Poverty remains, with a similar mix of hope and despair, but these are different streets. Most of the old tenements on Suffolk have been torn down, now empty lots filling up with eccentric, makeshift gardens of green vegetables and blooming flowers. Like any decent reporter, I hoped to find some old neighbor but there were none to be found. Rounding the corner of E. Houston St., I was struck with the ambivalent mix of growth and decay. Modern establishments like Kinko's and Blockbusters share blocks with dilapidated Matzo stores, aging Jewish monument shops, and even the famous Katz's Delicatessen (the proud originators of the saying, "Send a Salami to your Boy in the Army"). My eight-year-old son Ben grimaced and called the area "ugly." He's right. We stopped for a cup of shaved ice from a Dominican street vendor and happened upon a telling sight: A gutted, basement-level comics shop, long since closed, with fading pictures of Jack's Marvel characters peeling on the cracked window pane. On the store landing was a pile of still-bundled newspapers and for a fleeting moment, I imagined a modern newsboy, frustrated with his selling abilities, chucking away papers and setting off up Houston Street to dream of better, more fantastic possibilities.

The Lower East Side of the '20s and '30s – an era when it was foremost in the public's consciousness with Warner Brothers' gangster pictures and the Dead End Kids (who, under various names as the East Side Kids and the Bowery Boys, went on to be featured in 86 films) – has to receive co-creator credit when it comes to the King. Rose and Ben conceived and nurtured Jacob Kurtzberg, endowing him with a sensitivity and genius. But it was the streets that gave him resolve and fortitude enough to fight the Nazis, create publishing empires, and have the pure audacity to be Jack Kirby, the toughest comic book artist ever. ❍

1 The Lower East Side Tenement Museum homepage (http://www.wnet.org/tenement/ eagle.html).

2 Interview, *Will Eisner's Spirit Magazine* #39, February 1982.

3 Interview, *The Comics Journal* #134, February 1990.

4 *Cagney by Cagney,* James Cagney, New York: Pocket Books, 1977.

5 Samuel Goldberg interview, *How We Lived,* Irving Howe & Kenneth Libo, New York: Richard Marek Publishing, 1979.

6 Interview, *The Jack Kirby Treasury* Vol. 1, G. Theakston, ed., New York: Pure Imagination, 1982.

7 *Portal to America: The Lower East Side 1870-1925,* A. Schoener, ed., New York: Holt, Rinehard & Winston, 1967.

Special thanks to Ralph Hittman and Paul Doyle of the BBR. (The organization has produced a history that includes Jack's first published work. Please inquire at Boys Brotherhood Republic, 888 E. 6th St., New York, NY 10009, phone: 212-686-8888. Your help may just inspire another boy to greatness.) Also thanks to Nat Ronner and Sid Davis, old Kirby friends, and to Andrew D. Cooke and Patty Willett for getting Ben and I around town.

Tough Times, Hard Guys, & Gun Molls!

A look at Simon & Kirby's Golden Age Crime Comics, by R.J. Vitone

John Garfield and Lana Turner in The Postman Always Rings Twice.

"In a word, it was *tough*!"

Jack Kirby, from Greg Theakston's The Jack Kirby Treasury *Vol. 1, when asked about his childhood*

TOUGH! That was Jack's simple way of describing his youth. The simplicity belies the harsh reality. He was born August 28, 1917, amid the teeming cultural melting pot of Manhattan's Lower East Side. "It wasn't a pleasant place to live; crowded, no place to play..." he said in Mike Benton's *Masters of Imagination.* To escape, he read classics of literature from the local library. *Tarzan of the Apes, The Hunchback of Notre Dame, Treasure Island, The Three Musketeers, Robin Hood*; all these and others like them helped his mind to soar over the slum's rooftops. His imagination was fired by the grind-em-out pulp magazines of the era as well: Colorful covers, a handful of spot illustrations, and endless lines of words that ran page-to-page, issue-to-issue, month-to-month. These were the paperbacks of the time, and even at ten, fifteen, and twenty cents each (which must have been a small fortune to a Depression-era teenager), Jack managed to amass a stack that he kept most of his life.

Movies provided more escapist fare. Just going to the theater with family and friends was fun. But on the screen, a whole new wonderful universe of imagery unfolded: War movies, westerns, musicals, horror films, and more each week! "The Warner Brothers brought me up!" Jack told Theakston, and he was only half-kidding! The hard-edged studio look that Warners' pictures employed must have appealed to the street kid in Jack. There was plenty of "New York" there, too. Stars like Jimmy Cagney, Edward G. Robinson, John Garfield, and Humphrey Bogart snarled their way to the top in dozens of melodramas. Often their characters came from the streets. Often they died in the gutter. The message was clear: Crime may pay for a while, but in the end, look out! The cliché in most of these films went that, in order to get out of the ghetto, most kids had to pick up a pair of boxing gloves, or a gun, or a crucifix. Kirby picked up a pencil and started drawing. He got out.

Years later – a war later, hundreds of published comics pages later – Kirby "returned" to those streets.

Late in 1946, with the abortive *Boy Explorers* and *Stuntman* behind them, the Simon & Kirby team had moved to Crestwood Publishers with what Joe Simon called "...the best deal we ever had!" They began a variety of projects there, including their first fully-blown crime strips. (While crooks and thugs had been comics story staples since the start, few titles had been built around the crime theme. Book-length *Dick Tracy* newspaper strip reprints and publisher Lev Gleason's excellent *Crime Does Not Pay* comics, which began in 1942, were some of the few to fill the void.) With new pages to fill, Jack and Joe turned to crime. *Treasure Comics* #10 (Dec. '46) contained a six-page Kirby crime tale called "Tomorrow's Murder."

A few months later, Crestwood (under a "Prize Publication" slug) issued *Headline Comics* #23 and *Prize Comics* #63, both with new S&K crime stories. Almost simultaneously in early 1947, Hillman revamped *Clue Comics.* The stage was set. A new era in Jack Kirby's career had begun.

Headline #23 is notable for its content: Over forty pages (including cover) of top-notch S&K that paves the way for future issues. "The Last Bloody Days of Babyface Nelson" follows the gun-crazy last blasts of a doomed killer – seven dynamic pages full of tommy guns and car chases. "The Doctor Is Missing" is a period piece set in Boston during the 1800s. Done up in fine style with some slick visual touches (one panel shows the reflection of three men talking in a mirror), it ends on the gallows. "The Bear Skull Trail to Death" is a tale recounted by (occasional) narrator "Red Hot" Blaze to the editor of *Headline Comics.* Billed as "A True Tale of Double-Murder in the Okefenokee Swamplands," the story builds to an obvious end. A trademark double-paged spread opens the next story, a featured "Crime Thru The Ages" novelette – the career of Guy Fawkes, whose crime against the King of England resulted in conspiracy, torture, and death, as well as a national British holiday. Every year, poor Guy Fawkes is burned in effigy! The issue closes with a Kirby classic. "To My Valentine" is bylined by "Red Hot" Blaze, and opens with this caption: "In the Roaring Twenties, guns, bullets, and thugs ruled Chicago with a grip of steel..." From there we follow the trail of a thug on his way to an infamous event. We watch the St. Valentine's Day massacre occur, shown in a dramatic two-thirds-page panel, then wrap up the saga with some swift revenge, and a moral message from "Red Hot" Blaze (whose hair color changes from story to story): "The mad days of the St. Valentine Massacre are gone! It is up to all of us to be ever vigilant. To keep that bloody chapter closed!" Finally, a 5-page filler, "Killer in the Kitchen," invites the readers to match wits with a Scotland Yard inspector and prove the guilt of a murderous couple.

Do you get an idea of the overall sweep of that great package of material? Can you imagine how many directions this series could go

Prize Comics *#63 and* Headline *#23; Simon & Kirby's initial forays on each title.*

A spectacular two-page splash from Headline *#23. These "Crime Through The Ages" stories helped keep S&K from running out of criminals to write about.*

in from this early point? Instead of following a standard "booze-and-broads, shoot-'em-up" modern-day-gangster style, Simon & Kirby produced an anthology of crime through the ages. By broadening the scope of subjects, they not only would be able to present fresh, interesting settings for their stories, they would also avoid running out of ideas in a short time. It worked. In the years to come, the team produced a widely-varied slew of strips for the crime titles.

Sure, all the usual suspects were on display. Tales of alibis, arson, and black-market medicine were common. Crooked insurance scams, extortion, counterfeiters, and pick-pockets were covered. Political corruption, fake spiritualists, and fight fixing were not ignored. Murder, drugs, and crooked gambling seemed almost tame amid the carnage. And as expected, the range of stories did provide Kirby with the opportunity to again display his virtuosity. From the Old West to 1800s London, from Chicago in the Roaring '20s to the Florida swamps, Jack opened up his visuals to match the material. His pages became more miniature movies than ever before. The flow of the narrative was punctuated by dramatic closeups and frozen action. The violence, usually necessary in crime stories, became almost secondary, a part of the overall framework. Without a doubt, gunplay and fistfights were as explosive as ever, but the storytelling page structure led up to the outbursts. In most cases, the story would continue, exploring reaction or results of the activity. The wrap up would usually show the capture or death of the offenders, with a "Crime Never Pays!" banner prominently displayed. As in many of those Warner Brothers films, redemption for the guilty was a bullet wound!

Headline steered a steady course over the next couple of years. S&K supplied most of the covers and a story or more per issue. (*Headline* also ran a short series of photo covers starting with issue #36. These are so stiff, forced, and stereotypical that they are true classics. *Headline* #37 shows sneak-thief Jack Kirby caught in the act by very tall cop Joe Simon.) John Dillinger also got the Kirby treatment. "Public Enemy #1" (*Headline* #26) is born crying, grows to head a ruthless gang, then dies in a dark Chicago alley. "The Kansas City Massacre" in that same issue was based on actual events (and was "updated" in the 1971 DC magazine *In The Days Of The Mob*), but there were only so many well-known criminals to draw subject matter from. As mentioned earlier, the themes and situations in the S&K crime books broadened in scope. This variety kept the books fresh.

Women became more important than ever as characters – they were cover-featured and used inside as central story focal points. It became common to see a Kirby cover with a hard-bitten blonde holding a .38 on a hostage, or standing lookout during a crime. Stories like "I Was the Front For the Merciless Spirit Swindlers," "The Bobby Sox Bandit Queen" (both in *Headline* #27), "I Worked For The Fence" (#28), "I Was An Unwitting Accomplice to a Numbers Racket" (#30), and "I Was a Shop-Lifter in a Pick-Pocket Gang" (#31), all thrust women of varied degrees of morality into a life of crime. Sometimes they escaped. Sometimes they went to jail, even more determined to return to crime when they got out.

The amount of work Kirby produced for *Headline* decreased as time passed. Some issues featured a S&K cover, some a single story, or just loose layouts. After #37 (Sept. 1949), although a handful of issues would contain Jack's work, *Headline* was mostly left in the hands of artist/editor Mort Meskin. It continued on a successful run until 1956.

With the *Headline* formula set for the Prize line, *Clue Comics* at Hillman's was next up. Although S&K's main efforts were directed at the Prize packages, the team produced an impressive body of crime strips here as well. Overall, the material was interchangeable with their Crestwood output. In short order, Kirby covers blanketed the re-

Al Capone throws a party, as shown here in Justice Traps The Guilty *#1 (1947, above) and* In The Days Of The Mob *#1 (1971, below); although the details are different, the end result was the same.*

named *Real Clue Crime Comics.* Simon & Kirby's work on *Real Clue* ranged from short fillers ("Jailbreak," a four-pager in Vol. 2, #6) to epics (like the two-issue story featuring Gun Master, one of *Clue*'s stock heroes, from Vol. 2, #2-3). Lurid titles like "The Dummies Died Screaming" (Vol. 2, #5) and "The Mad White God of Palm Island" (Vol. 2, #7) and "Gang War" (Vol. 2, #6) were showcases for Jack's fluid storytelling. But by mid-1947, the team left Hillman's crime title. (The departure was possibly made to free up more time to work on Prize/Crestwood's new *Young Romance* book, which was released with a cover date of September 1947. The move would make financial sense, since they had a favorable set-up with that publisher.) *Real Clue Crime Comics* rode the wave of the crime trend and faded away in 1953.

Justice Traps The Guilty (Oct./Nov. 1947) marked the launch of a sister-mag for *Headline.* Built along the same lines – with a shocking "electric-chair" cover, and no less than five Kirby stories – at least some readers must have wondered why a second issue didn't appear for several months. "The Case Against Scarface" in that first issue tells the brutal, bloody story of Al Capone, without ever once mentioning his name. "Scarface" rules the Chicago mob, rubs out his opposition, and even tosses one of his own men out of a high-rise window. His own fall is quick and final. In one page, he's arrested for tax evasion, sent to jail, gets "ill," and is buried. On his tombstone: "Justice Traps The Guilty!" Real or not, this was good comics. (Jack resurrected Capone for *In The Days Of The Mob* #1. Naming names and pulling no punches, Big Al tears up Chicago in a wild fury. The 1971 story portrays Scarface as a hulking thug with phony "class." One outstanding sequence shows him beating a rival to death with a bat – a scene played with relish by Robert DeNiro in the '80s film *The Untouchables*.)

Justice Traps The Guilty returned to the newsstand early in 1948. S&K supplied most of the covers, plus one or two stories per issue. "Queen Of The Speed Ball Mob" (#4, May 1948) may be the quintessential Kirby crime story. Told in flashback from her prison hospital bed, Belle Munson lays out her confession to the policeman who captured her. Unknown to her, the teenaged girl's brother had headed a gang of high-speed getaway car drivers. Money came easy, and Belle's love for her brother covered any doubts. When her brother is killed in a police raid, the school girl bitterly takes over the operation. Suddenly transformed into a vengeful gang member, Belle becomes a driver for a mob boss! Enter Steve Crossman, Homicide Squad! She hates him at first (a sure sign of trouble ahead), but quickly develops feelings for him. Her anger and ambition overrule her heart. She drives getaway for a jewelry heist, and when the police show up, she grabs up a tommy-gun and starts mowing them down! She makes her escape, then kills the mob boss, barking, "I'm running this show from now on, get me? If there are any objections, I advise you guys not to voice them!" The election is unanimous. Belle was the boss, but Crossman confronts her. A wild car chase, a gun battle, a crash; broken and bloody, Belle raises her gun to blast the cop coming to pull her from the wreck. She can't. "Before I blacked out, I knew why I could never fire at Steve Crossman!" The flashback ends, and Belle orders the detective away. His indictment rings in her ears: "I tried to set you right, but you thought with a greedy mind and lived with a hating heart! Now you'll pay for your crimes!" As dramatic and compelling as any of those Warner Bros. films, this story sums up all the best that S&K brought to the crime comic genre. But the string was running out. As with the other crime titles, Kirby work in *Justice Traps the Guilty* declined over the next few years: Sporadic covers and a story or two after issue #10, then less. However, Jack and Joe never fully left. Issue #56 sports a cover showing Kirby, Simon, and other members of the Prize staff as shady-looking bums in a police lineup. In his book *The Comic Book Makers*, Joe Simon recalled, "In November 1953, when the Senate was preparing an investigation of the field, we had the gall to come out with the... cover showing our staff in a police lineup!" Amid some public outcry and a shrinking market, the title finally petered out in 1958.

Once the crime trend had run out, S&K moved on to other projects. Romance, westerns, and black magic fed the tastes of the day. Except for a handful of covers for *Charlie Chan* (Prize/Charlton) and a nicely-realized run of *Police Trap* (Mainline/Charlton, '54-'55), Kirby left the mugs and thugs behind. They went back to the silver screen of Jack's youth, back to being filler characters and handy plot devices. By the time *In The Days Of The Mob* came out in 1971, they had become gaudy curiosities of a nostalgic age, now remembered with a sort of sad, grudging respect.

"Tough"? Sure. But not bulletproof. ❍

A "Glass World" Full Of Criminals

Post-War Simon & Kirby Comics Noir, by Tom Morehouse

Hollywood tough guys: Richard Widmark and Victor Mature in Kiss of Death.

The years following the end of World War II were full of changes in American popular culture. In his *History of Narrative Film* (W.W. Norton & Co. Inc., 1981) author David A. Cook states: "After the elation of victory had passed... disillusionment and cynicism came over the nation which had at least as much to do with America's image of itself as with the distant horror of the war abroad." When they saw American motion pictures for the first time since before the war, French film critics coined the term *film noir* (literally "black film") to describe a mood and darkness of atmosphere in these movies that has much more to do with plot and character development than lighting technique. Grittier subject matter, graphic sexuality, characters who looked and acted like "real" people with all their flaws and desires, anti-heroes who acted like bad guys while they were doing good; after the war, in 1946 and '47, things got even darker! Movies such as *The Postman Always Rings Twice, The Blue Dahlia, Kiss of Death* and *The Big Sleep* thrived upon the unvarnished depiction of greed, lust and cruelty because their basic theme was the depth of human depravity and the utterly unheroic nature of human beings – lessons that were hardly taught but certainly re-emphasized by the unique horrors of World War II. Most of the films of the late Forties take the form of crime melodramas because (as Dostoievski and Dickens knew) "the mechanisms of crime and criminal detection provide a perfect metaphor for corruption that cuts across conventional

Gangland themes played a role in Jack's unused 1950s comic strip proposal King Masters. *Shown here are some of Jack's uninked pencil strips, and one strip inked by Frank Giacoia.*

Real Clue Crime Stories *Vol. 2, #4.*

moral categories...": A lesson not lost on the producers of comic books!

By 1947, the readership of Lev Gleason's *Crime Does Not Pay* had climbed to more than two million monthly! Part of the reason was the public's postwar appetite for hard-edged and realistic entertainment (such as *film noir*) along with the return to civilian life of American servicemen, nearly half of whom had been regular comic book readers before and during the war. No longer fascinated by patriotic hero fantasies, these ex-G.I.s were looking for a more mature type of comic book.

Enter Joe Simon and Jack Kirby.

Back from their service in the Coast Guard and Army respectively, Simon & Kirby were anxious to re-establish themselves in the marketplace. Joe and Jack convinced Hillman Comics editor Ed Cronin to give them a shot at doing stories that might appeal to this new audience of older readers – guys like themselves. An early attempt, "King of the Bank Robbers" appeared in *Clue Comics* Vol. 2, #1 (March 1947). An 8-page period piece set in 1860s New York, it's "A TRUE CLUE Crime Story" about the career (and eventual demise) of George Leonidas Leslie, who baffled police and bullied his cohorts for better than five years following the Civil War, until his deeds (and character faults) caught up with him, and he was killed by a former member of his gang. Simon & Kirby's "crime" career was off to a running start, and the next two issues of *Clue* contained more and more of their material.

In June 1947, after 3 issues *Clue* was changed to *Real Clue Crime Stories,* and the first cover (Vol. 2, #4, by S&K) featured a quote from Ralph Waldo Emerson as a slogan: "Commit a crime and the world is made of glass." Inside, along with the regular feature character, Dan Barry's "Gunmaster" (a carry-over from *Clue*), were three stories by Joe and Jack. "Come With Me and Die!" is about a killer who preyed on his victims during the London Blitz. The story utilizes a popular crime comic (and film) technique, and one which Simon & Kirby had used before, and did about as well as could be done. In the opening panels we're introduced to the story's narrator, Inspector Greeno of Scotland Yard, who, thanks to an I.D. tag conveniently dropped by the killer during a frustrated homicide attempt, cracks the case. "The Trail of the Gun-Loving Killer" tells the tale of a young man in the 1920s, Wilbur Underhill, who from a very young age is obsessed with firearms. After a seemingly charmed career of robbery, jail breakouts and murder, he dies with thirteen slugs in his body following a shootout with the police. It's the kind of story everybody's mom would tell if she saw her child playing with guns.

Everybody's mom, that is, except the narrator of the lead story "Mother of Crime" – Ma Barker, who we meet in the opening panels "in that fiery region which is supposed to be the last port of call for the wicked" (i.e. Hades). If the premise has a familiar ring to it, it should! Jack would use it again 24 years later in his black-&-white *In the Days of the Mob!* In the 1971 version called "Ma's Boys," some of the details have changed, but the basic tale reads the same. Ma Barker, the domineering mother of Herman, Doc, Lloyd, and Fred, trains her sons to be criminals – hating the law, shooting first and asking questions later. One by one her charges meet their doom, until the finale takes place in a house in Florida where Ma and Fred, her youngest, are hiding out. When confronted by Federal officers, Ma chooses to fight rather than surrender, but not before chastising her terrified son: "Stop it!" *(slap)* "I'll have no hysterics, Freddie" *(1947 version)* "Yuh do what yore Ma tells yuh! Do yuh wanna disgrace yore Ma?" *(1971 version)* After a furious gun battle, both Barkers are dead. For a guy like Jack who loved and respected his mother Rose, listened to her, and did what she said, this tale had impact. *Real Clue Crime Stories* had it too, lasting through Vol. 8, #3 (May 1953) – this despite having Vol. 3, #9 end up in *Seduction of the Innocent.*

Kirby's early home environment played an important role in the realism of many of the crime stories he would do throughout his life. Having been born and raised in a lower East Side neighborhood during the '20s, Jack recalled, "There were gangs all over the place. Gangsters were looked up to and feared. I'd see them in restaurants and they'd hold all these conferences. They weren't the stereotypes you see in the movies. I knew the real ones." If the autobiographical "Street Code" (*Argosy* Vol. 3, #2) is any indication, Jack had to choose early in life which side he wanted to be on. This might account for another storytelling technique he and Joe would use in many of their four-color "morality plays": the confessional narration, an example of which can be found in "I Was a Come-On Girl for Broken Bones, Inc." (*Justice Traps the Guilty* #1), where the lucky repentant says at the end: "Sure – I got off easy... I'm free now *(after serving 5 years)* and have a swell job... only 30 bucks a week, but I never felt better in my life." It doesn't take too much imagination to figure out that Kirby knew lots of folks who hadn't been fortunate enough to learn that justice traps the guilty. ❍

Jack chronicled the death of Ma and Freddie Barker twice – in the 1947 version (above), and the 1971 version (right).

KIRBY'S GANGSTERS NEVER GET THEIR DAY IN COURT

An examination of In The Days Of The Mob, *by Tom Field*

"Welcome to Hell!"

So spoke Warden Fry, the netherworldly host who greeted readers on the splash page of Jack Kirby's *In the Days of the Mob,* the black-&-white, one-shot magazine published in 1971 by DC Comics under the Hampshire Distributors Ltd. imprint.

But while Fry's intent was to introduce the gangsters and molls who populated his maximum-security corner of Hades, he might well have directed his fateful greeting at Kirby himself. For although Kirby invested extraordinary energy in this project, like so many of his efforts in his 1970-75 DC period, *Mob* died aborning – scaled back and then shot down before it ever had the chance to achieve Kirby's vision.

Ultimately, spotty distribution resulted in poor sales, justifying DC's decision to pull the plug on *Mob* after releasing but a single issue; but Mark Evanier – the comics/TV writer who assisted Kirby on *Mob* and several other early-'70s DC projects – says *Mob* really was cancelled before issue #1 even hit the stands. He attributes the decision to DC's inability to reconcile its corporate objectives with Kirby's creative vision. "DC never really knew what to do with Jack," says Evanier, who describes *Mob*'s rise and fall in a scenario so familiar to fans of Kirby's DC work:

- Like *New Gods,* which Kirby intended to be comics' first limited series – until DC balked and made it an ongoing series – *Mob* was to be the first *Heavy Metal,* a full-color, adult-oriented, comics and text magazine that would compete for newsstand space and readers alongside *National Lampoon* and *Mad Magazine.* In fact, Kirby envisioned – and prepared – an entire line of similarly adult titles, but only single issues of two of them – *Mob* and its ghostly 1971 companion *Spirit World* – ever appeared. And with both, DC pulled the plug on the color, toned down the mature content, and splashed the artwork with dull, gray tones that even Kirby abhorred.
- Like *Mister Miracle* and *Kamandi, Mob* was created with the intention (in Kirby's mind, anyway) that Kirby would be Editor only, turning over the writing and illustration to other creators under his supervision. But DC, realizing that Kirby the creator was far more bankable than Kirby the Editor, insisted that Kirby write and draw *Mob* himself, assisted by longtime Kirby inker Vince Colletta.
- Finally, just as Kirby's entire "Fourth World" epic was cancelled before he could bring the saga to a satisfying conclusion, *Mob* was D.O.A. – shelved after two issues were prepared, but after only the first was released.

"DC lost interest in the project very fast," recalls Evanier, who researched and wrote text features for *Mob* #1 and the unpublished #2. "DC just gave up – and I can't say they were 100% wrong. The newsstands just didn't know where to put (*Mob*) – I had trouble even finding copies on the newsstands in L.A. – and I don't think most fans even knew it existed."

Indeed, even if they were aware of *Mob,* Kirby fans couldn't have been prepared for it. Filled with gangsters, guns and Depression-era settings, *Mob* was a dramatic departure from the cosmic-powered super-heroes and space-spanning demigods that ignited Kirby's popularity in the 1960s. Yet, because Kirby was a child of the Depression, growing up quite literally *In the Days of the Mob,* these vignettes of Ma Barker and Murder Inc. remain some of Kirby's most authentic work.

"Jack had a certain amount of enthusiasm for everything he did," Evanier says, but *Mob* had a special place in Jack's heart. "He was a fan of that stuff. He had met a lot of people who knew the gangsters." And although Evanier and Kirby's other assistant, Steve Sherman, did a lot of research on gangsters and the Depression to help enrich Kirby's historical fiction, Evanier concedes, "Jack probably could have done these stories from memory and they wouldn't have been much different."

Uninked pencils from In The Days Of The Mob *#2.*

#1 spotlights the lives and deaths of several major underworld figures, including Ma Barker and Al Capone. The former stars in the 16-page lead story "Ma's Boys," detailing the life of the shrewish matriarch and her death alongside her ne'er-do-well brood. In the story's eerie conclusion, Ma Barker is reunited with her dead sons in the searing inferno of Hell. The Capone story that follows, the 12-page "Bullets for Big Al," actually was Kirby's first *Mob* effort, Evanier recalls (his first work on the project was this story's two-page spread depicting showgirls dancing atop a table). Depicting Capone as a modern-day Vlad Dracul, inviting his rival's messengers to a lavish dinner and then torturing them to send a "message" of his own, "Bullets" is both the most graphic and the strongest of the stories in *Mob* #1. The issue is rounded-out by text features prepared by Evanier and Sherman, as well as Kirby's eight-page "Kansas City Massacre" and two-page "Method of Operation" comics stories, plus two pages of gangster 'toons by Sergio Aragones.

Two features stand out in *Mob* #1, somewhat in contrast to some of Kirby's other DC work: The script and the inked artwork. Because these stories are of Kirby's era, the dialogue is much more believable – less awkward – than that found in many of his Fourth World strips. As scripted with Kirby's ear for Depression-era dialect, Al Capone is a much more credible character than, say, Flippa Dippa, who was supposed to be Kirby's take on a modern young Black man in *Jimmy Olsen.*

Likewise, where Colletta was criticized and ultimately removed from Kirby's DC work because of his somewhat scratchy inking style and "simplified" backgrounds (he's reputed to have erased some of Kirby's complex background pencils in the Fourth World titles), the collaboration very much works in *Mob.* In black-&-white, Colletta's sometimes-crude embellishment gives Kirby's pencils an edge that amplifies the raw work. Colletta's contribution especially shines in comparison to Mike Royer's more "slick" inks in the unpublished *Mob* #2.

Which brings us to the elusive, unpublished second issue of *Mob.* Although it's never has been released in its entirety, excerpts have appeared in such diverse publications as DC's mid-70s fanzine *Amazing World of DC Comics,* and in Robin Snyder's 1995 'zine *The Comics.* These stories, written and penciled by Kirby and inked and lettered by Royer, concentrate mainly on the misdeeds and miscreants of "Murder Inc." These stories place less emphasis on Warden Fry and the netherworld, but they continue to play up the historic personalities and pitfalls of the gangster era, including one curious feature that spotlights "The colorful, beautiful, pragmatic, inscrutable Ladies of the Gang!"

In some ways, Kirby's *Mob* work is ahead of its time, anticipating the mid-70s "mob revival" sparked by the films *The Godfather* and *The Sting;* but it's doubtful, even had DC supported the project whole-heartedly, whether *Mob* could have enjoyed sustained success. Logistically, retailers didn't know where to display the title – with other magazines or with the comics? – and the distribution industry, beset with its own reputed mob ties, wasn't wild about the subject matter, Evanier says. Creatively, Kirby lost his own enthusiasm for the project as DC skimped on production values and forced Kirby to tone down some of the mature content. "Jack never liked black-&-white comics, and he especially didn't like gray tones," Evanier says. "But by the time *Mob* came out, he had bigger problems than that. As the project developed, it just strayed further and further from his vision."

And so *In the Days of the Mob* came and went without fanfare. The first issue, a rare collector's item, has never been reprinted, and the second has yet to appear in its entirety.

Where, in the Kirby pantheon, does *Mob* fit? Somewhere in the middle. "It's not a major Kirby work – not a *New Gods* or a *Demon* or a *Kamandi,*" Evanier says. "It's a nice book, but it's not my favorite Kirby material. I admire the skill (in *Mob*) more than I do the imagination." ❍

A two-page comedy piece planned for In The Days Of The Mob *#2.*

Kid Gang Update

by John Morrow, with thanks to Stan Taylor and Frank Johnson

Way back in *TJKC* #7, we did a whole issue on Jack's (and Joe Simon's) Kid Gang groups. Since then, we've acquired new information on a couple of them, and since those were some tough little guys, we thought this was the perfect time to update you.

TJKC subscriber Stan Taylor brought to our attention that the first appearance of the Boy Heroes was in *All-New Comics* #6, dated 11/24/43. Since Jack and Joe were both already serving in World War II by that time, and the S&K studio was working on the backlog of work for the DC books, it seems unlikely that Boy Heroes was a creation of the S&K studio (although it's still possible the pages we printed were done later in the S&K studio). Also, Stan was unable to find any record of any collaborations between Jack and/or Joe and Al Avison or Al Gabrielle between the time S&K left Timely for DC, and when they started working for Alfred Harvey in late 1945. Unless Boy Heroes was discussed while Joe and Jack were still at Timely, it appears unlikely Joe or Jack were involved in the group's creation. If anyone can shed any light on this, please let us know.

In our feature on *Boy Explorers*, we missed one other minor appearance: They had a 2-page text feature in *Terry & The Pirates* #3 entitled "Mixed-Up Sounds." Also, subscriber Frank Johnson pointed out that the unpublished "Centropolis" plot (and possibly some of the art) was recycled and used in *Boy Commandos* #29's "City At The Center Of The Earth," not in #23 as we incorrectly stated. #29's story ends with the marriage of Feran and Alora (who look identical to the characters in the unused *Boy Explorers* page), and General Zort is a perfect match for Captain Khredo. Also, we mistakenly listed the unused *Boy Explorers* page on the back cover of *TJKC* #7 as being for issue #3; it was actually meant for #4.

Finally, a couple of new pages from *Dingbats of Danger Street* #3 have surfaced, and we'll feature them – and any others that turn up – next issue. ❍

Dave Gibbons inked this Boy Commandos pencil drawing for the cover of Jack Kirby Quarterly *#7.*

An unused panel from Boy Commandos.

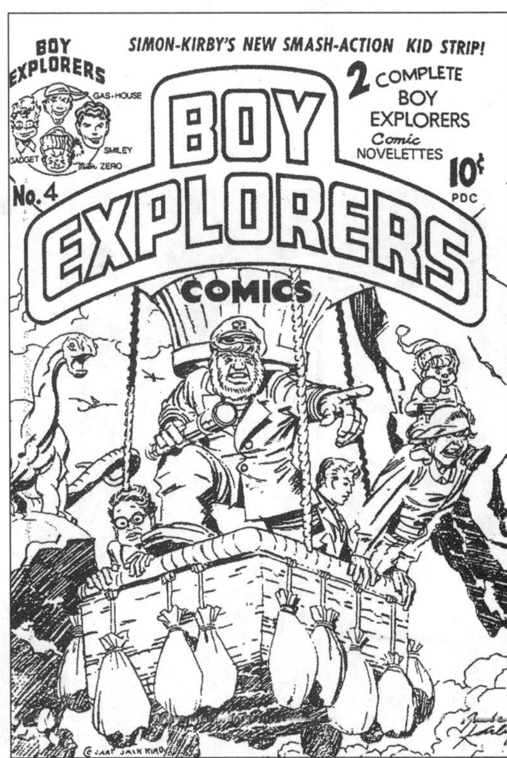

A 1980s pseudo-cover for Boy Explorers.

Will Eisner Speaks!

An interview by Jean Depelley

(In the late Thirties, Jack was looking for new editors as a freelance artist. In 1936, he started with the Lincoln News Syndicate, working on his first comic strips. Two years later, a more experienced Kirby was employed by Will Eisner & Jerry Iger's Art Syndication Company in New York. There, he produced three strips: Diary of Doctor Hayward, Wilton of the West, *and* Count of Monte Cristo *(finished by Lou Fine), published in the first issues of Fiction House's* Jumbo Comics *in 1939, and constituting his first comic book work. Jack left the studio the same year, going from Martin Goodman's Red Circle Company to Fox Features, where he met his long-time collaborator Joe Simon. Little was written about Jack's time in the studio apart from an interview conducted by Will Eisner himself for* The Spirit Magazine *in the Eighties. This interview with the Spirit's father was conducted on January 25, 1997 in Angoulême during the most important French comic convention. I'd like to thank Will Eisner for his time and his kindness. Special thanks also to Gerard Jean (Magazines de France) for the recording.)*

TJKC: In 1938, you created the Art Syndication Company with Jerry Iger. What was the purpose of this syndicate?
WILL EISNER: It was a company that I began with Jerry Iger, who was formally the editor of *Wow Magazine. Wow Magazine* was the first magazine that I did work for. I was a young freelance cartoonist. The magazine went bankrupt. It went out after two or three issues. So, I was out of work. I was very poor because it was still the Great Depression. Jerry Iger was broke; he was out of work, out of a job. But I saw something that was very obvious: You didn't have to be a genius to see that they were looking for new stories, original stories. Up until that time, the magazines that were beginning were using newspaper strips, which they pasted together. Then I said to Jerry Iger, "Something is happening here. Pretty soon, there won't be enough strips, and they will need original material; and I think we can do it." So I said, "Let's make a company."

We had lunch together in a little restaurant. He said, "No, I don't want to do that. Besides, we don't have enough money to start." So I said I would put up the money. It was my money: $15, which paid the rent for three months for a little office, a very tiny office. There was room enough for one little drawing board and a little desk, and that's all. That was why my name was first on the company: It was "Eisner & Iger." I was the financial man, you know! *(laughter)* So, I did all the drawings.

TJKC: How did you meet Jack Kirby at that time?
WILL: Within a few months, the company was successful. It was growing very fast, and we moved to a larger office on Madison Avenue and 40th Street. But you see, in that office we pretended that we had five artists, but actually it was all me! *(laughter)* I did five different stories with different names: Willis Rensie, W. Morgan Thomas, Spencer Steel, names like that. Iger was a salesman. He was not a good cartoonist, but he could do lettering, so he did lettering for me. He would be a salesman, he would go and call on the publishers, and he would say, "We have five artists. These are the names..." *(laughter)* Then we got so much business that we moved to another office, and I began to hire old friends. I went to school with Bob Kane *[at DeWitt Clinton High School]*, so I asked him to come work for me. He was looking for work. And then we began to hire people. Jack Kirby came in one day with a portfolio; he was looking for work. So we hired him and he was good. That's how he came.

TJKC: What other artists were working there, along with Iger, Kane, Kirby, Lou Fine and you?
WILL: Bob Powell. But these names you remember, they were different names! Bob Powell's real name was Stanislav Pavlowsky. *(laughter)* Jack Kirby's name was Jacob Kurtzberg. Bob Kane's was Bob Kahn. I was the only one that kept my own name! *(laughter)*

TJKC: Your production was to be sold to Editors Press Service, publisher of the British magazine *Wag.* Was your work, along with Jack's work, published then or was it first released in *Jumbo Comics* for Fiction House?
WILL: No, the first releases were to magazines that were starting out. The company was what's called a "packager." It's where you put everything together and deliver to the publishers what they call "camera-ready" and they would print it. The publishers who were coming into the business then had no experience with comics. They were all pulp magazine publishers and pulp magazines were dying. They were

An Eisner/Kirby "jam" drawing that accompanied Jack's interview in Spirit Magazine *#39. (top) Will speaks at Angoulême in 1997.*

looking for new material. So, we were not publishers, but we were producers.

First we began with Editors Press and there were a few other magazines. And then we went to Fiction House which then published *Jumbo Comics* and *Jungle Comics.*

TJKC: Do you have any anecdotes to share about Jack at work then?
WILL: Jack was a little fellow. He thought he was John Garfield, the actor! *(laughter)* Very tough, very tough. Everything you see here *[Will points to the cover of* The Jack Kirby Collector *#13]* was inside him. But he was a very little fellow; a very good fellow, but very tough. When we moved to a new office in a nice office building, we had a towel service for the artists to wash their hands, and we would buy a towel for each of the artists so they could wash up. The people who supplied the towels, however, were mafia! *(laughter)* They were charging more and more money, so my partner Iger said, "Look, let's find another towel service *[that's]* cheaper," because at that time we had ten to fifteen artists and it was beginning to cost money. So I called them and said, "Look, we would like to find another towel service." So I get a visit from their salesman. *(laughter)* He had a white tie, a black hat, a broken nose, y'know? Scarface! *(laughter)* And he came in and said, "Are you really not happy with the service?" I said, "Well, we want to find another..." He said, "There is nobody else that can service this building." *(laughter)*

We were beginning to talk loud, and from the other room, in comes Jack Kirby. He says to me, "Will, is he giving you a problem? I will beat him up." *(laughter)* This is little Jack Kirby, and this big guy! *(laughter)* I said, "Jack, go inside!" Jack says, "No, no." He says to the fellow, "Look, we don't have to take your towels! We can take other people's!" The guy looked at me and said, "Who is he?" And I said, "He's my chief artist. Don't get him angry, because..." *(laughter)* So this fellow said, "Look, we want to do this friendly. We don't want to have any trouble." And Jack said, "If he comes to see you again, call me and I'll beat him up!" *(laughter)*

TJKC: Did the artists work in collaboration on the same strips in the studio ? Did you ever work on Jack's pencils, or Jack on yours?
WILL: No, the way we worked in Eisner & Iger was that I would design a story in the very beginning, maybe sometimes in blue pencil, and then Jack would take it and do it, or Bob Powell would take it and do it. For example, I designed the character Sheena, Queen of the Jungle. So, I made the first drawing. Sometimes I would do the cover first, and then give it to somebody and say, "Here, you do it." That how we worked.

TJKC: Can you tell me what you did after the studio?
WILL: In 1938, the newspaper syndicate came to realize the importance of comic books. They wanted me to make a comic book for newspapers. At that time, it was a big risk! They gave me an adult audience and I wanted to write better things than super-heroes. Comic books were a ghetto. I sold my part of the enterprise to my associate and then began *The Spirit.* They wanted an heroic character, a costumed character. They asked me if he'd have a costume. And I put a mask on him and said, "Yes, he has a costume!"

TJKC: You met Jack again in the eighties *[1982]* for an interview in *Spirit Magazine* #39. Did you meet Jack after that?
WILL: After that, I would see him in places like San Diego. He moved to California. In America, up until a few years ago, artists didn't see each other very often, because they lived in different places. America is a very big place, and we didn't see each other. So I would see him when I got to San Diego; we would talk and say hello.

There is another thing I can tell you. I did a book called *The Dreamer [Kitchen Sink, 1986],* in which I showed Jack Kirby, and Jack said to somebody, "I didn't think Will liked me that much!" *(laughter)* He always called me "boss." *(laughter)* I said, "Jack, we're old men now, you don't have to call me boss anymore." "No," he said, "you're still my boss." *(laughter)* ❍

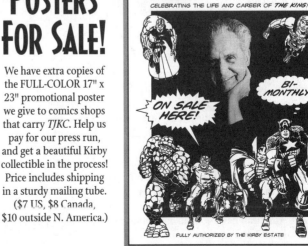

Jack Kirby Interview

by Juanie Lane and Britt Wisenbaker, conducted on September 15, 1984 with Jack and Roz Kirby at their home, for the Pepperdine University student publications magazine Oasis

JUANIE LANE: Well first off, just in terms of the hero... if you can just kind of give me your personal feelings in terms of the way that the hero has developed through America just in the past few decades.

JACK KIRBY: Well, the hero in America is very unique, because he's unlike heroes that have developed in the past elsewhere. The American has a distinct character. It's developed certainly over these hundreds of years, and of course, he's also unique abroad; you'll find that people abroad love American heroes... they love American comics and American movies, because of the kind of forthright characters we are. Of course, speaking about myself I say this reservedly, but the American hero is a guy that comes to the point... a guy that's not afraid to go over the line... he doesn't hesitate. He doesn't hesitate to help people, or to save people, or to avert some kind of danger. He's not afraid of confrontation. And that's the character of the American hero. He's a kind of a spontaneous character.

A hero somewhere else might be a little more subtle. He might be a little more... well, maybe suave, see? Or maybe debonair. Using corny words of course.

But the American hero isn't like that at all. He's just a guy... like Indiana Jones maybe, or Captain America, or like my own characters, the New Gods, which are coming out now, and they're being publicized. It's the first novel that's ever been done in comics and I've just finished it. And so, it's kind of a great thing for myself because I've done some experimenting in areas... in fact I've always done experimenting in areas that I felt were blank pages in comics and should be filled in. I felt that comics as a medium is a kind of visual literary medium – a kind of bridge between a novel and a film. It's a kind of visual art.

So I did the first comic novel, called the *New Gods.* And of course, I did that back in the early seventies, but now it's being reissued and republicized. And the characters are also being publicized, and you'll see them on Saturday morning TV; all my villains are being used in them. Of course, they're... the villains are like the heroes. They're also aggressive, and they're forthright in their own views. And of course they come in contention with the heroes, and the clashes are spontaneous, yet the effect of these clashes is powerful. And of course the issues are very dramatic. I think that Americans are a lot more dramatic than people elsewhere. They're a lot more, of course, spontaneous. So we see issues in a very dramatic way. We see ourselves in a very dramatic way. I don't think there's such a thing as an invisible American. I think that every American has a good image of themselves, because, possibly, he's had a lot of heroes to look up to.

Remember that Tarzan came from America, Superman came from America, and these are all characters that have had a dramatic in their own way... they didn't arise out of sources... out of sources that were awesome. They arose out of sources that were just dramatic, and perhaps mundane compared to, say, people like Hercules or Atlas or Samson. Tarzan, of course, was an update on all these things, but Tarzan was completely American. He wasn't really English, because although, you know, he has an English background, he's an American in nature. Superman, of course, is all-American. He's a classic. He's an institution, and he's timeless. The hero is always timeless, but he always reflects the character of the culture he springs from. If you have a culture where weather is a prime consideration, you'll find that the hero is a natural force. He's a natural elemental force, probably very mystic. But in America he's not mystic at all; he's got a family, he has a mother and a father, and he's the guy next door who suddenly acquires superpowers. And he skates, and he swims, and he surfs, and he does everything that every American boy does. Actually, he's an all-American character. And of course the people overseas won't see him that way. They don't see heroes in the light of the ordinary average Joe. So they'll see him in some overall overpowering image, where we have no need of that kind of thing. The American guy is self-sufficient; and he's got flaws, he's got virtues. He's very, very human. But of course, you give him a few super-powers... you're dealing with a really wonderful guy. So I pattern my heroes in that kind of way because I'm an American. It's just second nature to me, like any other guy. If you were doing a hero, if you were creating your own hero, well, she'd probably be an all-American girl, or an all-American young man; but with special characteristics. We all think of ourselves in that vein. When we go over to a video game, we go with the notion that we're going to beat this game, okay? And that's inherent in all of us. And we do beat the game.

I think Americans are winners. And I think those who think they're not underrate themselves. So my heroes are winners. And of course the evil people represent something with a flaw; something with a conflicting need. My villains are not specifically downright evil; I feel that they're people with problems who inflict these problems on others. And of course, if you do that, you come in contention with these others; and so you've got a story. Sometimes there are no villains at all.

ROZ: On to her next question... *(laughter all around)*

JUANIE: No, that's great. But one thing that I was going to ask is, you know you talked about the American hero as being the normal person in the basic context, with differences. Would you say that's always been true, pretty much throughout time, or is that just more so today?

JACK: No, that's always been true, specifically in Americans. You'll find that the Boston Tea Party was initiated by teenagers, who had never seen George the Third, who had only seen Englishmen as an occupying force, see. So, in order to show their own independence, they indulge in acts in which they risked their lives. That's history. And it's true. And so we developed this specific characteristic, and it

BARON VON THING

JACK KIRBY

(next page) Jack's uninked pencils to Fantastic Four *#91, page 16. Look, more gangsters!*

could be found in our origins. And so it's always been that way. You'll find that all our heroes are real people... all American heroes are real people. We go on in that vein because that's the way we are.

JUANIE: How are the heroes affected by time, in terms of the society of the day? For example, it's such a complex society that we have today; how does that affect the normal qualities of a hero?

JACK: All right... the hero is, of course, a product of his own time, but he will continue in the context of being a hero in contending with the problems of his own time.

ROZ: Like Captain America during World War II fought the Nazis.

JACK: Well, Captain America in World War II fought the Nazis, *[but]* we have different problems now; we have more dangerous problems, I think. And a hero today has to contend with these particular problems; he has to contend with people who don't... who might misuse things today that might affect everybody. It's the hero's job – at least it's my hero's job – to see that things continue. Not that they will never change, but that people are able to continue, and possibly improve themselves.

JUANIE: So what kinds of conflicts would you say we have today? I mean that are common to everybody.

JACK: Well, we have personality conflicts, we have national-international conflicts, we have high-tech conflicts.

JUANIE: So you're saying the hero, then, kind of enters into all levels of life.

JACK: Yes he does. In family life, in his individual family life, he won't hesitate to alleviate a problem... for his own people and, of course, his neighbors. He won't denigrate or back away from...

ROZ: I think she's trying to get like, exactly what are they fighting out here? Is that what you're trying to get?

JUANIE: Well, I'm just wondering the kinds of forces, you know; are these forces people or are they institutions, or...

JACK: They're all kinds of stories.

ROZ: Well, now they're worrying about the atomic bombs, and aliens.

JACK: All right? They're all kinds of stories. But the hero has to fight them on all kinds of levels. He fights them on a family level, he fights them on the international level. The atom bomb is a consideration. There are people who will tamper with it. And there are people who... we have toxic problems. Toxic waste problems. We have toxic waste that gives off radiation. We have to be careful with this kind of thing. That's a problem we haven't even solved yet. Of course, it's something the hero might tackle.

JUANIE: Would you say that the hero had to contend with all of these things on different levels before? You know what I'm saying?

JACK: Always. Always. We've had commoners and kings. We've had good ones and bad ones. But there's always been a hero to contend with these people. There's always been a hero to contend with problems on a national scale. There's Horatio at the bridge, right? There was El Cid in Spain. And there was King Arthur in England, who actually had a void to fill. Of course they say King Arthur is mythical; he might have been. But there's a gap in English history where the Romans left, and there was no law and order. England was like the Old West in the United States. Who was going to fill that gap? And they say that a character named King Arthur filled that gap, by creating a society with law and order. So King Arthur became a hero of sorts. Of course, he's a mythological hero, but I believe that somewhere there was a real person who helped create law and order in England, where there was none. The Romans

An unused Destroyer Duck *pencil panel.*

created the law and order, but when they left, their law and order went with them. So England needed a hero, and somebody filled that gap. In situations like that, there are problems that rise beyond the common man. I mean, how would you contend with living in a frontier town where there is no law and order? Where you haven't got a Wyatt Earp? Where just anything goes? You have a decent family, and you're making a living in this town, but the town has problems. It's not a personal problem, but it has problems. You have to survive in that town. The hero is a survivor.

JUANIE: Can you help explain how you actually go about creating a hero, in terms of the kinds of things that you try to pull from a specific generation knowing the kinds of needs that people may have in terms of a hero?

JACK: Well, I'm a storyteller essentially. After many years in this type of job, you become, I think, a very, very good storyteller. The only thing I can say about myself is that I'm thoroughly professional because I've been raised in an editorial atmosphere. I began... I was about eighteen years old, I worked for the Fleischer studio in the animation department animating Popeye. Of course, that wasn't the kind of thing I felt I wanted to do. I'm a believer in the individual. I feel that every individual has his own yearnings somewhere in the back of his own mind although it hasn't yet formulated. He knows; he instinctively knows what he'd like to do. If you gravitate towards machines you become an engineer or a mechanic. If you gravitate to storytelling you become a good storyteller, because you want to do your best at it. So, I did my best at it. I felt I could do it without supervision; I'd like to tell the story myself. And so I did, I began doing comic strips, I began doing editorial cartoons. Whatever I did, I put my own individual elements in the story.

ROZ: She wants to know how you create your characters.

JACK: Well, I create my characters out of people. No matter where they are. If it's a war story, my characters will be based on people, so the reader can relate to them. If it's a western story, my characters will be real people. But of course I'm not going to go into realism in the extreme. It's still a story; my object is entertainment, I'm not out to preach or to give my own particular views on any subject. My basic object is to entertain. In a war story, if I had a war story, there would be no enemies. Just people. Having gone through that experience myself, I found that was true. Here I was in a little corner of somewhere as a person, and there I was against people who were also persons – I found out they were persons. And there we were, in a situation that was very dramatic. I've written stories; I've taken just elements of the realism and these stories come across because there's power in these elements. And if there's power in any story, someone will read it.

JUANIE: You said that you're out to entertain and not to preach.

JACK: Oh, yes.

JUANIE: But would you say there's some central theme that you have throughout all your *[stories]*?

JACK: Yes, there is a central theme. And the central theme is compassion. I have as much compassion for my villains as I do for my heroes. And I feel that my villains are really tortured people, just as my heroes may be tortured people in a way. Because possibly my heroes don't like their job. Sometimes they don't like what they do. But they do it. For instance, possibly a hero might sacrifice himself to save an entire village, or to save a company of people, or to save someone personally. He might sacrifice himself. He might undergo... not necessarily physically, even mentally; he might have to undergo lots of stress. A hero will undergo lots of stress; and of course bring lots of stress to himself, and shoulder that stress in the cause of others. You might do that for your mother or your brother or your distant cousin, and of course you would be a hero. Because you would shoulder their problems.

ROZ: She wants to know, too, how you would create a particular hero.

JACK: Well, I'm trying to give you the basis for my heroes.

JUANIE: Well, you said that you use real people as your source to create a hero.

JACK: Not specific people. I use people in general as I know them.

JUANIE: Just individuals throughout your lifetime, but not necessarily, say, a political figure in the past or...

JACK: Oh, no. I believe that belongs in the realm of journalism and not storytelling. *(laughter)*

My people are fictional. I try to create an acceptable atmosphere but nothing more. So the stories are believable. In other words, for you to enjoy the story you have to believe it. If I tell you something that you feel is contrived, you won't read it. I never contrive a story. If I have a setting for it, you'll feel the atmosphere of that particular setting. If the villain is a certain type of person, you'll feel that there is that type of person about. Although he may have the trappings that entertain you, basically, you'll believe that somewhere there's probably a guy like that or a woman of that kind. I won't give you a contrived character that's made of wood, or made of any kind of metal; even if they were they would be people of flesh.

JUANIE: So, do you want these people, the readers, to actually be able to get something from your comics; to actually be helped, to be able to apply something in their life to what you're saying?

JACK: Uhh... no. My only object...

ROZ: Excuse me, hon... tell *[about]* the letter you got from the priest about the gods...

JACK: Yes.

ROZ: ...that's part of what she's asking.

JACK: There are people who want to analyze my characters, okay? And I had one character who was given to the king; I had an evil character who gave his son...

ROZ: Darkseid.

JACK: Yeah. This fella Darkseid is an evil character; he governs an evil planet, and it was in his interests to stop a war with this virtuous planet, who had a virtuous king. So what they did was something that they used to do in medieval times. In order to stop this war, that they couldn't stop any other way, the kings used to exchange sons, see, as hostages. Life-long hostages. And so this evil king gave this evil son to the virtuous king, and vice versa. And they have a problem immediately. There is this fella with an evil heritage who is raised in a virtuous atmosphere, and he doesn't know what to do about it. *(laughter)* But, he accepts these virtuous tenets, and of course he fights in their cause, but he fights as he is, see? Whereas, you have the good king's son who is raised in a very military atmosphere, in a very, well, savage atmosphere, who grows up and instinctively can't abide by these institutions, and so he escapes. And he escapes through what I called a "Boom Tube"; he escapes to Earth. And before he escapes, the evil king catches up with him and he says, "Well, you're brave for doing this, but remember some of this bravery is mine." And he says, "Come back with me and I'll destroy your character and make you over in my image." And he says, "I don't want your character, I want to find myself. I want to be myself." And, of course, that's an individual trait. We all want to be ourselves. There's a real element in that kind of story. That's part of the *New Gods.* Of course, I wasn't preaching religion at anybody, I'm just preaching... I'm not even preaching. I'm just telling a story about how people feel. I felt as an individual that I couldn't be part of a large organization. I had to do things for myself. I had to write stories that came from myself and nobody else. And so I became a writer/artist.

ROZ: Excuse me, but we still get a lot of letters where people are actually analyzing, because they're putting a lot into it...

JACK: Yeah, well... they analyze my characters. For instance, they wanted to analyze this character who was brought up on this evil planet, and yet on this virtuous planet, see. And they wanted to analyze him. And suddenly I found myself analyzing my own character. And so, I suddenly came to realize this character was my father. I didn't know what my father did on the outside. I didn't know what sort of problems he had at his job. I didn't know what he had to do to put bread on the table. But I loved my father, see? This man was my own father, and I... it was a young college girl that was doing this paper on my characters. I got letters from priests; I felt "well, here I go, they're going to give me heck," but they didn't! They felt that that's the way people are, and they got a lot out of it. In fact, they discussed my writing in the seminary, and they had a lot of fun at it. So, here I was, someone for them to practice on. They were analyzing me. And they said, "Well, Kirby's a human being. What makes him tick? That's our job. Our job is to understand people." And of course, that is the priest's job – the minister's job. He's supposed to understand us. And he's supposed to have compassion for us. And how does compassion arise? Well, compassion arises in contact with problems. And so, what I've done is form my own image of compassion. I love people. And I like to see them happy, and I like to see them well-adjusted. I have children of my own, and I know what makes them suffer or makes somebody else suffer. So in my stories, that kind of thing is reflected.

JUANIE: When these people write to you, and people communicate to you or one another that you've affected them, or that they've read more into what you've written, do you usually stay in touch with them or get back to them in any way?

JACK: No, I don't. I never do. And I feel that they have the right to analyze my characters in their own... they can define my characters any way they like. They're free to do that.

JUANIE: Could you explain the *New Gods* to me?

JACK: Yes. In the *New Gods,* I feel that I'm supplying a mythology for our own times. I feel that mythology is entertaining; it always has been. And that's what I do. What I'm doing is a parable on our own times. If you think upon it, you'll find that there's never been an academic god, and yet we have him. And this is the first time, I feel, that we have academic gods. And so I feel that's entertaining. I have a god called Metron.

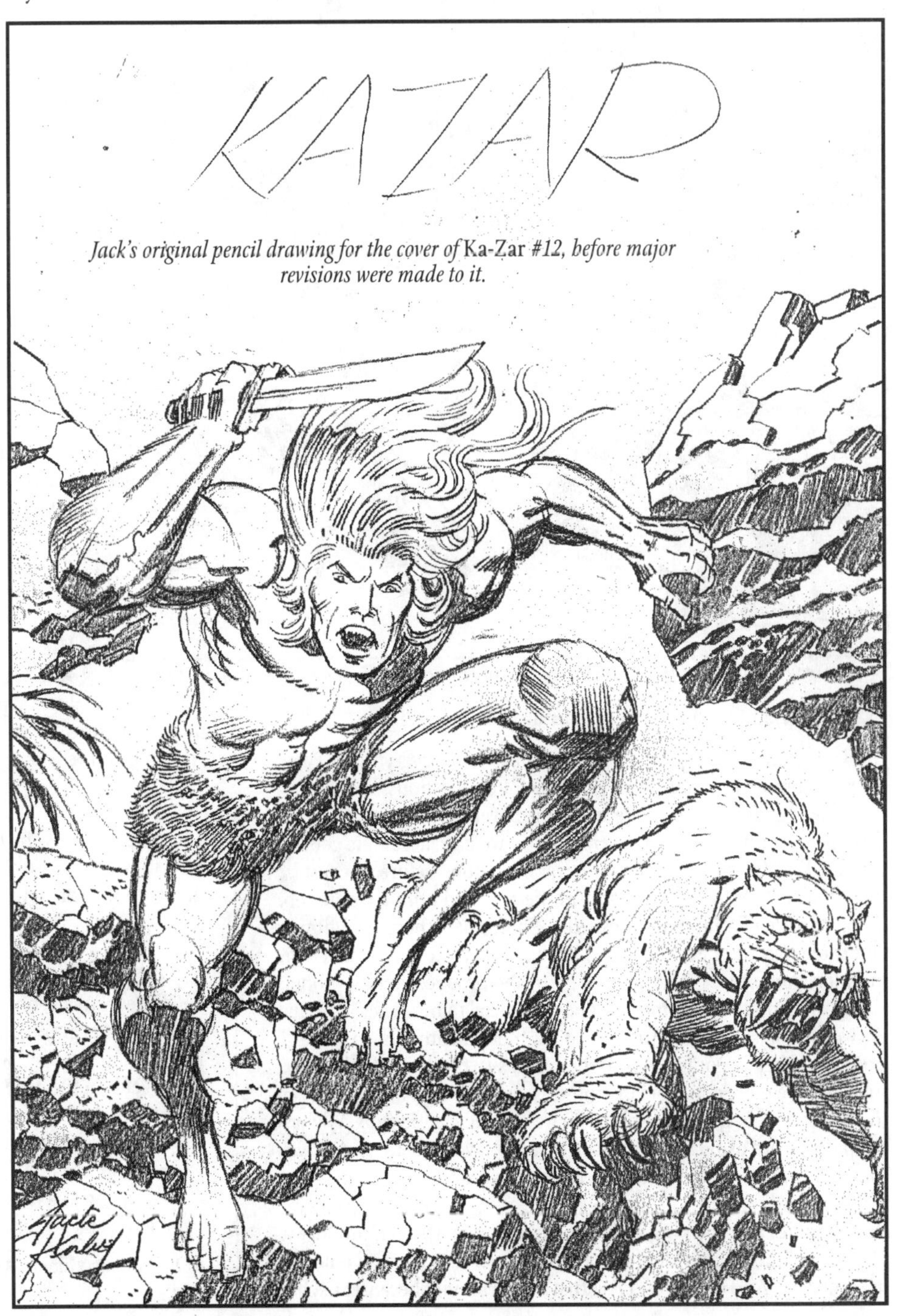

Jack's original pencil drawing for the cover of Ka-Zar *#12, before major revisions were made to it.*

An inked version of this drawing appeared in an issue of Pure Imagination's Buried Treasure.

JUANIE: What do you mean by academic gods?

JACK: Well... we have gods, our gods want to know everything. They want to know everything. We live with a lot of questions. We have a few answers, but I believe we're still in medieval times and that we have a lot more questions than answers. And so we have academic gods who are creating things that have never been done before, because they're searching for the ultimate knowledge. And I think we are too... we're searching for ultimate knowledge. Somewhere there's an ultimate; and there may not be an ultimate. We just don't know. And that's the question. And so we have academic gods who produce bombs, produce chemicals. And of course they produce beneficial things. They'll produce answers to our ailments. Answers to our mental ailments. And they'll produce... they're going out into the cosmos to find out what's there. And we have more and more instruments available that we're producing to answer a lot of those questions. So we have academic gods. We have people who are using instruments that are unavailable to us. And yet these are ordinary people. But they're doing extraordinary things. When we transcend ourselves in some way... we can transcend ourselves in the Olympics by becoming super athletes, people who can produce a "10" or an "11." I think all of us have the power to transcend ourselves in some way. And of course, I feel that's entertaining because maybe in that tiny moment when we do transcend ourselves, we become super images. Orion of the New Gods is a heavy character.

JUANIE: So the book that you're talking about is the completion of the series?

JACK: Yes, there's going to be also a Graphic Novel in which I get a lot more pages to produce more facets of my characters. And I've made the most of those pages. I have a Vietnam veteran there who was paralyzed; when death gives up his job, he goes to the Vietnam veteran. Who else would take the job of death? And it's his one chance to get out of bed, and jump on skis, and wear a flashy costume.

JUANIE: Would you say that film producers and other people involved in other types of media refer to some of the old comic heroes in creating their own heroes?

JACK: Yes, they do! Yes, they do, and in a way they try to update them. They try to keep them contemporary. We have a lot of contemporary heroes today, except they dress differently, and possibly have new personalities.

ROZ: And lots of them use comic books and they don't have to.

JACK: Well, yes. A lot of producers use comic books as sort of a springboard for their own films, and not necessarily using heroes that we know, but they're producing their own.

ROZ: Or taking ours and just making little changes here.

JACK: Like I say, comic books are very American, and that's why if they produce a hero from a comic book, you'll find a very dynamic and dramatic character. Because we haven't got time to... in comics we're given very little space to produce a well-rounded character. We have to do it in a certain amount of issues. It could take years sometimes. So we have a different problem than the average author, who is given two hundred, three hundred pages to round out his characters. Sometimes we'll have to take a year, two years, five years or ten years to produce a well-rounded character. The *New Gods*; I know we were going for about five years before I stopped. And I still hadn't finished with my characters or the central problem. And of course renewing the *New Gods* was a pleasure for me, because I love doing it. I love resolving whatever had to be done.

JUANIE: Is that with DC Comics?

JACK: Yes, that's with DC Comics, which is a fine organization. Business-wise we were able to cooperate with each other. I was able to regain access to my characters.

ROZ: But Jack's main association has been as a Producer-Consultant with Ruby-Spears.

JACK: Yes, I'm a Producer-Consultant with Ruby-Spears. I'm involved with Saturday morning animation on TV. I produce concepts for animation. I'm involved with *Mr. T.* I'm involved with *Thundarr,* who was a character in the distant future, and who has problems arising from a disaster period. And man has to lift himself up again. And Thundarr actually represents humanity in that kind of situation. I think somewhere along the line we've done that maybe time and time again. I'm only speaking as a novelist. My heroes are based on people of that sort. People who try to survive decently.

ROZ: You also like mythology; that's why your heroes are always godlike.

JACK: My gods are like that. They try to survive in awesome situations. They're awesome people, but they also survive in awesome situations. They live in galaxies far, far away, and maybe they feel that they're ultimates in their own way, but they're not. Like anybody in an average situation, I don't know if there's an ultimate, or where the ultimate lies. I feel that possibly I'm not equipped to ever answer that question. But the question intrigues me. I feel that it intrigues everybody. Like with everybody it's a question of faith. So, with me it's a question of storytelling and faith. That whatever the ultimate is, I have to have faith that it exists. And, of course, the hero does too; otherwise he would never lay his life on the line. Or the villain not only has free reign, but he would also live in fear; after all he's only human, or even super-human. He lives in fear; he's in fear of someone. And so he has to resolve that fear. And that's why he creates a problem and becomes a villain.

JUANIE: Would you say that your spiritual beliefs come into play as you're creating the storyline?

JACK: I don't know what spiritual beliefs are comprised of. I only know that I have senses; I have whatever senses that I have. And I bring them all into play. I don't know what these senses... I can't define them. All my senses are hidden from me. But they move me; for instance, your senses will move you. If you sit, say, for two hours and begin to think about things... if you're a storyteller, you have to take a little time out to figure out a problem. And the problem involves many, many facets of whatever surrounds us. I can't define spiritual. All I know is that I have my own senses as an individual, and I use them to pull whatever I have to. No more than we can define electricity; we don't know what comprises it, I don't know what comprises that. I wouldn't be pontifical and say I'm this or that. I just don't know. I have to have help. So I get that help from someone. I get it from myself, I can get it from my minister or rabbi, or I can get it from ordinary people who will reinforce my own senses. I'll say...

ROZ: You're always analyzing everything.

JACK: Yeah, well, I'm analyzing everything. And I think that's what we're all doing. We're analyzing everything around us. We're analyzing people. Essentially, we're all our own storytellers. Inside our own heads I think we don't know whether we're dramatizing or embellishing; we all have wants and needs. We'd all love to be heroes; some of us don't mind being villains, because we're in the process of analyzing ourselves. In doing so we make a lot of mistakes, and we have a lot of successes. And I think that's doing our best. I can tell you I've had a lot of both! *(laughter)* Just surviving is enough for me, and being on good terms with... trying to resolve things with other people is fine for me.

ROZ: (comment off microphone)...That's why I sit here... *(laughter)* ...he gets carried away.

JACK: I can only speak for my own character.

JUANIE: Well, you obviously seem to just be very, very enthusiastic and you have a real definite philosophy and energy towards the work that you've done. My only question at this point is where do you get all of this energy from, and imagination that it takes?

JACK: Well, I think basically *[it's because]* I'm small. *(laughter)* I've been a little guy all my life, and I come from an area where little guys get beat up, and little guys get to beat up on others. And, of course, if you're your own individual, you're a hero. *(laughter)* And so, I wanted to, maybe from the very beginning, I've wanted to find out what makes people do the things they do. And, of course, I don't know, see? But I

Jack even managed to work gangsters into Thor *#154.*

try to resolve it, and in doing so I tell stories. I get my dramatizations. I've seen people hurt, I've seen people bleed, and more than that. And basically I want to find out why. And in doing so, I tell a story. I've seen people on the wrong side deal with people on the right side, and I want to find out basically why. So I add a little more to my own character in doing so. And I add a little more to my own stories in doing so. And I feel that in not contriving to others, I am entertaining them and I'm telling them what I think, what I feel, basically about people.

JUANIE: Would you say that we can become – or people in general can become – heroes for each other, then?

JACK: I feel that... I feel that today people basically have to. I feel that there's another choice to be made. I feel that we have to make another choice. I don't know what that choice is. Maybe it's an end to power. We have to find some kind of an end to power. And whoever feels that he has power will eventually lose it. And in this kind of an age, I don't think we can afford power... of any kind. I feel that there's another road for us. I feel that the shopping mall has a lot more advantage for us than ammunition. And so it's a very dangerous age, and what the choice is, I don't know. But I'm certainly not a leader or anything like that. I'm a storyteller, and I feel that possibly we have a time in which we have to make the right choice.

JUANIE: So basically you would say, then, that the individual has all these forces or whatever within themselves.

JACK: Yes.

JUANIE: But like your stories, though, it's just an expression of showing that each individual has that power within themselves.

JACK: Yes, we do. And if we're sensitive to the world around us, we have to be sensitive to everything around us. That goes for objects, people, feelings, and we have to find a way... this is the atmosphere we live in! We have to find a way of keeping that atmosphere intact. We don't want to go through the... I'm certain the danger is going through the trauma of something that's outside our own orientation. We may have to go, you know... any dangerous situation that can develop into some kind of trauma which we don't know how to deal with, which we may or may not know how to deal with, and which we should not have to undergo.

JUANIE: Would you say there are certain age groups that need heroes more than others?

JACK: I think there are heroes for all of us. I think there are heroes for people of ninety; there have to be heroes for people of ninety. There have to be heroes for every age. They may have different personalities, because I believe each age is a sort of an ongoing personality change for all of us. Certainly I'm not the teenager that I used to be; I was another personality when I was a teenager, I was another personality when I matured. But I was maturing; not changing, just maturing. I don't believe I've ever changed, I don't believe that you will ever change, but you will mature. And you will mature in a way of dealing with your own surroundings and people.

JUANIE: You know, a lot of the time you hear people talking about the contemporary hero, saying that the hero is dead today, and that kind of thing. There was an article in *The Family Weekly* a week or two ago talking about the hero in athletics, and it said that the hero has died in sports; that he's become a more realistic person, which kind of ties in with what we are talking about. My question is, when people talk about the hero, and they're saying that they're dead today, it seems like a lot of the time they're just talking about the generation of today, and I wonder, do you think that our generation or that the young people of today really don't have heroes, or don't feel like they need heroes?

JACK: Well, I think the people of today, we've got to be our own heroes. I feel they have to be. We have to be our own heroes. Not in the manner of just being a hero, or not in the manner of dramatizing ourselves, but in the manner of... dealing with a lot of awesome problems that

A Kirby drawing of Conan The Barbarian.

weren't present, say, in your father's day. In my own case, I'm not going to jump up on some pulpit or bandstand or anyplace else and become a leader and say, "Well, this is how we should do it," or, "this is not how we should do it"; I would just go about my own business. I'm just speaking for myself. And say, "Well, this is the age I live in, and I'll just go about doing what I have to do, and I'll just be a hero for myself, and in doing so I may be for others."

Early cartoons done by Jack as a child, for the Boys Brotherhood Republic newsletter.

JUANIE: Would you have any kind of advice for young people today, in terms of confronting this complex world, because the young people are the people that you could say really have to deal with a lot of complex situations as they're growing up?

JACK: Well, I would say this. I would say, "Don't get excited." *(laughter)* I would just say, "Be yourself." Do the kinds of things that you would like to do. And there's nothing more you can do. Unless you have... if you're an ambitious person, you will do things that will satisfy your ambitions. If you're not an ambitious person, you'll do things that will interest you in some other way. I think there are unforeseen situations which none of us can foresee or answer; we're not andromedans.

JUANIE: What would you tell your grandson?

JACK: I would tell my grandson to be himself. And do whatever he'd like to do. I'm not saying that things can be resolved or not resolved. I'm saying situations develop. For instance, they develop outside of us; when I was dating my wife...

ROZ: Uh-oh. *(laughter)*

JACK: All right, when I was young, and I was dating my wife, I had no idea that some guy in Germany was coming out of a bar and suddenly discovered that he could speak at a union meeting, and suddenly get angry, and bring out all his prejudices, and not only that, but formulate those prejudices into a national institution. I had no idea that that was happening. There was nothing I could do about it. That situation was developing – and in the laps of the gods, so to speak – but here I was, doing my own thing, and just having a great time. And when that situation developed, I had to contend with that. And I did what I thought was right then; I went into the service and I was lucky enough to come back and build a family – and do what I've always done; so situations are not always expected. If you're at a ballgame, you'll notice that the customers never look at left field; they always look at what's happening in right field, see? And, of course, we can all have our opinions and say, "So that's what's going on," and, "This is what's going on," but we never see what's really going on and happening in left field, see, where the new plays are developing. And we can have people with titles who never watch left field. So we can't foresee everything. We can only be ourselves. And that's what I try to be. I'm basically an entertainer; a storyteller. So I tell stories, and I make my living at that. I create concepts and I make my living at that. That's my aim in life; to make my living and take the world for what it is.

JUANIE: Are you saying that as opposed to being overwhelmed by all the problems rather than just...

JACK: No. I'm not overwhelmed by them. In fact, I try to search...

ROZ: She means about young children...

JUANIE: Yeah, are you saying then to have the kind of attitude where you're just yourself and you're able to contend with situations rather than becoming overwhelmed by the complexities...

JACK: Well I think I... I think there are some parts of our character that we have no control over, and that our characters are shaped by events that we can't analyze. Some of us are more volatile; maybe more energetic. Or less energetic than others. Some of us spring from sources that are outside... for instance, why do we have people who think a little slower than others? People who think a little faster than others? We're shaped by our own experiences. And so we develop along those lines.

ROZ: I also think that if we have children, people fear too much what often could happen to the world; everyone's mind would just...

JACK: I don't think everybody does. I don't think I... no, I think you're wrong.

ROZ: No, I was just saying I don't think they could feel that way, otherwise they couldn't live the way they live, you know.

JACK: Oh... I can tell you in any traumatic experience, I turn myself off. In other words, I turn myself off so I can think out whatever situation I'm in.

ROZ: Well, if you feel that young people could turn off the world situation...

JACK: No, no. I don't say turn off the world situation, I just say become involved in whatever interests you. It may not be the world situation, but it's nothing that you have to worry about. It's something that you might become part of later on, but it's something that you had no part in developing. And it's something that could possibly be beyond yourself. I can only speak for myself; nobody's ever been able to mold me into part of a force of any kind.

JUANIE: Well, how does optimism as a characteristic play into all of this then?

JACK: Optimism is belief in myself. I've always believed in myself. I think everybody should believe in themselves. They're real! You're real! And you're a person. Male or female. You're real. You exist. In the final analysis, nobody can do your living for you. Nobody can do your dying for you. In the final analysis, you must do this all yourself. The other people are real too, but they're part of the outside atmosphere. Inside, you're yourself. And you can never escape that. You could never escape that. Inside, inevitably, you have to help yourself. No matter what kind of situation you're in. You're gonna react as the person you are. I don't believe that anybody can make you into any kind of person that's objectionable to yourself; some way you have an inner core that will reject, just like your physical body will reject an ailment... I think either your mental or spiritual body will reject anything that you yourself object to. You will reject it. And you won't be able to help yourself. And nobody will be able to make you do otherwise. ❍

Kirby's Rock 'n Roll Connections

by John Morrow, with help from Patrick Hilger, Carl Taylor, and Bill Wray

Sex, drugs, & rock 'n roll... and Kirby? It seems strange to add Jack's name to that expression; after all, he was approaching middle age when another "King" was helping to launch rock music by swiveling his hips and singing *Jailhouse Rock.* But although Jack's musical tastes probably leaned more toward Jimmy Dorsey than Jimi Hendrix, an entire rock generation grew up reading his comics. Since the "tough guy" image applies to many of the rock stars of the past few decades, I thought I'd document a few of Kirby's rock connections.

Back in *TJKC* #5 and #8, we published stories about Jack meeting Paul McCartney in the 1970s. Coincidentally, The Thing (who is perhaps the original "rock" star of comics) had a couple of earlier crossovers with The Beatles, compliments of Jack. On the cover of *Strange Tales* #130, he and the Human Torch meet the Beatles, and in *Fantastic Four* #34, a member of the Yancy Street Gang sends him a Beatle wig.

Many popular rock stars over the years have been Kirby fans. Graham Nash (of *Crosby, Stills & Nash*) has a huge collection of original comic book art, including Jack's work. Gene Simmons (of *KISS* fame) is a well-known comics fan – back in *Comics Interview* #2, he curiously mentioned Kirby having drawn a couple of old issues of *Superboy*. (Was he mistaken, or are these undocumented Kirby stories?) And the manager of the 1970s R&B group *The Silvers* was a big Kirby fan, so the entire group ended up visiting the Kirby home for an afternoon.

There are many other media celebrities who may be closet Kirby fans (a recent comment about Black Bolt by Tom Hanks on *The Tonight Show* sparked some interesting commentary on the Internet), but they seem to be especially plentiful in the music industry. Jack once had dinner with Frank Zappa, and I've even heard that Sting is a fan of Jack's work, but have been unable to substantiate this. If you know of any other Kirby rock connections, let us know! ❍

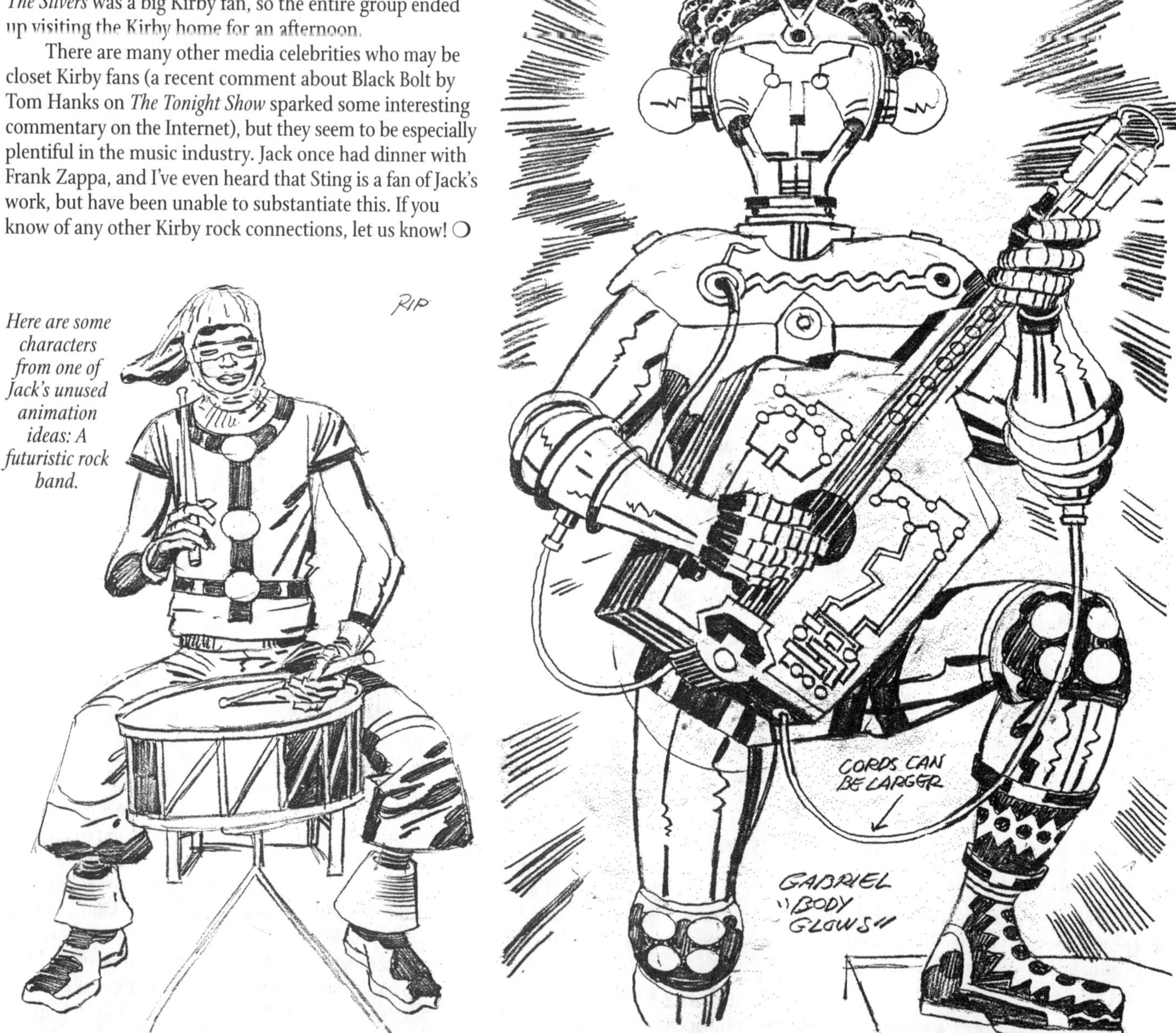

Here are some characters from one of Jack's unused animation ideas: A futuristic rock band.

LEATHER AND FUR SUIT..
BARE MIDRIFF
TIGHTS OVER PANTS
LEATHER PANTS.
OMAR
"FENDERELLA"
"ALLUSION"
"EGO"

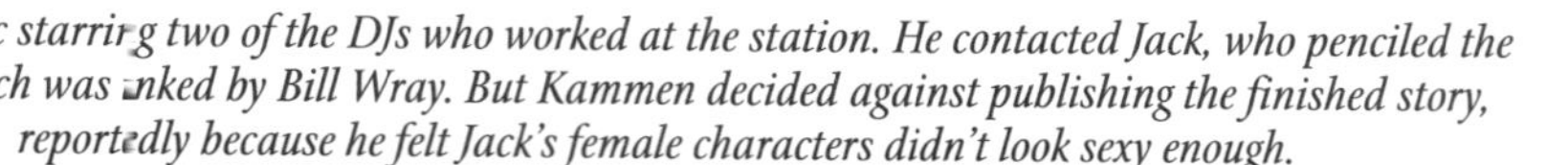

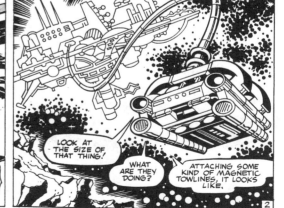

Here is a previously unpublished 4-page story Jack did sometime around the late 1970s. From what we've been able to piece together, it appears "The Astrals" was the idea of Glenn Kammen, a promoter for a Chicago radio station. In the wake of Star Wars, he conceived of doing a science-fiction give-away comic starring two of the DJs who worked at the station. He contacted Jack, who penciled the story, which was inked by Bill Wray. But Kammen decided against publishing the finished story, reportedly because he felt Jack's female characters didn't look sexy enough.

ALLOW ME TO INTRODUCE MYSELF. I AM KANDOR JASPERIAN. PERHAPS YOU'VE HEARD OF ME. I TAKE WHATEVER I WANT... AND I WANT MY OWN ROCK AND ROLL BAND. AND YOU'RE IT!
THEY'LL PLAY FOR ME AT TEN O'CLOCK TONIGHT. TAKE THEM AWAY UNTIL THEN!
WHAT ABOUT THIS THING?
PUT HIM IN THEIR BOBSLEDDER AND CAST IT ADRIFT.
GRRRR
LATER, ON BOARD THE BOBSLEDDER...
--AND HE WANTS THEM FOR HIS PRIVATE ROCK AND ROLL BAND? DOES HE REALIZE WHO HE'S DEALING WITH?
SET COORDINATES, KOWALSKI! --HEMISPHERIC PLAIN--ZERO ZERO POINT NINE FOUR. ATTITUDINAL PLAIN--BIAS FOUR FORTY POINT SIX.
THE BOBSLEDDER RACES TOWARD KANDOR JASPERIAN'S SPACE CITY.
THIS IS THE WEIRDEST GIG I EVER PLAYED.
COOL IT, OR OUR ROCK AND ROLL DAYS ARE NUMBERED!
I AM READY! LET THE ROCK CONCERT BEGIN!
YOU'RE RIGHT. THIS IS WEIRD! ONE--TWO--THREE--FOUR!
TELL YA WHAT, BABY SAY YA WANNA BE FREE OKAY, BIG DADDY THAT'S ALRIGHT WITH ME YOU GOT IT!
SAVE ME-- YOU DO IT EVERY TIME WE MEET SAVE ME TREAT ME LIKE DIRT BENEATH YOUR FEET
3
INSIDE THE BOBSLEDDER...
HOW DO I KNOW WE'LL FIND THEM? LISTEN FOR THEIR MUSIC, I SUPPOSE.
WHOA-OH-YEAH DO YOU KNOW HOW I FEEL? WHOA-OH-YEAH
KOWALSKI LISTENS FOR THE ASTRALS' MUSIC AS THEY HOVER ABOVE THE SURFACE OF JASPERIAN'S SPACE CITY...
WHOA-OH-YEAH DO IT LIKE IT REAL COOL! WHOA-OH YEAH!
HEAR ANYTHING YET?
MICRO NAVIGATES THE BOBSLEDDER THROUGH THE NARROW DUCTWORK OF THE SPACE CITY, FOLLOWING THE ASTRALS' MUSIC. THE BOBSLEDDER SUDDENLY BURSTS THROUGH AN AIR VENT --INTO KANDOR JASPERIAN'S THRONE ROOM...
THEY'RE GETTING AWAY!!
YOU CAN'T DO THIS TO ME! I AM KANDOR JASPERIAN!
YOU GUYS SAVED US!
HOW DID YOU DO IT?
QUITE SIMPLE-- WE FOLLOWED THE SOUND OF YOUR MUSIC.
SAVED--BY THE POWER OF ROCK AND ROLL!
THE END

FRANKY 'N JACKY ('N ME)

by Len Callo

Like many of you reading this mag, I grew up reading the work of Jack Kirby. I was about 7 years old when I was reading the adventures of the Fantastic Four and the Silver Surfer in *FF* #72 and beyond. Of course, at that age, I had no idea who Jack Kirby was. I only knew Reed, Sue, Ben, and Johnny. I knew the Hulk, Thor, Captain America, and Spider-Man. I didn't know or even care that there was an actual human being that "created" these characters. To me they weren't characters. They were real. They were my heroes.

By the age of 12 or 13 I became "too cool" to be reading comic books. That was kid stuff. I wouldn't be caught dead reading that kiddie krud. So, I threw all my comic books out and got into Rock 'n Roll! Man, that was "where it's at!"

As I explored and experienced various musical artists, I came upon one who was different than the rest. He wrote about things most never dared talk about, let alone sing about. He was blunt, brutally honest, and had a bizarre sense of humor. The more I heard of his music, the more fascinated I became. His name was Frank Zappa.

By the age of 16 or 17 I was scouring used record stores and flea markets looking for then-nearly impossible-to-find "out of print" Zappa records. By my mid 20s I had (and still have) well over 100 Zappa albums. I went to every Zappa concert I could. I began corresponding with people all over the world and trading bootleg concert tapes. I was lucky enough to meet Frank several times during various events. In fact, I used to write concert reviews and articles for a Zappa fan magazine not unlike the Kirby mag you're now holding.

It was about this time, in my late 20s, that I rediscovered comics. At first, I suppose it was to relive my childhood. I would see an old comic and say, "Oh! I remember that one! I had that when I was a kid."

As I began picking up these old comics I noticed that nearly all of them had the same man's name on them: Jack Kirby. As my comics collection grew, so did my admiration for Kirby. I now had a second hobby (obsession): following and collecting the work of Jack Kirby.

What an odd pair of people to admire: Zappa, who often wrote of the dirty underside of life; and Kirby, who wrote of everything heroic, noble, and wholesome. They were two men seemingly at opposite ends of the spectrum. Yet one thing they had in common was that they were totally honest. They were honest to themselves and honest to their art.

At a local comics shop I found a copy of *FF* #72 ("I had that when I was a kid!"). I took it home and started reading it, and there in the very center of the book was a full-page ad for Frank Zappa and the Mothers of Invention's second album (1967). My jaw hit the floor. Was Zappa a Kirby fan?!

Soon thereafter I saw an ad for a convention in L.A. where Jack Kirby was appearing. It was there that I first met Jack and bought my first piece of original Kirby art. Soon after that, a friend and I were invited to Jack's house.

And so it was, now at the age of 30, I was visiting the home of the man who created all my childhood heroes. It was a dream come true, a guided tour by the King himself. Anything you ever heard about Jack being a nice guy was a lie!

He was *the* nicest guy you could ever imagine. He may have been the sweetest, most sincere man I had ever met. It was only the second time we had met and he treated us like we were family. "Anytime you guys wanna go fer a swim, just come on up. It's an invite!" he exclaimed. He was dead serious.

He wandered through his halls and rooms with us following behind like wide-eyed puppy dogs. I can barely remember bits and pieces of stories he told about "this character" or "that piece of art." We walked by a splash of Fin Fang Foom: "Hey Jack,why does Fin Fang Foom have shorts on?" I asked playfully. We all looked at each other and tried unsuccessfully to hold in the laughter. "Well..." he replied coyly, "...we were modest in those days."

The last stop of the tour was his drawing room. That's where I saw *it* for the first time. Hanging on the wall, just to the left of his drawing board, was a framed photograph of Jack and Frank Zappa with their arms wrapped around each other

My eyes widened. My jaw dropped. I was staggered. I turned to Jack and asked a brilliant question. "You... know Frank Zappa?" Without a moment's hesitation Jack replied, "Oh, Frank's a wonderful guy. We went over to his house for dinner. He played us some of his music." "What did you think of it?" I had to know. "Well, he's a very talented man," Jack retorted.

My imagination ran wild thinking of Kirby and Zappa sitting down and breaking bread together. Our conversation went on to something else, and it wasn't till later that I thought of all the questions I would have liked to ask about that meeting.

I saw Jack many times after that but I never had the chance to bring it up again. It seemed such an insignificant part of the life of the man who, almost single-handedly (pun intended), made comics part of our American heritage.

In December of '93 Frank Zappa died of cancer. Less than 2 months later, Jack, too, was gone.

What a cruel twist of fate to – almost simultaneously – lose the two men that meant the most to me artistically. Both were part of my life for most of my life. I will live the rest of my life with my walls filled with the art of Jack Kirby, and the air filled with the music of Frank Zappa. They gave me (and continue to give me) countless hours of pleasure in many ways. I grew up with them. I learned from them. I laughed with them. They entertained me. They enlightened me.

They were my heroes. ❍

After meeting each other, Frank Zappa suggested to Jack that he create a comic strip based on Frank's song Valley Girl. *Maybe it's good this is as far as it got!*

Surf Hunter, *a 1950s strip idea likely inspired by the television show* Sea Hunt. *Shown here are two unpublished dailies (one inked by Wally Wood).*

Red Hot Rowe, *a 1940s strip idea about Justin Rowe, Private Eye. This brings to mind "Red-Hot" Blaze, who narrated some of the* Clue Comics *stories.*

S&K's Flying Fool

by Lou Mougin

One of the best strips to run in the *Airboy Comics* of the Golden Age was "The Flying Fool" in its Simon and Kirby incarnation. Joe and Jack worked extensively for Hillman Comics in the late Forties on crime, romance, and even funny-animal books, but this neat and short- lived little effort is my favorite of their Hillman work.

Link Thorne, a.k.a. The Flying Fool, debuted in *Airboy* Vol. 3 #8 (Sept. 1946). He was a troubleshooting pilot in the *Wings Comics* tradition, but he had little to distinguish him from much of the high-flying competition. After three unremarkable exploits drawn by Frank Giacoia, the Fool was shelved. Editor Ed Cronin must have asked Joe and Jack to do something with the strip after its initial crash. So, after a three-month hiatus, S&K rolled The Flying Fool out of the hangar again. This time, Link Thorne won his wings with gusto!

The first splash of Kirby's initial Flying Fool strip showed Link on a stepladder, painting the logo for the strip on a sign, with a note below it: "Will fly anything, anywhere, anytime – if it's worth my time –" He was facing a red twin-prop plane and surrounded by some curious Chinese. S&K had set his adventures in the Orient, and it made for a colorful, Caniffesque background.

It also provided him with one of his most winsome supporting characters: Wing Ding, Link's longsuffering Chinese secretary and Girl Friday. Wing, sheathed in silk, was pounding a typewriter when three tough guys walked into Thorne's office. The tallest of the three told Wing that they had come to offer Thorne "a golden opportunity!"

At that point, Link appeared and put in his two cents' worth: "Okay! I'll go for a golden opportunity... if there's enough gold in it!" Thorne, in jodhpurs and jacket, was told by his visitors that the new job would require working for Riot O'Hara. Since Riot was a competitor, he turned them down flatly. The hard guys came up with a solution: Riot would take over Thorne's outfit, and Thorne would be on her payroll. And Thorne gave out with a big grin.

At that point, Wing Ding reached up and grabbed a surplus US Army helmet and ducked behind her desk, lamenting, "Oh, poorly paid me!" A second later, one of the toughs was sent flying backwards right over her desk. Thorne took care of the other two with some knee action. The first hood, recovering, pulled a gun on Link. Wing Ding let fly with her helmet and tagged the baddie on the noggin. "Oh, Mister Thorne! This is most unfortunate occurrence!" moaned Wing Ding, looking upon the three fallen gangsters. "Office now resembles morgue!"

After thanking Wing, Thorne muttered, "I've got an appointment with Riot O'Hara!" After buzzing one of the planes at her private airport, the Flying Fool landed, made his way to O'Hara's office, and just avoided getting hit by an unlucky customer who came flying through the glass portion of the door. Thorne wasn't lucky enough to dodge O'Hara's next punch, delivered with brass knucks. When he woke up in the office, he was faced by a ravishing redhead. "That clout was a mistake, Thorne!" she apologized. "It was meant for an incompetent dolt I'd tossed out of my office! I'm Riot O'Hara!" Riot, who lived up to her name, was obviously based on Maureen O'Hara. She gave Link a chance to sign over his airline "before I break you!" Link drew a big X over the entire paper, and dared her to do her worst. She threw him out, and promised to do just that.

The rest of the story detailed how Riot's rather wimpish aide, Johnny Blair (whose name was probably taken from the "Johnny Blair in the Air" strip from *Captain Midnight*), conked Riot over the head during a flight to show he could pilot her plane, found out he couldn't, crashed it on a mountain, and necessitated Thorne coming to save his rival. After making a risky mountaintop landing, Thorne rescued Riot and took off with her in his plane. "I don't see how you can miss, Thorne!" said Riot, in an uncharacteristically gentle mood. "I hate to say this... but you're a good pilot!"

"I wonder if that build up is another approach to getting my airline?" asked Thorne, steering his plane as Riot laid her head on his shoulder. "Or aren't you as tough as you pretend to be?" Fat chance, Link. Riot was tough... but she had a soft spot for the Flying Fool.

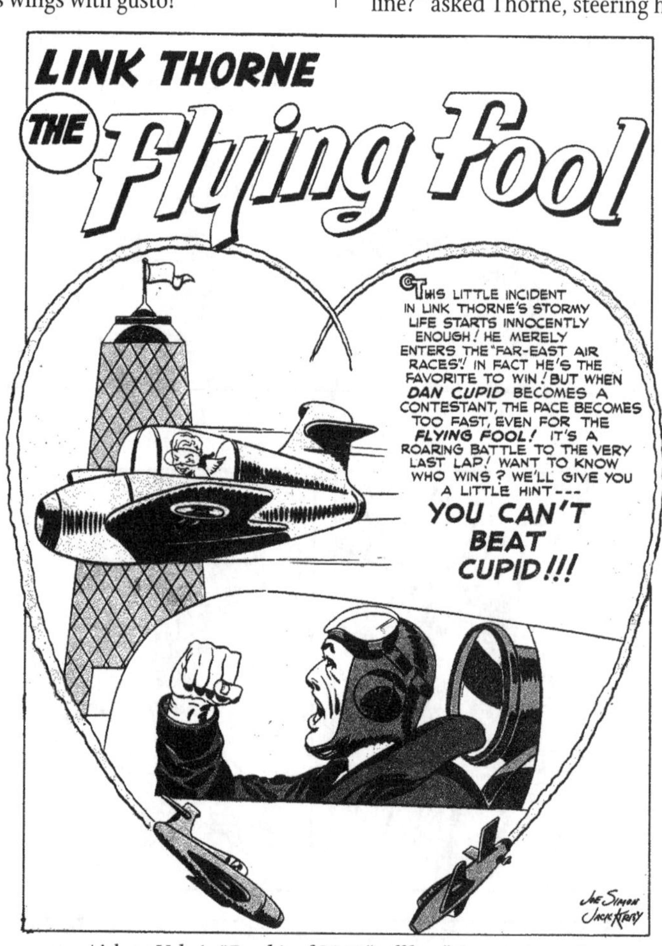

Airboy *Vol. 4, #7; a bit of S&K "tuff love" (see next page).*

Simon and Kirby piloted the Flying Fool through seven hard-knuckled outings (*Airboy Comics* Vol. 4, #5-11). The stories were laced with tough-guy heroics, airborne adventure, humor, romance, and a little pathos. They were impeccably paced, and made the other strips in the book almost standstills by comparison. One funny outing appeared in Vol. 4 #8, when Link encountered an Amish aircraft inventor. Aaron Grumm was taught by his hulking big brother Mordecai that flying was a sin, but he risked eternal punishment (or so he thought) by designing a hot new plane and giving it to Thorne. Mordecai appeared, cold-cocked Thorne, and dragged his brother back to their dairy farm... but not before he smashed up the plane with his bare hands. Inevitably, Link had a follow-up encounter with Mordecai, and knocked him flat. The Amish bully picked himself up and admitted, "You are the first man with enough courage to smite me, Link Thorne... I admire your courage!" In tribute, Mordecai allowed Aaron to continue with his airplane-building, and sent Thorne a big crate with a cow inside, which slurped him in the last panel.

But the most memorable of the Flying Fool stories has to be "The Face In the Storm" (*Airboy Comics* Vol. 4, #10, Nov. '47). It opened with a fascinating splash of Thorne in a plane, beholding the face of a beautiful woman in a thundercloud. A quote from Lord Byron compared a stormy night to the light in a woman's eye. After this intro, we fade into another stormy night, with Wing Ding and Link looking out their office window. When Link commented, "A storm in China can reveal many things to a man," Wing smiled and commented, "When Flying Fool cannot fly, he tell ghost stories, is so? Is perfect set-up, o' handsome employer! Outside, howling, noisy storm! Inside, lights are low! Wing Ding foresees next cue! So, give out, o' grounded eagle! Wing Ding paid to listen!"

Link's spots a friendly rival while waiting to meet his little sister Carol at an air race.

Link discovers Carol has grown up since he last saw her twenty years ago!

Naturally, Digger falls for Carol, and asks her to marry him.

So, lighting his pipe, Link Thorne related a story which he admitted he wasn't sure that he believed himself. "I remember that night in '43 – a flight of Jap Zeroes caught us on the Bombay-Kunming run – and I nosed the C-47 into an electrical storm as a dodge! Satan was on a spree that night! Beyond the storm, his grinning, yellow demons waited for us with loaded guns – while in the roaring darkness around us he battered us with thunderbolts!" The plane took a direct hit from the lightning. Thorne, semi-conscious, was shoved out the door to comparative safety by his co-pilot, who went down with the disabled craft.

Thorne awoke the next day, injured and unable to rise from the ground, surrounded by a group of curious onlookers in medieval dress. "Will one of you birds stop gaping and get a medic," gasped Thorne. "The pain is killing me –" A husky fellow in a green tunic picked up Link and carried him to a village nearby, and into a stone castle which, said Link, came straight out of the Middle Ages. There he met a beautiful black-haired woman named Auralie, dressed in ancient fashion, who spoke with a King Jamesian inflection ("Thou must rest. I'll give thee something to bring thee sleep –"), bandaged his wounds, splinted his broken leg, and saw to his recovery.

Carol is hesitant because of the danger of Digger's career, so he makes her a bet.

Digger's obsession with winning causes Link to crash! (He survives, though.)

Digger is all torn up about almost losing his friend, and lets Carol off the hook.

Of course, there was more to it than that. Their relationship progressed to the point that, one month later, a healing Link impulsively took Auralie in his arms and kissed her passionately. Breaking the kiss, she drew back. When Link admitted that he loved her, Auralie fled, and a barrier of fire appeared in the doorway through which she exited. Link attempted to follow, but the castle fell apart around him, and he was knocked unconscious by debris.

This time, Link awoke in a modern Army Air Force hospital, screaming, "Auralie! What happened to Auralie? Tell me! Tell me!" It took six soldiers to wrestle him back into bed, and three days' worth of sedation to calm him down. At the end of that, he was handed over to a new doctor, one Major Winters... a lady with a very familiar face.

"Auralie! Auralie, you're safe!" shouted a grateful Link Thorne – but the lady doctor assured Link that she had never seen him before. Still, Auralie was "an old family name" of hers, she admitted. Link slowly and regretfully came to the conclusion that Auralie was lost to him, probably forever, and, with a sigh, assured the doctor he would cooperate in her treatment plan for him.

"There it is, Wing Ding," finished Link, puffing on his pipe. "The mystery of Auralie – Perhaps the answer lies in the storm out there! – Maybe someday..." The Chinese girl sat straight-backed in her chair, making no reply. Link looked out the window again. "Looks like the weather's clearing up! Have my plane checked! I'm taking the Himalayan run as soon as I finish this smoke –"

Behind him, and unseen by him, Wing Ding wiped tears from her eyes. "Wing Ding attends to it at once, Link Thorne," she answered.

It was a story most Golden Age writers would have probably given one of their thumbs to have equalled. For Simon & Kirby, it was one more triumph out of many.

Jack and Joe wound up their Flying Fool tenure in the next issue with "Peril Paradise," about an island run by a lady pirate who offered her guests such fast-living pleasure that they literally burned away years of their life in a few weeks. Then they handed the strip to other capable hands, who took what they had given them and made the Flying Fool run another two years. Simon & Kirby had given Hillman what they gave so many others throughout their lives... a solid foundation to build on.

And they'd given us seven top-notch stories of The Flying Fool, to boot. ❍

Carol marries the big lug anyway.

Meanwhile, Link – stuck in the hospital – swears off love... for about two seconds!

KING OF THE WEST

by Tony Seybert

In the late 1950s, Jack Kirby created *Challengers Of The Unknown* for DC and *The Fly* for Archie Comics before returning to Marvel in 1959. As *Fantastic Four* did not appear until late 1961 and Jack did not create any lasting characters in this period, a harsh critic might be tempted to label this a barren time for Jack. Actually, Kirby was penciling hordes of great artwork for the company that was no longer Atlas and would again be Marvel; stories in every genre – horror, fantasy, war, romance, and westerns.

Many of the Marvel western heroes enjoyed great popularity and longevity, with several of the titles lasting well into the 1970s. Kirby was providing dynamic covers and amazing adventure tales, ensuring his place among the greats of the comic book western artists.

Rawhide Kid, dormant since the infamous Atlas Implosion of 1957, was resurrected and drawn by Kirby, resuming its old numbering with #17 in 1960. He was the primary artist on *Rawhide Kid* for several years as he contributed covers to all the western titles and drew numerous 5- or 6-page stories for *Gunsmoke Western Two-Gun Kid,* and *Kid Colt, Outlaw.*

There is very little blood, if any, in these stories. The Comics Code was still in force and the rampant violence of some of the early '50s westerns was almost eliminated. There were many fistfights and moral tales and desert pursuits. If there was a gunfight, the hero would shoot the weapon out of the bad guy's hands. It was wholesome entertainment for the Eisenhower years.

In *Rawhide Kid* #27's "The Man Who Caught The Kid," Rawhide is pursued through the desert by a very determined Sheriff and his posse. The Kid tries to escape on his faithful steed Nightwind, but the kind-hearted Rawhide Kid forfeits his chance to get away when he stops to prevent one mean hombre from beating a horse. The posse catches up, but the Sheriff lets him go, unwilling to believe the kid's reputation after witnessing this heartwarming scene.

"The Girl, the Gunman, and the Apaches" from the same issue is another story set in the desert, as the Rawhide Kid helps a family in a covered wagon escape from hostile Indians. The grizzled old wagon driver has a young son and a pretty, blonde daughter. She develops a crush on the handsome red-headed Rawhide Kid. They reach safety after a long, hard ride and a running shooting match with the Apaches, and the kid rides off. He's fallen in love with the girl but he thinks she'd never take a second look at an owlhoot like himself. She watches him ride into the distance and ponders how she could have thought the Rawhide Kid, with his exciting life, could ever love an ordinary girl. How tragic!

Kirby's Rawhide Kid may be short, but he's scrappy! The scenes in the desert are distinguished by mountains of sandstone, sagebrush, and cacti, illustrated by Kirby and Ayers. Nightwind and the other Kirby horses are magnificent, animated steeds. The cowboys are rough and unshaven and ready for a rumble. "The Girl, the Gunman, and the Apaches" is packed with the covered wagon, the driver, the pretty daughter, the wide-eyed preadolescent son, attacking Apaches, a knife-battle, and a buffalo stampede – and it's only six pages long!

Jack Kirby seldom drew the stories of the other western heroes, notably *Two-Gun Kid* and *Kid Colt, Outlaw,* but he did draw many of the covers, usually inked by Dick Ayers. He also drew the covers for *Gunsmoke Western,* Marvel's western anthology series in the late '50s and early '60s.

Many of the stories of this period did not feature continuing characters. It was a custom of the period for each book to feature one or two stories with the star and one or two stories about the Old West with a one-shot cast. For example, *Two-Gun Kid* #57 (Dec. 1960)

Original art to Rawhide Kid *#18, page 2 (Oct. 1960). Jack's handwritten word balloon (in pencil) is visible in panel one, indicating the likelihood of some uncredited Kirby scripting on this story.*

displays a pair of adventures of the Two-Gun Kid (art by John Severin) and a Kirby/Ayers story entitled "He Wore A Tin Star." In it, Ben Carter is sworn in as the newly-elected Sheriff of Dade City. He enforces the law strenuously and brings order to the town, but there is some grumbling among the citizens that the new Sheriff is too hard on them. Gunslinger and gambler Blackjack Bart gets the drop on the new Sheriff, confident that no one will help the unpopular Carter. The Sheriff risks his life to stop the villain, but he is saved by the grateful townspeople who realize that Ben Carter is a brave man and a good Sheriff.

The story is simple, but it has the power of all of Kirby's work. Ben Carter is a powerful, big-shouldered hero, almost a prototypical Ben Grimm. The townspeople are the regular bunch of Kirby's well-drawn stock characters. The white-haired Mayor slouches around in a top hat and offers advice to the Sheriff. One excellent sequence has the Sheriff hurling his lasso over a fellow riding his horse recklessly. The horse almost gallops off the page – a magnificent Kirby equine creation.

Gunsmoke Wester #64 (May 1961) features another Kirby story with a familiar title, "He Wore A Tin Star." This one is about a young hombre who belongs to a gang that's planning to rob a bank. The leader of the outlaw band persuades the young man, Joe, to become a Deputy under false pretenses and neutralize the Sheriff when the time comes. The plan doesn't work as Joe finds his conscience during his tenure as Deputy; by putting on the tin star, he has become a tool of the law. Again, the rather predictable tale is enlivened by the Kirby/Ayers art.

"The Betrayer" in *Gunsmoke Western* #69 (March 1962) is the story of Jeb Hart, a young man who joins his uncle's band of outlaws. When someone gets hurt during a crime, Jeb experiences a change of heart and turns himself in along with his uncle and the rest of the gang. "The Life And Death Of Ape Cantrell!" is a story of redemption from *GW* #71 (July 1962). Ape Cantrell is a big, brutish man who is hounded and jeered at and beaten up by the people of the town of Aces Wild, Texas. He practices with a pistol until he can whip anyone in the county and decides to become a ruthless gunfighter. Ape rescues a woman who falls in love with him for his bravery, despite his savage, loutish looks. He settles down with her on a farm and packs his guns away.

Both stories are simple and predictable, but the Kirby art endows each with the same power he contributed to the monster comics or the super-hero books. The misunderstood Ape is a sympathetic character much like the Thing or the Hulk. All the townspeople and the patrons in the saloon are possessed of their own personalities and it's a joy for the reader to read Kirby's characters and see the stories in their faces.

I think my favorite Kirby western story is "Red-Beard's Raiders!" from *Gunsmoke Wester* #73 (Nov. 1962). Red-Beard is a huge, ornery owlhoot with furry, red whiskers. He looks like Odin. He thrashes anyone who questions his authority among his band of outlaws. All the local people fear him for his ruthless attacks on ranches and towns. Red-Beard leads his bandits as they fly down from the hills and attack a ranch house. The white-haired proprietor refuses to surrender and puts up quite a fight. He shoots the gun from Red-Beard's grip, knocks him from his horse, and beats the hell out of the bandit chieftain with his fists. Their leader humbled, Red-Beard's Raiders slink away and disappear into the hills. The old guy turns out to be the retired gunfighter, Wild Bill Hickock.

My favorite of the Marvel western heroes is Kid Colt, Outlaw. Kid Colt was on the run for taking the law into his own hands and avenging the murder of his father. (This took place before the Code, of course, and when the origin was retold in *Gunsmoke Western* #72, it happened off-panel.) Kid Colt was a romantic outcast and everyone, bad guys and lawmen alike, always assumed he was a bandit and a mean desperado because he was wanted for murder. (The other Marvel western heroes were on the run for similar misunderstandings.) Kirby seldom drew any *Kid Colt* stories, which is a shame because he drew Kid Colt dozens of times on the cover of his own magazine and the cover of *Gunsmoke Western.* These are great covers, though they may suffer a little if compared to the covers Kirby was producing for the monster comics and the super-hero books. Colt was a tall, blond kid in a white hat, bright red shirt, black-&-white vest, and blue jeans. Kirby's Kid Colt is an animated, wiry fighter, a colorful adventurer in conflict with outlaws and lawmen alike. Some of his foes were super-villains of the Old West, as Marvel tried to find a way to duplicate the popularity of their super-hero comics in the Westerns. (Kirby only drew these Western super-villains on the covers as he was too busy creating one super-hero after another to draw any of the interiors.)

As the Marvel super-heroes became more popular, Kirby drew fewer covers for the westerns until he finally left them behind entirely. Later, Kirby would look far into the future (*Kamandi*), deep into other dimensions (*New Gods*), and way into the remote past (*Devil Dinosaur*), but he would never again look into the recent past of the Old West for inspiration.

Unless you count Serifan. ❍

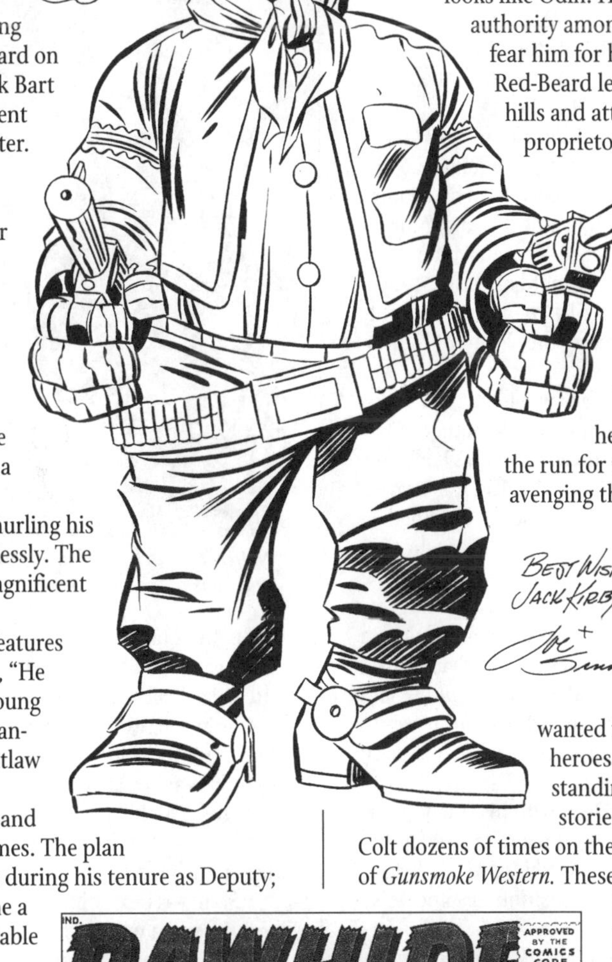

(left) Rawhide Kid *#17.*
(above) A fan drawing.

The King & The Kid!

An appreciation of Rawhide Kid, *by Jerry Boyd*

Sagebrush, snorting stallions, swaggering gunmen, cowering townsfolk, courageous lawmen, proud Indians, murderous outlaws, and a tragic young loner with nerves of steel and a draw faster than greased lightning... these all came together with the first Lee-Kirby effort on *Rawhide Kid* #17 (Aug. 1960).

Lee and Kirby had been out west before. Jack had done *Bullseye* and *Boys' Ranch* with Joe Simon and Lee and Kirby had done a good number of western yarns at Atlas, together and apart. Stan had edited, scripted and plotted stories for the original Rawhide Kid, a gunman more typical of that time's handling of the genre. That Rawhide Kid was tall, lean, and cut in the strong, silent-type mold of Gary Cooper and Joel McCrea. That kid was blond, frontier-hewn, and decked out in a buckskin-fringed shirt. He fit in well among the Clayton Moore- and Randolph Scott-type heroes of the '50s.

The '60s would be a new time. Stan and Jack would invigorate this "new" Rawhide Kid with nuances rarely seen previously in the genre.

Kirby took his successful Kid Gang formula from years back and gave this new creation a young, fresh-faced look. This Kid was drawn as a skinny teenager and at times a wide-eyed adolescent, horrified and repelled by the cold ruthlessness of the meaner gunmen who occupied the west.

But Jack also added a hawkeyed toughness to his character, showing an easy coolness that the little red-headed gunman could use to size up situations quickly and then attack or retreat. Perhaps Kirby had been impressed by James Dean's acting in the movie *Giant.* Dean's Jett Rink is a loner; a misunderstood hero/villain who is alternately kind, intimidating, charming, vulnerable, and anti-social. Rawhide is all of this and more.

One classic still from the film showed Dean with his cowboy hat pointed downward toward his nose and his feet up and crossed as he cooly sat in his employer's expensive car. One *Rawhide Kid* tale began and ended with him lounging in a very similar position in some noisy saloon (*RK* #31).

Kirby's character positioning and his brilliant use of panel design captures his young gunhawk's essence masterfully. The Kid is in a social gathering place – a noisy men's saloon – but he himself is quietly resting, with his head down and hat pulled over his eyes. His confidence in his gunslinging skills are subtly implied in that his arms are folded on his chest, away from his guns, while the other men's hands are close to theirs, even though their eyes and ears are open to sudden danger. Rawhide is a loner needing some social contact, but is tough enough for any type of trouble whether he is alert to it or not.

The Kid is small (5' 10", 155 lbs. according to a description in *RK* #18), but he's a coiled, two-fisted explosive who's more than a match for the hulking, unshaven, whiskey-guzzling bullies who try to manhandle him.

Kirby, ably inked by Dick Ayers, offered a gritty, unromantic view of the Old West. Prairie grasslands were wide and drawn with little linework. Townspeople were gossipy, fearful, and acted as a type of Greek chorus when trouble occurred. Indians, rattlers, and twisters leapt without warning

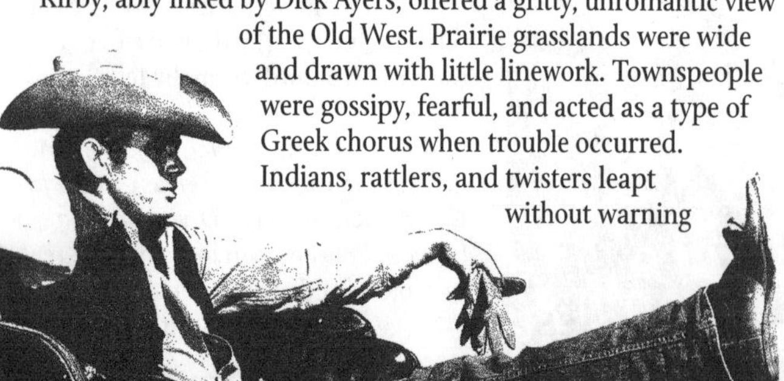

Notice how Jack positions the reclining Kid in the background, seemingly oblivious to the situation he'll soon enter. (below) James Dean in Giant.

into panels. Jack apparently had done some research. His characters often had the full, bushy mustaches, small stovepipe hats, derbies, and sugar-loaf sombreros true to that time.

Editor, writer, and Shakespeare fan Stan Lee put in a great deal of effort also. Rawhide, like Hamlet, is a good man thrown into a hostile situation when a close relative is betrayed and killed (in his case, his uncle Ben Bart). Like Hamlet, the Kid is dressed in mostly black attire. Also like Hamlet, he must avenge the murder though his life and reputation may forever be forfeit.

Stan was beginning to understand and use the appeal of the tragic hero; a person who sacrifices himself for the common good. (Silver Surfer's and Spider-Man's later characterizations would reflect this, among others.) Several stories presented situations in which Rawhide could've easily turned his back and ridden off. Instead, his sense of decency forces him to stay, exclaiming, "I reckon I sat thru all the bullyin' a man can take!" (*RK* #31) or something to that effect. Then the hard-fighting young firebrand twisted, punched, joked, and shot his way clear in some of Kirby's finest action sequences, in my opinion.

His being wanted as an outlaw for legal infractions, real and imagined, gave the Lee-Kirby team enough springboards from which to plot dilemmas for Rawhide. But the Kid (like Kid Colt) was no cold-blooded, gun-happy owlhoot like he was "painted up to be." Time after time, he confounded others with his selfless heroism and nobility. Stan would even have him disavow his guns and look forward to a day when he and other men wouldn't find them necessary. In this, he sent a fine message to those who found violent gunplay "cool."

The Rawhide Kid under the Lee-Kirby-Ayers team went from issues #17-32 (Feb. 1963). Under their handling, the spirit of the American Westerner, the rebelliousness of youth, and the "responsibility" of those with the "power to do good" was evoked. The stories were witty, sentimental, and action-filled.

Rawhide Kid #28 promoted two of Marvel's new mags, the *Fantastic Four* and the *Hulk.* Stan's writing and editing would take on a greater sophistication in the coming years and Jack' s co-plotting, inventiveness, and art would reach an incredible new pinnacle of excellence, but the fine storytelling they gave us out on the trail with *Rawhide* was and is an experience this fan will always cherish and never forget. ❍

Welcome To Dead Center!

The Western Saga of Bullseye, by R. J. Vitone

"When the legend becomes fact, print the legend!"
–from John Ford's The Man Who Shot Liberty Valance

Jack Kirby's vision of the Old West was as romanticized as his view of Suicide Slum from the Newsboy Legion strip. His imagination was fed by the flood of grind-'em-out "B" westerns that Hollywood relied on through the Thirties. In most, stalwart, jut-jawed heroes from Gene Autry to Roy Rogers to John Wayne galloped through endless dusty passes to head off hordes of less-than-noble redskins and assorted owlhoots. Showdowns at high noon climaxed with the roar of six-shooters. Often the honor of a comely damsel was at stake. It didn't matter. The guy in the white hat usually rode off with his trusty ol' hoss and a toothless Walter Brennan/Gabby Hayes sidekick at the end any-way. For the movie-hungry public, this was great entertainment. For Jack Kirby and a young generation of comic book creators, it was unforget-table imagery. When he became a comics pro, he drew on those images to enhance his work. Two of his first published strips were Westerns. *The Lone Rider* (a syndicated comic strip reprinted in *Famous Funnies*), and *Wilton Of The West* (reprinted in *Jumbo Comics*). While he and Joe Simon teamed in the early '40s to help develop the explosive super-hero market, Jack's western "reference library" was filed away.

When Jack and Joe formed their self-owned publishing house in 1954, a western was one of their first titles. *Bullseye, Western Scout* hit the stands with a cover date of August, 1954.

Simon & Kirby's company Mainline lasted only about a year, with its run of titles bridging the gap between the pre-code/code era. While they produced nothing dramatically new over this period, most of their books were as seminal to comics lore as any they had done before. In fact, over the lifespan of Mainline (Nov. '54 to Nov. '55), Jack and Joe would publish just about any comic genre you could think of. For Crestwood Publishing they did super-hero (*Fighting American*) and horror (*Black Magic*). For their own company they did war (*Foxhole*), love (*In Love*), crime (*Police Trap*), and western (*Bullseye*). They even found time to make a little comedy (*From Here To Insanity*) for Charlton. This would be an amazing display of versatility for *anybody*! For Jack and Joe, it was just business as usual.

And what a biz! Working out of studios in their respective homes and an office at Harvey Publishing, they assembled a crack team of revolving comics pros to crank out a steady stream of pages. It was the Ford "assembly line" concept on bristol board: Do it fast, do it right, do it well. Some were friends, or even friends of friends, but that didn't cut any slack. "We went through a lot of artists, " Jack said later. "There was a high turnover... most of them just could not do the work..." Joe Simon put it flatly: "If they didn't know what they were doing, they weren't working for us!" It's a delirious image: Jack hunched over his drawing board, smoke from his cigar billowing into the tiny room – a pause, and another penciled page (layout or finished) is tossed to a waiting artist or inker; Joe Simon on the phone, making deals as he points out details to a writer, letterer, or production assistant. Inked pages would be thrust back under Jack's nose, and he'd pick up a brush to "polish up" the product in order to maintain that famous S&K house look. Somehow, deadlines were met, and from this "controlled chaos," dozens of finished pages flowed to the waiting printers.

Bullseye rolled off of this frantic production line. Over its seven-issue run, at least three other artists would work on the title, but in the end, it was Jack Kirby who set the tone.

"HE NEVER MISSES!" promised the first issue's cover. In swift S&K fashion, the lead story introduced most of the elements that would form the basis for the entire series. The outpost town of Dead Center is wiped out by Yellow Snake and his renegades. Only grizzled old scout Deadeye Dick escapes with his infant grandson. Later, they return to the ravaged settlement and set up homesteading with Long Drink, a retired Sioux Indian scout. As the years pass, the boy learns the best of his guardian's frontier skills. He also earns the nickname Bullseye. (We never do learn his real name.) But Yellow Snake returns, and Deadeye dies in a treacherous ambush. A legend is born that day, as the enraged child battles the Indians to a standstill and scars Yellow Snake forever. In revenge, the chief brands Bullseye's chest with a target symbol, to show where his spear will one day claim the boy's life!

The second story starts where the first ends, as Bullseye and Long Drink mourn their lost friend. When Bullseye travels to nearby Long Horn Junction for supplies, he saves a timid wagon peddler from some town toughs. His magical gunplay silences the crowd, but the crooked town Mayor sees an oppor-tunity. He frames the youngster with crimes his own gang commits. The now masked and costumed youth becomes Bullseye, the outlaw. In time-tested comics tradition, he assumes the role of Panhandle Pete as a secret identity, using the now-departed

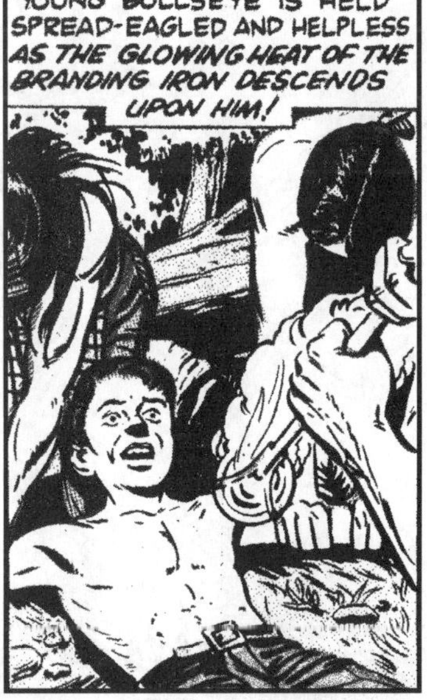

Despite some Kirby touches (left), Bullseye's origin in #1 was mostly drawn by other artists (right).

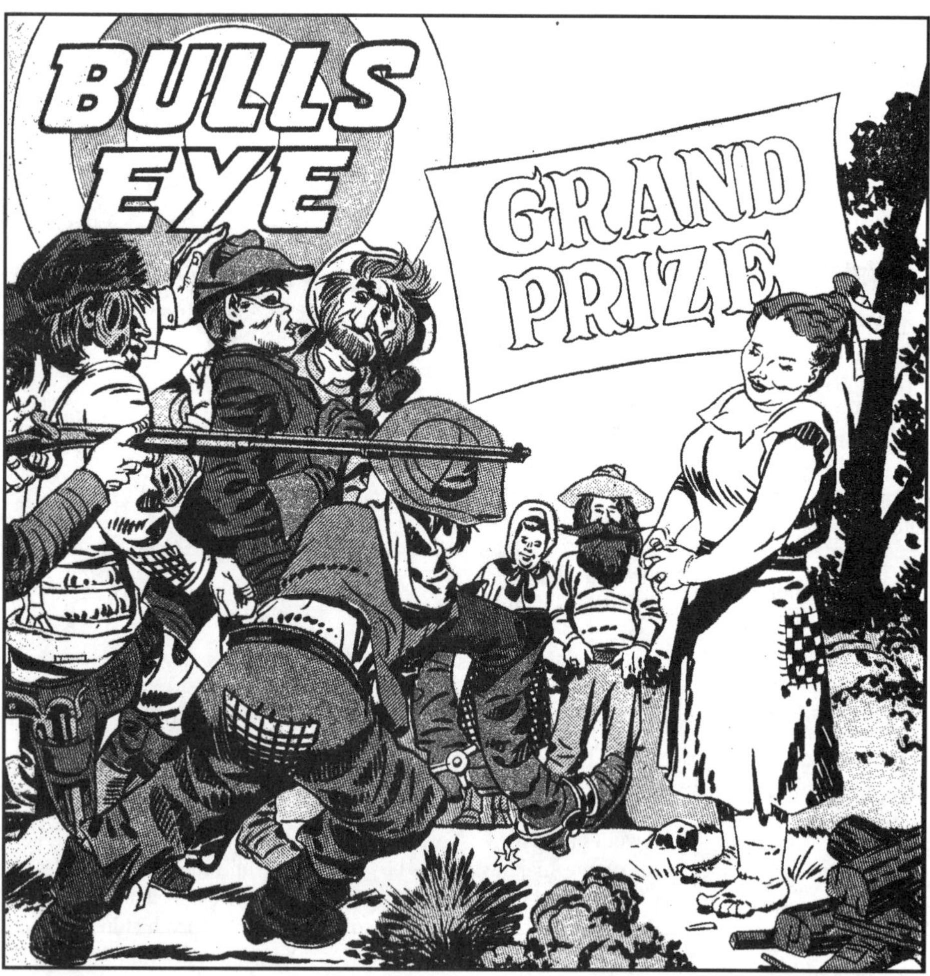

(above) Splash page from Bullseye *#2. This humorous story was the first one Kirby fully-penciled. (below) Splash from* Bullseye *#3.*

peddler's wagon as his base of operations. The issue comes full circle in the final story, as Bullseye encounters Yellow Snake and kills him during a cavalry ambush. Now respected by the army and feared by the red men, the new hero is ready for new adventures.

In most Kirby histories, *Bullseye* is either a footnote or just about ignored. Part of the reason for this may be the art in the first two issues. Jack's workload was heavy at this time, and his contributions to the premiere book are a first-rate cover, layouts for the origin story, then a great splash for story two, and another splash for story three. He may have had a hand in more, but the feel isn't there. While all the stories are well-written and rendered in adequate style by the S&K bullpen, there are few outstanding graphics to fire the reader's imagination. Issue two followed the same formula: An excellent Kirby cover promises more inside, but the promise falls short. The first two stories are stiff and rushed, with only a single Kirby splash panel to be seen. The final story, "Grand Prize," is literally another story. Not only does it veer off the beaten track of the semi-serious road traveled so far, it plunges right over a cliff! Bullseye stumbles into a shooting contest featuring odd characters right out of *Green Acres*. Names like Clovis, Dab Fuddley, Parson Pudgett, and the Beaglehorns populate the surreal scene, as everyone vies for a "grand prize." When he realizes that the hand of "beautiful" Lolly Beaglehorn is the prize, Bullseye throws the contest, then has to flee under a hail of angry hillfolk gunfire! If it sounds odd, it is! Drawn in a style similar to later *Fighting Americans*, this six-page story plays strictly for laughs, but it's pure Kirby, and the entire series takes off from this point.

Although issue three's cover shows Bullseye as the target of Indian torture, inside the tongue-in-cheek antics continue. "The Devil Bird" mixes prehistoric beasts and a crook's doomed greed for diamonds in a lost valley. "The Ghosts of Dead Center" pits Bullseye and Long Drink against a gang of land grabbers. Sight gags and swift action climax in a full-page nine-panel fist fight. Sure, there's pre-code violence (a "ghost" shot by a thug turns out to be a keg of TNT), but it's light-hearted and funny.

In the early '50s, *Boys' Ranch* had ridden the same trail. With a strong central character and an interesting "kid gang," that earlier strip offered Jack and Joe a wide range of themes to explore. The result was a series of stories that were multi-layered and engaging. *Bullseye* afforded a narrower field to develop dramatic stories around. Action, along with humor, took up some of the slack. (In the early '60s, Stan Lee would script *Kid Colt* and *Two-Gun Kid* strips drawn by Kirby, and he would employ a different "why me/not again" type of humor.) From wacky hillfolk, to the outrageous sight of the hero galloping along on a midget pony, to an irate Granny-lady thumping a horse with an umbrella, Jack found some unique ways to fill out the pages! *Bullseye* #4 continued the formula. "The Pinto People" and "Doom Town" feature classic Kirby action as well as more humor. Along for the ride is "Major Calamity," a cashiered Army officer considered bad luck by the townsfolk. When the town is raided, Bullseye has to battle giant "Big Red" Devlin to save it. When the matter is settled, Panhandle Pete gives the Major a lift out of town. (You know what has to happen!) The wheel falls off the wagon! Major Calamity earns his nickname.

The new Comics Code Seal of Approval appears on the cover of issue #5 (March/April 1955). It's hard to imagine now, but in 1955, the Comics Code Authority wielded real power. Original art from every story in every comic had to be previewed before printing. Changes in stories, art, and dialogue were outlined to the publishers. When the changes were made and gone over again, approval in the form of the CCA seal was granted. Bear in mind that even in a slow period for the comics industry, thousands of pages from hundreds of comics had to go through this time-consuming process! Issue #5's first story shows little tampering. It's a grim little tale of murder called "The Headhunter" that reads more like an Eisner *Spirit* story than a S&K product. Gunplay, fights, and mob confrontations show little code-dilution. But the next story, again, flies out the door! "Grandma Tomahawk" is "a scrappy old biddy" out to clean up her town. More Kirby touches make this a keeper. She busts windows, hits horses, smashes saloons, and (with Bullseye's help) blasts the pants off the owlhoots! The result? With the bad guys trounced, she turns on Bullseye and chases him out of town!

That ending was ironic, because that's just about what the Comics Code did to Mainline. Distribution problems (along with *many* ripple effects of the Code) forced Jack and Joe to virtually close up shop. Simon made a hasty arrangement with Charlton Comics to print and distribute Mainline's titles. *Bullseye* would end its run under the Charlton slug, along with Mainline orphans *Foxhole, Police Trap,* and *In Love.* The house that Simon & Kirby built, the one that should have been the crowning achievement of the team's long career, instead crumbled and fell to ruins.

The two issues that fill out the *Bullseye* run are the best of the series. Issue six features a long chapter-structured story of twin Indian chiefs: One (The Prophet), peaceful; the other (Scalp Taker), warlike. It's a filmic Kirby epic that features ambushes, raids, and some Code tampering. At one point, Bullseye battles Scalp Taker in a tomahawk match, but the Code has magically made the weapons disappear! A climactic Army/Indian battle may also have been edited clean out as well, replaced by a simple caption. The story turns full-circle and ends where it began, with the warlike brother forsaking his violent ways to take up his fallen twin's peaceful path. It's as satisfying an ending to a morality play as comics can present.

Bullseye #7 (Aug. '55) closes the series on a high note. "Duel in the Sky" mixes hostile Indians, a search for a gun-running Army deserter, and an all-out fist fight in an airborne hot-air balloon! The final *Bullseye* story, "The Stolen Rain God" opens with a terrific two-page Kirby spread. Against a backdrop of what looks to be Monument Valley, a thundering horde of war-painted braves ride to battle. The lone figure of Bullseye tries desperately to head them off. It's a visual *tour de force* that only Jack Kirby could produce, and even though the story that follows doesn't measure up to the splash, it's a solid enough entry to finish the saga of the man who "never misses." (There's a 4-page "Sheriff Shorty" filler by Kirby in issue seven, the only time he drew anything other than the title character.) Reprints of *Bullseye* stories later show up in Skywald's 1971 *Sundance Kid* #1 and #2, as well as in "odd-lot" publisher Super Comics' 1963 *Blazing Six-Guns* #12.

So *Bullseye* (and Mainline) rode off into the sunset. Falling sales, a shrinking market, and the demise of their publishing company was the beginning of the end of the Simon & Kirby team. What should have been a stretch of rewarding stability had turned instead into a tenuous period of professional uncertainty. Kirby faced the future as he always had – he picked up his pencil and went back to his drawing board! ❍

A virtuoso action page from Bullseye *#3.*

KIRBY'S WAR COMICS

by David Penalosa

One of the most pivotal events in Jack Kirby's life was World War II. For those of us who were born after the war, it's hard to imagine the profound impact this global conflict had on those boys – barely men – who had to travel off to foreign battlefields. World War II shaped an entire generation. The world would never be the same afterwards.

Rifleman Kirby of Company F set foot on the coast of Normandy about two months after D-Day. In late 1944, his unit was involved in a protracted battle near Bastogne, in which they took heavy casualties. Jack himself needed to be hospitalized for severe frostbite on both legs and lower feet. After recovering in a hospital in France, he was sent home in January, 1945. Jack spent the rest of his six months of duty at Camp Butner, North Carolina. On July 20, Private First Class Jack Kirby was honorably discharged with a Combat Infantry Badge and the European/African/Middle Eastern Theater Ribbon with one Bronze Battle Star.

Jack's war stories were famous. I never had the privilege of hearing them firsthand. What I know about the stories comes from what I've read and the few secondhand accounts that I've been told. From what I understand, his stories were gradually embellished over the years. It's easy to imagine the master of fantasy taking liberties with the re-telling of his life experiences. In a way, the type of war comics Jack did took on more of a fantasy quality as time went on. The gritty stories of the 1950s and early 1960 contrast considerably with the less-credible war stories of the 1960s and '70s.

I consider the first true Kirby war comic book to be *Foxhole* #1 (October 1954). This was his first cover depicting regular soldiers in combat. However, for historical perspective, it's worth mentioning the more fantastic war-oriented comics published while the Second World War raged. During that era, it was very common to see comics featuring the Nazis as villains. The Jack Kirby/Joe Simon team produced such stories even before the United States was officially in the conflict, *Captain America* being the most famous example.

The first Kirby series that starred soldiers of a sort was his collaboration with Simon, the *Boy Commandos.* Most people think kid gang comic rather than war comic when they think of *Boy Commandos.* The first issue had a cover date of Winter 1943. This comic has to be one of the most unrealistic war mags ever. After all, we're talking about children here, children who were an elite commando unit. As fantastic a fantasy as that was, it no doubt had great appeal to those pre-pubescent boys (a prime comic book audience, after all), who were too young to worry about being drafted into a real bloody war, but would have little trouble fantasizing about being boy commandos. *Boy Commandos* was a hit throughout America's involvement in the war. Today, the comic still retains an attractive charm in both its art and stories.

In the early '70s, DC reprinted quite a bit of Simon & Kirby's Golden Age work, including *Boy Commandos.* In 1973, DC released two *Boy Commandos* comics consisting of reprints. Perhaps DC will someday reprint these classics in hardcover form. More *BC* reprints can be found in issues of *Mister Miracle* #4-9.

In the mid-1950s, Simon & Kirby's own company Mainline produced books within a variety of non-super-hero genres, amongst them war stories. *Foxhole* was the label's war comic. *Foxhole* #1 has one of the most outstanding Kirby covers of all time. Unlike the more typical war comics which glorified war, *Foxhole* #1 depicts the suffering in the aftermath of battle. The text at the top reads: "You dig in – you fight and maybe you die! This is war as seen by the guys in the *Foxhole*." In the bottom lefthand corner, taking up a good third of the cover, is a soldier writing a letter home. His helmet is dented and most of his face is bandaged, with blood soaking through just below his ear. The wounded soldier's letter reads: "Dear Mom: The war is like a picnic! ...Today we spent A DAY AT THE BEACH!" In the background, we see the beach, which is a littered battlefield. There are two dead soldiers lying face down in the surf, a burning landing craft, another soldier advancing up the beach, and three medics attending a wounded soldier who is clearly in pain. After the bandaged soldier writing the letter, your eye is drawn to the suffering soldier being helped by the medics. The coloring on the cover of *Foxhole* #1 is superb. You can see an unused cover idea for *Foxhole* #1 in *The Art of Jack Kirby* and *The Jack Kirby Treasury* Vol. 2. It's a pencil drawing

Jack had the Losers meet George Patton; in WWII, Jack himself served in the General's army.

depicting a squad being mowed down by gunfire.

The second issue of *Foxhole* (December 1954), while having a more typical heroic-type cover, is very grim. The color scheme, done by Jack himself, is extremely dark: Indigo sky, red smoke, green soldiers and yellow earth. The scene involves American soldiers advancing on what appears to be dug-in Chinese positions. The center of the cover consists of a Chinese soldier standing up in a foxhole, seemingly surprised by an American, his hands up in the air, a sub-machine gun in his left hand. The American who has taken the Chinese by surprise is gritting his teeth and about to drive the bayonet on the end of his rifle through the skull of his opponent – gruesome stuff. The first three issues were pre-Comics Code, and the gritty nature of these books is reminiscent of the EC war comics of the same era. On the inside, *Foxhole* #2 has an outstanding two-page story of a bomber being shot down, called "Hot Box" (see *The Jack Kirby Treasury* Vol. 2.). The other story Jack drew was a six-pager entitled "Booby Trap."

The third issue of *Foxhole* features a soldier tramping through mud with a wounded or dead buddy carried on his shoulders. The original Kirby cover for *Foxhole* #4 was rejected by the Comics Code. Taking up most of that cover was a dead Japanese sniper, hanging upside-down, with his lifeless eyes staring open at the viewer. In the lower lefthand corner stands the marine who killed him.

From January 1956 to September 1958 (cover dates), Harvey's *Warfront* was graced by Jack's dramatic covers. Issue #28 (Jan. 1956) shows a bomber engulfed in flames, with one of its parachuting crew members taking up most of the cover. He's firing what looks like a cross between a carbine and a sub-machine gun at unseen enemy fighters. This would be a very unrealistic act for someone bailing out of a plane. *Warfront* #29 (Sept. 1957) shows a marine firing his tommy gun into a destroyed pillbox, killing the remaining survivors.

Jack's next stint with the war genre was Atlas' *Battle.* Not only did he do the covers for issues #64 (June 1959) through #70 (June 1960), Jack drew at least one story in each. In addition, the King's pencils were inked by such "Bullpen" artists as Steve Ditko and Joe Sinnott. The art from this run has the same quality as the pre-hero monster books of this era. The stories are concise little gems.

Marvel's *Sergeant Fury and his Howling Commandos* debuted in May 1963. I've heard a rumor that Stan Lee chose the name of this mag on a bet that he could turn any comic into a success. I guess it was a pretty silly name when you think about it. It's not hard to imagine that the cigar-chomping Sergeant Nick Fury was a creative rendition of Jack Kirby himself. Fury remains an important character in the Marvel universe.

By the time *Sgt. Fury* appeared, Marvel was well into the first phase of its new line of super-hero comics. The Marvel Age of Comics had begun. It's in this context that we can understand the far-out fantasy slant of *Sgt. Fury.* Sgt. Fury and his Howling Commandos were, in essence, Marvel super-heroes. Their adventures required the same suspension of logic that was required for the rest of Marvel's super-hero line. For instance, inside the first issue, we're treated to a scene where the Howlers are floating down to earth in parachutes while shooting down German planes with tommy guns. As a young boy, I had no problem accepting these type of scenes. After all, there were other examples of super-heroes like the *Avengers'* Hawkeye, who had plenty of skill, but no super-powers. One thing I always wondered about, though, was why Fury's t-shirt would be torn to shreds, while his men's shirts remained fairly intact.

Jack drew the stories for the first seven issues, and the covers for nearly all of the first twenty-five. As with nearly all of Jack's covers, the ones he drew for *Sgt. Fury* were spectacular! Of special note is the story in issue #3 which featured a cameo appearance by OSS Officer Reed Richards. Jack also drew the story for *Sgt. Fury* #13, entitled "Fighting Side by Side with Captain America and Bucky!" Here we see the Howlers where they belong, within the Marvel super-hero pantheon. This is an incredible issue with inks by Dick Ayers. The story begins with an envious Nick Fury watching news clips of Captain America and Bucky. Next, Fury's nemesis Sgt. Bull McGiveney is bullying private Steve Rogers in an English pub. Fury comes to Rogers' aid, and a riot then breaks out between the Howlers and McGiveney's men. Later, Cap, Bucky and the Howlers kick some Nazi butt in France. Both *Sgt. Fury* #3 and #13 are available in reprint form in *Marvel Special Edition* #5 and #11 respectively. You can find this obscure title in the bargain bins at comic book shops or conventions. Check them out!

An animation character design.

The stories in *Sgt. Fury* were full-book length, which means that they had a beginning, middle and end, leaving lots of room for the kind of action scenes Jack drew so well. These are classic Kirby/Lee books.

Jack's last stint in the war comic genre was the Losers (Captain Storm, Johnny Cloud, Gunner and Sarge), featured in DC's *Our Fighting Forces* (#151, Nov. 1974 – #162, Dec. 1975). According to *The Art of Jack Kirby,* some of the stories in this comic were the closest to Jack's own wartime experiences. I would love to hear from anybody that ever heard the stories which these yarns were based on.

The mid-Seventies were a period when Jack created far-out fantasy titles like his Fourth World, *Kamandi, Demon* and *OMAC.* It's interesting that he worked on a minor title like *Our Fighting Forces,* dealing with characters which he didn't create. Having said that, I do feel that Jack did a commendable job on the series. The Losers were drawn, written and edited by Jack, with most of the inking and lettering done by Mike Royer. It was pure Kirby. Like the Howlers, each member of the Losers had a distinctive hat or helmet which made the individual characters easily identifiable. The Losers series was almost as much in the far-out fantasy realm as *Sgt. Fury*; however, the Losers didn't beat odds nearly as overwhelming as the Howlers, and Jack's dialogue was far more down-to-Earth than the wise-cracking verbiage Stan Lee wrote a decade earlier in *Sgt. Fury.* Kirby's run of *Our Fighting Forces* is readily available and inexpensive. They're worth checking out. ❍

Pencils from another unused 1950s comic strip idea, Chip Hardy.

Kirby's Nightmare

An examination of Jack's unfinished novel The Horde, *by Sibley Carlyle*

Before he conjured up a Fantastic Four or dreamed of a big green ogre named the Hulk, Jack Kirby pondered the real world threats to humankind. "Humans are their own worst enemy," he once explained. "It's our nature to balance our ambition to build with our potential to destroy."

This preoccupation likely resulted out of his experiences serving in the US Army during World War II. Among the first wave of American soldiers to hit Omaha Beach in 1944, Kirby saw raw warfare at its worst. But the most lasting impressions came from witnessing the throngs of refugees that were swarming away from the battlefield and into newly-liberated cities. He saw them clogging the roads in endless lines of pained humanity. They slowed his unit's advancement, allowing him time to study their faces and fix an indelible image of the pain and powerlessness of their struggle.

Kirby commented in *The Art of Jack Kirby* (published in 1992), "It was quite a mess and I still remember parts of it like it was yesterday. It was a horrible, horrible thing to see."

Author and publisher Ray Wyman, Jr., recalls, "During our interviews I could tell that the memory of what he had seen still disturbed him deeply. Fifty years after returning from Europe and Jack was still dreaming about it. Roz told me that Jack would sometimes yell things in German in his sleep."

At the height of his career in the 1960s, Kirby rediscovered *En Masse* suffering resulting from the many new changes occurring in the world. Through television and publications he had read, Kirby became aware of exponential population growth throughout the world and the appalling living conditions in which most people were forced to live.

"He extrapolated from what occurred in pre-WWII Europe and his personal experiences there," says Wyman, "and rightfully speculated that somebody could come along and rally billions of starving and angry people into open revolt."

What Kirby envisioned was an unstoppable horde that would consume Asia and Europe – and even the Americas.

The first draft of a novel entitled *The Horde* was completed in October 1977. In it, Kirby foretells the end of all civilization on earth – not by nuclear fire, but at the hands of large, aimless mobs, "searching for nothing and seeking out anything that will burn." Essentially, his story is about the darkest kind of war. It tells of a crusade of hatred driven by the revenge of a single man and eventually leading to the collapse of the world's most populous country: The People's Republic of China. Ensuing riots and wanton destruction trigger the forced migration of hundreds of millions of Chinese over land and sea. As the chaos explodes into a human stampede, all armies and nations unfortunate enough to be in its path are consumed.

Kirby had a clear vision of what these people would be like. Their faces were among the thousands he watched numbly plodding past his jeep. Closing his eyes, he pictured them as one great herd of humans streaming out from the smoldering skeletons of burned-out cities.

Two years after completing the first draft, Kirby invited Janet Gluckman, then a publisher's agent, to help him edit and package his new project. But as the story took shape, world headlines convinced him that his story was no mere fairy tale. He was suddenly struck by the realization that it might actually occur. "It was a nightmare I couldn't escape," he admitted.

In 1982, Kirby took on various consulting jobs, and quit working on extra projects, including *The Horde.* Gluckman went on to write four short stories based on her earlier work with him, publishing them in various anthologies and magazines. Kirby later claimed that he stopped working on *The Horde* because the reality of the story had become too frightening. In essence, his own contemplation of this dark human calamity scared him into silence.

The manuscript was eventually shuffled into a closet and there it languished until Wyman discovered most of it during one of his forays into "the King's archives."

"I was instantly attracted to the story," Wyman recounts. "As Jack first described it to me, I was struck by its simplicity and relevance to historic trend. Something like this has happened before; it could happen again."

After completing *The Art of Jack Kirby,* Wyman showed Kirby new story treatments to bring *The Horde* back to life and give it a contemporary setting. Kirby responded enthusiastically, even if a bit reluctantly, and invited Wyman to continue working on it.

"We talked a lot about the story; what the main character, Tegujai Batir, was like and what the Horde might look like coming down the road," Wyman comments. "We got this picture of a tank commander on the border frontier of some unfortunate country, waiting for the Horde to come. When they do come, they are a rabble so large that they stretch for as far as the eye can see. Armed only with farm tools and clubs, this huge mass of people descend onto their position like locusts. The tank commander orders his unit to shoot. The bodies pile up, but more of them keep coming. Finally the tanks run out of ammunition, and all the soldiers, including the commander, are slaughtered; and then, the Horde marches on."

After Kirby died, Wyman felt compelled to pursue the work in earnest, if for no other reason than to fulfill Kirby's dream to publish the novel. But Wyman also wanted to show a side of the comic book legend that his fans rarely saw.

"At the core of this story is a fascinating blend of horror and reality: The tale of a mass of people becoming a monster, backed by conjecture that the affairs of this planet may have reached a point where it could happen. This is where Jack and I instantly connected."

Meanwhile, Wyman was pursuing other projects with writing partner Peter Burke, a music publisher and producer known for his work in pop and historic Hawaiian music. Wyman and Burke often shared story ideas and discussed writing problems in mutual as well as personal projects.

"I started telling Peter where I was getting stuck in my writing. He'd offer a suggestion or two, then more and more. Soon it became apparent he was helping me write it," says Wyman.

The two solidified a partnership on the project and signed a contract with the Kirby Estate late in 1996 to write a novel and script versions of the story for a Graphic Novel and film.

"Ray and I worked pretty well together in the past," comments Burke, "but this project really changed things. It has its own life; maybe it's Jack's spirit. Sometimes we feel as if Jack is still around, figuring out the problems with us and offering story twists. I'm glad I'm on his team."

"It also helps that Roz has given us creative autonomy," adds Wyman. "We couldn't do this if we had the family standing over our shoulders. We're using as much of Jack's original manuscript as possible – where it makes sense, and no more. That's my agreement with Jack, and we're holding to it."

"Is *The Horde* merely mythological apocalypse?" Kirby asks rhetorically.

In his original story outline, he explains, "Consideration is given to the present-day situation. This is not a science-fiction war. Its slogans, weapons and political posturing can easily stem from sources familiar to us all. At its heart are the great issues of our time. About its feet is the common understanding that periods of great change are inevitable."

In the end, Kirby wants us to realize that *The Horde* is not an event outside the margins of human behavior but, rather, is a part of the very fabric that makes us human. The over-arching question becomes: How factual does the imagination have to be before we begin taking the real threats seriously? How real must it be before we are all scared? ❍

NYPD BLACK & BLUE

by Robert L. Bryant Jr.

Sgt. Daniel Turpin doesn't eat quiche.

Or tofu. Or pasta. Or broccoli. When we first spot him in *New Gods* #5 (1971), "Terrible" Turpin has one fist wrapped around a steaming cup of java, and his other paw is shoving a sandwich down his gullet. The sandwich looks like maybe a quarter-pound of roast beef on rye: A cop's lunch, wolfed down at a cop's desk.

Turpin's tough. He looks like a gorilla whose DNA got crossed with J. Edgar Hoover's. Turpin's tough. He fought the Mob as a young cop. Turpin's tough. He wears derby hats and smokes Kirby cigars. Turpin's tough. His pinstriped suit is bright orange, and nobody laughs. Nobody... even... chuckles.

Turpin might have been little more than a bit player on the crowded stage of Jack Kirby's Fourth World series, just another bemused urbanite rubbernecking at a battle of gods. But one story – "The Death Wish of Terrible Turpin," in *New Gods* #8 (1972) – made the aging cop an unforgettable character. When the gods kick his ass, he kicks theirs right back.

"King Kong on a rooftop is no more dangerous than a nervous punk with a pistol!!" Turpin tells one of his men as they race toward a showdown with Kalibak. "The idea is to give as good as you get!!" Thirties movies, a Thirties mindset for this Metropolis cop about to retire.

Turpin corners his Kong on an apartment roof ("I've got some stuff that might stop this ape!") and works his way up the ladder of deadly force – machine guns, shock grenades, and finally, the world's biggest set of jumper cables, which zap Kalibak into dreamland. "I'm the law – understand?" says the brutalized sergeant, his face like hammered meat loaf. "No super 'muk-muks' are gonna use this town – as – a – fight arena!! ...This town – belongs – to – us – !"

And then, the tough guy swoons, just as all tough guys do when their job is done and their town is safe. Sweet dreams, Sarge. You're not forgotten. ❍

Bryant is a newspaper copy editor in Columbia, SC. He doesn't eat quiche, either.

The character designers for the Superman Adventures *animated series based the look of Sgt. Dan Turpin on Jack.*

FRANK MILLER INTERVIEW

by Jon B. Cooke

(One of the leading creators in mainstream comics, Frank Miller was outspoken in his support for Jack Kirby in the King's fight to get his art from Marvel Comics during the 1980s, and was given the honor of delivering a eulogy for Jack at the funeral. Miller's creative achievements are widely celebrated, from the revitalization of Daredevil, Ronin, *the radical updating of the Batman mythos in* The Dark Knight Returns, *and memorable collaborations with David Mazzuchelli (*Daredevil: Born Again, Batman: Year One*), Geof Darrow (*Hard Boiled, Big Guy*), and Bill Sienkiewicz (*Daredevil: Love & War, Elektra*). Frank has, since 1992, devoted much of his writing and drawing energies to the series* Sin City, *a crime comic published under the Legend imprint by Dark Horse. He was interviewed via telephone on April 25, 1997.)*

THE JACK KIRBY COLLECTOR: When did you first get exposed to Kirby's work?
FRANK MILLER: I first saw Kirby's stuff when I was probably about nine years old. I'd been reading comics since I was six, which was when I decided I wanted to do them. Then one day one of my brothers showed me *X-Men* and a Kirby *Fantastic Four,* and I entered a whole new dimension.

TJKC: So you really witnessed Kirby at his height in '65.
FRANK: Well, I place Kirby's height in the '70s. He had so many heights, it's like talking about the Alps! I remember seeing *Fantastic Four* and the *X-Men,* first through friends passing them around, and finally going out and haunting the drugstores myself – of course, back then, there weren't any comic book shops.

TJKC: So what were your favorite Kirby comics?
FRANK: Jeez, there were so many. I loved the general sense of weirdness and alienation in the *X-Men.* But I suspect that for me, the transforming stuff – the stuff that showed me that comics could go much further than I thought they could go – was everything from the Galactus Trilogy onward in the *Fantastic Four.*

Some of Frank's gritty, black-&-white crime work from Sin City.

TJKC: Did you follow his work over to DC?
FRANK: Oh, yes. As a matter of fact that was about the time I was losing interest in comics, and when I saw a cover of *Jimmy Olsen* by Jack Kirby, I said, "This I gotta see." For me, I have to say, the Fourth World stuff is my favorite.

TJKC: So you followed the Fourth World even as you were dropping other comics?
FRANK: Comics go through periods where they grow stale and then they get interesting again, and it seems that when they got interesting decade after decade was usually because Jack was around.

TJKC: Why were you losing interest in comics? General adolescence?
FRANK: There was always the discovery of girls. *(laughter)* Various social things like that, but also comics come and go as being interesting or not; fallow periods and very rich periods. In the '70s, what became interesting was when Neal Adams was taking off, with all his wild stuff – and when Jack came to DC.

TJKC: Were you disappointed with the books' cancellation? What was your reaction?
FRANK: Furious, but what could I do?

TJKC: Did you stick around for *Kamandi*?
FRANK: Oh, I stuck around for the works.

TJKC: To me, I see a Gil Kane influence in your figure work, and increasingly a lot of Eisner and Krigstein. But only with *Dark Knight Returns* do I see an overt Kirby influence. Did you think about Kirby at that time? What was his influence on your work?
FRANK: That's kind of like asking a musician if he's influenced by Beethoven. The work is so seminal that I think it affects everybody who has come along since. I think that *Sin City* owes more to Kirby than *Dark Knight* does because the use of shape is much bolder. But I can see what you mean, because the figure work was much more Kirbyesque in *Dark Knight* – so blocky and chunky. To me, he's just a constant influence – always has been. He had a rather manic, citizen-on-the-street view of what was going on with all these grand characters that brought an immediacy that really hadn't existed ever before. It's easy to talk about his explosive power because that's what people understand most about Kirby, but his virtues went far beyond that – into the concepts, into the various genre he either reflected or brought about himself; so many more subtle values he brought to storytelling. He had a way of drawing things wrong that looked so right. Reality didn't look right anymore. When you see a drawing by Jack Kirby of someone holding a pipe, it looks like the way someone should hold a pipe, even though it isn't a way someone holds a pipe! It's fascinating!

TJKC: Increasingly, you were looking at the work of Hugo Pratt and Alex Toth?
FRANK: Hugo Pratt, Vereccia, Muñoz, all kinds of folks – I love to drop names, it makes me sound really smart – and, of course, Eisner and Johnny Craig – my two huge, most abiding influences. I looked at everything I could get my hands on.

TJKC: When you first came to New York, you first sought the advice of Neal Adams?
FRANK: Neal ran almost a halfway house for comic book artists; an advertising studio where people would do commercial work. He would offer advice, counsel, instruction and work for people. Back then in the late '70s, it was very, very difficult to make a living doing comic books. The page rates were so low, there were no royalties, and it really was pretty dreary pay. Neal helped a lot of us get along by providing us with work that would pay better, even though it was less than creatively satisfying. He also was very generous of his time with me. I would come in every few months with another stack of pages, and he would tell me one more time to give up for all time because I had no prayer, and he would do the same thing again the next time!

TJKC: And yet you persisted and finally even moved to New York.
FRANK: Yeah. Well, it was either that or going back to driving trucks, which I wasn't very good at.

TJKC: Did you consider going to Joe Kubert's school?
FRANK: I've never been a good student. Sometimes I wish I had gone to art school and stuff, but I barely got out of high school. I was so eager to become a professional, so I had to learn on the job. It's been the only way to make a living.

TJKC: Jack pretty much drew what was asked of him for a number of years. If super-heroes sold, he drew super-heroes. If love comics were in order, well, he invented them. He did westerns, war, etc. You seem very enamored with crime stories. What keeps you in the crime genre?
FRANK: I have to answer that at two different directions at once, if you don't mind. First, I grew up reading crime stories, everything from Mickey Spillane to Raymond Chandler to Dashiell Hammett. It's always been my favorite kind of fiction. So naturally, I wanted to do comic books that were like that. I grew up not knowing the wealth of great crime comics that had been done in the past. But I loved comic books, and I loved crime stories, so the next logical thing was to do comic books about tough guys, beautiful women, and great cars. I got more encouraged when Warren Publications started re-releasing *The Spirit,* which I had never seen. This was just before I became a professional. They were just mind-expanding. The brilliance of that work is still staggering. Eisner's gone on to bigger and better things since, but still, even that young, he was producing stuff of extraordinary depth and quality. And as time passed, I got to study Johnny Craig and, in particular, his *Crime SuspenStories* for EC Comics. I became more and more convinced that crime comics were what I most wanted to do.

Jumping back in time, when I first showed up in the late '70s at Marvel Comics, DC, and Gold Key, I waltzed in, not having read any comic books in years, and showed them all my samples. My samples were all stuff like *Sin City,* and they all looked at me like I was completely insane because they didn't publish anything like that. A nineteen-year-old's arrogance. It took me a while before I got the freedom to do what I really wanted to do.

TJKC: You're from Vermont – the country – and yet you tell stories about dark, urban violence; this film noir kind of setting? Why?
FRANK: (laughter) You know the old phrase "Write what you know"? I don't entirely agree with it. I think you should write where your mind takes you. I can testify that I never shot anybody. I've been through some things but certainly not as extraordinary as my characters have been through. But I was always compelled by stories of the city where people are pressed close together, and tested by one another constantly. Someone else might want to do stories about something like, say, marriage, which is another case where people are packed together and tested by each other. Any romance story is essentially that. Different venues attract different people. I've always had a violent imagination and it's kind of like asking Stephen King why there are so many monsters in his stories. His answer is the perfect one: "That's the kind of stories I come up with." Also, I can now say, after living twenty years in the two biggest cities in the country: I know whereof I speak.

TJKC: You say that *Sin City* owes a lot to Kirby in its approach.
FRANK: You don't look into the eye of the sun and forget it. He really is the most profound genius to ever work in the field. There's Before Kirby and there's After Kirby, and the two eras are just not the same. Everyone since Kirby has had to absorb and interpret his work. He was that good. You mentioned Gil Kane earlier, whom I did study to beat the band. He helped me understand dynamic anatomy by his example. Gil has often remarked that much of what he did was to intellectualize and analyze Kirby, to take what Kirby had done – by seeming intuition or by divine gift, whatever it was – and turn it into something that

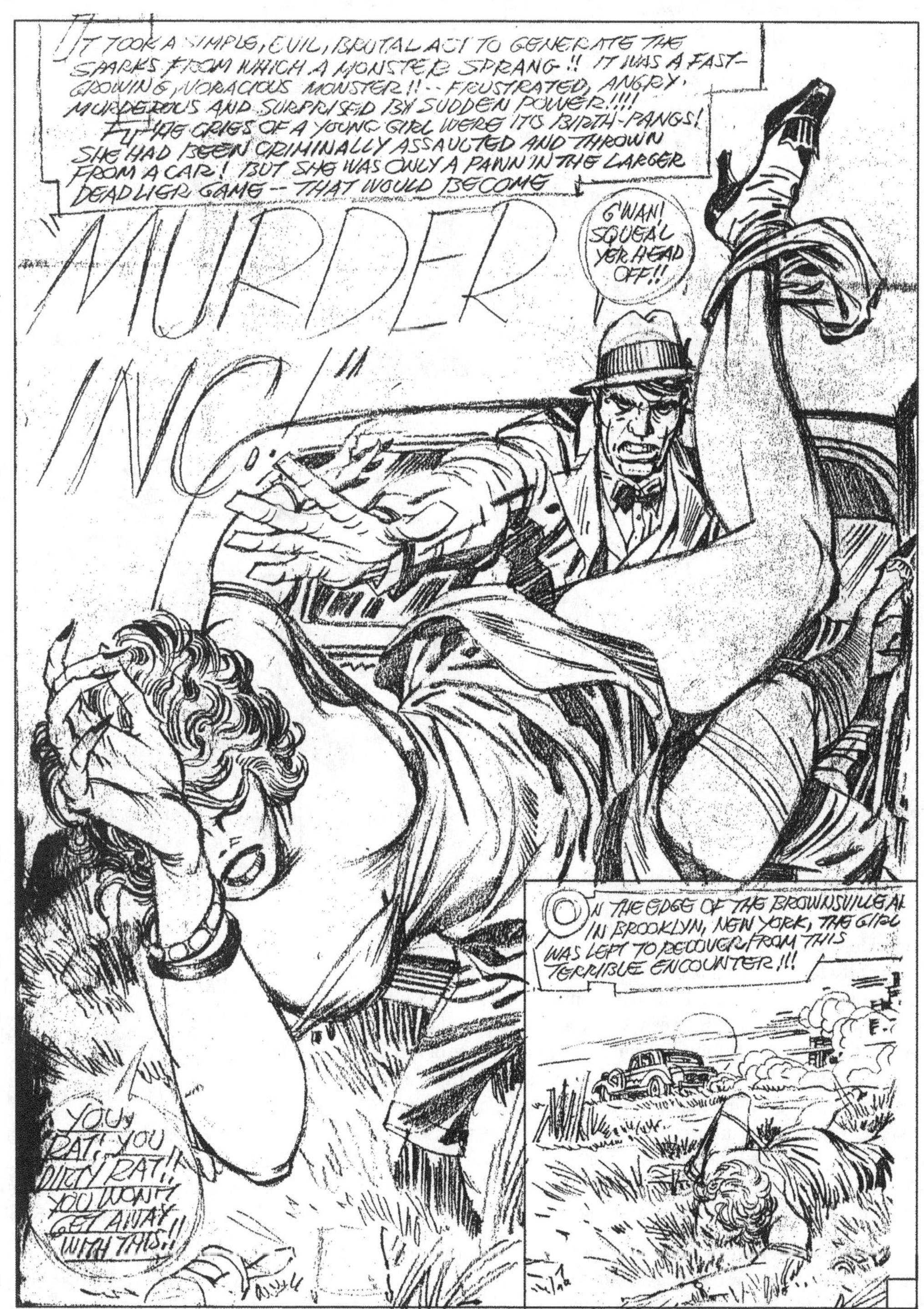

Jack's splash page from In The Days Of The Mob #2, *which Frank was kind enough to ink for this issue's cover.*

could be understood. Gil was a terrific source because he is such a clear thinker, such an analytical artist.

TJKC: You seem to have a continuing manga influence in your work.
FRANK: Now more than ever.

TJKC: Do you see yourself doing even more overt Japanese work?
FRANK: It's funny. I think of *Sin City* as being my most Japanese work, even though it has the least to do with content. Sure, I'll do samurai stories one of these days. Between American comics and Japanese comics, there's this enormous schism in terms of the use of time. American comics tend to have everything packed very tight, almost like a slide show or home movie – you want it to be over as quickly as possible. Whereas Japanese comics have a sprawling, undisciplined approach to time, as if they just won't let you leave the room! I like to mix the two; let time contract and expand. Manga is of great use for me for understanding the sense of letting the eye dwell on a moment.

TJKC: Some critics have perceived your work over the years as having a fascistic subtext. How do you respond to that?
FRANK: (laughter) I laugh a lot. To my mind, a fascist is someone who tells someone else how to think, and that's something I never do. I don't care who people vote for; I don't try to control people's minds a bit. That's one of the reasons I don't have a staff of assistants. I'm a very independent operator. My stories are morality plays, explorations of various subjects such as good and evil. I'm not a propagandist. These days everything is regarded as propaganda and reviewed as such. I've got no taste for propaganda and have no interest in doing it. I really think that anyone with half a mind who has read my stuff and thought that it was the work of a fascist really should go out and learn what fascism is. I also have to say that it's a word that's tossed around with abandon; it's insulting, it's offensive, it's like being called a rapist, and I take great offense at it.

TJKC: Like Woody Allen in that movie – when the aliens come down and say they like his earlier, funny stuff – does it get wearing sometimes when people say they wish you would return to super-heroes?
FRANK: (laughter) Well, no, I understand that. Maggie Thompson really said it beautifully: "The Golden Age of Comics is twelve." When you're twelve years old, and you see comics for the first time, comics are never quite magical again. The same dynamic exists with people who come to like the work of certain artists. Will Eisner is haunted by *The Spirit* fifty years later. I'm going to be honored by *Daredevil* forever, or for people who came out just a little later, by *Dark Knight.* And then there's people who think *Ronin* was the best thing. And all that I can allow myself to think is that is when they first gained affection for the work itself. And there's nothing like falling in love for the first time. But I've got to move on and go my own way. I've got to believe that what I'm doing now is the best work of my life or I won't be able to get up in the morning and do it. I understand how people can feel that way. I'm already getting mail from people saying the first *Sin City* was the best one, and that I should do nothing but stories about Marv. It just means that people are connecting, and I have to enjoy it for what it is.

TJKC: But you've previously said that you don't focus on the audience, but on what you want to do.
FRANK: There's some give and take with the audience, especially now that I'm doing my own stuff. It's always fun to have that give and take. But I can't take my cues from the audience because otherwise, why would I be here? I've got to be challenging my audience or I ought to be doing some other kind of work.

TJKC: When did you first meet Jack?
FRANK: At his seventieth birthday party in San Diego. We never really knew each other very well. I may have met him briefly at one other time, but it was in the midst of a crowd. We never had so much as a meal together.

TJKC: When did you first become aware of Jack's plight with Marvel?
FRANK: Almost from the onset, because I knew there had to be a reason so many people on staff at Marvel were bad-mouthing the guy. Kirby

was bad-mouthed by many of the Marvel staffers at the time, but not the ones I got along with.

TJKC: Around the time you were doing *Ronin*, Jenette Kahn and Paul Levitz offered Jack a lucrative deal that gave him a percentage of the *New Gods* licensing. Do you think it was part of a public relations plan to not only do the right thing, but also to appeal to creators like yourself and say that DC is a home that will treat freelance creators fairly?
FRANK: Why shouldn't they? It was both good business and good ethics to have moved in that direction at that time. DC did take the lead over Marvel in terms of such issues. They showed flexibility. They showed creativity. People don't get the history right, but I was there: DC announced its royalty system to the total surprise of Marvel. Marvel had up to that time maintained that a system could not possibly have been done without putting the company out of business. Once DC announced it, Marvel scrambled to match it. It was very fast and I was there. The sequence was DC first, Marvel second. It was clearly the brainchild of both Jenette and Paul. It was really the first time I saw that; given it was essentially a two-party system – the other publishers were not nearly as strong as they've become since – it was a major breakthrough to have one of the Big Guys listening. It was an important step. I can say in retrospect now that it was a half-assed step, or I could criticize it top-to-bottom, but it was so very important that the door actually opened. It would figure that Jack would be a part of it.

TJKC: You came out, guns blazing, in support of Jack to get his art back.
FRANK: Why not?

TJKC: Well, Marvel was one of the Big Two. Where did you get the chutzpa to do that?
FRANK: I wasn't raised to think that someone who wrote me a paycheck earned my silence. I just don't think that way. I always felt that my dealings with Marvel are fair on both ends but I didn't owe them anything beyond the work I did. And when they were wrong, I said so.

TJKC: Did you ever consider a boycott?
FRANK: Of Marvel? More like a strike, you mean? There was much talk for various reasons – at the time there was almost a guild of comic book artists, that Neal Adams had tried to bring into being – but the problem with the notion of a strike is that it seemed tactically stupid. Basically we were throwing away our clout if we stopped working. I think I was a much more effective voice cajoling Marvel when they were publishing my work, than had I been off pouting in the corner.

TJKC: What, in essence, did Jack's fight represent?
FRANK: To me, it represented the dignity of our craft itself. Here we had our greatest talent being treated like a nuisance who was irrelevant. He was treated disgracefully, whatever the contracts said – and I haven't read them. The guy who built the house deserved to at least collect a little rent here and there, or at least get paid for his work. To me, the fight over Jack focused everybody's mind on what our craft is and what we are trying to do with our art. Does it have any dignity? Does it have any meaning? Are we just slobs mashing out McDonald's burgers, or are we doing something that is actually valuable? If we were going to allow our greatest talent to be so disgraced without a peep, than that is essentially a passive declaration that we are worthless.

TJKC: What response did you get from your peers?
FRANK: The people who agreed with me said so, and the people who disagreed just smiled. You understand that any time I've been in any of these fights, the enemy has always been silence, not debate. I've always wanted more debate, and I always run into silence.

TJKC: Did you ever debate John Byrne?
FRANK: Only in private. *(laughter)* John and I are good friends and we only disagree on a few things, such as the shape of the planet.

TJKC: What do you think of Byrne's statements that Jack always knew what the rules of the game were, and deserved no better treatment than anyone else?
FRANK: Saying that the rules were different back then doesn't make the rules right. We live in a country where we don't depend on our

(this page, previous and next pages) Unpublished art from In The Days Of The Mob *#2, inked by Royer.*

laws to decide right and wrong in every instance. We don't live in Socialism or Communism, where you have so many laws that every mode of behavior is controlled. It's up to us to define what's right and what's wrong. Surely we all have to abide by contracts we've signed. That's why I've never challenged Marvel's ownership of Elektra, for instance, because I did consciously agree that they were the authors of her. That said, some things are just plain wrong. There was a law at one point in a certain European country that Jews could be shoveled into ovens; that law didn't make it right. The mistreatment of Kirby was so outrageous and so ridiculous and of such questionable legality, that it was certainly worthy of a protest that has come since. And Marvel has even copped to half of that. Even Marvel has made concessions. The point is that Kirby was a prodigious talent who kept his eyes on the drawing board, and was punished by people who were a little quicker with the legal document than he was. But as far as the contract where Kirby signed his rights away, I still haven't seen it. Whether he signed one or not, right is right, and wrong is wrong.

TJKC: It's been twelve years since the fight, and Jack's been gone for three years now. Why do you think a demeaning attitude persists with even former employees of Marvel?

FRANK: When so much is based on an untruth, people sit uneasy. The basic philosophy of the company is that Jack Kirby was nobody and, in fact, Stan Lee was nobody, and that these characters just kind of created themselves. All the work that folks like me and them did was just done by replaceable hands. You're seeing that literally fall apart before your eyes right now, as this bad philosophy is collapsing on itself.

TJKC: Industry-wide or just with Marvel?
FRANK: With Marvel more than anybody. DC has made certain concessions, mostly cosmetic, but certainly they've come to recognize that the talent involved is very important. It was only a symbolic move, but they cancelled *Sandman* after Neil Gaiman left, and that is something that wouldn't have been done ten years ago. It would have been unthinkable. Cancel a good-selling book just because the writer leaves? Whereas Marvel just cavalierly fires Chris Claremont after 17 years. That's where you're seeing the philosophy played out. DC's got a different point of view. DC is also based on a wider range of artists. Obviously there was Siegel and Shuster, who were profoundly fundamental to the company, but they're older. With Marvel, it gets down to Stan, Jack, and Steve: The people who essentially built the whole house.

TJKC: Marvel used to be a house of personalities in the beginning, with Stan pushing that attitude. It's turned into something that seems a complete denial of personalities, as if the stuff is done by machine.
FRANK: In a way, Marvel reminds me these days very much of DC in the '60s: Lost. The last truly visionary publisher was William Gaines. He had Feldstein, Kurtzman, Wallace Wood, Johnny Craig, all who brought powerful visions of their own to make it happen. But Marvel was an interesting case in that it was Jack Kirby and Stan Lee who were the creative volcanoes who made it happen – and I do believe that Stan deserves a lot of credit for his part in it. As far as now, I see things more in a state of atrophy, more a state of confusion, but something better will emerge. The structure itself needs to break down, and it is breaking down. The current confusion is a reflection of that. There aren't any ground rules anymore. The old factories are just sputtering, dying their empty deaths, and nothing new has really emerged. But I think looking for a brand name to save the industry is looking in the wrong direction. Do you think Berkley Books is going to save the book industry? Or Stephen King?

TJKC: The creators over at Image take a lot of flak for the present demise of the industry bought on by insane speculation, inflated circulation figures, etc.
FRANK: Yeah, like no one else was riding that same gravy train for a while there!

TJKC: You're in Legend, then, because you own the work. You profit through the umbrella of the group.
FRANK: The Legend thing has been really nothing more than a bowling club; a mutual admiration society is what I call it. We don't profit from each other's work; we don't share contracts, nothing like that. But mainly I think Image began as something that seemed to represent artists working independently.

That was what I liked about them. Now that most of them are factories of their own, I've lost a lot of interest.

TJKC: A pivotal issue of *The Comics Journal* (#105) brought Kirby's fight to get his art to light, and the section started off with a letter from Jenette and Paul that was devastating. It stated, basically, "All we did before was wrong. We were wrong and we're trying to be right. The other guy should be right, too." Word is that you were involved in having that letter see the light of day. Is that true?
FRANK: I can't talk about it. Draw your own conclusions, but they made their own decision and that's the important thing, and they should get full credit. I didn't ever put my own services on the line to try to get a document out of anybody.

TJKC: In 1985, just a couple of months before one of the most extraordinary years in comics, you wrote: "While numerous inequities remain, and the field still faces the task of preventing the further stagnation and the eventual collapse of the industry, there is cause for cautious hope. The old days of despair and resignation are fading into memory, a dark age best forgotten." That was written 12 years ago. How do you feel about that now?
FRANK: My, wasn't I an optimistic young fellow! *(laughter)* I still stand by that, but unfortunately I have to update it. It's just all taking so much longer than I thought it would. That's the main thing; I haven't become cynical nor weary of the struggle. In fact, this is my favorite period of my career. Without question, as much fun as I had all through the Marvel years, doing *Dark Knight* – those were glorious times – this is my favorite period because I'm finally seeing my own generation in the position to take the reins of the industry. We've finally stopped acting like petulant children, stopped squealing about creator's rights, and this and that, and actually shown 'em. Part of what I want to do is arrogant and audacious – but you gotta be arrogant and audacious when you do this kind of work. It's to set the goal of trying to top the old guys I adore so much. I'm sure there'll be failures ahead, but what a fun time it'll be trying!

TJKC: Can you give us a hint at what's coming in the future?
FRANK: Right now, I'm finishing up a 126-page *Sin City* one-shot; damn the market and full speed ahead. I've got tons more *Sin City* ideas and I've also got a variety of other projects I want to get to, but more and more I'm drawing my own stuff, so it takes a while. So it's hard to predict when things will come out.

TJKC: Will you ever work for Marvel again?
FRANK: There isn't a Marvel. It's ceased to exist – haven't you heard?

TJKC: Marvel Entertainment Group.
FRANK: I only work for comic book companies. *(laughter)*

TJKC: I saw a devastating cartoon by you, of Marvel goons digging up the grave of Elektra, her rotted corpse in their hands, with another goon trotting off, exclaiming "Hey, I think there's a Kirby one over here!" *That's* a statement.
FRANK: (laughter) As far as "would I work for Marvel again," I'm always careful never to say "never again." I mean, yup, before I had to pump gas. Absolutely. Were everything to change and everything to be so different and were I to be in the mood? Yes. But right now, why go back in time? Jack himself – who would always say to all of us, when one of us would rush up with a drawing of Captain America and say, "Jack, I was thinking of you" – would always say, "If you're thinking of me, make something up. That's what I did."

TJKC: You were involved in *WAP [a newsletter devoted to creator's rights]*, which seemed a continuation of Neal Adams' guild concept. Do you think the field can ever get organized?
FRANK: I wonder if it needs to. Conditions for the talent are better than they've ever been, by and away. One could make the argument after certain things have happened that talent's powers had even swung too far the other way. I think mainly we have to proceed and make work possible. Of course there will always be instances of corruption and malfeasance; bad debts that will happen in any industry, but by in large, the ground rules have gotten pretty good and I don't see any reason to keep storming the barricades that have already fallen down.

TJKC: Should Marvel give Jack co-creator credit in the books that he co-created?
FRANK: Absolutely. There's something called the truth. The fact that they haven't means they're standing in a lie.

TJKC: What's your assessment of Jack's influence on American culture?
FRANK: Jack, in many ways, epitomized a certain generation, with a genius and talent, and was able to give his art his fullest expression in a form that was so much under his control; he was able to do it freely. While he was obviously absorbing the movies and trends of his time, regurgitating a certain number of them, they were all coming through Jack Kirby's filter; and that kid from the Lower East Side who fought the Nazi Bund members was able to deliver consistently something transcendent, and his work has obviously a gold mine that many people have mined a little too vigorously, for a little too long.

TJKC: Do you think rage was an important factor in Kirby's work?
FRANK: Without question. But also constant hope. There's violence in his work, but his heroes were always impeccably heroic. Even his most ambiguous character – which had to be Orion from the *New Gods* – was much more good than evil. ❍

Jack at home in 1974. Photo by Dave Stevens.

THE JACK KIRBY COLLECTOR #16

A TWOMORROWS ADVERTISING & DESIGN PRODUCTION IN ASSOCIATION WITH THE KIRBY ESTATE
EDITED BY JOHN MORROW ASSISTANT EDITOR PAMELA MORROW ASSOCIATE EDITOR JON B. COOKE
DESIGN & LAYOUT BY JOHN & PAMELA MORROW PROOFREADING BY RICHARD HOWELL COVER COLOR BY TOM ZIUKO
CONTRIBUTORS: TERRY AUSTIN JERRY BOYD ROBERT L. BRYANT LEN CALLO SIBLEY CARLYLE JON B. COOKE STUART DEITCHER JEAN DEPELLEY WILL EISNER TOM FIELD PHILIP FRIED RUSS GARWOOD JAMES GUTHRIE DAVID HAMILTON CHRIS HARPER PATRICK HILGER TOM HORVITZ FRANK JOHNSON KARL KESEL MARK MARDEROSIAN FRANK MILLER TOM MOREHOUSE LOU MOUGIN MARK PACELLA DAVID PENALOSA KEVIN PHILLIPS STEVE ROBERTSON TONY SEYBERT FRANCIS ST. MARTIN ED STELLI DAVE STEVENS CARL TAYLOR MARVIN TAYLOR STAN TAYLOR GREG THEAKSTON MIKE THIBODEAUX R.J. VITONE BRITT WISENBAKER BILL WRAY RAY WYMAN
SPECIAL THANKS TO: JON B. COOKE JEAN DEPELLEY WILL EISNER MARK EVANIER MIKE GARTLAND RUSS GARWOOD D. HAMBONE RANDY HOPPE RICHARD HOWELL KARL KESEL FRANK MILLER TOM MOREHOUSE MARK PACELLA STEVE ROBERTSON ARLEN SCHUMER GREG THEAKSTON MIKE THIBODEAUX R.J. VITONE TOM ZIUKO & OF COURSE ROZ KIRBY MAILING CREW D. HAMBONE GLEN MUSIAL ED STELLI PATRICK VARKER AND THE OTHER KIRBY FANS IN RALEIGH, NC

COLLECTOR COMMENTS

Send letters to: The Jack Kirby Collector
c/o TwoMorrows • 1812 Park Drive
Raleigh, NC 27605 or E-mail to: twomorrow@aol.com

(I absolutely HAVE to start this "Tough Guys" column with the following excerpt from a letter I got from one of my favorite Kirby afficionados; the first two paragraphs beautifully sum up the most basic, primal appeal of Jack's work:)

Jack's male characters can be beautiful and graceful, sometimes markedly so, but Jack never pulled back from facing the ugliness of extremity, the testosterone drive of passion and obsession and consuming rage. His best characters lived in bodies that could sweat and bleed and make ungraceful love, even if he never drew a line of it. Sometimes the ferocity to live that he portrays possesses the near-terrifying quality that you see in open heart surgery – the mass of the heart endlessly beating, a red, knotted muscle that is beyond all grace and beauty, wanting only life and endless, savage movement.

Jack's unique genius is that he could somehow romanticize that quality, and make it a conscious part of our own life. Beyond everything else, I believe this is what made him so overwhelmingly popular for so long. Other artists ignored the testosterone drives of adolescence or pretended they didn't exist or were ashamed of them. Jack acknowledged them. He delivered the goods.

Reading the excellent articles on *Machine Man* by Jaret Keene and *The Eternals* by Charles Hatfield – both outstanding and insightful – I was struck by how easy it could be to see Jack somehow creating his work in an emotional vacuum – that is, to see this period as a good one, and that one as a poor one, as though one were discussing a natural phenomenon, like the weather. But every story a man tells comes out of his inner life, and I suspect that if you look back over Jack's life and Jack's art you'll see very close connections.

The *New Gods* trilogy, for example, not only uses the human face as an image and a mask, but is actually about the loss of face. Loss of face is the subject of the series from beginning to end, in all three books, concluding with Esak's transformation *[in Hunger Dogs]*. In the "Glory Boat" story, the young man completely loses his face. There is nothing but smooth flesh where his features once were. (The colorist didn't understand and colored his whole head a confusing metallic shade, as I recall.) Again and again, loss of face, partial or absolute, occurs – this from an artist and writer who had just left Marvel, where his work had been re-written by his editor, who had also effectively denied him creative credit for two of the most successful comic books of their time (certainly a metaphoric loss of face) and is now confronted (faced) with the loss of face at DC if he should fail there.

So is it really surprising that *Machine Man* grew out of *2001*? Jack was back with Marvel. The DC period had been disastrous, and now he was drawing somebody else's creation. *2001* was, like *Kamandi*, a "template" book, where Jack created a formula story that effectively never advanced. This is what he'd done before he'd left Marvel the first time, presumably so that Marvel (and later DC) couldn't benefit further from his creations. And here he was, putting the best face on the situation, but really worse off than before – his greatest creative ambitions shattered with the cancellation of the *New Gods* series and all the other problems at DC, and with no clear creative future, his own self-image damaged by years of editorial interference and mistreatment and misunderstanding. If he saw himself as a drawing machine whose self-image had been taken from him, wouldn't he be likely to create out of a mechanical series, *2001*, a man who is a machine, and who is without any protective mask to show to the world, but who is still a man?

Now, these things may not be really germane. But it seems to me we should look deeper than we have if we want to know more about Jack's stories.

Jack was a genius. He had maintained his inner world against enormous pressure – I am astonished that he, or any creative person, could have his heart's desire cancelled, and then without a pause create, write and draw two new series at a very high technical level, one of which, *The Demon*, is exceptional. But there has to be some time when the outer world becomes too intrusive, and the struggle supremely difficult. If *The Eternals* is less than one would hope, is it the consequence of the diminishment of Jack's powers – or is it the result of the bitter and private realization that there was no future for his gifts at Marvel?

And, beyond DC and Marvel, where was there?

"The Great Kirby Science Fiction Concepts" is excellent, although it occasionally pushes mechanistic ideas too much – the Mother Box, for example, is clearly Freud's superego given material form.

Mike Thibodeaux's interview was really exceptional, with a number of valuable insights. Especially notable is his assertion that Jack's pencils should be what is printed. I hope it will come to pass, perhaps when computer programming technology is so advanced that the xeroxes of Jack's pencils can be reconverted to look like his original work.

This is absolutely not to be taken as a criticism of Mike's own work or any other Kirby inker's. As wonderfully gifted as some were, and as talented as each of them was – even Colletta – the essence of the man is still in those pencil drawings.

Richard Kyle, Long Beach, CA

(I think this letter speaks for itself, so I'll shut up.)

I have a mystery for your "tough guys" issue. I have an old comic without the cover. The title of the story is "Booby Trap." It takes place during the Korean war, and involves a platoon getting ambushed because of a foul-up named Jake Loomis. It is classic Kirby with a lot of action, and great dialogue. In the story the Chinese soldiers hid beneath the floor of a farmhouse where "the Koreans light fires to heat their homes." Imagine my surprise years later when I visited a palace in Seoul and found out an outer building at the palace was heated this exact way – just another touch of realism that was Jack Kirby!

My question: What the title of the comic? When was it issued? What company issued it?

John Rutter, Hong Kong

(Sounds like this is from Foxhole *#2, published by Jack and Joe's Mainline Publishing Co., Dec 1954. See David Penalosa's article on Kirby war comics elsewhere in this issue for a rundown of* Foxhole*.)*

"The Story Behind *Sky Masters*": So *THAT's* why Kirby left DC. SHEESH! But who knows – if not for that mess, we might never have had *Fantastic Four*, etc.!

Henry R. Kujawa, Camden, NJ

The graph on page 25 of #15 really shows the relationship of the *Sky Masters* litigation with Jack's output at DC Comics. Keep up the good work!

Kevin L. Cook, Bronxville, NY

I really appreciate your efforts in keeping the Kirby legacy alive. I got to see Mr. Kirby at two conventions; he told me a story about how in the Forties he had gotten a call from a couple of Bundists who were in the lobby where he worked. They were threatening him for drawing Captain America kicking Hitler on one of the covers.

"Oh, yeah? Well, I'll be right down!" Jack told me he answered them.

Jack saw the horrified look on my face, smiled and said, "Whatta ya want? I was young and stupid back then. Luckily when I got down there, no one was there."

Still horrified at what could have happened to him, I said that if I had been him, I would have run down to the lobby, said, "Mr. Kirby will be right down," and high-tailed it out of there!!

He looked at me for a second, smiled and said, "Hey... I like that... that's pretty good..." at which point he was called away and I just stood there, still in awe that I had actually spoken to him.

John L. Montero, Bergenfield, NJ

(Thanks to you, John, for taking that great photo of Jack talking to Al Williamson from issue #15.)

There used to be a radio show about comic books, *Star Trek* and the like on my local college station. When Jack died, someone called in and told the following story:

As a young boy living in Long Island, he and his friend discovered Jack Kirby also lived there. They looked up his name in the phone book and, to their amazement, found his address. Riding their bicycles there, they knocked on the door and a man answered. They asked if he was Jack Kirby; he said 'yes' and the two boys started asking dozens of questions. He politely told them he was busy at the moment, as it was his daughter's wedding day. Crestfallen, they started to leave, but Jack called them back and asked if they could return the following week. They said 'no' and never went back.

Just kidding!

Of course, the two of them went back the next weekend and Jack welcomed them into his home. He showed them his drawing board and one of the pieces he was working on for an upcoming *Fantastic Four*. Dr. Doom's face was to be revealed and only be slightly scarred, not horribly disfigured, as Doom saw himself.

John Parrett, Bethpage, NY

(This is fascinating, since I don't hear too many stories of people visiting Jack at his Long Island home; most of the tales of visits take place after Jack moved to California in 1969. It sounds like it probably was Fantastic Four *#85, page 19 Jack was working on at the time; the Bullpen page in FF #87 announced that Jack was moving to California, so the timing seems right. But if this story is true, the scene mentioned here got altered, so we never actually saw Doom's unmasked face. Perhaps this was yet another instance of Jack's and Stan's directions for a character not converging.)*

Here's my usual message to (a) say that your new issue is superb as always and to (b) amplify on a few matters mentioned within. I hope this isn't getting monotonous...

The Watcher drawing that Al Williamson inked for your back cover is an example of something that occurred with increasing frequency during Jack's last few years at Marvel. Many times, he would draw one of those full pagers and then decide he couldn't bear to send it in. Often, Roz would come in and say, "That's too good for them! I want that page." Their complaints were many and legendary, but at the root of it all was that Jack did not feel he was being properly credited or compensated for his work for Marvel, and one does not easily send a masterpiece to a patron who is not appreciating you...or, as in this case, giving your work to an inker who will spend as little time as possible finishing it.

It was probably a feeble gesture but what Jack would do – and he did this at least a half-dozen times – was to give the penciled page to Roz. Then he would sit down and draw a new page that was just as good (if not better) to replace it. In this way, I guess he felt that he had saved a little piece of his artistry from disappearing into the Marvel machine.

I am curious/skeptical about the dating on *Starman Zero*. What is the source for placing this material as "late '40s?" (If it's me, I may have been wrong.) The work is lettered by Ben Oda, in what looks to me like the kind of lettering he was doing around the mid '50s. For that matter, can we peg exactly when Oda started lettering for Simon & Kirby? And do we think that Mr. Simon had any involvement in this strip and, if not, how come? I'm afraid this strip represents a kind of Negative Zone in my Kirby expertise. Somehow though, it feels more to me like something Kirby would have done in the latter months of his partnership with Joe.

Regarding the Lee-Kirby *Silver Surfer* Graphic Novel... I have come across a batch of notes and story concepts, typed up by Jack, which really do show that Stan and Jack were not of like minds on this project. Kirby clearly saw the characters and story from a different POV that Stan and, while no one can say for certain whose vision was superior, I think the book would have benefited from being done wholly Stan's way or wholly Jack's. The end-result strikes me as a series of compromises, serving the ideas of neither man. One cannot help but wonder if – had Kirby stayed with Marvel in '69 – if this is the way all subsequent Stan/Jack stories would have gone.

I must admit to mixed feelings on Jon Cooke's article on the *Sky Masters* lawsuit. Jon did a helluva good research job but I don't think he had access to enough to present Kirby's side of the case well. Jack had radically-different recollections of the events described in Schiff's side, and ample reason (he felt) to view Schiff's demands for money as a shakedown. About this, Kirby may have been dead wrong but, given his version of events, and in the context of an industry where other editors DID extract kickbacks from freelancers via threats, Kirby's position is a bit more understandable. I'll try to state both positions, as I understand them, in this much-awaited book I keep touting.

For the time being though, I'd like to note that the chart on Jack's income from DC is kinda misleading. Stories – especially for anthology titles like *House Of Mystery* where much of his work was appearing – could be bought way ahead, so charting when stories were published might not give one a true picture of when Jack got the work. The truly relevant thing to note is simply that, at a time when he doubtlessly needed the work, Kirby stopped working at all for DC. It is not a question of his assignments declining but of them ceasing... at a time when he could not possibly have been occupied full-time by the newspaper strip. In fact, he was picking up lower-paying work from Stan Lee at the time.

It's theoretically possible that the DC anthology titles were simply over-bought at the time (though Schiff did not claim this). The question is why Bob Brown took over drawing *Challengers Of The Unknown,* which was a regular assignment. Schiff does not, in his affidavit, claim, "I had to give the book to another artist because Kirby was too busy." Instead, the suggestion is that Kirby got less work from DC (actually, NO work) because he simply stopped coming around. Schiff may have been in the right with regard to his contractual claims, but I find it hard to believe that Jack – at a time he needed money – abandoned a regular assignment for DC to draw monster comics for Martin Goodman's company for less money.

The end result of the whole brouhaha was, of course, a lose-lose situation for all sides. Kirby lost his ability to get work from DC, which made him virtually a "prisoner" at Marvel. Schiff lost the services of Kirby, which his books could have well used in the years that followed. And DC, of course, lost. The whole Marvel Age of Comics might never have happened if Kirby had stayed at DC, doing *Challengers* and, doubtlessly, inventing other books. The ones who really "won" in that lawsuit were Martin Goodman and Stan Lee.

Mike Thibodeaux's interview was very good, and I wanted to affirm that Jack and Roz really did come to view Mike as part of their extended family, and that Jack was very happy with Mike's inkwork. I don't think it's still there but for years, Jack kept Mike's airbrushed Thor painting (which you reproduced) on the wall of his studio. I don't think Kirby considered it his own work; I think it was there because he was proud of Mike. Kirby fans everywhere owe Mike an enormous debt for all the help he gave Jack and Roz over the years.

Lastly, I wanted to call everyone's attention to something that may have been overlooked but which I was reminded of by your reproduction of that *Captain Victory* splash – one of Jack's last – on page 48. Jack penciled in the credits, misspelling Mike's name, but including that of Janice Cohen, colorist. It's a nice bit of closure to recall that Janice colored so much of Jack's last work in comics. I wonder how many people know that Sol Brodsky – who functioned as production manager and occasional inker and colorist for Kirby's early-60s Marvel work – was her father.

Mark Evanier, Los Angeles, CA

(I got the Starman Zero *date from KIRBY UNLEASHED. However, since Jack was cranking out so many strip ideas/proposals in the mid-50s, it seems more than reasonable that it might've been done then, with King Masters, Surf Hunter, etc. As for Simon's involvement, I have no idea. But it would reason that Jack saw the writing on the wall with the "Wertham" comics biz, and was hedging his bets by aiming toward strip work. Plus, having the resources of the S&K shop behind him to get it done – inks, lettering – probably made him feel that much better about producing a daily strip on schedule.*

By the way, Mike Thibodeaux called to say he didn't ink the Hulk drawing we ran on page 41 of #15. Royer also says he didn't ink it, so who did is anyone's guess.)

It's fascinating to see what different interpretations can be inspired by a single work. Case in point: the responses to *2001* #7 shown in *TJKC* #15. First, Robert Bryant reads the conclusion of this story as uncompromisingly bleak: "Heroics die anonymously in the mud, and the future is as cold and mysterious as the rocky surface of the Monolith." This fits with Bryant's thesis that Kirby's *2001* concedes nothing to the demands of its publisher or audience. But then, two pages later, Jon Cooke sees #7's end as another expression of Kirby's constant theme, "that humanity can rise above the adversity of injustice and hatred and achieve a life of peace and love."

Perhaps this tug-of-war between despair and hope characterizes Kirby's work as a whole? From the sunlit optimism at the end of *Bicentennial Battles,* to the fierce anti-nostalgia of "Street Code," from the utopian visions of Supertown to the bleak dystopia of *OMAC,* Kirby's stories seem to veer back and forth between hopefulness and battle-weary fatalism. The fact that one story can support two variant readings suggests just why Kirby is an inexhaustible subject for discussion.

I enjoyed #15 immensely, from the little things (e.g., the *Eternals-style* logo on page 3) to the big things—foremost among which is Jon Cooke's well-researched and scrupulous treatment of the painful *Sky Masters* incident. This incident is one of the under-explored areas in the history of Kirby's career; it is by no means a minor one. In fact I see it as a crucial turning point in Kirby's career.

Consider: Here was a man who had enjoyed considerable success. Kirby was a founding partner in one of the most successful comic book studios. He had co-created some very popular characters and titles. He was accustomed to working as an editor, layout artist and even publisher for the S&K operation. After S&K he succeeded in gaining the much-envied position of syndicated newspaper strip artist, the grail of most comic book artists. Yet by the close of the 1950s he was working at industry second-stringer Atlas, under the editorship of a man who had scarcely been more than a boy when Simon & Kirby scored their first big hit in 1941. Why?Jon's article helps to answer that question, and the answer, though unpleasant, is fascinating. I thank him for digging up the dirt, and you for publishing it. This is easily the most valuable piece of history in *TJKC* #15, and is a journalistic coup to rival any *TJKC* has pulled off so far. Jon's use of court records shows a rigor to which we should all aspire.

Charles Hatfield, Storrs, CT

NEXT ISSUE: #17 is the one many of you have been waiting for: Our DC THEME ISSUE! The front cover is of KAMANDI inked by MIKE ROYER, leading into our lengthy section on the Last Boy On Earth! We'll also feature a new interview with NEAL ADAMS, as he discusses DC in the 1970s, and interviews with Kirby inkers D. BRUCE BERRY and GREG THEAKSTON! Our back cover is inked by STEVE RUDE! There's also a rare KIRBY INTERVIEW, plus articles on Jack's '40s DC work on SANDMAN and MANHUNTER, through CHALLENGERS and GREEN ARROW in the 1950s, up through 1970s work like OMAC, ATLAS, KOBRA, THE LOSERS, SANDMAN, and on to his 1980s SUPER POWERS books. And throughout, we'll show unpublished Kirby art including unused pages, published pages BEFORE they were inked, and more! We're taking an extra month between issues to attend summer conventions, so we'll see ya in mid-October! Deadline for submissions: 8/15/97.

SUBMIT SOMETHING-GET FREE ISSUES!

The Jack Kirby Collector is a not-for-profit publication, put together with submissions from Jack's fans around the world. We don't pay for submissions, but if we print art or articles you submit, we'll send you a free copy of that issue or extend your subscription by one issue.

Here's a tentative list of upcoming issues, to give you ideas of things to write about. But don't limit yourself to these – we treat these themes very loosely, so anything you write may fit somewhere. And just because we covered a topic once, don't think we won't print more about it. So get creative, and get writing! And as always, send us copies of your Kirby art!

#18 (DEC. '97): MARVEL ISSUE

We'll cover Jack's 1970s Marvel books like *Captain America* and *Black Panther,* and delve back into the 1960s, with interviews from several surprise Bullpenners! If it's Marvel, we want it! **Deadline: 10/1/97.**

#19 (FEB. '98): ART ISSUE

We'll examine the artistic worth of Jack's comics, exploring the subtleties and nuances of his storytelling techniques. Plus we'll take a look at the ins and outs of original art collecting, discuss the merits of Jack's various inkers, feature fan art (including the winners of our inking contest), and spotlight the colossal Kirby art holdings at the Words & Pictures Museum in Massachusetts. If you want to weigh in on Kirby's artist value, send us your criticism and commentary. **Deadline: 12/1/97.**

#20 (APR. '98): KIRBY'S WOMEN

From Mother Delilah to Big Barda, the Invisible Girl to Granny Goodness, we'll explore Jack's heroines and villainesses, including a lengthy section on Simon & Kirby's romance comics. **Deadline: 2/1/98.**

#21 (JULY '98): JACK'S WHACKIEST IDEAS!

Nobody's perfect, and even Jack managed to lay a few eggs in his otherwise stellar career. So from *Red Raven* to those crazy Atlas Monsters, Arnim Zola to the Fighting Fetus, we'll have fun finding redeeming qualities in Jack's wildest, weirdest, hokiest, lamest, and most preposterous ideas, including gizmos and gadgets! **Deadline: 4/1/98.**

#22 (OCT. '98): VILLAINS

From the big guns like the Red Skull, Doctor Doom, and Darkseid to all the also-rans in-between, we'll take a closer look at what makes Jack's bad guys so darn good! If there's a Kirby villain you love to hate, write something about them! **Deadline: 7/1/98.**

SUBMISSION GUIDELINES:

Submit artwork in one of these forms:

1) Clear color or black-&-white photocopies.
2) Scanned images – 300ppi IBM or Macintosh.
3) Originals (carefully packed and insured).

Submit articles in one of these forms:

1) Typed or laser printed pages.
2) E-mail to: twomorrow@aol.com
3) An ASCII file, IBM or Macintosh format.
4) Photocopies of previously printed articles OK.

We'll pay return postage and insurance for originals – please write or call first. Please include background info whenever possible.

Jack Kirby
KESEL
4-11-97

FULLY AUTHORIZED BY THE KIRBY ESTATE

THE JACK KIRBY COLLECTOR

$5.95
In The US

ISSUE #17, NOV. 1997

A NOT-FOR-PROFIT PUBLICATION
CELEBRATING THE LIFE & CAREER OF THE KING!

A *"KING"-SIZE 68-PAGE* ISSUE ON JACK'S WORK AT *DC COMICS!!*

A RARE 1971
KIRBY INTERVIEW

INTERVIEWS WITH
NEAL ADAMS
GREG THEAKSTON
D. BRUCE BERRY

1997 KIRBY TRIBUTE PANEL, FEATURING
MARK EVANIER
STEVE SHERMAN
MIKE ROYER
MARIE SEVERIN
AL WILLIAMSON

SPECIAL FEATURES:
FOURTH WORLD, KAMANDI, MANHUNTER, CHALLENGERS, GREEN ARROW, SANDMAN & MORE

UNPUBLISHED ART
INCLUDING PENCIL PAGES *BEFORE* THEY WERE INKED, AND *MUCH MORE!!*

1996 & 1997 EISNER AWARDS NOMINEE
BEST COMICS-RELATED PUBLICATION

1997 HARVEY AWARDS NOMINEE
BEST BIOGRAPHICAL, HISTORICAL OR JOURNALISTIC PRESENTATION

KIRBY + ROYER '97

ISSUE #17 CONTENTS:

Front cover inks: Mike Royer
Back cover inks: Steve Rude
Cover color: Tom Ziuko

THE JACK KIRBY COLLECTOR

Handwritten on the back of this Kamandi drawing were the words "The Real Mr. Sacker." Our thanks to Mike Royer for taking time to ink this issue's cover.

Mike's selling his inked art to this issue's cover for $700; contact TJKC *if you're interested.*

The Jack Kirby Collector, Vol. 4, No. 17, Nov. 1997. Published bi-monthly by & © TwoMorrows Advertising & Design, 1812 Park Drive, Raleigh, NC 27605, USA. 919-833-8092. *John Morrow*, Editor. *Pamela Morrow*, Asst. Editor. *Jon B. Cooke*, Assoc. Editor. Single issues: $4.95 ($5.40 Canada, $7.40 elsewhere). Six-issue subscriptions: $24.00 US, $32.00 Canada and Mexico, $44.00 outside North America. First printing. All characters are © their respective companies. All artwork is © Jack Kirby unless otherwise noted. All editorial matter is © the respective authors. PRINTED IN CANADA.

On The Trail Of Manhunter

by John Morrow

"He stalks the world's most cunning and dangerous game... Man!" So began Joe and Jack's first Manhunter tale in *Adventure Comics* #73. Simon & Kirby did relatively few stories, but each concentrated on cramming as much action as possible into a few pages. I discovered Manhunter through 1970s reprints, and I assumed they'd created the character from scratch. A little research showed me I was wrong.

Way back in *Adventure Comics* #58 (Jan. 1941), a strip called "Paul Kirk, Manhunter" debuted. Paul was a "tracer of missing persons" who did favors for his old friend Tim Holden, Chief of Police. He sported the same dull green double-breasted suit for most of his adventures, and got involved in ordinary murder and robbery cases, tracking down crooks. *Adventure* #58 gives a byline to Ed Moore for the story, so I assume he created the character. The run from #58-72 was reasonably entertaining stuff, but nothing spectacular.

Enter Simon & Kirby.

A look at the original version of *Adventure* #73 ("Secret of the Buzzard's Revenge" from April 1942) shows a number of interesting changes during S&K's first outing. For this one issue only, Paul Kirk was called Rick Nelson (it was corrected and relettered when reprinted in *New Gods* #4). He's now labeled a "young sportsman" (and later, a "big game hunter"), and Police Chief Holden was replaced by Inspector Donovan, whose death at the hands of the bizarre Buzzard sparks Nelson/Kirk to don a super-hero outfit and use his tracking abilities to hunt down the killer.

Adventure #74's "Scavenger Hunt" is the story of a little runt who must bring in Public Enemy #1 to win the hand of his girl. Naturally, Manhunter is behind-the-scenes helping out. #75's "Beware of Mr. Meek" involves timid Myron Meek, a soft-spoken crook with a diamond heist on his mind. #76's "Legend of the Silent Bear" revolves around a bear statue that holds an old man's life savings, and the crooks who want to steal it. (Manhunter needs the help of a Boy Scout to track down the crooks!) #77's "The Stone of Vengeance!" spotlights a cursed jewel that passes through the hands of crook after crook, leaving a trail of bodies behind. In #78's "The Lady And The Tiger," Manhunter hunts a crook called The Tiger, who takes after his feline namesake. These stories are reprinted in *New Gods* #5-9.

Adventure Comics #79's "Cobras of the Deep" is the highlight of the series, with stellar art and writing. No wonder; Jack and Joe had Manhunter face a group of Nazis in a U-Boat! Given the war fervor of the times, this story must've been a lot of fun to do. (It was reprinted in *Detective Comics* #440.)

Adventure #80's "Man Trap Island" (the only S&K Manhunter that was never reprinted) is the one time S&K fully utilized Paul Kirk's background as a hunter. Manhunter tracks a gang of escaped convicts to a remote island, but the tables turn, and the convicts end up hunting him. Weaponless, Manhunter must use his trapping skills to capture the crooks (with a little help from an orphaned Indian boy); a fine finale for S&K on the series.

Without S&K aboard, the strip limped along with lackluster art and stories from #81 through #92. Throughout its run, Manhunter played second fiddle to Sandman in *Adventure*, both on covers and story position in each issue (Sandman's "dream" motif lead to much stronger story ideas). But luckily, all but one were reprinted in the 1970s.

Which leads us to 1975's Manhunter revival in *First Issue Special* #5. Despite some pretty nice art (beautifully inked by D. Bruce Berry), the series didn't go anywhere (although Jack's text page gives the idea that it was intended to be an ongoing series). In it, Public Defender Mark Shaw is recruited to be the latest member in a centuries-old sect of lawmen (*à la The Phantom*). The costume is very similar to Paul Kirk's 1940s version, and perhaps Jack planned that the old Manhunter who passes the torch – or baton, in this case – to Mark was an aged Paul Kirk (in direct contradiction to Archie Goodwin and Walt Simonson's earlier Manhunter revamp). Whatever the case, Manhunter continued its second-tier status, never receiving its own book, but based on the holes in Jack's X-List (shown elsewhere in this issue), I suspect there might be a couple of unpublished *Manhunter* stories floating around somewhere. With time, hopefully we'll uncover them, so we can all see Kirby's last contributions to the character. ★

Page 13 of First Issue Special *#5. Is that an aged Paul Kirk in panel one?*

Kirby Was Here

by Chris Knowles

As bad as the mid-'70s were for the comic book industry, they were worse for Jack Kirby. Lured by promises of artistic and editorial control, Jack jumped ship to DC Comics and found himself working for people who neither liked nor understood his work. In five short years, Jack went from being the single most celebrated creator in the comics field to a perceived has-been, doing journeyman penciling in the service of less-celebrated writers and editors.

Much has been written about the cancellation of the Fourth World books that Jack Kirby created for DC Comics in the early '70s. After signing a lucrative contract to develop new characters, Kirby soon found himself having to do the work he intended for others. Initial successes for his *New Gods* family of books resulted in inflated print runs, and once sales fell beneath expectations, DC killed *New Gods* and *Forever People.* Despite the crushing humiliation Kirby felt, he soldiered on with two new series, *The Demon* and *Kamandi.* He also continued to work on *Mister Miracle,* the last remaining series in the Fourth World troika.

A sick and dying legacy of the Fourth World, *Mister Miracle* was allowed to limp to its 18th issue and then was mercifully euthanized. It seemed as if all the spirit of the Fourth World had left Kirby with the cancellation of *New Gods. Mister Miracle* seemed carelessly written and drawn in its death march, finally ending with issue #18, which featured cameo appearances by most of the Fourth World cast.

The Demon was clearly intended to cash in on the resurgent horror genre of the early '70s. Viet Nam and the other convulsions of the '60s had given America a dose of all-too-real horror, and by the '70s, these ruptures in the nation's psyche were being channeled into over-the-top escapist fare. The Hammer horror films were revived at drive-ins and midnight movies; rock bands such as KISS and Alice Cooper – who traded in Grand Guignol imagery – were wildly popular, and such grisly fare as *The Last House on the Left* and *The Texas Chainsaw Massacre* were scarring young minds across the country. Predictably, the comics field dove into the gore sweepstakes, and such books as Marvel's *Werewolf by Night, Tomb of Dracula,* and *Tales of the Zombie* hit the stands, along with the constant stream of blood and guts from the Warren books and other, more downscale publishers. DC had its long-running mystery anthologies and the newly-debuted *Swamp Thing,* and Kirby was pressed into service with his *Demon.* Eschewing gore and guts, Kirby headed for the mythology of ancient Europe. Etrigan the Demon was Merlin's (of King Arthur's court) pit bull and was given an alter ego in Jason Blood, the immortal occultist. In contrast to Alan Moore's poetic Demon (from Moore's later run on *Swamp Thing*), Kirby's Etrigan was somewhat less verbose. Kirby's Demon rarely spouted lines more poetic than "Die! Die!" while pummeling his foes into the ground with tree trunks and boulders. Kirby also harkened back to the horrors of the Golden Age of cinema, retooling ghoulies like *Frankenstein, The Werewolf* and *The Phantom of the Opera.* However, Kirby's style seemed ill-matched to these occult adventures. His heroic proportions and minimalist drawing style did not evoke the mood that pen and ink stylists like Wrightson and Tom Sutton specialized in. Royer's line was uncommonly sensitive and light-handed on *The Demon,* but even that couldn't save it from the axe.

Kirby's other post-Fourth World creation, *Kamandi,* was criticized by many fans for being a carbon copy of *Planet of the Apes.* There is certainly some truth to this accusation. DC was unable to secure the rights for the *Planet of the Apes* comics, so Kirby was enlisted to do a book that would vie for its audience. Kirby revived a name from a failed comic strip pitch from the late '50s and *Kamandi* was born – but Kirby being Kirby, *Kamandi* took the premise of the *Apes* films and ran for the end zone, through the stands, out the stadium door and down the Interstate. *Kamandi* was a rocket ride of near-hallucinogenic fervor. Every conceivable form of wildlife had sentience and speech in *Kamandi,*

Unused cover to Demon *#15.*

Kirby's Great Disaster was never really named as a nuclear war, like in the *Apes* films. It was simply an excuse to do bugger-all with everything imaginable. Giant insects, walking plants, cities of dolphins, talking killer whales, serpentine capitalists, *X-Men*- like super-heroic mutants, giant killer bacteria, mutated cosmonauts and demon-possessed leopards all stampeded through *Kamandi*'s pages. Kamandi himself was a half-civilized teenager who navigated this bizarro world with his fists and his wits. He was given to shooting randomly at anyone who crossed his path.

Early Kamandi illo; despite its initial similarity to Planet of the Apes, Kamandi *veered wildly into its own direction.*

Kamandi's world was Kirby's America: A land where the certainties of Europe were supplanted and tossed away; where roving bands of tribes of unassimilated savages fought daily for parcels of a ravaged wasteland, as did the various ethnic gangs in the hellhole of New York's Lower East Side in the early 20th Century. In Kamandi's world, the Tigers were nominally in charge. They were regal and aloof and worshiped their own military might. Could the tigers have been anyone but Kirby's image of the WASP hierarchy? Kamandi himself was yet another incarnation of Kirby in Nordic drag. Outnumbered and embittered, he fought every day just for the privilege of existing. This was Kirby, both in the old neighborhood, and in the newly-hostile landscape of the '70s comics field. Kamandi often railed against the beastly usurpers who had stolen mankind's legacy. A parallel could be drawn between Kirby and the untutored newcomers who were taking over the comics business at the time. In *Kamandi,* Sacker the Snake sold the artifacts of mankind's glory as "funny animal pictures." Sounds like a nightmare vision of a comics publisher.

Perhaps anchored by a strong, identifiable lead character, *Kamandi* long outlasted any of Kirby's other post-Silver Age creations in its original run. Kirby's art was more tightly focused than his earlier DC work; and in much the same way Colletta's inking lent a fairy-tale quality to *Thor,* D. Bruce Berry's strange, obtuse approach to inking Kirby's pencils gave *Kamandi* a dreamy and detached feel. In a landscape of psychedelic wannabes, Kirby showed who was boss when it came to four-color fever dreams.

Encouraged by *Kamandi*'s success, DC publisher Carmine Infantino reportedly told Kirby to do another "futuristic" book. Kirby went in the exact opposite thematic direction with his next creation, *OMAC.* A futuristic Captain Marvel, *OMAC* was way ahead of its time, and in the end, too far ahead. OMAC's world was a large-scale Singapore, a corporate New World Order, policed by faceless "Global Peace Agents." High above, the omniscient "Brother Eye," an orbiting super-computer, watched over Earth and created OMAC, the One Man Army Corps, to do what its GPA's could not. In other words, OMAC's "World That's Coming" was a Militia-type's worst nightmare. Kirby focused on futuristic menaces with the evil Mister Big, the Body Banks (later appropriated, along with a Darkseid-like villain, in Marvel's *Micronauts* series) and a couple more prosaic menaces in *OMAC*'s eight-issue run. *OMAC* fell by the wayside with such short-lived DC series as *Claw, Hercules Unbound,* and *Stalker*.

As the DC brass watched new book after new book die in its effort to catch up with Marvel, Kirby floundered. He was given a number of work-for-hire assignments to fill his 60-page-a-month quota. All talk of Jack taking the reins of other DC Universe characters died along with the Fourth World. Kirby was put in service for books like the *Justice Inc.* revival, the *Sandman* revival, and the third-tier war book *Our Fighting Forces.* Jack's work on the dismal *Justice Inc.* was predictably uninspired. Jack was known to dislike working with other writers to begin with, and Denny O'Neil seemed similarly dispirited to work on a moldy old pulper like the Avenger. The misery continued with the *Sandman* revival. Originally slated to be a Simon-Kirby one-shot, accounting practices at the distributor led Carmine to believe *Sandman* was a hit. By the time the sales figures were in, Simon was long gone and Mike Fleisher was pressed into service to do something with Simon's ideas. Ernie Chan was called in to do some Kirby-like art while the King was unavailable. By the time Jack returned, the house of cards collapsed and *Sandman* was on its way to the graveyard. *Sandman* was only redeemed by the final reunion of the classic Kirby- Wally Wood team in its final issue.

Kirby's tenure on *Our Fighting Forces* was something else altogether. "The Losers" was a throwaway concept from the Bob Kanigher stable: Four mismatched soldiers from different branches of the service who launched raids behind enemy lines. Having actually served in combat in World War II, Kirby used *Our Fighting Forces* as a forum for his

This OMAC *#6 page includes a previously unpublished panel that was replaced by the shrunken-down two-page spread from that issue, due to shrinking page counts in the '70s. Inks by D. Bruce Berry.*

WWII memories, free of the hoo-hah of *Sgt. Fury.* The grit and weight of real war experience gave Jack's "Losers" a somber tone, and the horrors of the Nazi reign of terror were more clearly depicted than in the other DC war books. In his short run, Kirby took the Losers from Europe to the Pacific to the homefront. Carmine gave Jack a forum to do some of the best work he had ever done for DC.

That being said, the fact that Carmine would relegate Jack to a dog like *Our Fighting Forces* showed just how far Kirby had fallen out of favor with the DC brass. How exactly Kirby got the assignment is unknown (for all we know, Jack may have asked for it), but one thing is certain: By working on a low-selling war title, Jack was slipping away from the DC mainstream.

DC lurched from failure to failure in the waning days of the Infantino regime. The comics field on the whole was seemingly in its death throes. Only Marvel, Archie and DC had any significant presence on the racks. Second-tier publishers like Charlton and Gold Key were in their last days. The old pros at DC did their best, but they were no match for the young turks at Marvel in the eyes of the fans. Panic set in as one short- lived series after another died. No one at DC could seem to get a handle on what the fans wanted to read. Taking a cue from the old *Showcase, First Issue Special* was launched. Theoretically, *First Issue Special* provided a safe forum for DC to test drive new series without the expense of ordering a number of issues of a series and waiting for the sales stats to drift in. But it also acted as a clearinghouse for series that had been pitched and then aborted. Kirby was roped in to try out some new ideas. Perhaps inspired by the *Sandman* revival, a new "Manhunter" appeared. "Atlas," a sword and sorcery concept, also got an airing, as did an attempt at a kid gang, "The Dingbats of Danger Street." None of these ideas went anywhere, but DC used *First Issue Special* as a launchpad for a revival of *New Gods* once Carmine had left.

Though it was unknown to comics fans at the time, Stan Lee was deeply hurt when Kirby left Marvel for DC. Rumor has it that, almost from the time of Jack's departure, Lee had been making overtures to Kirby through intermediaries. As the situation at DC worsened, Kirby apparently began to take these offers quite seriously. In 1975, as the expiration date of Kirby's contract neared, an announcement was made that Jack would be returning to Marvel. It is unlikely many tears were shed on either Kirby or DC's side.

When notice was given, *Kamandi* was taken over by Gerry Conway, first as Editor, then as writer for the title. When Kirby left *Kamandi* with #40, old Marvel hand Chic Stone took the penciling reins, and Royer stayed on board to smooth the transition. Soon the book passed from team to team until it got the axe in the DC Implosion.

So why did most of Kirby's DC books fail? The grim realities of the market at the time cannot be ignored. Very few new series went anywhere for any publisher. Dozens of new titles were launched in the '70s; hardly any survived – but it must be said: Kirby's books were just plain weird. Untempered by Stan Lee's showmanship, Kirby took off into the conceptual ether. Nothing like the Fourth World books, or *Kamandi,* or *OMAC* had ever been seen in mainstream comics before. Jack's scripting was off-putting to many older fans, and many fans were not used to the unpolished rendering that Royer and Berry provided under Kirby's direction. DC, the staid and slick house, was simply not ready for Kirby unleashed. DC wanted blockbusters and Jack's cosmic/heroic ruminations must have seemed like rubbish to the DC brass.

And so must have much of what a new generation of readers wanted. Weaned on the "us-versus-them" turmoil of the counter-culture '60s, many comics readers did not want their father's – or even their big brother's – comics anymore. The DC staff must have been supremely frustrated to find themselves on the wrong side of the generational gap, especially since Carmine promised a bold new start for the line in the late '60s; but, with its army of pure and noble heroes and its stable of middle-aged journeyman craftsmen, DC simply was out of step with the times. For one reason or another, DC's attempts to jump on board the relevance bandwagon were aborted, and Marvel took up the slack. Although Kirby stood in stark relief to the rest of the DC line, fans were abandoning the DC line in droves, and Jack found himself thrown out with the bathwater.

Jack was the first real superstar of comics fandom, and the movement came of age just as Jack was reinventing comics over at Marvel. Many fans might have felt betrayed when Jack jumped ship, and many were disappointed when Jack simply did not do Marvel-style comics over at DC. Further compounding Jack's problems was the rise of the "New Young Turks" like Neal Adams, Mike Kaluta, Barry Smith and Bernie Wrightson. As these slick young artists emerged, old pros like Jack found themselves back-dated. Fandom is notoriously fickle, and each generation of fans finds its own heroes and turns against the heroes of their predecessors. Jack was simply the first to fall.

Ultimately, DC wanted characters to hand over to licensing agents for exploitation. The difference in the amount of revenue generated on the newsstand by a top-selling comic and a low seller was not all that significant. However, the huge windfalls of the Batmania craze of the mid-'60s made corporate overlords suddenly realize that comics could be more than a low-brow, money-losing appendage to their publishing concerns. The money in comics is in the trademarks to the characters. By licensing those trademarks to TV, movies, toys, lunchboxes, beach towels – what have you – comics become a great medium to develop properties for exploitation. Carmine had seen how Kirby had transformed Marvel from a dying concern to a powerhouse and he wanted some of that magic at DC; but Kirby had grown tired of the Marvel formula. He wanted to sail off into uncharted territory. He wanted to push back the envelope of the form, with new concepts and new formats. The old line at the old DC did not share his ambitions. ★

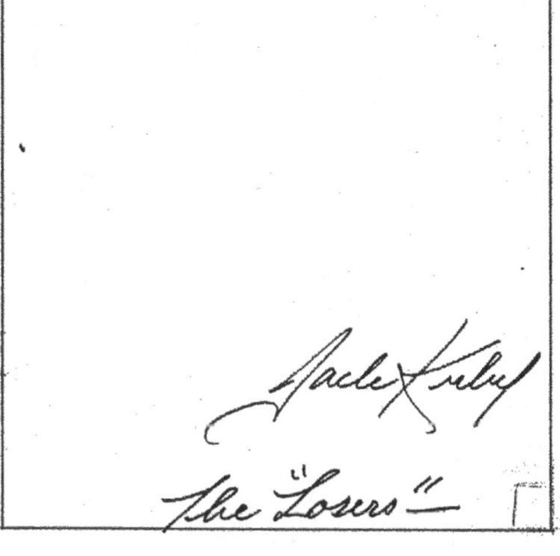

FROM THE WORDS & PICTURES MUSEUM:

This unfinished Losers page is part of the permanent collection at the Words & Pictures Museum in Northampton, Massachusetts. Museum founder Kevin Eastman remarks:

"When I first moved to Northampton, I tried to sell some of my artwork to a magazine called Scat. *They were moving onto other things at the time, but said I should hook up with this local artist who was into the same kind of stuff, artwise, I was into. His name was Peter Laird. So I called Pete, and the next day I go over. He invites me in, and the first thing I see on his wall was the Kirby Losers piece! I freaked out! It was the first Kirby original I had ever seen! We ended up talking about our all-time hero Jack and our favorite panels, covers, and stories for hours! Years, and a bunch of Ninja Turtles later, Pete gave me that beautiful page as a birthday gift!"*

The Museum is going through a financial crisis, and is in the midst of a campaign to raise the necessary funds to keep its doors open. The museum is non-profit, and serves as a valuable resource for the preservation of comic art, including a huge collection of Kirby originals (which we'll spotlight in our upcoming "Art" issue). Please do your part to sustain it by sending a tax-deductible contribution in any amount to The Words & Pictures Museum, 140 Main St., Northampton, MA 01060. ★

Golden Age Adventure With S&K's Sandman

by R. J. Vitone

Before Jack Kirby had even met Joe Simon, The Sandman was a star in the comics. An early entry in DC's attempts to duplicate the success of Superman and Batman, he arrived full-blown as the cover feature of *Adventure Comics* #40 (July 1939). The original concept was trite even then: A bored, wealthy playboy seeks anonymous thrills disguised as the dashing Sandman. The trappings are familiar as well: A baggy business suit, slouch hat, cape, gas gun, and scuba-style mask made up the working clothes of the first Sandman. Credited to writer Gardner Fox and drawn by Bert Christman, the strip lived up to the comic's name: *Adventure,* as the Sandman ranged the world as a mysterious troubleshooter. Although competent and entertaining for its time, the strip must not have generated much response from the readers. Christman left the series (reportedly to join the Air Force in search of his own excitement) and DC artists such as Craig Flessel, Gill Fox, and Paul Norris took over. Although Sandman rated highly enough to appear in *World's Fair/World's Finest* and to sit at the fabled Justice Society table starting in *All-Star* #1, clearly he was falling, not rising in rank. The Hourman debuted in *Adventure* #48, bumping Sandman off the cover. The Manhunter jumped on with issue #58. Starman was added in #61 and finally the Shining Knight rounded out the cast in #66. *Adventure* became crowded with heroes fighting for space, and Sandman moved to the back of the book. Something had to be done!

Joe Simon must have had the same thought, but over a different matter. Working at Timely Comics with his partner Jack Kirby on the immensely-popular *Captain America* had become a losing proposition. Money poured into the publisher's coffers, who in turn squeezed just a trickle into S&K's hands. Using the clout of Cap's popularity, Jack and Joe met with the "big men" at DC. As recounted in Simon's memoirs, *The Comic Book Makers,* a deal was quickly struck and ironed out. The team would work at the most successful publisher of the Golden Age. They would continue to produce work at Timely while developing new concepts. This stressful situation ended when a furious Martin Goodman (Timely's publisher) found out about the deal, and fired them.

Just as they had left *Blue Bolt* to work on *Captain America,* S&K were faced with a fresh start at a new home base. Sandman would be their first assignment. In a 1983 interview, Jack was asked if revamping the established hero was his idea. "Yes," Kirby replied. "I felt that each man has a right to innovate and to guess at what the character really represents, and the Sandman would represent something entirely different to me than he would to another guy. To me he represented something entirely different, and I'd get him into dreams and nightmares, and to me that's what he meant." So the stage was set. Sandman was ready for his new creative team – but first some changes were in order.

A Kirby fan drawing done during WWII. (below) A Simon drawing done around the same time.

Adventure #69 (Dec. '41) pits Wes Dodds (wearing a new "super-hero" costume) against giant insects. He also gains a new partner, Sandy, who "likes to pretend he's Sandman." The boy is drawn in a 1941 Bob Kane/Jerry Robinson style (*Batman* #8 is advertised in this issue). A story has grown among collectors that Kane had something to do with the "new look" and sidekick. While Sandy sports the "look" of Robin in some panels, in others he and the rest of the art bear little of the *Batman* look. It seems unlikely that Kane, riding the crest of his comics popularity at the time, would write (or draw) a 3-issue unsigned series of stories. Kane himself (never timid about accepting credit) makes no mention of the Sandman strip in his autobiographical book *Batman and Me* (Eclipse Books, 1989). Even when commenting on the flood of imitators that followed the introduction of Robin, Kane fails to mention Sandy, but does bring up Bucky (and the Young Allies), Toro, Speedy (from *Green Arrow*), Dusty (from *The Shield*), and even Roy, the sidekick of the Wizard. That alone does not mean that he didn't contribute some of the changes, but it does appear highly unlikely. *Adventure* #70 and #71 continue in the same vein; standard super-hero hijinks, interchangeable with most other strips of the day. But that day was over!

Adventure #72 still cover-featured Starman, but above the title, bold lettering called out "NEW SANDMAN!" What an understatement! A new legend headlined the strip, one that would appear frequently through the S&K run:

> *"There is no land beyond the law,*
> *Where tyrants rule with unshakable power.*
> *It is a dream from which the evil wake,*
> *To face their fate—their terrifying hour..."*
> *The Sandman!*

"The Riddle of the Slave Market" is an unsigned epic that may as well have been in *Captain America* #11! (In fact, it looks like Timely staffer Syd Shores did some "under-the-table" inks on the story.)

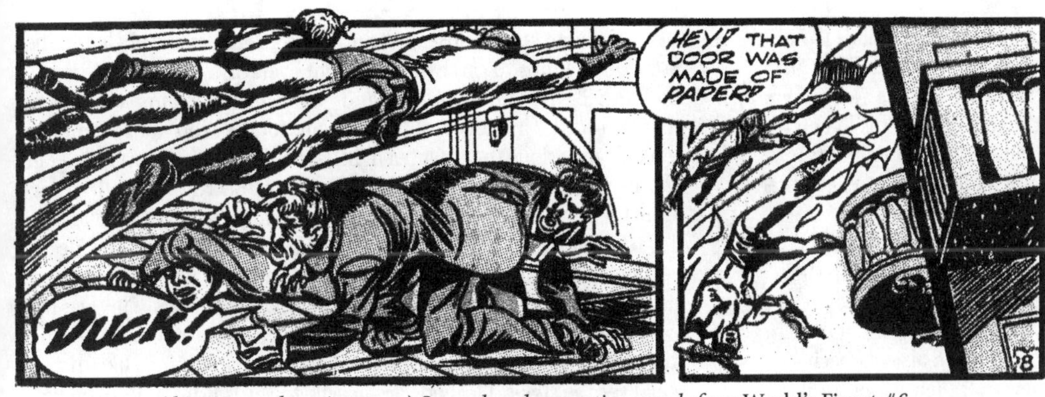

(this page and previous page) Some slam-bang action panels from World's Finest #6.

Larger panels with explosive fights or important action became more frequent. Kirby's fabled sense of exaggerated motion almost began to look confined! Other inkers' (supposedly DC staffers) styles showed up, signaling a decrease in S&K input in the months to come.

"Dreams of Doom" in *Adventure* #77 added little of merit to the series, but a classic cover team-up of Sandman, Sandy, and Manhunter on *Adventure* #78 promised a great story. "The Strange Riddle of the Miracle Maker" comes close. The *Captain America*-style splash takes us to familiar Kirby territory: A carnival, where Magno the Mystic works his wonder, aided by a gang of well-known felons. Sandman cracks the riddle, and Magno, too.

Included in *Adventure* #78 was an ad for *World's Finest* #7 (Fall '42), featuring the second and final S&K Sandman story in that quarterly title (the Boy Commandos would start a run in #8). "A Modern Arabian Nightmare" follows the trail of a priceless, cursed statue of Gori, the Protector of Thieves. Rich collectors die trying to obtain it, and Sandman has to unravel another mystery. (At one point we're treated to a "cut-away" view of Sandman's wire-poon gun, complete with detailed descriptions. This diagram style would become a recurring Kirby device.) The statue of Gori winds up in a museum showcase, and Wes Dodds speaks its epitaph: "Protection for criminals is a dream that never comes true..."

"Footprints in the Sands of Time" (*Adventure* #79) opens with a great splash of Sandman trying to free Sandy from the inside of a giant hourglass. (Jack must have liked the idea. The hourglass shows up on issue #81's cover.) Also shown in the splash is a green-skinned

Included in the package are stylistic flourishes that Jack and Joe had begun to fully develop at Timely: Bold inking to express power; exaggerated figures bursting out of panels to emphasize speed and motion; receding backgrounds that thrust the figures in the foreground into the reader's face; dramatic, filmic "under-lighting" of characters to portray evil, greed, or villainy; and of course, round panels spotted on pages, large 1/4-page panels for wider action, tilted angles, jagged borders, symbolic splashes, and good old knock-down, drag-out fights as only Kirby could visualize. Armed with his "Wire-poon" gun, Sandman is presented as the scourge of evil-doers, so powerful that he haunts their very dreams! Sure enough, nightmares haunt the Slave-Master, and Sandman puts his operation to sleep.

A classic Manhunter cover, signed by the team, adorns *Adventure* #73. The Sandman story, "Bells of Madness," looks just a bit rushed (the inking varies from page to page), but it's a good melodrama as Sandman foils a plot to swindle a girl out of her inheritance (Sandman's new costume finally appears in *All-Star* #10, advertised in this issue). *Adventure* #74 (May '42) would begin a string of Sandman covers, reflecting his "star" status. He would be featured on every cover (but one) through the end of the actual Sandman series in #102. The only exception would be another classic Manhunter cover on #79! "The Man Who Knew All The Answers" is another fine entry in the run. *Adventure* #75, however, is a cornerstone in the Kirby saga. "The Villain from Valhalla" is indeed Thor, the mythical Norse God of Thunder. When he sails into New York harbor aboard an ancient Viking ship loaded with warriors, quite a stir results; but when he cracks a cop's skull with his magic hammer Mjolnir and proceeds to loot banks, only Sandman and Sandy can save the day! Rallying the dispirited police into a raiding party a near-riot ensues. The "Vikings" turn out to be well-equipped thugs, and a wild free-for-all erupts. An electrifying full-page battle scene is the climax, and the wrap-up shows "Thor" battered and bandaged in the hospital. *World's Finest* #6 (Summer '42) went on sale about the same time as *Adventure* #75. In it was a great S&K Sandman story, "The Adventure of the Magic Forest," featuring a vaguely Vision-esque green-skinned foe called The Nightshade. His magic forest is crawling with some favorite S&K vegetation: Deadly living weeds! A burst of flame takes care of the threat.

"Mr. Noah Raids The Town" (*Adventure* #76) opens with another nightmare, causing a man to imitate the biblical Noah and to preach destruction to skeptical masses. He seems a harmless crank until a car full of talking animals shows up in town. An ape, a vulture, and a tiger rob the bank, then battle Sandman and Sandy to a standstill. Like the Vikings, the "animals" turn out to be costumed crooks, and Mr. Noah a con man. In an odd twist of fate, the villains are killed by the real animals gathered for the "ark." The story closes with a blurb for *Boy Commandos*.

By this time, S&K were turning out Sandman and Manhunter for *Adventure*, Newsboy Legion for *Star-Spangled*, Boy Commandos for *Detective* and *World's Finest*, and even Sandman chapters for *All-Star* #14-17 and #19. Despite the workload, Jack's art maintained a high level of quality. Slowly, from this point on, some "shortcuts" crept into the mix. Backgrounds were simplified or eliminated. Seven and eight panels per page became the norm, with more "decorative" round panels included.

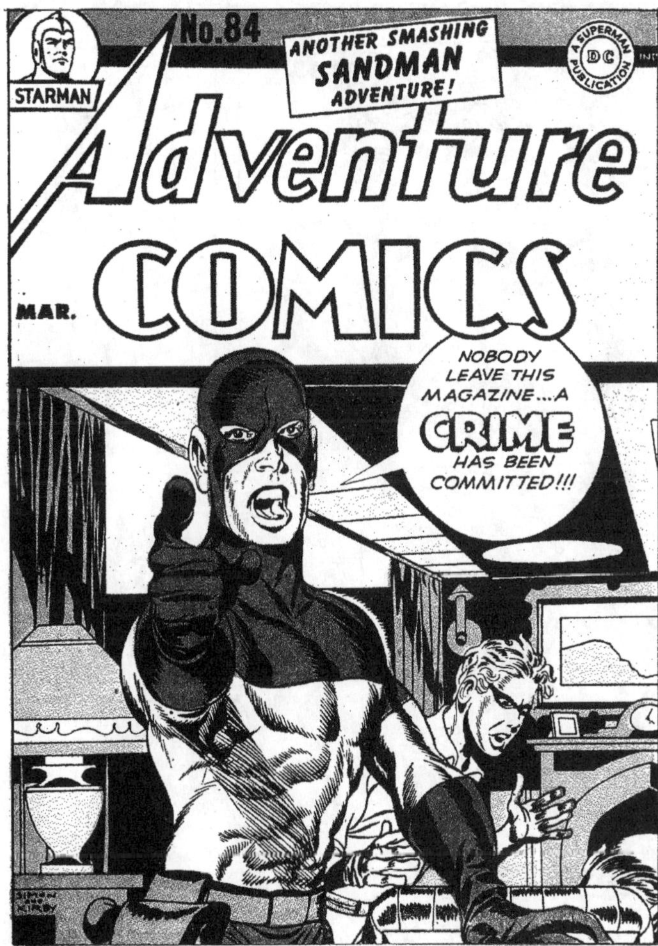

gent who bears a bit of resemblance to the villain Nightshade from *World's Finest* #6. But two odd points: 1) The guy is called "The Curio Man" and 2) He isn't even in the story! As presented, the story offers a slick premise. Mortally wounded, Sandman fights for his life on an operating table. He finds himself in "a strange world of unreality" where he learns that an hourglass holds a secret formula to make water burn. Greedy thugs plot to sell the formula to the Axis, but a revived Sandman and Sandy crush their plan. Over a heap of the criminals' stacked bodies, the heroes deliver a ringing patriotic appeal to their readers to buy more war stamps and bonds.

This call to action was a sincere one. WWII was raging, and a clear outcome was not in sight. Many comics heroes had already been fighting the Axis for years. Publishers knew that their young crop of male artists and writers were ripe pickings for the wartime draft. At DC, a decision was made to work up an advance inventory of S&K material. Covers and features were cranked out and stockpiled. When, in fact, Jack and Joe were drafted and left for duty in mid-1943, their stories continued to appear for months to come.

Sandman stayed close to the urban front. It was mainly left to the Boy Commandos to carry the S&K fight overseas. "The Man Who Couldn't Sleep" (*Adventure* #80) and "A Drama in Dreams" (#81) were standard entries in the series. "Santa Fronts for the Mob" (#82) combines some dead-serious thugs with a lighthearted Christmas story. It's a tale of Yuletime redemption for "Man-Mountain" Bearde, a wrestler rung in by the gang to scope out rich victims while acting as a popular department store's Santa. When he realized the full price of his deeds, he helps Sandman capture the crooks and ends up a hero to the cops and to the underprivileged kids he previously called brats. This was the kind of story that Joe Simon liked to produce. In a 1990 interview, he said, "If you look at them, the Newsboy Legion and things like that, you'd see the styles. I leaned very heavily towards Damon Runyon type of writing. And those stories were really cute." "The Lady And The Champ" (#83) runs the same track. The elements are simple: A boxer, a female fight announcer, a crooked fight manager(!), some nightmares and some schemes. Add Sandman, start a riot in the ring, and end up with a new heavyweight champ who's engaged. Fun. Simple. Effective.

Sandman *#1, page 20. Jack must not've thought it was a one-shot, since he gave a "next-issue" title.*

"The Crime Carnival" (*Adventure* #84) returned to familiar Kirby stomping grounds: A traveling carnival, filled with colorful crooks named for specialties; Samson, Stretcho, Presto, and Midge. They tout the sticks robbing banks and committing varied mayhem. Some strange situations have to be overcome before this one wraps up. "The Unholy Dreams of Gentleman Jack" (#85) opens with a tormented prisoner's dreams. When he's released, he uses the nightmares as blueprints to avoid Sandman. But his lust for revenge is too much. He challenges fate and almost wins. Almost. He winds up back in jail, with the Sandman's motto scrawled above him to remind him of his folly.

Adventure #86 (July '43) brought us "The Boy Who Was Too Big for His Breeches" – the story of a kid who wants to wear long pants! (I think it's better that we move on.) *Adventure* #87 takes the premise of #80's story, where a man turned to crime because he couldn't sleep, and reverses it to present the plight of Silas Pettigrew who claims "I Hate The Sandman!" Why? Because he always falls asleep – anywhere, anytime, even when he witnesses a murder, then runs afoul of the thugs. It's up to Sandman to wake him up! *Adventure* #88 takes us to the edge of the world, in a *Boy Explorers*-style high seas fable called "The Cruise of the Crescent." Fired by his "Gramps'" salty tales of high adventure, young Jerry dreams of sailing with the old man on a magnificent schooner. Pirates attack, and the plank is the kid's fate. But Sandman and Sandy appear to repel the boarders. When he awakes, Jerry is thrust into an actual adventure, and Sandman really does have to save the day. Gramps, of course, doesn't believe a word of the kid's story! "Prisoner of His Dreams" (*Adventure* #89) covers the curious crime career of timid Archibald Shelby, an accountant who "dreams up" perfect crimes, then hires a gang to carry one out as a lark. The crooks force him to continue dreaming up schemes for them. Some high-speed chases and a wild *melée* wrap-up the case.

"Sleepy Time Crimes" (#90) is a flashback story. Prominent society folks are "put to sleep" and robbed. But Wes Dodds and Sandy are among the victims. The story has more thugs and fights than usual, but not much of an ending. The art to this point had remained mostly Kirby. Not so in *Adventure* #91 (May '44). "Courage à la Carte" has the look of being patched together from frenzied layouts. Styles vary from page to page, and at least two inkers put their two cents worth in. Jack's work here was minimal, much less than half the finished package. Perhaps the inventory had run out by this time (mid-1944). S&K covers would appear through the end of the Sandman run in #102, skipping #98 and #99. *Adventure* #100 sports a striking S&K cover, and a 10-page Kirby laid-out story as well. Cover-dated Oct./Nov. 1945, "Sweets for Swag" marks the return of Jack's pencils from war service. Although the art is smothered heavily by the inker, Jack's style shows through more than half of this mystery tale. "No Nap for No Nerves" (*Adventure* #101) shows just the barest traces of any Kirby involvement; a face here, a pose there. It's generally left off any list of Kirby work, and should be. *Adventure* #102 (Feb./Mar. 1946) closes the Golden Age Sandman saga on a high note. "The Dream of Peter Green" is a quiet, good-natured tale of a do-gooder trying to build a modern, safe place for kids to play. Hardhearted businessmen and grafting politicians block the project. Sandman steps in to open the eyes of the money men. It's nicely handled, done in an understated, professional manner. Jack and Joe moved to other projects, leaving Sandman behind in the sands of time.

But Time Is A Circle...

Early in 1974, Joe Simon teamed with Jack for the final time on a newly-revised Sandman strip. Changes were again in order. A new costume (red mask, cape, shorts and boots), new sidekicks (the hulking Brute and a meatball with tiny arms and legs named Glob), and new powers and paraphernalia formed the basis of the revival. The Sandman was tagged "the master of dreams and nightmares." The legend that headlined the series went, "Somewhere between Heaven and Earth, there is a place where dreams are monitored. This is the domain of a legendary figure, eternal and immortal, who shares with man and beast all the secrets of the ages. He is... The Sandman!" Now our hero watches over humanities' dreams on a multi-screen viewer (the Universal Dream Monitor) and flashes to the aid of people in dream danger. Armed with the ability to enter and influence dreams, some real-life "weirdies" force Sandman to "hurl himself into his dream ejector tube" and enter the mortal world. "General Electric," a crazed Japanese WWII vet with a see-through cranium crammed full of state-of-the-art computers, leads a group of ex-Axis soldiers bent on revenge. Brute and Glob pitch in, unleashing an army of nightmare demons, and Sandman's supersonic whistle shatters the General's skull. Case closed – back to home base!

As presented, the book was neither vintage Jack nor solid S&K. The story is stiff and stale, while the art is almost as mediocre (despite some decent Royer inks). Originally intended as a one-shot, the letters page in issue #2 (released almost a year later) explained that the first issue sold extremely well, and "several hundred" letters of approval were sent to the DC offices, assuring a new series. Issues #2 and #3, however, were produced by scripter Michael Fleisher and artist Ernie Chua. Mike Royer remained to ink in some Kirby touches. (Jack did supply covers for these two issues, as well as for the rest of the series.) Fleisher tried to maintain a blend of humor and dream drama, while providing some Kirbyesque touches. (#3 featured gorillas with see-thru heads.) By #4, Jack had cleared his slate and returned to the strip as artist only. Fleisher would script the rest of the series.

#4's "Panic In The Dream Stream" contains some notable material. A group of "hyper-space" aliens decides to conquer the Earth by destroying humans in their sleep via their dreams. To do this, they must capture the "Nightmare Wizard" who supplies monsters for dreams. (The evil aliens, plus several of the Dream Stream creatures, are reminiscent of past Kirby creatures from his pre-hero Marvel days.) Needless to say, Sandman flies to the rescue, and leads the attack on the aliens. ("Oh boy," yells Brute, "It's clobberin' time!") *Sandman* #5 presents "The Invasion of the Frogmen!" Sandman helps series regular Jed cope with the death of his Grandpa by taking the kid on a dream mission against the terrible Frogmen (more comical versions of *Hulk* #2's Toad Men!). They win, and Jed returns to his dreadful new family with at least some relief.

Jack's cover from Sandman *#3.*

The plug must have been pulled by the time Jack finished issue #6, but it's a nice ending. Wally Wood did the inks, and the combination of the two old pros is a nostalgic treat. "The Plot To Destroy Washington" is a simply-told tale. Dr. Spider wants to blow away Washington using Sandman's fabled supersonic whistle, but Jed, Brute, and Glob manage to save the day. Jack's final regular-issue work on The Sandman closes as the hero and his help argue ethics! This was the final issue of the series, but not the last story. "The Seal-Men's War on Santa Claus," an 18-page epic by Fleisher/Kirby/Royer, showed up in *Cancelled Comics Cavalcade* and *Best of DC Digest* #22 (March 1982), titled "Christmas With The Super-Heroes." The unpublished strip (planned for #7) follows Jed on another Sandman mission. Together with Santa (and Mrs. Claus and some elves), they battle the Christmas-denied Seal-Men to save the holiday. That done, they also save charity a million dollars by proving to an old man that Santa does exist!

Overall, Jack's art on the short series is competent and fairly interesting, done in the style of his later *Captain America* run at Marvel. The Wood inks in #6 produced some nice backgrounds and enhanced the dynamic action sequences. Royer's work throughout the series was sure and steady, some of his best efforts. This version of Sandman went into comics limbo, closing the door on a super-hero style run that began back when Jack and Joe took over the character back in *Adventure Comics.* ★

S&K Golden Age Sandman Reprints

- *Christmas With The Super-Heroes* (Treas. Edition) C-43: (rpts. *Adventure* #82)
- *Wanted* #9: (reprints *World's Finest* #6)
- *Superboy 100-pg. Super-Spectacular* #15: (reprints *Adventure* #81)
- *World's Finest* #226: (reprints *Adventure* #87)
- *Forever People* #4 and *Adventure Comics Digest* #492: (reprint *Adventure* #85)
- *Forever People* #5 and *Adventure Comics Digest* #495: (reprint *Adventure* #84)
- *Forever People* #6 and *Adventure Comics Digest* #499: (reprint *Adventure* #75)
- *Forever People* #7 and *Adventure Comics Digest* #491: (reprint *Adventure* #80)
- *Forever People* #8 and *Adventure Comics Digest* #496: (reprint *Adventure* #77)
- *Forever People* #9 and *Adventure Comics Digest* #498: (reprint *Adventure* #74)
- *DC All-Star Archives* Vol. 3 (reprints Sandman chapter from *All-Star* #14)

(The entire S&K Sandman run from Adventure *and* World's Finest *is available on microfiche from Microcolor International, PO Box 243, Ridgewood, NJ 07450.)*

THE "MARVEL"-OUS CHALLENGERS

by Chris Lambert

Much has already been said about the similarities between the Fantastic Four and the Challengers of the Unknown – the two most popular comparisons being that both teams were partially or wholly created by Jack Kirby and composed of four members who formed a team after surviving an air crash. Both teams also sported single color uniforms (blue for FF and purple for the Challs). The two different team comics also presented a decisive leader (Ace and Reed), a strong man (Ben and Rocky), a young hothead (Red and a literal Human Torch, in this case), and a rather nondescript member (Sue, the veritable Invisible Girl and Prof, who while supplying the scientific knowledge *à la* Reed, was often portrayed as the blandest member of the group).

But I'd like to take the time to delve into a deeper contrast and analysis here: Story content. This is where I think you'll find an amazing degree of similarity going on in that short time span between the late 1950s and the early '60s. For comparison's sake, I'll be using *Fantastic Four* #1-30 (the first team book of the Marvel Age) and the Kirby Challengers issues: *Showcase* #6, 7, 11, 12 and *Challengers* #1-8 (the first team book of the Silver Age; hmm, yet another item in common).

The Challs cheat death, in their origin from Showcase *#6.*

Starting with the Challengers' first appearance in *Showcase* #6, The Death-Cheaters faced "The Secret of the Sorcerer's Box." The purple-clad heroes fought their share of sorcerers and alchemists as they solved the "Secret of the Sorcerer's Mirror" (first story, *Challengers* #3). Of course, what was Dr. Doom, but a sorcerer who combined his talents with that of super-science?

And speaking of Doom, in his first appearance in *FF* #5, weren't we introduced to his time platform? And a time cube was just the device the Challs ran across when they met Tico in *Challengers* #4 ("The Wizard of Time"). But before we get too far away from the sorcery, weren't Miracle Man (*Fantastic Four* #3) and Diablo (*FF* #30) also-ran, fake magicians that made things appear from nowhere? That's exactly what happened to the Challs when they ran across the evil Roc in the second story of *Challengers* #2 ("The Monster Maker"). Heck, even honorary member June Robbins turned into a magician in *Challs* #6 ("The Sorcerers of Forbidden Valley!").

The Molecule Man had a similar power and much stronger abilities when he used his atomically-altered body and focusing wand to create matter from the molecules in the air (*FF* #20, "The Mysterious Molecule Man"). The Challengers fought someone very similar in the evil Drabny who used a thought machine to spring solid menaces from his mind (first story, *Challengers* #8, "The Man who Stole the Future").

Robots are a common menace in sci-fi and comics, and the two groups met their share as the FF tackled many a Dr. Doom look-alike robot (countless issues) and Kurrgo's robot in *FF* #7 ("Master of Planet X"). Meanwhile, the Challengers faced the giant robot Ultivac in *Showcase* #7 ("Ultivac is Loose!") and the robot Kra, from *Challengers* #8 ("Prisoners of Robot Planet").

Is it alien races that make your comic book a perfect read? In *FF* #2, the "World's Greatest Comic Magazine" featured the first appearance of the Skrulls. The Challs, too, had their share of extra-terrestrials when they met the Tyrans in *Showcase* #11 ("The Day the Earth Blew Up!") and when they met the Plutonians in the first story from *Challs* #7 ("The Beasts from Planet 9").

Once in a while, heroes have been known to be captured in the comics and made slaves. That very thing happened to both groups. In *FF* #19, the FF became helpless slaves back in the land of the pharaohs, when they were at "The Mercy of Rama-Tut." Likewise, the Challs became helpless circus freaks in *Challengers* #6 ("Captives of the Space Circus").

On the back of this glued-down Surf Hunter *panel (left, inked by Wood) was this unused pencil panel from* Challengers *#4. Jack must've reused it to keep from wasting paper! Note how similar it is to the published, Wood-inked panel (shown on the next page).*

The two groups even found themselves shrunk to tiny size, as the FF fought Doc Doom in the 16th issue of their own mag ("The Mysterious Micro-World of Dr. Doom!"). That story appeared four or five years after the Challs found themselves made tiny, in the second story from *Challengers* #7 ("The Isle of No Return!").

One of my favorite plot twists occurred when both teams met an almost omnipotent alien only to have the entity thwarted when its parents came to collect the poor thing. That story line took place not only in *FF* #24, "The Infant Terrible," but also in the second story of *Challengers* #1 ("The Human Pets").

But as I did the research for this article, I couldn't help but wonder: What would have happened if Kirby had not had the argument and lawsuit with Jack Schiff? What would have happened had he stayed at DC through the 1960s, instead of going over to Marvel? It's been stated many times that Jack kept to himself the characters that would eventually become the Fourth World heroes, as early as 1965. Had Schiff not been at DC, would Kirby have been introducing the New Gods as early as 1966 or '67?

More importantly, would the Challengers have counted Dr. Doom among their rouges gallery? Would the Death Cheaters have faced the Inhumans, the Black Panther, the Kree and the Skrulls, Him,

the Watcher, the Silver Surfer, or Galactus? Counting some of the other books that Jack worked on at the House of (Jack's) Idea's, would the Challengers have travelled to the Negative Zone, Ego the Living Planet, fought against the Super-Adaptoid, Mangog, the Wrecker, or the holder of the Cosmic Cube?

Although they had no super-powers, I'd like to think that in the talented hands of Kirby, Ace, Prof, Rocky and Red could have held their own. They might have been a bit more "Marvelized"; but then again, without Jack in place, there probably would have been no Marvel. Yep, the Challs would have become Kirby "Cosmic" by 1966, and the Death Cheaters would have gone on to become the "World's Greatest Comic Magazine." I think the title of the comic says it all, though. For Kirby created not only the Challengers, but with his many concepts, he also created the Unknown. ★

(Editor's Note: Most of Jack's Challengers stories are available in inexpensive 1970s DC reprints. Don't miss these great stories!)

Kirby's Challengers Checklist

by Harold May

Challengers of the Unknown

#1 (14-page "The Man Who Tampered With Infinity" – never reprinted, 10-page "The Human Pets")

#2 (10-page "The Traitorous Challenger," 14-page "The Monster Maker")

#3 (12-page "Secret of the Sorceror's Mirror," 12-page "Menace of the Invincible Challenger" – never reprinted)

#4 (25-page "The Wizard of Time")

#5 (25-page "The Riddle of the Star Stone" – never reprinted)

#6 (15-page "Captives of the Space Circus," 10-page "The Sorceress of Forbidden Valley")

#7 (13-page "The Beasts From Planet Nine" – never reprinted, 12-page "The Isle of No Return")

#8 (12-page "The Man Who Stole The Future," 13-page "Prisoners of Robot Planet" – never reprinted)

#64 (reprints first 12-pages of "Secrets of the Sorceror's Box" from *Showcase* #6)

#65 (reprints other 12-pages of "Secrets of the Sorceror's Box" from *Showcase* #6)

#75 (reprints 24-page "Ultivac Is Loose!" from *Showcase* #7)

#76 (reprints 10-page "The Traitorous Challenger" from *Challengers* #2 and 12-page "Secret of the Sorceror's Mirror" from *Challengers* #3)

#77 (reprints 24-page "The Menace of the Ancient Vials" from *Showcase* #12)

#78 (reprints 12-page "The Isle of No Return" from *Challengers* #7, and 10-page "The Sorceress of Forbidden Valley" from *Challengers* #6)

#79 (reprints 14-page "The Monster Maker" from *Challengers* #2, reprints 10-page "The Human Pets" from *Challengers* #1)

#80 (reprints 24-page "The Day The Earth Blew Up" from *Showcase* #11)

DC Comics Presents

#84 (Superman/Challengers team-up)

The Essential Showcase 1956-1959 (DC trade paperback)

(reprints 24-page "Secrets of the Sorceror's Box" from *Showcase* #6, reprints 24-page "The Day The Earth Blew Up" from *Showcase* #11)

Greatest 1950s Stories Ever Told (DC trade paperback)

(reprints 24-page "Secrets of the Sorceror's Box" from *Showcase* #6. This book also reprints two Kirby Green Arrow stories: 6-page "Mystery of the Giant Arrows" from *Adventure Comics* #252, and 6-page "Prisoners of Dimension Zero" from *Adventure Comics* #253)

Secret Origins

#1 (reprints 6 pages of "Secrets of the Sorceror's Box" from *Showcase* #6.)

Showcase

#6 (24-page "Secrets of the Sorceror's Box")

#7 (24-page "Ultivac Is Loose!")

#11 (24-page "The Day The Earth Blew Up")

#12 (24-page "The Menace of the Ancient Vials")

Super DC Giant #S-25

(reprints 12-page "The Man Who Stole The Future" from *Challengers* #8, 15-page "Captives of the Space Circus" from *Challengers* #6, 25-page "The Wizard of Time" from *Challengers* #4)

Notes:

The never-reprinted story "Menace of the Invincible Challenger" from issue #3 is the story in which the Challs are asked to help test a chemical substance of extra-terrestrial origin, which may allow astronauts to adapt to hostile environments in outer space. Rocky takes the chemical, and is sent up in a rocket, to test his reactions. When he crashes back to Earth, he is found to have developed super-powers as a side effect of the chemical. He can radiate fire from his hands, or extreme cold, depending upon his need. He can grow to the size of a giant, make himself invisible, or generate electrical impulses. In effect, he has the powers of 5 different super-heroes... all of whom later were part of the Marvel Universe. Rocky, however, loses his powers at the end of the 12-page story.

Ace Morgan is identified in the first Challengers adventure as "...the man who shot down nineteen of the enemy in the Korean fighting —" This language appears in all of the reprints of that story, except in Secret Origins *#1, in which the wording is altered to read: "...the man who's tested more planes than any man in the world!" No explanation is known for this change.* ★

Challenging The Unknown

by Ken Penders

I suspect that when people back in 1956 picked up a copy of *Showcase* #6, few if any realized what a landmark issue they held in their hands. Even today, very few comics historians are quick to acknowledge the seeds of Marvel Comics and much of writer-artist Jack Kirby's later work are sown here. To understand why this issue – indeed, the creation of this particular series – is of importance, it is necessary to start with the man himself.

If we examine Jack Kirby at this point in time, circa 1956, we find a man who will later come to be recognized as a creative genius – and one of the driving forces of an entire industry – barely able to support his family. After years of being one-half of a team recognized throughout the comics industry as among the premier creators, Kirby is now on his own, forced to act on his own behalf, without any guidance or supervision from his former partner, Joe Simon.

Whereas Simon had previously handled all matters regarding contracts – spelling out details such as credits, royalties, and other pertinent matters while his partner concentrated on the primary task of creating comics – Kirby now found himself handling matters he had demonstrated neither the interest nor the ability to do so. Clearly, all Kirby wanted to do was work in a field he excelled at in order to provide a living for his wife and children.

The record shows that prior to going solo, a Joe Simon/Jack Kirby byline would be prominently featured on every Simon & Kirby story, whether it was Timely's *Captain America,* DC's Newsboy Legion or *Boy Commandos,* Headline's *Fighting American* or any other series they worked on. Afterwards, Jack's lack of negotiating skills would prove his downfall numerous times, resulting in not only a loss of rights, but – for years – of recognition as well.

Looking back through the benefit of hindsight, one can see Kirby's work leap through the pages of *Challengers of the Unknown,* but at the time, a young boy sitting back to read *Showcase* #6 would be hard-pressed to say who wrote and illustrated that issue, for there are no credits to be found anywhere, save that of the Editor in the indicia. Not only that, but that same boy would not be able to find any Kirby credit or acknowledgement in any issue throughout Kirby's entire run, nor was there a letters page of any kind to provide that information.

(Regarding the Editor credit in the indicia, apparently it was about this time that DC started listing individual editors on whichever books they handled, but this was not implemented on all the books at the same time, which is why Editor-In-Chief Whitney Ellsworth's name appears on books he didn't edit. Jack Schiff was listed in the indicias of the *Batman* books published in the late fifties, but not everything he handled was so indicated, as *Challengers* issues can attest to.)

Because the typical reader of the day had no idea who created that first appearance of the Challengers, that same reader would also be unaware of the fact that this issue shows us the birth-pangs of Kirby maturing from the style many readers were familiar with during the so-called Golden Age, to the style many readers would become familiar with during his period at Marvel. If anything, even today, debate rages over who did what in regards to Challengers, especially over that first *Showcase* appearance.

Recently, Joe Simon has gone on record stating he had a hand in the initial development of the COTU, and he may very well have, along with writer Dave Wood. What may have happened is that COTU was probably one of the last, if not the last, concepts being developed at Mainline, the publishing house Simon & Kirby ran, and when the assets were divvied up, Jack ended up with the *Challengers.*

In researching the years 1954 through 1956, one can see those were hard years for both men, as well as the comics industry as a whole. Most accounts seem to shy away from talking in detail about a period of time they'd rather forget about. In his book *The Comic Book Makers,* Joe talks of maintaining ownership of copyrights when discussing another publisher putting out books he and Kirby prepared for Mainline, but even Simon admits he wasn't above accepting a check that didn't

Splash page from Showcase #7.

HESSE'S STORY IS SUDDENLY INTERRUPTED BY ROCKY...
OKAY...YOU BUILT THE MACHINE! GET TO THE POINT... WHAT HAPPENED?
SOMETHING STRANGE AND UNCANNY...SOME-THING INSIDE THE MACHINE! AN ACCIDENTAL PROCESS BEYOND OUR SCOPE!

WE'RE THE MASTERS NOW, EH, HESSE? HE'LL MAKE MILLIONS FOR US!
WHY NOT? AS HIS CREATOR, I KNOW WHAT WILL STOP HIM AS WELL AS MAKE HIM TICK!

(left) Showcase *#7, page 6, inked by Stein. (right)* Showcase *#7, page 15, inked by Jack.*

amount to much more than a pittance for the material he was supplying the publisher with. As for Kirby, a record of his workload indicates he must have spent many a sleepless night wondering how he was going to put food on the table for his family. Of the comics with a cover date marked May of 1956, only one book released featured his work, while only two books with a June cover date could boast the same. Considering his productivity, unless he had non-comics work available, the lack of work would very much motivate his priorities. Credit and copyrights be damned. A steady paycheck was more important.

The gestation of the Challengers most likely occurred during this period, as Kirby scrounged around for whatever work he could find, accepting anything and everything that came his way, with little regard for the future. In those days, not many creators gave consideration to credits, copyrights, ownership of original art, or other matters that have since become important issues to today's creators. To Kirby, Challengers represented a project he could market to a prospective publisher as a means of simply creating employment for himself.

When he approached Editor Jack Schiff with COTU, chances are Kirby had thrown out Wood's script and submitted his version along with his art. Most accounts credit Kirby as the solo creator, whereas it's only been in later years any mention of Dave Wood or Joe Simon's involvement surfaces. Kirby in later years was quick to downplay Stan Lee's contributions in creating Marvel's line of characters, but he hadn't been so quick to dismiss Joe Simon's involvement in their collaborations. Since Simon doesn't present any evidence regarding his contributions, nor has he been linked through any records in DC's possession, I think it fairly safe to say his input was minimal at best. (Referring back to *The Comic Book Makers,* there isn't one mention of Challengers. Considering Simon didn't hesitate to point out who created what, especially his own contributions to any particular creation, this tends to lend further credence to Kirby being the primary, if not sole creator of COTU.)

In examining the script for the premiere adventure, the text reads very much in the style closely associated with Kirby that he used on all his books upon returning to DC in 1970.

"WHAT"S OUT THERE? Places we cannot see! Things we fear to touch! Sounds that do not belong to this world! Riddles of the ages lurking beyond the bridge without a name! Only men living on borrowed time would dare cross that bridge! Here are such men and the incredible adventure of... The Secrets of the Sorcerer's Box!" Surely, this is copy that could just as easily have been found at the beginning of a *Demon* story, or any book Kirby worked on in the '70s, for that matter. The rest of the story continues in a very similar fashion.

(In fact, all the *Challengers* stories up to Kirby's last (*COTU* #8) read as though written by the same writer, with one notable exception. "The Man Who Tampered With Infinity" in the first issue of *COTU* reads as though written by a different person. Either Editor Schiff was incredibly heavy-handed with the editing pen, or he used a story commissioned by someone else, which makes absolutely no sense at this point, unless one takes into account difficulties Kirby appeared to be having with Schiff around this time in late '57-early '58.)

As for the art, the opening pages appear to be rendered in ink by Marvin Stein over Kirby's pencils, but then Kirby steps in to handle a page here, some panels there, with Stein evidently completing whatever Kirby didn't. (As for Roz Kirby's credited involvement, most sources seem to indicate she spent time helping out filling in the large black areas and assisting with minor line work; thus her contribution could be described as minimal at best.)

Once you begin to examine the *Showcase* issues more closely, the interesting aspect of Kirby's style, storytelling, and panel arrangement comes through, representing a gradual departure from a look and style many readers had been familiar with in his earlier work. Comparisons with early issues of the *Fantastic Four* become unavoidable, due not only to content of the story and the series' concepts, but also because of the look presented. Kirby's art appears cleaner, less cluttered, and the finished art looks more like early Marvel than an issue of *Stuntman* or *Boys' Ranch.* (Because no one inker has been

HE HAD A SMALL PLANE WAITING-- WITH A SELF-LAUNCHER! WE'LL GO AFTER HIM IN OUR WHIRLYBIRD!

A question of inking: (left) Challengers *#3, page 4, supposedly inked by Wood; (right)* Challengers *#7, page 4, definitely by Wood.*

identified in regards to *FF* #1, one could be forgiven if they believed Stein inked that issue as well. The look is that similar, and not just because of Kirby's pencils.)

Panel arrangements evolve rather quickly from the various shapes Kirby employed on all stories prior to *Challengers* to the rather strict grid format he would come to use exclusively after. By *Showcase* #11, featuring the third COTU adventure, only three pages at best use anything other than the normal grid format Kirby usually employed, and of the three, one of those pages was original art first seen in *Showcase* #7, which described the Challengers and their abilities in one neat, concise page. By *Showcase* #12, there are no signs anywhere of circular panels, panels with curved or jagged edges or anything of the sort. From here on in, if not for the DC trademark displayed on the cover and interior pages, the rest of Kirby's run in terms of visual appearance could easily have been published by Marvel in the early '60s.

Where the controversy usually arises concerns the finished art, which brings up an interesting point. If the company didn't keep records over who did what, to all intents and purposes, any attempt at crediting a writer, a penciler, or inker years after the fact is pure guesswork at best. For instance, in *Challengers* #75, which reprinted the COTU's second appearance from *Showcase* #7, DC finally acknowledged Kirby as the writer and illustrator of the story. However, upon examining the art closer, there are clear indications of a different style in various panels throughout the story. It is quite possible that Marvin Stein helped out for whatever reason Kirby needed him to at the time. (An interesting side note about this story concerns the character of June Robbins. In the original *Showcase* issue, her hair is brown, not black as depicted in the reprint, and I daresay she bears something of a resemblance to Kirby's beloved wife Rosalind.)

Subsequent adventures have only intensified the credit debate. DC credited Wally Wood in *COTU* #77 for inking the fourth installment printed in *Showcase* #12, yet the finished art for that book bears a closer resemblance to the work seen in *Showcase* #11 – which DC now credits to Bruno Premiani – than it does to any of the stories that Wood clearly inked for *COTU* #4-8. The same also applies to stories featured in the first three issues of *COTU*. In the reprints, DC credits Wally Wood as the inker of those stories, yet the style bears little if any resemblance to the work Wood would turn in on the following five issues. It's hard to accept the premise that Wood would be asked to submerge his style so thoroughly, and then given the green light to ink in the style he always had. The comparisons are that jarring.

The series concept itself, as well the scope of the adventures contained within any issue, were also somewhat of a departure for Kirby, reading more like a blueprint for things to come not only at Marvel in the '60s, but DC in the '70s as well. Where prior to *Challengers* Kirby's characters were more grounded in reality – including those like Captain America, who was basically a soldier wearing the flag fighting the Nazis – *COTU* was a step forward into the realm of the fantastic, even more so than such genre books as *Black Magic*, which he co-created.

In the Challs' first *Showcase* appearance, Kirby wastes no time in getting us through the origin. By page 4, we're well underway into the initial adventure, which begins with a nod to the mythology of our past that transitions into a portal of tomorrow, mysticism giving way to super-science. To hammer this home, the villain Morelian, depicted as someone who evokes images of a medieval past, meets his destruction by failing to heed the warning signs of a technology he didn't understand.

Like other series most closely identified with Kirby – *Captain America, Boy Commandos, Fantastic Four, Thor, New Gods, Forever People* and *Mister Miracle* – *Challengers* was very much a vehicle he used to express his vision of how he saw the world. While story after story would deal with amazing (at the time) concepts – such as sentient artificial lifeforms, technologically advanced aliens bent on conquering the Earth, a cloned criminal, telekinesis, time travel, space exploration, atomic mutations and other subjects equally fantastic – a personal philosophy was beginning to emerge. Technology could only be trusted up to a certain point. What triumphed over all was the indomitable spirit, strength, courage and compassion of man. Kirby was very much preparing for the future, but he was by no means embracing it. He saw warning signs all over the place.

This splash from Showcase *#11 has an EC-feel to it.*

Many readers have long since pointed out the similarities in the origins of both *COTU* and the *Fantastic Four*. What many fail to recognize are the significant differences. *Fantastic Four* is a more hopeful series, while *Challengers* is a more pessimistic one. The Challs didn't have the benefit of cosmic powers enabling them to survive the horrible crash they experienced. It's clearly spelled out that they should have died, but didn't. Every mission from here on in could be their last, and they know it. The FF, on the other hand, look forward in wonderment to the next adventure. Thus, we can plainly see how the attitudes of Jack Kirby and Stan Lee each affected their approach to writing their stories.

If *Showcase* #6 was a portent of things to come, *Challengers* was also a flashing red light heralding danger ahead. From every indication, Kirby was bristling with ideas waiting to be told. Eventually differences between him and Editor Jack Schiff, to say nothing of other editors at DC Comics (as a result of an unspoken company policy – that other editors would not touch a freelancer associated with a certain Editor, especially if these differences resulted in a freelancer losing an assignment) resulted in a parting of the ways. He took those ideas and translated them into Marvel Comics with Stan Lee. Years later, differences between Kirby and Lee would result in Kirby withholding new ideas and taking them back to DC, which would go on to publish his most personal creation, the Fourth World.

As for the *Challengers*, when Kirby returned to DC, I suspect he didn't do new material for the series for much the same reasons as he hadn't for *Fantastic Four* when he returned to Marvel years later: He had already done that. He was ready to explore new vistas, always venturing forth in search of the unknown. ★

Jack Kirby's Train Of Thought

Excerpts from the Kirby interview in Train Of Thought *#5, 1971.*

(Editor's Note: This interview was conducted just after Jack launched the Fourth World books, and offers a fascinating glimpse into his thoughts at this early stage of the characters' development.)

JACK KIRBY: The idea of the Anti-Life Equation is that all Darkseid has to do is say a word and you become a slave. That's what he's after. He likes that and the fact that he likes that makes him valid, see? Because he exists and his idea exists, so why the hell shouldn't that be valid? That's the way Darkseid looks at things, and he's going to get what he wants in his own way. He's very ruthless and he's very smart.

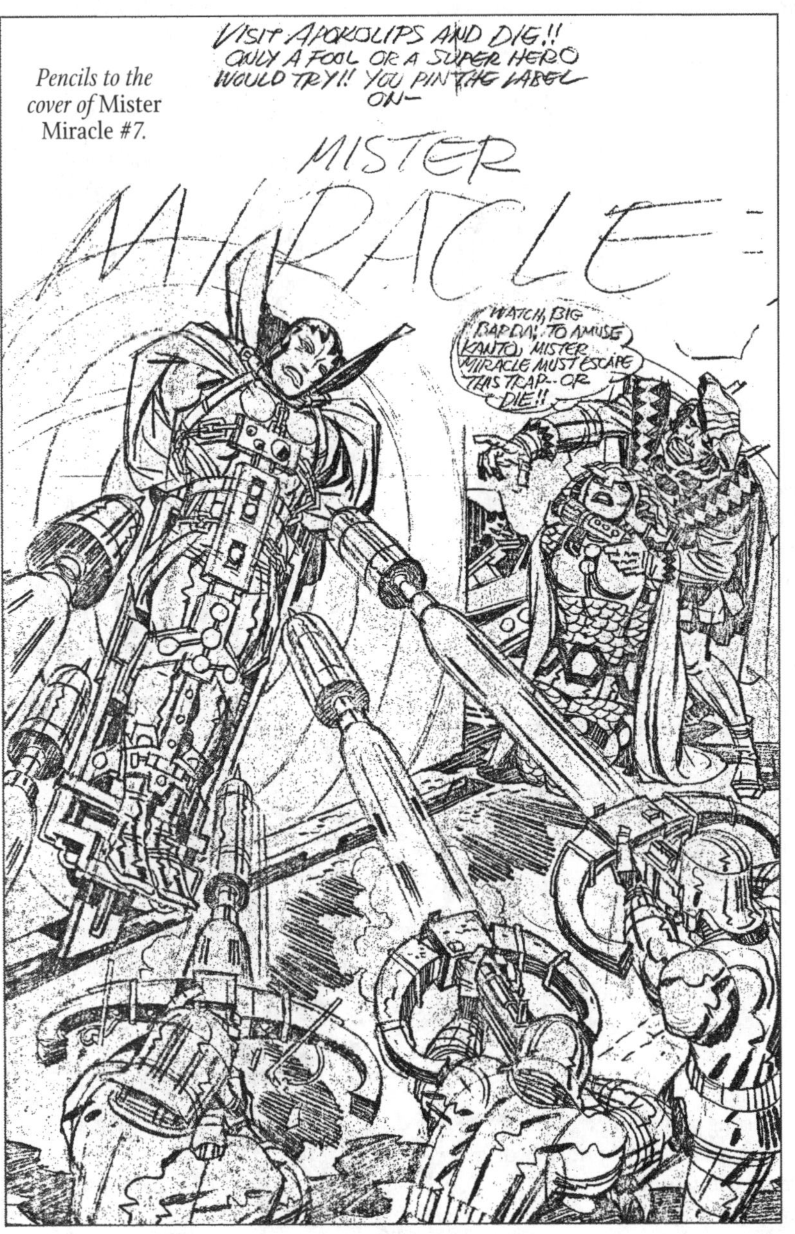

Pencils to the cover of Mister Miracle *#7.*

TRAIN OF THOUGHT: Infinity Man seems as powerful as Darkseid, and even a lot more powerful than Superman.
KIRBY: No, he's not as powerful as Darkseid. Well, he has intense power, but Darkseid is, as the story unfolds... I mean, his powers are almost as great as Darkseid's, but there's something about Darkseid that is universally overpowering. He is evil itself, or what we consider evil.

TOT: Is Infinity Man more powerful than Superman? There's one scene where those robots pound Superman into the ground (*Forever People* #1).
KIRBY: But remember, they had the strength of entire galaxies; heavy mass galaxies.

TOT: But that other guy just sorta tossed them around.
KIRBY: Well, Superman might be able to throw him around, but just not as easily as he throws everything else around. Power is relative.

TOT: In about three issues of *Jimmy Olsen,* you've changed the entire image of Superman. Are you going to continue to use Superman?
KIRBY: Yes I am. Superman will continue as a character in many of these stories. In the first story we thought that it would be important to use him and see how relative he would be to that kind of thing. And Superman is relative. Superman has, despite the fact that he is a super-being, emotions just like everyone else. He's not a robot. If I were a super-being, I'd just be a human being with super-powers, which is the way I see Superman. He's a human being with super-powers and he can be lonely; he has emotions, he can be in love, he can hate people. He hates evil.

TOT: That would be the same idea as at Marvel wouldn't it? You know, that super-heroes have feelings and all that.
KIRBY: Yes, but Superman is invincible, and Superman is the first super-being to come into literary life. There he is alone. That's the way I see him. If I were a Superman among two billion people, despite the fact that I was a super-being, I'd feel pretty insecure. For instance, say I was a white hunter in Africa and I were to walk into a cannibal village. Despite the fact that I had a gun and they didn't, despite the fact that I had ammunition and they didn't, I'd feel pretty insecure, despite the fact that I could probably shoot my way out. Superman is alone in our world.

TOT: What about the other super-people like Supergirl and Kandor?
KIRBY: That's very little help in a world of two, three billion people. If suddenly two, three billion people developed a psychosis – say they felt you were a danger. What if Superman didn't want to be good? What if Superman wanted to be evil? What if Superman wanted to impose his power on us? That's the way human beings think. Did you ever feel that although you gave authority to some people they might abuse it? Suppose that someone said that Superman might abuse his powers and have reason to harm us? Suppose you believed him? What would you do? You'd try to kill Superman. That's what Superman faces. Superman faces three billion inferior people; and not only inferior, but Superman has to make sure they don't feel insecure about the fact that they're inferior to him. That's a Superman's problem, or else he'd better take off for the moon.

TOT: What's this new change in Superman? Is he going to be weaker than he used to be?
KIRBY: No, not weaker, but he's going to be a real person with super-powers against other people with super-powers. And there's not only going to be other people with super-powers but ordinary people who, although they don't have super-powers, may have to make super-efforts. Which I think is a good thing. I think the noblest part of man is the fact that he could transcend himself if he really tried. I mean, man is a very pliable object. It's been proven that you can put a man in 120 degrees of heat, hold him there for a certain amount of time and this guy – he's not going to walk out chipper, but he's going to walk out. Man has been subjected to what they might call 'killing stress' and he's walked out of that. In fact, I underate stress. Man can do something we might consider a super-act. Man can bend steel, and under stress

he might be able to bend some even more intractable object. Man with training can perform super-acts. In other words, man can transcend himself in many ways. You take a man like Leonardo Da Vinci, who transcended the ordinary by so many different accomplishments in so many different fields because he was a curious man who made a super-act out of his own curiosity. He was a master painter, a master architect, and I'm not talking about an ordinary mechanic. He was a master at everything he did because he had that transcendent quality of making a super-act of whatever he did, because he had insatiable curiosity.

Who is to say that man hasn't got the power to become a super-being because we happen to be in a time period where men certainly aren't super-beings? The possibility exists mentally, physically, and possibly even other ways. We just can't see right now. So why not ordinary people contending with Superman? That's what I've got in the stories. I'm going to have ordinary people engaged in great efforts that make them more than they are, and super-beings with super-powers deciding that it may be more fun to be a human being. There may come times when it's wrong to use a super-power, or weak to use a super-power. Darkseid himself – the villain of the piece – at one point decides not to use his power because he's a professional and he feels that he's using his powers on a second-rater, and it would demean his own profession to use that power, so Darkseid will not harm him. Darkseid lets his victim go saying that it would denigrate his own abilities to destroy that man. Darkseid, although he's evil, is too much of an admirer of his own power or his own stature to denigrate himself. He won't do it.

TOT: It seems like you've created another character like Doctor Doom; he's evil, but he has his own code.
KIRBY: Of course. Some of the most virtuous men are murderers by the fact that they stick to their own principles. Hitler was a virtuous man in the context of his own principles. He initiated a pretty dirty hour as far as humanity was concerned, but the idea is that he did it for his own reasons. They were mad reasons, but he felt that he was sticking to his principles. So even an insane man may have an insane code of ethics. Some people will kill for second-rate reasons and that makes their act even more monstrous. The fact that a man will kill for a little money or kill for unnecessary reasons as the thrill of it might be looked down upon by a professional killer. He wouldn't kill for a few dollars or for the thrill of it. The professional murderer would kill for good money and good reasons and he would consider himself a craftsman. As Darkseid does. Darkseid is very evil. He's the equivalent of a mass murderer, but he wouldn't waste his super-powers on just one individual. He wouldn't go out of his way just to kill one man; it would be ridiculous. He wouldn't do it. He'd just walk away. That's how my villains think.

TOT: Why is Earth so important to him?
KIRBY: Because Earth becomes a testing ground. This is where we have thinking animals, and there's the principle of Anti-Life. If someone took control of your mind and you were not able to think as yourself any longer, you would no longer be yourself. You'd be something in his command. You as an individual would be dead. That's Anti-Life. In other words, if you gave yourself to some cause, and gave up everything as an individual and you were at the beck and call of some leader, you would be dead as an individual. And that's what Darkseid wants. He wants control of everybody. If it was snowing outside and you weren't wearing any shoes and it was 38 degrees below zero and this guy says, "Go out and get me a bologna sandwich," you have to go through all that; you obey him automatically, you obey him meekly. You walk out without a coat and you freeze to death. He doesn't care. You do it anyway despite the fact that you don't want to do it. You're dead as an individual. You have no choice. You can't object and you have no stature as a person. You're dead. A slave is a dead man. That's what Darkseid wants. Darkseid wants complete subjugation of everything at a word – his word. He wants every thinking thing under his control.

I believe it's an evil concept but he doesn't think so. Not if he's Darkseid. If you had the power you might not dislike the idea. Everybody sees the world from where they sit. It may be uncomfortable for the next guy but you think it's great. The right idea to Darkseid is anything that benefits him. He isn't going to worry about you. He sees the world from where he sits, and of course what he sees is big. He's a big man. Darkseid is a tremendous, powerful, evil figure, and he's going to see everything in a cosmic view. He's not going to see a view of the candy store around the corner or what's playing at the Palladium next week. Darkseid is going to see everything in an over-powering cosmic view, and of course what else would he want but complete subjugation of everything? Earth is included in that everything, and my concept is that somewhere on

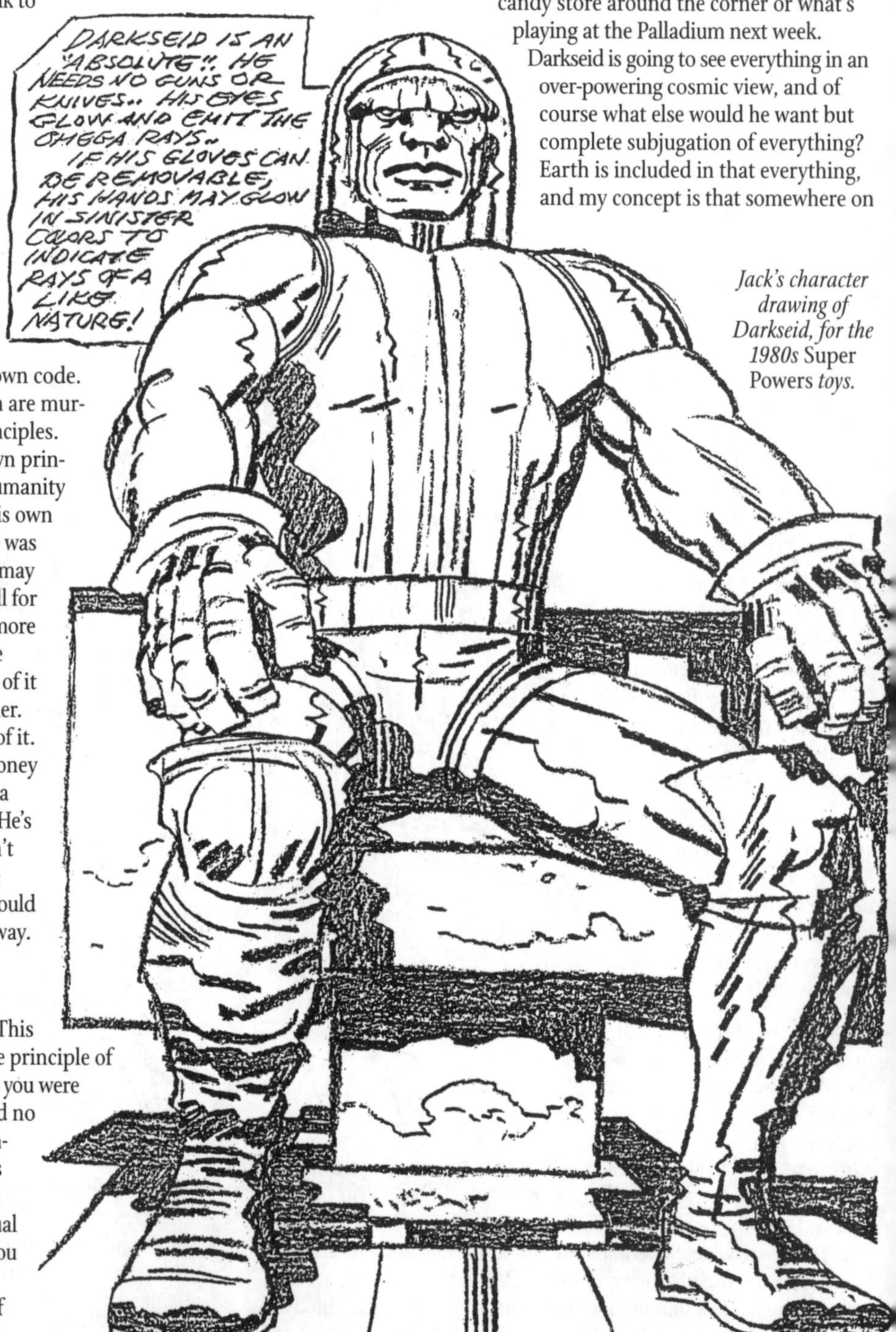

Jack's character drawing of Darkseid, for the 1980s Super Powers *toys.*

A ghoulish shot of Desaad, from the early 1970s.

Earth is someone who can solve the Anti-Life Equation, and Darkseid is after that poor soul. He shakes up everything. He shakes up cities and creates all kinds of plots.

TOT: Does he have any equal, or is he the most powerful?
KIRBY: No actually, he's not the most powerful, but he's the most relentless. In other words, Darkseid is strictly a first-rater. I don't classify gods as far as their power goes. I classify them as far as their personality goes. Each god, if he used his power right, could defeat another god. If I used my power right I could defeat anyone on Earth if I wanted to. As a man, if I used my physical strength at its best, I could overpower anybody I wanted to. If I did it right. It's the same way with the gods. If they used their super-powers right, they could defeat any other god. Darkseid is no different except that Darkseid is an evil guy with a lot of class. He's the kind of guy that might outthink you, and with super-powers involved it could be in a very dangerous and earthshaking way.

TOT: Have you ever thought of creating a hero that was nonviolent?
KIRBY: The Forever People are nonviolent. The Forever People are a challenge to comics, I feel, because although they're engaged in violent activities, they never fight. The nearest they come to fighting is this fella, Big Bear, who is just so strong that he could lean against a pole and that's it. The Forever People are a challenge to see how nonviolence can work in comics. I feel that nonviolence coupled with some kind of sustaining influence can work in comics. I don't feel that you have to show blood and gore and guts. I think it's repellent. I've seen enough of it in its reality, and it's just as repellent when it's drawn as in reality. I see nothing of any value in anything that has what you call shock value. I see nothing in that except using that sort of thing to prove a point. In other words if you're making an anti-war document or if you're trying to tell the truth about a certain subject, and the blood and gore was a part of that subject, I wouldn't omit it. If I were going to make an *exposé* on anything I would show anything connected with it. For instance, in a gangster movie I would show the results of being a gangster—the life activities as well as the end and death. I would show exactly how it is they ended. I would show the bullet holes because it's part of the picture, but I wouldn't exploit it for its value alone. I see no entertainment in that sort of thing.

TOT: Do you think you'll be able to appeal to the little kids as well as the serious readers?
KIRBY: Of course, it's a problem. I know I might fail at it, but I'm trying to make it a universal thing if I can. That's a challenge in itself. It's a heavy subject. The god stuff always was. I'm trying to put something into it to give it an affinity to the times themselves. I feel these are times when that kind of thing is felt. These are times when we're all operating on the edge of holocaust, Apokolips, and everybody is living with the bomb. It's a strangelove kind of time, so I felt that the characters might reflect that sort of thing. There's the problem of making all your characters different. There's the problem of making them reflect everything that is good or bad inside of us. Our weaknesses and our strengths, and our potential for good and evil. It's enormous. I'm trying to get all that across in an entertaining sort of way. Of course I can't do it all in three or four issues. At Marvel it took five years, and my problem was that I couldn't do a simple story – I had to create an instant world in each magazine. An instant world with everything in it to get the ball rolling. Say, if I had done a foreign intrigue story. Just a story say of a stolen diamond or a stolen national secret of some kind. The hero would have to go after it and there would be a lot of gimmickry and a lot of shooting. Yet to have an individual story you'd establish a single character. You wouldn't know where he came from, or what he was really like. You might have to wait out an entire series of books until you really knew anything about him. I could've gone that route, but I was forced to go the other way. I'm coming in from the other end. I'm coming in with the whole ball of wax, which I have to unravel. I could've come in with just one character and developed his friends, but from what I've done here you know everybody. You know where they came from. You don't know exactly what kind of world it is but you know it isn't like Earth. You don't know what kind of powers they have but you know they have powers. You know there's a war going on between good and evil. You've got that all in one issue. What I have to do is separate the individual action from the mass action. In other words, there might be an adventure with just Darkseid or one of the Forever People, but you'll know

Jack at the 1972 San Diego Comic Con.

them. You'll know what kind of people they are from the first issue.

TOT: On the way up here we were talking about the Forever People and the way I see it, when you consolidate these kids they become Infinity Man. But the message is: Join together in brotherhood and you become one solid force of good.
KIRBY: Yes. And of course there could be a solid force of evil too. These same people can have equal, evil counterparts. A poet doesn't always have to be good. You take Ezra Pound; he was a poet in the classic sense, he was a fine poet. Nothing wrong with his poetry except he was a Nazi. He had a different view than we did. You have a picture there of a poet, but a different type of poet. Of course with other types of people you've got corresponding types. That's what the New Gods and the Forever People will try to say. That there's good and bad in all of us. We have to face them both, and sometimes we have to make a decision between each. It's nothing we can avoid. It's nothing we can rant against. Each individual has to make his own decision on it.

The *Forever People,* as I said before, is a reflection of our times like the *New Gods.* We live in a time where we have the bomb and the apocalypse all around us. Somebody is always talking about holocaust and about the whole thing blowing. Then we live in the kind of time where everybody says, "Well, that doesn't have to happen. We're gonna do great. We're gonna take all of these things that we make for destruction and we're going to do good things and build up some kind of universal brotherhood." Now that may happen too. I think that's a good thought. I have these two worlds, Apokolips and New Genesis. There could be a New Genesis for all I know. That's the way I see it. It's heavy stuff of course, but I think it's going to have to unravel to become the kind of thing it is. I'm going to have to unravel all the characters so that you really get to know them and know what their powers are. For instance this kid in a cowboy hat, Serifan, isn't just a kid in a cowboy hat because it isn't a cowboy hat. The others have other gimmicks. What I've done is come in with the whole ball of wax, plopped it down, and I'm going to ask everyone's patience to allow me to unravel it.

TOT: Is Mark Moonrider Mark Evanier?
KIRBY: No, nobody is any definable person that I'm acquainted with.

TOT: Earlier you were talking about how anybody, if they had the training and really put forth the supreme effort, could do almost anything. Is this the kind of character you want to show in this Mister Miracle guy?
KIRBY: Yes. Mister Miracle is a superbly professional craftsman. He's a superb escape artist. He's a cool character. He'll play it cool to the very end. I have a scene where it looks like he's going to get killed, and it's going to happen in seconds, but he just lays there deliberately trying to see how fast he can get out of there. He wants to see if he can beat those few seconds because he's a professional. That's what makes him a super escape artist. He'll put his life on the line to see how well he can do his craft. That's the kind of guy he is. He'll bet you $10,000 that he can get out of any trap you devise. If you lose you pay him ten thousand bucks. He puts his life on the line, but that's his trade.

TOT: Is this Supertown that the Forever People come from directly related with New Genesis?
KIRBY: Supertown is New Genesis. It's just that the children are young and they have their own terms for things.

TOT: And is Mister Miracle part of the New Gods too?
KIRBY: Mister Miracle, strangely enough, comes from Apokolips. He's a defector from Apokolips. Mister Miracle is a nice guy. He just doesn't think evil. He feels that he should have a good time. He'd like to live

Mister Miracle drawing done for the Masterworks *portfolio; thanks to Steve Rude for his back cover inks!*

Mike Royer inked this pencil drawing for a San Diego Con program book.

life cooly with tongue-in-cheek, and just playing it for the experience. They don't like that on Apokolips. Of course, they come after him.

TOT: Is Supertown going to be like the New Jerusalem concept which is all peace and happiness, or is it going to have good and evil?
KIRBY: It has good and evil in it because it has real people in it. Orion is a real person. Orion is a fearful god because he is afraid of himself. He wasn't born on New Genesis. Orion is a very fierce god because he has an inner hostility. He fights himself constantly because he knows that he's not from New Genesis and that he's capable of tremendous evil.

TOT: We consider Darkseid evil and ourselves good. Does Darkseid consider himself good and the other way of life evil?
KIRBY: Yes. Darkseid considers anything evil that's going to stop him. If you stop me, I consider you evil.

ROZ KIRBY: I'm stopping you, you've got to eat.
EVERYONE: You're evil, you're evil.

TOT: Why have they been redrawing some of your pictures of Superman?
KIRBY: Nobody up there is used to me. In other words they're afraid of what I'm going to do, and I don't blame them. They know what Murphy Anderson can draw and Neal Adams and the rest, but they don't know how I'm going to treat a thing like Superman, which has made maybe a hundred-twenty million dollars for them. Now I do it their way and I feel they were right. ★

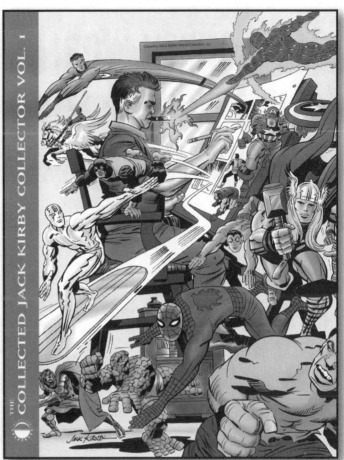

The Fourth World (And Beyond): Some Minority Opinions

by Adam McGovern

Jack Kirby's Fourth World series, and much of what came after, were sweeping sagas which can prompt a variety of readings. Mine may contrast with some which have long been held, but the essence of Kirby was to look at familiar ideas in different ways.

The Asgardian Connection

For one thing, to conclusively view the *New Gods* as heirs to the Aesir, even if that's what Kirby intended in a strictly narrative sense, is to impoverish the full scope of his vision in creating the series. First of all, many old sources and new inventions converged in these characters' formation. Their unspecific familiarity is just what gave them resonance, and helped make Kirby one of the few artists to successfully create modern myths for an age without mysteries.

Second, the series had just as many roots in the Jewish experience (a legacy which both Kirby and I share, behind our Irish-sounding names) as in Norse tradition. Apokolips' ideology resembles a triumphant Third Reich, and its visual presentation is unmistakable as a planet-wide concentration camp. Much of New Genesis' names (Isaiah, Esak) and imagery (Highfather's patriarchal raiment), its codes of vengeance and inherited burden, its times to love and times to kill (the pacifist Lightray's transformation into a kind of warrior, and Isaiah/Highfather's opposite course), its characters' reliance on prophecy, are straight from the *Old Testament* and other Jewish lore. Interestingly, this specific reference makes the series more universal, in that the living religions of Judeo-Christianity are open to more interpretations than the closed circle of Norse myth.

Kirby's Crystal Ball

Surely Kirby's foresight about his medium cannot be over-emphasized. This would not be the first essay to note the Fourth World's introduction of such then-unappreciated but now-commonplace concepts as limited-run series and overlapping narratives in simultaneous publications – not to mention Kirby's rejected plans to present the saga as a series of what would much later be known and embraced as "graphic novels." The King was equally perceptive of current events, from his early assimilation of countercultural motifs (The Forever People, Jimmy Olsen's "Hairies") to his exploration of late-'70s millennial anxiety in *The Eternals,* to his astute and witty wordplay: Delicious puns and non-sequiturs like "Boom Tube" and "Fourth World" itself show him to be second only to George Clinton, among '70s artistic figures, in his keen ear for social psycho-babble.

But Kirby's insight goes way beyond the fact that Darth Vader is identical to Doctor Doom and "The Force" is "The Source" and the Death Star looks like Kamandi's Tracking Site and the entire end sequence of Close Encounters is lifted directly from the coming of the Celestials in *Eternals* #2, and so on. What interests me most is not Kirby's pop-culture contributions, but his social predictions.

The idea of swapping children between New Genesis and Apokolips to suspend their cosmic conflict would be seriously proposed by peace advocates for the rival US and Soviet union in the mid-'80s. The New Gods' practice of patching into the spirits of their ancestors with what would one day be familiar as hand-held computers accurately anticipated both the electronic toys and the new-age mysticism of our own decade. The high-tech Hairies indeed find their match in Jaron Lanier ("The

Steve Rude inked this piece for the deluxe hardcover collection of History Of The DC Universe.

Father of Virtual Reality") and today's other freak mathematicians and scientists.

Likewise, the image of the defeated dictator Kafka standing for a mug-shot during the *OMAC* series eerily approximates similar real-life photos of Manuel Noriega after the Panama invasion. (Of course, unlike George Bush, the One-Man Army Corps did it clean, never having actually employed Kafka and hauling him in without sacrificing thousands of innocent civilian lives. But Kirby was tapping into the same popular fantasy, and much sooner.) In many other ways, from its advance depiction of late-'70s/early-'80s video-arcade hysteria (a scene in the "New Bodies for Old" storyline) to its envisionment of the Mohawk's return (the title character's "warrior god" hairstyle), *OMAC*'s "World That's Coming" came sooner than anyone expected. These lowly comics held keys to our near future that no one noticed, during or since.

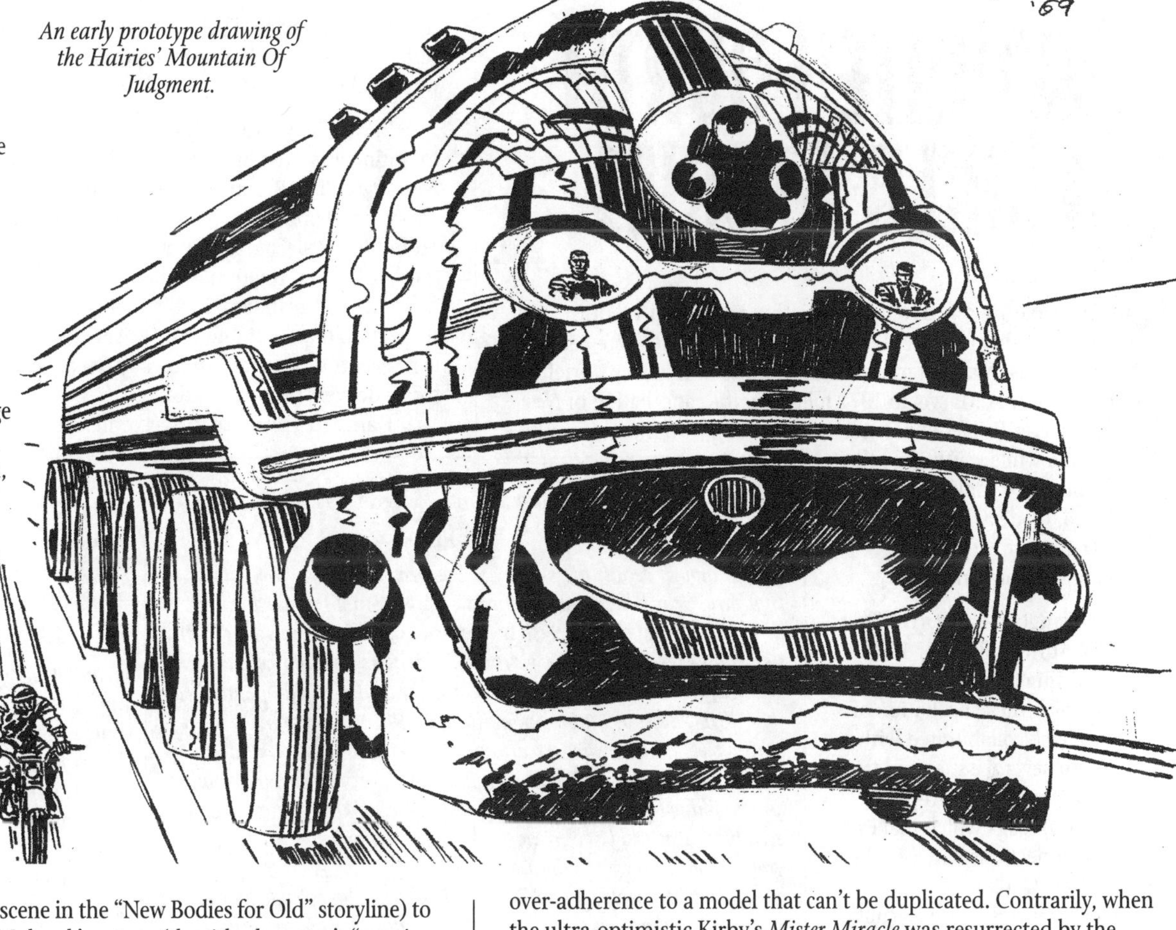

An early prototype drawing of the Hairies' Mountain Of Judgment.

The Gods, Ourselves

Notwithstanding the generations of readers who have cherished and identified with the Fourth World series, I would caution us not to look for too much of "ourselves" in these heroic beings. In an era of "relevant" comics, Kirby jettisoned a certain measure of realism, thereby making the medium show an uncommon honesty about itself. Kirby understood that gods, and super-heroes, and celebrities, are projections; anyone who accused him of hokey dialogue and broad gestures was off the mark because the New Gods' very unreality is what made them ring true. We relate to them as personified abstractions (to borrow Charles Hatfield's definitive phrasing from *TJKC* #6), not as familiar peers.

That said, Kirby did – innovatively – humanize these deities to the extent of imbuing them with the very qualities that make us uncomfortable about ourselves and our society. In their murderous inter-generational conflict, the New Gods are the ultimate warring, fragmented family; many protagonists, particularly Orion, have no worse enemies than themselves. These characters' deeds were larger than life, but so were their dysfunctions – another way in which Kirby was ahead of the societal times, by anticipating the confessional pop culture and public discourse of the '90s.

When The King's Away...

It may come as a surprise that I also don't believe Kirby's creations have been mishandled in his absence. Not exactly, anyway: I believe they haven't been mishandled enough. Nearly every Kirby revival by other hands has been an unqualified travesty, but the main cause is over-adherence to a model that can't be duplicated. Contrarily, when the ultra-optimistic Kirby's *Mister Miracle* was resurrected by the ultra-skeptical Steve Gerber (significantly, a later Kirby collaborator) for a handful of issues in the late-'70s, the results were unexpectedly wonderful. The audacity of the mismatch suited Kirby's own sense of adventure, and it worked. (Unsurprisingly, it got cancelled even quicker than Kirby's original.)

Similarly, subsequent *New Gods* scenarists have neglected to explore unfamiliar territory, endlessly reassembling the elements left by Kirby in his handful of issues, rather than moving on from the Orion/Darkseid conflict as Kirby most likely would have by now. How about bringing that storyline to a long-overdue conclusion, and proceeding to an epic civil conflict between the "Bug" society and the pious gods of Supertown? (The condescension that even Orion and Lightray show toward Forager of the Bugs is one of those grand dysfunctions I was referring to.) Or a crusade for Orion's soul after the ferocity of the final conflict makes him crack and take the place of his father as the head of their hellish world? Enduring so many rash cancellations, Kirby had to learn how to leave things behind, and so should his would-be successors; but I guess new action-figure molds can only be minted so fast.

What Happened Next

One view I hold which is no doubt shared by the majority is that Kirby's post-DC, non-*Eternals* work does not rank among his best. The short-sighted powers that be cancelled such a large number of his great books that eventually even the King had to start straining for ideas. Nonetheless, I'm not so bothered by the incompletion of his magnum opus. I'm even satisfied by it, in a way. Like the Dead Sea Scrolls (an apt analogy, given Kirby's subject matter), the Fourth World's unanswered questions enhance its mythic stature; the empty spaces let it loom all the larger in our imagination. What we have should be enough for us. And what Kirby needed – recognition – was, thankfully, largely his before the end. His failures were really the industry's, but the triumphs were all his. ★

Favorite Fourth World Stories

by Joe Magee

When people are asked to name their favorite Fourth World stories, they invariably include "The Pact" along with other "pre-cancellation" tales. Alas, I started reading comics during Jack's brief eight-month stay at Marvel in 1972 following the cancellation of *New Gods* and *Forever People.* Those stories, beginning with the *Thor* multi-parter he did while waiting for the opportunity to continue the Fourth World saga, made a deep impression on me. Here are my favorites, chronologically presented.

1. "Strangers in Asgard," *Thor* #210-215, April-September 1973. After returning to Marvel immediately following the cancellation of *New Gods,* Jack collaborated with Stan Lee for several issues and then wrote and drew this multi-part "hypothetical" saga which makes clear the connections between the Old and New Gods.

The epic begins with Karnilla, the Norn Queen. Driven by her love for Balder the Brave, Karnilla attempts once again to create a magic spell that will give her control over the minds of men and gods. Intrigued by the new technologies of humans, she mixes some scientific laws into her magic. The resultant spell mysteriously sets off the Odinsword, and both Karnilla and the Odinsword are transformed. Ragnarok has begun.

A stunned Odin soon has Karnilla, her growing army of mindless slaves, and a mutating Odinsword to worry about. While conflict escalates between Karnilla and Odin (with Balder as the bone of contention), three disguised strangers appear in Asgard. The strangers are, of course, Orion, Lightray, and Metron (although for copyright reasons they are called Ikarus, Makarri, and Domo) and they are fleeing a disaster in their own universe that has its origins in Asgard.

It falls to Thor and Loki (on Odin's command) to form an alliance and track down the strangers. As the plot unfolds, we learn that the strangers are here to witness the final days of Asgard, where a great weapon (Anti-Life) will first appear. As the strangers desperately search for clues to the "Great Weapon," Karnilla continually tests Balder's loyalties in a series of confrontations between her army and Odin's. Soon Asgard is destroyed and Ragnarok in full bloom. But before the end occurs, the strangers join forces with Thor, out-scheme Loki, confront Karnilla, and finally disappear into the Odinsword's new shape. And just before the very, very end, Balder and Karnilla also vanish into the Odinsword's final form. There they are given a choice to redeem the carnage. Their choices, and the deep love they both tragically profess for each other, echoes throughout eternity, and paves the way for the New Gods.

2. *New Gods* #12, November 1973. This was Jack's first issue after Infantino was fired in June and Jack had returned to a now-monthly *New Gods.* "The Promise" is one of his "tapestry" issues which filled in background on major characters. Focusing on Darkseid, this story is set in the Royal Court of Apokolips during the reign of Darkseid's mother Heggra. It alternates between Darkseid's romance with the delicate Suli (including the birth of their son Kalibak), and Darkseid's realization that Anti-Life truly exists. (Metron's discovery of a way to view events on Earth – specifically the actions of 20th century dictators – delivers proof of Anti-Life.)

Darkseid's promise to keep Suli safe from the deadly intrigues of Heggra's court fails because of his growing obsession with Anti-Life. With Suli's murder, Darkseid experiences his own struggle with the Source, which ends with his acquisition of the Omega Effect.

3. "If This Be Infinity," *Forever People* #17, September 1974. Another tapestry issue, this one filling in background on Infinity Man and the Black Racer. Few people suspected the true nature of Infinity Man and how Jack connected "Infinity" with space/time points which overlapped the Final Barrier between our universe and the Source. This was Jack's initial foray into the Source's outer domain, an area ruled by the Black Racer.

4. "Orion Among the Hairies, *New Gods* #27, February 1975. One of the most offbeat of the Orion stories, this issue showed just how out-of-place he is in a civilized setting; specifically, among the cerebral and pacifistic Hairies and their Mountain of Judgment. The story is an intricate mystery involving a shape-changing villain, but it is the character of Orion – unsure, intimidated, and thoroughly real – that takes center stage as he makes mistake after mistake in pursuit of his enemy.

5. "The Maze," *Forever People* #21, May 1975. While four of the Forever People are put in jail for not paying their rent, Darkseid finds a comatose young woman whose mind has strung together in proper sequence the nine archetypical symbols that form the Anti-Life Equation. With Desaad's help, Darkseid enters her mind only to find himself in a struggle to survive. Meanwhile, Mark Moonrider has his pacifistic ideals tested in a battle of wits with the cornered Desaad.

6. "The Survivor," *New Gods* #40, March 1976. Exploring the ruins of New Genesis, Lonar discovers an Asgardian child who survived the death of the Old Gods (thanks to the sacrifice of a mysterious figure who is clearly Thor). The child tells her tale to Highfather, Lonar, and Metron, and they begin to connect the Death of the Old Gods with Anti-Life.

7. "The Truce," *New Gods* #41, April 1976. Another tapestry story,

(*from* Rocket's Blast Comic Collector *#94, 1972)*

KIRBY LEAVES DC:

Although details are sketchy, it has been learned by this column that Jack Kirby has severed relations with National Periodicals. His three books, Mister Miracle, The Demon *and* Kamandi *will be given to Dennis O'Neil to edit. New artists and writers have not been chosen yet, but probability is high that two or all of the titles will be cancelled.*

Kirby, beset by a number of disappointments during his two-year stay with National, is reportedly again working for Marvel and Stan Lee. The exact details, as we mentioned before, are unclear and nobody seems willing to commit themselves at this time. We have heard, however, that Kirby will be given the X-Men *book and possibly his own small group of books to write, edit and draw.*

The Kirby contract with National, we are told, provided for an easy "out" in the event that Jack became disillusioned with his work at the company. The actual reasons for the split are many and have not been made public, although speculation has been made in a number of areas. Kirby was supposedly to have been given a number of comics to edit (with no creative responsibility), which never came about, plus the fact that his living in California obviously left much to be desired in the way of communications. Nothing, however, has been made public and most likely will remain personal unless one side or the other brings it out.

There is a hitch... or rather could be. It is understood by this corner that DC and President Carmine Infantino have considered holding Kirby to his contract (which has at least two years to run yet) by paying him a salary to do nothing. Jack would not have to turn anything out for National under this arrangement, but he would also be prohibited from working for Marvel or any other major comic book company.

The official break was announced August 23rd, but very little additional information has been forthcoming since then. Each side is obviously weighing the legal aspects and we should have further to report by next issue. What this will do to the proposed New Gods *paperback project is unknown, but National owns the rights to the entire series.* ★

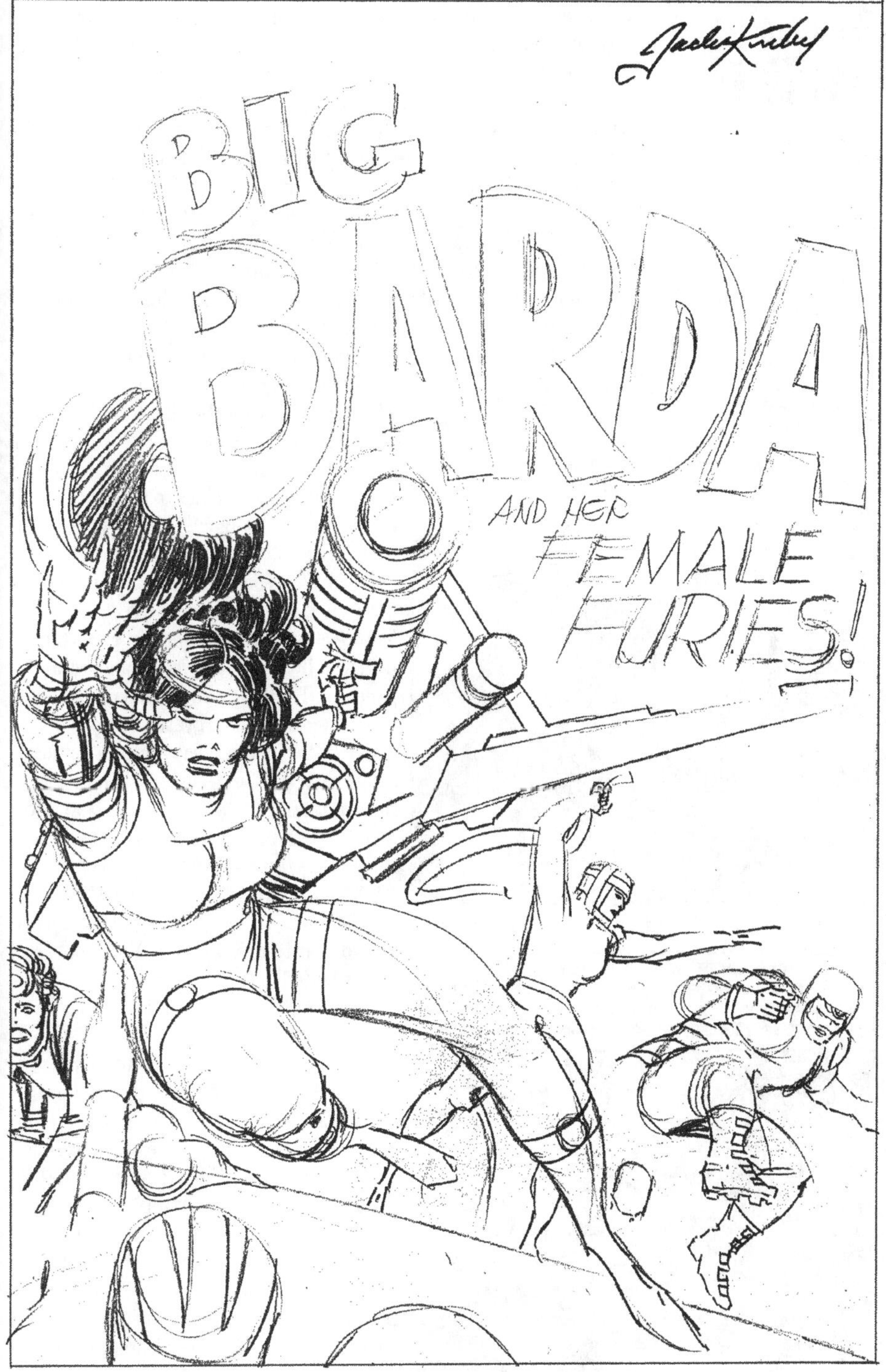

Cover sketch for a proposed Big Barda *comic, which was never realized.*

this one details Orion's adolescence on New Genesis, and how he won the Astro-Force from Kalibak in an athletic competition between New Genesis and Apokolips. This story also shows Orion's brief time on the Council of the Young and his friendship with Lightray.

8. *New Gods* #50, January 1977. As a confident Darkseid closes in on the last three symbols of the Anti-Life Equation, Metron and Infinity Man journey to the galaxy of the Promethean Giants and cross "The Final Barrier" to the Source. After encountering Seagrin and other New Gods who have died in battle, they flee from the Black Racer into the Inner Domain of the Source, where Balduur and other mega-gods exist. Balduur communicates with Metron, and gives support to Metron's suspicion that the Anti Life Equation first came into existence during the Death of the Old Gods.

Balduur also elliptically accounts for his transformation from a warrior god to his present state and – under Metron's prodding – hints at a dangerous path through the intersecting domain of the Old Gods' Land of the Dead that might take the travelers into the time/space coordinates of the Old Gods.

9. "When the Universe Ends," *Forever People* #33, May 1977. Here's the big one: Darkseid's acquisition of the Anti-Life Equation and the shutdown of the universe. Only a few people – the "Immunes" – are left to help the Forever People hide.

10. "Among the Dying Gods," *New Gods* #56-64, June 1977-February 1978. Moments before Darkseid acquires Anti-Life, Metron scoops up Orion and Lightray and the three gods flee through the Final Barrier, unaware Devilance the Pursuer is following them. They journey recklessly through the Outer and Inner Domains of the Source, but skirt the unknown center-most area. They then find the opening into the Old Gods' Land of the Dead – Valhalla – and narrowly escape Hela.

Orion, Lightray, and Metron finally reach DC's version of Asgard, but are separated by space/time disturbances caused by their own traveling. Although this saga is a retelling of *Thor* #210-215, the emphasis now has switched to the New Gods. Metron slowly pieces together the origins of Anti-Life (as the war between Odin and the "Sorceress" worsens). Orion and Metron end up fighting Thor and other Asgardians, dealing with Loki's schemes, and then finally confronting Odin and the "Sorceress." Meanwhile, an injured Lightray arrives weeks earlier. He falls in love with an Asgardian goddess who nurses him back to health.

At the end, during the final moments of Ragnarok, a battle to the death between Orion and Devilance is halted by the appearance of a gigantic, fiery "Moving Hand" which emerges from what was once the Odinsword and is now simply "the Wall." This blazing hand pulls Orion, Lightray, and Metron into it. Inside the Wall, the Moving Hand asks (in burning letters) if Orion will become the Living Embodiment of the Life Equation. Orion agrees, is transformed, and then emerges (along with Metron and Lightray) not into the Ragnarok of Asgard, but the Ragnarok of New Genesis (which has been split in two). Supertown is in ruins, the dead are everywhere, and Highfather has just been killed by Darkseid.

The whole series comes down to this moment: Can Orion control the savagery and hatred inside himself and use the civilizing and peaceful principles of the Life Equation to nullify Darkseid's control of Anti-Life? During the battle, Orion's monstrous physical appearance and violent nature is revealed to all. He suffers immensely before he gives himself to the Source and to Life. Thus, Darkseid is defeated, Anti-Life is nullified, and the universe returns to normal. ★

(Editor's Note: Although the snippet from RBCC *#94 and the Big Barda cover are genuine, obviously, none of these comics actually exist. But I felt this was a beautifully thought-out hypothesis of how Jack might've continued the Fourth World, had he been given the chance. I hope you enjoyed it as much as I did, and I extend my thanks to Joe for his patience in waiting over two years for me to publish it.)*

A King For A Queen

by Rich Morrissey

Jack Kirby's involvement with one of DC's oldest characters came unexpectedly, but briefly, in 1958. Green Arrow had been around for seventeen years, having first appeared in *More Fun Comics* #73 (November 1941) in a story by Writer/Editor Mort Weisinger and artist George Papp. Many other writers had handled the series since then, most notably Ed Herron and Dave Wood, both frequent Kirby collaborators over the years. But Papp, except while in the Army during World War II, had remained the sole artist until Weisinger decided to switch him to *Superboy,* on whose stories he would remain until 1968.

Green Arrow and Speedy showed the definite influence of DC's most successful non-powered crimefighters, Batman and Robin. Oliver Queen was a millionaire playboy like Bruce Wayne, and also the guardian of a young teenager, Roy Harper, who doubled as his partner. As Batman had his Batmobile, Batplane, Batcave, and Bat-Signal, so did Green Arrow have his Arrowcar, Arrowplane, Arrowcave and Arrow-Signal. Weisinger himself always maintained Green Arrow was inspired by Robin Hood (who had also been cited as the inspiration for the name and costume of Batman's boy sidekick) and the source of the name was never given. (Still, another successful DC hero of the time, Green Lantern, was said by creator Martin Nodell to have been inspired by a colored subway lantern. Could Green Arrow have owed his name to a traffic light?)

At that time, Green Arrow's feature was unusual in appearing in two different DC titles. Kirby took over the strip from Papp as of *Adventure Comics* #250 (July 1958) and *World's Finest Comics* #96 (Sept. 1958). According to stylistic analyst Martin O'Hearn, Kirby not only drew but wrote (or at least rewrote existing scripts for) his first two *Adventure* stories, both of which displayed particular Kirby touches. "The Green Arrows of the World" in #250 featured the crime-fighting archers of many different countries. Possibly inspired by a similar *Batman* story a few years before, it seemed rather limited in its theme, but Kirby's imagination enabled him to create several fascinating variations on a theme – none of which, regrettably, ever made a comeback.

Panels from Adventure *#255 (above) and #256 (below).*

With #251, Kirby began to delve much farther into science fiction than Green Arrow's adventures normally did. In "The Case of the Super-Arrows," Green Arrow and Speedy acquired a quiver of trick arrows from the future – enhancing their crimefighting skills until the arrows fell into the hands of criminals. Needless to say, the battling bowmen ultimately prevailed with their traditional arrows combined with their superior skill.

Probably the most famous of the Kirby Green Arrow stories appeared in *Adventure* #252 and #253: "The Mystery of the Giant Arrows" and "Prisoners of Dimension Zero." The use of a two-part story was itself a departure for DC at the time, but Kirby seemed to be frustrated by the 6- and 7-page length of Green Arrow's stories, and took full advantage of the extra space to bring Green Arrow and Speedy into a dimension where people were "a mile high" (dramatic exaggeration; they couldn't have been more than 80 feet high), and even toy arrows sent across a dimensional barrier could cause havoc on Earth. With the aid of yet another counterpart archer – the giant dimension's Xeen Arrow – Green Arrow and Speedy were sent back through the passageway – silent but otherwise identical to the "Boom Tube" of Kirby's later Fourth World series – arriving on Earth just before it closed. Ed Herron scripted this and most of the rest of Kirby's Green Arrow stories (although Dave Wood, his brother Dick, and Robert Bernstein may have written one or two each), but in all probability Kirby continued to have a hand in the plotting.

Perhaps the Editors (Mort Weisinger, Jack Schiff, and reportedly George Kashdan) considered these stories a bit too far-out for the character. The four stories in *World's Finest* #96-99 were more in the strip's traditional direction, involving a kidnapped man's clues to his location ("Five Clues to Danger" in #96) and a ruse to preserve Oliver Queen's identity ("The Unmasked Archers" in #98). #97's "The Menace of the Mechanical Octopus" did feature a very memorable crime machine which sadly was destroyed in a mere six pages, and #99's "Crimes Under Glass" featured a battle in a Kirbyesque futuristic location, but neither was quite as unique as the early *Adventure* stories. Kirby's remaining run in *Adventure* #254-256 also focused on other facets of Kirby's skill as the archers faced Western bandits in #254's "The Green Arrow's Last Stand" and Japanese sailors unaware of the end of World War II in #255 ("The War That Never Ended").

Kirby ended his run on the character with, literally, a new beginning—"The Green Arrow's First Case" in *Adventure* #256. Asked by the Editor to write an origin for Green Arrow, Kirby and writer Ed Herron came up with the version that has been followed ever since (superseding the original, Golden Age version), in which playboy Oliver Queen, marooned on a desert island, first made a costume of leaves, and developed some rudimentary trick arrows he anonymously put into use against pirates. Fittingly, although quickly gone from both Green Arrow and DC itself, it was Jack Kirby who established the definitive background for one of comics' oldest heroes.

Green Arrow's art was turned over to Lee Elias, a talented artist but hardly in the King's league, and within a year he had lost his feature in *Adventure Comics.* His *World's Finest* feature was relegated to alternating issues with #134 and dropped entirely after #140, leaving only his status as a Justice League member to keep him in DC's lineup at all.

Yet it was his JLA membership that led to his renewed success, as former Marvel writer Denny O'Neil – taking over the *JLA* in 1968 – was inspired by Kirby's character development in Marvel's team books to develop the one character in the book *not* hampered by a solo series. Green Arrow quickly became one of the most interesting characters in the book, soon becoming a co-star in *Green Lantern* in an acclaimed series by O'Neil and artist Neal Adams that renewed his popularity. In that way, the King's influence on the Emerald Archer proved far more enduring than his actual work on the series itself. ★

GREG THEAKSTON INTERVIEW

Interviewed by John Morrow

(Greg Theakston was born November 21, 1953 in Detroit, Michigan. Besides inking a number of Jack's final comics stories, Greg founded Pure Imagination, publishing a numerous books on Jack and other comics artists. He also developed his Theakstonizing process, which bleaches color from published comics pages, leaving only the black line art for use in reprinting classic strip art. Pure Imagination has recently released the first volume of The Complete Jack Kirby, *an ongoing project that will ultimately reprint thousands of pages of Jack's work. This interview was conducted by phone on August 28, 1997 – Jack's birthday.)*

THE JACK KIRBY COLLECTOR: Did you grow up on Jack's work?
GREG THEAKSTON: Yes, my older brother Pat would scout down great stuff and introduce me to it – including Jack Kirby comics, among other things. He brought home the Green Arrow appearances in *World's Finest* and *Adventure,* Harvey's *Amazing Adventures, Black Cat Mystery, Double Life of Private Strong* and the first couple of issues of *The Fly* as well.

TJKC: So you grew up on Jack's solo work more than on Simon & Kirby?
GREG: Yes, basically it was after they'd separated. *Challengers of the Unknown* was another good one. Jack's style was so potent that you could tell his work from company to company, even though you didn't know who the artist was. It wasn't long before my brother started bringing home the Marvel monster books, which cleared up the mystery.

TJKC: I've always felt your inking style was more reminiscent of the Simon & Kirby house style than any of Jack's later inkers.
GREG: Joe Simon once looked over my inking and said, "Where were you in 1948?" *(laughter)* I was very flattered. If I tend to emulate the Simon & Kirby period, it's because I'm really trying to ink the way Kirby inks his own stuff. By studying his old comics, I've kind of figured out how Jack likes to ink his own stuff, and I use that as my touchstone. But there's a huge chunk of Wally Wood in there, as well as Joe Sinnott and Frank Giacoia.

Greg with Jack at the San Diego Comic Con.

TJKC: What's the Kirby work you were most impressed with?
GREG: As a kid, the *Fantastic Four* was my favorite. It was a really good time to read comics. There was just no doubt that Kirby was the king.

TJKC: How do you think the 1960s Marvel books hold up now, with a little hindsight?
GREG: I still find them terrifically entertaining; very, very formulaic. One of the reasons they went over so well was the colorful villains and the bizarre set-ups. Lots of that's due to the Ditko and Kirby influence in the work.

Greg's inks on this unused Kamandi *#1 cover; the pencils are reproduced elsewhere in this issue.*

TJKC: When did you first meet Jack?
GREG: I'd been interviewing Kirby since around 1970 and finally got to meet him in 1971 in New York at one of the Seuling comic conventions. Roz, Jack, the kids and I went across the street to Howard Johnson's and had some chocolate sundaes, which Kirby always dug. *(laughter)* I was in awe! I was 16 or 17, and it was pretty mind-boggling.

TJKC: How did you first get into comics?
GREG: My history goes back to 1969. There was an organized fandom in Detroit where I lived. It was a terrific place to be interested in comics, because Jerry Bails was there, and Shel Dorf was living in the city at the time. Shel did the first Detroit Triple Fan Fair comics con, and I worked on them for years; ultimately I ended up owning the show.

In 1969 I published my own fanzine, the *Aardvark Annual* #1, which had an interview with Stan Lee – it was hot stuff for that period. *(laughter)* I printed it in the laundry room of our house on a mimeograph. There were probably 25 copies of this six-page fanzine. But it brought me to the attention of the founders of FFCG (Fantasy Fans and Comic Collectors Group) in Detroit. The FFCG had planned to do a book on Jack Kirby, and I had been accumulating a checklist of his material. I'd spoken to Kirby, so it became my project for the club.

I spoke to Steranko at a 1970 convention, and invited him to write something for our book. Jim was thinking about doing his own book on Kirby, and he said, "Work with me, and I'll absorb whatever you guys have done so far, and I'll publish the book." So I pitched my efforts in with him. We got to know each other better and he invited me to come to Reading, Pennsylvania to help him found SuperGraphics. I graduated high school in June of 1971, and eight weeks later I was helping Jim refurbish a three-story row house, and helping him move into his new building. Ken Bruzenak moved in after I got there. I spent a hot August steaming all of the wallpaper off every room in the house on all three floors. *(laughter)* The deal was, if we worked for him during the day, he'd give us art lessons and room and board. He would give us comics theory and make us practice in the evening hours. It was kind of like a school and a boarding house. Steranko had just quit Marvel Comics, and his new company SuperGraphics was getting a lot of attention. It was a very exciting place to be. I learned an awful lot about how to treat employees, a healthy approach to your work, and what you should and shouldn't allow companies to do to you. Jim was and still is a very dynamic individual, and was my mentor for a long time.

I stayed with Steranko from August 1971 to Ash Wednesday of 1972. After that, I went back to Detroit, and this new kid named Jim Starlin was looking for someone to ink his samples. He didn't ink, so I inked four pin-ups for him, and it helped him get work in the comics.

Jack's note to Greg read: *"I'm still a bit vague on Green Arrow's hat. If you could help further, please do."*

TJKC: Did you ever try to break in at Marvel?

GREG: By high school, I was interested in working at Marvel, and Frank Giacoia was the art director in the early 1970s. I had sent a bunch of inking samples in, and Giacoia wrote back and said, "As soon as you're out of high school, come to New York and you'll be working for Marvel Comics." This was at a time when breaking into Marvel was a difficult thing to do. Giacoia was willing to train me, but he left and John Romita took over.

A guy named Al Hewetson left Marvel around then, and as a going-away gift, John Romita did a drawing of Mary Jane with nothing on. We called up Romita and said, "Hewetson sold us a bunch of stuff, including the nude. Can we print it?" He said, "Absolutely not. Hewetson never should have sold that stuff to you. Send it back to me." But we'd used FFCG funds to buy this stuff; if Romita was pissed off, we wouldn't print it, but we weren't going to send it back to him. So I never got an inking job for Marvel.

TJKC: At the time you were looking for work at Marvel, Jack was over at DC. How'd you feel about the Fourth World stuff?

GREG: It's difficult to say, because of Vince Colletta's inking. It had structure like the Marvel stuff in terms of the scope of the story, and revealing so many new characters at once, but I'd have preferred something with single stories that built to make a bigger story. Too much too fast; but it was remarkable work.

TJKC: When did Pure Imagination come into being?

GREG: Around 1974. The money I made from a 1972 convention paid my way to New York to try to break into professional illustration. I did men's magazine illustrations and the occasional commercial art assignment, which didn't prove particularly profitable. So I moved back to Detroit, and founded Pure Imagination with illustrator Carl Lundgren.

TJKC: What were the first things you published?

GREG: We reprinted Frazetta's *Johnny Comet.* I had published a book called *The Bernie Wrightson Treasury.* We did a pirate book on Frazetta, which sunk my ship with Frank forever. *(laughter)* I called him up and said, "I want to do a checklist on you, and run some of your more interesting art." It never got past Ellie, who had just cut a deal with Ballantine for the big full-color Frazetta books that reprinted all of his paintings. She said, "Unless you've got $30,000, we're not interested in talking to you." So being a couple of young bucks who should've known better, we said, "Screw this. Most of this stuff is public domain anyway." A few years before, I had called Frazetta up and invited him to come to the Triple Fan Fair. He declined, but the calls turned into these long interview discussions. I had an interview and a checklist and public domain art, so I printed it. It's unfortunate, because I admire the man and his work. I'm sorry something I did so long ago set this path of Frazetta being angry at me for years.

The same thing happened on a book on Wally Wood. I was under the impression that Wood didn't care. I said, "Do you want to do a book together?" He said, "No, I've got my own projects. Do whatever you want to do." I took that as a signal to do it, and the next thing I know, Wood's pissed off that I'd done a fanzine on him.

On the other hand, I did the *Neal Adams Treasury* Vol. 1 and 2. Neal and I worked very well together, and it made a lot of money for the two of us. Then I published some more Frazetta in *The Comic Strip Frazetta,* and a *White Indian* reprint. I printed the *Stuntman* book, *Buried Treasures* #1-3, *The Betty Pages,* and others.

TJKC: Did you have plans to do more than one volume of *Stuntman*?

GREG: Sure, but it didn't sell very well. Once I split the pie three ways with Jack and Joe, what was $2400 became $800 for each of us. It was a lot of work for $800. I'd planned to do a comic book called *The Simon & Kirby Reader,* reprinting old classics. It too fell to a mediocre reception. The market was too glutted with product for it to make an impression.

TJKC: Why was there such a big time lapse between *The Jack Kirby Treasurys*?

GREG: I was pursuing my career as an illustrator, so that put the project on a hobby level. As you know, producing a research book is an extremely difficult thing to do. I had certain dissatisfactions with the first one, and I wanted to make sure the second one did the job. Kirby was gracious enough to do a nice big wrap-around cover.

TJKC: On the pencils to that cover, there's a handwritten note *(see above)* by Jack saying something like, "I can't remember Green Arrow's costume; you figure it out." Was that pretty common with Jack at that point?

GREG: It was uncommon for him to leave me a note. The only other time was on a page from the Vagabond Prince story in the *Stuntman* book. Simon had all the original art except one page, so it seemed like a terrific opportunity to reunite Simon and Kirby for one last piece of art. So Simon wrote it, Kirby penciled it, and I inked it. There was a panel where the hero is supposed to be jumping over some bushes into a house, and Kirby left it blank and wrote: "Greg, have fun!" *(laughter)* So I had to draw that panel.

But frequently during *Super Powers,* Kirby was drawing characters that he had no empathy for whatsoever. Green Lantern was consistently wrong. He didn't memorize the costumes; it was torture for him. At this point in his career, Jack was getting pretty tired of doing comics. He was used to a regimen of single concept illustrations for television cartoon episodes, done three times up; enormous drawings. He was back now to doing six to eight panel comic book pages, with 22-page stories. He swore he would never do a regular comic book again after

Super Powers. It was a big grind on him. The pages would come to me in batches of three or four pages at a time. The first page was always very strong; the last page was weak. He was losing steam; he couldn't do three or four sparkling pages a day, but that was the schedule.

TJKC: How did the opportunity to ink Jack on *Super Powers* come about?
GREG: I had been pestering Kirby to ink some of his stuff since *Captain Victory.* I had inked a couple of sample pieces that were never used; one sample page for *Silver Star,* and a *Captain Victory* cover. When Jack went to DC, I went in and showed Andy Helfer my stuff. Helfer was Assistant Editor to Joe Orlando on the *Super Powers* series. I showed him samples and they let me ink one of the covers – the one with Superman as the brute (Vol. 1, #4). *Super Powers* Vol. 1, #5 was the issue Jack penciled. I inked it during the San Diego convention. I was going to the convention during the daytime, and at night I'd go back to the hotel room and ink pages. *(laughter)* It was kind of a blast.

TJKC: Can you add anything to what we know about the background on *Hunger Dogs*?
GREG: There had been a comic book created that would set up the conclusion of the *New Gods* series. When it was turned in, the powers to be at DC did not like it. Kirby was slated to do the *Hunger Dogs* Graphic Novel, so they said, "Take this book you've already written and incorporate it into the *Hunger Dogs*." It was done in a comic book format, which was 150% larger than the size it was to be printed; Graphic Novels were being done at 200%. So there was a discrepancy in the sizes. Somewhere along the line, the pages were photostatted at the same size they were drawn, and glued to the 200% Graphic Novel paper. So Kirby had to fill out the top, bottom, and side margins. If the Editor had instructed the production department to blow up the pages to Graphic Novel size, Kirby wouldn't have needed to draw out the panels on all four sides. It ruined his compositions. If you look carefully in *Hunger Dogs,* all of the pages where the type falls to the center of the page are the pages from the original comic book. Any page that has dialogue all the way to the border was done specifically for the Graphic Novel.

D. Bruce Berry ended up inking the new Graphic Novel pages. In the photostatic process, the Royer pages were photostatted rather dark, so the line weight beefed up. You had pages with beefy *(Royer)* linework on a photostat, and incredibly light *(Berry)* feathering filling out the margin. There was a big discrepancy visually.

So I was looking at this mismash of style, and Helfer says, "Do you want to color this?" And I said, "Absolutely. In fact, would you mind terribly if I took these with me and worked on them?" And they said they'd love me to do whatever I could to help align the clash of the two styles. So for five or six days, I worked for free, trimming back some of Royer's linework so the weight was a little bit lighter, and beefing up some of D. Bruce Berry's work. In some cases I simply reinked the material. It was just a coordinating project that I didn't get paid for. *(laughter)* I got paid to color it.

Some of the precision of Jack's work was weaker than it'd previously been. Eyes were sometimes askew; some of the perspective was a bit off, and so on. Kirby had a rule with his inkers that they were not to change anything, so based on Kirby's instructions, the inkers were rendering things that needed to be fixed. Nobody ever told me that I was not allowed to change anything, and to the very end, whenever I inked Kirby's work, I had *carte blanche* to do whatever I pleased on it.

Greg inked these Kirby pencils from DC Comics Presents *#84.*

TJKC: After *Super Powers,* what else did you ink?
GREG: After *Hunger Dogs,* Julie Schwartz contacted me and said, "Would you ink this *Challengers of the Unknown* thing?" (*DC Comics Presents* #84) So I got to ink Toth as part of the bargain; what a cool deal. Toth had started a job that wasn't big enough for a full book, and had never done the second half, so they got Jack to do a wraparound on it. Jack seemed to care about that one; he did a good job on it.

TJKC: How did your Theakstonizing process come about? I've heard Joe Simon used to do something along those lines to bleach old comics pages for reprinting.
GREG: Simon had been experimenting with various processes for removing color from printed comics, and not having much luck, as evidenced by the reinking of several *Fighting American* stories originally planned for the *Fighting American Annual* #2 from Harvey. He had somebody trace off three or four *Fighting American* jobs; if you go into

Jack's Atlas cover pencils for First Issue Special *#1.*

the hardcover, you'll see those jobs. But Simon definitely gave me the clues. I went home and immediately began experimenting with what he had told me, and came up with a system by way of his recommendations that worked for both of us.

TJKC: At what point did you get really close to the Kirbys, and start visiting often?
GREG: The early 1980s, I guess. What happened was I started traveling to the San Diego Con with Julius Schwartz. We would travel to Los Angeles, go see the Kirbys and have dinner with them, and the next day I would drive them to San Diego; I got to be their chauffeur for about seven years. It was a real honor and pleasure. I always brought old time jazz tapes, and both of the Kirbys and Schwartz love old music. I'd hear Kirby in the back seat saying, "Gee, I haven't heard that song in years."

TJKC: In the midst of the whole original art controversy with Marvel, I remember reading that the Kirbys wanted to send you into the Marvel vault to categorize what was there. Whatever happened?
GREG: Marvel refused to let me anywhere near it. They wouldn't even let Al Milgrom, who was an Editor at the time and offered to do the same thing. Right around that time hundreds of pages were stolen by an office employee. Jim Shooter had called back a waist-high stack of classics pages from the vaults to look at: The first ten *X-Men,* most of the Steve Ditko *Spider-Man*s, and so on. Milgrom told me he and some of the other editors were looking at them in Shooter's office when it was on Madison Avenue. When Marvel moved to their Park Avenue offices, rather than storing the original artwork in Shooter's office, I've been told Jim asked for it to be stored in the concession room – the commissary, with the vending machines. *(laughter)* As I understand it, a very high-ranking Editor was fired around that time, and the Editor decided to come in that weekend and get his "retirement fund." Using the keys he still had, this Editor whisked away all of the originals sitting so vulnerably in the commissary. Soon after, an art agent called and offered me *X-Men* #9, *Sgt. Fury* #5 – the entire books of original artwork. So I called up Marvel and left a message that said, "Hey, Shooter, I don't know if they knocked the doors off the warehouse and there's nothing left, but I've been offered a large amount of original Marvel artwork that belongs to the artists. Somebody stole it." I got no answer.

I called again on Thursday. This was just before a big summer convention. I said, "I can guarantee most of this art was going to be at the show this weekend; I'll help you pin the guys, and we can get this artwork back." So Shooter said, "All right, I'll be there with the police." So I got to the convention, the doors open at 10:00, and sure enough, people start buying and leaving with original art pages. It's all stolen art. So about 12:30 or 1:00, I'm real irritated. Shooter shows up, and says, "In the move, we've lost the list of the original artwork we're supposed to have in the vaults, so we couldn't be sure we weren't seizing something that didn't legitimately get out through some avenue." So he completely washed his hands of the whole thing. It wasn't until later that I learned Shooter had called all that stuff back, then left it unguarded. Cadence, *(Marvel's)* parent company, decided not to do anything about it. Ultimately, it was Shooter's responsibility all that stuff was stolen. It was heartbreaking, because Ditko lost all but two *Spider-Man* issues. Kirby lost hundreds of the most valuable pages he ever drew. All of that was gone. Early *Fantastic Four* material was gone. Prime issues like *FF* #50 were gone. It was sad and infuriating. Marvel wouldn't return it, or properly guard it. I sometimes wonder if it wasn't just a ploy to avoid giving Kirby his art back, thereby setting a precedent for ownership. If they decided to dispose of it, rather than giving it back to Kirby... well, it would be a truly rotten thing to do.

TJKC: At the time, did you call Jack and tell him all this was going on?
GREG: I called and discussed this with their lawyer, but there wasn't much they could do. Marvel wasn't budging. Ultimately, it probably shortened Kirby's life, with all the angst it put him through.

TJKC: Do you think the theft of this art convinced him to settle the case sooner than he would've otherwise, thinking that sooner or later it'd all be gone?
GREG: It must've played some part. I think it wore them down; it wore them out. Morally, everyone was outraged, but you simply can't address a faceless corporation. It's like there was no villain other than the legal department, who insisted that if Kirby was returned his artwork, that might set a precedent for him owning the characters. That was the key thing they were trying to avoid. In fact, I'm surprised no one has ever pointed out that all of the changes that took place that year in the Marvel Universe were in an attempt to not lose their trademarks and copyrighted characters. They made the Hulk gray. They changed Dr. Strange's outfit. They rearranged the Fantastic Four. Spider-Man was in his black costume. It was not the same universe there. Why do you think all those changes happened that summer? Because Marvel was afraid they were going to lose their characters. They couldn't lose something Kirby had not designed, so as best they could, they redesigned all the characters. When Kirby's threat passed, most of them were switched back. Exactly 28 years was coming up *(the time when copyrights come up for renewal)*, and if Kirby was going to sue at all, his grounds would be lessened, because none of the characters looked anything like what he had designed.

TJKC: Give me a little background on the pencil version of *Jack Kirby's Heroes & Villains.*
GREG: Well, what a fabulous sketchbook. For years people were after Roz to let the book be printed. She said, "You're the only person I trust to take this book and return it to me safely." It was this huge honor to be entrusted with "The Book" so that it could be reprinted. I shot all the negatives myself, and retouched them all myself. Because Kirby was less interested in a pristine drawing than a good one, frequently, the righthand side of his drawings were smudged; he was never shy about pressing hard on the lead or touching the paper with the side of his hand. The challenge was to drop out the gray of the graphite that had rubbed off, yet maintain the very fine linework. So frequently I had to shoot it heavier to keep the fine linework, and retouch it. I shot some of those pages eight to ten times to get the right balance. I spent a week in the darkroom nursing the negatives in the developing tray until I had the best shot that could be had. This was a time before computers and scanners, and Photoshop techniques; it took a week to retouch 130 negatives by hand.

When it came time to print the book, I mixed a combination of high grade black ink with a metallic ink until I achieved the exact shade of a #2 pencil lead. The printed images shine the way a penciled piece does. I really went all-out on that project.

TJKC: How many copies of that book were printed?
GREG: I printed 1000 copies, and bound one-third. Those were signed and numbered, but they do not have the decorative endpapers. The binder sent the box of endpapers back with the bound books, saying, "What is this for?" *(laughter)* I've had rotten luck with printers and book binders. They tend not to be very bright.

So I put the 666 unbound volumes in my storage room, and told my brother to call the recycling place to come get the scrap that was sitting out in the front of the print shop. And when I went to have the other 666 sent for binding three or four months later, they said, "The paper guy took all that stuff." I ultimately reprinted the missing 666 volumes as a second printing, with a continuation of the numbering. That was the edition with the endpapers; those were also signed and numbered. It was a terrifically fun book to do, and Steranko's intro was a sweet tribute to our hero. It's a book I'm proud of.

TJKC: How about the inked "Black Magic" edition?
GREG: As big a let-down as the penciled volume was a thrill. I thought at the time it couldn't lose; get every popular inker in the business to ink over Kirby. He's pretty indestructible; nobody could do that much damage to his work. I took a full set of pencil Xeroxes to the San Diego con and passed them out to potential inkers. Of the 100 pages I distributed, some 15 or 20 guys took their jobs, and I never heard from them again. Right down to the week before it went to press, I was hounding artists for their assignments. I'm not saying this to scold people, just to point out the difficulties I've had producing products like this, and why some of them seem to fall short. A friend of the Kirbys had said, "Don't worry, I'll write the introductions to all these characters." He procrastinated, and weeks turned into months; all the while he was insisting that he could turn the job around in a couple of days, so hold tight. Three or four days before the book was to go to the printer, he said, "I'm sorry, there's a crisis here. I simply can't do it." So Richard Howell and Mark Evanier and myself each wound up doing a third of the intros.

When I got my proof copy back from the printer, I provided corrected copy to replace the errors on several pages. Tim and Greg Hildebrandt's name was misspelled. Tim Bradstreet's was my biggest regret; he didn't sign his work, and I simply couldn't remember his name. I put it down as 'Blackwell.' When the book came out, those corrections were not made; the book is full of errors they simply didn't correct for me. We were going to do a hardbound edition with all the inkers signing. I sent the signature plates to two or three guys to sign, and one of the inkers still has 500 plates half-signed, and the book is dead in the water because this joker won't send them back. And I don't know who it is, because I didn't give them to him; one of the other inkers passed them along. So whoever's got the damn plates, send them back! *(angry laughter)*

I offered a rate of $75. A couple of big name artists came up to me later at a convention and said, "You never paid me for my work." Everybody who billed me got paid. A large number of people said they'd do it for nothing, but some people said they'd take the $75 rate. So anybody that sent a bill got paid, and anybody that didn't, I assumed didn't want to be paid. If any of the inkers on this book think I stiffed them, I must say in my defense: As with any professional, you must

Page 12 of the unpublished Dingbats of Danger Street *#3. Inks by D. Bruce Berry.*

More unpublished Dingbats *art, from #3, page 14.*

bill for a job before you can get paid.

Kirby died before *(the inked) Heroes and Villains* came out. As it was, he saw large numbers of the drawings, and he was truly flattered and amazed that so many diverse styles were being used on his work and looking so good. I suppose I could've only used the top professionals, and give two or three pieces to each, but it made more sense to me to give 132 or so people – who might not ever get a chance to work on Kirby – a once-in-a-lifetime shot. I can't say I'm satisfied with everybody's renditions; in a better world I might've sent some back and said, "Try again." But as it was, Jack was pretty pleased, and I think there were some remarkable combinations in there.

TJKC: How's *The Complete Kirby* series progressing?
GREG: It's expanded. My original concept on Volume One was 136 pages. It came in at almost 200 pages. There's a 10-page Fiery Mask story by Joe Simon; I could've cropped that and saved 10 pages, but I think it's important that readers see Simon on his own and Kirby on his own, and see the two of them together to see where each of these artists is coming from. It makes it easier to detect who does what when they work together. A number of biographers have suggested that Joe Simon was this terrific layout man, and taught Kirby all kinds of stuff about layout. It's simply not the case. By the time they met, Kirby had produced 1500 published panels; Simon's count hovered at something like 150. If you look at Fiery Mask, and the work that surrounds it by Jack, it becomes very evident that Jack was not just the superior draftsperson – he was the superior storyteller. However, Simon's stuff was infused with a terrific energy, and there is a similarity in styles that's unmistakable. There's probably a lot of cross-pollinating there. But Kirby definitely had the inside track on drawing and layout, and taught Simon an awful lot. And by including the Fiery Mask story, the readers will be able to discern that for themselves.

I hope that *The Complete Kirby* resolves once and for all what jobs Kirby worked solo on. It's not the instant team people think. Jack produced a number of stories by himself – right down to the lettering – long after he met Joe Simon. At Marvel, some Vision stories are strictly by Kirby. Hurricane, Tuk the Cave Boy, and Comet Pierce are all Kirby solos.

TJKC: So this is all work that's in the public domain?
GREG: Yes. But it's Joe's work, and Jack's work, and a percentage of the profits from the book will go to both Joe and Roz.

TJKC: I've gotten lots of letters from fans saying, "Is Greg really going to chronologically reprint everything Jack did?" How can you get around publishing old stories of copyrighted characters?
GREG: There was no problem with the first volume, because none of the characters are currently in use. Marvel doesn't use Red Raven or Mercury, so that's not an issue. The second volume will have the Mr. Scarlet story from *Wow,* all the Captain Marvel stuff, the Black Owl stories, the Ted O'Neil stories. What may be a problem with the next volume is the Vision. I'm going to see if I can license the Vision stories from Marvel, and if not, I'll reprint the splash pages, a synopsis, and two or three of the juiciest panels. So although you're not getting every panel he ever did, chronologically this is what he was doing that month, and a basic idea of what the story was about. It still encompasses all of his work, if not reprinting every single page. But I'm optimistic.

The big problem is Volume Three, which picks up with *Captain America* #1. Here's the question I pose to the readers of *The Jack Kirby Collector:* If I can get permission to reprint that material, should I reprint the *Captain America* stories? They've already been reprinted once; everybody who cares about Kirby probably got a copy of the hardcover set. Should I just print a splash page, with plot synopses and a couple of panels? Should I print the entire thing again in black-&-white, in its chronological order if I can get the rights? Or do I simply skip ahead to 1946 and pick up the post-war work? I wouldn't have any trouble reprinting material from Prize Comics or Hillman Comics. I've got a book outlined that goes from 1947-48 that might be the next one to do; that would have most of the Flying Fools, most of the Lockjaws, a good sampling of *Real Clue Crime.* It would have the first romance comic; it's really a terrific slice of all this public domain material. Do I jump ahead? That's the question. The quality of the work's really far superior to the stuff they were doing in the Golden Age. *(Editor's Note: Greg has just announced that the third volume will jump ahead to Jack's work from 1947, and will be the first of three books covering Jack's work from Hillman Comics, including Lockjaw the Alligator, Earl the Rich Rabbit, the Flying Fool, plus crime stories and other prime Simon & Kirby work. Look for it in February*

PURE IMAGINATION'S NEW PERMANENT ADDRESS IS:

PO Box 5810
Atlanta, GA 31107
E-mail: teasemag@mindspring.com

Write Greg and tell him what you want to see published!

1998, and be sure to order yours directly from Pure Imagination, so Greg can keep this worthwhile project going.)

TJKC: Can you explain how public domain works?
GREG: Traditionally, 28 years is the first crack at renewing copyrights. If you renew, you get another 28 years, for a total of 56 years; after that anybody can use it. If that's the case, everything from 1941 and before is now in public domain ideally, but not always. Theoretically, every year I could do a new year's worth of stuff. I could reprint Sandman and the Guardian, and all the Golden Age DC stuff simply by waiting. But my guess is, I'll jump ahead and go back later and cut a deal with DC and Marvel to fill in those spots.

TJKC: When will future volumes come out?
GREG: I want to do it twice a year if possible. Of the 400 people I had gathered names from to pay for the printing, only 250 coughed up their money. There may have been some misunderstanding that they not just buy the book, but they buy it from me. If there are enough people who agree to buy the next book from me, and I can build the list up to a solid 400, I can publish anything on Kirby. I can publish *The Complete Sky Masters*, or anything that was in the public domain. If 400 people want to see all four issues of *My Date,* I could do it. It's up to the readers.

TJKC: Will there ever be a *Jack Kirby Treasury* Volume Three?
GREG: That's a good question. The story I told in *Pure Images* #1 and #2 – the birth of Spider-Man and Marvel – is in essence where the next volume picks up. If I were to do a third volume of the Kirby book, it would include all that material, and be amended and extended. In the interim, I've picked up all kinds of neat related stuff that would flesh it out nicely. But again, if 400 people will write me, it's not a big deal to put that one together.

Whatever they ask for, 400 is my golden number. If they'll buy 400 copies from *me,* and they'll send the money when I'm ready to go to press, then whatever those 400 Kirby fans bid me to do, I'll be their Jack Kirby genie. *(laughter)*

TJKC: Back when we were doing our Kid Gang issue, you said someone had offered you some *Dingbats Of Danger Street* stuff for sale. There was some talk that it might've been a fourth and fifth issue.
GREG: Frank Giacoia made me the offer, for Vinnie Colletta. When Colletta was fired from his art director job, he apparently took them with him. They were being offered through Giacoia. He said they were pencil stories, but I'm thinking perhaps they were the two inked jobs (*Dingbats* #2 and #3), and Giacoia was simply wrong. I was going to buy them, but thought better of it. I wish I'd asked for a set of Xerox copies, but that's hindsight.

TJKC: A lot of our readers are curious about the pencil Xeroxes Jack kept, and what there is in the files.
GREG: For the most part, the files begin right where Royer's work picks up. Jack's son worked for a copy machine company, and managed to snag one for his old man. So when Jack was penciling stuff from that point forward, they would make copies of it and file it. From that point forward, virtually all of Kirby's pencils exists in copies. There's a variety of quality; some of the Xeroxes are very light and almost worthless. Some of them are almost as good as real pencil art.

A handful of the Marvel stuff still exists, mostly because – and this is my guess – when they moved from New York to California, that material was missed when they threw away everything else. Marvel used to do digest-sized photostats of the material and send it to Jack, so he'd have reference for costumes, vehicles and so forth when he began penciling the next issue. So there's a handful of stuff left over from the Marvel days, probably no more than 200 pages total. Then it picks up when Royer begins to ink, which is really sad. Royer was extremely faithful to the pencils, and what we need to see is material that Syd Shores inked, or Vinnie Colletta inked, where there was a distortion in what Jack was trying to say. Not that it's great, or it stinks, but that it's no longer the Kirby manuscript that was underneath it. I continue to archive the material.

TJKC: Anything you'd like to add?
GREG: Just that working with Kirby was a dream come true. Some kids fantasized about being a major league ballplayer, or an astronaut, or a rock star, but never realized their dreams. As a child I fantasized about working with Kirby, and being his friend, and ultimately my dream came true – a rare thing in the real world. Jack was like a second father, and Roz was my Yiddish momma.

TJKC: Finally, what's the most important thing you learned from working with Jack?
GREG: I learned that you can be a genius and an average, nice guy. All the talent in the world doesn't make you a superior person. He was a remarkable model for being a wonderful human being. ★

(Greg is now taking orders for the second volume of The Complete Jack Kirby, *which will feature the Mr. Scarlet story from* Wow, *the S&K Captain Marvel stories, the Black Owl, Ted O'Neil, the Vision, and more. Shipping in late November, it costs $25, and people who order directly from Pure Imagination also receive the second issue of his special newsletter, containing rare Kirby art that's not included in the volume – including many of Jack's pulp illustrations – plus letters of comment from Kirby fans, details about upcoming projects from Pure Imagination, and more! Greg currently has only 150 copies of Volume One left for $25, which also includes the first issue of his newsletter, while they last. Finally, Greg also has 10 copies of the* Jack Kirby's Heroes & Villains *sketchbook; this is the signed and numbered pencil version, and is available for $150 per copy. The address is: Pure Imagination, PO Box 5810, Atlanta, GA 31107. E-mail: teasemag@mindspring.com)*

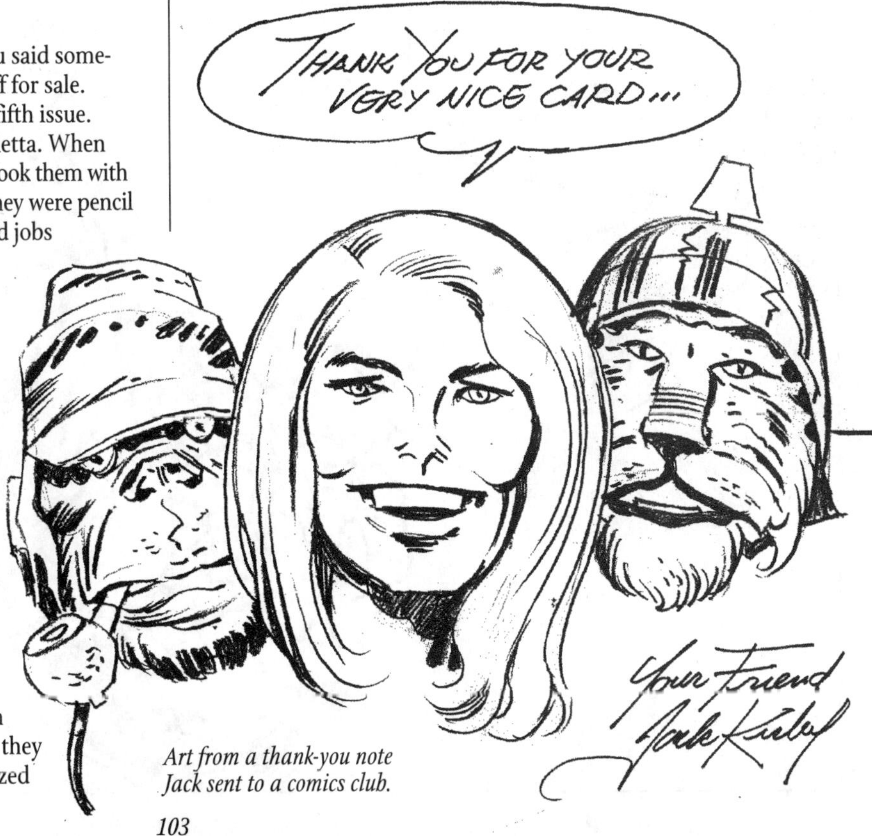

Art from a thank-you note Jack sent to a comics club.

THE INSECT HORDES OF MANTIS INVADE
EARTH- THE DOOMED DOMINION!
READ THE
NEW GODS

Uninked cover pencils from New Gods *#10.*
This – and other photocopies of uninked pencils from Jack's published comics that we show in TJKC *– are reproduced courtesy of the Pure Imagination archives. Our thanks to Roz Kirby and Greg Theakston for their continued support.*

D. BRUCE BERRY SPEAKS

Conducted by mail in August, 1997 by John Morrow

(D. Bruce Berry was born on January 24, 1924 in Oakland, California. After a stint in the Air Force as a sign painter, he went on to a career in advertising art. He got involved in 1960s comics fandom, and went on to ink much of Jack's 1970s work for DC.)

THE JACK KIRBY COLLECTOR: How'd you get started in a career in art, and later in comics?

D. BRUCE BERRY: What originally attracted me to artwork was the appearance of *Flash Gordon* in the early 1930s. As a kid, I had all kinds of daydreams and misconceptions about the cartooning business. There were no comics fan groups in those days. There weren't even any comic books. There was no way in the world that I could find out what the comics business was really like. However, by drawing my own cartoons, I gradually developed a good artistic ability. After the war, that experience served me well. I have never been to an art school, so that was my only training. With a little searching, I found the only type of art job that was available to me: An advertising agency.

I became a merchandise artist, and that was my main profession for the rest of my working life. I was what was known as a "hard-lines artist." I drew anything that was made of metal: Jewelry, pots and pans, and machinery. You can never get rich at that sort of thing, but it was a steady business. To sum it up, I know more about advertising than I know about the comics business.

Shortly after the war, I wandered into a bookstore in Oakland in search of science fiction reading material. That was where I met Richard Kyle. He was the clerk behind the counter. After I visited the store a couple more times, he offered to introduce me to some other people who were interested in science fiction. That was the beginning of a somewhat erratic connection with science fiction fandom. What made it erratic was the fact that I had no idea what the group really was. It was apparently a very serious group that had its origins among Hollywood writers. I did not find that out until twenty years later. It was not actually a 'fan' group in the accepted sense of the word; it was a 'literary' group.

In the 1950s, I moved to Chicago where there was more work in advertising. I teamed up with a freelance art director and worked with him as a one-man studio. I did art, paste-ups, photo-retouching and finished layouts from the art director's roughs. Around the end of the '50s I came into contact with one of the last of the old pulp science-fiction magazines. It was called *Imagination*. I illustrated it for the last year of its existence. It was shortly after the magazine folded that Richard Kyle brought me into contact with comics fandom. I did quite a bit of work for fanzines. However, toward the end of the 1960s the art director I was working with moved to another city. The art business was getting shaky. Photography was beginning to replace line drawings in merchandise promotion. For various other boring reasons, I decided to return to California.

TJKC: How'd you get the job of inking Jack's work?

D. BRUCE: On my arrival in Long Beach, Richard Kyle – who knew the city – helped me to locate an apartment. In the following weeks, he drove me around and introduced me to some of the pro cartoonists in the Los Angeles area. One of the people I met was Mike Royer. Mike and his family lived in a very nice ranch-style house. Behind the house was

Berry's inks (and lettering) from page 10 of the unpublished Dingbats of Danger Street *#3.*

his well-equipped, air-conditioned studio. It was obvious that he was quite successful. In his filing cabinets he had a fabulous collection of old originals of cartooning art.

As it turned out, he was loaded with other work besides Kirby. I began helping him out by inking some backgrounds. The amount of backgrounds increased and finally resulted in *Kamandi* #16. Mike did the main figures and the faces on the background figures. It was about this time that he decided that his work load was getting too heavy. I did some sample inks for Jack and met him at his house in Thousand Oaks. Jack liked what I was doing, and I took over all of his inking. *Kamandi* #17 was probably the first book I did; definitely my first full entry into professional cartooning.

TJKC: Did Mike Royer offer any help or suggestions to you when you started?
D. BRUCE: Before I took over Jack's work, Mike said to me, "You won't have any problems. Just follow the lines." Keep in mind that I came out of the advertising business. When an advertising art director tells you the way a thing should be done, it's the rule of the game. Mike said 'follow the lines', and that is exactly what I did.

Throughout my association with Jack Kirby, I inked every damn line that he drew! Nobody ever bothered to tell me that I could ink the books any way I wanted to. I ended my cartooning career completely exhausted!

TJKC: How'd you first meet Jack? Did you go up to the Kirby home often to pick up work?
D. BRUCE: Richard Kyle introduced me to Jack. Jack mailed the work to me, and I mailed back the inks.

TJKC: How old were you when you started inking Jack's DC work in the 1970s?
D. BRUCE: About forty-eight years old.

The original, unaltered splash page to the Hunger Dogs *Graphic Novel, inked by Berry.*

TJKC: How fast did you have to ink and letter the DC work? Was it difficult keeping up with Jack?
D. BRUCE: I had to work like hell. I have already told you the reason; I was inking every line. That left me two days off between books every month. I worked ten hours a day.

TJKC: What was your favorite Kirby series that you inked at DC?
D. BRUCE: My favorite book was OMAC. It was the only book without slum backgrounds.

TJKC: What was your opinion of other Kirby inkers before you, like Sinnott, Giacoia, Stone, Wood, etc.? Was there one of them whose approach was what you were striving for in your inking?
D. BRUCE: Before I inked Jack Kirby, I had no idea that those other artists were connected with him. The only Kirby connection I knew was Mike Royer. I knew about the others only from their individual work. Wood had a great style. Personally, I was not trying to emulate anyone. I was too busy going out of my mind!

TJKC: When Jack went back to Marvel in the mid-1970s, you only inked a few stories. Why didn't you do more of that work?
D. BRUCE: Because of a decision that was made in New York. They wanted all of the inking done there. They called me and asked me if I was coming to New York, and I said 'No'. That was the end of that. I'm a native Californian, and I like it here. Big cities drive me up the wall. I was tired of traveling. That was the end of my cartooning career.

TJKC: What were you doing between the mid-'70s and early-'80s when you weren't inking Jack's work? Did you ink any of his animation art?
D. BRUCE: I did artwork for an educational publisher in Carson, California. I had no connection with Jack's animation work.

TJKC: How'd you get assigned to in the 1980s New Gods finale that appeared in the 6th issue of the *New Gods* reprint series – and how did you happen to end up with copies of Jack's pencils from it?
D. BRUCE: It's really quite simple. Jack and I were working on *Silver Star* for Pacific Comics when he slipped that in to complete his contract with DC. Jack had his own copy machine, on which he made copies of the pencils before sending them to me. It just happened that his machine broke down when we were working on *New Gods*. He phoned me and asked me to make the copies in a local printing place. To play it safe, I made two copies and mailed him one. It got through okay, so I simply filed the other copy with my stuff. It eventually ended up in a suitcase on the back porch.

The existence of those pencil prints is a minor miracle. They were just a spin-off from an ordinary day's work. I do not have a filing system. In fact, I have never had a studio. My entire equipment is a drawing table and the tools to use on it.

TJKC: What are you doing today?
D. BRUCE: I am completely retired. I might add that my communication with you was the first I heard of the death of Jack Kirby. Since I retired, I have been totally out of contact with fans and pros alike.

TJKC: Lastly, what was your impression of Jack?
D. BRUCE: Always diplomatic. I found him to be a perfect gentleman. ★

Kamandi's Origins

by John A. Modica

Jack Kirby's most enduring character for DC was *Kamandi.* With Jack's forty-issue run, it was arguably his most commercially successful strip in the 1970s. But by understanding the roots of *Kamandi,* perhaps we can understand Kirby on a deeper level. For *Kamandi,* like Kirby, was rather complex.

Convention sketch, with Royer lettering.

When *Kamandi* first appeared, DC had just recently cancelled Kirby's Fourth World saga. They were attempting to secure the rights to the popular *Planet of the Apes* movies. They failed, so Carmine Infantino suggested creating a new series based on a future world following a cataclysm. Kirby wanted to start a strip to be written by Mark Evanier, and illustrated by someone else. To appease the dejected Kirby, Infantino offered him creative control over the new book. But who came up with the concept of *Kamandi*?

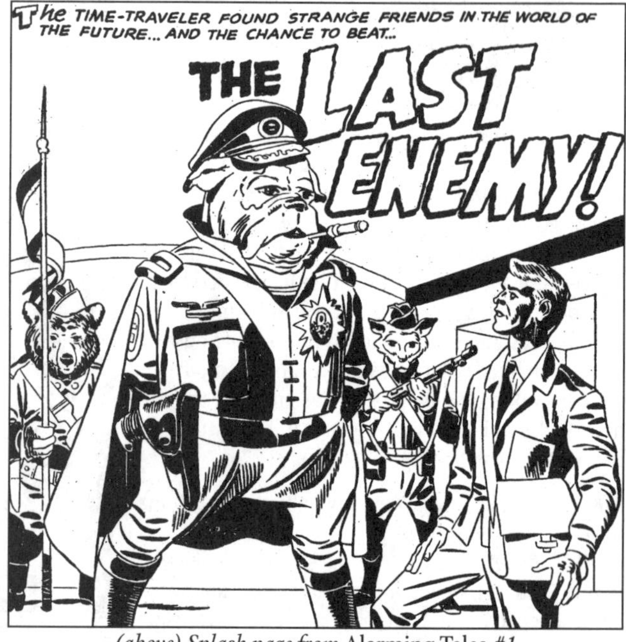

(above) Splash page from Alarming Tales *#1.*
(below and next page) The unused Kamandi of the Caves *strip.*

"I created Kamandi and plotted that for him. Of course, he took credit for those. I didn't care. I didn't give a damn. As Editor, it was my job to create things."

Carmine Infantino (in Comic Scene Spectacular *#6, July 1992)*

Kirby never threw away any concept or idea. Around 1956, he attempted a newspaper strip called *Kamandi of the Caves.* Shortly thereafter, Kirby drew a story about a time

KAMANDI OF THE CAVES

traveler who journeys to a future world where talking dogs and rats dominated the landscape ("The Last Enemy," *Alarming Tales* #1). *Kamandi* is a combination of ideas from both Kirby's *Alarming Tales* story and his failed newspaper strip. It is therefore obvious that Kirby, not Infantino, created the concept that became *Kamandi* 16 years later.

Some readers felt the "Great Disaster" implied Kirby's feelings about Infantino's massive cancellation of his Fourth World series. This makes sense, and would lead to deeper implications within the body of Jack Kirby's work; but to better understand the *Kamandi* series, the Great Disaster must be logically explained. This writer believes *OMAC* was a sort of prequel to the *Kamandi* stories. There are various clues found in both series to warrant such a theory.

In the opening issue, Kamandi is seen paddling his way through the world that have been ravaged by a disaster. Later he sets down in hollowed-out buildings and encounters his dying grandfather, who informs Kamandi he is one of the last remnants of the human race. Kamandi recalls his grandfather's tales of the events leading up to the Great Disaster. His grandfather dies in the first issue, thus leaving Kamandi alone in "Command D," the bunker he was named after.

In *OMAC* #1, we are introduced to Buddy Blank, an employee of the Pseudo-People Company. His only friend, Lila, is revealed to be one of the Build-A-Friend units manufactured by the company. These artificial beings are living bombs, used to destroy people. Buddy becomes OMAC, and must destroy Lila and all the other Build-A-Friends. The first *OMAC* story ends where it began, with OMAC walking through the destruction of the area known as "Section D."

It's easy to make a simple connection between *Kamandi* and *OMAC*. Could the "Great Disaster" have been the great environmental disasters that were presented in the last two issues of *OMAC*? After all, if Brother Eye was able to release all the water in the bars that Skuba had, would it not cause an environmental disaster? Assuming Buddy Blank survived the destruction that occurred, wouldn't he return to the only safe haven he'd ever known; the one where he'd met his only friend (albeit an artificial one)? In light of this "Great Disaster," wouldn't a One Man Army Corps set up a command center in New York? Later, wouldn't that old man attempt to start a family in order to restart the human race? Then the former Section D would become Command D, where OMAC would live out his days with his grandson Kamandi. And there lies the simple explanation of the origins of *Kamandi*.

Kirby left *Kamandi* and the DC Universe after the forty-issue run. We were never shown Kirby's explanation for the Great Disaster, from which Kamandi's origin is found. Instead, like all good art, it would always be open for interpretation from critics and fans for years to come. ★

(Editor's Note: This article raises some interesting questions in my mind. First, Kamandi *#27's letter column hints that links exist between* Kamandi *and* OMAC. *Might Jack have eventually revealed that most, if not all of the sub-literate humans Kamandi encountered were really leftover, broken Build-A-Friends, thereby truly making Kamandi the last boy on Earth? If his grandfather was Buddy Blank, who was his father? Could he have been the son of the blond-haired Apollo from OMAC #7-8? Or could Kamandi have been a Build-A-Friend unit himself, constructed by an aging OMAC to cure his loneliness? Although* Kamandi *#16 revealed how the animals acquired human intelligence, we never learned how humans got dumbed down, or just what kind of a "natural" disaster occurred, so we'll probably never know how Jack would've brought the story to a climax.)*

Unused cover from Kamandi *#1.*

The 1997 Kirby Tribute Panel

featuring (from left to right) Mark Evanier, Mike Royer, Steve Sherman, Marie Severin, and Al Williamson
Held at Comic Con International – San Diego on July 19, 1997
Transcribed by John Morrow

(Editor's Note: Due to bad acoustics and problems with the PA system in the hall, large parts of my tape of this panel were inaudible. I've transcribed it as close to verbatim as possible, but in some instances I had to fill in stray words that didn't pick up, while trying not to alter the speaker's intent. My apologies to our speakers for the sections I had to omit entirely, and particularly to Marie Severin and Al Williamson; most of their comments didn't pick up on tape.)

MARK EVANIER: In the way of announcements, DC is putting out a collected edition of the *New Gods.* It was supposed to be out next month; they decided that stark black-&-white looks too unfinished, so they're adding some gray tones to it. That should be out in a couple of months. *(Editor's note: It's rescheduled for December release.)* They're poised and ready if that thing sells at all to do the other Fourth World books in that format.

I'm currently working on a biography of Jack which I hope will approach the word 'definitive.' It's now at 120,000 words and still growing. I keep finding things in my files and notes. I came across notations for a *Jimmy Olsen* story that was never finished. There was a sequence of *Jimmy Olsen* where Morgan Edge was plotting to blow up the Daily Planet building, but it never paid off, because DC vetoed what Jack originally planned to do with it. So I found this plot, and I called up Steve Rude and said, "Do you want to draw it?" He said yes, so we're doing it as a *Jimmy Olsen Special* next year. A big credit line will go to Jack, and a lot of the money will go to Roz. *(applause)* Jack's still got more new comics coming out than a lot of people in comics. *(laughter)* DC is hoping to release a reprint volume of *Jimmy Olsen* material to coincide with that, so we could have a very Kirbyish year.

In the meantime, I think we finally have solved the legal problems on the *Kirby Tribute Book* which has been looming out there for some time. Frank Miller is now... I've done my end of it. From now on, you nag Frank! *(laughter)*

That's all the Kirby news for now, so I want to take this moment to introduce Roz Kirby to you all. *(applause)*

ROZ KIRBY: Mark, this is my grandson Jeremy. *(applause)*

MARK: Also, there's a few other people in the audience. One of my favorite things Jack did was a story called "Street Code" for a magazine called *Argosy.* The publisher who commissioned that work is here; Richard Kyle. *(applause)*

The person I think whose association with Jack dates back the most is Al's. You had the experience of inking Jack at a time when you weren't an inker.

AL WILLIAMSON: That's correct. I went up to Harvey Publications around 1957, give or take a couple of years. The Editor, Joe Simon, didn't have any work for me, but he had a Jack Kirby five-page science fiction story, and asked if I would like to ink them. They inked themselves; I had no problem. I took them in, they liked them, they gave me three or four more, and that was it. I don't think they were printed right away, because I never saw them until the 1960s.

MARK: You were familiar with Jack's work already?

AL: Oh, sure. I lived in South America, in Bogota, Colombia. They didn't do any comic books, but they imported a lot of comics from Argentina and Mexico. The very first Jack Kirby work I ever saw was a black-&-white reprint of a character called Cosmic Carson, and I thought it was just great, just wonderful. It was translated into Spanish. Then I discovered American comics, which didn't get down there too often, maybe one or two a month. I picked up my first American comic book, which was *Famous Funnies,* which had a one-pager called "The Lone Rider." That was the second strip; I knew it was the same artist. I discovered two friends who loved comics, and

A Demon drawing from a 1975 NY convention. That day, Jack would draw any character you requested for $20!

they were visiting from Panama, where they could get American comics much easier. They sent me two comic books: One was an issue of *Young Allies.* It was just incredible. All I remember about it was a double-page spread of the most exciting, exquisite fight scene I've ever seen. I've never seen that comic book since; I don't know if it exists, or if it's my imagination. If anybody has it, I'd love to see it.

Y'know, he just grabs you, right from the beginning. I think he and Wally Wood are probably two of the finest comic book artists that ever lived. Inking his work was quite a thrill for me, because first of all, he was the first artist I ever inked. He did all the work for me; I had no problem at all. I've been credited with inking a couple of covers and some jobs that I didn't ink. The only jobs I ever inked of Jack Kirby's were those science fiction stories: "The Three Rocketeers." So my apologies to whoever inked those panels or those covers; they should've gotten credit.

MARK: Did you find that anything in Jack's work applied directly to your own work?

AL: He, from what I understand, credits Foster and Raymond as two of the influences he had. The funny thing is, I can see in the early work of Jack's a little bit of the Alex Raymond; just a little bit, especially the legs. But I have to confess something. Nobody can draw a fight scene like Jack Kirby, and I was stuck for a fight scene one time, and I *(whispering)* swiped Jack Kirby. *(laughter)* I did it a little differently, but Jack came to my rescue. I have a feeling about Jack that he never looked back; he always went forward. I've found every real, true artist does that: Wally Wood, Alex Raymond, Foster, on to the next one. And Jack just kept going; I don't think he looked back. He just wanted to do the next drawing. I don't know how he did it. And prolific; if I lived to be 300, I don't think I could turn out the work he did in ten years. And it's all good. The proof of being so good is that, the more you look at it, the better it gets. You don't see mistakes. It looks better every time. He's up there with the greats, there's no question about it.

MARK: Marie, when did you first meet Jack? At Marvel?

MARIE SEVERIN: Yeah. I'd heard of him, and I'd seen some of his work; wow, this guy was powerful! I'd say it was in 1964. I was in the Bullpen – well, I *was* the Bullpen – and I came tearing around the corner and I almost banged into him, and Sol Brodsky said, "This is Jack Kirby." And I said, "Oh, hi!" And he looked at me and said, "Judy Garland!" *(laughter)* And I was so upset because I always wanted to look like Mary Astor. *(laughter)* And that's a far cry from Judy Garland!

MARK: That's the same thing he said to me! *(laughter)* I was wearing red shoes at the time.

MARIE: When I first came there, Stan didn't even look at my portfolio; he threw me into the Bullpen to do paste-ups. When I started drawing, Stan said, "Get the feel of Kirby." And maybe, maybe, maybe I could get the feel, but I'll never draw like that; he's so powerful! And as a woman, I recognized this tremendous strength – and talk about fight scenes! It was great to color it; I loved coloring the stuff. It brought out emotion. It was like you were part of it. So I finally tried to figure out *why* he drew it that way, and it came together. I was never skilled enough to draw the anatomy the way he did. People tried to copy him, and it looks awkward to me. He did it and it worked.

When he left Marvel, Stan nearly had a heart attack. *(laughter)* It was supposed to be a big secret. And there was some sort of a convention the day Jack came back, and it was supposed to be an even bigger secret. I came up to the office and I saw Jack, and Stan put a page in front of my face and said, "You did not see any of this!" *(laughter)* And I said, "Okay, I did not see any of this" and I went out in the hall and yelled, "Kirby's back!" *(laughter)*

MARK: Mike was reminding us that you had one of Jack's cigar butts.

MARIE: When he left, I put it on my wall. *(laughter)* I should've had it bronzed.

Dingbats *#3, page 17.*

MIKE ROYER: It was the first thing I saw on my first visit to Marvel Comics. I walked through the reception area, and there it was in plain view: "Kirby Was Here." *(laughter)*

MARK: Steve, what do you remember about meeting Jack?

STEVE SHERMAN: I remember when he moved out and he lived in Orange County, and going up the stairs; there in this empty bedroom was this drawing table, and nothing else in it except Jack's taboret. And Jack was just drawing away on a *Thor* story. It's Jack Kirby; wow! He was the nicest guy you'd ever want to meet.

One funny story though; Jack really wanted to start a West Coast division of DC, and he had to do it without any money. The staff consisted of himself, Roz, Mark, and myself. At the time DC was going to reprint old horror, mystery and romance stories. They asked Jack, "Can you handle that?" "Yeah, yeah." So they sent Jack these comic book-size pages of old DC stories. What we had to do was white-out the clothes they were wearing, white-out the faces, and update everything. We got a bunch of white-out, and went back to Mark's house and we started whiting out the faces, the dialogue balloons, and everything. That was a big mistake, because there's no way you can draw over the white-out. We tried, and they looked horrible. We were tearing our hair out, going, "What have we done?!" So sheepishly we went back to Jack, and he said, "Okay." And that's when he called Mike. You had to put those things on the light box, right?

MIKE: I must've had a dozen romance stories, all drawn in the late 1940s and '50s, and my job was to put bell-bottoms on them, *(laughter)* and contemporary hairdos on all of them. So I drew it all on the light board on typing paper, inked it, and rubber cemented it down over the other pages. But it was the most godawful assignment. I felt I was performing this vile operation on these patients who hadn't asked for it. *(laughter)* It just didn't work! I still have in my closet, copies of this giant romance annual I did, and it's just godawful!

MARK: Jack decided that, having started romance comics, he would now end them. *(laughter)* Steve, do you remember the dinner when Jack created *The Demon* sometime between the time we ordered and the time we finished? *(laughter)*

STEVE: That escapes me. The thing with Jack is, it'd come so fast to him. I remember one evening just sitting with him, and I'd just read the book *Rendezvous With Rama.* I'm sitting talking to Jack about flying saucers and things like that, and Jack always claimed he could see UFOs from his picture window in Thousand Oaks, and you'd believe it. And in the space of about 45 minutes, Jack'd come up with 13 different stories about flying saucers and people meeting them; an entire series. Complete stories, telling me about the characters, the beginning, the middle, the end, the whole thing. It was just amazing.

MARK: We did a couple of things for Jack where he'd officially let us write an issue. So we'd spend three of four days working on a plot, we'd take it out to Jack, tell him the story, and he'd say, 'That's great. Now add this. That's great." And he'd add all these other things into it, and we wound up with a completely different story than we'd started with. *(laughter)* Then we'd go off and write it up and take it out to Jack, and he'd go, "This is great. This is absolutely perfect. You guys did a great job." And he'd sit down and use absolutely none of it. *(laughter)* Then he'd figure out he hadn't used any of it, so he'd go back and find one line of dialogue we'd written, and he'd put it in. *(laughter)* And when we came back to look at the pages, he'd go, "See, there's your line there." *(laughter)*

STEVE: It all came from his head. Maybe occasionally there was a scrap of paper with something written on it; a name or descriptions, but other than that, when he sat down at the table and started to – I shouldn't say 'draw', because he was writing and drawing at the same time. The pencil would go down, and he'd start, and maybe an hour-and-a-half later there'd be a page. And it would be all broken down into story, and he'd go on to the next page. And he always ended up with 22 pages. It always had a beginning, a middle, and an end. When he was at DC, you have to remember he did that seven days a week, four weeks out of the month. He'd do one book, 22 pages, in seven days, finish it and go to the next book with entirely different characters and different stories, and the next one, and the next one, and go back, and keep knocking them out.

Early Kamandi *sample art.*

MARK: Steve and I at the time were enormous fans of Don Rickles. Like many people at that time who were our age, we all went around doing Don Rickles, insulting each other. Rickles used to say, "I never picked on a little guy, I only pick on big guys." Somehow this gave us the idea that we should have Don Rickles make a cameo appearance in *Jimmy Olsen* to insult Superman. It was gonna be like a three-panel thing. So we wrote out a couple of pages of Don Rickles insults. One of them was, "Hey, big boy, where're you from?" And Superman says, "I'm from the planet Krypton." And Rickles says, "I got jokes for 8 million nationalities and I've gotta run into a hockey puck from Krypton." *(laughter)*

So we took these out to Jack; Jack was a big fan of Rickles. And he says, "That's great, that's terrific." And of course he used none of it. *(laughter)* He said we've gotta get permission from Don Rickles for this. So Steve contacted Rickles' publicist, and they gave us permission to have Don Rickles do a cameo. Then Jack tells Carmine Infantino about it, and Infantino thinks this is great, this is something promotable, it's gotta be a two-issue story arc. So instead of us writing two pages, it's now Jack writing two issues. And you all saw the end product was Goody Rickels. And if you look over the entire story, the one thing that's missing is there's not one panel where Don Rickles meets Superman. *(laughter)* He somehow never got that into the story.

MARIE: Nobody's mentioned Jack's romance stuff. I remember one story, it was great, it was so different. Even with the romance, it had such a life force to it. It really impressed me. He put life into everything he did. *(to Roz Kirby)* What'd you feed him? *(laughter)*

MARK: I don't remember ever going anywhere with Jack that he didn't have a hamburger. *(laughter)* Wherever we took him, he ordered a hamburger. If we went to a restaurant that didn't' have hamburgers on the menu, he's say, "I want a hamburger," and they'd say okay, and go in the back and jury-rigged up a hamburger for him. *(laughter)* Let's throw this open to questions.

AUDIENCE: There's a rumor that Jack was doing a romance book for DC. What's the story behind that?

MARK: Jack's contract for DC called for 15 pages a week minimum; he usually exceeded that. But he didn't want to be sitting there cranking out pages. He wanted to create new books. Steve and I were brought in because he wanted to have a staff of young people, local people, West Coast people. One of the ideas he had was a series of things he called the Speak-Out Series. It would be a series of magazines, as Jack envisioned them, that were going to be like *Heavy Metal* magazine, with full-color, real advertisements. He was very interested in getting into photo comics, too. He wanted to get name authors; get Norman Mailer and Truman Capote, to adapt their short stories. And DC looked at this concept, and essentially said, "Oh, this is a chance to do *Creepy* and *Eerie*," and turned it into black-&-white magazines which Jack would draw by himself. The first one he did was *In The Days Of The Mob*, and then he did *Spirit World*, which Steve and I did this weird photo-thing for; to this day we don't understand what we did with that thing. *(laughter)* And then they did the romance stuff. It was called *True Divorce Cases. (laughter)* An anti-romance comic. Steve and I wrote one story for it, and Jack wrote the rest. The one we wrote, he actually used about 10% of. *(laughter)*

He handed it in, and DC hated it. They hadn't figured out *True Divorce Cases* would be about divorce. *(laughter)* There was one story in it about a black couple, and somehow this evolved into a new comic called *Soul Romances*, or *Soul Love*. We did three more stories; the idea was we took one story out of *True Divorce Cases*, so we didn't do two complete books; one story was common to both books. Jack wrote most of it. We got him copies of *Ebony* for reference, and it was some of his best art of the period. He sent it in; the first thing he got back was negative feedback that DC didn't feel they could market it unless the book was done by black writers and artists. They were talking about putting a pseudonym on it; like somebody else would want it. *(laughter)* Every book had to have a pull-out poster in it. *In The Days Of The Mob* had this poster of John Dillinger that I pasted up on my drawing board. It's a total fraud poster, *(laughter)* but it looked pretty good. So, they showed *Soul Love* to some distributor who said, "I can't handle that, it's too ethnic." *(laughter)* The poster that was gonna be in it was going to be of Roberta Flack, who at that time had an album coming out on Atlantic Records, which was affiliated with DC somehow. I'm not making any of this up! *(laughter)* So they sent the stats of the comic to Roberta Flack's manager, and either the manager, or Roberta, or her publicist, or someone from her end of things came back and said, "We think the black people look too ethnic; the lips are too big." And they were perfectly fine. So they gave the book to – you'll excuse the expression – Vince Colletta, *(laughter)* and said, "Make these people white." He used to leave out buildings; here he left out lips! *(laughter)* Colletta was told to make the men more like Sidney Poitier, and to make the women more like Diahann Carroll. I'm not sure if he had inked the book before this order came down and he then went back and retouched the pages, or if he merely inked with this in mind. In either case, he knocked down the black characteristics. In my opinion, the final art was very bland compared to what Jack had penciled. When we got through it all, DC said to us, "Okay, this is great, we'll schedule it right away," and they never mentioned it again. *(laughter)* In the meantime they put out *Spirit World* and *In The Days Of The Mob*, and before the first ones even came out, they decided not to continue the project.

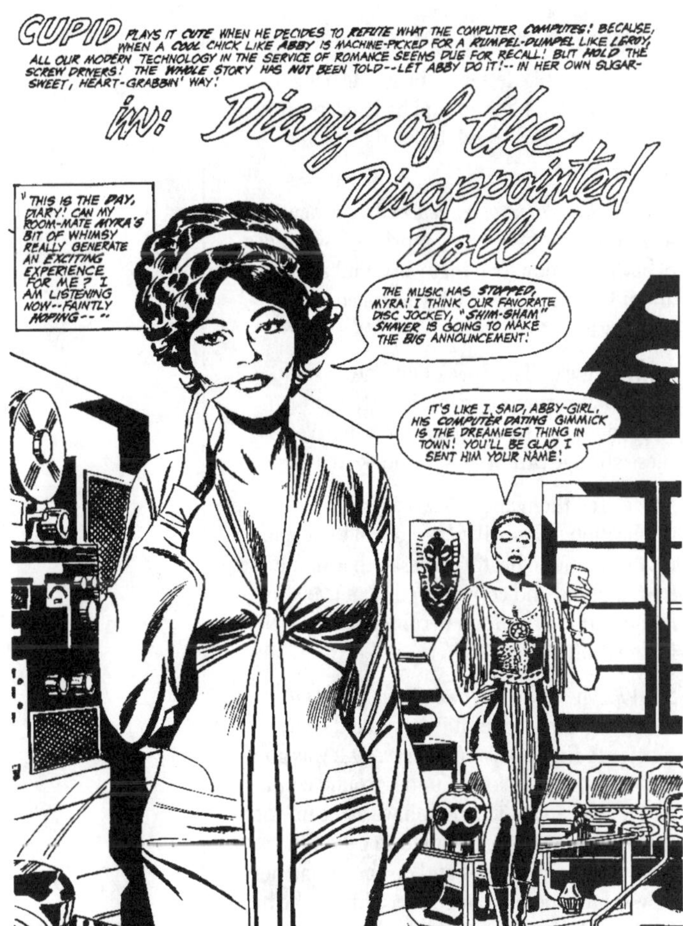

Splash page from the still-unpublished Soul Love *book.*

MIKE: I had a blast inking (*In The Day Of The Mob* #2), and I went nuts making sure all the lettering for each title page was cool. And when it was eventually printed in some DC fanzine *(Amazing World of DC Comics #1)*, they relettered it all.

MARK: At that time, the star letterer at DC was John Costanza. John Costanza was slanting his body lettering slightly. Mike called me up and said, "Do they do that at DC?" I said, "John Costanza does it." And Mike said, "It'd save me a lot of time if I could slant the lettering slightly."

MIKE: I could letter it twice as fast.

MARK: So, Mike lettered the whole book on a slight slant. DC blew up, and had it all relettered back in New York. And to this day I don't understand it.

SCOTT SHAW (from audience): In the new *Jack Kirby Collector* (#16), they reprinted two pages of a *Mob* humor strip that wasn't inked by you, and it looked to me like it was inked by John Costanza.

MARK: It was. The Speak-Out line was also going to have a humor comic by Sergio Aragonés called *Shriek-Out.* We still have all these strange prototypes for books that...

MIKE: Tell them about *Super World.* This publication – *Super World* – had all these names that were in the prototype issue that should be trademarked and copyrighted. Can't you just imagine the script for a heroine named "Helen Damnation"? *(laughter)*

STEVE: The full name was *Super World Of Everything.* At one point it was called *Uncle Carmine's Fat City Comix. (laughter)* It was going to be a cross between an underground comic and *Rolling Stone.* The reason we came up with that was because Jack wanted to get off the comic book newsstand and on the magazine newsstand, and he wanted everything to be big. So the only thing we could think of was to do it Sunday newspaper size, tabloid size. It was gonna be the size of *Kirby Unleashed.* And we figured out a way they could print it on the DC presses just like a comic book, but without the color covers, and just one fold and one cut; something like that. Anyway, we did it and it was very economical, and we figured out a way they could get advertising from Coca-Cola and people like that who weren't advertising in comic books at the time. We did a mock-up, and Jack did *Galaxy Green*; Steve Ditko did a strip called *Gemini.*

Jack's unused cover for In The Days Of The Mob *#2. The circle in the center would've been a photo.*

MARK: Marie was going to do a strip. Steve and I had this idea about an old retired silent movie star. And Jack came up with the greatest name for it: "Emile Fadeout." *(laughter)* We just made up these little mock-ups; two or three pages each. A bunch of DC people were at the Beverly Hills Hotel, and we presented it all to them, and they looked at us like we'd grown antlers. *(laughter)*

STEVE: Jack had a great sense of humor, too. The cover for *In The Days Of The Mob* #2; remember that cover? Jack drew it up; it was gonna be a photo cover of a gangland killing. We actually shot the photo, using us and Jack's son Neal and his daughter Barbara. We lined them up, and they all had guns to Mark's head. *(laughter)* Mark was bound and gagged and was going to be killed in the fields of Thousand Oaks. *(laughter)*

MARK: I have a photo of Jack with me in a Red Skull costume. I'm holding a gun on Jack, and he's sitting there drawing with one of those feisty looks: "I don't care, I'm gonna finish this story, Red Skull." *(silence, pause)* Yeah, we were really young and foolish in those days. *(laughter)*

AUDIENCE: I was wondering if Marie could elaborate, since you were around when Jack left Marvel the first time, what that was like. How much notice did Marvel have? It seemed like it happened overnight.

MARIE: Being in the Bullpen, I was not privy to any of the stuff that went on. There was the surge of, "Well, he's gone. Did you see what he's doing? It's terrible, it's terrible. It is terrible, isn't it? Oh my God, please let it be terrible." *(laughter)*

STEVE: It had to have happened pretty fast, because when Jack stopped drawing for Marvel, he had to immediately start drawing for DC. There was that three-month gap, so as soon as he finished that last *Fantastic Four,* he just immediately started drawing the new stuff.

MARK: He mailed in an issue, and he called Stan on a Friday that coincided with the arrival of the issue. Stan's unpacking the package and hears, "Jack's on line two." And he started at DC the following Monday.

The first time Steve and I went to DC, the first issues of *New Gods, Forever People, Mister Miracle,* and *In The Days Of The Mob* had already been turned in, and they were keeping them under lock and key. Carmine calls us into his office and closes the door, because the other people at DC were not allowed to know about the books. It was an absolute secret, what they were about. Julius Schwartz stopped us in the hall and said, "What's this new Kirby book about?" So we called Jack that night and said, "They're doing a wonderful job keeping your books secret. They're keeping them under lock and key at DC.

Nobody knows what's going on." The next day we're up at the Marvel offices, and there are *(Jack's)* pages pinned all over doors. Vince Colletta had been xeroxing them and taking them up there. *(groans, laughter)* And about three months later, Jack needed a page from *Forever People* that he'd already sent in for reference; this was before Jack got his copier. And we called DC and said, "Can you send out page two of *Forever People* #2?" And they could not do it, so I called the secretary at Marvel, and she pulled it off the wall, xeroxed it, and mailed it to me. *(laughter)*

AUDIENCE: Could you talk about why he left Marvel, and why he came back?

MARK: In the biography I'm doing, I devote about forty pages to it. When he was working for Marvel, he created this wonderful empire, and he was not being credited or compensated adequately in his opinion, and in almost everyone else's opinion as well. When Jack went to DC, he hoped things would be better; they certainly couldn't have been worse for him. I don't know if was any happier, but there was no place else.

STEVE: I think what Jack realized at the time was that Marvel was suddenly getting very, very big. The Goodmans were going to sell out to a corporation, and Jack sort of saw himself getting pushed farther and farther away from what he'd done. And there wasn't anything he could do about it, because he'd had a personal relationship with Martin Goodman, but once he was out of it, Jack was basically a freelancer.

AUDIENCE: What about when he returned later?

STEVE: Well, personally he'd settled something, but that was just a matter of it was the best job offer. Jack really loved comics. He could've done anything; we used to talk to him about advertising. He just didn't want to do it, because it meant he'd have to redo things, and he hated redoing things. And it meant giving up a lot of the freedom he had, because really, he could just sit down and do what he wanted to do and send it in, and any changes they would do at the office.

MARK: Also, he felt that he did comics really well. Jack had a very healthy ego about it; not overly excessive. He was very proud of what he did. When he was doing *Jimmy Olsen,* and he knew they would be redrawing Superman heads, he still drew them full. Even knowing an inker was going to leave stuff out, he still put it all in. He was very happy to finish the job, it was all there. He did some advertising stuff, and he was very happy with the money, but it didn't satiate a certain need he had to tell stories.

I have a theory that in the course of Jack's work in the 1970s, the one thing that he was totally disinterested in was covers. I think his covers became increasingly afterthoughts. He'd finish a story and it was done; it was anticlimactic to him. He was generally doing them after the stories, and opposed to the sixties when they were done before the stories.

RICHARD KYLE (from audience): Jim Steranko told me that when Jack left Marvel, they called all of the artists in to the office and held up the Kirby covers to all of the comics, and everybody was trying to figure out how the covers worked; why this cover was a good cover as opposed to that one. Apparently during that time, Jack was really into the cover art; it meant something to him. When he went to DC, occasionally there's a very strong cover, but most of the time there isn't. And he changed his dynamics for covers. The focal center of the pictures change and he never went back to that.

STEVE: I think a lot of that is because at Marvel, he was pretty much left alone about what to put on the covers. Whereas at DC, Carmine was very much involved in the covers.

MARK: Carmine did the layouts for those covers. You see a lot of unpublished Kirby DC covers; Jack drew a cover, then Carmine designed his own cover for the same issue. I always felt Carmine and Jack were at the opposite ends of comic art; totally different approaches. Carmine never drew a figure leaping out at you, straight-forward. When he did fight scenes, Carmine's characters were always sort of after the punch, whereas Jack's would always throw the punch. I don't think it was possible for Jack to do a good cover over a Carmine layout; they were too diametrically opposed in their composition.

One time Carmine sent Jack an advance proof of a cover, and said this was the greatest cover ever done in the history of comics. It was a Neal Adams cover for one of those 100-page specials, with all the characters they ever had, all standing there posed. *(Editor's Note: See the Neal Adams interview in this issue for a look at that cover.)* Jack told Carmine on the phone he thought it was a dreadful cover, because you had all these action heroes standing around with their hands on their hips. *(laughter)* "They should be leaping out and jumping and fighting, and punching and smashing. And they all had the same physique, too. All your characters look alike." Carmine was very upset about that.

Early Kamandi *concept drawing.*

Darkseid sketch done for a fan.

AUDIENCE: I noticed in *The Jack Kirby Collector* that a lot of later *Thor* covers were rejected. Why were they rejected?

MARIE: Because Stan didn't like them. *(laughter)* I didn't hear much about it, because I wasn't privy to the conversations; I was just doing my job. As for as rejection would go, it might be that a new Editor was helping Stan out. I don't know. It could be that Kirby drew some situation that was already appearing on another cover that month, a situation I try to solve by putting all the covers up on the wall, so we wouldn't be duplicating. Sometimes you could have a helicopter coming out of five covers, because all these guys worked at home. Maybe that's how it happened; a similar situation or a similar layout, or something like that. Because I couldn't imagine what would be wrong with his covers; he didn't do bad design.

MARK: As I go back over my old notes for the book, I find that Jack predicted the entire direction that comic book industry was going to take. Jack was the first guy to predict the size this convention would eventually be. He was always thinking we should start a bookshop, before the direct market was invented.

STEVE: Jack was going to start a comic book shop. Remember, Roz? We went to look down in Florence, in a place called Old Town. He wanted to open a comic book shop.

MARK: I think he knew the impact the direct market would have one day. He'd already done *Captain Victory,* and he gave Pacific a legitimacy. It's one thing to bring out a new comic; it's another to have a Jack Kirby comic as your cornerstone. He really believed the next generation had its right to take over.

MIKE: Especially if they weren't trying to imitate him. He wanted everybody to do their thing as well as they could, and they could study his kind of design, his kind of grouping and the dynamics, but not draw *like* him.

STEVE: After we did *Kirby Unleashed,* we were trying to figure out what to do next. Mark and I asked Jack, "Why don't we do *Jack Kirby: How To Draw Comic Books*?" Jack just went, "NO!" *(laughter)* Just adamantly, because he said, "Whatever anyone has to learn from me, they'll find it in the books. Just look in the books, because it's all there."

MARK: When kids came to Jack for drawing tips, he was always metaphysical. He never gave them anatomy lessons. He told them how to think about the work, the work ethic behind it, the philosophy behind it; be true to yourself. He never once told anybody, "Use this pen, look at this reference point on the perspective." He figured that was the easy part. Anybody could learn to draw, but not everybody could realize a vision, and have a personal stake in the work.

AUDIENCE: How would Jack feel about Rob Liefeld using his character Fighting American?

MARK: If Roz is getting money, I think he'd be tickled pink. *(laughter)* Jack always viewed his work as closed-ended. It's very hard to explain this to readers who see *Fantastic Four* as a series of issues that are all numbered. To Jack, *Fantastic Four* ended with issue #102. If somebody else did a *Fantastic Four* comic, it was their *Fantastic Four* comic. It had no more to do with his *Fantastic Four* than... now that Mike (Royer) is doing Winnie The Pooh, it doesn't make him a collaborator with A. A. Milne. They're separate bodies of work, like a remake of an old movie. It's a new work, not a continuation of it.

(Editor's Note: To supplement the discussion of Jack's 1970s DC work, here are a series of messages Mark Evanier posted on the Internet over the last couple of years.)

1970s SANDMAN

Carmine Infantino brought Joe Simon into DC to do a number of projects. They were old pals and had the same lawyer, and Infantino thought Simon might come up with some projects that would succeed for DC. One of them – a weird book called *PREZ* – was, I think, an unrealized masterpiece, which never gained a following due to inappropriate artwork.

Anyway, at that point, DC pretty much considered Kirby a flop as a creator of new characters, at least for them, and there was the belief that he needed a writer. Simon proposed a new Sandman, and Infantino decided to have Kirby draw it, in the hopes that the old magic would reunite. As far as I know, Simon wrote it all by himself, possibly with a few suggestions from Jack, but more likely, not.

Mr. Infantino seems to recall the book as a smash hit but actually, Simon and Kirby did the one issue together, and DC had so little faith in the project that they put it out as a one-shot at a time when most new books were being started as bi-monthly or even monthly books. Apparently, there was some reason to believe it was a sales hit. (With newsstand distribution, it was difficult to tell how a one-shot sold, because a lot of newsracks would just keep them on sale until they sold, instead of returning the unsold copies when #2 came in.)

Anyway, it was suddenly put back on the schedule, by which

time Joe Simon was out of DC. They gave it to Michael Fleisher to write, with Ernie Chan and Mike Royer imitating Jack on the insides, and Jack himself doing the covers. One wonders why, if the Simon & Kirby *Sandman* was as much a hit as Infantino now claims, he didn't put Simon or Kirby back on it, or why it only lasted six or so issues. Jack did a few of the latter issues when he was in the later stages of his DC contract and they needed to find work to keep him busy.

Morgan Edge

Jack intended Morgan Edge to be a bad guy. He wanted to explore the theme of organized crime gaining a foothold in corporate America – particularly a giant media conglomerate. Given the shady background of the company that acquired Warner Brothers and DC, it was something of an inside joke but obviously, they couldn't tolerate it.

When Jack introduced Morgan Edge, he intended there to be one and only Morgan Edge, and for him to be a bad guy. The decision was made in New York to convert Edge to a non-Mafioso.

I don't know for a fact that Jack didn't suggest the Evil Factory twin explanation but, if he did, it was because DC was insisting on the change in Mr. Edge. It may or may not have been Jack's idea. I vaguely recall that Nelson Bridwell came up with the storyline that would convert Edge, which is why it was done in the book he edited, *Lois Lane.* But I'm not completely certain on this one.

Collages

The collages were done before the inking. Jack would do the collage and send it in, along with a separate page on which he would pencil the figures to be placed over the collage. The inker would ink those figures, then someone in the production department would combine them. Usually, they shot a screened, black-and-white velox stat of the collage, then statted the figures, cut them out and pasted them onto the velox. Then the page was "shot" from the stat.

The collages were usually done in color, using clippings from magazines. I believe that in most cases, Jack did the collage, then later decided how to work it into the story.

He usually did not plan them. He'd leaf through magazines in his sparse spare time and cut out shapes that were of interest to him. When he felt he had enough, he'd paste them into a collage. Some involved some drawing on Jack's part, but most were just built through instinct.

The reproduction was poor; that was one of the reasons Jack stopped doing them. (Also, they were more work than drawing pages.) He was very enthused by the technique and always hoped to find a venue in which he could do a story primarily (or completely) in collage and get decent printing.

I never saw Jack do a collage that filled an entire wall. I think he *wanted* to do things like that but never had the time nor facilities.

He did most of them on illustration board around 22" by 28." I think he did one that was like a fold-out – three of those placed end-to-end – but designed so they could be viewed as one big collage or three separate ones. I think that would be his biggest one.

He didn't do many of them in his last few years. One of the reasons was that most of the magazines he used for material – *Life, Look, Saturday Evening Post* – had gone out of business. I remember he had Steve Sherman and me get him a pile of old ones at a second-hand bookstore at one point. But I think his interest in the form declined largely because there didn't seem to be any real market for them. ★

An example of the art Jack would supply with his collage pages. This is from the two-page spread in Kamandi *#9.*

Neal Adams Interview

Interviewed by Jon B. Cooke

(Neal Adams is one of the most highly acclaimed artists in the history of comics, inspiring nearly as many imitators as Jack Kirby. Since starting at DC as an artist for Robert Kanigher's war books, Adams immediately rose to the top and became an instant fan favorite, drawing such classic series as The Spectre, *Deadman, and the lauded* Green Lantern/Green Arrow. *His graphic redefinition of the campy Caped Crusader into The Batman, dark avenger of the night, remains the quintessential version that exists today. Between 1967 and '72, Adams was the house cover artist, working on – among virtually every other title published by the company – Kirby's* Superman's Pal, Jimmy Olsen *and the occasional Fourth World title. This interview was conducted by phone on September 2 and 3, 1997. Special thanks to Arlen Schumer for facilitating the conversation.)*

THE JACK KIRBY COLLECTOR: Did you grow up reading Jack's work?
NEAL ADAMS: I guess everyone who read comic books more or less read Jack's work. I must admit that I wasn't a Jack Kirby fan as a kid. People seem to think there were the same number of Kirby fans in the '50s before Marvel as *after* Marvel, but in general, Jack Kirby worked for the secondary companies. I mean, he did *Fighting American* and worked for DC at various times, but essentially Jack was put into the same category as guys like Bob Powell – not necessarily the mainstream of comic book guys like Alex Toth, Kubert, and the DC guys. He was sort of a "B" brand. When I grew up, as much as I bought comic books and recognized Kirby's stuff once in awhile, I really wasn't a fan.

I got to be a fan later on – boy, a *big* fan when I realized what was under all that! In Jack's early stuff – and even later on – Jack had a style that was just a little bit crude. He always had people with big teeth, screaming and yelling; drawings that you weren't used to seeing in the other comic books which were much more sedate, much more heroic and much more pretty-boy. Jack's stuff came off as a little bit odd.

TJKC: Were you into the EC stuff?
NEAL: Sure.

TJKC: Would you say you were a big comics fan?
NEAL: I don't think so. In those days there were Fan Addicts for EC, but I was just a reader of comic books, a reader of comic strips, and went to the movies. My mother didn't keep me from comic books, so I guess I was something of a collector, but not a big one. I certainly *did* read comics. Because of my early interest in art, I tended to keep some comics that were well drawn. I wasn't looking for the artist necessarily, but I also had favorite comic *books.* I was a big fan of Supersnipe. And Captain Marvel, Superman, Batman. There's hardly a comic book you can bring up that I don't remember reading, because when we were kids we traded comic books. That's how I got to read all the comic books. *Powerhouse Pepper* and all these oddball comics were traded back and forth. Even if it wasn't the greatest comic, we read it. That's pretty much the way things happened until I was ten or twelve years old. That's when the sh*t hit the fan in the comic book business, and I went off to Germany as the son of a sergeant in the army.

I didn't know what was going on back in the states with Congress attacking comics and so forth. I just got incidental comics from the Army PX. By that time I had become a Joe Kubert fan. I was a big fan of *Tor: 1,000,000 B.C.*, and 3-D comics. Then they died. When I came back to America I just started in again, and this time I realized that a lot of the guys had disappeared, just gone away. Somehow there weren't that many comic books out. It started to dawn on me that this was a different time. It was as if only DC comics were available. So with Jack Kirby, what I did – along with all the other kids in America – I would notice that every once in a while Harvey Comics or Archie would come out with a series of super-hero characters that were spearheaded by Jack Kirby and Joe Simon. So I started to realize that this is a guy out there who was trying to make something happen, and I began to recognize this guy from before. I started to follow what Jack was doing – not so much as a fan, I must admit, but more as a person I recognized who was trying to crack the business back open again, though I didn't quite know why it was closed down. Here was Simon & Kirby going to Harvey comics doing "Space Commandos" or whatever the heck it was called, and then going to this company doing a series of books for them, and then this company, disappearing and reappearing somewhere else. It was fun! Suddenly there would be Jack Kirby, Al Williamson, George Evans – all the old guys being pulled together and trying to make

Neal gives his rendition of some classic Kirby characters in these pencils from Avengers *#93.*

Another unused Kamandi *#1 cover. The blurb in the top left corner would seem to indicate that Jack viewed the term "Fourth World" as a catch-all phrase for all of his new ideas, not just books related to the New Gods.*

something happen.

When I was a later teenager, Joe and Jack did *The Fly* and the *Shield* for Archie Comics, which lasted for a certain period of time and then went down the tubes. They were down in the trenches. It would seem that Jack would go to Timely and do work, and later blast out to work with Joe again. At Marvel, Jack would work on the standard Stan Lee five plots: "Mogaam," "Fin Fang Foom,"... *(laughter)*

One really high point in the '50s was when Jack went to DC and started to do *Challengers of the Unknown.* That was probably when Jack Kirby's artwork really hit me right in the face, big, big, *big* time. Not so much in the first couple of issues inked by that guy...

TJKC: Marvin Stein.
NEAL: ...but suddenly his pages would hit me. Now I was a big Wally Wood fan, and Jack inked by Wally just blew everything away. Jack's perspective, Jack's attitude towards composition, Jack's storytelling with Wally Wood's delicate inking with the blacks just knocked me out, blew me away. I guess they just did three or four issues of *Challengers,* and then they did a comic strip called *Sky Masters.* It was in a New Jersey newspaper, and I would go down to an out-of-town newsstand and buy it every Sunday just to get that page.

TJKC: How did you find out that it was in that paper?
NEAL: I scouted around. You find stuff when you're a teenager. I would haunt these secondhand book stores to buy science fiction books for 10¢. At this point, I was in high school and interested in art, so I was tracking this stuff and looking for what was going on. *Mad Magazine* was where Wally Wood found a home, and Mort Drucker went there after wasting his time being ignored by DC. Things were starting to happen, but it wasn't happening very much.

TJKC: At this time you were starting to get professional aspirations?
NEAL: I was in the School of Industrial Art, now called the School of Art and Design, and I was certainly interested in drawing comic books. But in those days, people who drew comic books really were interested in drawing comic *strips.* In the '50s you didn't draw comics *unless* you wanted to draw comic strips. That included Jack, Joe Kubert, everybody. The idea was to get a comic strip. So you did comic books in the meantime. From 1953 on, comic books were considered toilet paper, and anyone who was producing them was considered less than human. It was not a good thing to do. This aspect was piled on you when you spoke to people in the business. The best example I can give you is the fact that there is no one in this business that is five years my junior or five years my senior. So really, what I heard was, "Oh, what a terrible place to be," and people were getting crushed all around. And yet in the middle of it, there was Jack trying new experiments here and there, and then, by golly, he did land a syndicate strip – and thank goodness for the rest of us in comic books that it fell apart!

TJKC: You actually drew a sample *Sky Masters* strip.
NEAL: I did when I was in high school. I did a Sunday page. I became a fan of the Kirby/Wood combination so that even when I did it, I was doing Wally Wood lines and I was trying to do Kirby drawings. I realize now that I was failing at the Jack Kirby drawings more than the Wally Wood lines. There you go. It's hard to see past that now. Yeah, I was a big fan of that strip. I don't know what happened to my collection, but I had every Sunday page until I got out of school.

TJKC: You worked for a syndicate on *Bat Masterson* and *Ben Casey.*
NEAL: I did backgrounds for a guy named Howard Nostrand on *Bat Masterson.* Later on, after I had done a whole bunch of stuff – it seemed like an eternity – I landed a comic strip with Jerry Capp, an adaptation of a TV series called *Ben Casey,* when I was 21. A lot of things happened in-between. I worked over at a place called Johnson & Cushing, a studio that did comics for advertising. Illustrations, comic booklets, all kinds of stuff. I worked 24 hours a day.

TJKC: When I was a kid, one of my favorite magazines was *Boy's Life,* and I remember a bunch of your half-pages.
NEAL: There was a guy named Tom Schauer (who is now Tom Sawyer, head writer for *Murder, She Wrote*) and he did *Chip Martin, College Reporter* for Bell Telephone. In the middle of it, he decided to quit, and they looked around for someone else; and of course I was there, big

grin on my face, saying, "I can do it! I can do anything!" I continued to do the pages for a couple of years. Very, very difficult work. It really allowed me to arc my abilities. Very demanding with lots of reference. It required lots of discipline.

TJKC: So what got you into DC?
NEAL: Well, I had the syndicated strip for three and a half years. Instead of going into comic books, I decided to be an illustrator. I spent six months painting samples and I took them to various places to try to get some illustration work. One place I dropped them off and when I came back, they were gone. So I realized that although I may have had a syndicated strip, reality says you're not going to pick up a lot of spot illustrations; people aren't going to do you a lot of big favors, so maybe I should look for some comic book work. So I went over to *Creepy, Eerie,* and *Vampirella.* Archie Goodwin was the Editor over there when they started to do the Warren horror books, so I did work there in a number of styles.

The best other comic books out there were the war stories over at DC Comics, so I went over to try to get some work. Coincidentally, I had helped Joe Kubert get a comic strip, *Tales of the Green Berets,* so maybe they were looking for kind of a Kubert thing. So I went over and met Bob Kanigher and nearly got into a fistfight. I never would ever hit anybody, but if I ever did, it would have been Bob. So he gave me work!

It was a big shock to me *(to get work at DC)* because when I had just gotten out of school I had samples to show, and they were pretty good. I would have to say that out of desperation perhaps, they were professional. And when I took them to DC to show them, they wouldn't let me past the lobby. They just sent out some guy to tell me to go away. It was a very, very bad time. So at this point, Marvel had started to give DC Comics a little bit of a run for their money. I didn't even know that they were called Marvel yet, but I could see that Jack Kirby was kicking a little butt. I don't think Kanigher cared one way or the other. I think he just probably missed Kubert, and thought that I could turn out some decent war stories.

TJKC: You actually got an opportunity with Kubert's war books because you got Joe the syndicate job?
ADAMS: Isn't that weird? *(laughter)* It never ended up that way because I went to see Kanigher; having heard some horror stories about him – hearing that he gave Johnny Severin a hard time, which I can't imagine anyone giving Johnny a hard time. I thought that he would have some work for me because Joe was not there; it was very clear to me when I picked up the books that he had people drawing them. So it wasn't like he needed me, but I don't know; I made the appointment like a professional, went up to see him and he gave me a script. Then he started to art direct me. So, ho-ho, that was it.

TJKC: So you did about three war stories?
NEAL: Y'know, I didn't count the stories but I think it was more than three. Maybe five. There are people who keep track of that stuff who can probably tell you.

TJKC: Actually those are about the only stuff of yours I'm missing. I just bought your run of *Jerry Lewis.*
NEAL: Yeah, hard to get.

TJKC: (laughter) There's only a little of you in them.
NEAL: Jerry Lewis was the best money I ever made in comics. I penciled ten pages a day! You can't do that with the realistic stuff. It was tough to give them up. People ask me, "Why did you do those?" Boy, golly, ten pages a day! You can't beat that. You're talking about $35 a page, but at ten pages a day, that's decent pay. If you do it the regular style, you're doing two pages a day.

TJKC: You just went back and started doing work for Murray Boltinoff?
NEAL: Well, it kind of jumped around. I thought I was going to get myself canned out of there because I confronted Kanigher for art directing my stuff – I basically told him, "I don't tell you how to write, so don't tell me how to draw." But he was cool. I think that Julie Schwartz might have thought that I had spunk because he hadn't quite seen anybody stand up to Kanigher before. He offered me an Elongated Man story, and I think I did more work for Julie after that, *The Spectre.* It is kind of a jumble. Bob Oskner was going off to draw *Dondi* or he was having some trouble with his eye, and he couldn't draw the *Bob Hope* stuff. So I was there, and I said, "I can do *Bob Hope.*" So Murray, who was always unsure of everything, called Sol Harrison in, and said, "Sol, do you

Uninked pencils from issue #152 of Jack's most personal war series, Our Fighting Forces.

Shown here at an early 1970s convention are (left to right) Jack, Mark Evanier, and Carmine Infantino.

think this young man can draw *Bob Hope*?" So Harrison said, "He can draw, so what's your problem?" Murray said, "Okay, okay." So he gave me those books. It kind of spread. It seemed as though anything they gave me wouldn't stop me, so basically I started getting split up and shared with people. But it wasn't bad.

TJKC: At the time, Carmine Infantino, Arnold Drake and Jack Miller invented Deadman in *Strange Adventures.* You came on the second issue and in a very short period of time you started kicking butt.
NEAL: I thought I was kicking butt on *The Spectre.*

TJKC: Yeah, I remember some great double-page spreads. Were the production problems on some of those spreads frustrating to you?
NEAL: My problem, to a certain extent, was that I had done a lot of work in the advertising business. When I was 18, I started doing brochures for advertising agencies and studios, and I had learned a lot of reproduction techniques. I was one of those guys that when you ran the film from school on printing techniques, I paid attention. I was one of those people – a geek. I knew about this stuff, and when I could, I'd do dropouts and all kinds of stuff. I understood the techniques of what you could do. When I came into comic books, it dawned on me very quickly that what was worse than the comic strip business was the comic *book* business. It was as though they were in the dark ages. They didn't know anything, yet you had very smart, clever people like Jack Adler and Sol Harrison. In the production room at DC, I couldn't believe that these bright guys didn't keep up with the techniques that were available. It seems as though that not only was it a closed shop as far as writers and artists were concerned, it was a closed shop as far as *time* was concerned. They were locked into a very strange era. It was 1952 and they just kept on moving forward and DC stayed 1952. Even though they were moving into the '60s, even though Marvel was biting at their butt, DC was still staying the same.

So I would say, yes, I was frustrated. For example, the obvious thing of putting Zip-a-tone on comic books to create more colors didn't start with me doing it at DC Comics. It started at EC Comics! Anything that I ever did at DC was done at EC long before me. To me it's a joke to hear people talk about all the "innovations" that I brought in because it's not true. I just did what they used to do, and I brought it back. I was pumped enough to say, "No, I'm going to do it, leave me alone, I'll make the mechanical for you; I will provide it in a negative acetate form if you need it, but please, let's do this." So people started to pay attention, and Carmine started to act like I was brought in by Carmine. *(laughter)* So I got to be Carmine's guy to some extent.

TJKC: When Carmine became Editorial Director in '67, when Kinney bought the company and gave him a management role, do you recall the writer's strike at all, when Arnold Drake, Bill Finger, Gardner Fox, and a number of writers were suddenly not being published at DC anymore, because they demanded health benefits?
NEAL: I sort of remember it, but not really. I wasn't paying attention.

TJKC: Jack Miller, who was writing Deadman, was suddenly off the book.
NEAL: Well, what they said at DC Comics was that Jack had done some double-billing. *(The "strike")* certainly wasn't publicized, certainly wasn't talked about. I never heard anybody refer to it as a "writer's strike." I heard of it as some guys were looking for some more money so basically they really kept a lid on it. In those days, it was a terrible time when things should have changed but things didn't.

TJKC: How did things change with Carmine in a management position?
NEAL: Carmine had nearly nothing to do with the changes that took place. This is not a criticism of Carmine, but he was interested in being publisher and advancing himself. From an art director point of view, he felt he had something to contribute. But when it came to creator's rights, he lived through the worst of times and he was quite happy with the *status quo.* He liked the idea of having new people coming in for him to take credit for, and that was great. But essentially, Carmine did what he was told. I'd like to say that Carmine was a total ally in all the rights battles, but it really wasn't quite that way.

TJKC: There was an influx of new books that suddenly appeared. Dick Giordano came over from Charlton.
NEAL: That's the thing that Carmine did that I thought was so good. Basically everybody at DC was saying that we have to have new blood. Once I got there, everyone realized that gee, maybe things *can* change. But they still kept the doors closed! In fact, I had a room there and I was constantly hiding people in there, finally introducing them to editors. It was a rather rowdy time, but it was Carmine's feeling that to bring new people in was a good idea and Neal was the proof. So he hired Dick who brought all the people over from Charlton, starting as a new Editor who turned out new stuff. Then Joe Orlando, who had a heart attack, I believe, was put on as an Editor to let him sit down and relax a little bit from the more frustrating times of his life. Carmine did indeed hire some people and start things up. Some of them worked out but others of them didn't. Giordano was potentially somebody who

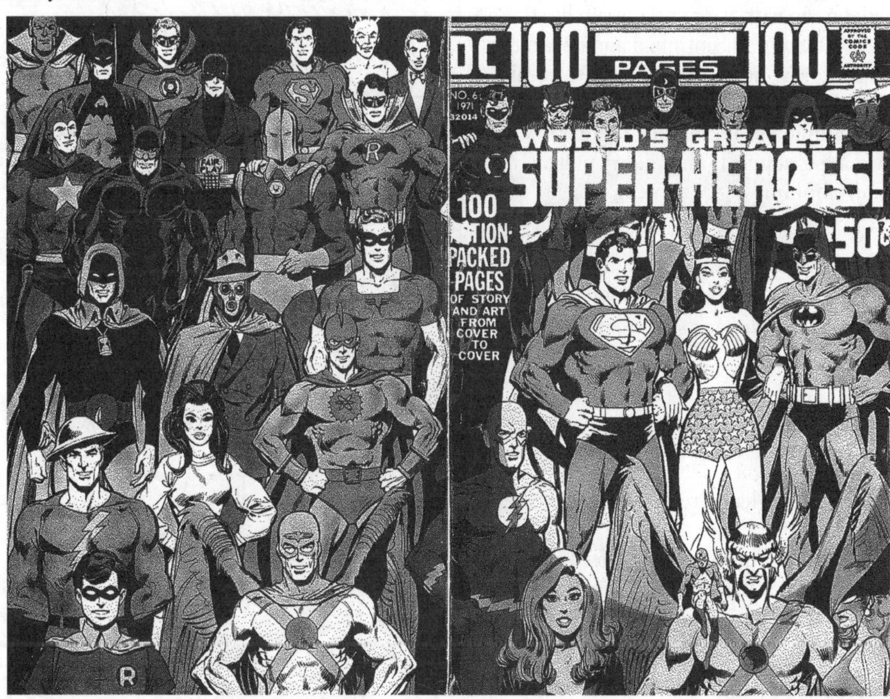

Neal's cover to DC 100-Page Super-Spectacular *#6; Carmine Infantino told Jack this was the best cover DC had ever done. Jack disagreed, as related in this issue's Kirby Tribute Panel.*

could do Carmine's job, I think, better than Carmine. After a while, there got to be a little bit of a realization of that, and I guess you'd have to say that Dick's days were numbered. I would say that Carmine brought Dick in and Dick brought everyone else in.

TJKC: Any truth to the rumor that the *Green Lantern/Green Arrow* story with the depiction of Spiro Agnew and Richard Nixon as villains upset Southern distributors, and led to the book's cancellation?
NEAL: I don't know about the distributors but I can tell you that there was a letter from the then-governor of Florida – I remember seeing and reading it but I don't have a copy – that said how offended they were that the Vice-President was so maligned in the comic book, and that if DC Comics were ever to do such a thing again, he would see to it personally that DC Comics were not distributed in the state of Florida. What's interesting about it is that he never noticed that the little girl in the comic was based on Richard Nixon. We had a good time with that. *(laughter)* It's not like it was a big secret, pointing a finger at Spiro Agnew. I guess some people were afraid of it, but my goodness, what a terrible person he was!

TJKC: Carmine tended to cancel books at the drop of a hat.
NEAL: I probably know too much about that! *(laughter)* Sometimes people rule from their head, sometimes from their gut, sometimes they rule from their passion. I think that Carmine tended to rule from his passion.

TJKC: Carmine not only brought Dick over but he also brought Jack Kirby over to DC.
NEAL: Jack brought Jack over. I think Jack was ticked off. He wasn't thrilled at the way things were going and he wanted to prove that he could do everything all by himself.

TJKC: What was the atmosphere like when the announcement was made that Jack's coming over?
NEAL: It was great! Everybody thought, "Boy, the millennium's here!" *(laughter)* Indeed, it was! It seemed as though DC was going to kick out. I don't know if DC quite knew what to do with Jack, and therein lies the story. If Jack had continued and gotten the support that he needed over at DC Comics, I think he really, really would have done something. But I think that there was a waning of support. They didn't pull out the stops for him.

TJKC: At the same time, you were doing work for Marvel. How was it working with Stan?
NEAL: Stan is affable, gregarious, avuncular, terrific! *(laughter)*

TJKC: How about his art direction?
NEAL: Oh, I don't think that Stan knows exactly what art is. His brother Larry Lieber does.

TJKC: Did you have problems with the covers you did?
NEAL: Not with Stan, to be perfectly honest. I think that Stan was a good administrator and listened to what other people said. When I did my first *X-Men* cover, Stan was fine with it, but when he took it over to the publisher – I believe his uncle – he said, "No, I can't read the title. You gotta do it over again." There is a tendency for people to say that Neal didn't do as good covers for Marvel as he did for DC. I was given quite a bit of artistic freedom over at DC, but there's a tendency for people to think that after my first experience I was oppressed, but I really wasn't. Maybe I just didn't do very good covers. *(laughter)*

TJKC: John Romita would redraw your faces.
NEAL: Not a lot. I would say hardly any at all. When you take somebody whose work you like a lot and he gets slapped in the face once, the echoes reverberate around the room, so you tend to think that it was a lot. I did one *Man-Thing* story and Stan insisted that Johnny redo the faces and figures of just the girl. My figures in the original were fairly realistic and I thought that they were pretty good. They tended to look an awful lot like Johnny Romita figures when they were done. An awful lot of people saw that. Johnny was embarrassed by it, but he had been given his instructions and he did what he was supposed to do. And I believe that it was his job. So I'm not upset with Johnny.

The only other time that I really experienced such a thing was by Marie Severin. The last *X-Men* book that I did *(#65)*, I did a creature

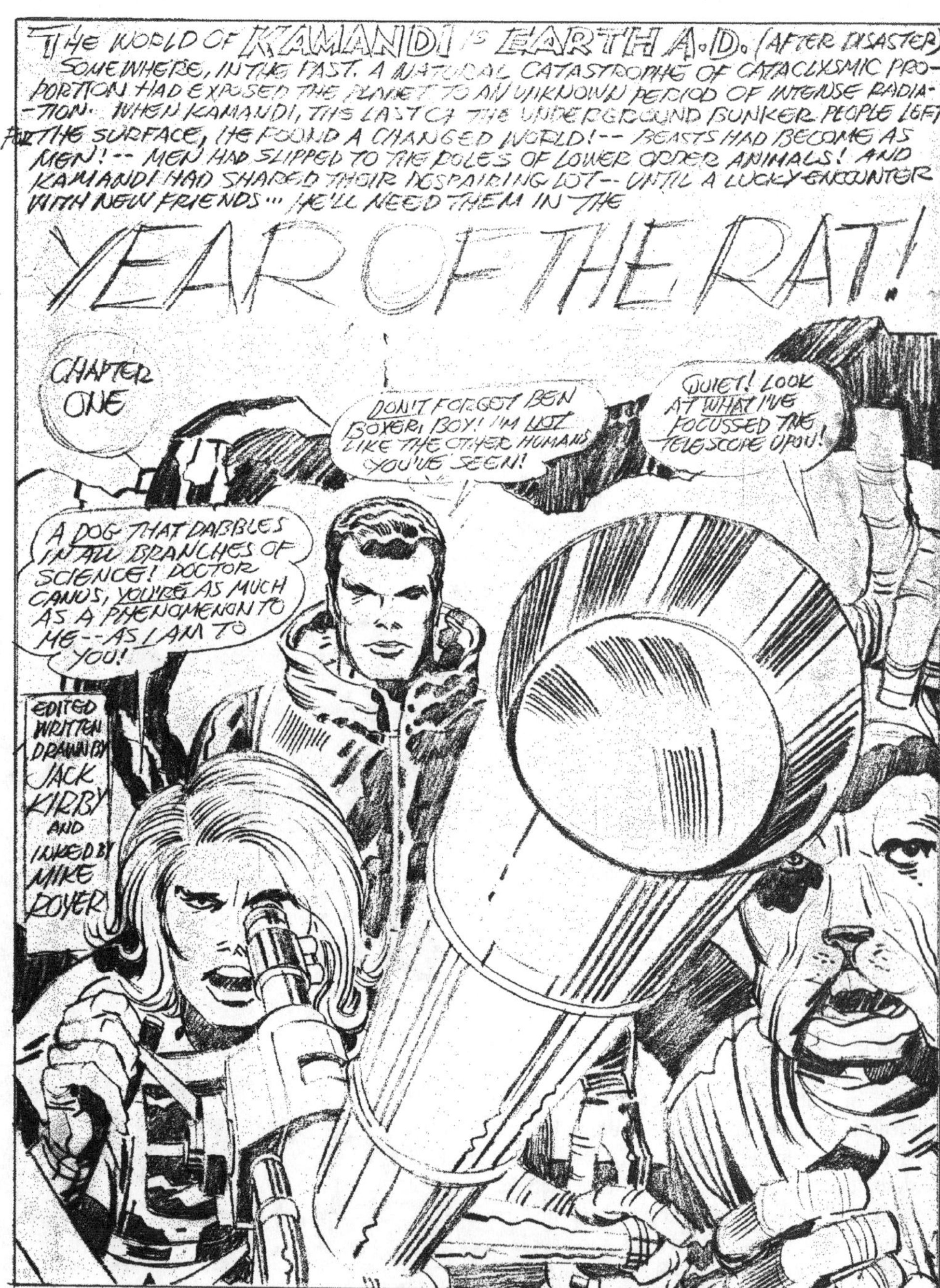

Splash page pencils from Kamandi *#2.*

Splash page from Demon *#9.*

that wandered the halls of the Z'Nox spaceship, a doglike creature. Stan felt that it should be a manlike creature. So he insisted that Marie Severin redraw the creature in the panels that it appeared. Well, Marie had a problem because the new creature had to be as big as the old one. The old creature walked on all fours, so to draw a manlike creature she actually had to draw one that had scales and walked around on his hands and knees. So if you look at that book, you go, "Why is this thing on its hands and knees?" When I came in one day subsequent to that being done – I didn't know that it had happened – Marie met me at the door and said, "Neal, Neal, Neal. I just wanted to tell you I had nothing to – they *made* me do it! It was not my choice, I *had* to do it, they *made* me do it!" I thought, "What was she made to do? What is she talking about?" So, of course, when I finally saw it, it was just ludicrous. I guess that Stan hadn't quite thought it out exactly that this creature would have to walk on its hands and knees. It was very silly. Beyond that, they really didn't play with my stuff very much – maybe a cover here and there. Except for that creature thing, they didn't mess with my *X-Men* stuff or my *Avengers* stuff. I even did two issues of *Thor.*

TJKC: What did you think of the Joe Sinnott inks?
NEAL: I liked them. People don't necessarily understand what you do when you do what you do. I thought I was going to do a "Marvel Story." I wanted to do a "Marvel Story" so that you almost couldn't tell if it was done by John Buscema, John Romita, Neal Adams, or whoever. I wanted it to look like a "Marvel" – or Jack Kirby – story. So they inked it like Marvel, which was *exactly* what I wanted. People said, "Gee, it doesn't look like Neal Adams," and I said, "I didn't *want* it to look like Neal Adams!" I was quite happy with it but people kept coming up to me saying, "We don't like that inking." The same thing happened on the Inhumans with people saying that John Verpoorten did a lousy job, but no, no! He did a *great* job! It looks just like a Marvel job! I had a good time with that.

When you do nice stuff, people care about what you do. They're looking out for you, so you really can't be offended. You can't be upset with people because they have all the good wishes in the world.

TJKC: I think we were all spoiled by the dead-on Tom Palmer inks.
NEAL: Yeah, sure. And I appreciate that. How can I argue with that point of view? It's a part of the experience. People have a right to be angry and upset. But after all, it's *comic books.* When you think about it, people are being paid money to draw pictures. It's an entertainment. Hey, listen, I'm offended when people do bad sh*t on other people! I'm never quite so upset when they do it to me, but when they do it to other people, I get pissed. I like to see good work. I'm one of those people who think that Vinnie Colletta ruined more comic books that any five artists could have drawn in a lifetime.

TJKC: Do you remember your experience inking Kirby on those Fourth World covers? What was that like? His anatomy's a lot different than yours.
NEAL: I wouldn't call what Jack does anatomy. He does an impressionistic thing and he does it because he pencils very fast and he's a storyteller. You don't sit Jack down and say "Here's an anatomical study, Jack. Do this." What you get is the impressionistic quality that is in many ways superior to someone who draws realistically the way I do. I would tend to fall short, because I don't have that freedom in the work. I would have to put aside a certain discipline to jump into what Jack does. What I thought my contribution was on Jack's stuff – if you can call it a contribution, and it's hard to say that with Jack – was that there were certain people who inked Kirby that harken back to the Wally Wood thing, that made Jack look different than he did on something else. I thought, "Well, if I just inked the lines, I wouldn't be adding much and you could just give them to anybody else. If they asked me to do it, what they're saying is, 'try it with a little something else.'" I tended to make the muscles a little bit more real, a little bit more three-dimensional, trying very, very hard not to take away the Jack Kirbyness of the drawing. They were obviously looking to me to add a little sales potential, because they gave me covers to do. They thought, "Well, we don't want to drive away all the *Jimmy Olsen* readers, so let's keep a little edge on it and maybe we can wean them away from the standard Curt Swan stuff." The thing that I was upset about in certain cases was they got Al Plastino to redo Superman figures in place of Jack's. No, please, not *that!* No offense, Al, but those were putty guys! Not right! They looked so out of place. What I was striving to do was not make my style intrude so much that you

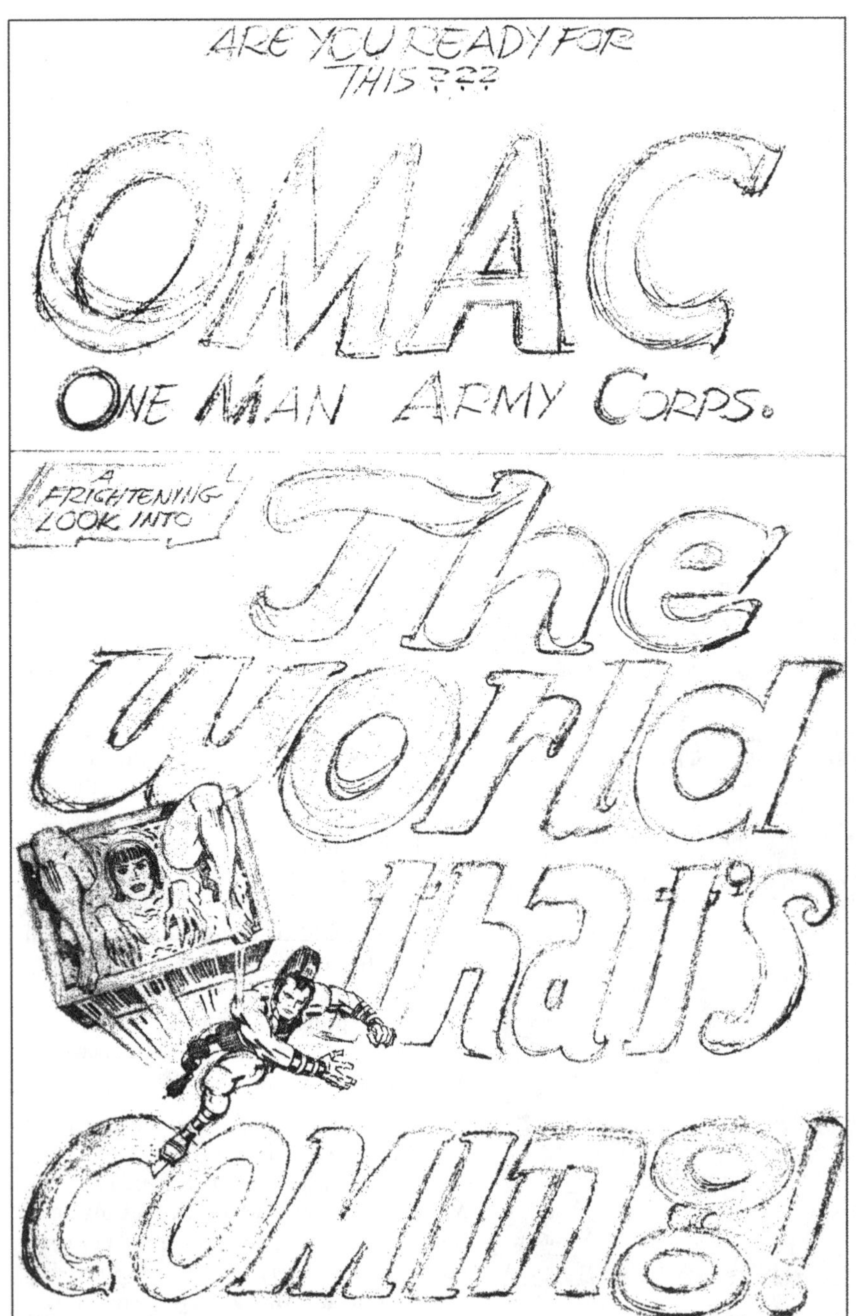
ARE YOU READY FOR THIS???
OMAC
ONE MAN ARMY CORPS.
A FRIGHTENING LOOK INTO
The world that's coming!

The original version of the OMAC *#1 cover. DC flopped the image and repositioned it.*

TJKC: Was it routine for Carmine to ask for a lot of cover changes? Jack had a lot of rejected *Jimmy Olsen* covers.
NEAL: Yeah. The excuse that I got was, after all, *Jimmy Olsen* was one of the Superman titles and you can't take the Superman audience and immediately turn it into a Jack Kirby audience. You had to wean them away. So they decided to wean readers away with the covers – and I guess some of the insides by having Plastino work on stuff. I didn't think this was a good idea. But on the other hand, I felt that by accepting the commissions to do the covers, at least I would try to keep enough of the Kirbyness with it that perhaps I could protect his rear if I could. Otherwise it would have been Al Plastino or Curt Swan or whoever.

TJKC: Did you respect Carmine as a cover editor?
NEAL: I respected Carmine more when I was younger, when I really liked his work that he inked himself. Then he got other people to ink it and that kind of sketchy line that suited his style so well disappeared. We lost Carmine and had his layouts left. They had a certain vastness about them, empty spaces going off into nowhere. But the style wasn't there. Carmine had a limited number of layouts that he did and a certain way of handling things: The dead body splayed out, one way or another. I accepted his covers to a certain extent because there was a certain workability to them. His layouts were simplistic in nature.

TJKC: There seemed to be a change for the better at DC after Carmine left, and you seemed to be a part of that. The Siegel & Shuster settlement was getting good publicity, Jenette Kahn came in, and almost overnight the image of the company changed. There seemed to be a chemistry going on between you and Jenette.
NEAL: Jenette Kahn and I lived together for a year.

TJKC: Well, there you go! *(laughter)*
NEAL: There was a chemistry going on! *(laughter)*

TJKC: I liked the *Muhammad Ali* book a lot. I thought that it was the best thing you did.
NEAL: It's very tough when people ask me what the best comic book I ever did was and I reluctantly say *Superman vs. Muhammad Ali.* Part of the reason is that there was an awful lot of things that I liked in it. Also it harkens back to an awful lot of things that I believe in and feel strongly about. It didn't do well in the United States, strangely enough, but it did very, very well around the world.

would not get any impact of the Jack Kirby drawing, even though you might miss some of the Jack Kirbyness of it – that you get the *power,* the *impact.* I tried to keep that as much as I could. But those Plastino paste-ups...!

Carmine had a lot to do with some things I didn't necessarily agree with. I didn't think that I should be working on the *Jimmy Olsen* covers. I thought that Jack should do them. It may have been the Editor combined with Carmine who insisted that I do them, but I put up a big fight to get off of them. I didn't feel right about it.

Jack Kirby did good comic books for DC. But he was sabotaged along the way. Jack was getting too much attention. I know that people criticized the writing and all the rest of it but, y'know, the stuff he did at Marvel somehow got better with time, but the stuff he did at DC got worse with time because he wasn't supported. The team around him didn't bolster him up. There were some people there who were Kirby fans, but basically he was let down. It came from the top. The *New Gods* could have been one of the best things that DC ever had, but it would mean that maybe Jack Kirby would become the Publisher eventually. And that wasn't going to happen.

TJKC: Did you ever have the desire to ink a full Kirby book?
NEAL: Sure. Wouldn't that have been great? I would have loved it. It's one of the experiences that I missed in those days, never having a shot. The opportunity was never there. They were always busting me to do something else at DC and I always had my own books to do. But, boy, it would have been nice to take a job aside. In all honesty, I would not have done it unless I was sure that it was okay with Jack, and the communication didn't exist.

TJKC: Were you aware Jack was using Deadman in the *Forever People?*
NEAL: Yeah. It was all right with me. I had a proprietary interest in the character but I didn't feel that it was exclusive. It was a DC Comics character.

TJKC: Was Deadman a favorite character of Carmine's, too?
NEAL: No. He didn't give a sh*t about it.

TJKC: He allegedly ordered Jack to put the character in *Forever People,* and it just doesn't work.
NEAL: Well, there you go. I can't tell you why. Maybe it was a power thing. Once I started doing Deadman, as far as I know, Carmine didn't

want anything to do with it. He did the first issue but I don't think that Carmine thought it was much of a comic book.

TJKC: You helped Siegel & Shuster get a credit line and a pension from DC Comics in the late '70s. Any advice on how to get a similar co-creator credit line at Marvel Comics for Jack?
NEAL: Ask them. I would ask them whenever possible, as much as possible. I would ask people to ask.

TJKC: You made some comments in an old *Comics Journal* interview that Jack refused to sign work-made-for-hire agreements. Can you expand on that?
NEAL: Jack went to Pacific Comics, remember? He did *Captain Victory.* I don't think that Jack was into the work-made-for-hire thing so much as he was for supporting the idea that you can work for independents and you can own your own property. He wanted to own his own property for years. The effort that I made, as small as it was, was to let people know that there were comic artists out there, and if you wanted to print your own comic book, and you're willing to let them have their own rights to the book and maybe be willing to pay them a royalty, then there's a distribution system out there and, strangely enough, these artists might do work for you. I guess it hadn't occurred to anybody. If there's only DC and Marvel and some guy has a distribution system and would like to print some comic book, it doesn't occur to him that he can hire Jack Kirby to do it. Because Jack Kirby, Neal Adams, and Sergio Aragonés are being paid sh*t. Pacific Comics got ahold of Sergio and Jack, the two people with the most balls in the comic book business, perhaps besides myself, and said, "Look, you can own your own property if you'll do a comic book for us. How about it?" Those are the two guys who basically cracked the whole thing open, worked for an independent, did their own characters and essentially broke the back of the work-made-for-hire business in the industry. Now, there's still work-made-for-hire and it's not going to go away until we change the copyright law – which should have happened ten years ago. Jack was one of those guys that went out and, devil take the hindmost, did comic books for independents. He showed the way.

TJKC: Did you ever socialize with Jack and Roz?
NEAL: Just at conventions. I liked Jack and Roz. I think that Roz is the stuff that held Jack together. There's less said of Roz but I think that she is indeed the other half of Jack Kirby. I'd say it's the "Roz & Jack Kirby Show," not the "Stan Lee & Jack Kirby Show."

TJKC: What's the most important thing you learned from Jack Kirby?
NEAL: That there are other ways of doing things; not just my way, or the way of people whose stuff I appreciate. I learned that from Will Eisner, too. There's a lot of wonderful things out there, and my favorite thing is enjoying the work of other people who don't do what I do. My favorite thing about Jack Kirby is that he didn't do what I did, and yet he did what I did. He gave a new look to it, a new feeling about it, and made me realize – as with all great creators – that there are always new worlds to conquer.

If you think about what Jack did: Jack created Marvel Comics. Jack *could* have recreated a good 50-80% of DC Comics if they let him. He is 50% of the creative stuff in comic books today. What do you say about somebody like that? Me, I just did some characters; I may have picked the right ones. The truth of the matter is that I brought a quality to comic books; Jack *made* comic books. There's just no comparison. I'm just one of those guys out there who tries to do his own thing. Jack is a giant. Jack created worlds. Universes. Now we think of them as part of what we do and we go out and try to build on top of them and fail miserably. He really held them together – and all in his head. It's incredible.

TJKC: Did you have any opinions at the time in the fight to get his art back?
NEAL: I wasn't even aware of it. I'd been spoken to about it. I learned later on, before Jack died, that there was indeed some effort being made to get his artwork back, but I was unaware of what Marvel's response to it was. There was a time when I was volunteering to help, but I was rebuffed. It seemed to be in the hands of people who were pursuing it legally. I really am not in favor of pursuing things legally. I'm

Jack took his turn at Neal's signature character, Deadman, in Forever People *#10.*

in favor of pursuing things morally and ethically, and I believe that's the stand that should be taken. I don't like much about the law or much about lawyers who seem to able to use law to their own advantage. Morality and ethics are a much stronger argument, I believe, and they're very hard to argue with. You can see the greys more clearly with morality and ethics. You can't see the greys very clearly with the law. I believe that it would have been better pursued in perhaps a less legal, more straightforward level. At a certain point, I made an effort to volunteer my help. I even called Stan on a personal basis and asked him to step in, and he basically told me that it was out of his hands. I could've worked it out between me and Stan, I think, because there was nothing wrong with it from Stan's point of view. So we were thwarted by the legal putzes in the world and stopped from doing what we should have done. We should have put our heads together and figured out a way how to get this stuff returned.

TJKC: Did you approach the Kree-Skrull War with Jack in mind? It felt like Jack, it felt cosmic.
NEAL: Of course, it is. If Jack was the influence that made me do the Kree-Skrull War, then I say hats off to Jack. Probably because he wasn't there *(was why)* I would do such a thing. The Kree-Skrull War was really intended to be a freewheeling, kick-out thing that I really didn't see an end in sight for. There were always this politics and crap that was going on over at Marvel; personal problems that people have. But it would've been fun.

TJKC: You did Jack's quintessential character, Captain America, but only for a few panels.
NEAL: I tell ya, I think that I can do a better Captain America than almost anybody. Because I really believe the sh*t that he spouts. I am such a naive shmuck, but I tell ya, I really believe that sh*t.

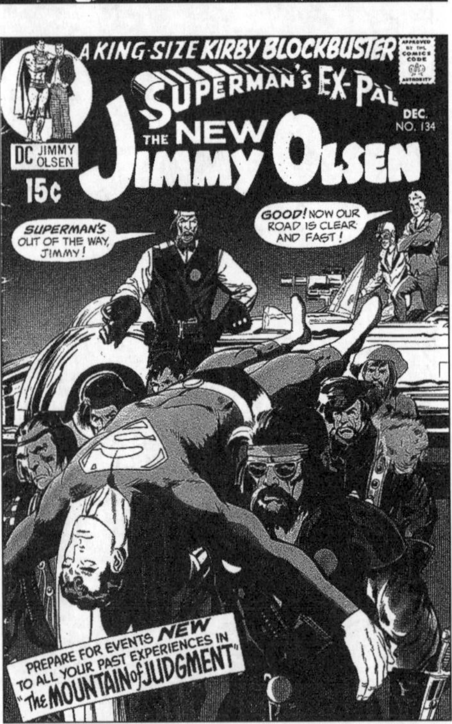

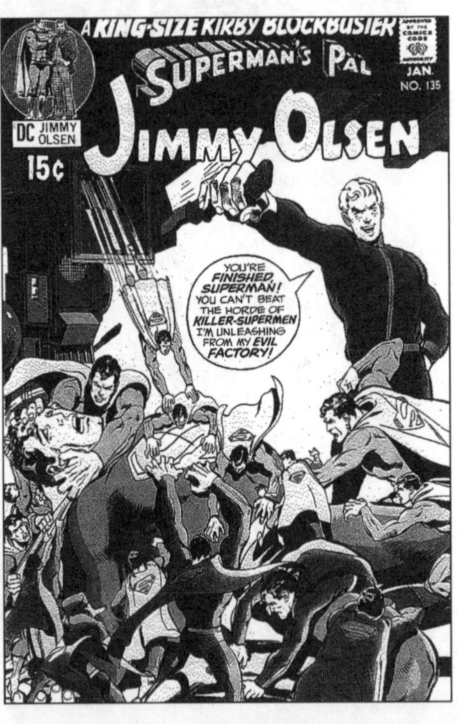

Cover Discussion:

New Gods #1: I don't believe I had anything to do with this cover directly. Jack was fairly aware of tints and stuff. And I had introduced the idea to the production room that they should go out and buy tints of various sorts to put into their photostat machine. Whether Jack had gone out and had it done on the outside, or Jack Adler influenced that and had volunteered to shoot a mezzotint with a halftone for the planet, I really don't know. By that point I had managed to educate the production department enough to do that sort of thing.

Mister Miracle #5: Isn't this weird! Y'know, I *know* I did that sword! I'll be damned if I didn't do the bomb. Now you have me spooked! I have a feeling I did that contrivance on the right, with the axe. Sure, I did! I'll be damned! It seems to me that they were done as an afterthought. It's possible that we couldn't tell what the bomb was. Maybe I reangled it or something. The more that I think about it, some issue came up that things were not clear, and the more that I look at it, it looks like they were just added. Maybe they asked Jack if they could just add some stuff in.

Superman's Pal, Jimmy Olsen #134: There is something reminiscent of Carmine in this. The bloom hadn't gone off the rose yet, but Carmine had decided that Jack wasn't going to do the covers on *Jimmy Olsen.* I had looked at the story and thought that *(Jack)* ought to *(draw the cover)*, so I took an image out of the story. Probably my layout, though there are certain Carmine-isms to it. The corpse does look like one of those Carmine things.

Superman's Pal, Jimmy Olsen #135: That's all me. It's a Carmine Infantino layout and I think what happened was he rejected Jack's cover, I believe, and there's maybe something of Jack's layout there. In this kind of situation usually they had no time, and basically they would come to me at the last minute and say they needed a cover. All the Superman figures were a really big pain in the ass. Jack could have done it a lot faster and a lot better, but for me it was at best a pain in the ass.

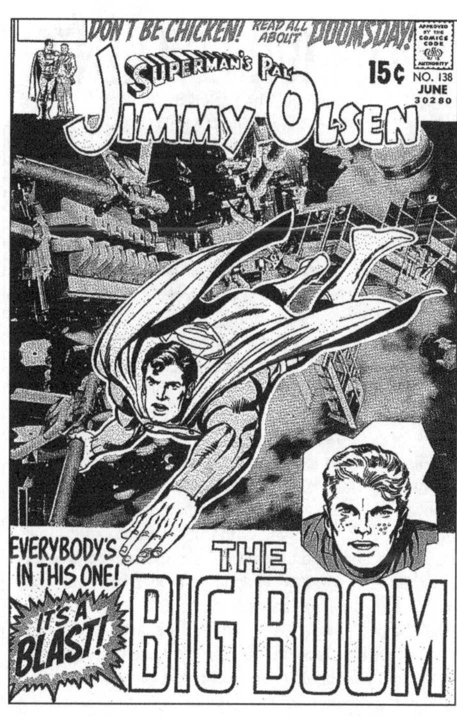

Superman's Pal, Jimmy Olsen #136: There's a lot more of me in there than I would hope. You'll note that the Jimmy Olsen is a Carmine Infantino kind of figure. He did these log-like figures with the fists busting out. His old *Batman* stuff looked like that. All that was left of Jack's was the *(Newsboy Legion vignette)* in the back. Carmine decided it was going to be a totally new thing, and he had laid this thing out, and I pointed out to him that you couldn't see Superman's face. I changed the form of Superman so it looks more like a Neal Adams figure. A mishmosh of a cover, a piece of crap.

Superman's Pal, Jimmy Olsen #137: The perfect match between the two of us. I think for a time there I was convincing people, "Just let me ink the covers and we'll be fine." An example of someone who knows how a cover layout works. He does it on several levels, not just the one big figure concept. The argument, "Let Jack do the covers and I'll ink them – they'll be fine," won out. If you had to satisfy the Editor to make the books look more like DC Comics – by having me ink them – that would do it. That philosophy lasted for a little while.

Superman's Pal, Jimmy Olsen #138: Jack's collage and my inking over his figure. Jack is the collage man. When I did collages, I tried to integrate it more clearly into the art so that your eye might go over it. Jack made it into an art form with some of those double-page spreads he did.

Superman's Pal, Jimmy Olsen #141: Totally Jack Kirby drawing and one of the most fun ones I inked.

Superman's Pal, Jimmy Olsen #142: *(The Superman figure is)* an ink of a Jack Kirby drawing. The question was, should we give this to Plastino to redo the Superman? And I said, "No, I'll do it." It was presented to me in such a way that I had to make a choice. We could give this to Al, but I said, "No, just let me do it. I'll ink it and if you like it, we'll use it. I don't want to have to redraw it."

Superman's Pal, Jimmy Olsen #148: Carmine did the layout and I did the cover. I attempted to make it look as much like a Jack Kirby cover as I could, but you can see by the speed in which I did it, I really didn't succeed. Couple of the faces look like Kirby. ★

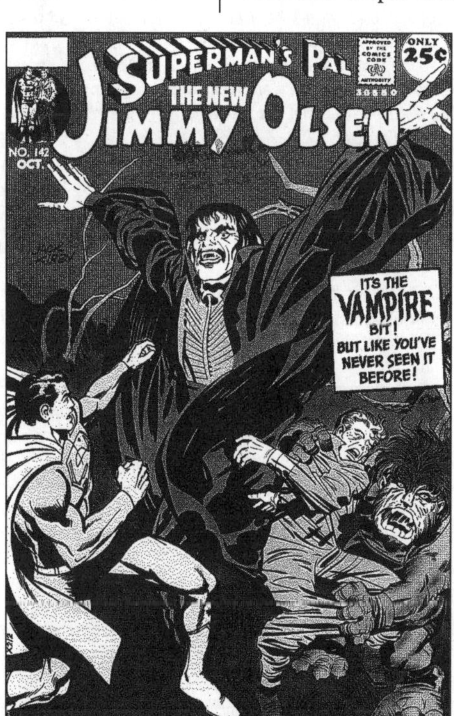

COLLECTOR COMMENTS

Send letters to: The Jack Kirby Collector
c/o TwoMorrows • 1812 Park Drive
Raleigh, NC 27605 or E-mail to: twomorrow@aol.com

(Well, gang, sorry you had to wait so long for this issue, but we take an extra month between the Summer and Fall issues, so we can attend comic cons to promote TJKC. *Since we just moved to our new address, that extra time sure came in handy! Now, on to your letters on* TJKC *#15 and #16:)*

Having just gotten *TJKC* #16, I appreciate the lack of time that you undoubtedly have for many things, including e-mail. I thought I would send you a very brief message on a few topics, however.

First, I wanted to let you know that I thought #15 was, if not your best issue, then certainly the one I have enjoyed the most to date. As a child of the '70s, I first "met" Jack through many of the books described in that issue, and I enjoyed the appreciative look at books (e.g., *Machine Man, Captain Victory*) that older fans may find not up to Kirby's standards from the '60s and early '70s. In particular, however, I would like to commend Charles Hatfield for his piece on the *Eternals*: I find his articles to be among your best, in terms of thoughtfulness, comprehensiveness, and balance.

Second, as I said above, I just received #16, and I must say that I think it has the most striking and well-done cover of any *TJKC* to date (if it doesn't get you more subs, I don't know what will)! It was also a pleasure to read about much of Jack's work that I had not seen to date.

Steve Fontana, North Haven, CT

P.S. I find it interesting that Jack returned periodically to the word "Tiger" in his work: You discussed "Tiger 21" in the 1950s, while Black Panther's (tentative) first name in the 1960s was, I believe, "Coal Tiger," and, of course, Captain Victory's ship in the 1980s was the "Dreadnaught Tiger."

(I was amazed at the number of younger fans in San Diego who came by our booth and, upon seeing Frank Miller's inks on the cover, said, "Look, Sin City!*" Let's hope that Frank's wonderful inks and interview helped expose some youngsters to Jack's genius.*

*Charles Hatfield had to bow out of any articles for this issue, but he promises me he'll have the second part of his Marvel/*Eternals *piece ready for next issue. Speaking of Charles...)*

This issue seems less focused than usual, since "tough guys" is a pretty vague hook. At first I was put off by the seemingly haphazard mix of topics – crime comics, westerns, war, rock'n'roll, and others – since I think most of these topics merit special issues unto themselves. A crime issue, for instance, would be great; ditto the western and war books. Once I dived in, though, I noticed some welcome overlaps between essays– most notably, between Jon Cooke's biographical intro and the two S&K crime surveys by R.J. Vitone and Tom Morehouse. All of these combine knowledge of Kirby's books with a strong sense of the cultural and personal contexts surrounding those books (e.g., in Morehouse's article, postwar film noir *and* Kirby's own biography). Likewise the trio of western-themed articles, one of which – Vitone's on *Bullseye* – gave me a really vivid mental picture of the frantic S&K shop. Only war comics seemed to be given short shrift, though the connection between Kirby's wartime experience and *The Horde* got me to thinking.

Once again, Jon Cooke deserves special mention for his historical spadework. His research into the Lower East Side and the Boys Brotherhood Republic, when taken alongside Kirby's "Street Code," really establishes the milieu of Kirby's childhood. An excellent choice to open up the issue.

I also think R.J. Vitone deserves a hand for setting forth so much information about S&K in such readable form. There's a wealth of background detail there in addition to the expected (and needed) plot summaries.

Richard Kyle's comments about looking at Kirby's work in biographical context are well-taken–though we should guard against the temptation to *always* go this route, as the work has much to offer readers who know nothing about the cartoonist's background. Incidentally, I agree with Richard's suggestion that the intrusions of the "outer world" compromised and ultimately wrecked *The Eternals.* What a shame.

Two questions: 1) Jon Cooke gives Kirby's birthdate as August 25 (page 4), while Vitone gives it as August 28 (page 6). Which is it?

2) On page 37, Vitone seems to imply that S&K's "distribution problems" were among "many ripple effects of the [Comics] Code." What distribution problems are we talking about, exactly, and how can we demonstrate that these were ripple effects of the Code? It's become fan gospel that the Code ruined everything in comics, but I remain skeptical. What source can we go to, to get the lowdown on this distribution shakeup? No doubt the Code had a disastrous long-term effect on the general perception of comics, but how did the Code cause immediate distribution problems?

Any light we can shed on this – any details we can glean from the record, as Jon and R.J. and other *TJKC* contributors have – would be most welcome.

Charles Hatfield, Storrs, CT

(Jack's birthday is August 28th. Sorry for the error. As for the distribution problems, I'll leave it up to more knowledgeable readers to enlighten us. Anyone out there got some details they'd care to share?

As for having separate issues for Jack's crime, war, and western work, I'd love to, but we're limited by what material we have available. While I'm sure we could get an issue full of articles on those topics, there's very little rare or unpublished art in those genres. All we'd have to show was inked panels from printed comics, and I think fans would be disappointed if they didn't get their usual dose of rare pencil art. But we'll definitely feature more articles on those books in future issues.)

I used to own the original artwork to Jack's original concept drawings for Atlas. I had two pages (there may have been more) and it was clear from these drawings and descriptions that Jack had more than a one-shot in mind.

The concept drawings describe in detail not only Atlas, but Chagra the Seeker, Kubla the Oppressor, Atlas' battle with the Headless Idol, as well as talking about the Crystal Ball and Crystal Mountain.

There is also a description of future Atlas stories, including "The Gorgon Masks" (which is worn by an army of Zombies) and "The War-Women of Nefra!!" (who are according to Jack, "Amazon Sea Raiders").

Anyway, it seems that Atlas was one of Jack's unrealized series that we were lucky to get a glimpse of in the *First Issue Special.* It's a shame more wasn't done with the character.

David Schwartz, Agoura Hills, CA

P.S. Originally, the published issue of *Dingbats* #1 had a double-page spread on pages 2 and 3. When the book was published, they reworked the artwork, to make it fit onto a single-page splash.

(Thanks for the info, David. Chris Harper ran those Atlas drawings in Jack Kirby Quarterly *#8. And hopefully all you* Dingbats *fans will enjoy the unpublished pages we ran this issue.)*

Thanks for the *Collected Jack Kirby Collector* Volume 1. I got a real smile out of seeing the old *Comic Reader* cover back in print after so many years hanging on a wall... and another one from seeing the NY Con luncheon interview from a con program book I edited for Phil (Seuling). So much of what we did is ephemera... it's great to see some of it still matters.

The *Kirby Collector* remains a wonderful piece of work.

Paul Levitz, DC Comics, New York, NY

(For those unaware, Paul published The Comic Reader *back in the days before he was VP at DC Comics.)*

I read "Kirby's Rock 'n Roll Connections" (*TJKC* #16) and a few corrections are needed to the "Silvers" story. First, their name is spelled "Sylvers," and second, it wasn't their manager who was a Kirby fan, but their group leader (singer, writer & producer) Leon Sylvers. Leon produced, through his company Sylverspoon Productions, hits for Gladys Knight and the Pips, The Whispers, and at least 15 other R&B groups. His studio was across the street from the newsstand I first saw him at. Jack was appearing at the American Comic Book Company comics shop to promote his 3-D book at the time, and I called Leon to tell him where Jack was appearing.

When I called Jack two weeks later, Roz answered. I mentioned to her about Leon Sylvers, and she said, "Oh, the Sylvers? They were all up here just the other day!"

Carl Taylor, Los Angeles, CA

(Sorry for the mix-up, Carl. When you told me the story over the phone, I never thought to ask the spelling of the group's name.)

Re: Inking Contest Guidelines. Two categories, professional and amateur, with the best overall piece featured on the cover.

Gee whiz, John, I wonder which category the cover winner will be from?! Give us non-pros a break, man! I can't compete with someone who sits at a drawing board 7 days a week. As someone who very much wants to start a career as an illustrator, being featured on the cover of an international magazine would be a great coup, and I'll bet lots of others in my position feel the same. I'll hold my own with anyone at my level, but if people like Sinnott, Rude, Stone, etc. submit, forget it! Your magazine was created for Jack's *fans* – give *us* a chance to be on the cover of Jack's zine!

Mark Alexander, Decatur, IL

(Sorry for this confusion, Mark. I'd planned to use the winners from both categories on some future cover, but there's only room for one winner on the "Art" issue's cover, since I've got big plans for the other cover that issue. But I've amended the wording of the rules this issue, and we will feature the Amateur Winner on a cover at some point.)

Issue #16 knocked me right off my chair! Frank Zappa hung out with Kirby?! No way! They are two of my favorite artists. Along with Fellini, they make up a trio of artists who carried 20th century art to new heights in their respective fields. Len Callo's article knocked me out. PLEASE, PLEASE, PLEASE talk to Mrs. Kirby and see if you can PRINT THE PHOTO!

Jason Sandberg, Eagan, MN

(Mike Thibodeaux was going to run that photo in the tribute book he was working on awhile back, but the book's up in the air, so we'll try to run it in TJKC at some point.)

I found I enjoyed #15 less than usual, and I think I know why: The overviews. I can understand the desire for some of this, considering much of Jack's work was done 20, 30, and 40 years ago. #14 had 4 pages on his 80 issues of Thor, and that's fine. This issue, though, had two 6-page overviews. Was that really necessary? There was very little here that any reader interested in Jack's work wouldn't already know, even if they had never actually read many of his earlier books. I really can't see its value. A simple checklist taking a third-page column could have given the relevant issue numbers.

Then there was the *Eternals* overview – again 6 pages. Now, these 19 issues aren't all that hard to find, or expensive to buy. And even without the actual issues, I reckon 95% of *TJKC* readers would know this stuff or enough about it to make such an overview fairly pointless. But I don't think it's only familiarity with the material that is the problem (for me, anyway). I don't know much about Jack's pre-FF monster material, but still didn't find the "Classic Monsters From TOS" in #13 of much interest. Are you sure other readers do?

Of course, the *Eternals* piece was more than just overview; it contained a lot of opinion. And that brings me to my second dislike for the issue: The opinions. The opinions of Jack's professional colleagues and family make great reading. What Mark Evanier and Joe Sinnott and

Mike Royer thought of working with Jack is fascinating. Chic Stone commenting on Frank Giacoia inking Jack and Al Williamson's comparison of Jack to Alex Raymond blew me away. But if I tell you my opinions, who cares? I realize it's hard to write without giving one's feeling, but I believe such opinions are irrelevant and should be kept to an absolute minimum.

I haven't meant to be rude to anyone here, but since I love this book so much, I thought I'd see if other readers might ultimately agree.

Shane Foley, Australia

(You ask who cares if you tell your opinions, Shane? Well, I for one do, which is why I'm running your letter here. I don't doubt that Kirby fans would love a magazine filled with nothing but page after page of unpublished art, behind-the-scenes interviews and previously unknown secrets about Jack's career; I know I would! But unfortunately, there's only so much intrigue to report – or at least that we've currently uncovered – and there's only so much unpublished work out there as well. Besides, this is a magazine by and for fans, and I feel everyone's voice deserves to be heard. As an Editor, I try to weed out repetitive pieces, and keep from running too many "gosh-wow-Jack was the greatest" articles in each issue, but I think those have a place alongside the more factual pieces. Also, learning other fans' opinions of Jack's work has helped me view some of my least favorite Kirby work in a new light. I won't run an article unless there's something in it that touches me – as a Kirby fan, I've got to rely on my own judgment to decide what gets published – but ultimately, even though not every article is about a subject I'm personally interested in, there's somebody out there that cares about that subject; otherwise, the piece would never have been written.

Also, there are a lot of fans out there who aren't familiar with, say, Jack's pre-Kamandi work. Some only know his Pacific Comics work, believe it or not. Still others are youngsters raised on Image Comics, and are just finding out about Jack's amazing career. So I try my best to get a healthy mix of material in each issue; that's why we treat our themes so loosely. I can't guarantee this approach will please everyone all of the time – of course it won't. But hopefully, you'll continue to find something of value in each issue, as will all the other Kirby fans out there, who each have different tastes.)

THE JACK KIRBY COLLECTOR #17

A TWOMORROWS ADVERTISING & DESIGN PRODUCTION IN ASSOCIATION WITH THE KIRBY ESTATE EDITOR: JOHN MORROW ASSISTANT EDITOR: PAMELA MORROW ASSOCIATE EDITOR: JON B. COOKE DESIGN & LAYOUT: TWOMORROWS ADVERTISING PROOFREADING: RICHARD HOWELL COVER COLOR: TOM ZIUKO CONTRIBUTORS: NEAL ADAMS D. BRUCE BERRY MARK BLACKNEY LEN CALLO JON B. COOKE BOB COSGROVE PAUL DOOLITTLE KEVIN EASTMAN MARK EVANIER LANCE FALK JOE FALLON MIKE GARTLAND GLEN GOLD DAVID HAMILTON CHRIS HARPER PHILLIP HESTER ALEX JAY CHRIS KNOWLES CHRIS LAMBERT JOE MAGEE RUSS MAHERAS MARK MARDEROSIAN HAROLD MAY ADAM McGOVERN JOHN MODICA RICH MORRISSEY MARK PACELLA KEN PENDERS PHILIPPE QUEVEAU MIKE ROYER STEVE RUDE FIONA RUSSELL DAVID SCHWARTZ TOD SEISSER MARIE SEVERIN STEVE SHERMAN JEAN IVES SIONNEAU DAVE STEVENS GREG THEAKSTON MIKE THIBODEAUX KIRK TILANDER WILLIAM UPCHURCH R.J. VITONE PETER VON SHOLLY TOM WATKINS AL WILLIAMSON CURTIS WONG TOM ZIUKO SPECIAL THANKS TO: NEAL ADAMS JIM AMASH D. BRUCE BERRY JON B. COOKE KEVIN EASTMAN MARK EVANIER MIKE GARTLAND D. HAMBONE RANDY HOPPE RICHARD HOWELL PAUL LEVITZ MARK PACELLA MIKE ROYER STEVE RUDE FIONA RUSSELL ARLEN SCHUMER STEVE SHERMAN GREG THEAKSTON MIKE THIBODEAUX TOM ZIUKO & OF COURSE ROZ KIRBY MAILING CREW: D. HAMBONE GLEN MUSIAL ED STELLI PATRICK VARKER AND THE OTHER KIRBY FANS IN RALEIGH, NC

KIRBY COLLECTOR BULLETINS

LATE BREAKING NEWS!

ITEM! This just in: The "Beta" version of the updated KIRBY CHECKLIST is now ready for distribution! Rascally RICHARD KOLKMAN has finished compiling all the changes you fans have been sending in, and the whopping 48-page version is ready for spot-checking by anyone's who interested. Download a FREE COPY from the TJKC WEB SITE (**www.fantasty.com/kirby/**) or we'll send you a hard copy for a measly $3.50 in the US ($4.00 Canada, $6.00 elsewhere), which covers our copying and postage costs. Everything that's been changed from the original checklist in Ray Wyman's THE ART OF JACK KIRBY has been highlighted with an asterix, and we're asking all interested fans to get a copy of this trial version and double-check all the highlighted entries. Any changes you send in must include documentation to support it (a photocopy of a page from the issue in question will do), and a blue ribbon panel of Kirby experts will review all the final changes. To keep this from dragging out forever, we're setting the deadline to send in corrected lists at FEBRUARY 14th, 1998, so get your copy today and start checking! Once we've gone through this last round of revisions, we'll post the final, updated checklist on our web site, and make a printed version available for ordering. So let's all work together to make this the most accurate checklist possible!

ITEM! Once we got started on this issue, we saw there was so much good stuff that we'd have to make it 68 pages just to hold it all! So we upped the cover price a little, but subscribers get this super-size issue as part of their regular subscriptions, at no extra charge. (One more perk of getting TJKC directly from us!) Next issue is another 68-pager for $5.95 (subscribers get that one for no extra charge too), and then we'll revert back to our usual 52-pages for $4.95 unless you want the larger size to continue. If so, we'll have to increase the subscription price to $30 for six-issues in the US – $40 Canada, $55 elsewhere. So let us know if you'd be willing to shell out a little more for more Kirby each issue. (Because this issue shipped late, #18 won't ship until January. But when you see it, we think you'll agree it's worth the wait!)

ITEM! We got a sneak peek at some sample art by Sturdy STEVE RUDE for the JIMMY OLSEN SPECIAL he and Mighty MARK EVANIER are doing for DC (as discussed in this issue's Kirby Tribute Panel). Steve's renditions of Jimmy, Superman, the Guardian, Morgan Edge, Dubbilex, Simyan, and Mokarri are dead-on, and he's just getting started! We'll keep you posted as things develop.

ITEM! Just a quick note to thank Reclusive RICHARD HOWELL for his usual great job of proofreading. (There, Richard; now you've got a "Bullpen" nickname!)

NEXT ISSUE: #18 is another 68-pager, featuring a MARVEL THEME! We start off with cover inks by Joltin' JOE SINNOTT on an unused FANTASTIC FOUR cover, plus some SURPRISE ART for our other cover! Then we'll roll up our sleeves and start the interviews with every Bullpenner we could find, including Mirthful MARIE SEVERIN, Happy HERB TRIMPE, Fabulous FLO STEINBERG, Rascally ROY THOMAS, Jazzy JOHN ROMITA SR., and (tentatively) STAN THE MAN himself! There's also a rare KIRBY INTERVIEW, plus articles on Jack's '40s Timely work, his '60s work on everything from A to Z (ANT-MAN to ZURAS), and his 1970s work on CAPTAIN AMERICA, BLACK PANTHER, THE ETERNALS, and others. We'll also reveal the oldest existing Kirby fan drawing, show unpublished Kirby art including unused pages, published pages BEFORE they were inked, and more! Our recent move has us running a little late on next issue, so we'll see ya in mid-January! The deadline for submissions: 11/15/97.

SUBMIT SOMETHING- GET FREE ISSUES!

The Jack Kirby Collector is a not-for-profit publication, put together with submissions from Jack's fans around the world. We don't pay for submissions, but if we print art or articles you submit, we'll send you a free copy of that issue or extend your subscription by one issue.

Here's a tentative list of upcoming issues, to give you ideas of things to write about. But don't limit yourself to these – we treat these themes very loosely, so anything you write may fit somewhere. And just because we covered a topic once, don't think we won't print more about it. So get creative, and get writing! And as always, send us copies of your Kirby art!

#19 (MAR. '98): ART ISSUE

We'll examine the artistic worth of Jack's comics, exploring the subtleties and nuances of his storytelling techniques. Plus we'll take a look at the ins and outs of original art collecting, discuss the merits of Jack's various inkers, feature fan art (including the winners of our inking contest), and spotlight the colossal Kirby art holdings at the Words & Pictures Museum in Massachusetts. If you want to weigh in on Kirby's artist value, send us your criticism and commentary. **Deadline: 1/1/97.**

#20 (MAY '98): KIRBY'S WOMEN

From Mother Delilah to Big Barda, the Invisible Girl to Granny Goodness, we'll explore Jack's heroines and villainesses, including a lengthy section on Simon & Kirby's romance comics. **Deadline: 3/1/98.**

#21 (JULY '98): JACK'S WHACKIEST IDEAS!

Nobody's perfect, and even Jack managed to lay a few eggs in his otherwise stellar career. So from *Red Raven* to those crazy Atlas Monsters, Arnim Zola to the Fighting Fetus, we'll have fun finding redeeming qualities in Jack's wildest, weirdest, hokiest, lamest, and most preposterous ideas, including gizmos and gadgets! **Deadline: 4/1/98.**

#22 (OCT. '98): VILLAINS

From the big guns like the Red Skull, Doctor Doom, and Darkseid to all the also-rans in-between, we'll take a closer look at what makes Jack's bad guys so darn good! If there's a Kirby villain you love to hate, write something about them! **Deadline: 7/1/98.**

SUBMISSION GUIDELINES:

Submit artwork in one of these forms:

1) Clear color or black-&-white photocopies.
2) Scanned images – 300ppi IBM or Macintosh.
3) Originals (carefully packed and insured).

Submit articles in one of these forms:

1) Typed or laser printed pages.
2) E-mail to: twomorrow@aol.com
3) An ASCII file, IBM or Macintosh format.
4) Photocopies of previously printed articles OK.

We'll pay return postage and insurance for originals – please write or call first. Please include background info whenever possible.

HAPPY 75TH BIRTHDAY, ROZ KIRBY!

Jack Kirby '79
—and the Dude '96

$5.95
In The US

ISSUE #18, JAN. 1998

A *"KING"-SIZE 68-PAGE* ISSUE ON JACK'S WORK AT *MARVEL COMICS!!*

A RARE 1970
KIRBY INTERVIEW

A 1975 INTERVIEW WITH
STAN LEE

INTERVIEWS WITH EVERY BULLPENNER WE COULD FIND, INCLUDING:
ROY THOMAS
JOHN ROMITA
JOHN BUSCEMA
MARIE SEVERIN
HERB TRIMPE
FLO STEINBERG
GEORGE ROUSSOS

SPECIAL FEATURES:
ANT-MAN
THE ETERNALS
BLACK PANTHER
& MORE

UNPUBLISHED ART
INCLUDING PENCIL PAGES *BEFORE* THEY WERE INKED, AND *MUCH MORE!!*

the AMAZING
SPIDER-MAN

JACK KIRBY

An early 1980s Captain America drawing.

Issue #18 Contents:

Back cover inks: Joe Sinnott
Front cover inks & colors: Jack Kirby
Back cover color: Tom Ziuko

Photocopies of Jack's uninked pencils from published comics are reproduced here courtesy of the Kirby Estate and the Pure Imagination archives. Thanks to Roz Kirby and Greg Theakston for their continued support.

JACK KIRBY COLLECTOR

Our front cover is an unused Marvelmania poster drawn and colored by Jack, circa 1969. Our back cover is an unused Fantastic Four #71 *cover (pencils shown above), which Joe Sinnott graciously agreed to ink for us.*

The Jack Kirby Collector, Vol. 5, No. 18, Jan. 1998. Published bi-monthly by & © TwoMorrows Advertising & Design, 1812 Park Drive, Raleigh, NC 27605, USA. 919-833-8092. *John Morrow*, Editor. *Pamela Morrow*, Asst. Editor. *Jon B. Cooke*, Assoc. Editor. Single issues: $5.95 ($6.40 Canada, $8.40 elsewhere). Six-issue subscriptions: $24.00 US, $32.00 Canada and Mexico, $44.00 outside North America. First printing. All characters are © their respective companies. All artwork is © Jack Kirby unless otherwise noted. All editorial matter is © the respective authors. PRINTED IN CANADA.

The Great Atlas Implosion

by Jim Vadeboncoeur, based on a story uncovered by Brad Elliott

(Brad Elliott was originally hired to produce the Marvel 50th anniversary book that eventually became Marvel: Five Fabulous Decades *by Les Daniels, instead of the true history that Brad had envisioned. Brad had full access to all Marvel records for well over a year and here's what he learned about Marvel/DC and the late '50s.)*

If you pay any attention to the names in the Ownership Statements, you'll notice that up until 1952, Robert Solomon is listed as the Atlas Business Manager. In that year a new name appears in that position: Monroe Froehlich, Jr. Remember him; he created comics as we know them today. Honest!

For those of you who may not be completely aware of the magnitude of the events of 1957, let me explain exactly what the evidence of the comics shows.

In 1957 (cover-date time), Atlas published 75 different titles — monthlies, bi-monthlies, and one-shots — during the July through October period. In November and December of that year they put out 16 (all bi-monthly). So what happened? And who the heck is Monroe Froehlich, Jr.? Here's the script.

The Set-Up:

Atlas, as you may have known, was not really a comics company, but was in fact a distribution company. The comics were published by Martin Goodman's various corporations (Chipiden, Timely, Red Circle, etc.) and distributed by Atlas Magazines, Inc.; all legitimate incorporated entities. Atlas Magazines (wholly owned by the Goodmans, Martin and Jean) was paid a fee to distribute Goodman's comics — profits, profits, profits.

The Catalyst:

Monroe Froehlich, Jr. was Goodman's golfing partner who somehow finagled himself into the business manager position. He pretty much had a free rein with the comics, the pulps and the newsstand magazines, but he was kept out of the distribution end of the business. Being apparently an ambitious sort, he wanted to expand his political base in the company to include some measure of control over distribution. Arthur Marchand was the man in charge of Atlas Magazines, Inc. and exerted every effort to prevent this.

The Ploy:

As Froehlich was frustrated in his attempts to gain control over the distribution arm, he eventually resorted to some subtle business maneuvering to accomplish what office politics had failed to do. He somehow renegotiated the contract between the publishing arm and Atlas Magazines so that the latter received a lesser percentage of the price of each publication for the distribution service. On paper, Atlas Magazines, Inc. began to lose money.

The Sting:

Froehlich exploited this apparent change in the distribution situation to convince Goodman that he needed to switch to a national distributor. In the summer of 1956, when Goodman gave the go-ahead, Froehlich negotiated a five-year contract with American News Co. (the ANC on the covers of so many comics in the early Fifties) to distribute comics, magazines and Lion paperbacks. Goodman disbanded his distribution system and Froehlich was apparently "king of the hill."

The Zinger:

American News Co. was Mafia-connected and under investigation by the government for less-than-legal transactions of some sort. (ANC was into a lot more than periodical distribution — restaurants, for example — and it was there the troubles lay.) Rumors flew that ANC would soon be out of business. Even before the contract, Arthur Marchand had tried to warn Goodman of the potential problems, but he was viewed as merely playing in office politics against Froehlich.

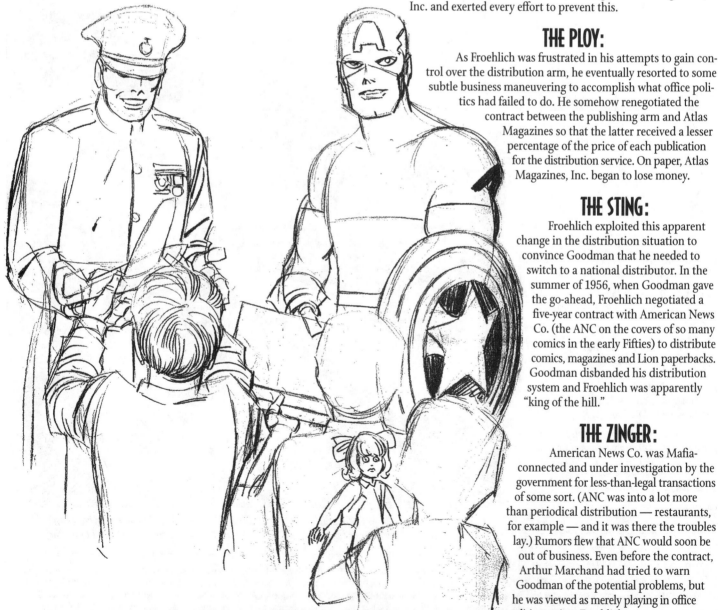

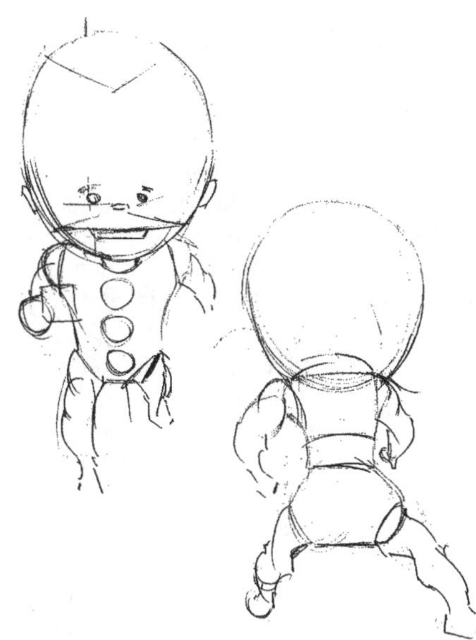

THE CRASH:

American News Co. assumed the distribution of the Goodman line Nov. 1, 1956. Six months later, American ceased operations. Not having time to re-establish his old network, Goodman was forced to lay off the entire staff with the exception of Stan Lee, while he searched for an alternative distributor. It took about a month (corresponding to the October 1957-dated books).

(Note: Brad Elliott has discovered records which show that the cover dates of Atlas titles were not totally accurate. During any given month, shipments could include books with cover dates spanning three months. We hope to eventually show that books like *Dippy Duck,* which has an October 1957 cover date, were actually shipped with the August and September books.)

THE AFTERMATH:

Goodman did find himself a distributor. It was DC-owned Independent News Co. They agreed to take him as a new account, but the terms were tough indeed: Independent would handle all of Goodman's magazines, but Lion Books had to go (Independent News was already handling New American Library), and since DC wasn't about to support its biggest and more successful rival, Independent News insisted that only eight comics per month could be accommodated.

Goodman and Lee opted to use that allotment to publish 16 bi-monthly titles. The first eight (*Gunsmoke Western, Homer the Happy Ghost, Kid Colt Outlaw, Love Romances, Marines in Battle, Millie the Model, Miss America* and *My Own Romance*) came out dated November 1957, the second batch (*Battle, Navy Combat, Patsy and Hedy, Patsy Walker, Strange Tales, Two-Gun Kid, World of Fantasy* and *Wyatt Earp*) in December. With inventory on hand to fill 75 titles, Lee simply cancelled 59 of them and hardly bought a story for over a year. Most 1958 material was produced in 1957.

In the mid-1960s, Jack was asked to create poster art for the "Toys For Tots" campaign put on by the US Marine Corp. The annual campaign collects donations of toys and distributes them to needy children at Christmas. On the previous page is his original preliminary pencil rough for the poster; on the back of that art, still in pencil, are rough drawings of several little elf-like creatures (an example is shown on this page). Shown below is the final art from his first attempt, and above is the final art that was eventually used on the poster.

Jack did this sketch in late 1964 for the cover of the fanzine Super-Heroes Anonymous *#2, which had a circulation of 35 copies!*

(You can get some idea of just how dominant Atlas was in the comics industry by reading interviews with artists who were working at the time. Every one of them makes a comment similar to Al Williamson's in a 1969 *Heroes Unlimited* interview: "...because by 1957, things were pretty grim," as if industry fortunes rose and fell with those of Atlas — which they *did*. I have some excerpts from the Ayers publishing guide that lists total monthly comic sales by company by year that show Marvel heading the list in 1952 with 15.2 million issues — twice that of any company except Dell's 10 million. In 1957, their position falls to 4th with 4.6 million, with Dell now 14 million and DC still about 7.5 million. Assuming these numbers reflect the '57 fall, comics circulation took a big hit that year. Thanks to Mark Carlson for the data.)

It wasn't until December 1958/January 1959 that Lee gathered around him the core of what was to be Marvel Comics: Kirby, Ditko, Heck, Ayers, and Reinman. This lends credence to Kirby's claim to have found Lee despondent on his desk, ready to throw in the towel. If the inventory was depleted and sales were down and growth was restricted, what was a man to do but give it all up?

THE RESULTS:

Over the next few years Goodman was free to publish whatever he liked, but whenever he wanted to introduce a new title, another had to be sacrificed. (*Battle* dies June 1960 to make way for *My Girl Pearl* in August, which fades away in April of 1961 to allow *Amazing Adventures* a slot in June.) They finally added a 17th title in 1961 and ironically enough it was *The Fantastic Four.* But with the exception of annuals and reprint titles, that number — though Goodman had managed to upgrade most of them to monthly — held until early 1968.

It was time to renegotiate the contract with Independent News. At that point Marvel Comics was a force to be reckoned with in the industry and Independent didn't want to lose a good client. The restriction on the number of books was lifted and Marvel exploded. The three split books (*Tales to Astonish, Strange Tales,* and *Tales of Suspense*) spun off into six individual titles (*Iron Man, Captain America, Doctor Strange, Nick Fury: Agent of SHIELD, Hulk,* and *Sub-Mariner*) and *The Silver Surfer, Captain Marvel,* and *Mighty Marvel Western* were launched. A year later, Independent lost Marvel anyway — to Curtis Circulation Corp., a subsidy of Marvel's new owner Curtis Publishing — and Marvel really went wild!

HISTORICAL INTERLUDE:

In 1957, Atlas was simply the largest comics company that had ever existed, but they had never been a leader or innovator. Goodman's empire had been built on selling paper, not innovation. If one western comic was good, ten were better. If super-heroes were selling, you can bet your boots that Atlas would have been publishing them indiscriminately.

Lee had resurrected the Atlas heroes in 1954, dropping most after three or four issues. In fandom lore, DC has been credited in 1956 with bringing super-heroes back from their oblivion in the dark ages with the appearance of Flash in *Showcase* #4. The reality is that it had been less than seven years since the original *Flash* comic was cancelled, *Batman* and *Superman* had continued uninterrupted during that time, and the marketplace was not clamoring for more of them.

DC was giving their heroes tryouts in *Showcase* and as back-up features, but none were setting the stands on fire. It wasn't until Atlas self-destructed in 1957 that rack space opened up for a potential resurgence of the genre. It would still be over a year before Flash got his own book.

THE LEGACY:

Monroe Froehlich's abortive attempt to manipulate Goodman's empire left Goodman with a scaled-down operation. Its size was artificially held at a level where it was feasible for one man (Stan Lee) to actually control the content of all the books. He couldn't get bigger, which had been the goal for the previous seventeen years, so he ended up getting better.

The pre-super-hero Marvel stories were done originally with tongue in cheek, but they soon developed a moral stance reminiscent of EC. Lee was getting interested in comics again. When Goodman asked him to develop a super-hero team, he could easily have brought back all of the old Timely characters with which he was so familiar — just as he'd done back in 1954. Instead, he expended some creative effort to think of something innovative for a change. Those early Marvel super-heroes were indirectly created by Froehlich, whose actions allowed Lee and the Bullpen to devote the time and thought necessary to the creation of interesting characters. If Atlas had continued to expand through the late Fifties, it is extremely doubtful that comics as we know them today would exist. Stan Lee would probably just be a name in an Ownership Statement, as it is only with hindsight that the occasional story he wrote and signed takes on any significance. Lee, or more properly his writing staff, would have continued to churn out a full spectrum of Romance, Teen, War and Western books (just look at the list of titles that continued after the implosion), and super-heroes wouldn't exist in the same sense they do today. Oh, we'd have heroes aplenty, but they'd be the same stale commodity they had been, with only slight variations on the theme.

There would probably be no 'continuity,' no 'angst,' no 'universes,' nothing but that formula which had served so well for decades... until a coercive business contract, precipitated by the actions of Monroe Froehlich, Jr., put spare time into the hands of Stan Lee for the first time in his life. Thanks a lot, Monroe. We owe you one.

(Addendum: It's interesting how history repeats itself. Marvel and distributors today seem to be an unhealthy mix. Maybe after all the current dust clears, Marvel will have to scale back and start creating interesting comics again.)★

FROM THE WORDS & PICTURES MUSEUM:

This unused cover for Captain America *#105 (circa 1968) is part of the permanent collection at the Words & Pictures Museum in Northampton, MA. Jack originally penciled Cap with left foot forward. John Romita had Jim Steranko re-position the leg as it appears now, but then the background characters needed to be rearranged to balance out the cover. Romita worked up a new cover concept, changing Cap's position and rearranging the background characters. Not quite satisfied, he brought in Dan Adkins to do yet another composition of the background characters before approving the design (shown below).*

The Words & Pictures Museum is going through a financial crisis, and is in the midst of a campaign to raise the necessary funds to keep its doors open. The museum is non-profit, and serves as a valuable resource for the preservation of comic art, including a huge collection of Kirby originals (which we'll spotlight in next issue's "Art" theme). Please do your part to sustain it by sending a tax-deductible contribution in any amount to The Words & Pictures Museum, 140 Main St., Northampton, MA 01060. ★

A CAP RARITY

by Will Murray

In the Spring of 1995, I had the good fortune to have lunch at the Society of Illustrators in Manhattan with no less than Stan Lee's brother, Larry Lieber. I had interviewed Larry by telephone, but this was our first face-to-face meeting. Accompanying me was Mark Evanier, whom I had just met for the first time and who like me had never met Larry before.

With his thick salt-and-pepper beard, Larry Lieber looked every inch the artist; all he needed was a jaunty beret. He reminded me a lot of the 1950s Stan Lee captured in so many photographs — vital and healthful and happy. I always thought of Larry as the forgotten man at early Marvel — after all, he scripted the earliest episodes of Thor, Human Torch, Iron Man, and my personal favorite, the Ant-Man — so I took particular pleasure when the waiter came up to Larry and respectfully whispered that someone at an adjoining table would really appreciate an autograph from the artist of the *Spider-Man* daily newspaper strip. Larry was only too happy to oblige.

Our lunch was very pleasant. Larry regaled us with gentle tales of early Marvel and his transition from fledgling scripter of love stories to super-hero co-creator, then full-fledged artist/writer on *The Rawhide Kid.* How much he disliked Matt Fox's heavy-handed inking of his earliest fantasy tales came up when I presented one for autographing. But especially, Larry spoke of how much he loved the art magic of Jack Kirby, with whom he collaborated on all those big monster stories for *Tales of Suspense, Journey into Mystery* and *Strange Tales.* It's still not widely known, but it was Larry, not Stan, who scripted the bulk of Kirby's monster stuff, and that their early super-hero collaborations alone make Larry one of the most prolific and important Kirby collaborators, third only to Stan Lee and Joe Simon. Jack, Larry recalled, drew so fast that he had a hard time writing scripts fast enough to keep Kirby working!

As we talked of Kirby, the conversation came around to a meeting Mark and I had with Jack's original collaborator Joe Simon the previous day.

"Joe Simon," Larry mused. "I met him — I think...!"

"Think?" we asked. When Larry's name had come up with Joe, the response was: "I don't think I ever met Larry."

So Larry told us the marvelous story of his first meeting with Joe Simon and the artist with whom he would collaborate twenty years later.

It seems that one day in 1941, Stan decided to take his younger brother Larry up to the offices of Timely Comics and show him around. Larry was then ten years old. Stan was still in his late teens. There was quite an age difference between the two of them.

Larry admitted he doesn't remember the visit at all. But he knows it happened because to this very day there hangs on his wall a pencil sketch of Captain America and Bucky, saying, "Hi Larry!" and signed by Joe Simon and Jack Kirby.

"So," Larry concluded, "I must have met them."

This electrified us. A Kirby fan sketch from 1941? Such things weren't known to exist. We wondered if Larry could honor us with a copy. Graciously, he did.

The sketch — which is reproduced here for the benefit of Kirby posterity — is remarkable. It's almost without question the earliest known surviving Kirby fan sketch, but it's unique in another respect: The Cap bust is purely Simon's work. Clearly Joe executed a quickie sketch of the good Captain, and Kirby came in after the fact, added Bucky's head, the "Hi, Larry!" word balloon in his distinctive Kirby-esque lettering, as well as the "To My Pal Larry." It's interesting to note the difference between Joe's smiling, almost airy Cap and Jack's heavier, more rough-and-tumble Bucky. Probably nowhere is the basic difference in their approach to their art better displayed.

But the thing I carry away from this story is that in 1941 a ten-year-old boy met his future artistic idol and collaborator and completely forgot the experience — or would have, had not Joe Simon and Jack Kirby bestowed on a wide-eyed boy a simple pencil sketch to immortalize that fateful first encounter.★

THE HIGHS AND LOWS OF HENRY PYM

A Look at Kirby's Ant-Man/Giant-Man, by Mike Gartland

When I was asked to write an article on Ant-Man, I realized I never really gave much thought to the character — and neither, it appears, did anyone else. Therein lies the basic flaw in the character of the Ant-Man: Fans were interested... but not very.

First of all, why make a super-hero out of a character the size of an insect? I'm sure anyone familiar with Ant-Man already knows that he started out as scientist Henry Pym, who shrank himself down, and got trapped in and escaped from an anthill in a then throwaway fantasy story "The Man in the Ant Hill," published in *Tales to Astonish* #27, Jan. 1962 (approximately the same time *FF* #2 appeared). Lee plotted the story and the art was by Kirby/Ayers. (Dick Ayers remembers sending Stan a note back with this story, telling him he found the concept of a man in a world of insects intriguing.) But the scripting (dialogue and captions) was by Stan's brother Larry Lieber, one of the unsung heroes of early Marvel. Lieber scripted many of the early Ant-Man stories.

Shortly after this story was published, Lee began the task of converting his "monster comics" into super-hero magazines. Perhaps it was due to fan response to the anthill story, or the fact that during this time Lee (or Kirby) was in a "bug" kind of mood (there was also "The Man in the Beehive" story in *Suspense* #32 and the debut of Spider-Man approximately one month before the Ant-Man introduction), or the fact that DC had successfully re-introduced the Atom, a six-inch super-hero, in *Showcase.* Since the artwork is submitted approximately (but not always) six months before the cover date/month, the Ant-Man story would have been drawn shortly after *Showcase* #36 — the end of the Atom's debut run — and Lee may have wanted a tiny super-hero in his growing stable of stars.

Dr. Pym's first appearance from Tales To Astonish *#27.*

In any event, the Ant-Man debuted in *Tales to Astonish* #35 (Sept. '62), on the rack with *FF* #6, *Hulk* #3, and *Journey into Mystery* #84 among others. The Ant-Man costume was clearly a Kirby creation, and it never looked as good as it did after the first splash page. The chest emblem was designed to resemble a huge ant, complete with head, thorax, and legs. The helmet was beautifully reminiscent of an ant's head with antennae and mandibles. The boots were also unique inasmuch as they appeared to be designed for treading underground, and were never used again after the first issue. Sadly, over time (and with the frenetic pace Kirby was working under), the costume became a diluted version of the original, with the boots resembling the gloves, the helmet sometimes without antennae, and the ant emblem becoming simply a large black ball on the hero's chest.

According to Lieber, Stan named the character Ant-Man, but Larry came up with Henry Pym — just as he came up with Don Blake, Tony Stark, and other characters whom I grew up with, never realizing the creative input of this quiet man. Larry Lieber was the principal scripter not only in Ant-Man's introduction, but also in Thor's, Iron Man's, and the Human Torch's in *Strange Tales.* Stan gave Larry the scripting chores on the monster comics that became hero comics, not to mention the many westerns, romance, and fantasy stories he was scripting at the same time. If anything, this should make him just as important in launching these characters as Stan and Jack were; remember when you go over these classic stories, the words were by Lieber.

Perhaps the reason Ant-Man had problems finding an audience was the premise; a super-hero the size of an insect was interesting, but not sustainable over the long run. The early Ant-Man stories were a good read and Kirby's visuals were entertaining; it had to be a challenge to

Splash page from Tales To Astonish *#35. Note the ant-like symbol on Ant-Man's chest.*

Ant-Man fought his share of Communists, as shown here in Tales To Astonish *#36.*

effective use of art.

Kirby drew the first six issues (#35-40) to get the character started; of this run, the best story to me was issue #39, "The Scarlet Beetle" — a definite throwback to the pre-hero stuff, but a fun twist having the insect human-size and vice-versa. With #41, Don Heck took over the art chores and coincidentally was drawing Iron Man's first appearance in *Suspense* #39 at the same time, so Heck was starting his super-hero run jumping in with both feet. Lieber continued to script up to #43; by then either it was determined that sales weren't good enough, or Lee wanted another female hero at Marvel (or people were getting tired of having Ant-Man converse one-sidedly with a bunch of ants). So by his tenth issue, it was decided to give him a partner.

With #44, Kirby was back and the Wasp was with him. Heck backed Kirby on inks, but the scripting was done by one H.E. Huntly, a pseudonym for Ernie Hart, who was an editor under Stan from the Atlas days. Lee was still getting credit as plotter, and this is evident because this story has Commie-villain elements in it. We find out that Pym had a wife, Maria, who came from and died behind the Iron Curtain. Janet Van Dyne, whom Pym transforms into the Wasp (via Kirby), also loses her father in this story, so the two are united to avenge his death. Ant-Man ends up with a partner, Pym ends up with a love interest, and Lee ends up with another Kirby-designed character. Up until this time, Ant-Man fought mostly common criminals, spies, saboteurs and the like; it wasn't until #48 (his 14th issue) that he was given a costumed super-villain. Perhaps the introduction of super-villains or lagging sales (probably sales) prompted Lee to re-vamp the character.

Kirby returned in *Astonish* #49 (once again backed up by Heck) to turn Ant-Man into Giant-Man. The name may have been picked because of the play on Gi-Ant Man, because the Ant-Man angle was not to be abandoned. This issue also introduced a one-time menace called "The Living Eraser" whom Les Daniels in his book *Marvel: Five Fabulous Decades* goes out of his way to showcase as one of those unique Lee creations. Yes, the character is unique and imaginative, but that's my point of contention: Kirby was on the book! One should notice that whenever revisions or additions were made to the Ant-Man character, it was Kirby who worked on that story, and it was in a decidedly different vein than was being done when Kirby wasn't involved.

guys like Kirby, Ayers, and Heck because the skillful use of perspective was key with this type of character. I like to think of Lieber's early Ant-Man stories as *Scooby-Doo* enders, because they all had a mystery solved with an unmasking at the end. Of course, there were the inevitable anti-Commie stories (Lee peppered his comics with this stuff during this time). Unlike Kane's stylized Atom, where hero and villain were always perfectly physically proportioned, Kirby's Ant-Man looked like he lived in an almost surreal world; villains loomed over him like mountains. Kirby's approach was both cinematic (as usual) and striking — almost frightening. You saw things from the perspective of an insect — an

Kirby made good use of the insect idea, with Ant-Man constantly hopping around, as shown here from Astonish *#38 and 40.*

DON'T YOU TRY ANYTHING LIKE THAT AGAIN! I DIDN'T SAY I WAS QUITTING! I'VE JUST GOT TO FIND A WAY TO FIGHT THAT THING! AND I THINK I'VE FOUND IT NOW!

Don Heck's inks/finishes over Kirby's layouts created a beautiful, polished look; it was some of Heck's finest work. This panel is from Astonish *#44.*

Kirby stayed on for #50 and #51 and helped launch The Human Top, who was being groomed to be Giant-Man's arch-villain. To my knowledge these issues have never been reprinted (which holds true for many of the Ant-Man/Giant-Man stories) and that's really a shame, for they have some very imaginative Kirby fight scenes. It was also an early two-parter, but even more interesting is that the first part of the story is inked by Steve Ditko, and the pairing of these two on super-hero stories was rare indeed. The second part (#51) was inked by Dick Ayers, probably to help introduce him to the character, for he was to become the primary Giant-Man artist. Issue #57 guest-starred Spider-Man (published around the time of *Spider-Man* #14), and issue #59 had The Hulk, probably to introduce the character to new readers since he became Giant-Man's new "roommate" in the next issue.

Beginning with *Astonish* #60, the book was split between Giant-Man and The Hulk, and while The Hulk was looking for an audience, sadly, Giant-Man was losing his. His stories seemed to be slipping back to the Ant-Man run-of-the-mill villains (Lee was credited as writer by this time). In issue #65, one last chance was tried with "The New Giant-Man." He was given a slight redress, a new cybernetic helmet (the original was discarded when he went from Ant- to Giant-Man), and the new ability to control the size of others, with some very nice Bob Powell artwork thrown in too; but it was too little, too late. Having never really known what to do with the character, Lee threw in the towel. The hero decided to "retire," another unique approach for a super-hero and a first for Marvel, so by issue #70, The Sub-Mariner debuted in place of Giant-Man.

Stan, refusing to say die, brought back Pym and Van Dyne for cameos in The Sub-Mariner story in *Astonish* #77 and #78. In it, The Wasp decides to tail Namor, which leads to her being captured by Attuma in *Avengers* #26, which in turn brings Giant-Man back to the Avengers in #28 with yet another new costume and name: Goliath. (True Marvelites remember Ant-Man was a founder of The Avengers, appeared as Giant-Man with issue #2, and left the group in #16. Goliath went on to become one of the "angst-ridden" Lee heroes, developing size changing-induced psychoses, and finally marrying The Wasp in *Avengers* #60 as yet another incarnation, Yellowjacket.)

Ant-Man/Giant-Man has always gotten a bad rap from fandom in general. In comics-related anthologies he's either listed as an "OK" character, one who "never seemed to cut it," or simply as a "joke." Ironically, he was held up to national ridicule, and practically no one knew who he was when it was being done. I'm referring to the classic *Saturday Nite Live* sketch with the super-hero party, where Garrett Morris as Ant-Man gets razzed by a John Belushi Hulk and a Dan Akroyd Flash. He became the Rodney Dangerfield of Marvel super-heroes; frankly, he deserved a little better. To me at least, Henry Pym, The Astonishing Ant-Man was, all in all, a decent hero for his time.★

Excerpts From The 1975 Stan Lee Panel

Held at the 1975 San Diego Comic Con
(Special thanks to Kevin Shaw, and especially Carl Taylor for providing a tape of this panel)

(Editor's Note: We weren't able to bring you a new interview with Stan this issue as we'd hoped, so we're presenting this panel, which was held shortly after the announcement that Jack was returning to Marvel in 1975.)

Unused Kirby art for MarvelMania International.

STAN LEE: Thank you, culture lovers. *(laughter)* I hate to listen to speeches; that's one of the reasons I hate to *make* speeches. I don't want to make this any more unbearable for you than it has to be. I'm equally inept at any kind of speaking; it doesn't matter what I talk about, I do it badly, so I might as well talk about what you'd like to hear. Does anybody just want to shout out something they'd like to hear about, so at least I'll know I'm saying something that at least *somebody* wants to hear?

AUDIENCE: What about the Silver Surfer?
AUDIENCE: How did you get started?
STAN: All right, let's do it that way. How did I get started, and then we'll *segue* into the Silver Surfer. *(laughter)* When I was a kid, many decades ago... just to show you how things never work out, I wanted to be an actor. They had something called the WPA Federal Theater; it was part of Franklin Roosevelt's NRA New Deal. It was to keep guys off the streets from stealing hubcaps and so forth, and they set up little theatrical groups. I joined one; Orson Welles was also a part of this thing, and many other big names. The only thing is, the other guys stayed with it, but I had to make a living and it didn't pay too well, so I got a lot of very, very exotic jobs in writing, because I was always pretty facile at it.

I got one job writing obituaries for a news service; obituaries of famous people who are still alive. When a celebrity dies, an hour later there's a special issue of a paper, and his whole life story is in the paper, and you've probably wondered, "How did they ever write this so fast?" Well, that thing's been on file for years. Guys like me have been writing them. I kept the job for a few months, and I quit because it gets very depressing writing about living people in the past tense. *(laughter)* I gave that up, then got another very glamorous job writing publicity for a cancer hospital. *(laughter)* I gave that up after a few months.

Then I heard there was a job open at Marvel Comics, which was then called Timely Comics, for a reason that nobody's figured out. Jack Kirby and Joe Simon were practically the whole staff, and they... I better watch what I say, 'cause I never know; Jack may be here. I'm not noted for always telling the truth, but at least people don't usually catch me at it. But Jack may remember this, so I'll be careful. *(laughter)* Anyway, he and Joe were virtually the whole staff. Jack sat at a table behind a big cigar, and he was drawing. Joe stood up behind another big cigar, and he would ask Jack, "Are you comfortable? Do you want some more ink? Is your brush okay? Is the pencil all right?" And then Joe would go out and yell at me for awhile, and that was the way we spent our days. I was a gofer; I'd go for the coffee, for the broom, for Jack's cigars. They also let me write some copy. Little by little, when they found out I could spell, and I knew which end a sentence to put a period at, they started exploiting me, *(laughter)* just the way I've done with Marv Wolfman and everybody else over the years. *(laughter)*

After awhile, Joe and Jack, for reasons that history will one day record, left Timely Comics. The publisher, a stalwart named Martin Goodman who owned the company and all that his eye beheld — namely me at the moment *(laughter)* — looked around at his vast empire. He saw this one skinny kid with a broom in one hand, and a typewriter in the other, and he said, "Hey, where's the rest of my staff?" And I said, "I'm it." At that time I was about 16½, and he said, "Somebody's got to edit these books. Stan, can you hold down the job until I get somebody else?" I think I was offered a half-dollar more a week, and to me that was like gold — it still is — and I said, "I'll take it." So he went off into the outside world to seek another editor, and I was now Stan Lee, Boy Editor *Pro Tem*. It's lasted ever since then.

I'm going to tell you a story there's really no reason to tell, except I've got to kill a few minutes here somehow. Years ago, I was doing some work for a film, and a guy from the *Hollywood Reporter*, which is a motion picture trade magazine, came to hear me. Now if you think I'm dull standing up here, you should've heard this guy! He's doing an interview that's going to be published in the *Hollywood Reporter*, and these are the questions he's asking me: "How do you spell you name? When were you born? Where do you live?" and other stimulating facts like that to intrigue and entrance the reading public. I said, "I've got to jazz this up somehow." So he asked, "Where did you get your start?" So I told him this fascinating and enthralling story about Martin Goodman, and Joe and Jack Kirby, and me being the only one there. And I saw him writing half asleep, and I wanted to jazz up the story a little bit, so I said, "About thirty years ago, I was told the job was temporary. He never told me it was permanent, so as far as I know, Martin's still out there looking for another editor." Ha-ha. *(laughter)* So the guy wrote it down. *(laughter)* This'll teach you never to try to liven up an interview when some dullhead is writing it. This is the way it came out in the *Hollywood Reporter*: "Stan Lee lives in New York City and is the editor of Marvel Comics. He's been there for 30 years, and presently his publisher is looking for a new editor." *(laughter)* So that taught me, "Stan, a comic you'll never be."

There was another deep, meaningful question hurled at me; in quivering tones, I heard someone say, "What about the Silver Surfer?" I would like to answer in kind: What *about* the Silver Surfer? *(laughter)* Actually, the Silver Surfer is one of my really true great loves, next to being up here talking to you. *(laughter)* I did not really create the Silver Surfer. Those of you who are historians or archivists, take note. Jack and I were doing the *Fantastic Four*, and we came up with this plot; something to do with Galactus and our usual crazy stuff. I was telling Jack, he wasn't listening, and I wasn't paying attention to what I was saying. He went off and drew something. The way we worked, for those of you who don't know, is not the way they work at other companies, where the writer writes a script, and it's given to an artist, and the artist draws it, and that's the end of it. With us, it's a *marriage* of talents. *(laughter)* The artist and the writer will discuss the plot together, then the artist goes off to his little nook where he works, and he — without benefit of script! — only with this vague, ridiculous plot that he's discussed, goes and draws the whole story all by himself.

In the early days, I was writing scripts for virtually all the books, and it was very hard to keep all the artists busy; poor little frail me, doing story after story. So I'd be writing a story for Kirby, and Steve Ditko would walk in and say, "Hey, I need some work now." And I'd say, "I can't give it to you now, Steve, I'm finishing Kirby's." But we couldn't afford to keep Steve waiting, because time is money, so I'd have to say, "Look, Steve, I can't write a script for you now, but here's the plot we'll use for the next *Spider-Man*. Go home and draw anything you want, as long it's something like this, and I'll put the copy in later." So I was able to finish Jack's story. Steve in the meantime was drawing another story. Then Don Heck would come over and say, "Hey Stan, I need something to do." I'd say, "Well, I can't write it for you Don, but here's the plot for *Iron Man*, you go and draw it, and I'll put in the copy later." That way I could keep five, six, ten artists busy; they were drawing, and as they'd bring in the strip, I'd put in the copy. Okay, it started out as a lazy man's device — or maybe a guy who just didn't have enough time — but we realized this was absolutely the best way to do a comic. Because any artist who really belongs in this field — and of course our artists do — is a storyteller himself. He tells stories with pictures; he has imagination, he knows continuity, he knows how a story should be told. So if he just knows what the general plot is, the idea is: Let him go home, let him draw the things that he thinks are the most interesting. Don't have the writer say, "Panel one will be a long shot of Spider-Man walking down the street." The artist may see it differently; maybe he feels it should be a shot of Spider-Man swinging on his web, or climbing upside-down on the ceiling or something.

So following the basic plot, the artist draws it. Then, when the writer has to put in the copy, just imagine how much easier it is to look at a drawing and suit the dialogue perfectly to the expression of the character's face — to what the drawing represents — than to try and write perfect dialogue when you're looking at a blank sheet of paper, trying to imagine what the drawing will be like. So it worked out as the fastest way to work. It also gives us the best results. And you're all sitting there thinking, "What does this have to do with the Silver Surfer?" *(laughter)*

Here's what it has to do. Jack and I had discussed a story dealing with Galactus. All I remember is we were saying, "We've already had Doctor Doom, we've already had Sandman, and all these powerful villains. What can we do to top what we've done? The only thing to do is get a villain who's practically a god... who doesn't want to *conquer* the earth; a villain who destroys whole planets!" Well, that sounded good.

Unused page from either Fantastic Four *#17 or #23, based on the mention of "Dr. Doom's robot" on the page. It's inked by George "Bell" Roussos, and if it's from #17, this was probably his try-out for the inking chores.*

It was easy for me to say it; now it was up to Jack to go home and draw it. *(laughter)* I don't remember; Jack may have come up with the name Galactus, or I might've. I probably wanted to call him Irving. *(laughter)* The thing came back, and lo and behold, Jack had Galactus, and I loved it. Well, I love everything Jack does. I'd look at these drawings and I couldn't wait to start writing the copy. All of a sudden, as I'm looking through the drawings, I see this nut on a surfboard flying in the air. *(laughter)* And I thought, "Jack, this time you've gone too far." *(laughter)* And under his cigar, Jack said, "No, no, Stan. I figure anybody like Galactus, who's that big and powerful and travels through space, needs a herald." That was about as logical as anything else we've ever done, *(laughter)* so I figured the Silver Surfer will be the herald. But now comes the part that makes Marvel Marvel! We didn't make him a herald who said, "Hey, there's a nice place. I think I'll sit down there and have a smoke." *(laughter)* We made him a herald who said, "This planet is a virtual paradise. Why don't men realize the glories that they have all about them? Why do they wage war when they should make love?" and other typical Stan Lee profound sentiments. *(laughter)* Somehow this naked, nutty character... I didn't even realize he was naked until the third issue, y'know? *(laughter)* Who pays attention? He was naked in a very unique way, which we'll get into later when we have our adult session. *(laughter)* Anyway, I figured if we could get away with this, we could get away with anything.

Well, the readers loved the Silver Surfer, they loved Galactus, they loved everything. After awhile... my memory is bad, and Marv can probably tell you later on if you stay after class. I don't know how it happened, but Jack was doing his *Fantastic Fours* and his *Thors* and this and that. And we were getting mail: "Why don't you give the Silver Surfer his own book, his own movie, his own world, his own everything?" *(laughter)* John Buscema had joined us prior to that, and we were looking for a new script for him, and we decided to do a whole book just of the Silver Surfer.

Here's what happened: The older readers loved the *Silver Surfer.* He became a cult figure. Every time I'd lecture at colleges, one of the first questions was, "What about the Silver Surfer?" But the younger kids, the very young ones... we still need a lot of young kids to buy our books, because we have to sell 72 million a year, and there aren't enough intelligent older readers to keep us going. *(laughter)* So I'm dependent on the intelligent younger readers. We lost a few sales. It didn't sell as well as our other books. We got more fan mail on the *Silver Surfer* than on virtually any book we had. It was mostly from older readers. So I had a conference with my then-publisher who said, "Y'know, we ought to downgrade the stories a little. Let's make them a little more simple. Stop using thirty-syllable words, Stan. Let's make the stuff simpler, and get more action and fighting and stuff, and then it'll sell better."

For once in my life, I was ethical and true to my convictions, and I said, "Aahh, to hell with it. I don't want to change the Silver Surfer; he's too pure and beautiful. Let's wait until we've upgraded the tastes of the whole human race, and then we'll bring him back again."

(laughter, applause) Thank you, ye of great faith. *(laughter)* I think you'll admit we've been making great progress, as evidenced by this overflow crowd. Pretty soon, we'll probably bring the Surfer back. I don't have the time to write it, and I'm too rotten a person... I'd just as soon nobody else do it, because it'll probably become a big hit, and I don't want anybody else to become more famous than I am. *(laughter)* I was talking to Jack about it. Maybe we'll do a big super-special one-shot issue; maybe a 200-page Silver Surfer story. We'll sell it for five bucks, and print it in hardcover, and exploit the hell out of the public like we always do. *(laughter, applause)* You know, the usual: Silver Surfer t-shirts, Silver Surfer toothbrushes. *(laughter)* We'll probably take a year or two to do it. Jack'll do ten pages an hour as he usually does, and I'll probably write ten pages a week. Sooner or later, we'll get it finished.

Actually, I have a terrible problem. I don't know what I am. Sometimes when strangers say to me, "What do you do?", my first

Pencils from Machine Man *#6, page 3.*

impulse is to say, "I'm a writer," or "I'm an editor." Now I've got to say, "I'm a publisher," but I'm not really anything, because publishers are guys who just handle the business end of a business. I don't really just handle the business end. The company that owns us has 50 million businessmen who check numbers and charts and graphs, and do all of that. I'm not an editor anymore, because I'm lucky enough to have Marv, and Archie Goodwin doing the black-&-whites and so forth. So I'm not the editor, I don't do any more comic book writing, so I'm not really sure what it is I do. I know I go to the office every day, and I'm busy as hell.

AUDIENCE: Barry Smith!
STAN: What's the question: *Is* there a Barry Smith? *(laughter)* Oh, where is he? I had seen him in New York at the Marvel Convention in April. Barry is a funny guy. *(laughter)* He's a great talent as we all know. But he seems to want to be — and I'm not putting him down for it, he's got every right to — an entrepreneur. He doesn't just want to write and draw comic strips. He wants to own his own business. So he'd like to publish his own things, be they posters or books or underground papers. Every time I see him, I give him the same line I gave Kirby all the time: "Hey, when are you coming back to Marvel, where you belong?" *(laughter)* And with Kirby, who's impressionable, it worked! *(laughter, applause)* I will admit I'm pretty good at it, and Barry got all misty-eyed, but he persevered. I hope someday he comes back to us, because let's face it: Marvel is like the Mecca of the comic book world; sooner or later, though they may stray, we'll always get them back. *(laughter)*

AUDIENCE: Kirby!
STAN: Kirby? I just spent a half hour talking about Kirby! *(laughter)* There's nothing anybody can say about Kirby that the lyricists haven't lyricked about, and the sonnetists haven't written sonnets about. *(laughter)* We need a whole separate lecture about Kirby, but I don't have the heart to inflict that on you right now.

AUDIENCE: What about your second *Origins of Marvel Comics* book?
STAN: I thought you'd never ask. *(laughter)* As you know, *Origins Of Marvel Comics* has advanced the cause of literature to a great degree. *(laughter)* Actually, there's over 100,000 in print now; I think they've sold three. *(laughter)* In its own way, it's a quiet best-seller; it's becoming a cult book. Just to prove that even big companies can make mistakes, Simon & Schuster said, "Hey, Stan, how about writing a sequel?" And just to prove that money will accomplish anything, I said, "Sure." *(laughter) Son of Origins* will be coming your way in October of this year, and I expect all of you, to whom I have poured out my innermost longings and secrets, to support this book, because we did it. Next year, there will be another book about the Marvel villains; it might be called *Brother-In-Law of Marvel Comics*. *(laughter)* We'll go right down the line with the whole family. But it seems we've really started something, because the book is a great seller.

AUDIENCE: What about Spider-Man and Superman?
STAN: I have an agent, a very great young man, who sold the book *All The President's Men*. He made so much money, he got hysterical and said he'd represent me too. *(laughter)* He came to me one day, and said, "I was out on the coast last week, and a little kid walked up to me and said 'How come Spider-Man and Superman aren't in a movie together? Boy, I'd like to see that.' " So I said, "Look dumbhead, they're not in a movie together because Spider-Man is owned by Marvel, Superman is owned by National, and you can't do things like that." But my agent, David Oaks, is the type of guy who would've discovered gravity. He said, "Why *can't* you do it? What if you agreed to it, and Superman agreed to it?" *(laughter)* The idea, I must admit, was a little bit of a grabber, so I said, "All right David, I agree." So he went to talk to the powers that be at Superman; I will not mention their names, because why should I plug the competition? *(laughter)* They were very interested in doing this movie too, but unfortunately they were already doing a *Superman* movie, and legally they weren't authorized to do another one, and the deal fell through. But David Oaks, my agent said, "If you can't do a movie, what about doing a comic book?" I said it's all right with me, so he went over to National, and Carmine Infantino, who was in one of his rare good moods I guess, *(laughter)* said it sounds okay to him. Before you knew it, we had signed a contract to do a book called *Superman vs. Spider-Man*. Now here's the problem: There is no way that Marvel Comics is going to let the title of this book be *Superman vs. Spider-Man*. *(laughter, applause)* Instead of being smart enough to know that the mere mention of the name Superman with Spider-Man will do them a world of good, they too feel they don't want it to say *Spider-Man vs. Superman*.

Bumper stickers sold through the Mighty Marvel Marching Society.

So, you've heard about the legend where King Solomon said, "Cut the baby in two"? I came up with what was probably my most Solomonish decision of all time. I said, "Let there be two covers." And there shall be two covers. One cover on half of the books will say *Spider-Man vs. Superman*. The other cover on the other half will say *Superman vs. Spider-Man*. *(laughter, applause)* Now, Carmine Infantino, the estimable and noteworthy publisher of Superman, not to be outdone, then said, "Maybe on one we can draw Spider-Man looking like he's winning, and on the other draw Superman looking as if he's winning." I think this is going to be a very interesting situation, but in my own greedy way, I realized we've even accomplished something else. I know we're going to sell twice as many books. Why, you ask? Can you imagine any collector not wanting both editions? *(laughter)* I think we ought to do two covers on every book! *(laughter)*

AUDIENCE: Neal Adams!
STAN: Is he here? No? Neal Adams is a strange person. *(laughter)* I've been told he has a modicum of talent, *(laughter)* a certain amount of charisma, and can draw a pretty good story. All right, let's face it, he's one of the best artists in the business. But Neal Adams — who I'd like to call my discovery, except if I tell the truth, I can't *(laughter)* — has a funny code. He doesn't believe in giving his loyalties to any one company. He feels something like Neal Adams should be shared by all; *(laughter)* he's too great a commodity to keep. Well, he was always a tough guy to give a steady feature to. Another thing about him, he's terrible with deadlines. I guess it's because he works so hard and puts so much into the books. But our books have to go out at a regular frequency, or else readers commit suicide. Can you imagine, on the 14th of the month, you're waiting for a new issue of *Iron Man* or *Howard the Duck, (applause)* and the book doesn't arrive? Can you imagine: Husbands don't talk to their wives, children don't go to school, people don't eat? *(laughter)* We can't do this to the human race. Not Marvel! *(laughter)* So it was always difficult to give Neal Adams a steady book to do; he couldn't make our deadlines. At the moment, if you ask what he's doing, as far as I know it's an occasional thing for *National Lampoon,* where they can do it seven months in advance, and a lot of advertising work. And as many stories or covers as we can get him to do, which aren't too many.

The name Stan didn't want to divulge was The Eternals; *shown here are pencils from #4, page 17.*

To anticipate your next question, generally the same answer goes for Jim Steranko, who I wish was working for us on a full-time basis. Jim is a combination of Barry Smith and Neal Adams. Jim was not the greatest with deadlines when he worked for us, and he too has entrepreneurial tastes and ambitions, and more power to him. He's one of the most talented, nicest guys I know. And maybe some day, just for sentiment, he'll want to do another strip with us. I hope he does.

AUDIENCE: How many books will Jack Kirby draw?
STAN: He's doing *Captain America* on a monthly basis. *(applause)* Considering the guy created Captain America, it's the least we could do. *(laughter)* He's doing *A Space Odyssey*, which I think he's just finished. He may do a sequel to *A Space Odyssey*. He's doing a new "gods" thing. You know the *New Gods* he did for National? That was only a prelude. *(applause)* That was just to give you sample of the way his mind works. Now he's getting down to the serious business of explaining what the world is, and why and where it's going. If you keep your eyes peeled, you'll soon be seeing a series called... should I say it? There might be a guy from National here. Very seriously, it's very possible somebody might come out with the title ahead of us, and I don't want to ever go through life suspecting that one of you wonderful people will have divulged the secret. *(laughter)* Believe me, you'll know it when you see it.

Now, let me close by saying that if you've enjoyed this half as much as I did, you had a really good time. So I want to compliment you on your choice of speakers. *(laughter)* Excelsior; thank you all very much. *(applause)*★

Roy Thomas Interview

Interviewed by Jim Amash

(Roy Thomas was born November 22, 1940. His involvement at the beginning of 1960s comics fandom led to his eventual employment as Stan Lee's assistant editor at Marvel Comics in 1965, and a lengthy career as one of comics' most prolific writers. This interview was conducted by phone in September 1997.)

THE JACK KIRBY COLLECTOR: When were you first aware of Jack's work?
ROY THOMAS: It must've been fairly early after the war, when Joe and Jack started up again in 1946 or '47. I recognized the names "Simon & Kirby" along with Joe Kubert's name as artists; I recognized both their styles, although Jack was imitated by more artists. And who knew what was Simon and what was Kirby, or still does exactly? I felt their stories were better written than most, and they certainly had their own unique style.

TJKC: Did you read their romance comics in the late 1940s?
ROY: I'm sure I saw the artwork and recognized the style, but I wouldn't necessarily have picked those up, just like I didn't generally pick up Joe Kubert's war comics, although he is my favorite artist in many ways.

A mid-'70s fan drawing.

TJKC: When did you get into fandom?
ROY: Comics fandom only really got started in early 1961, with Jerry Bails starting *Alter-Ego* and Don and Maggie Thompson starting *Comic Art* at almost exactly the same time. It began to get going in late 1960 when Jerry and I got in contact, even though the real impetus was him, not me. I was like Robin to his Batman, Tonto to his Lone Ranger. *(laughter)*

TJKC: Did being involved in fandom lead to meeting people like Kirby?
ROY: No, not really. I did exchange letters with a few people here and there, including Julie Schwartz, Gardner Fox, and Otto Binder, whom I call the three patron saints of *Alter Ego.* I was only helping Jerry by writing articles, so I wasn't doing a lot of corresponding with other professionals. The first pro I ever met — in the Spring of 1965 — was Wendell Crowley, who had been the editor of all the Captain Marvel comics. He'd gone into the family lumber business after Fawcett folded its comics line. He came through St. Louis and called me up, because we'd exchanged one or two letters. I skipped school, *(laughter)* and we split a pizza that day. He told me I was an old man, getting into the business at age 24, *(laughter)* compared to him and all the people that started in the forties. I guess at 24, maybe I was. I'd already had four years of another adult career.

TJKC: You were a teacher, right?
ROY: Yes, which I think is kinda good. I think too many people nowadays wander into comics as writers and artists, and they have no idea what the rest of the world is like, and I had a little of that anyway.

I remember my only contact with Stan Lee in those days was a letter I wrote him; I'd missed an issue of *Spider-Man* (#4 or #5), and mentioned that I was going to hunt it down, and he kindly sent me a copy and a little note. It was the only contact we ever had up until I went to work for him. He was aware of who I was and what *Alter Ego* was, but he wasn't the same kind of correspondent as Julie and Gardner. They'd write occasionally, and that was all I'd expect; I understood they were busy with other concerns.

TJKC: Stan was busy being an editor, too.
ROY: Yeah, editor and writer; he was working pretty hard. That's one reason I didn't ask him for a job. Who'd have thought he needed any help? He looked like he was happy doing everything himself.

TJKC: How'd you finally get that job with Stan, and meet Jack?
ROY: I only worked for DC for a couple of weeks in 1965, and I jumped ship to Marvel when Stan offered me a job, because I was unhappy working for Mort Weisinger. Of course, people didn't come into the office that much, and at Marvel, much less than DC. Marvel didn't have much in the way of offices; just three or four little rooms. Stan's office was as big as everything else put together, and Sol Brodsky, Flo Steinberg, and Marie Severin were crowded into two other little rooms. There was somebody else who was working on commercial comics, who was sort of half a comics person. Steve Skeates had been working there a week or two before I came in, and was soon gone. That was really about it. There were not many people working there, so people just brought in their work. Ditko and Stan weren't speaking by that point. So Ditko would come in, deliver his stuff to Sol, Sol would take it in to Stan; it was a very weird, strained atmosphere. Jack and Stan were still getting along pretty well. They'd go out to lunch together occasionally when Jack would come in. I was introduced to him, but I don't remember "the day I met Kirby." But I was well aware of his importance, and from the first issue of *Fantastic Four* I was aware that he had been half of the Simon & Kirby team, even though the original credit in *FF* #1 was only for "J. Kirby," and Stan Lee had his whole name credited. Jack's name got abbreviated for some reason.

TJKC: We see a lot of that. We saw a lot of "S. Ditko" too. *(laughter)*
ROY: Some people said Stan did it because his name was so short, and he didn't want anybody's name to be longer than his, *(laughter)* but I don't think so. I don't know how it happened; it wasn't happening when I came there.

There were only a couple of Kirby-related incidents I really remember about that first year or two. One of them was a lunch, and I don't think Stan was there. I may have had lunch once or twice with Stan and Jack and a couple of people, but never with Jack by himself. I remember this one lunch with Jack, and probably Sol Brodsky and John Romita and Frank Giacoia; five or six of us. This was one of the relatively few times Jack had lunch with us, as opposed to Stan. The only thing I remember from that lunch, besides nice anecdotes and being with an entertaining guy, was somebody asking, "What's going to be the next big thing in comics?" Super-heroes had been going for years; what's next? Jack said, "I don't know any more than anybody else, but the one thing I can tell you is, it's not gonna be me, and it's not gonna be Stan Lee. It's gonna be two guys in a garage somewhere, coming up with something, just like Siegel and Shuster did." I think of that from time to time, when I see something like *Teenage Mutant Ninja Turtles* come out. There's a certain amount of truth to that, that these things come out of nowhere. And it's as likely to be done by an unknown as it is by an established professional.

The other incident I remember was one of the seminal problems that I know Stan has always felt led to — not exactly a final break between Jack and Stan, but heaping more coals on the fire of animosity that Jack felt, I think more than Stan, probably because Stan's position was more secure. Jack was the key artist. No one was going to replace him, but on the other hand he had no real secure situation like Stan. There was a big article in the *New York Herald-Tribune,* where some reporter came in and interviewed Stan and Jack. For some reason, I was called in to be a witness or whatever, because I certainly took no part in it. We're talking within six months or a year of when I started there. Stan is always "on," and he's promoting Stan, but he's also promoting Jack. I saw that, y'know? And Jack would jump in with his own pronouncements, and Stan strides around, and Jack just kind of sits there, but he was eloquent enough in his own way. And the reporter is more interested in Stan, but at the same time is talking to Jack. And then the article came out, which of course Stan didn't have any prior approval of. The article is somehow very unfavorable toward Jack. It talks about him sitting there in a Robert Hall suit, and Stan saying something, and Jack falling off his chair in glee. It sort of put down Jack in a way that made Stan very embarrassed, and Jack very upset. Stan always had the feeling that Jack felt Stan had somehow maneuvered that. And other than Stan being Stan, and Jack being Jack, and this reporter having his own agenda, I just didn't see any of that. There was no jockeying between Stan and Jack as to who was the top person, but of course Stan was the editor, and he's the person who was doing the writing, and he's a little more eloquent in speaking, maybe, than Jack was. But it was just one of those unfortunate situations that I think really did heap a lot of coals on the fire, and Stan always considered it an important turning point in his relationship with Jack. But there's no way to prove that or straighten it out. How do you say, "I didn't do it. I wasn't responsible for what this reporter wrote."?

Within a few years, Jack had moved out to California, as one of the first comics people to do that. His status was such that he could afford to do that, and Marvel would keep working with him, even if Stan was probably reluctant to see him leave, for the lack of personal contact. Once Jack moved out to L.A., I didn't have much more contact with him. I do have this weird memory that I'm sure about, though it's a bit vague. It was after Jack moved out to L.A. At some stage, Stan called me into his office, and told me Jack had some new characters he wanted to do, some new concepts and ideas. And Stan was very happy wanting to keep Jack on *Thor* and *Fantastic Four.* I've always had the feeling that it may have been Jack thinking of offering Marvel things like the *New Gods.*

It was not that much longer after that that he quit. I know Stan was very upset, and a little depressed when he called me and Sol into the office to tell us Kirby had just called to quit. When he quit, he was already working for DC. He had already set up everything else before he even told Stan he was thinking of quitting. I think this is because Jack bottled it all in, so when he quit, he had to do it as a clean, total break, with no niceties. You can see where almost anybody would be upset in that kind of circumstance.

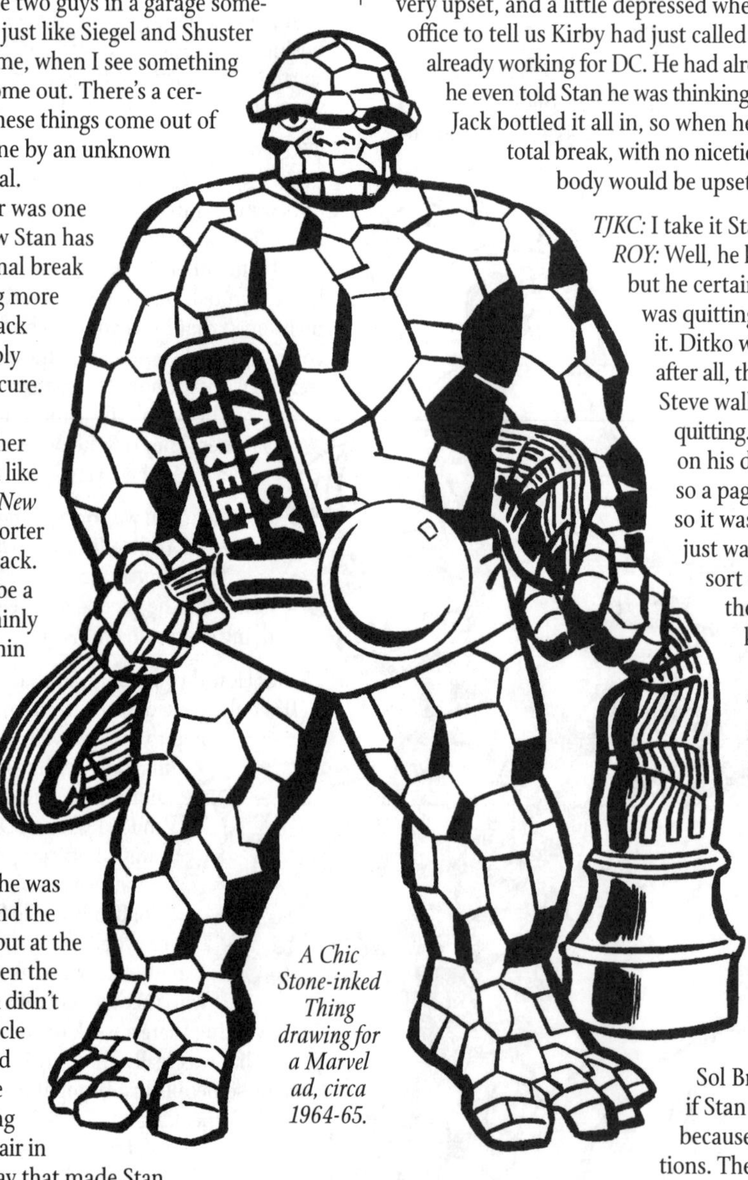

TJKC: I take it Stan didn't see it coming.
ROY: Well, he knew there were some difficulties, but he certainly didn't see it coming that Jack was quitting, or I never got any indication of it. Ditko wasn't a great surprise, because after all, they weren't speaking, and one day Steve walked in and just told Sol he was quitting. Sol was sitting there with a memo on his desk to give Steve a raise of $5 or so a page, or whatever they could afford, so it wasn't a matter of the money. He just wanted to quit. But with Jack, he sort of bottled it up, and Stan knew there were problems, but he didn't know how deep they ran.

Some of the problems were about what should be done, or shouldn't be done, which is a matter of opinion. Some people are so rabidly pro-Jack that anything Stan does is automatically seen as being the work of the devil. *(laughter)* Stan is being castigated for every time he asked Jack for a correction, like it's automatically wrong. And it isn't. Stan was the editor; he was responsible for quality control. Production manager Sol Brodsky would get very frustrated if Stan wanted Jack to do a correction, because Jack just wasn't good at corrections. The thing about Jack is, he had seen the thing already in his mind before he drew it. To him, drawing was almost like photographing the strange, realistic world that he saw inside, which was his genius, his talent. For somebody to tell him, "Can you change this facial expression?" or do a different arm or something; it's like telling Jack to forge a photograph, almost. It just wasn't the way he saw it. That's why John Romita and other people would be asked to do faces on Jack's art.

I know I was happy when Jack finally did one *Conan* cover for a

YANCY STREET

A Chic Stone-inked Thing drawing for a Marvel ad, circa 1964-65.

reprint that had Conan and Elric on it. Stan had John Romita do the face over, so it still wasn't quite a Kirby drawing. It's annoying; as much as I love Romita, I wanted to have a Kirby face on that cover. I know it wasn't me who had it changed. It was usually either Stan who had a drawing changed, or Romita might change it on his own, knowing that Stan would want him to change it. John was very good at anticipating Stan, and sometimes when people thought Romita was changing it on his own authority, he was doing it, yes. But he was very good at anticipating what Stan wanted him to do, which is why he stayed art director until the time he retired.

Aesthetically it's impossible to say "Stan was right" or "Jack was right." Maybe sometimes it wasn't handled as tactfully as it could have been. Mostly, Stan would just have people do it. If Jack had been there, they might have talked. But because Jack was off in California, I think these things festered more than they needed to, because they never got together to talk it over. The distance didn't help that situation.

TJKC: Especially on *Thor,* a lot of 1960s covers Jack did were rejected.
ROY: Stan didn't talk to us when he had a cover done over. Stan had his own ideas of the covers, and he was ultimately responsible for them. So it was his right, and maybe if Jack had been there they could have talked it over, but increasingly, as Jack was out of the area, they couldn't even do that.

TJKC: So you think the distance led to the deterioration of the relationship?
ROY: I think it did, although the fact remains it could've gone to pieces anyway. After all, Jack went to work for another company and was equally distant from them. Within a couple of years, *that* relationship floundered as well. Despite Funky Flashman, Houseroy, and the whole thing in-between, when I was out there in the summer of 1974 for the San Diego convention, several people — Jack and their son Neal and probably Roz and maybe someone else — got together with me to my surprise to talk about the possibility of Jack coming back to Marvel then, about a year before he actually did. It didn't quite come to anything just yet, but it was obvious that within that three or four years, the bloom was definitely off the rose at DC, too, and Carmine was now the enemy, as he was to many other people. Again, I'm not saying whether Jack was right or wrong; at some stage, when Jack got tired of trying to talk to people, or he didn't feel he could, he'd just move on to something else. And all I could say to Jack was, "The only thing between you really is that Stan was a little hurt about the way you left, but that's not a big deal. And the Funky Flashman stuff bothered him a little bit, because it seemed, to Stan at least, somewhat mean-spirited." I said to Jack, "I don't take the Houseroy stuff that personally, because you don't know me. My relationship to Stan was somewhat like what you said, and partly it's just a caricature because I was there. And the name 'Houseroy' is clever as hell, and I kinda like it." I'm even a sympathetic character because I got tossed to the wolves. *(laughter)* But I said, "We can get past that. Stan would love to have you back; he never wanted you to leave." The only thing is, a month or two later I left myself, and it took several more months, and I was gone by the time Jack actually came back.

TJKC: There was a mention in *Rocket's Blast ComiCollector* that Jack was thinking about coming back as early as 1972, and would take over *X-Men.*

Pencils from Thor *#147, page 4.*

MOMENTS LATER, THE PRISONER FINDS HIMSELF AIRBORNE. THE VILLAGE BELOW HIM HAS COME TO LIFE. A VARIETY OF PEOPLE WALK THE STREETS, INTENT ON DESTINATIONS OBSCURE TO HIS CURIOUS EYE...
THE VILLAGE SEEMS BUSTLING WITH ACTIVITY.
YES, IT'S THE PEAK OF THE DAY.
FURTHER FLIGHT REVEALS WHAT "NUMBER SIX" HAS FEARED: THE VILLAGE IS LOCATED ON SOME UNIDENTIFIED ISLAND. IT IS THE KIND OF PLACE WHICH WILL NOT BE EASY TO LEAVE...
THIS WORLD BE AN IDEAL TIME TO MAKE AN ESCAPE ATTEMPT--I COULD TAKE OVER THIS HELICOPTER AND--
HAHAHAH--THAT'S INCREDIBLY NAIVE!! I'D NEVER HAVE INVITED YOU IF THAT WAS POSSIBLE--
OUR WEAPONS ARE CONCEALED--NOT MISSING--

NO DOUBT--OLD CHAP--YOU WILL FORGIVE MY FANTASIZING!!
OF COURSE--OLD CHAP! I SUGGEST THAT YOU CONCENTRATE ON THE VIRTUES OF THIS THIS PLACE--
IT'S REALLY LIKE A VACATION SPOT... WE CERTAINLY DON'T FROWN ON WATER SKIING--

WE HAVE THE CAFE AND OUR GENERAL STORE--WE ALSO PUBLISH OUR OWN LITTLE NEWSPAPER... THE FELLOW WHO RUNS IT WAS QUITE A BRILLIANT JOURNALIST--!
YOU MUST SEND ME A COPY..
THE HELICOPTER TRIP IS SHORT BUT QUITE THOROUGH. THE PRISONER HAS ALSO BEEN SHOWN A GRAVEYARD, A SWIMMING POOL AND A FEW ATTRACTIVE GIRLS DISPORTING THEMSELVES IN THE SUN...

Page 16 of the unpublished Prisoner *adaptation Jack did for Marvel. See* TJKC *#11 for details on this story.*

ROY: Well, it could be. I was at two early '70s conventions in San Diego, one in 1972. The Summer of 1972 was just about the time I became editor-in-chief, so it could've been '72 instead of '74. I won't swear to it. Whatever it was, it didn't come to anything for awhile, and I'm not certain which of the two years it was.

By 1975, when Stan would talk about him coming back, one or two of the editorial people there weren't sure it was a good idea. I was delighted; I thought it was a great thing to have happen.

TJKC: Did that come about through Jack having contact with Stan himself, or was that through an intermediary?
ROY: I'm not quite sure how it happened. By that time I was a writer/editor, and I only came in two or three days a week. Stan called me in and told me, and I didn't hear any details. I don't know if Jack contacted Stan directly or if he went through Len Wein or Marv Wolfman. I can't imagine that he did, but he may have had an intermediary do it. It had been set up, because of course I had reported my conversation to Stan, and there may have been others. The pump was primed, which is probably partly why Stan told me when it actually happened, because he knew I had been wanting to bring it about myself.

TJKC: Do you have any idea what triggered the Funky Flashman thing?
ROY: No. I knew nothing about it until it came out. I think it was just the resentment Jack had built up, some of it based on the differences between his personality and Stan's. Each of them would find the other to be an alien being in some way; they were so different, y'know? This is true with many partners, and Stan and Jack were such different people; they had such different lifestyles, such different outlooks on things. Of course, Stan had a higher position, so Jack would see him as not only being a partner, but his superior, and he didn't like that. He remembered Stan as some kid who, when he was eighteen years old, inherited the editor's job because Simon & Kirby left Timely. I think there was some resentment coming out, and I think it was an unfortunate thing that didn't need to happen; it might have been better left undone. As much as I admire Jack, even I was a little bothered the first time I saw the Houseroy thing, because it's a reading of me that's only partly true; sure, I was Stan's right-hand man, a flunky. Maybe he would've tossed me out the window to save himself. *(laughter)* But Jack was such a gentleman, such a nice person, and I hated to see what a lot of us felt — not everybody, some people thought it was greatly justified and clever as hell — what I felt was a cheap shot at Stan, and I would've felt that whether Houseroy existed or not; because I felt the Funky Flashman stuff was just so obvious. If it'd been a little more disguised, you might've put it down to something else. Jack of course said, "Well, y'know, I was just making stories" when I talked to him that time, but we all knew it was a little more than that. But we all do things like that; sometimes we regret them later, sometimes we don't. I have no idea how Jack came to feel about it later. Stan said he never let it bother him, but the relationship was never quite the same. Stan, as much as he admired Jack's talent, would never again think of him as the automatic number one guy artistically, because by that time John Romita was working there, John Buscema was popular. Jack would come in and be respected and be admired and be liked, but it wasn't going to be the same as it had been up to 1970.

TJKC: Were there efforts to get Jack more into the company in the late

1960s — more than just as a freelance artist?
ROY: I don't think so. I don't know if Jack ever asked. The one thing Jack wanted was the idea of saying "By Stan Lee & Jack Kirby" instead of differentiating them as writer and artist, because Jack felt he contributed more. That was his idea, but I don't think Stan resisted it, because he knew Jack contributed more. None of them was getting paid so well for what they did; even Stan wasn't getting any super-high page rate. Stan's better pay came as being editor, which was his job alone. None of us really thought that much in those days about who's writing and who's drawing. After all, I'm not the artist, but I'm telling people what to draw, so I doing some of their thinking for them. If they feed me back an individual line in the margins that might be good, or an extra idea that's good, well, okay. I take credit for some of that, but on the other hand I take the blame for some things that maybe they drew that I wouldn't have wanted them to draw. It's only later — and this happens a lot with artists — suddenly 20 years later they start deciding they were the only person that was important in the team. This happened with Stan, this happened with me, and it's happened with several other writers who suddenly had artists who felt the writers were holding them back. And generally that's bull.

TJKC: Ditko demanded credit as plotter and got it. Do you think if Jack had insisted on something like that, he would have gotten it?
ROY: I don't know. He might have. The closest thing to anything like that happened around 1976. I came up with this deal where I was going to write *Fantastic Four,* and I wanted to get Jack back as artist. I called Jack up and we talked for awhile. I was editor, but I said if Stan and the other people would OK it, I was willing to have Jack get plotting credit even if I came up with the original idea, because he would do more plotting, and I had plenty of other work to do. He wasn't going to get paid a lot extra for it, but he'd have the freedom. He'd get the credit for the plot, he'd have his name first. But he wasn't too interested, so I had to settle for the one thing I could get him to do, which was his last Fantastic Four comic story, the *What If?* issue — "What If The Fantastic Four Were The Original Marvel Bullpen?". I was going to write it myself, and then decided to get Jack to do everything. The only changes we made in it were that Stan didn't like how Jack would refer to him as "Stanley." I don't think Jack meant anything by it, but every place that he was called Stanley in Jack's script, I had to change it to Stan. *(laughter)* But other than that, it was fine; an offbeat kind of story, but I just wanted to see what Jack would do with it, and get him to draw the Fantastic Four again. I was real happy that I did, even if it didn't lead anywhere.

TJKC: Were you around when Stan and Jack were plotting together?
ROY: I remember times where they'd talk briefly, but I wasn't around for much of that. I remember Stan talking about how he and Jack had been in a car stuck in traffic and had plotted an issue that I think became the first Diablo story, one of the ones he most hated. I was called in more for him and John Romita, to take notes. Remember, since Jack was doing a lot of the plotting, there wasn't any reason for me to take notes, because Stan would talk to Jack, and Jack would go off and draw and plot. Before I even moved to New York, I saw the plot from *Fantastic Four* #7. That was a two-page plot that Stan wrote, and everything was kinda there, but there was a lot of room for expansion by Jack. But still, the story is initially Stan's. Later I saw Stan's plot for *Fantastic Four* #1, but even Stan would never claim for sure that he and Jack hadn't talked the idea over before he wrote this. They may or may not have; he just didn't recall because he didn't think it was important at the time. At the very least, Jack took that plot and added these initial events at the beginning, where the Torch is working on a car and burns it up, and Sue's trying on clothes and disappears, and the Thing goes rampaging through the city. Stan started it more directly with the origin itself. Again, was it an idea Stan had verbally, or was it totally Jack's idea of doing it? I don't think anybody knows anymore. I wouldn't trust either Stan's memory or Jack's memory totally in these

Jack did this Silver Surfer drawing in the early 1980s at the San Diego Con.

cases, because people tend to remember things differently after years. All partners do at least 90% of the work; we know that. *(laughter)*

TJKC: We've all seen interviews where Stan and Jack maybe both claimed more of the credit than they deserved.
ROY: I think once Jack left, there was a natural tendency to mentally downgrade his contributions, just from a practical viewpoint. Otherwise, you're giving a competitor credit. I won't say how much of that was conscious and how much was unconscious, but it's a natural tendency. At that stage, you're doing it for hype, for publicity purposes, and to do that, you don't necessarily play up the guy who's quit and gone to the competition.

TJKC: A lot of people were really upset about *Origins of Marvel Comics,* because it seemed like Stan had really downplayed Jack's contributions a lot there.
ROY: The problem there may also have been the legalities. Back in the 1960s, both Joe Simon and Carl Burgos initiated lawsuits, about Captain America and the Human Torch. They never came to very much, and Jack of course made some depositions on behalf of Marvel about Cap at that time when he was still there. It led to Bill Everett, who had created the third big 1940s character — Sub-Mariner — being given a loan by Martin Goodman that wasn't going to have to be paid back, so he wouldn't sue, which he never intended to do, anyway. I don't know how the Burgos thing was settled, but it was probably settled reasonably amicably. But once these things happen, you don't necessarily want to play up the other person. Stan would always talk about Jack as being this great artist, but he didn't always play up Jack's other contributions. Yet from the very beginning, he's always been clear about the fact that Jack invented the Silver Surfer, and just tossed him into a story where Stan had not suggested any character like that. I know for a fact, having seen the pages in pencil when they came in, that the character was just called "The Surfer" in the border notes, not "The Silver Surfer." The name "Silver Surfer" at the very least was Stan's, and the speech patterns.

Jack wrote all these border notes, and they were great. They told the story, and would've made a nice comic book sometime. But Stan didn't tend to use much of the dialogue from those notes, because he had his own style. I think he sometimes deliberately veered away from Jack's notes; not out of resentment or disrespect for Jack, but because he had his own way of doing things, and he was the writer. Sometimes he was changing the emphasis of the story; even without changing the pictures, he would change the emphasis and some of the motivations from what Jack had. And Jack would resent that, and I can understand it. Sometimes I wonder if Jack read the stories carefully enough to notice Stan had written totally new dialogue and changed the motivation. Jack may have thought Stan just took his notes and turned them into dialogue, which was almost never the case.

TJKC: In that period when Marvel introduced the Inhumans, Galactus, and the Black Panther, would you say those were all co-creations, or did Jack come in like he did with the Silver Surfer and say, "Stan, I have these characters"?
ROY: From what little I heard from talking to Stan and Sol Brodsky, the Silver Surfer was kind of an exception, although there may have been a few villains that were created by Jack. I think Stan had an initial idea for quite a few of them, but I wouldn't say that there couldn't be some individual characters that Jack didn't come up with the idea for. When two people are kicking ideas around, later on, who can remember who came up with this or that? Unless you remember that *you* did it. *(laughter)* It's like all the mish-mash about Spider-Man, where everybody from Joe Simon to C.C. Beck seems to have created him, because they all created something on the road to Spider-Man. I saw Spider Spry in the *Fly* comic years ago, and then you see this other stuff by Beck. As I once said, "Everyone who didn't create Bugs Bunny

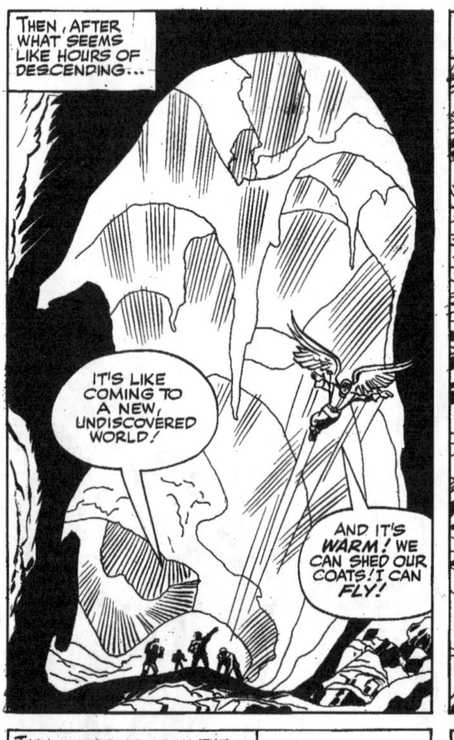

Original art to X-Men *#10, page 6; some of Jack's margin notes were trimmed off, but we typeset what was left of them, so you could compare them to Stan's finished dialogue.*

Page 17 of The Prisoner; *Stan supposedly scrapped the book because there wasn't enough action in it.*

created Spider-Man." *(laughter)* I wouldn't say that Jack didn't have the initial ideas in some cases, but the point is, they should all be considered co-creations.

I remember Stan and I got into a good-natured argument about it ten years ago in L.A. I wasn't even working for Marvel at the time, and we had lunch. He talked about people like Stephen J. Cannell and television, saying if Cannell comes up with a general idea, and wants a few people running around doing this and that, and calls them the A-Team, he's created that. It says "Created by Stephen Cannell." And I said yes, but that's a function of *power,* not of creativity. It means Stephen Cannell has the power to say he created that thing alone, and other people buy into that by agreeing to sell their work for work-for-hire, or for other financial deals. But it doesn't mean he *really* created the whole thing just because it says so on paper. That's a legal thing. It's caused by his power; you either play by his rules or you don't play. It doesn't mean he really created the A-Team all by himself.

TJKC: How did Stan react to your point?
ROY: I think we agreed to disagree in a friendly way. He knew I always felt he got a raw deal from the more Kirby-oriented part of the press. I sometimes felt they just didn't want to listen to his side of it. He didn't like to be vocal about it, because he felt no one could win that kind of argument. Not that Jack was a small man, but it's the old thing about "never fight anyone smaller than you, because if you win you're a bully, and if you lose you're a bum." Here, fighting Jack was fighting the guy who left Marvel Comics and did not own a piece of these characters. To the extent that Stan ever said anything, he looks like he's trying to bully Jack, or take advantage of his position; and if Jack got the better of him, then he *really* looks bad. *(laughter)* I think he really just preferred to keep out of it, but I know he was hurt by the situation sometimes because of his admiration for Jack. I'm sure that sometimes he was resentful, too. Neither Stan nor Jack were perfect human beings. Neither were any more godlike than the currently-deified Princess Di.

TJKC: Do you think the problems between Stan and Jack were strictly business, or personal?
ROY: It was mainly business. Nobody was trying to take any more advantage of Jack than of other people. In fact, if anything, because of his talent Jack got special treatment, but maybe it wasn't as special as he might've deserved in the long run. If Jack hadn't left Marvel, I think he would've eventually gotten a real good deal out of them when they got bought out by conglomerates. But once he left, suddenly he wasn't so essential anymore. You don't come back in the same way you left, unless you'd done something between that's so great, they can't ignore you. And the fact remains that Jack's stuff at DC, however inventive and creative it was, had not been such a huge success that Marvel needed to accommodate him. They were glad to have him back, but there wasn't any objective reason to make him suddenly a part of the company any more than any other artist/writer. There was probably still a little feeling of, "Hey, you shouldn't have left in the first place." Of course, Jack had a perfect right to leave.

TJKC: Was Jack under any sort of contract at Marvel in the 1960s?
ROY: I don't know what his relationship was, but I think probably he wasn't, because they didn't really have contracts much in those days. They had sort of an informal arrangement; he may have even gotten paid by the week, but it's one of these things that could be cancelled at a moment's notice. There wasn't anything in writing that they had to give him notice. He would've eventually gotten things like that, but unfortunately he left and went to DC instead.

TJKC: It's pretty common knowledge that when Jack returned to Marvel in the mid-'70s, he felt a lot of people were out to get him, and there seemed to be a lot of changes made to Jack's work.
ROY: I can't understand that. He was welcomed home, though there was a little guardedness because he had left. So he didn't come in with a position of real power, but after all, they gave him *Captain America,* which was a major book. I remember being the one who suggested

that he be given *Black Panther,* which maybe didn't work out well in certain aspects, but it seemed to make a lot of sense. He had co-created Black Panther; his Coal Tiger character was the basis for it originally. I went out of my way to get him to do all the *Invaders* covers I could, *3-D Man, What If?,* or anything I could get him to do. Stan didn't work with him that much, but he wanted him to do important books — *Captain America* being one of them. It just seemed as if the combination of Jack's writing and drawing together didn't grab the Marvel readers as much as the combination of Stan and Jack had before. Times had changed, and Jack had been in the field a long time, and maybe was slowly winding down, even though certainly the work looked great. I loved the concept of the *Eternals.* In some ways I liked it better than *New Gods.*

TJKC: What stories did you work with Jack on?
ROY: Only two. In the early days before he had left, it was an Iron Man/ Sub-Mariner fight (*Tales To Astonish* #82). Stan and Jack had plotted it, and I think that's when Stan took one of his rare vacations on a train to Florida, probably typing the whole way. I was asked to do the dialogue for it. Now of course, my name comes first, because at that time we didn't talk about plot. Otherwise it would've said "Plot and Art by Jack Kirby."

The other one was right before he left. Jack did a couple of those Ka-Zar lead-ins in *Astonishing Tales.* Again, I dialogued one of those. I'm listed as writer, but it was really his plot, just like the couple of *Dr. Strange*s I did with Ditko. They're really Ditko's plots, not mine; it's just the way we did it, and we didn't question it at the time. Neither did Jack or Ditko. We weren't worried about the credits, because there wasn't any money involved. It's only later you begin to say, "Hey, why didn't I take credit for this or that? Why didn't I put my name down as plotter?" Whenever *Tomb of Dracula* #1 is reprinted, Gerry Conway gets all the royalties, and I did the whole plot! *(laughter)* But I didn't put my name on it. I plotted one or two *Spider-Man*s with Gil Kane for Stan to dialogue, but I didn't put my name on them. But then, Gerry and others anonymously plotted a few stories for *me,* too!

TJKC: Right before Jack left Marvel in 1970, he finally got writing credit on the Inhumans (*Amazing Adventures* #1-4) and a couple of mystery stories (*Chamber of Darkness* #4-5). How did that come about?
ROY: I think he probably wanted to write these stories, and Stan was trying to keep him happy, even though he wasn't as enamored of Jack's writing as of his art. But he thought, "We've got other people writing, let's see what Jack can do." Jack had certainly written a lot of great stories in his day; there was no doubt about Jack's talent as a creator. He'd written stuff that back in the '40s and '50s was well above the level for the field. It didn't seem to traffic quite as well in the '60s. Certain aspects of it did. There's a certain poetry about Jack, in concepts and phrasing. Other things could be a little bit clumsy, but you just take them all together, and they make a very interesting read, especially his Fourth World stuff at DC. I'd look at it, and I'd see these words in quotation marks, and weird things that bothered me, but at the same time there's this kind of poetic feeling. He wasn't the only person who'd go to the *Bible* and other places for inspiration. Stan did, I did, we all went to the classics for inspiration. But Jack was certainly one person who did that. He was a sensitive guy, a poetic guy, an intelligent guy; and that was bound to be reflected in the work.

His work wasn't tremendously successful sales-wise his second go-round at Marvel, but that doesn't necessarily mean it wasn't good. A lot of things that were very good failed at various times: *Conan* almost, the early *Silver Surfer*s, Neal Adams' and my *X-Men,* and Steranko's *SHIELD* didn't do that well.

TJKC: How did Jack's involvement on the 1970s *Fantastic Four* cartoon come about?
ROY: Stan was in that arrangement with Depatie-Freleng. Jack did these storyboards from a general plotline, so it was like working Marvel-style in animation. I was real happy with the cartoons that were turned out. Despite Herbie the Robot, they came out more or less like I wrote them. My working relationship with Jack wasn't direct at all. They gave me the stuff; I never talked to him about it at all. I'd turn in my plot, he turned in his drawings, and I wrote the script based on his drawings. They probably didn't make the best storyboards for animation, because Jack wasn't trained in that way, and was thinking differently,

Jack's cover pencils to Avengers *#156.*

but for a writer they worked out just fine, and I thought the shows turned out pretty well.

TJKC: When Jack did covers for you in the 1970s, did you have direct contact with him?
ROY: Yes, I did. I'd come up with a general idea, and usually we'd send him some art, so he'd know what the costumes looked like. Even the one I own the original art for, with Union Jack; in that case, I designed Union Jack. I drew a picture of the guy in the Union Jack costume and gave it to Frank Robbins, and probably to Jack, too. We'd just give him the general idea, and Jack would do a slam-bang cover. He sometimes did submit a cover rough, but they were almost always accepted right away. Sometimes there wasn't time to do a cover rough.

TJKC: Should the Marvel characters be equally considered co-creations of Stan and Jack?
ROY: It's hard to divide things and say "equal." Sometimes it's 50/50, sometimes it's not, but they are co-creators of almost everything they did together. Sometimes if there had to be only one creator listed, it would have to be Stan, because he probably came up with the idea of the Fantastic Four and the characters. If you had to say there was one creator of the Silver Surfer, it was definitely Jack. But look at the Human Torch; was that created by Jack Kirby? Stan Lee? In many ways it's just a revamp of the Carl Burgos character. In collaborative mediums, the credit that says "Created by..." is usually some sort of legal lie. *(laughter)* But if you had to choose one creator, quite often Stan would have to be that person, simply because he got there first, and said, "Let's do a character called Thor," if that's what happened. It wouldn't make any difference if Jack had once done a character named Thor at DC. But that doesn't mean Jack shouldn't be credited with co-creating the character. It's very rare that things are nice and neat and simple. I think what happens is, the people that like Marvel or Stan will say Stan was the main creator, and the people that buy into Jack's particular situation will say it's all Jack. The truth is not always, but usually, in-between.

These guys were so talented and so valuable to the company; it's really a shame some of these things had to happen. They were both indispensable. I don't think Stan would've created Marvel Comics — and certainly it would not have been created in the same way or taken off the way it did — without Jack being there to realize these early stories; Ditko too, but especially Jack. On the other hand, there's no evidence Jack would've done this by himself either. It was a collaboration. Stan was maybe the man on the spot, and the guy who guided it, but... is it the jockey or the horse that wins the race? *(laughter)* What you really want is for the jockey and the horse to become a centaur, but the centaur is a very unstable life form, *(laughter)* who'll slip back into being a jockey and a horse.

Cover pencils to Avengers *#158.*

TJKC: What kind of influence did Stan and Jack's plotting have on you when you started taking over books like *Avengers* and *Thor*?
ROY: Powerful. I was influenced by Stan's writing even more, but with Jack it was the excitement Stan wanted. Not to imitate Jack, but it was that type of excitement he wanted, and he used Jack as the template for years to come. "Do it like Kirby would do it!" he would say. If we could all do that, we'd be in great shape. *(laughter)*

TJKC: Was Stan actually saying to the artist, "Draw like Kirby?"
ROY: No, he wanted them to *think* like Kirby, and do that kind of excitement. He didn't want Gene Colan to imitate Kirby. Once in a while it'd come off close to that, and he'd influence Buscema and people to get a little closer to Jack's style. But it wasn't so much the drawing as it was certain ways of telling the story, and thinking, to get the excitement in. I think sometimes it went too far. Like with Buscema; it brought out his Kirby aspect, but it stifled his illustrative aspects. I think the changing point for Buscema was *Silver Surfer* #4, with Thor. Afterwards, he started drawing more like Kirby, because that seemed to be what Stan wanted. I think his better work artistically was before that. On the other hand, he probably became a more commercial artist after that. *(laughter)*

TJKC: How would you describe the legacy Jack leaves behind?
ROY: Jack was one of the giants of the field, and he continues to cast a long shadow. I don't think you have to worship him in a way that says he was always right, and Stan or whoever was always wrong, in order to do him justice and give him proper respect. If there are a handful of people in the comics business in the last half-century who deserve the title of genius, Jack would definitely be in that very small grouping. How much more can you expect from anybody?★

Super-Heroes With Super Problems

by Nat Freedland

Originally published in the New York Herald Tribune *Sunday Magazine Section on January 9, 1966*

(Editor's Note: This is the article that, as mentioned in this issue's Roy Thomas interview, was a turning point in the relationship between Jack Kirby and Stan Lee. The interview for this article probably took place in November or December 1965, due to Stan's comments about Federico Fellini returning "in January." The art that accompanied the article was from the cover of Fantastic Four *#49, and the page mentioned in the first paragraph is from* Fantastic Four *#50, cover-dated May 1966, which would have been on newsstands about the time this article appeared. The plotting conference at the end of this article was for* FF *#55, an issue just after the most prolific period of new character creation on the series. Steve Ditko also quit Marvel Comics around the time this article saw print.)*

On the drawing board is a big oaktag sheet recording the Fantastic Four's last-ditch struggle to save Earth from being "drained of all basic elements" by the godlike villain Galactus. One picture shows cosmic force rays bombarding Manhattan. Stan Lee, chief writer-editor of Marvel Comics, tells production man Sol Brodsky, "It's not clear that the rays are hitting now." He thinks for a few seconds and then pencils in "ZIK, ZIK, ZIK" at the points of impact. No other comic book writer would have wasted that few seconds to think what cosmic force rays sound like. They would have just written "Pow" or "Zap" or something equally conventional.

Stan Lee, 43, is a native New Yorker, an ultra-Madison Avenue, rangy lookalike of Rex Harrison. He's got that horsy jaw and humorous eyes, thinning but tasteful gray hair, the brightest-colored Ivy League wardrobe in captivity and a deep suntan that comes from working every Tuesday, Thursday, Saturday and Sunday on his suburban terrace, cranking out three complete Marvel mags weekly.

He is also a good mimic and does a fine reproduction of that rolling, Continental voice we were hearing on the class TV interviews back in October. That voice got on the phone to Marvel Comics at 625 Madison Avenue and said, "Hello, this is Federico Fellini. I like very much your comics. In one hour I come see you, yes?"

No, it wasn't a put-on. Somebody had shown Fellini a couple of Lee's Marvel masterpieces while the great Italian film director was racked out with a virus at the Hotel Pierre. Fellini turned up at Stan Lee's office with a medium-sized entourage his first day out of sickbed. "He's my buddy now," says Lee. "He invited me to come to see him at his villa any time I'm in Rome. I'm supposed to take him to the cartoonists' convention when he's back here for the *Sweet Charity* opening in January."

1978 Hulk fan drawing.

Stan Lee drew a bigger audience than President Eisenhower when he spoke last year at Bard, one of the hippest schools on the Eastern Seaboard. Co-ed dormitories! From the Ivy League to the Pacific Coast Conference, 125 campuses have their own chapter of the "Merry Marvel Marching Society." The M.M.M.S. is at Oxford and Cambridge, too.

Pre-college Marvel fans at times have taken to assembling on the corner of Madison and 58th Street, waving wildly with homemade signs whenever anybody appears at the second-floor windows of Marvel's three workrooms. "Like we were the Beatles or something," Lee muses.

In terms of the real world, all this adulation means that Marvel circulation has tripled in three and a half years. With an annual circulation of 35 million, Marvel (which puts out 17 super-type comic books) is now a comfortable number two in the comics industry, gradually edging up on the long-established Superman DC line. No other comic book publisher can show anything like Marvel's phenomenal sales growth in the Sixties. A secondary harvest of promotion tie-ins is starting to bloom, too. Forty thousand Marvelites have come up with a dollar for their Merry Marvel Marching Society kits. In the works are plastic models, games, a Spider-Man jazz record, and a television cartoon series.

"We really never expected all of this, you know," Lee admits. "I mean it started out as a gag, mostly. I just thought maybe it would be worth trying to upgrade the magazines a little bit. Audiences everywhere are getting hipper these days. Why not the comic book audience, too? And then all of a sudden we were getting 500 letters a day about what great satire these stories were, and how significant. We used to get about one letter a year... before."

Before Stan Lee dreamed up the "Marvel Age of Comics" in 1961. When Lee went to work for the comic book division at Martin Goodman's publishing outfit he was 17 years old. By 1961 he had been manufacturing comic strips at the same stand for 20 years. It was getting to be tiresome.

Nostalgia about old comic books is a large item now, what with Pop art and Camp riding high, but fond remembrance of childhood joys is one thing, and actually reading that stuff is something quite different. It's no accident most adults outgrew the comics of their day at puberty. The carefully selected samples in Jules Feiffer's *Great Comic Book Heroes* anthology give pleasure because they are perfect examples of their form. But as the same old tired stories and stiff drawings were trotted out year after year, they couldn't keep up the pace. "Have some punch," Batman would quip as he decked a bad guy; idiot puns were the height of old comic book humor. "What th'?" and "Huh" were as expressive as Captain Marvel ever got. Superboy, on returning from a recent adventure in the ancient past, said, "Bye now, Hercules and Samson." This is hardly an example of super-conversation, points out John Butterworth, Class of '64, in his Colgate Maroon study: "Spider-Man strives for status in Competitive Comic Book World of Insincere Super-Heroes."

Comic book super-beings had mighty powers but no personality — not until Stan Lee tried out the Fantastic Four in October, 1961.

The whole new tone of Lee's vision to bring human reality into comic books was set in an early FF appearance. (All Marvel characters quickly pick up affectionate nicknames.) This super crime-fighting team was evicted from their Manhattan skyscraper HQ because they couldn't get up the rent. The stock market investments that paid their laboratory bills had temporarily failed.

The Fantastic Four, who appear in their own comic book and guest star in other Marvel publications, are beset as much by interpersonal conflicts as by super villains. Invisible Girl, Sue Storm Richards, is always bugging hubby Reed Richards, Mr. Fantastic, to leave off with the world-shaking inventions already and take her out to a discotheque. One sometimes wonders how much the phallic implication of Mr. Fantastic's body-stretching power has to do with holding this stormy couple together. Sue's kid brother, Johnny, is the Human Torch. He flames, flies, and swings off-duty in a Corvette Stingray. The grumpiest, most complex, most ambivalent and most popular member of the Fantastic Four is the Thing. "Bashful, blue-eyed Benjamin J. Grimm" as the Thing likes to refer to himself in more lyrical moments — usually just before issuing his clarion cry, "It's Clobberin' Time" — has actually deserted to the side of the villains on occasion.

Lee calls Ben Grimm "a tragic" monster who cheers himself up by acting the clown... "a good man with a bitter heart." The Thing talks like Jimmy Durante and has good reason to be bitter. A moon rocket mishap with cosmic rays gave the rest of the FF super-powers that can be turned on and off at will. But it left him looking like a human-shaped rock formation "covered with broken pieces of orange-colored flowerpots," an apt description from Jennifer Stone's Hunter College Meridian analysis, "Hark, the Hulk Hurtles into Your Heart."

The Fantastic Four rapidly became one of the hottest things in comic books and Lee followed up with the most off-beat character he could think of — his masterpiece Spider-Man.

Spider-Man is the Raskolnikov of the funnies, a worthy rival to Bellow's Herzog for the Neurotic Hipster Championship of our time. "If Charlie Brown wore a skintight costume and fought crime, he would be Spider-Man," concludes John Butterworth in the Colgate Maroon. According to Sally Kempton in the *Village Voice,* "Spider-Man has a terrible identity problem, a marked inferiority complex, and a fear of women. He is anti-social, castration-ridden, wracked with Oedipal guilt, and accident-prone." In short, "...the super-anti-hero of our time."

The saga of "your friendly neighborhood Spider-Man" began

Sorry, we have no idea who or what Cap is referring to in this drawing.

when orphan Peter Parker, a brilliant but friendless high schooler from Forest Hills, Queens, got accidentally bitten by a radioactive spider at a science fair. This made him the equal of a gigantic spider in: Speed, Agility, Climbing Prowess, Strength to Body-Mass Ratio, and Sixth Sense. He also invented a web-shooting wrist apparatus as an extra aid.

Peter immediately sewed himself a disguise costume, so as to avoid shocking kindly old Uncle Ben and Aunt May, and then he went into show biz. His super acrobatics got him instant television stardom. But this triumph, like most of Spider-Man's brief tastes of victory, soon turned to ashes.

To keep his secret identity a secret, he had to accept a paycheck made out to Spider-Man... The TV producer insisted he couldn't give out cash because of the tax records. So Spider-Man went to a bank and...

Bank Clerk: I'll have to see some identification!
Spider-Man: What about my COSTUME?
Bank Clerk: Don't be silly! ANYONE can wear a costume! Do you

have a social security card or a driver's license in the name of Spider-Man?

Wandering off in a blue funk, Spider-Man just shrugged unconcernedly as a burglar ran by. When he got back home to (a regrettably unauthentic rural-looking) Forest Hills, of course it turned out that the burglar had just murdered Uncle Ben.

Spider-Man duly vowed to be more public-spirited in the future. But now, he really had money problems. Aunt May would not hear of his quitting school. But how could he support the household with a part-time job and still find time to catch crooks? He tried to solve everything by going on salary with the Fantastic Four. (All Lee's characters are located around New York and tend to run into each other on the job.) But the FF wanted to keep their nonprofit foundation status and turned him down. "You came to the wrong place, pal" said the Thing unsympathetically. "This ain't General Motors."

A rare Kirby Daredevil sketch; this was done for a Marvel t-shirt.

At the moment, Peter Parker has a science scholarship to State College and supplements it by freelancing news photos. His specialty is delayed-action pix of his spider self in combat. It's not much money — Peter Parker is a lousy businessman — but at least it picks up the tab for Aunt May's many hospitalizations.

The Hulk is the most unstable character in the history of comic books. At first, scientist Bruce Banner and the jolly green monster had a gamma-ray induced Jekyll-Hyde co-tenancy. But now the Hulk is in permanent possession, having absorbed some of Banner's I.Q. but none of his peaceable ways. Hulky will bash anything that gets in his way — including Marvel's other super-heroes and the US or Soviet Armed Forces.

Thor, the Norse thundergod, recently had to take an elevator to the top of a midtown skyscraper before he could fly off to Asia to stop a rampaging super witch-doctor — because a cop wouldn't let Thor whirl his magic hammer on a crowded street. A woman in the elevator looked up at Thor's shoulder-length blond curls and mused, "That REMINDS me — I'm due for a PERMANENT at noon."

Practically every costumed hero in Lee's new Marvel Comics mythology displaces enough symbolic weight to become grist for an English Lit. Ph.D. thesis.

The unremittingly tragic Iron Man usually has to schlep home his transistor-powered armor for recharging after a fight. Since his heart (chewed up by Viet Cong bullets) is also transistorized, this tends to become a tricky business. Daredevil, revival of a famous comic book name, is now the world's only blind masked hero. He struggles through with his indomitable will and "radar senses" acquired by getting run over with a truckful of uranium. Equally indomitable is the unshaven, cigar-chomping Nick Fury, who functions simultaneously in *Sgt. Fury and his Howling Commandos* and *Nick Fury, Agent of SHIELD.* A black eye-patch distinguishes the post-war Fury from his military self.

However, Captain America, that fighting hero of World War II, comes on more like Captain Anomie these days. Returning to action in 1963, after 18 years of suspended animation in an iceberg, he does more brooding over his destiny than any Captain since Ahab. "The TIME I live in belongs to others... The only thing that's rightfully mine is my PAST. Can I ever forget BUCKY, the teenager who was like a brother to me? What has become of Sgt. Duffy?"

Lee always provides full backstage credits for these epics:

Bombastically Written by... Stan Lee
Brilliantly Drawn by... Jack Kirby
Beautifully Inked by... Vince Colletta
Bashfully Lettered by... Artie Simek

He has to. No detail of the month's output is too minor for Marvelites to single out for praise in the letters pages...

"The art was great, especially page 5, panel 3, which was a perfect rendition of the beam's effect. "

No error is too minor for complaint...

"...and Cap had an 'A' where his star should have been on his chest."

Young dreams of romance appear often in these pages...

"Please don't make Sub-Mariner lose his dignity. He reminds me of 'The Sheik.' ... If Sue and the Scarlet Witch don't want him, I do."

Contemporary problems may also break in...

"Could you maybe publish a letter to parents or something? I'm tired of getting static from my mother about how ridiculous it looks for a Rice U. sophomore to stand in front of a drugstore haggling with an eight-year-old kid over the last copy of *FF* or *Avengers.* (I got them, but it cost me 30 cents and I had to let him read them first!)"

"It's ruining my eyes," says Lee about the avalanche of mail. "I never wore glasses before this thing started." He tries to read as many of the letters as possible. "That's the kids telling us what they want." His private life has also been somewhat curtailed by the demands of success. "I take my wife out to dinner with friends three or four times a week. That keeps her reasonably happy, even though I'm working every day and haven't been able to take a vacation in three years." The chic blonde Mrs. Lee is a former British model. Daughter Joanie, 15, is a talented artist, but not particularly excited about comic books.

Princeton University's Merry Marvel Marching Society sent up a delegation to meet the master the other day. Fabulous Flo Steinberg, the secretarial star of Marvel Bullpen Bulletin gossip notes, ushered the group into the Presence. "Here I am fellows," said Lee. "I guess it's a pretty big disappointment, huh?"

They assured him it wasn't.

"Don't tell me what you like about the books," Lee requested. "It's more help if you tell me what you don't like."

"There's a schism in the cult over Spidey's personal life," said one. "Factions are forming about all the play Peter Parker's adjustment problems are getting lately."

Lee hastened to explain. "I don't plot *Spider-Man* any more. Steve Ditko, the artist, has been doing the stories. I guess I'll leave him alone until sales start to slip. Since Spidey got so popular, Ditko thinks he's the genius of the world. We were arguing so much over plot lines, I told him to start making up his own stories. He won't let anybody else ink his drawings either. He just drops off the finished pages with notes at the margins and I fill in the dialogue. I never know what he'll come up with next, but it's interesting to work that way."

A 1980s commissioned drawing.

Actually, Lee hardly ever writes out a standard picture-by-picture script any more. (He recently hired three assistant writers, after 200 applicants flunked a sample *Fantastic Four* assignment. But he doesn't think the boys are ready yet for anything more demanding than *Millie the Model* and *Kid Colt*.)

Lee arrives at his plots in sort of ESP sessions with the artists. He inserts the dialogue after the picture layout comes in. Here he is in action at his weekly Friday morning summit meeting with Jack "King" Kirby, a veteran comic book artist, a man who created many of the visions of your childhood and mine: The King is a middle-aged man with baggy eyes and a baggy Robert Hall-ish suit. He is sucking a huge green cigar and if you stood next to him on the subway you would peg him for the assistant foreman in a girdle factory.

"The Silver Surfer has been somewhere out in space since he helped the FF stop Galactus from destroying Earth," begins Lee. "Why don't we bring him back?"

"Ummh," says Kirby.

"Suppose Alicia, the Thing's blind girlfriend, is in some kind of trouble. And the Silver Surfer comes to help her." Lee starts pacing and gesturing as he gets warmed up.

"I see," says Kirby. He has kind of a high-pitched voice.

"But the Thing sees them together and he misunderstands. So he starts a big fight with the Silver Surfer. And meanwhile, the Fantastic Four is in lots of trouble. Doctor Doom has caught them again and they need the Thing's help." Lee is lurching around and throwing punches now.

"Right," says Kirby.

"The Thing finally beats the Silver Surfer. But then Alicia makes him realize he's made a terrible mistake. This is what the Thing has always feared more than anything else, that he would lose control and really clobber somebody."

Kirby nods.

"The Thing is brokenhearted. He wanders off by himself. He's too ashamed to face Alicia or go back home to the Fantastic Four. He doesn't realize how he's failing for the second time... How much the FF needs him." Lee sags back on his desk, limp and spent.

Kirby has leaped out of the chair he was crumpled in. "Great, great." The cigar is out of his mouth and his baggy eyes are aglow. His high voice is young with enthusiasm.

Here's the esprit that makes this the Marvel Age of Comics. You can bet Stan Lee hasn't lost the touch that won him three first prizes in the Herald Tribune's "Biggest News of the Week" teen contest back at old DeWitt Clinton H.S.★

The Never-Ending Question: Lee or Kirby?

by R.C. Harvey

Much as I admire Earl Wells' attempt in *The Comics Journal* #181 to solve the question of authorship of the Marvel Universe by using the analytical methods of literary criticism, I think his deployment of those methods is based upon an erroneous premise and therefore leads him astray. Wells examines Jack Kirby's work on the *New Gods* series at DC in the early 1970s and compares it to the work he did while at Marvel in the 1960s. So far, Wells is on solid ground. Then he loses his footing; noting that the spirit of the *New Gods* books is antithetical to the spirit that animates the Marvel books of the previous decade, he concludes that the same man could not have written both — ergo, the true author of the Marvel books was Stan Lee, not Kirby.

While it is true that the whole body of work produced by any creator such as Kirby should be taken into account when examining any aspect of that work, the examination must also recognize that the creator may change his mind or attitude over the period of time that his work is produced. Wells, I think, overlooks this possibility entirely; and there is ample evidence to support the notion that Kirby viewed heroism differently at different times in his career. In the common parlance of literary criticism, this sort of change is called "growth." In short, Kirby grew as an artist and as a storyteller; and as he grew in technical proficiency, he also grew philosophically, and that growth, in turn, is reflected in the themes of his work.

Wells writes that "it is difficult for me to believe that the same man, an adult professional with years of experience, over the course of only five or so years *(the span between, say, the birth of the Marvel Universe and the genesis of the New Gods),* could have written with such deep feeling about two such widely divergent themes — on the one hand, that great power requires responsibility, sacrifice, and suffering, and on the other, that great power is so dangerous that even a philosophy of responsibility, suffering, and sacrifice can be twisted into an obsession with death and *(be)* made to serve anti-life."

But if we assume that a creative artist grows and matures during his career, we can find in Kirby's growth the explanation for the difference between the New Gods and the Marvel heroes.

Wells says "Kirby was writing about war" in the *New Gods.* I agree. And Kirby had written about war before — in the early 1940s, when, with Europe plunged into the Nazi maw, he and Joe Simon created Captain America. The character personified patriotism, pure and simple. And that's what patriotism was during the years of that war — pure and simple. It was uncomplicated, uncompromised, unequivocal devotion to the principles for which the nation said it stood; and Captain America was not a complicated personality. He embodied those high-sounding principles.

Kirby was scarcely alone in embracing these ideas at that time. Indeed, most Americans embraced a kindred idealism—and they did so unquestioningly. So did Kirby. For Kirby, the struggle was between Good and Evil, and the heroes of his fictions were the Good Guys.

Kirby continued to subscribe to this idealism through the war and into the post-war era. But by the time he reached *Boys' Ranch* in 1950, his understanding of the nature of Good and Evil had achieved a more nuanced balance than before. If we consider only the "Mother Delilah" story in #3, we find a seriously flawed hero (the long-haired kid Angel) and a villainess (Delilah) not altogether bad. I examined this story in great detail in a book of mine called *The Art of the Comic Book* (published in January 1996), so I won't go into it here. Suffice it to say that the tales in *Boys' Ranch* are markedly different from the patriotic epics of World War II.

But then, none of us were as simple-minded about our country or about good and evil in the 1950s as we'd been in the 1940s. Working with his long-time partner Joe Simon, Kirby nonetheless tried to revive the clarity of war-time patriotism with another super-powered patriot,

Jack's margin notes from Avengers *#16 show he had major input on the story. We've relettered the top set of margin notes only for easier reading.*

1975 drawing of Odin.

hearing a story-development session from the back seat of a car, John Romita reports: "Stan would plot the *Fantastic Four* with Jack, and they would both come in with their ideas, and they would both ignore each other. Each one would have their own ideas, and I could see that the other guy was countering with another idea... So when Jack got the story in, sometimes Stan would say, 'Gee, Jack forgot what we talked about.' And I'm sure Jack thought the same thing, that Stan forgot what they talked about."

The pages of art that Kirby turned in transformed Lee's story ideas into dramatic action; and Lee embellished the action with his verbiage, writing captions and speech balloons that gave the stories a self-deprecating patina. Kirby could not have injected any such mocking tone into the tales; but Lee's contribution was as lyricist, refining the creative output of his collaborator. This is no small achievement. But the creative workhorse here was — in my view — Kirby, not Lee.

Despite the mockery, the stories were still celebrations of the heroic, as Wells maintains. So how did Kirby get from the Marvel ambiance to the *New Gods* ambiance? The latter shows that Kirby, once a believer in the redemptive and triumphant power of heroism, had lost his faith — or, rather, had tempered it with an almost cynical realism. He did what all of us did as we progressed from World War II through the Korean War to Vietnam.

Kirby was as fond of his audience as he was of drawing and storytelling. Any comic book reader who spent any time with him can testify to that. And Marvel's success with the college crowd (slightly older readers than he'd been working for prior to that time) doubtless made Kirby more aware of the blighting impact of Vietnam on American youth than he had been before during either of the other conflicts he'd witnessed. His readers were being marched off to a war they despised for reasons that seemed wholly irrelevant. Kirby could scarcely have ignored what was going on around him — and around his readers.

This was another war. But by now, we had all learned something about how war works in a purely political context, a war fought not to win but to make a political statement; an endless war. But this time — in sharp contrast to the World War of the 1940s — many Americans viewed war as futile and, ultimately, meaningless. Kirby, I believe, came to share that view, and he incorporated his attitude into the *New Gods* books; and heroism in that context was certainly less heroic.

That's the route I think Kirby's thinking took — and that's why the *New Gods* books, although produced by the same creative personality as the Marvel Universe, seem so anti-thetical. The *New Gods* books represent just another step in the philosophical and psychological evolution of Kirby's thinking about life and heroism. *The New Gods,* as Wells says, were not 1960s Marvel heroes. They were, rather, 1970s Kirby heroes.

That Kirby attempted such a mature and nuanced treatment of heroism was due, probably, to his understanding that comic books could be made for older, more mature readers than before. His experience with the Marvel books had shown him that. With the *New Gods* books, then, he simply took the next step. Kirby's entire career can be seen as a progression. I've indicated some of that progression here; in my book, I indicate other aspects of it. For now, however, it is perhaps enough to say that if we view the creative artist as a growing, developing consciousness, we can easily explain what Wells finds so inexplicable: The conflicting views of heroism and human nature found in the Marvel Universe and in the New Gods universe.★

Fighting American, in 1954. An unabashed attempt to cash in (this time) on a patriotic creation like Captain America, Fighting American was a crusader against Communism, which, in the McCarthy atmosphere of that time, was a noble thing to be. Unhappily (as I point out in *The Art of the Comic Book*), the timing was wrong: McCarthy and his minions were discredited just about the time *Fighting American* hit the stands. Simon and Kirby quickly revamped their concept and attempted to produce a satirical book. Alas, neither of them was much good at satire.

But perhaps in the foundering satire of *Fighting American* we have the seeds of the self-mockery that distinguishes the early Marvel creations. Couldn't Kirby have brought that notion with him to Marvel? Suggested it to Stan Lee as a novel approach to heroism? And Lee, the man who scripted *My Friend Irma* and other similarly juvenile humor titles, seeing in the concept a place where his penchant for humor could be exercised, immediately pounced upon it. Why not?

It's pretty clear from the testimony quoted in Wells' article and in other places in the same issue of the *Journal* that Lee ginned up plot ideas and that Kirby accepted some of them and rejected others as he fleshed out the ideas that Lee rained down upon his head. Over-

George "Inky" Roussos Interviewed

Interviewed by Jon B. Cooke

(Familiar to modern fans mostly as a colorist, George Roussos has had a career in comics which spans back to the dawn of the art form, beginning as a background inker for Bob Kane's studio on Batman. *Working for nearly every comics publisher, George earned his keep as penciler, inker, letterer, and correction artist beside a veritable Who's Who of the industry and, astonishingly, after 57 years he still works in the business today as staff cover colorist for Marvel Comics. This interview was conducted by phone on May 27 and November 26, 1997.)*

THE JACK KIRBY COLLECTOR: When did you start working in comics?
GEORGE ROUSSOS: In 1940, I started work with DC Comics. First, I worked directly with Bob Kane on *Batman* in his studio, but the character became very popular and he couldn't produce the work fast enough — he was very slow — so they decided that Jerry Robinson and I would go into the office several months later.

I was doing the backgrounds and lettering on *Batman* and Jerry was doing the figures. Bob would send us the pages. This way the office was able to keep tabs on us.

TJKC: In those early years, did you like working on *Batman*?
GEORGE: I liked it, but it's hard for me to explain it. At this moment I see it in such an odd way. I imagine it was mostly in the economics — I needed a job — and that was the emphasis primarily in whatever I did. That's why I've never succeeded like others did. The others threw themselves in totally and I was never able to do that.

TJKC: Did you work at Timely in the '40s?
GEORGE: There was a guy by the name of Bernie Klein (who later got killed in the Army) who was a sports cartoonist, and he wanted me as an assistant. (They all wanted to use me because of the technique I developed on *Batman* for the backgrounds.) Bernie got a job from Jack Kirby to do some inking on *Captain America* and I did the backgrounds on it. I think it was the third issue.

TJKC: Did the fact that Simon & Kirby were going over to National have any effect in the office?
GEORGE: Yes, everyone was impressed with Simon & Kirby. We were all impressed with Jack's very unusual, terrific style.

TJKC: When did you first meet Joe Simon and Jack Kirby?
GEORGE: I met them at DC, while I was on staff, when they began bringing in their *Boy Commandos* pages. I spent more time with Jack. For some odd reason, Jack penciled a drawing and he asked me to ink it. I inked it very quickly and he was very pleased with it because I followed what he had penciled; his pencils were quite precise. Joe I remember vaguely. I do remember that the artwork was on illustration boards — it look liked they brought in the Ten Commandments — there were so many pages and they were so thick! *(laughter)*

TJKC: Do you remember how they worked?
GEORGE: Joe was the writer — he never trusted Jack with the writing — and Jack would do the penciling, which Joe would ink. Sometimes both of them pitched in to ink.

TJKC: When did you get the nickname "Inky"?
GEORGE: It was given to me by Bob Wood because I was doing a lot of inking. He wrote a story using me as a villain named "Inky" Roussos in one of his books. And then Jack Kirby picked it up and he

(this and next 3 pages) Pencils from pages 10-13 of Journey Into Mystery #101, *which George "Bell" Roussos inked. We ran the first nine pages of pencils from this story in* TJKC #14.

always called me "Inky" every time he saw me.

TJKC: So Simon & Kirby named their newspaper strip after you?
GEORGE: No. I believe there was a play on Broadway about a cartoonist. I don't know if Bob swiped it or whatever.

TJKC: Did you enjoy the work of Mort Meskin?
GEORGE: Oh, Mort I liked very much. He lived just downstairs from me in the Village. I worked with Mort and, in fact, helped him out of a very difficult situation that he got into. Mort was a very uncertain guy, extremely sensitive. He got in trouble with the office for some reason, with Whit Ellsworth — some kind of disagreement; probably the artistic temperament out of control — and they asked me to take over his work. (Mort did "Johnny Quick" and "Vigilante.") I tried to get him back again. They were doing the movie serial of Vigilante and we were to do a 16-page giveaway for the movie theatres, and I told Whit that this was a bit too much for me to handle. I could ask Mort to do the penciling and I would finish it off. So I was able to get him back.

TJKC: Was Mort heavily influenced by Kirby?
GEORGE: No. He was influenced by the artist who drew *The Shadow;* the pulp illustrator. It was line drawings with crayon shading of grays.

TJKC: Mort's work always reminded me of Kirby's, what with all the action.
GEORGE: Mort's work was more graceful. Jack's was exaggerated action and dramatic — one leg would be about ten feet away from the other. Mort was a gymnast so it had an influence on his Johnny Quick and Vigilante. Mort was graceful, but Jack was dynamic. Later on, Mort left comics and went into the advertising field.

TJKC: Besides the *Captain America* story, did you work for Simon & Kirby in the '40s?
GEORGE: No, but later on I worked on some mystery stories or something — nothing very important. I inked a few jobs of Jack's but I don't remember them.

TJKC: Did you go into the office when they worked up at Crestwood?
GEORGE: Yes, in fact I worked in the office sometimes. They were up somewhere off Broadway. It was not bad, a small outfit, a lot of fun. Ben Oda, the letterer was there. Carmine Infantino's younger brother worked there for awhile; very nice guy. Marv Stein and Mort Meskin were there. I was working there on a freelance basis. I liked working with Joe and Jack. Joe was the real business manager; very clever, efficient guy, and also an excellent artist. He was the brains.

Jack was there at the drawing board. He hardly talked; he just *produced.* So there was a lot of energy inside of him that he didn't waste on talking and kidding around. He'd do six or seven pages, starting from the left side and go right across, the next line and the next line... *(laughter)* amazing guy, really. It was a very pleasant atmosphere and I enjoyed working there.

When some difficulties arose at Crestwood, a few artists weren't paid. This caused a lot of resentment toward Joe and Jack, and they avoided them. I met Jack later at an art store at Grand Central Station. He was happy to see me, and I sensed he wanted to talk. So we walked to Stan Lee's office and back to Grand Central. He was talking away. I wish I had that dialogue today, but who would ever think that someone would come along and ask questions! *(laughter)* We covered every subject, only he did all the talking. I guess it was a pent-up energy and he was rather hurt that people took out their anger on him — unnecessarily he felt.

TJKC: Were the troubles tied to Wertham and the downfall of comics?
GEORGE: I don't know if it had anything to do with that. I was surprised because prior to the situation, the books were selling as much as 95 percent. I don't know what happened to bring them down. Their books were nice and clean. They weren't doing the weird things Gaines was doing, and shouldn't have been criticized. Gaines and Bob Wood's books — they're the guys who created the monster.

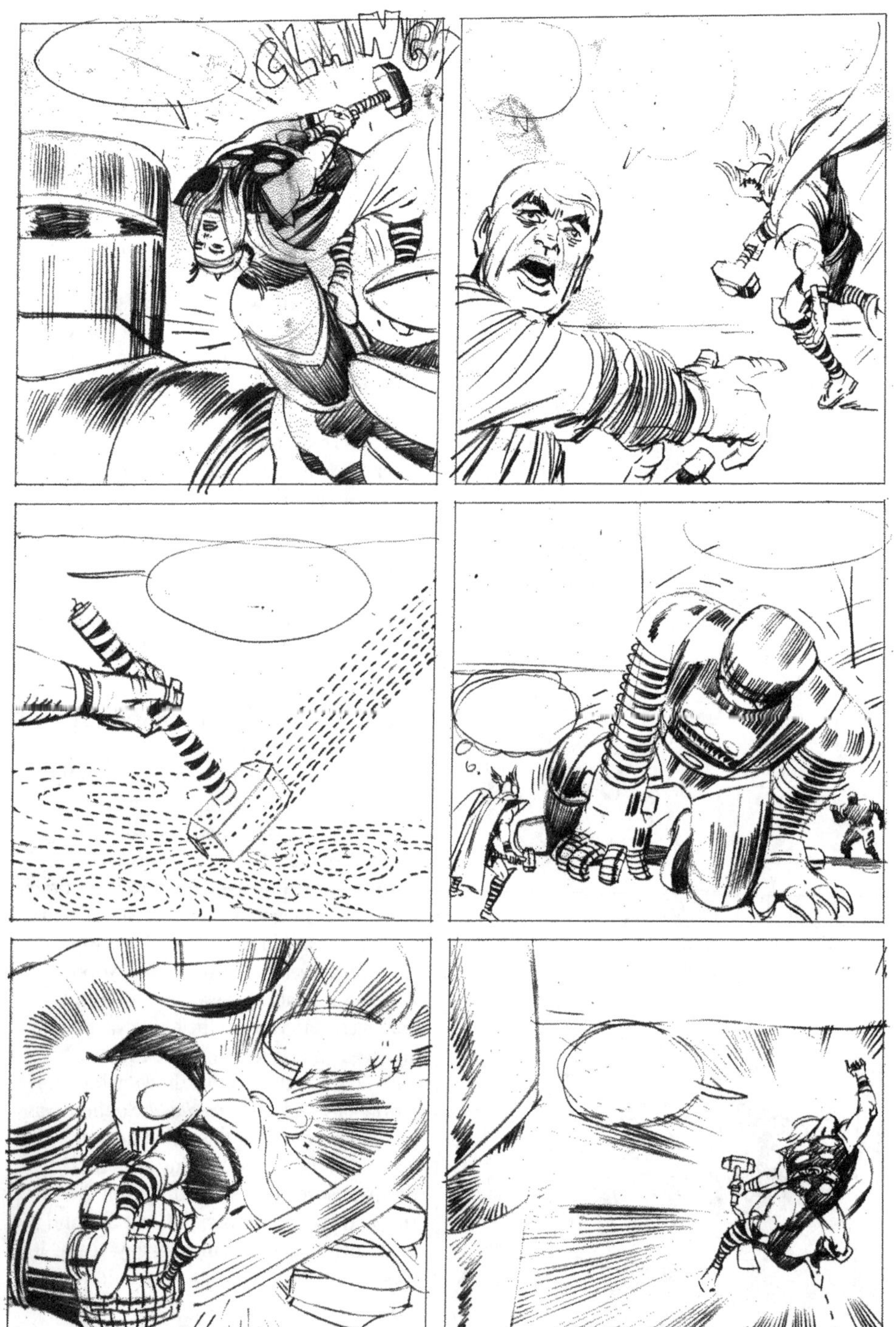

TJKC: During your conversations with Jack, what did you make of him? Was he a deep thinker?
GEORGE: He was a very intelligent guy, but not what I call depth. There's a difference between wisdom and intellect. I asked him, "Do you do any painting, Jack?" He said, "Yes." And I asked him what kind of paintings he did. He said, "I paint Captain America, Iron Man, and all that." I thought that was interesting and I asked him, "What kind of paints do you use?" He said, "House paints. They're pretty good." That gave me the impression of not much depth beyond comics; but a bright guy, no doubt about it.

TJKC: Did you see any problems between Jack and Joe?
GEORGE: I don't know the extent of what really took place, but there was a point when they split up when they were working at Crestwood. Joe took the business end of it and Jack would do the artwork. That didn't work out very well, because when you split up two people in the same room...

TJKC: Backing up a bit — were you aware of their success with the romance books?
GEORGE: Yes. I knew that the sales were 95 percent — but I couldn't understand how this thing could have folded up. I never dwelled into the business end, I just knew the superficial end. I knew the results of what happened, but I didn't know what brought it about. I knew that they split up while in the same room because I was there. There were differences but I was never around when they had any particular argument.

TJKC: Did Jack ever comment on your work? Did he ever give you advice?
GEORGE: No. Jack was never like that.

TJKC: Did Joe?
GEORGE: I don't remember. Because my work wasn't so outstanding, I guess Joe didn't see the practical uses for my work. Joe saw things from a practical aspect — on whether he could use an artist for a particular publication. I guess I fit the bills for specific types of stories, doing certain jobs.

TJKC: You worked on *Black Magic* — what about any of the romance stuff?
GEORGE: I don't think so. I was more for the mysteries.

TJKC: Did you work for Atlas at all?
GEORGE: Yes, I did mystery stories when they were up in the Empire State Building.

TJKC: What did you think of Stan?
GEORGE: I liked Stan right away. There's something *alive* about him, and I always felt that he would amount to something. He always gave me work and I always had a feeling that someday he was going to be successful. That's the reason why when Jack came over, I said that those two are really going to go places. I even told that to Stan, who said, "When I see the sales figures, I'll believe you, George." When sales went up, he never said a word to me. I always call him "The Sign of the Sun." Y'know how we all reach for the sun when it comes out? He's got the same kind of energy. When we were all half-asleep, he would come into the office, and you could feel the energy. It was a stimulating place to work. You need an environment of that kind.

TJKC: Stan was enthusiastic and positive?
GEORGE: Yes, totally. A ball of energy.

TJKC: And you went back to Stan in 1964?
GEORGE: I was getting less work over at DC, and when I saw Jack move over to Stan Lee, I jumped ship, and started asking for work. I worked for peanuts. He couldn't afford to pay much, but I inked everything — or ruined everything! *(laughter)*

TJKC: In that year, you inked quite a bit for Marvel.
GEORGE: I did everything, because some inkers were very slow, as they inked much neater than me. Neatness takes a lot of time. My style is bold, more than anything else. It reproduces almost as good as theirs. I was able to ink an entire story overnight — 22 or 24 pages. I would outline it quickly with a pen, and then throw the blacks in. By the time I got off the drawing board, I could hardly stand up because

I was up for 12 or 13 hours. I would bring it in the following day. I didn't want them to think that I had rushed it. *(laughter)*

TJKC: You would ink an entire page in a half hour?
GEORGE: Well, I would start slow and I'd warm up all through the night, without going to sleep for sometimes more than 12 hours. I wouldn't sleep until I finished the job.

TJKC: Do you remember working on Jack's Marvel work?
GEORGE: Yes! It was easy because it was nicely penciled. No matter what I did, it held up because it was beautifully drawn out. Stan was pleased and he said, "You're Mr. Marvel now, all these books are on time!" No one can produce books like me — for $11 a page, of course. *(laughter)* I was happy to do it and happy to be a part of it. As I began to see myself sinking — the fact that I didn't have the energy or the interest — I asked for a job on staff and I got it.

TJKC: Did you realize that these books at Marvel were different?
GEORGE: Yes. It was Jack's work. I never read any of the stories, but by looking I could tell. I would see certain things that Jack would do; like when the Thing would lean against a building, it would be crumbling at the spot his shoulder would touch. I thought that was cute and very humane. Different from what people did before. Jack had his quiet humor which I liked.

TJKC: Why did you use the name "George Bell"?
GEORGE: At the time I was inking for Stan Lee, I didn't want to lose my contacts at DC. I didn't want to irritate the DC editors. I wasn't getting that much work from them anyway — I was more or less on the way out. I never got along too well with Carmine.

TJKC: All of the sudden you weren't inking the books. What happened?
GEORGE: Stan began to afford the best inkers. They were much more efficient than I was and Stan liked their work. Stan always liked the crisp line work of Joe Sinnott, and mine was not like that. He could afford to pay more because the books began to sell, whereas I was only getting $11 a page, which I didn't mind. I thought it was a good rate for me. I had a very strong feeling that DC was getting submerged, sinking, and this guy was coming up.

TJKC: Did you ever meet Steve Ditko?
GEORGE: Oh, I still see him occasionally and when we have discussions, though not heated, I'm right and he's wrong all the time. *(laughter)* He's very strong-headed about his ideas, and that got him into trouble with Stan Lee. Very stubborn and very pleasant. I liked Steve.

TJKC: So you eventually started working in the bullpen?
GEORGE: Yes, in 1972. Roy Thomas was the assistant to Stan. Artists John Romita, Sr. and Herb Trimpe, department head John Verpoorten, and cover colorist Marie Severin were there. The reason I got my job was that John Verpoorten would call me in to do corrections. They'd give me a whole story and in a few hours I would finish it. Roy Thomas would say, "Gee, when George comes in, the book is finished." So they could get the book out on time. Eventually I asked John Verpoorten if I could work on staff. In a short time I came to do the cover coloring when Marie Severin decided to do artwork. I've been coloring covers ever since.★

Most margin notes were obscured on these pages, except for a few of Stan's notes, as shown here.

Excerpts From The John Romita Panel

Held at Comic Con International: San Diego on July 19, 1997
Transcribed by John Morrow

QUESTION: When did you start working on *Spider-Man*?
JOHN ROMITA: I started it in 1966, but only because Stan absolutely conned me. *(laughter)* Before I actually agreed to pencil any stories for him, he took me out to lunch and hit me with everything in the book. I told him I had taken a job at *(advertising agency)* BBD&O. He said, "Do you want to be a little fish in a big pond, or a big fish in a little pond?" I've been in this little pond for 46 years now, and I've always made a living, so I guess I made the right decision. I don't have an ulcer, and I've got a wonderful son that works in the business, so I'm very grateful to all the fans who care and remember. I'm still amazed that people remember my artwork from the Sixties.

QUESTION: What's your favorite issue of *Spider-Man*?
ROMITA: There was a two-story arc having to do with Flash Thompson returning from Viet Nam, where some Southeast Asians were out to kill him because they felt he had desecrated their temple when he was a GI. It was my plot, a lot of it was my idea. Stan injected Dr. Strange into the second half, which was great. That second half is in the book *The Art Of John Romita,* the whole story. It's my favorite because I like the story, and also because I was a *Terry and the Pirates* freak when I grew up. I used to absorb it through my pores every Sunday, and in that storyline I had a big Chinese chauffeur who was based on Big Stoop.

QUESTION: Was there a scramble when Steve Ditko suddenly quit *Spider-Man*?
ROMITA: I had heard a couple of times that he was thinking of leaving. He and Stan didn't get along; they disagreed on plotting, they disagreed on motivations for the characters, and I found out later on they disagreed on the identity of the Green Goblin — and I think that's what broke the camel's back — but there wasn't a scramble. Stan asked me to draw Spider-Man as a guest star in *Daredevil* #16 and #17. That was sort of like a try-out. But frankly, I thought Ditko was just going to leave for a few months until he got over his anger, and then come back. If I had created a character like Spider-Man, and he was getting bigger and bigger every year, I wouldn't have given it up. I don't care if I was working for Godzilla, it wouldn't have mattered. I always got along with editors because I let them have their way. I always figured my obligation was to give him everything he wanted, as close to what I liked as possible, but more what he wanted than what I wanted. I thought that was the obligation of a paid artist.

Ditko was really ahead of his time; he was like the young artists today. They want to inject their own feelings and their own version of everything. When I took it over, my generation felt the obligation to ghost a book. If you look at my first few issues, they look like Ditko. I tried to make them look so much like Ditko that nobody'd notice. I thought that's what a guy should do when he took over a successful book. It was a failure, but I figured they wanted to see Ditko — and let me tell you, young fans were absolutely cruel to me for at least eighteen months. Every time I ran into fans, they would say, "When is Ditko coming back?" It hurt me, but I also understood it. Frankly, up until maybe 1968, I felt like a stranger on that book, ghosting for somebody else temporarily. I never quite lost that sense of being out of place all during my run on *Spider-Man.*

QUESTION: But sales rose.
ROMITA: Well, that's the reason I'm here. *(laughter)* I'm credited everywhere as the man who brought *Spider-Man* up to number one; *Fantastic Four* was our best-selling title before that. When I first saw the book, Stan gave me the first 33 issues to look over, and I said, "Gee, it looks silly. It looks dumb." By the time I reached the twenties, I realized Ditko was really rolling. I had an interview once that just quoted the first part of that statement, that I thought it was silly and crude. That's all that ever got into print, and it's a wonder Ditko ever talked to me after that. They never put in the other part that said how much I loved it and respected it after I got into the run.

The first thing today's artists want to do is change the costume, the characters. They want to make it scary and heavy and

(this page) 1970s Romita Spidey art.

(next page) Romita & Steranko made face changes to this Captain America *#102 page.*

dark. Stan always wanted it lighthearted with laughs. The reason we killed people like Gwen Stacy and Captain Stacy was because Stan made it so lighthearted, people were starting to take it for granted. Nobody would ever get hurt, nobody was getting killed. So we killed Captain Stacy, and then Gwen, because we wanted the readers to see, every issue, they don't know who's gonna survive.

QUESTION: Where did Mary Jane come from?
ROMITA: She was in the book about three or four issues before I took it over; but this is another reason they disagreed — I don't know if Ditko wanted her to be unattractive, and Stan wanted her beautiful, or vice versa — but they never could agree on what she looked like, so in her first few appearances it was a suspenseful gimmick where Peter Parker is supposed to meet this girl, and he kept breaking the appointment. There was this scene where this huge flower was blocking her face; all you could see was the back of her hair, and you saw her in silhouette and shadows. They couldn't decide on her look. So when I took over the book, after we decided that Norman Osborn was going to be the Goblin — Stan decided, I didn't decide; he just told me; that's why I was on the book *(laughter)* — the second thing he did was ask me what I thought about Mary Jane. I thought she should really be a knockout, and really oooh him. This way, he'd be ducking her for a year, and when he finally sees her, he'd say, "What, was I stupid?" He went along with that, and I did a sketch which I still have, the first sketch I ever made of her. It was based on Ann Margaret, with dimples and a cleft in her chin, and red in her hair.

When it came out, it didn't come out as good as I wanted. My first pencil sketch was much better, and my first penciling on that page looked better than the final inking. I almost went nuts because I didn't like what it looked like, and I tried two or three times to improve it, and I never could get it to where I wanted it. Slowly but surely I learned how to draw her.

I gotta tell you something about Stan and his terminology. He gave us all nicknames in lieu of money. *(laughter)* Martin Goodman was very tight with page rates. But when it came to nicknames, he had two names for me, and all the nicknames were based on your first or second initial. So I was "Ring-A-Ding" Romita sometimes, and I was "Jazzy" John sometimes. When my mother saw that, she said, "What's this 'Jazzy' John?" I said that was just one of the nicknames. She said, "You tell Mr. Stan Lee everybody can't be as fancy as he is." *(laughter)* She took it wrong, like it was a condescending wisecrack about the fact that I was a square, and that "Jazzy" was like a joke.

QUESTION: Who did Steve Ditko originally want the Goblin to be?
ROMITA: From what I've gathered — and this is secondhand information, because I never asked Steve this — he wanted it to be someone unknown. And his theory was sensible; this is the reason Stan and he disagreed a lot. Ditko had a feeling that more real life should be put into the strips, and I thought he was a pioneer that way. He wanted politics in the strip, he wanted sociological upheaval in the strip; that's why there were riots on the campus in the strip and all that stuff. He was a very political animal, and he was very conservative too, as you probably know. He wanted all this stuff to look real, and he said, "In real life, if there's a masked criminal, and you unmask him, 99 times out of 100 it's going to be someone you never know." And Stan's like, "What are you talking about? We're not doing real life here; this is a guy who crawls on walls." *(laughter)*

QUESTION: What was the reaction when the Comics Code didn't approve the drug issues?
ROMITA: I plotted those stories with Stan, thinking I was going to do them, then he yanked me off them to do *Captain America* or *Fantastic Four* or something. Gil Kane always got the biggest issues, and I wanted to kill him. *(laughter)* I never got a chance to do one landmark issue.

We plotted that because we got a letter from a government agency asking us to put in some anti-drug storyline in one of the books. I swear, it was a government agency request! We sat down to do it, and if you ever saw any of our message books, you probably didn't even recognize it, because we tried to bury the message behind the entertainment. DC did a similar thing after we did those two issues. They did a very strong drug series. But they made the drugs too heavily the message, and it became a documentary; at least that's my opinion. Ours were a little more entertaining; the characters were involved, Harry almost jumped off a building. We did that as a direct public service. We should have been given a medal, and the Code turned on us like a snake, and said they won't put the Code stamp on that because it's bad. If you saw those issues, there wasn't one bad thing in it. We certainly didn't show paraphernalia, there wasn't an instruction manual, nobody was happy. I don't think there was even a happy drug dealer in it. It was done carefully and with entertainment in mind. I thought it was a giant accomplishment, and we got slapped down.

The upshot of the whole thing is we ended up getting good publicity out of it. We had the guts to go without the Code. Martin Goodman, or whoever was in charge, could've said, "We won't put the books out." I was very proud.

QUESTION: Could you do a little self-analysis of your work, and talk about your strengths and weaknesses as compared to those of other artists?
ROMITA: I used to get very hurt when people in the office and at conventions would say, "Jack Kirby, I love your artwork. John Buscema, we adore your artwork." No one ever told me they liked my artwork. Now, I was a success; I was selling books, more than anybody else on any other title. And everybody was happy, but I always felt that sadness because, gee, why doesn't somebody tell me they like my artwork?

AUDIENCE: I love your artwork! *(laughter, applause)*
ROMITA: I learned a great lesson. I suddenly realized after a couple of years that everybody who came up to my table or up to the office would tell me, "We loved what Peter Parker went through. We loved what happened to Aunt May. We loved that storyline, that double issue, that cover." They were complimenting me, and I was too stupid to understand. I suddenly realized that it was the greatest compliment of all. Now, that's my philosophy when I teach young artists: Every time you do a flashy drawing — and you know how many flashy drawings have been in comics in the last five years — they do not do the job. You can do the most fantastic drawing in the world, but what you're doing is telling the reader, "This is only a drawing. Don't worry about it." Nobody's going to get hurt; it's a drawing, a piece of paper, it's two-dimensional. What I strive for is something in my work makes people forget it's a drawing. I don't do photographic work; I certainly don't do work as well as a lot of other guys. The only thing that I have going is that, after the splash page maybe, people forget about the drawing, and care about what's happening to the character. What you've got to do is check your ego at the door, and don't try to show off with your artwork. The artwork is only a tool to tell the story. If you make your drawing so clearly a drawing, as a storytelling comic book artist, you're a failure.

I remember I used to recommend some of my favorite artists to Stan Lee, and he said, "If the guy's a great artist, I don't want him at Marvel Comics." In fact, I think maybe Neal Adams was one of those guys. Even though he worked for us, Stan always felt, and rightfully so — as much as everyone loves his artwork, and I admire his work; Neal Adams is a wonderful artist — his artwork gets in front of the story. And I think a whole generation of Neal Adams clones compounded that felony. I think for years they lost themselves. The Image guys do spectacular artwork, but frankly, their characters suck and their storylines suck, because the artwork is so sensational. It's like getting hit in the face with a pie every two seconds. After awhile, you can't see through the whipped cream. *(laughter, applause)*

QUESTION: When you took over from Steve Ditko, and you were drawing the cover to *Amazing Spider-Man* #39, did you feel pressure to do the cover of your life, or did that great cover just come out?
ROMITA: I don't think I felt any pressure. I thought I was on it tem-

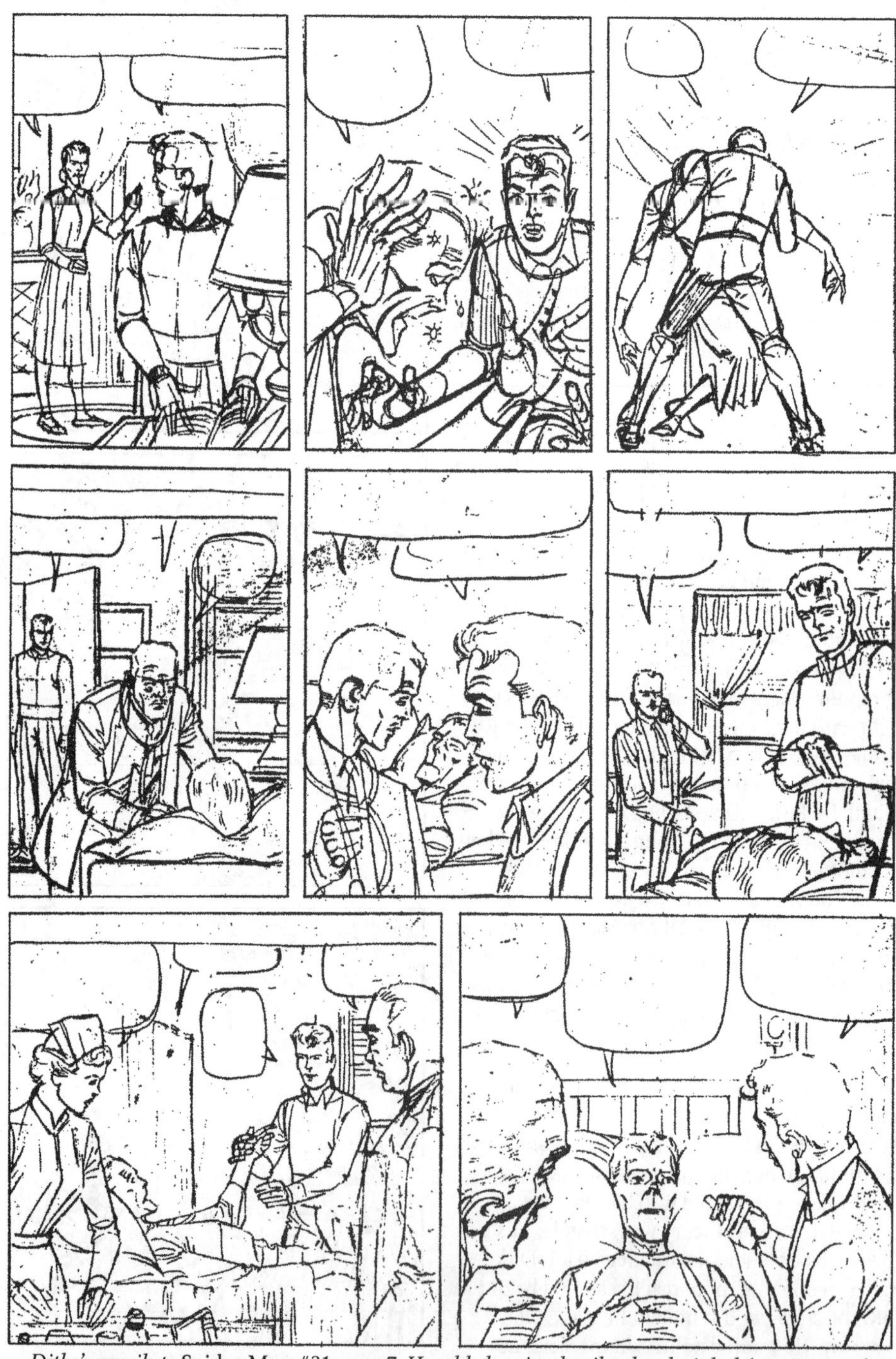

Ditko's pencils to Spider-Man *#31, page 7. He added major details when he inked (see next page).*

porarily, and I didn't feel I was in competition with Ditko. I think that's what saved me; I had no fear. That one just came to me.

QUESTION: Did you purposely change your style over the years, or did it just evolve that way?
ROMITA: My first five or ten years in the business, I thought I was without a style. To me it was a mish-mash; half Jack Kirby, half Milton Caniff. I always felt like a man without a style, which helped me in a way, because when I went to Stan in 1965, I could jump in on any strip and ghost it. Then I found out later on people could recognize my artwork anywhere. Every time I did a replacement head on a Jack Kirby story or a Barry Smith story — everybody hates me for that — people would write in and say, "Tell Romita to stop putting his heads on everybody else's bodies!" *(laughter)* But I have changed, but I think I've only changed in an endeavor to keep it current, so automobiles and buildings look like today.

QUESTION: When you're doing your artwork, do you ever have anything sitting in front of you? Not just other people's artwork, but...
ROMITA: Sometimes it is other people's artwork. When I did *Fantastic Four,* I had about five of Jack Kirby's books spread out in front of me at all times. I didn't feel like anybody should ever touch *Fantastic Four* but Jack. In fact, my first thought was that, when he left to go to DC, that we were going to cancel *Fantastic Four.* That's how stupid I was. I went in to Stan and said, "What are we going to do? We can't get anybody to do *Fantastic Four.*" He said, "You're gonna do it." I said, "You're joking! *(laughter)* I just told you I didn't think anybody should do it. You're gonna give it to me?" My opinion was nobody should've ever touched that book again. Although John Buscema proved me wrong. He did Jack Kirby with a nice veneer of slick drawing on top. John Buscema's *Fantastic Four* still stands out as one of the best. Those four issues I did were just to keep the ball rolling until somebody else could come in, and John saved my skin. I had Jack Kirby books all open; I wanted to make it look just like his stuff — and if you look at those books, they're absolute swipes of Jack Kirby everywhere, and I'm not embarrassed by that at all.

QUESTION: During the period when you were in New York, did you ever carpool with other Marvel artists?
ROMITA: No. I used to take their work in, though. I was their delivery service. *(laughter)* I lived halfway between the city and where most of the guys lived. Frank Giacoia, Gene Colan, and Al Milgrom used to use me regularly as a delivery service. I saved the company millions of dollars carrying that stuff in. *(laughter)* And they gained an extra twelve hours to do their artwork and get the deadlines done, so I used to save them a lot of trouble.

Gene Colan and I used to meet at Stan Lee's house on the island at three in the morning, and one time we almost got arrested for looking like burglars. We drove into Stan's driveway, and this cop stops outside the driveway to watch what we were doing. We were both putting pages of artwork into Stan's mailbox. *(laughter)*

QUESTION: How did you get to be art director at Marvel?
ROMITA: Stan Lee got tired of telling people what he wanted. Once he heard me telling somebody everything that he had been telling me, and you could see the light turn on above his head. *(laughter)* "Sonofagun, I've got this guy who can do my spiel for me, and I don't have to do it anymore." So I ended up doing his indoctrination speech, which was: "This is what we want. We want excitement on every page. I want every double-spread to have something exciting on it. And I want it to be so good that when a kid flips through a book, he finds something interesting every time he stops." That's the Marvel Way. Jack Kirby used to have sinews that didn't exist running through the arms of every character — but boy, they worked! *(laughter)*★

A 1970s Romita rendition of the FF.

Marie Severin Interview

Interviewed by Jon B. Cooke

(Marie Severin is renowned for her humor, friendliness, and generosity, not to mention her exceptional capabilities. Best known for her satirical work on Marvel's Not Brand Echh, *Marie is also an accomplished penciler, colorist, breakdown artist, and cover designer, achieving critical success with her brother John on the lauded* Kull the Conqueror *series in the early '70s. She also served as Marvel's art director for a brief period in the late '70s. This interview was conducted via phone on November 10, 1997.)*

THE JACK KIRBY COLLECTOR: How'd you get started in comics?
MARIE SEVERIN: John, my brother, was at EC and they weren't happy with the coloring. He suggested me to *(Harvey)* Kurtzman for the war books and I passed muster. Then Bill *(Gaines)* and Al *(Feldstein)* gave me the science fiction and horror. I did most of the covers but Harvey always did his own.

They were chopping people up and doing all kinds of icky stuff... I figured it wouldn't be quite so offensive if I muted some icky stuff with darker colors — they called me a censor but they never would have let me hurt the storytelling.

TJKC: Was it a riotous atmosphere working with Bill Gaines?
MARIE: Oh, it was fun, but it was quite intense work. Guys didn't sit all day and talk to the editors. Al wrote intensely most of the day — Harvey, too. He brought in tons of layouts for all his books. We had breaks where they fooled around. One day, Al came to me with a push pin pasted on his palm, with some red ink. It looked painful, but being practical me, I just yanked it out and then saw the glue and the pin had no point, and the guys were just disgusted with me... the unshockable. Kurtzman was very intense and he knew what he wanted. I hated tramping around the city doing research with a duffel bag — this was 1953, and it wasn't in fashion! But he made me laugh a lot. He'd try out a little scene from a *Mad* story, and he would turn into one of his cartoons.

I learned a lot there. It was my first experience in comics. Al Williamson and I were the youngest. They paid well, and they paid right away. The workers *worked* and were respected.

I remember Williamson and his baseball team coming in; y'know, Frazetta and Torres and all of those guys. They were funny; they really were. They were so ahead of their times; they came in wearing dungarees and stuff, and in New York, all the guys had on shirts and ties. These guys were the forerunners of the '60s styles.

TJKC: What happened in 1954, when Bill went down to Washington to defend horror comics?
MARIE: That was awful. We were in the office, and it was on a poopy little black-&-white TV set. I was just annoyed. I remember saying to Johnny Craig, "Jeez, poor Bill. He's all alone there!" And then they held the cover of the book with the *(severed)* head on camera, and Johnny was saying, "Why *my* art?" *(laughter)* Years later, Bill was honored on TV with an award from the Horror Hall of Fame. He felt it vindicated EC. He was very proud of EC and his gang.

(above) Marie's cover for Thor #175; *strangely enough, it's signed by Jack. (next page) Jack's original, unused version of the cover.*

TJKC: When did you go over to talk to Stan about working for Atlas?
MARIE: The Comics Code knocked out the EC color books and I was working on *Mad.* But there wasn't that much to do. I didn't think *Mad* would last; ha-ha! I followed John to Stan, who was doing a wannabe *Mad*-type thing. He hired me as one of his production people. It was a big bullpen with Stan's office up front. John, Bill Everett, Joe Maneely, Danny Crespi, and a great bunch of letterers all worked together. Except for two proofreader ladies up front, I was the only gal. It was fun being in the middle of a bunch of guys, *except* when it got into exhaustive baseball discussions. Once I yelled at Artie Simek because he had not shut up for 40 minutes about the darn Yankees.

TJKC: How long did your initial stay with Marvel last?
MARIE: I think about a year and a half. The newsstands had more comic titles than they could handle, and with the overly strict Comics Code, the covers and stories were dopey. I went to work for the Federal Reserve Bank after getting laid off from Marvel and did a lot of their graphics. I also did a comic called *The Story of Checks.* John did the finished art. It was a classy-looking little book. I was hired away from there to do educational film strips for about a year.

Then I heard that Stan was reviving stuff, so in 1964 I brought my portfolio in. Stan said, "Marie, I'm so glad to see you! Sol needs someone to help him in production. Sol! Look who's here!" And I said, "Stan, I'm..." A couple of months later, *Esquire* magazine wanted to have an article on Marvel Comics on college campuses, or the Marvel-type art dealing with dope on campus. Anyway, Sol didn't want Kirby to endanger a deadline — which I'm sure would *not* have happened as Kirby could pop off the *Esquire* spread in an hour or two — so Sol sent me, as I had started doing penciling as well as production and coloring. When Martin Goodman saw the printed version, he said, "She shouldn't be doing paste-ups, she should be drawing." Ditko had just quit, and Bill Everett was getting sick, so I took over *Dr. Strange.* I was on staff all those years because I wanted something steady. I didn't want to be walking around New York in heels with a portfolio.

TJKC: Did you ever see Martin Goodman in the office?
MARIE: Sure. I'd pop into his office to thank him for a bonus. Once, when I knew he was out for the day, I took a nap on his couch. Nancy Murphy — the longest continual employee except for Stan — admired him a lot. Nancy handled his contributions to a big charity. Flo, Nancy and I keep in touch; we plan to blackmail the lot in our old age.

TJKC: Was Goodman involved in day-to-day operations of the comics?
MARIE: I don't really know. In the beginning, Stan had to check in with him about what was going on. When the company was sold, Stan was a free man. He had proven himself, and Martin didn't interfere, to my knowledge.

TJKC: What was Stan like when you met him?
MARIE: Oh, just the way he is now; a mixture of Jack Benny and Errol Flynn. He's funny and he's charming, and he's interesting. I like Stan. He was always a gentleman. One time he corrected me in front of the

Bullpen, and I went into his office and gave him heck — he wouldn't have yelled at one of the *guys* in public! Later he came back with a big thing of flowers and put it on my desk. He goes back into his office, and I followed him in with the flowers and I said, "And you wouldn't give the guys *flowers,* either." *(laughter)* You could talk to Stan — he was not aloof — like you could talk to Bill Gaines.

Once I started working with Stan as a penciler, I really started learning the pacing he liked, and the way he liked to work. He'd go over a story with you, and you'd rough it out, and then he'd dialogue it. He wasn't able to do that later on, because he was too busy. John Romita, Herb Trimpe, and I were the last artists whose pencils he had the full time to review. Roy Thomas, then Denny O'Neil were hired; that was the beginning of Marvel making it big, and there were many additions to the staff.

TJKC: What was Flo Steinberg like?
MARIE: Oh, she's fun, she's a doll. She was Stan's secretary; she had to do everything for him. He used his secretary like a wife: "Sew this. Could you fix that? Would you exchange this?" *(laughter)* In those days, that's what a secretary did. She used to go, "I don't want to do that on my lunch hour! *(laughter)* Marie, he sent me over to exchange a stupid bathing suit!" *(laughter)* But she was a darn good secretary. And smart.

She left early on. They wouldn't give her a raise, which was so stupid. The office was never the same without her. She got a better job; she did the right thing. Secretaries in those days weren't appreciated.

TJKC: Did you see Jack when he'd come in?
MARIE: Yeah. He wasn't one to hang out in the office, to my knowledge. He was pretty business-like. He dealt mostly with Stan. Jack was always pleasant; his conversation was always worth listening to — and always the cigar.

TJKC: What do you remember about Stan and Jack's story conferences?
MARIE: I worked two offices down. It was 1964 and I guess by then they had a smooth routine. Flo said that she did have to holler "Keep it down!" as she couldn't hear on the phone.

When I started penciling, it was quite a show when Stan would get into character — leap about or die or gesticulate in wild abandon. I doubt Kirby needed much of that. I imagine they bounced off each other. Just look at the results.

TJKC: Did you keep up with all the new books as they came out?
MARIE: I knew I had to if I was going to work there. When someone put the wrong costume on, I was making corrections and things. You never knew if Stan was going to say, "I want another balloon in there," for whatever reason. Often he'd say, "Turn the head around." In those days, it took forever to get a photostat, so you'd usually redraw it and paste it up. Swipes, y'know? It didn't happen often, and a lot of times you could do it freehand, but a lot of times you'd hit a snag. I remember in the Inhumans, that dog Lockjaw was hard to draw. Kirby is a hard act to follow.

When Roy Thomas came, we had a guy who knew all the characters and we got fewer "No-Prizes" going out to fans — and more corrections — but that was okay.

TJKC: You must've been aware that media attention was starting to hit Marvel. Did you understand why it was happening?
MARIE: The books were getting exciting-looking, and Stan had a hands-on approach with it. He was writing stuff that was different than what had gone before: The indecision, and the fears, and the fallible characters — and the wide range of characters had a broad audience. In those days, sales figures were hush-hush, but the fan mail was heavy, and all of a sudden, we could order art supplies without flak!

TJKC: Roy said that back in 1966, an article in the *New York Herald Tribune* made Jack sound bad, and that Jack might've felt like Stan orchestrated it.
MARIE: That may have been the beginning of the rift. I think the reporter just wanted to make it sound controversial. At the time, I

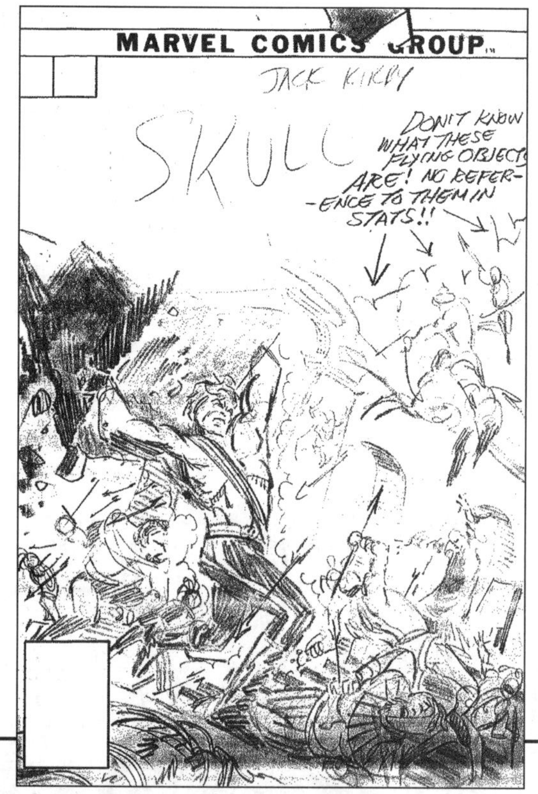

remember people saying, "Wow, Kirby got treated really lousy." But I can't *imagine* Stan doing that intentionally. I just don't think Stan would *talk* like that. It might've been the guy trying to add a little juice to it. You know how Stan is: "Everybody's swell, everybody's great." I don't think he would ever dis Jack. I think that was unfortunate. I think we *all* were stunned when Kirby left.

TJKC: What was it like when Ditko left, as opposed to when Jack left?
MARIE: I thought that no one could replace Ditko's *Spider-Man* — but Stan made Romita work on it, and John turned his version into the Marvel trademark — but *Dr. Strange* was never done better than Steve. Stan must have been uneasy when Ditko left and, though I never heard him talk about it, when Kirby left, I imagine he felt awful. *But* when Kirby returned, he was jubilant!

TJKC: Did you ever meet Ditko?
MARIE: Yeah. I like him. I got along fine with him. It's a shame he doesn't take advantage of the money he could make on drawings and those recreations like so many pros are doing. When Kirby left, the books were sailing. Many artists were now drawing most of Kirby's characters — the line was growing — so even though our big hits like *Fantastic Four* and *Captain America* were associated with the Kirby look, it was not the end of the world as far as getting the books out.

TJKC: What was the hierarchy at work?
MARIE: Stan was the boss and you knew it. Sol Brodsky was production chief and passed on Stan's instructions. Many times Stan would want to talk to me directly, especially in '64 about cover coloring. You could always go to Stan, and if he had the door closed, he was "big busy." He was not aloof.

TJKC: Did Sol just make sure the books got to the printer?
MARIE: That's a big job! He sometimes influenced who would get assignments. Sol had a lot of sway, because he got the books *out.*

TJKC: Did you study Jack's stuff, and apply it to your work?
MARIE: Yes. I started to get an idea of sort of why he did that, and I could at least try to think like him — and I started to get the sense of impact. Nobody's like Kirby, but you try to get the essence of him, because that's the way Stan wanted the books to be. So it was sink or swim. I enjoyed it. It helped to use that direction in storytelling. Jack could do a "talk" page and it was still better than a lot of people's action shots. His art is like a camera thrown about the situation; moving, telling, and fun to look at.★

Marie comments on this *Skull The Slayer* #8 cover:
"The Skull cover is an example of my days of cover sketches. We did that for a time when Stan got too busy to discuss each and every cover. I'd do a sketch and when approved, it was assigned to whomever. Stan was hands-on with the books for quite a while. He wanted the masthead colors to rotate each month so the display in newsstands was not confusing — also it was easier to have someone sketch them who had access to the rest of the books, so we didn't duplicate situations and designs.

When Skull was assigned, I guess we didn't send reference to Jack for the flying guys, so I penciled them in."

Marie's cover rough and Jack's pencils to the cover of Skull The Slayer #8.

Interview With The Invisible Woman, Flo Steinberg

Interviewed by Michael Kraiger

(Hardly invisible herself, Flo Steinberg was there from the start as Stan Lee's loyal secretary/girl Friday. Stan gave her the moniker "Fabulous Flo" and if you meet her you'd know why. What has this to do with Jack Kirby? Well, in 1978, Jack Kirby wrote and penciled Marvel Comics' What If? *#11 featuring a story entitled "What If The Original Marvel Bullpen Had Become The Fantastic Four?" The idea was Roy Thomas', who offered the concept to Jack Kirby. Jack took it and flew with it, returning to the Fantastic Four after eight years, not only to pencil the new story but, for the first time, to receive writing credit as well. In the story, Stan Lee becomes Mister Fantastic, Jack becomes the ever-lovin' blue-eyed Thing, production man Sol Brodsky becomes the Human Torch, and Flo Steinberg becomes the Invisible Girl.)*

THE JACK KIRBY COLLECTOR: What does it feel like to be turned into the Invisible Woman?

FLO STEINBERG: It feels great! It's such a wonderful compliment, it's such a great story and I'm utterly flattered to have been immortalized by Jack. He's the best!

TJKC: When *What If?* #11 came out you were no longer working at Marvel. How did you find out about your role in the story?

FLO: It was 1978 and I was working at *ARTS* magazine. I was still connected to comics through friendships. Jim Shooter called me up and told me the whole premise — what Jack was doing — and he asked for my permission. I said, well, if Jack wants to do it, that's great! I'd be very pleased. I had to sign something, which I did, and they promised to send me some free comics, which they did. It was all done properly, so I wouldn't sue.

TJKC: What was your friends' reaction at the time to you becoming a member of Marvel's original super team?

FLO: Oh, my friends in comics thought it was a riot and just loved it. I got a wonderful kick out of it, too. My friends who weren't in comics didn't quite get it, but they thought it was funny. I reread it every once in a while and I'm just amazed at how Jack captured everybody's speaking patterns. Sol was just that way, very practical. Sol would have looked for the practical side of things, and figured how to get out of the situation. Rereading it, I find it a very warm and loving thing. I don't see any of those problems that developed years later which I wasn't party to. I'm sorry that happened.

This is so funny, this one *(pointing to page 37, panel 3)*. It just cracks me up every time I read it, that one panel. I mean that's just... *(In the panel, Flo Steinberg as the Invisible Girl is pleading with the Sub-Mariner.)* "Oh, please listen to us, Prince Namor! We're simply aching to be our old selves again! We need your help so badly!" *(laughter)*

It just amazes me that he wrote this great copy that captured everybody so well, and I think it's done with affection and respect.

TJKC: What did you think of Jack's depiction of you? Do you think he got a good likeness?

FLO: Physically, yes, it's me, but I think he really caught me in my office mode so well. So many of the things that I said in there, I actually did say; Stan and Sol and Jack also. It really was how we all talked. You know, sometimes I was a little whiny when I needed to get things done.

TJKC: I don't know if he was working from memory or a photo, but I think he caught your eyes. I look at it and see Flo's eyes.

FLO: It's just the way we were in the office, and the way we talked. The way Stan speaks and writes, it's really the way he is. People really did say things like "honestly," and I did call them boys. Stan was always telling me to pipe down when I'd be bothering them about something. On page 15, where I bring in the box, I'm sure I actually did say things like, "Surprise, Stan! I've got something here that will brighten your day." And he would have said, "That's what I was lacking — a brighter day!" Jack caught the way we talked. I think he got our personalities perfectly.

TJKC: According to an editorial in that issue, this was Roy Thomas' idea, and he was meant to play the Human Torch, with either you or Marie Severin playing the part of the Invisible Girl.

FLO: That would have made Roy very happy, but I guess Jack was more comfortable with Sol, whom he had known forever.

TJKC: The story takes place after you open a mysterious package in the office. How typical was it for Jack to be in the office?

FLO: Well, he was in there at least once or twice a week, delivering work. This was before FedEx and out-of-town messengers and stuff like that; you either mailed it or brought it in. People mostly lived in the metropolitan area. It was a nice break for the guys to come in because they were all working at home, alone; everyone worked in the basement or the attic or some such place. Most of the artists were supporting families, so they didn't have the discretionary income to spend on a studio. Jack would come in and sit around and talk; then he'd go into Stan's office and they'd go over plots, make sound effect noises, run around, work things out. Then he'd go back home to work some more. Jack would usually have his wonderful cigar. He always had it; I don't know if it was always lit.

TJKC: How was Jack on deadlines?
FLO: Oh, excellent. He never missed a deadline as far as I know — nobody did then. If you were a professional person, this was part of being a professional. There had to be something really bad for you to miss your deadline. People at that time didn't think that they were the stars; their work was what mattered. They did a professional job and got it in on time and they got paid. This is what being a professional is about, not being a prima donna. It was really basically unheard of for people to miss deadlines. It was not an issue. If someone didn't show up when they were supposed to, we just assumed they were in a terrible accident. There was no fabricating, people were very honest; if they couldn't get in or needed an extra day they'd call and we'd work around it — or we would call and track them down. Once Don Heck didn't show up and we tracked him down on Fire Island. We just assumed something dreadful happened because he hadn't come in when he said he would. People were very dependable — it was part of the work ethic. It's not so much a part of it today, unfortunately for the business. It was just a different work ethic.

TJKC: Opening and reading the mail was one of your jobs.
FLO: Oh yes, my main job.

TJKC: Do you remember a general sense of what the readers thought of Jack's work?
FLO: Oh, everyone loved Jack's work; it was very heroic, very physical, three-dimensional. People who were reading it could grasp the characters and identify with them. They really loved the characters.

TJKC: Did you get any unusual requests through the mail?
FLO: So many people would write in. They often wanted sketches, autographs, or to know why this happened, why that happened. We wouldn't send sketches but we'd certainly send autographs or explain why things happened or didn't happen.

TJKC: In individual letters?
FLO: Yes, we acknowledged all the fanzines and anything in that genre. If people sent in art samples, we'd write and say it's fine, finish high school first, go to art school, work hard and practice. It was very personal — the fans were a very important part of it all. There weren't the huge conventions there are now, so the fans rarely met these artists.

TJKC: Did artists like Jack have a sense that the fans appreciated their work? Did they see the letters coming in?
FLO: They knew they were doing a good job because the books were selling and they had work. They didn't seem to need this constant patting of their egos. They knew they were good and took pride in that. They didn't need strangers telling them they were good. If it was an unusual letter we would make a copy for them or put it in a letters page. Everyone was happy and sort of amused by all these fan letters coming in. But most decisions were determined by whether the book sold or didn't sell.

TJKC: What happened to the original art?
FLO: Oh, good question! When I was there, no one ever expressed interest in getting their original art back. It was like an old script; once it was done, it was done. The printed copy, that became your work. When shelves got too crowded, I'd just throw it out.

TJKC: That's likely to make people cry.
FLO: Nobody asked for it back. After a while, when people seemed to realize it was a commercial commodity, the art started disappearing. Eventually, after I had left, Marvel began returning art to the artists.

TJKC: You would throw it out when the shelves got full?
FLO: This is in the Sixties, mid-Sixties. Yes. Sorry!

TJKC: Being Stan's secretary/girl Friday has gotten you a bit of notoriety in the comics world. What's your take on the world of comics?
FLO: I'm so grateful to it; if not for all this I wouldn't be working now. I actually only worked in the office in the Sixties, although I was connected with comics afterwards in different ways, mostly through my friends. A few years ago I was between jobs. Not being computer-literate, it was pretty hard. It happened that Jack Abel *(Marvel Comics' proofreader)* was going on vacation. Virginia *(Romita, Marvel's production manager and John's wife)* called and asked me to fill in for Jack. So I did, and somehow I just stayed on. For the past few years I've been earning my living as a proofreader at Marvel, so I'm eternally grateful to something that happened over thirty years ago. Some people think I've been at Marvel all this time. I haven't. I'm very grateful to Stan for hiring me in the first place. I'm a very lucky person and Jack Kirby was a darling man.★

Herb Trimpe Interview

Interviewed by Jon B. Cooke

(Herb Trimpe, best known for over 100 issues of the Incredible Hulk, *also worked in the Marvel Bullpen from 1966-'70. An accomplished biplane pilot, Herb is also recognized for outstanding work on Ant-Man, Killraven, and* War is Hell *stories during his freelance days in the '70s. He is now doing freelance art while studying to be an art teacher in New York. Herb was interviewed via telephone on November 12, 1997. The interview was transcribed by John Morrow and copy edited by Herb and his wife, Linda Fite.)*

THE JACK KIRBY COLLECTOR: How did you get started in comics?
HERB TRIMPE: I came out of the Air Force in 1966; I'd just spent a year in Viet Nam. I had worked prior to entering the Air Force for a year or two for a man named Tom Gill who did mostly Gold Key and Dell comics. I did backgrounds for him, right out of art school, on western stuff like *Bonanza* and *The Lone Ranger.* Then I went into the service for four years. While I was in, a friend of mine who I went to art school with, John Verpoorten, was working at Marvel. When I left the service, John said, "Hey, you oughtta bring your stuff up, because we're looking for people." So I got some samples together. I had art school stuff; I'd gone to the School of Visual Arts after high school. I took some material up there and talked to Sol Brodsky, who was the production manager at the time. He gave me some inking work; for about eight months I worked on Werner Roth stuff, *Kid Colt, Rawhide Kid.* This was 1966. Kirby was already taking off, and all the big characters were already in place. I came in between generations. Barry Smith came in around the same time. It was a great atmosphere. Marie Severin was in the Bullpen.

Sol called me one day and said they didn't have enough work for me, but they did have a job in the production department coming up, operating the photostat machine. It'd be a full-time job, and I could pick up some freelance. So I said sure, great. I started at $135 a week, which was okay in those days. I worked for about six months doing that, during the period I did the Phantom Eagle with Gary Friedrich for *Marvel Super-Heroes* #16. That was the first pencil and ink job I did.

TJKC: Were you hoping the book would take off?
HERB: In those days, artists weren't really linked with the creative effort as a package the way they are today. It was a very loose arrangement. If a book failed, it wasn't a black mark on any of the creative people. They considered the people that did the books to be competent professionals. If a book failed, they cancelled it and started up another, and you got another assignment. There was no such thing as failure. Roy and Stan might've felt like failures if a book failed, but as far as the creative people go, there was little attachment.

I wanted to draw like Jack Davis; I had a very cartoony adventure style. That was my natural style. When I got to Marvel, that all went out the window. Stan didn't say, "Draw like Kirby," but he was always throwing his storytelling style at me. Everybody had to look toward Kirby in the mid-Sixties.

So I worked in production for six months, and then the Hulk was in *Tales To Astonish.* Marie was doing the Hulk, and when it switched to his own magazine, that was the first regular pencil assignment I got. Basically Stan said, "You want to draw the *Hulk?*" Marie was pretty much exploited, as we all were, I guess. To this day, she's one of the most versatile and talented artists — and I mean *artists,* not just comic book artists — I know. She can do anything. She's just astounding.

So I wound up on the *Hulk.* On that first issue, I did a couple of pages and took them in to show Stan, and he said, "No, no, no, no. Let me get Frank Giacoia in here." I always had very good storytelling ability, but I was used to the EC stuff. I liked Jack Davis, so there was a lot of in-close stuff; the subtle, weird stuff that he does. There wasn't enough slam-bang going on. So Frank laid the story out, and Stan said, "Do it like this. Watch Frank." I penciled over Frank's layouts. Frank laid the story out, and I followed it.

When I started on the *Hulk,* I basically worked there for another six months, and since I wasn't doing production anymore, there really wasn't any need to work in the office. So Stan says, "Why don't you work at home?" From that point I was a salaried quota person.

TJKC: Marie Severin said you were the last person who received direct attention from Stan.
HERB: Yeah, I was. Stan understood the whole philosophy of Marvel,

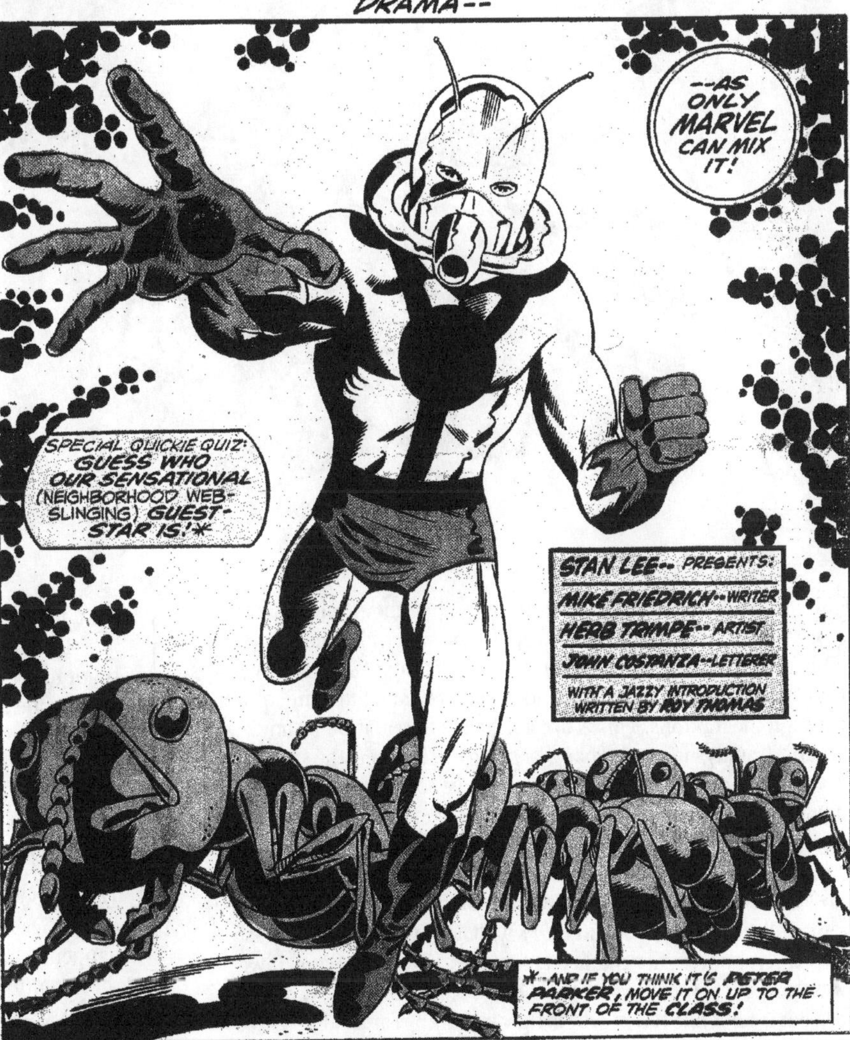

You can really see the Kirby influence on Herb's Ant-Man, from Marvel Feature *#4.*

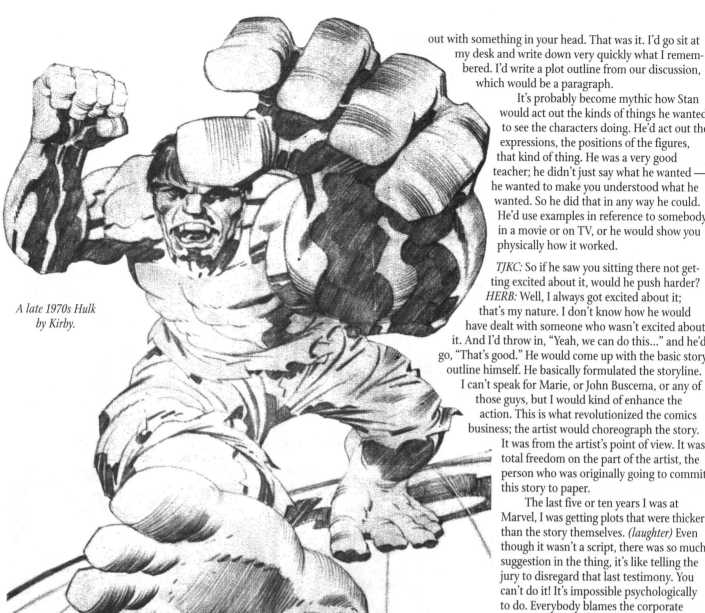

and I think the basis of their success was when they decided not to work from scripts. They would work from a story idea that was ostensibly conceived by the writer and the artist combined. In reality it was basically Stan that did it; you kind of sat there and Stan kind of went through the motions. This is not a negative observation by any means; frankly, he knew what was going on, he knew the storylines from all the other books. He knew what we could use and what we couldn't, so it worked out fine. When an issue would come up, you'd go into the office and go, "Stan, we've got to get together on a story." And he'd say, "Ok." And he'd shut the door, and he always ordered grilled cheese and tomato sandwiches; that's what he ordered every day for lunch. *(laughter)* And he'd say, "Okay, what happened last month? Who were the characters?" and we'd go from there. If we introduced a new character, you'd do it right there. They'd be conceived; it's not like today, where they kick things around for three months, and it's gotta be an executive decision. Things happened very quickly. You'd be in there maybe half an hour, and you'd walk out with something in your head. That was it. I'd go sit at my desk and write down very quickly what I remembered. I'd write a plot outline from our discussion, which would be a paragraph.

It's probably become mythic how Stan would act out the kinds of things he wanted to see the characters doing. He'd act out the expressions, the positions of the figures, that kind of thing. He was a very good teacher; he didn't just say what he wanted — he wanted to make you understood what he wanted. So he did that in any way he could. He'd use examples in reference to somebody in a movie or on TV, or he would show you physically how it worked.

TJKC: So if he saw you sitting there not getting excited about it, would he push harder?

HERB: Well, I always got excited about it; that's my nature. I don't know how he would have dealt with someone who wasn't excited about it. And I'd throw in, "Yeah, we can do this..." and he'd go, "That's good." He would come up with the basic story outline himself. He basically formulated the storyline. I can't speak for Marie, or John Buscema, or any of those guys, but I would kind of enhance the action. This is what revolutionized the comics business; the artist would choreograph the story. It was from the artist's point of view. It was total freedom on the part of the artist, the person who was originally going to commit this story to paper.

The last five or ten years I was at Marvel, I was getting plots that were thicker than the story themselves. *(laughter)* Even though it wasn't a script, there was so much suggestion in the thing, it's like telling the jury to disregard that last testimony. You can't do it! It's impossible psychologically to do. Everybody blames the corporate mentality, they blame Perlman, they blame management. Yes, this is a piece of the pie, no question about it. But I tell you, the editorial levels are just as culpable. Most of these people are not leaders, they're not professionals in the sense of the business. There's no vision; they're basically fans. There were very few people in those editorial positions who could stand up to those people above them and say, "Look, this isn't going to work."

I noticed over the years that the place went to a bunker mentality. It got to the point where, even if you were working there, you couldn't get anyone on the phone, and they wouldn't return calls. Or if they did, it'd be days or weeks, and you had to keep calling. Barry *(Windsor-Smith)* used to call up that place every week, and he told me, "It was a damn answering machine again, and I just cursed for ten minutes into that thing, and I finally got a call back the next day." *(laughter)* You can't run a business like that.

TJKC: Do you think that was connected with Marvel going public?

HERB: Yes I do. Dan Green and I talked to each other the day that happened, and we both sort of looked at each other and said, "This is the beginning of the end." Once the motivation is outside the creative process, you've got a serious problem. You might be able to do that if you're selling soap or cereal, but you can't do it when you're selling comics. The comics, in my opinion, thrive on the ability to not only

A late 1970s Hulk by Kirby.

create spontaneously, but to have the process be extremely flexible, so if one avenue of approach doesn't work, you can immediately back out and try something else. That all changed. My editor on *Fantastic Four Unlimited* told me, "When we come up with an idea, it takes three months to implement it by the time it gets back to us. It's a nightmare." They were all living in fear.

But working with Stan, I came out of the office with this plot, and I was free to pencil 18 or 20 pages exactly the way I wanted. Then you'd finish the job and bring it back, and go in the office again, and you'd go over it page by page, and he'd make corrections. The changes were always very minimal. There were never major, drastic changes. On the work I handed in, the basic storyline was acceptable, and it might be tweaking it up here and there. It was a very pleasant thing to do.

TJKC: How long was it fun doing the *Hulk?* It seems like there were inherent limitations in the character.
HERB: I drew the character for eight years. I was living in England for about a year, and I just got tired of doing it. There were new guys coming in, and a lot of creative stuff going on, and I wanted to get involved in it. I'd done the *Hulk* for a long time, and I thought I was getting stale. Going to conventions and talking to fans about this stuff makes me like the work I did. I never liked the work I did on the *Hulk.* I hated it; from day one I was dissatisfied. It was not the way I saw myself as an artist. How can you match Kirby, with his facile approach, his speed, how he created these massive panels and really tiny spaces? I looked at guys like Al Williamson, and the old EC guys. I hated my stuff.

TJKC: Do you like it now?
HERB: I talked to these fans, and they have given me a new appreciation for that stuff. They have allowed me to look at it in an objective way in terms of style and content that I was never able to do before — and I like it a whole lot better. The downside is, I sold 90% of this stuff about 15 years ago, and I regret that immensely.

TJKC: You worked with some good writers.
HERB: Stan was good. I loved Roy; Roy was good. In later years, I talked to Roy extensively on the phone, especially around the time things were going bad at Marvel, and there was no more work. He called me to see how I was doing. He exhibited a very kind and sensitive approach. Roy to me is an ace guy. He's a comic book freak and a comic book fan from the word 'go.' And the guy's got a heart, and I really appreciated that — and he tried to get me work when I didn't really want it. I finally had to tell him, "I'm outta this. I'm not gonna do it anymore."

Jerry Siegel worked for a brief time as a proofreader at Marvel — the guy who started it all! The thing is, DC was crapping all over him, and he came up to Marvel, and Stan gave him a job. That's all that really was available, and he took it. He was getting into some of the writing, but I'm not sure he really wanted to. He was a very kind man — and if I have any unfinished business, it's that I would have liked to have done a Superman story in the old style. Maybe we're all getting too old. I hate to look back and say, "Everything was the best then." Everything wasn't the best then; there were conflicts, there were problems, there were professionals coming in who couldn't get work. But it was better all around from the creative point of view, in terms of the freedom.

TJKC: Did you see Jack come into the office at all?
HERB: Yes! My wife used to imitate his stance; he'd rock back and forth from one foot to the other with his cigar in his mouth. He had a style. *(laughter)* When he went over to DC, Marie had an old burnt-out cigar of his taped up; she made a little plaque out of it. But the thing I remember about Jack is, he came in one day and we were all talking to him. He came right into the Bullpen and we cleared a desk for him. There was a cover he'd done; I don't remember if it was a *Thor* or *FF* cover. Stan wasn't satisfied with it, and he wanted another cover, and he needed it quick. So Jack came in to pencil it. And we just kind of stood around and BS'ed while he penciled this cover. It was one of those "learning experiences," as they say. *(laughter)* He knocked this thing out in about an hour, and he's talking the whole time, munching on his cigar. And he pencils this cover with all this great dynamic stuff in it. It was great, a real treat.

TJKC: Did you talk to him?
HERB: Oh, yeah, I always talked to him. We were in a very small office then, so when you entered the office,

The Hulk goes to a cocktail party; Trimpe pencils and Severin inks from Hulk *#142.*

Unused Kirby Machine Man *panel. Herb assisted Barry Windsor-Smith on layouts for his* Machine Man *mini-series.*

you came in past the receptionist, and walked down a very narrow corridor, and the Bullpen occupied one side. He walked in, and he came right into where we were. There were only about five or six of us there. It was very familial. It's different now with these large offices. You have to wander around to find people.

TJKC: Did he hang out at all?
HERB: Occasionally he would come in for lunch and things like that. I don't believe he was a 'sticker.' He'd come in, do his business, and go. He was working; the guy was drawing a lot of books.

TJKC: Did you get any sense of the relationship between Jack and Stan when he was in the office?
HERB: I really wasn't privy to what went on when they separated, but they had a great relationship as far as I could tell. I don't know what Marie's take is on it, but my sense was that it was a very good relationship. I never heard how their story conferences went, but it was very good.

TJKC: How did you hear that Jack was leaving?
HERB: I think it just popped up one day. You walk in and somebody says Kirby is leaving, he's going over to DC. There was really no warning as far as I'm concerned.

TJKC: How did the office take it?
HERB: It really had no effect on me; a lot of people were stunned, but life went on. In those days, there was a debate as to whether characters could survive without the creators. In those days, the fan input wasn't as great as it is today. It was a general readership.

I never was "inside the loop." Every generation of artists has its key people, and I never was inside one of those loops. I didn't get involved too much with conventions; I had other interests. I had an airplane for fourteen years. I was raising a family upstate, and I spent a lot of time doing things with my kids. While I worked for Marvel all those years, I did a lot of outside freelance. I did a lot of animation design, storyboarding. Remember the Crest toothpaste campaign with the Cavity Creeps? I did that.

TJKC: What did you think of John Severin's inks on your work?
HERB: I'm an EC fan, y'know? He makes it John Severin. But what can you say? The guy is John Severin! *(laughter)* I was thrilled to have him work on the stuff. I got to talk to him; John's a nice guy. He's like Marie; he's nuts! *(laughter)* He's a big old bear of a guy.

TJKC: Did you ever meet Wally Wood?
HERB: Yeah, Wally was an interesting guy. Flo Steinberg did a one-issue underground called *Big Apple Comics.* I did two stories in it, one of which Wally inked. Wally was at a couple of parties at our apartment. He was very good friends with Flo. We saw him pretty regularly. He was a nice guy; very quiet, a very depressed character. He loved to sing folk songs; he played his guitar at our apartment, and sang in a down-home, simple manner.

TJKC: Did you have any dealings with Bill Everett at all?
HERB: Yes, I loved Bill Everett. Bill Everett was a sweet guy. I called him the last time he was in the hospital, and then a couple of days later he died of cancer. I liked him immensely. Wally was a cynical character, and Bill wasn't.

TJKC: Why did you stop working for Marvel?
HERB: When *FF Unlimited* was cancelled, that was all she wrote. When Tom DeFalco went, I knew it was over. (Tom was a very big booster of mine and he kept me working.) I was terminated via a Federal Express letter. I had tried to call, right up until the time I was canned; I hadn't heard from anybody for a month or two. Then I got a FedEx letter from upstairs saying, "We can't supply the work, your quota's in the hole, blah, blah, blah." Nobody ever called; I haven't heard from anybody since, except for Holly Rondeau in Human Services, bless her heart. Thirty years; nothing.

Luckily though, I had begun my schooling six months prior. I finished my BA in art, and went straight into a Masters program. So I go to school full-time, and I do art for a couple of local companies.

TJKC: You inked Jack on *Silver Surfer* #18.
HERB: You could ink Jack sleeping! *(laughter)* Just put the brush in the ink, and away it goes. Jack is the easiest person in the world to ink, no question about it. I had an excellent brush technique, which nobody has anymore. One of the things we did was a lot of brush inking in those days. It was a very skillful thing; you couldn't just come in with a pen and hack away. Of course, Vinnie *(Colletta)* inked with a pen, and he was criticized in those days because of that sort of noodling style he had, but I liked it; but I also liked the brush style, like Frank Giacoia. John Verpoorten would ink some of Jack's work once in awhile, and the few occasions I got to ink, I loved it. It was just great.

TJKC: Did you learn any lessons from Jack's work?
HERB: Working at Marvel probably destroyed for a long time to come any sort of individual initiative I had. I never felt like I developed a style. I felt like I was always chasing somebody else's style. The only time in the last couple of years where I broke out of that mold was when I was out of a job, and I started to paint around the house, and went out into the fields and did oils and acrylics. I did stuff that was core stuff; it wasn't great, but it was me at least.

What you learn from Kirby is that you'd better develop your self first. Self-development is the most important aspect of life in no matter what you do, whether you're an artist, engineer, or whatever. All in all, it was the best of all possible jobs. I got to work at home, develop with my family, and I worked when I wanted to, setting my own time schedule. What I do regret is that stylistically, I never felt I gave myself enough space to zero in and develop my own style.★

John Buscema Interview

Interviewed by Jon B. Cooke

(John Buscema came to join the Marvel Age of Comics in 1966, first working on Nick Fury *and the* Hulk. *His exceptional artistry is fondly recalled on his repeated* Avengers *runs,* Conan, *the early* Sub-Mariner *issues, and the* Fantastic Four. *His* Silver Surfer *series is considered by some to be the finest super-hero comics ever to appear from the House of Ideas. John was interviewed via telephone on November 18, 1997.)*

THE JACK KIRBY COLLECTOR: Did you read comics as a kid?
JOHN BUSCEMA: Yes, I think I started around age 12. The first comic I ever saw blew my mind; it was *Superman.* By 14 or 15 I stopped reading comics. That was back around 1939-41.

TJKC: Do you remember seeing Kirby's work when you were a kid?
BUSCEMA: No. I probably did, but I saw Kirby's stuff, just a bit of it, when I started working for Marvel back in 1948. I saw one or two pages of pencils that he had done, that were laying around the studio there. I was very impressed with the drawing. It was a different style than he had later — very loose.

John took over Thor *after Jack left Marvel; here are Jack's pencils from* Journey Into Mystery *#112.*

TJKC: Were you an avid reader of comic strips?
BUSCEMA: I was never really interested in the stories, but I was always interested in the drawings. The three artists I followed were Hal Foster, Alex Raymond, and Burne Hogarth. I don't know how many years of Sunday comics pages I saved, but then in 1957, I threw everything away. *(laughter)* I was angry. Comics were in a bad situation. I couldn't buy a job in those days. I'd worked for Marvel, I worked for Western Printing; I don't know how many different outfits. They all folded; it was like a domino effect. I just got ticked off, and all those strips and anything comic related that I'd saved, I threw out. When I think about it, tears well up in my eyes. *(laughter)*

TJKC: Did you have aspirations to be a comics artist?
BUSCEMA: No, I never really wanted to. I wanted to be a painter. But who could make a living at that?

TJKC: How'd you get into comics?
BUSCEMA: Funny, I never got anything making the rounds, until I read a "wanted" ad in the *New York Times.* Timely was looking for cartoonists. That's the first time I met Stan Lee.

TJKC: What was he like?
BUSCEMA: Like he is today, except he had a little more hair, I guess. *(laughter)* He was a very energetic guy, very personable guy. At the time I thought he was a genius, because I knew nothing about comics. He gave me a staff job, my first job in comics. I worked in a large room with a group of artists: Carl Burgos, Syd Shores, Danny DeCarlo, and Gene Colan were there. Bill Everett worked there too, but he wasn't on staff. There were many others, but I can't recall their names.

We worked on the 14th floor of the Empire State Building. They had half the floor, and there were several rooms. I started in 1948 with crime comics, and I graduated into westerns. We bounced around to whatever was popular at the time.

I worked for Timely for about a year and a half, and that's when they put everybody on freelance. The story I heard is that one day, Martin Goodman opened up a closet and found hundreds of pages piled up that had never been published. These were stories that the editors were unhappy with, and they just tossed them into the closet. So Martin Goodman decided, "No more staff, only freelancers." And we all were put on a freelance basis. I loved it; I was working at home, and I started working for other publishers. I was working for so many different publishers at one time, I had guys working for me. I was just roughing it in, and they were doing the tightening and inking.

I always had in the back of my mind that I was going to get out of comics. And after 48 years, I got out. *(laughter)* I never really was happy with comics. I think if I were paid enough that I could turn out a page every two or three days, maybe I would've been happy. But I always pushed, turning out as many pages as I could in a day.

Jack Kirby lived it. He breathed it, it was his life. Everything that he did was comics-related. He was constantly thinking of plots, of characters. I had no interest in comics. The only interest I had was how much I can earn, and how fast I can make it. At one time I averaged three to four pages a day. I knew artists who were always having a financial problem; it's a common thing in this business. You've got to have that discipline to get up in the morning, and turn out 'X' amount of pages a day.

TJKC: How did you first meet Jack?
BUSCEMA: Back in 1965 or 1966, I got a call from Marvel. They wanted me to go back. I'll be honest with you, I was afraid, but it was appealing to me because I wouldn't have to commute. I could work at home. It was a tremendous effort for me to make that decision. But I started working for them in 1966, and I met Jack one day in Stan's office. Stan and I were working on a plot and Jack walked in. As far as meeting Jack, I think I can count the times on one hand; just for short periods. I saw him at the convention out in San Diego; we exchanged a few words, pleasantries, whatever. We drove home together once; he lived on Long Island, and Don Heck drove us home. That's about the extent of it; I didn't have that much contact with Jack. Although I would not have been able to survive in comics if not for Jack Kirby. When Stan called me back in 1966, I had one hell of a time trying to get back in the groove. You can do illustration, you can do layouts, but that doesn't mean you can do comics. It's a whole different ball game. Stan gave me a book to do; I think it was the Hulk. I did a pretty bad job — Stan thought I should study Jack's art and books so he gave me a pile of Kirby's comics. Well, everybody was given Jack Kirby books! *(laughter)* It was the first time I'd seen his work. I started working from them, and that's what saved me.

TJKC: What did you learn from them?
BUSCEMA: The layouts, for cryin' out loud! I copied! Every time I needed a panel, I'd look up at one of his panels and just rearrange it. If you look at some of the early stuff I did — y'know, where Kirby had the explosions with a bunch of guys flying all over the place? I'd swipe them cold! *(laughter)* Stan was happy. The editors were happy, so I was happy.

TJKC: Did you get a step up in pay when you went into comics?
BUSCEMA: It went up, but not that much. What I was wary of was, how long was this going to last? But Stan was very convincing. He said, "John, things are different today. We're making a big comeback. Things are picking up, we're making tremendous strides."

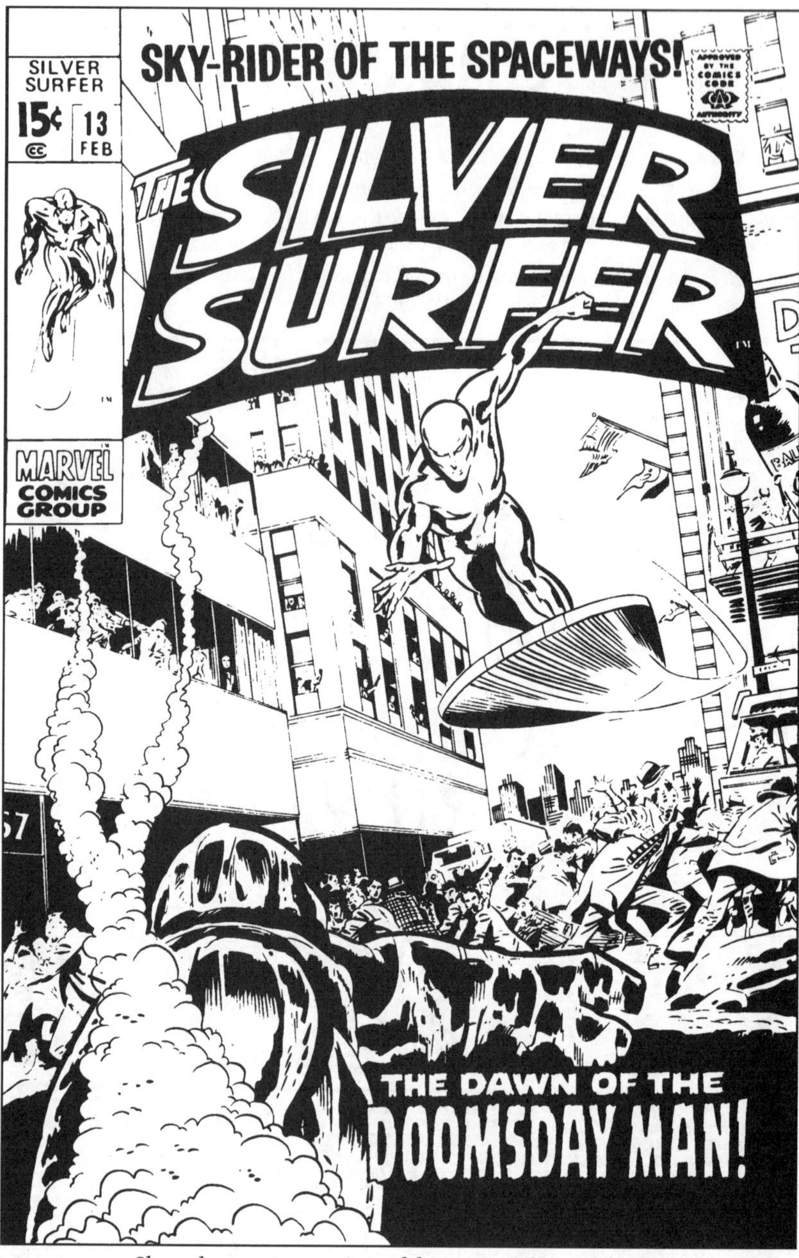

Shown here are two versions of the cover to Silver Surfer *#13.*

TJKC: Did you go into the office every week?
BUSCEMA: The first few books I brought in as I did them. After a few months, I'd go in whenever I felt like it. There were times I'd only go in three or four times a year. I mailed. I very rarely went into the city.

TJKC: Did you ever lose anything in the mail?
BUSCEMA: No, but Don Heck did. He lost a job once in the mail, and at that point he decided he would xerox everything.

TJKC: Were you close to Don?
BUSCEMA: Yes. He lived about fifteen minutes away from me. We were pretty close. I made a lot of friends in this business, but some have died and most have retired and moved away.

TJKC: What kind of story conferences did you have with Stan?
BUSCEMA: At the beginning I'd go in and discuss the story, and we would throw ideas back and forth. When Stan became more confident in my ability to do stories, he'd call me up, or I'd call him up and say, "Stan, I'm ready for a plot. What have you got in mind?" The last time

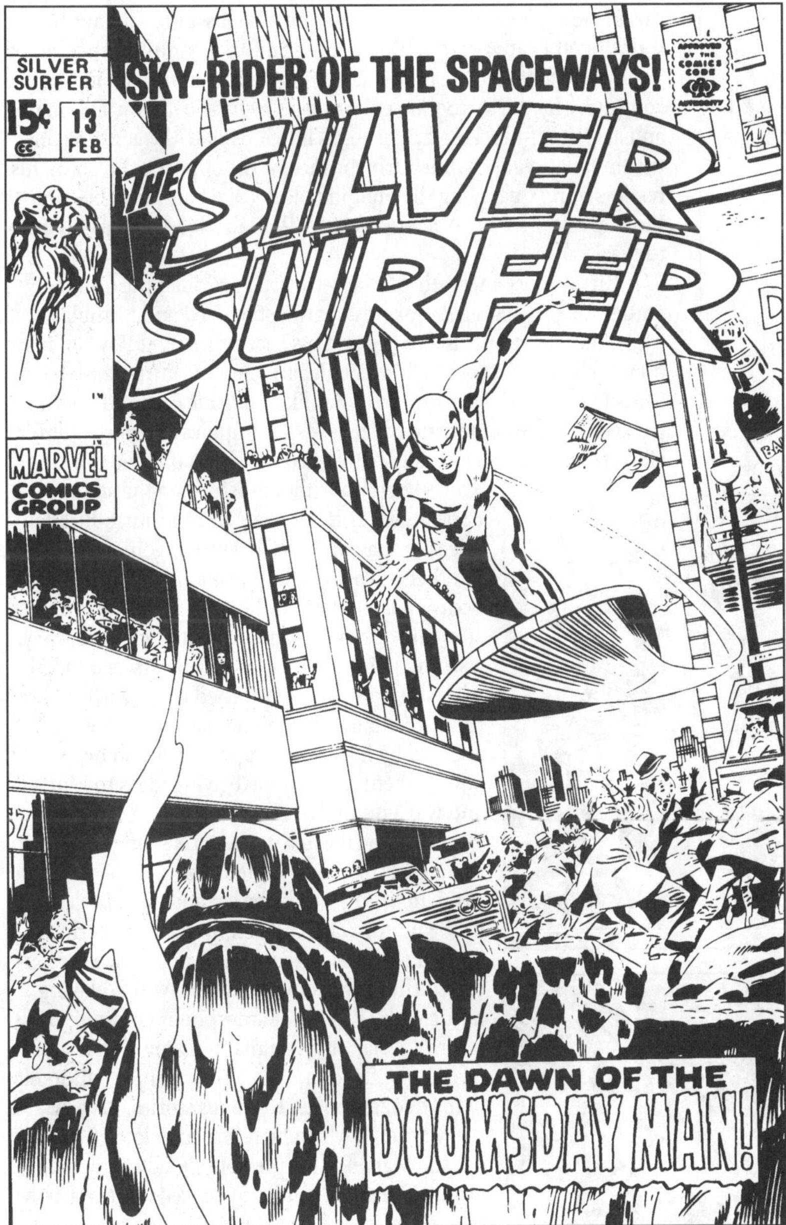

Nitpicking over cover details apparently wasn't enough to help sales on the series.

I worked with Stan was on the *Silver Surfer.* After that I started working with Roy Thomas. I worked with a lot of different writers.

TJKC: I understand there was a problem with *Silver Surfer* #4.
BUSCEMA: Yes. We worked on the plot, Stan and I. I was very, very excited about doing the book. I thought, "This is one job I'm going to get away from the Kirby layouts. I'm going to try something different," which I did. I think it had a different look about it from the previous stuff I'd been doing. People were congratulating me on this particular issue. Stan tore the book to pieces! He started with the first page: "Well, okay, not bad." On and on and on. Every second page he ripped to shreds. "This is not good, this should be done this way..." I walked out of that damn office of his; I didn't know which way was up or down. I was completely demoralized. I walked into John Romita's office; John looked at me and saw that I was very upset. I said, "John, how the hell do you do comics?"

Maybe seven or eight years had gone by; I get a call from Stan one morning. We usually exchanged pleasantries — Stan said something; I think he called me an SOB or something *(laughter)* — and I said, "What's up, Stan? What'd I do wrong?" He said, "John, do you remember that book we worked on, the Silver Surfer and Thor book?" I remembered it very well. "John, that was the greatest thing you've ever done, the greatest comic ever done, the greatest thing you and I ever turned out!" Well, I thought he was pulling my leg, and I didn't say a word.

Stan says, "Johnny, you still there?" I said, "Stan, are you kidding? Are you serious?" He said, "No John, really, seriously." Well, I tried to refresh his memory. He said, "I don't remember ever saying anything like that. I don't remember ever telling you that; the book is beautiful, how could I possibly...?"

Well, I tell this to many, many people. How many guys have been destroyed by an editor — some editor who just happened to get up on the wrong side of the bed, and does this to some guy who's put everything into his job? I know it happened to Don Heck. I remember Don coming to me and saying, "John, help me. I don't know what the hell to do anymore."

TJKC: Did you have to redraw it?
BUSCEMA: No! The book was published. But what happened was, in those days, for some reason the *Silver Surfer* just didn't click. The number one issue sold well, but each succeeding issue lost sales. It just went down, which was probably what was bothering Stan. Many years later, Stan told me at lunch one day, "John, I just didn't know what the hell to do with the damn thing. I didn't know what direction we were going."

TJKC: It's been said that Jack was upset about the *Surfer* series, because he had his own vision of the character.
BUSCEMA: Yes, I could understand Jack's resentment. This was his thing, his idea, his creation — and it's being taken away from him and given to me.

TJKC: Do you think Jack was treated fairly at Marvel?
BUSCEMA: You know the story better than I do. What I know is secondhand. We all know how Jack was treated. They cut his page rate; you know the story?

TJKC: No.
BUSCEMA: This is again something told to me; I don't remember by who. Well, Jack Kirby was very fast. Martin Goodman was upset that Jack Kirby was making so much money. He felt, "Kirby's turning out so much work, let's cut his rate." That's when Jack left Marvel and went over to DC. This is the story that was told to me.

I'll never forget when I walked into Stan's office and heard that Jack left. I thought they were going to close up! *(laughter)* As far as I was concerned, Jack was the backbone of Marvel.

TJKC: Did you have to hustle fast to work on books Jack left behind?
BUSCEMA: I didn't have to work any faster. I was given the *Fantastic Four.* That was very intimidating, following the best! *(laughter)* I worked on *Thor* and *Fantastic Four.*

TJKC: Did you have any favorite inkers?
BUSCEMA: Frank Giacoia. My brother *(Sal)* did a fabulous job. Tom Palmer did some absolutely unbelievable stuff on early *Avengers.* George Klein I was never happy with; he had a very heavy hand.

TJKC: Were you one of your own favorite inkers?
BUSCEMA: Naturally! *(laughter)* I know exactly what I want. But I never inked that much. I would ink occasionally. If you don't keep doing it, you lose it. I think Joe Kubert is the smartest man in the business. He pencils and inks himself, and nobody can do a better job than Joe.

TJKC: What was it like doing *How To Draw Comics The Marvel Way?*
BUSCEMA: That came out of the workshop I had. I had invited Roy Thomas, Gil Kane, and Stan Lee to come up and give a talk. I had about 30 students in my class. Stan was very impressed, and thought that we should do a book together. And we did.★

On Kirby's "Unexpected Constants"

The Problem of Marvel Continuity in The Eternals
by Charles Hatfield

If *continuity* bears a special meaning for readers of corporate super-hero comics, then that meaning dates from the revitalization — indeed, thoroughgoing reinvention — of that genre in the early 1960s.

Granted, the genre first sparked with new life in the late 1950s, under the editorship of National's Julius Schwartz, a former SF fan-editor who boosted super-heroes into the streamlined Age of Sputnik. Yet it took Marvel's Stan Lee and Jack Kirby to stoke these new fires into something like a roaring, four-alarm blaze — the former trumping the already pungent ironies of the genre with his witty and hyperbolic scripting, the latter responding to Lee's editorial oomph with a raft of absurd and splendid creations, all organized into one grand, interactive continuity by the cartoonist-editor pair. Lee provided topical humor and a wry, self-mocking cynicism, as if to inoculate the genre against the threat of reality, while Kirby pushed in the opposite direction, his restless mind quarrying the building blocks of what would become the Marvel Universe — a corporate mythos absolutely insulated from the real.

Kirby, most energetic of Marvel artists, provided the protean matter for this aggregate cosmos, matter-stabilized and formularized by promoter extraordinaire Lee and his successors (first Roy Thomas, then such fan-scripters as Steve Englehart, Gerry Conway, and, later, Chris Claremont). Kirby-driven titles like *Fantastic Four* and *Thor* yielded a surplus of terrific conceits — geographical, cosmographical, allegorical — which virtually reinvented the world inhabited by the Marvel heroes, without disturbing the stable appearance of *status quo.* Concepts introduced in one title spawned arcs — even ongoing series — in other titles. Continuity no longer consisted of occasional cross-promotions and the rare extended story arc; it now became a point of great urgency, a selling point, as the Marvel Universe exploded with story possibilities opened up by Kirby's brainstorming and Lee's management. Yet Kirby, angered by his loss of proprietorship in his creations, eventually stopped giving ideas to Marvel, and walked.

Jack's uninked pencils from Eternals *#4, page 4.*

Between the first moments of Marvel continuity in the early '60s, and the fetishizing of the principle in the mid-'70s, Jack Kirby left and came back again. In the interim at DC, he enjoyed a brief period of limited editorial autonomy, during which he conceived the sadly-aborted Fourth World, playing havoc with DC's as-yet-amorphous continuity. His return to Marvel, presumably, came with a similar promise of freedom: Kirby would enjoy editorship of his books, and get to tell *his* stories, his way. But the Marvel to which he returned in late 1975 was not the Marvel of the previous decade, and, to him, its now-Byzantine continuity proved more restrictive than generative.

Scripters, rather than cartoonists, now held the reins, an ironic reversal of the situation in the early to mid-'60s. Moreover, these scripters had colonized concepts birthed by Kirby a decade before, and invested them with their own meanings, via long, elaborate arcs (e.g., Thomas' Kree/Skrull war in *Avengers,* and Englehart's *Avengers vs. Defenders* crossover). Characters worked up by Kirby had become vehicles for cultural arguments alien to Kirby himself: Englehart had worried the issues of patriotism and duty, post-Vietnam, in *Captain America*; while Don MacGregor, in his Black Panther run (in *Jungle Action*) had spotlighted issues of race and racism blithely ignored by the Panther's creator. The *X-Men,* fallow for years, had just been revived, and were about to become Claremont's vehicle for an elaborate take on xenophobia and prejudice — one hinted at by Kirby & Lee, yes, but brought to the fore by Thomas and crucially underscored by Claremont.

Marvel was now a scripter's world, its continuity anxiously defended by writers both fannish and professional. From its pell-mell origins, the Marvel Universe had grown into stability under the scripter's touch, with the once-radical ideas of yesterday curbing creativity in the now. Continuity, as well as editorial mass, pressured production at Marvel, and the stars of the moment were *writer/editors* as opposed to cartoonists.

Under Thomas and subsequent editors, verbiage had hemmed in the visual; Stan Lee's star was in ascendance, despite his virtual retirement from comic-book making years before. Indeed, Lee had progressed from publisher to icon (*Stan Lee Presents:*), leaving behind a flock of writers determined to work in his name. In this fannish environment, a succession of editors-in-chief sought to give shape to Marvel's still somewhat anarchic enterprise — until Lee's hand-picked *wunderkind,* ex-fan Jim Shooter, succeeded to the chief spot in the late '70s, centralizing editorial power and placing more and more stress on continuity. Yet even before Shooter, continuity and organization went hand in hand, constraining the work and the art.

Of course, some writers had produced spirited work under these constraints — after all, they loved the complexity and depth of the company's universe — but Kirby, brashly imaginative, had never had a taste for the yeoman-like upkeep of continuity, and his new creations at Marvel fit poorly into the very cosmology he had midwifed years ago. Case in point: *The Eternals.* Like the Fourth World before it, *The Eternals* threatened to make a wreck of corporate continuity, and suffered for it.

The Eternals upholds Arthur C. Clarke's dictum that technology, sufficiently advanced, seems like magic. Like Clarke, Kirby took this insight as far as it will go, re-imagining God as a host of technologically advanced extraterrestrials. Updating the premise of the Simon & Kirby five-pager "The Great Stone Face" (*Black Cat Mystic* #59, Sept. 1957), folding in Clarke's *Childhood's End* (1953), and cashing in on the popularity of Erich Von Däniken's archaeological humbug *Chariots of the Gods?* (1968), *The Eternals* not only posits a potentially apocalyptic future — a Last Judgment, if you will — but also rewrites the past in one fell swoop: Humankind, we are told, is but one of three related hominid species created by the godlike Celestials. Beneath the sea lie the Deviants, genetically unstable upstarts driven into hiding by the gods as payment for their world-conquering hubris; while above the clouds, and hiding among us, are the graceful, immortal beings known as the Eternals, friends and protectors of humanity. Though Kirby's original working title, *The Return of the Gods,* was nixed in favor of *The Eternals* (due to editorial caution?), the series' premise in fact unites all three species in their hour of judgment, going *New Gods* one better in apocalyptic urgency. (For fuller treatment of this premise, see my essay in *TJKC* #15.)

The Eternals, then, offered (to quote "The Great Stone Face") "something so important that all the history books would have to be rewritten." This re-visioning of history, predictably, threw a wrench into Marvel continuity, already brim-full with gods, demigods, secret histories, and hermetic lore. Indeed, the matter of whether to slot *Eternals* into Marvel continuity — and if so, how — spawned a debate within the very letter column of the book, a development which Kirby could hardly have foreseen and to which he could not adapt. In the "Eternal Utterings" column of issue #3 (Sept. 1976), fan and soon-to-be Marvel staffer Ralph Macchio uncorked the issue with a letter at once eloquent and puzzling, addressed to "Jack" but in fact talking of Kirby in the third person (an inconsistency typical of the fan letter genre; after all, these things are addressed as much to editors and other readers as to any creative presence). While praising *Eternals* as "a new excursion into myth" and a "perfect vehicle for exploration" of the great ontological issues, Macchio urges (not Kirby, presumably, but the editors) to "keep the world of the Eternals separate from the Marvel Universe, and let each evolve separately."

Macchio's reasoning is threefold: Kirby's cosmology threatens to "contradict already established laws of the Marvel Universe"; Kirby's answers to the big questions posit "unexpected constants" which will not allow other writers "sufficient latitude in storytelling"; and, conversely, the Marvel mythos will not allow Kirby to flex his imagination "to the fullest extent." In sum, the collision of Kirby's vision with Marvel's long-tended mythos will sacrifice both *continuity* and *verisimilitude,* two goals which, Macchio argues, "make Marvel Marvel"; while avoiding such a smash-up will liberate Kirby editorially. Thus, it's "imperative" to separate the two.

Eternals *#4, page 7.*

As an eleven-year-old Kirby devotee with only a patchy knowledge of Marvel continuity, I could hardly follow Macchio's reasoning — much less share his anxiety — in 1976. Nor did I even notice when, in the time between issues #3 and #7, Macchio (called Marvel's "correspondent from Cresskill, NJ" in #3) arrived at the company as a professional, where he has promulgated Marvel continuity ever since. Indeed, to this reader letter columns were some far-away, exclusive province, populated by readers aloof to my concerns, caught up in their own obscure worries. It would be years before I sought entry to such a space.

But credit Macchio with a degree of prescience. If his argument struck me, and still strikes me, as irrelevant to my enjoyment, it does recognize, to a degree possible only to the most devout fans in the mid-'70s, the pressures of "continuity," pressures all the more evident in the wake of such corporate crossover "events" as *Crisis on Infinite Earths, Zero Hour,* and *Heroes Return.* Macchio must surely have been at the vanguard of fandom based on continuity; like the late Mark Gruenwald, co-founder of the continuity-driven 'zine *Omniverse,* Macchio represents the influx of *continuity fans* into the comic book's editorial sphere.

And he was right; bracketing off *The Eternals* from the Marvel Universe would have served Kirby, and the series, better.

Macchio was not alone in his concerns. Indeed, the very same issue contains a letter from Dennis Millard of Southington, CT who dubs *Eternals* a "new classic," yet hopes that "the Eternals stay in their own universe and away from the other Marvel heroes." While the unnamed lettercol host doubts that "our newly-revealed race of Eternals will contradict any of the already established Marvel Universe" — a claim which had already been proved wrong by #3 — he does invite other comments on the issue from "Marveldom Assembled." In fact many letters in subsequent issues continue to pick at this topic, building on and responding to Macchio's initial points.

One letter in issue #4 raises the issue, very briefly, while in #5 two correspondents assume, and indeed hope, that *Eternals* will join Marvel continuity — the opposite of Macchio's view. (Yet one of these, Kurt Cruppenink of Westville, IL, worries that Kirby's stories may not mesh with "the more realistic Marvel Universe"!) In #7 the floodgates open, as Marveldom Assembled takes the editorial bait in #3: Seven letters weigh in on the continuity problem — three in favor of Macchio's suggestion that *Eternals* take place in a parallel "dimension," three against, and one undecided.

Jana Hollingsworth of Port Angeles, WA nicely distills the pro-Macchio argument: "It would hurt both "continuities" if either Kirby had to curtail his mythologizing, or the rest of the Marvel Universe had to warp itself around Kirby's mythos." Curiously, the opposite camp — in favor of folding *Eternals* into the Marvel Universe — also grounds its arguments in the conservation of continuity; "alternate worlds," they say, are too messy and confusing. As Ryan Hollerback of St. Genevieve, MO complains, this solution "smacks too much of what DC did to their characters...." On either side, no one seems to consider the possibility that *Eternals* might be wholly *unrelated* to the Marvel cosmology.

Paul Carlsen, of Stamford, CT finally realizes this possibility in #9, as he urges the editors "to keep the Eternals off in a world of their own — the real Earth, not another dimension." Other letters in #8-10 try to reconcile Kirby's world with Marvel's, though one reader demurs in #10 (a little too late). In #11, Scott (here misnamed Sam) Taylor of Portland, TX expresses dismay that *Eternals,* "the best thing (Kirby's) ever done in comics," has apparently been jammed into Marvel's already overcrowded "mess." Mike W. Barr (another fan destined to turn pro) advises Marvel to simply let Kirby "have a totally free reign,"*[sic]* with no thought to "inconsistencies" or "contradictions."

Dennis Mallonee (another pro-to-be) sounds the clarion of consistency in #12, calling the inclusion of *Eternals* in Marvel continuity a "mistake." Other posts in #11-12 continue to fret over the issue, though by this time only the pro-Macchio position is voiced, the other viewpoint having been satisfied, presumably, by tentative nods to Marvel continuity in #6-7 (of which, more below). The anonymous host attempts to "officially" ring the debate to a close in #14, but the problem resurfaces in #16, and, inevitably, in #18, as baffled and disappointed readers respond to #14's failed crossover, "Ikaris and the Cosmic-Powered

Eternals *#4, page 16.*

Hulk." At this point Kirby seizes the reins of the lettercol, inviting mail directly to his PO Box in California — a sign of increasing tension between the artist and Marvel's NY-based editorial establishment.

No matter. Only one issue of the series remained.

Here, in the letter column of *Eternals,* a principle already erected in super-hero fandom tardily enters the editorial discourse of the comics themselves: Continuity becomes comics' first, most important principle. This debate over *Eternals* was not a matter of grubbing for no-prizes, or nitpicking minor editorial gaffes, but rather of negotiating different visions of a universe, competing visions — a conflict invested with a religiosity which, depending on your perspective, is either laughably inappropriate or strangely fascinating. In the end, the anonymous editorial vision prevailed: *Eternals* was part of the Marvel Universe — never mind the contradictions.

Not-so subtle hints of continuity troubles hit, as shown here from Eternals *#6 (top) and #7 (bottom).*

Perhaps Kirby wanted it this way, or did not understand just how snugly the straitjacket would fit? In any case, the loser in this instance was Kirby's vision of the series — his greatest conception after the Fourth World.

Marvel continuity exerts an increasing, distorting force on *Eternals* as the series progresses. Issue #6 tosses off a gag about the FF's Ben Grimm, though it's not clear whether *this* Grimm is regarded as a real or fictional character. Moreover, issues #6-7 refer pointlessly to Marvel's SHIELD, as three secret agents come face-to-face with Kirby's Celestials; their identification as "Nick Fury's men" seems gratuitous, and one is left to wonder whether Kirby came up with or simply acceded to this idea. Worse yet, issues #14-16 sidestep the series' apocalyptic premise entirely, offering the aforementioned crossover with the Hulk, an aimless, ambiguous concession which serves neither Kirby's creations nor the high-profile guest star (who is an android Hulk, as it turns out, not even the genuine article). This crossover effectively scuttles the larger storyline, yet does not satisfactorily answer the question of whether *Eternals* is actually canonical, in the Marvel sense. With this episode, the series self-destructed (though it limped along for three more issues).

The "Hulk" story trashes Kirby's own continuity in such a way as to confirm Marvel's intellectual ownership of the property but not to actually make sense. Though Kirby winks satirically at Marvel fans in one sequence (#15), in which a crowd of onlookers wonder whether other super-heroes will arrive to fight the ersatz Hulk, this mild raspberry does little to redeem a thoroughly expendable, and crucially mis-timed, story arc. By the last two issues of *The Eternals,* a hollowing out has taken place, much like the loss of depth evident in the last handful of *Mister Miracles* — after DC had pulled the plug on *Mister Miracle*'s *raison d'être,* the overarching Fourth World storyline. The collapse is perhaps less noticeable than in that abortive experiment, since here Kirby is limited to one title, but the dropoff in energy and inspiration is nonetheless comparable, and just as disheartening. By the end of the series, *The Eternals* has been evacuated of almost all of its grandeur and terror.

Note that the phrase *has been evacuated of* does not assign agency; it is a passive construction — the kind of phrasing endemic to bureaucratic life, as it denies agency and makes everything a matter of vast, impersonal forces which no one person can contravene. I try to avoid such mystifying phrases, but in this instance I cannot, because I do not know quite *why* Kirby attempted to bridge the gap between his mythos and Marvel's. That is to say, I don't know *who* was involved. From whence did the pressure come? Kirby devotees have spoken of editorial gerrymandering in the letter columns, of staffers who conspired to fill Kirby's mid-'70s Marvel titles with a disproportionate, misleading load of fan criticism, of an editorial imperative to rein in Kirby's expansive vision. Why this should have happened, if indeed it did, is beyond me — a matter of loose conjecture at best.

As ever, I'm tempted to cite editorial mediation or interference, of a sort which compromised Kirby's nominally free, West Coast-based editorship of his own work. Yet it seems clear that the ambivalent reception of Kirby's mid-'70s work, both among readers and among pros, had as much to do with the centripetal force of continuity as it did with any shadowy aspects of Marvel's editorial culture. One need not envision a conspiracy to understand why Kirby's free-wheeling talent ill-suited the Marvel of the mid-'70s; the conservation of continuity increasingly defined both fan taste and the editorial environments into which fandom led. Kirby had supplied so much raw material to Marvel in the 1960s that he had virtually crowded himself out of his own neighborhood, leaving behind a flock of preservationists who, confronted by his return in the mid-decade, worried that his newest plans might call for nothing less than the wrecking ball.

The history of *The Eternals* post-Kirby has been one of creeping revisionism, with scattered guest shots and a twelve-part series (1985) leading to the thorough absorption of Kirby's Celestials, Deviants, and Eternals into the Marvel world-scheme. Prerequisite to such absorption, of course, was their diminution. All of these later stories, even the well-intentioned, Peter Gillis-scripted series,give the impression of someone batting cleanup, trying to make the most of a mess. A long run in *Thor,* climaxing with issues #300-301 (Oct./Nov. 1980, scripted by Gruenwald), effectively put the apocalyptic claims of Kirby's original to rest — it's an earnest but numbing example of continuity-splicing, reducing the awesome to the mundane through relentless exposure. Dutiful but dull, such episodes hardly seem worth the cataloging.

We await further research to show us, from the inside, just what the editorial interface between Kirby and Marvel was like in 1976. Until then, we have a splendid series, *The Eternals,* compromised by bad choices that apparently reflect both editorial pressure and Kirby's unwillingness or inability to engage with Marvel continuity on a more substantive level. In *Eternals,* as in *Captain America* and *Black Panther,* Kirby discovered that, in truth, you can't go home again — even if you built it.

(Thanks to Jon Cooke for loaners, and to Garrie Burr and Pat Hilger for leads that haven't been followed as far as they should — yet. And thanks, as ever, to John Morrow for patience!)★

In Gods We Trust

by Robert L. Bryant Jr.

Things finally came to a head in the letter column of *Eternals* #6. A fan had taken offense to the storyline and philosophy of Jack Kirby's newest cosmic opus for Marvel, and the House of Ideas laid down the law on this poor soul from Warwick, Rhode Island: "*Eternals* is not about theology, but rather... about mythology! ...It is not the Bullpen's intent to get embroiled in theological debate — everyone's entitled to his/her own beliefs, right?"

Heavy stuff indeed for something sold in a rotating metal rack at the Piggly Wiggly in 1976.

The Eternals is mostly remembered as little more than a footnote to Kirby's second stint at Marvel; another short-lived creation, another trip to the well of cosmic mythology he exploited more skillfully at DC with the Fourth World series — but conceptually, "Eternals" ranks as the King's most daring work ever. In the series, Kirby posits "three divergent species of man":

- Plain old homo sapiens, or regular folks.
- Eternals, immortal humans who were the basis for ancient gods and even Incan deities.
- Deviants, mutated humans who became the root of our legends of devils and demons.

No aliens here, despite appearances; these are all long-lost brothers, born of the same world as you and I and Captain Kangaroo — and this is only the foreground.

The background is the arrival of the *real* gods — giant, silent aliens who have visited Earth before to do good or ill, screaming in for landings at the same ancient spaceports Erich von Däniken depicted in *Chariots of the Gods?* Only in this case, they fly neato, energy-crackling, big-shadow-casting Kirby starships. "They planted intelligent life on this planet," an Eternal muses. "The crop has matured. The Celestials will test it and weigh its value!"

Cover pencils to Eternals *#4.*
(above) Jack's original drawing of Ikaris.

What's remarkable about *The Eternals* is its strong atheistic overtones — common enough in science fiction, but damned rare in 1970s comics. It was not the Christian God who created mankind and washed it away with the flood; it was the space gods. It was not a heaven-sent seagull that led Noah's Ark to safety; it was Ikaris the Eternal. "I suppose those humans mistook me for some kind of bird," he confesses.

The Deviants' straw boss, Kro, remakes his Silly Putty cellular structure in the image of Satan to play on human fears and superstitions: "To this very day, this image lingers like a virus in their brains! Give the humans a real devil and they'll destroy the galaxy to be rid of him!" (Which leads to the single best line of dialogue in any Kirby comic, as a helmeted cop takes aim at Kro's Deviant army: "You can't reason with space devils, Inspector! Just back off so we can blast 'em!")

All this, of course, owes something to Hammer Studios' *Five Million Years to Earth* and Arthur Clarke's *Childhood's End* ("scientific" explanations for devils), as well as von Däniken's speculations and Kirby's own *New Gods.* And there's a certain tiredness here, as if Kirby knew he'd milked this cow once too often.

The standout characters are not the Eternals, but the supporting players, like Karkas, the Deviant monster whose raw-hamburger body is topped off with a buzz saw mouth and a poet's mind (Kirby didn't draw the Thing for a decade without learning some lessons about ugly being only skin deep), and the Deviants' bloated master, Great Tode, lolling in his mutant-filled chambers, may have provided George Lucas a template for Jabba the Hutt in 1983's *Return of the Jedi.*

Ultimately, what sticks in your mind about the series is the gleeful way Kro and his army dress up in "devil" attire to wage war against their brothers — us. "The devil remains your fear," Kro exclaims, "and my weapon!" Would Kirby disagree?★

THE MONARCH OF WAKANDA

Why Black Panther *is my favorite Kirby Marvel series of the 1970s*
by Alejandro Martinez

When Kirby returned to Marvel in the mid-Seventies, the fans welcomed the idea enthusiastically, but I had my reservations. Would the King's work have the same magic that it had in the '60s? I was afraid I'd be disappointed, but even so, I avidly followed his new creations, and I must admit that Kirby's new work disappointed me a little. *The Eternals* had great potential, and they were without doubt very interesting characters, but the development of the adventures was inadequate, and the close of the series left many questions open. *Machine Man* and *2001* gave me the same impression. The ideas were excellent and the characters were original and full of force, but the plots didn't seem to have a clear destination. I disliked *Captain America* on principle. After Steve Englehart's wonderful run on the series, the new adventures by Kirby seemed out of place, though I must recognize that *Captain America's Bicentennial Battles* was a stupendous adventure that compensated me in part.

In spite of this, I maintained my faith in Kirby. I was secure in the belief that the characters the King was creating would become an important part of the Marvel Universe, as it would be demonstrated afterwards. But I was still searching for work of Kirby that I really liked as a whole, and I found it in *Black Panther.* The work of Don MacGregor with the character had been excellent, but Kirby, as opposed to his *Captain America* series, understood how to change the character's style perfectly.

Kirby ignored the storylines that MacGregor created. Wakanda would be free of the threat of civil war, and T'Challa would abandon his struggle against racism for the moment. The King would bring us pure and dynamic adventure, and I was fascinated immediately. Without forgetting that he is the monarch of his land, with all that it entails, T'Challa took part in adventures that even Indiana Jones would envy. In the first issue, characters like Mister Little and Princess Zanda create a saga around the mysterious King Solomon's Frog, which turned out to be a time machine that was responsible for the legend of Alladin's Genie and the Loch Ness Monster. Kirby knew how to involve us in a delicious and imaginative adventure that finishes with the arrival of a grotesque and dangerous being from the future. The action didn't stop with the first issue; the following ones continued in the same way with the introduction of more characters like the rest of the royal family of Wakanda, Kiber the Cruel, and other important concepts like the mountain of Vibranium, almost forgotten in the Marvel Universe in those days.

Unlike other Kirby series from that period, I held my breath while reading *Black Panther,* and I could hardly wait for the next issue. In this series, the King set aside large concepts and long cosmic sagas that never seemed to end. Here the characters and the situations were presented and the adventure immediately carried out. In a few issues, when one adventure finished, another started. The plots were simple — nothing cosmic or magnificent — but very entertaining.

Unfortunately this change arrived too late. In spite of the quality of the series, one of the last that he did for Marvel, Kirby left the company, leaving me with a real feeling of sadness. I was convinced that the King had finally found his way at Marvel, but the sales and office politics at Marvel put an end to my hopes.

Over the years the Eternals have been converted into one of the most important groups of characters of the Marvel Universe, and Machine Man has had excellent adventures. Of course, Black Panther has experienced a number of exciting sagas, but those adventures never had the freshness and the epic action that Kirby brought us in the Seventies. However unlikely it seems, I really miss Mister Little and his deceiving King Solomon's Frog.★

Jack drew this Black Panther drawing for the 1977 All-American Comic Convention.

A Talk With Artist-Writer-Editor Jack Kirby

Interviewed by Bruce Hamilton, and originally published in Rocket's Blast ComiCollector *#81*

(Editor's Note: This interview was conducted shortly after Jack left Marvel in 1970 to realize his Fourth World series at DC.)

BRUCE HAMILTON: Do you care to discuss your main reasons for switching to DC?
JACK KIRBY: I don't mind at all. I can only say that DC gave me my own editing affairs, and if I have an idea I can take credit for it. I don't have the feeling of repression that I had at Marvel. I don't say I wasn't comfortable at Marvel, but it had its frustrating moments and there was nothing I could do about it. When I got the opportunity to transfer to DC, I took it. At DC I'm given the privilege of being associated with my own ideas. If I did come up with an idea at Marvel, they'd take it away from me and I lost all association with it. I was never given credit for the writing which I did. Most of the writing at Marvel is done by the artist from the script.

BRUCE: Was the concept of the Fantastic Four your idea or Stan Lee's?
JACK: It was my idea. It was my idea to do it the way it was; my idea to develop it the way it was. I'm not saying that Stan had nothing to do with it. Of course he did. We talked things out. As things went on, I began to work at home and I no longer came up to the office. I developed all the stuff at home and just sent it in. I had to come up with new ideas to help the strip sell. I was faced with the frustration of having to come up with new ideas and then having them taken from me. So, I was kind of caught in a box and I had to get out of that box, and when DC came along and gave me the opportunity to do it, I took it. I believe working for DC can lead to other experimentation and a better kind of comic book, and the kind of comic book that could lead to all sorts of different things.

BRUCE: What do you feel is your single greatest creation in 30 years of working in comics?
JACK: Well, there's no doubt that Captain America became some kind of an institution with some kind of a legendary status. I accept that as probably the big one.

BRUCE: Is it true that some of the things signed by Simon & Kirby actually contained work by other people?
JACK: Yes. We had, for instance, Eddie Herron, the man who created Captain Marvel. He was an editor for Fawcett who later became a writer for DC. He also created the Red Skull, which I used in an early *Captain America*. Compared to Captain Marvel, that became his biggest hit. In fact, the Red Skull stands out as a kind of an all-time villain. He proved to be a great character — but I didn't create him. And I used him to good effect. We had things like that from time to time.

BRUCE: There's been a continuing controversy whether you or Beck drew *Captain Marvel* #1 and who drew the *Special Edition* that came out before that. Did you do either one?
JACK: I did the *Special*. I originated the costume and all that business. I did that for Eddie Herron.

BRUCE: Let's talk about the future. Is it true that Superman is really from New Genesis?
JACK: No, it's not. The people from New Genesis are not the kind of people who are made into persons of Superman's class, although they are super-beings in their own right. They don't stem from that kind of an origin.

BRUCE: John Clark of Phoenix came up with the idea the other day that maybe Superman was really the son of Highfather and that he'd been kidnapped by Darkseid and injected with a false memory of his origin. We thought it was interesting speculation.
JACK: There is a concept in the strip that the true son of Highfather is going to be brought out, but it's not Superman.

BRUCE: In your many years of collaboration with Joe Simon, we were wondering who usually wrote, who penciled, and who inked? Or did it sometimes vary?
JACK: Joe Simon is a very very competent man and he is quite capable of doing all those things, but I wrote them and I penciled them... and *(laughing)* I inked them half the time! It was a lot of fun doing them, though.

BRUCE: Is he still active in comics?
JACK: I don't know what Joe is doing. I haven't seen or talked to Joe in about five years.

BRUCE: You were quoted in an interview six or seven years ago as saying you didn't think the Alley Awards for the Best Artist were given to enough people. Would you care to comment on that?
JACK: Yes. I believe the Alley Awards were sewed up among a few people and were handled in a sort of clique fashion. In other words, they were dominated by one group, which gave it to one group. It became a kind of an overall self-promotional, which I thought was wrong. I feel that the people who handed out the Alley Awards stayed within their own likes and dislikes. They didn't give enough study to the other artists in the field who were doing pretty competent work for other books. This was because of the clique situation.

BRUCE: Are you familiar with this new publisher Skywald? Do you know the story behind some of the old comics they're reprinting?
JACK: Well, it's probably a simple story. I don't know the story behind it, but I've done the same thing in the past myself. Purchasing old artwork cuts down on costs. I see they got hold of some of my old *Bullseyes*. I don't know how they did that, but I'm quite sure they bought it legitimately; but I don't know from whom.

1970s Cap drawing.

BRUCE: Do you feel comics are here to stay in their present form?
JACK: No, they're not. I feel that they're going to change. I feel there's being a lot of experimentation in that respect. I feel the change will

come. I can't say what the format will be or what the books will look like, but I think it's going to have to change. I call for it to change.

BRUCE: Do you think there's any way a magazine format that takes comics out of their own bins and puts them with adult magazines will keep the kid audience?
JACK: It all depends on what kind of a book you put out. You can't keep a kid audience with an adult book. That's the way I feel about it.

BRUCE: What do you feel about the Code? Do you think the Code is here to stay?
JACK: Yes, I think the Code is here to stay. I think the Code is very valuable. I think you can operate outside the Code, but if you operate within it you should adhere to its regulations.

BRUCE: Marvel has made one attempt recently to operate outside the Code. Do you think that was a mistake? Do you think it will hurt the industry?
JACK: Yes, I think it could hurt the industry, and I think it was a mistake. I think these comics are vulnerable to all the people who make a point of knocking comics, like the people who've done it in the past who've had an ax to grind, or someone with a book to write. Comics have been a victim of that sort of thing. I feel the Code is its own protection, and tampering with it is very foolish in that respect. I would never do it.

BRUCE: Do you feel the prospects are optimistic for the future, and if there is any reason for alarm, what could be done to revitalize the industry?
JACK: I think it's in need of revitalization. The industry is... just there. In other words, it's just like the movies or any other media; it's just there... and it's going to take competent people to make it big or keep it small. I think it's up to the people who handle the industry. It's available to everybody, and I look forward to people maybe coming in and doing things for them that I haven't seen done before and taking it in several directions. I don't know...

Pencils from Black Panther *#9, page 2.*

BRUCE: What do you feel we the fans can do to help?
JACK: I think the fans, whether they're movie buffs or science fiction buffs or whether they are comic buffs, should make their likes and dislikes known. I think they should stick with the industry and point out things people close to the trade can't see. I think that's where the fans are valuable. I appreciate the fans in that respect and that they are really loyal. They should correspond as to their likes and dislikes now and what they'd like to see in the future. They're our barometer. And I think they should always remain that way.

BRUCE: Do you think the rapid increase in comic conventions around the country is helping?
JACK: Yes. I think conventions are fine. I feel that they haven't been done well, but that if they are, they could be quite a force. I think they could be a great cultural force, if they're managed right. So far, I haven't seen any proper coordination. I've seen good intensive planning, but somehow I feel that the most hasn't been made out of conventions. I think they can be run much better than they are.

BRUCE: What would you suggest to correct this fumbling?
JACK: I think the intents haven't been made public. I don't look at it as fumbling. I look at it just as inexperience and doing something new. I think as conventions continue and experience is gained, they're going to improve greatly, to a point where they can really be enjoyed by a large amount of people. I feel that experience is going to do the trick and this thing about conventions is really going to blossom. I would welcome *any* conventions and bigger and better ones.★

Why Marvel Should Credit Kirby

by Adam McGovern

It surprises me to think that either Marvel in general, or Stan Lee in particular, might believe they'd be giving anything up by belatedly granting Jack Kirby co-credit for the creation of the Marvel Universe and many of its classic stories. Instead, to do so would help secure Marvel's — and Lee's — place in history, and restore their status on the cutting edge.

Nobody can begrudge Lee his guiding managerial vision. He was the Marvel Revolution's entrepreneurial engine. In this postmodern era, the concept of artist as overseer is gaining acceptance, and rightfully so. (It's not just for reasons of rank that hip-hop artists, whose innovative work largely recontextualizes that of others, call themselves "MC"s.)

By no means is this to say that Lee was nothing but the boss. His witty narration and dialogue set a new and enduring standard for pop culture, and his irreverence was just as much a part of Marvel's soul as Kirby's heroics were — but he was every bit a *collaborator,* as was Kirby.

One of Marvel's major contributions was to make strict distinctions like "writer" and "artist" obsolete. The credits boxes which read simply "By Stan Lee and Jack Kirby" were closer to the truth, and to the increasingly communal and cross-disciplinary nature of American arts in the late 20th and early 21st centuries. Marvel innovated a creative synergy whose importance to popular culture is completely obscured if all parties aren't simultaneously given recognition.

As time goes by and people pass on, old rivalries become more meaningless (as I hear they have for Lee and the Kirby family), and accurate history becomes more important a legacy. It was probably Lee himself who gave "The King" his title. Give it back its full meaning, and everybody wins.★

Jack and Roz Kirby at home in the 1980s.

Will Jack Be Credited On The Silver Surfer Series?

by John Morrow

There's no question Jack Kirby single-handedly created the Silver Surfer. Stan Lee's gone on record saying as much (this issue's panel is one of many times he's said so). So why is there any question as to whether Jack will be credited as creator (or even co-creator) on the new *Silver Surfer* animated series, scheduled to air in January?

Some might think it has to do with finances. Marvel Comics recently filed for federal bankruptcy protection, and is currently trying to reorganize. A Marvel press release stated that creator royalties owed for projects created prior to the bankruptcy have continued to be paid, but it's questionable whether royalty payments will continue. But we're not talking about any sort of payment here, just a simple name in the show's credits. Any talk about payments (or lack thereof) is just a smokescreen.

Others insist that it would open Marvel up to a lawsuit by the Kirby estate for ownership of the character. But the precedent was set years ago at DC, first with Siegel and Shuster getting credit on Superman, and now with Jack getting credit on his creations like the New Gods. After years of DC giving Jack a credit line, no one's ever sued them. Roz Kirby tells me she has no desire to sue Marvel, and I believe her. She just wants — finally — for Jack to get a little bit of credit for his creation.

The folks I've talked to at the animation studio are big fans of Jack (and Stan), and are all for giving Jack a credit line. They've even based the character designs and the look of the animation on Jack's drawing style (something else he should get a credit line for), but they tell me the final decision is in Marvel's hands.

So the only thing stopping Marvel from crediting Jack on the *Surfer* series is Marvel. Someone there — be it Joseph Calamari, or Stan Lee, or someone else — has the power to make that decision and do what's right.

I for one am anxiously awaiting the airing of the first episode of the *Silver Surfer* animated series early in 1998, but regardless of the quality of the animation or stories, it's the credits I'm waiting to see; and if the name 'Jack Kirby' isn't to be found somewhere in the first episode, you can bet I'll find something better to do than watch any future ones.

I urge all of *TJKC*'s readers to do the same.★

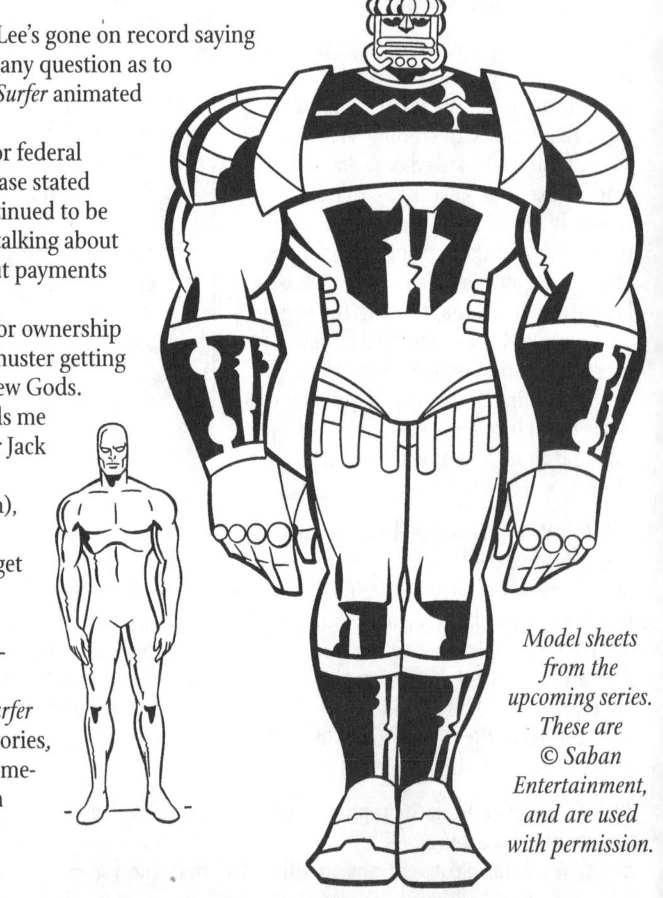

Model sheets from the upcoming series. These are © Saban Entertainment, and are used with permission.

COLLECTOR COMMENTS

Send letters to: The Jack Kirby Collector
c/o TwoMorrows • 1812 Park Drive
Raleigh, NC 27605 or E-mail to: twomorrow@aol.com

(Let's get started with a letter I felt was particularly appropriate to run in this issue:)

To say you are doing a FANTASTIC job is an INCREDIBLE understatement. Simply AMAZING how you keep us in SUSPENSE month after month awaiting each ASTONISHING issue. Thanks for being DAREDEVIL enough to provide us with a bi-monthly JOURNEY into the realm of Kirby X-travaganzas!

David Robbins, Rogue River, OR

Y'know, TJKC #17 took me two days to read—almost as long as it takes me to digest a new COMICS JOURNAL! A very rich, very filling issue, as befits Kirby's DC work. Love that centerspread, both covers, and, again, Jon Cooke's outstanding research and interview contributions.

I agree with Adam McGovern that the link between Asgard and the Fourth World has been over-emphasized. The mythologies are quite distinct, and, yes, NEW GODS boasts a much more Biblical/Hebraic feel, in contrast to the Norse connections of THOR.

On a similar note, John Modica's suggested link between OMAC and KAMANDI seems tenuous at best; I suspect that, in Kirby's mind, the two series were unconnected. If the aforementioned THOR / NEW GODS link is justified by both internal and external evidence, the OMAC / KAMANDI link strikes me as wholly speculative, and heedless of the huge differences in tone and subtext between the two series. Whereas KAMANDI posits a world of chaos and endless variety, OMAC assumes a world of chilly order, a dystopia in which variety has been replaced by sameness and anonymity.

Of course, one could be viewed as chronological sequel to the other, but why? These are distinct visions, and I don't think Kirby intended to splice them together. The idea that they must be connected seems to stem from the recognition that both series are, in a legal sense, DC's intellectual property. Okay, but what has that to do with Kirby?

The OMAC / KAMANDI connection reflects DC's position in the late '70s, not Kirby's design. After Gerry Conway's arrival at DC in the early mid-70s, and their resultant attempt to bring a Marvel-like consistency to the line, various efforts were made to ensure that all Kirby series were connected, not only with each other, but to the DC Universe as such. Conway launched HERCULES UNBOUND, for instance, cashing in on the mutant animals from KAMANDI, and Paul Levitz (if I recall rightly) authored an article for the in-house zine THE AMAZING WORLD OF DC COMICS, establishing, for official continuity's sake, a chain of links between disparate series: NEW GODS, HERCULES UNBOUND, OMAC, KAMANDI, "The Atomic Knights," and so on. (This was to have been an alternate future timeline— alternate, that is, to DC's favored future with the Legion of Super-Heroes.) Based on this would-be future, KAMANDI #50 (scripted by Denny O'Neil) made it clear that OMAC—or Buddy Blank, rather—was Kamandi's grandfather; but the crossover was perfunctory, the explanations scant, the whole affair rather pointless.

These *ex post facto* attempts to bridge Kirbydom and DC continuity seem just that: Efforts to shore up and extend DC's then-chaotic universe, not products of Kirby's own brain. (A similar observation might be made of the recent GENESIS: the Fourth World has become the crux of the DCU, it seems.) Granted, such continuity-building can be fun, but it doesn't seem to have much to do with what went on in Kirby's head as he crafted the series in question.

One more thing: I'm afraid I don't understand Shane Foley's letter. On the one hand, Foley complains that the overviews in TJKC #15 offer nothing beyond well-known facts; on the other, he complains that these articles are infused with too much "opinion." These two complaints are, if not mutually exclusive, then at least at odds, for an essay which mixes known fact and fresh opinion is, inevitably, an essay which offers new information. Opinions ARE information, just as documentary facts are, and can influence and inform, provoke and inspire, just as facts can.

May I point out that there is no fact worth noting which is not also worth having an opinion about? Opinions matter; I read TJKC for opinions as well as documentary evidence and terrific artwork. All I ask is that the opinions be interesting ones, well-grounded in evidence.

It occurs to me that Foley may object, not so much to the presence of opinion *per se*, but to the CONTENT of certain opinions in TJKC #15. If so, he should be encouraged to submit his own contrary opinions to TJKC, and to let the fur fly! Let's get a debate going—that's what it's all about.

Charles Hatfield, Storrs, CT

(In regards to the OMAC / KAMANDI link, it was stated in KAMANDI #27's letter column — well before Jack left the book — that there were ties between the two series, and I don't think it's that far of a stretch to think that, based on the success of KAMANDI (another letter column said that KAMANDI was officially one of DC's best-selling books), Carmine asked Jack to create another "futuristic" series, possibly relating to KAMANDI in some way. The fact that Jack never got to fully explore the links himself shouldn't, in my mind, exclude the possibility that he had plans to do so at some point, or the evidence that hints at it. But then, if Jack had managed to conclude every dangling plot thread he ever created, we probably wouldn't have these fun debates!)

GREAT issue! Joe Magee's article was fantastic, though when I first glanced at it I thought "My God!! There are issues of THOR that connect with the NEW GODS and I never knew it!!!" Joe's stories sound interesting and appropriate to Jack's arc of stories.

I have a question that I would like you to open up in the mags letter column if you think it's appropriate. WAS BILLION DOLLAR BATES THE ONLY PERSON TO REALLY HAVE THE ANTI-LIFE EQUATION? When I picked up the Fourth World series as back issues in the early 80's, I was most interested in the FOREVER PEOPLE and issue 8 (wouldn't you know it) was the last one I found. It seems to me that at the end of that issue, DARKSEID seems to clearly realize that the equation is lost to him forever. BUT—I was never sure what those folks who Orion saves in NEW GODS #1 had to do with the anti-life equation (and why those people specifically?), and I thought in one of the interviews you published I read that Jack never intended Darkseid to get the anti-life equation because it wouldn't work the way he thought it would. So, between Mark Evanier and all the other people out there, can we get a chronology of how Kirby's ideas about the anti-life equation developed?

Bill Meisel, Jacksonville, FL

(Glad you liked #17. As to Billion Dollar Bates, the sense I got was that, once he died, the Anti-Life Formula was somehow transferred to the mind of another human somewhere on earth, so Darkseid would have to start all over. As to the connection with the humans in NEW GODS #1, I think they all held a small part of the formula in their minds, so Darkseid was supposed to get it from them. And I believe Beautiful Dreamer was the only person who could string the formula together and make sense of it (as told in FOREVER PEOPLE #1). But I'm ashamed to say I'm writing this all from memory; I need to get out my Fourth World books and check it out, but I'm trying to get this issue wrapped up so you guys won't start sending me nasty letters if it's late!)

I would go as far as to say that your collected efforts fall into the indispensable category, for any fan of Jack Kirby or anyone with an interest in the artform. Having been with you since #6 (and having acquired the previous five issues) I feel that TJKC offers a unique view of the greatest, most prolific comic book creator, and it brings the works of a great many others into sharp focus.

Furthermore, it is valuable to reflect on the growth of interest in Jack Kirby over the past 4-5 years, and the increase in the publication of related material; a trend that must be attributed, in no small part, to the efforts of Chris Harper and yourself.

Paul Osborne, Congresbury, N. Somerset, ENGLAND

(I'm sure I speak for Chris as well when I say "Thanks!")

Rather than gush on about how great the magazine is, I wanted to bring up a question or two! I was surprised about your note at the beginning of this issue regarding artwork (or the lack thereof). Surely the Kirby Estate wouldn't hold back access to the originals they still have! Judging by the back page advertisement alone, there seems to be a lot of artwork out there still — and even if it's inked I think it still deserves to be showcased in the magazine.

I was completely blown away by the 1972 press release you published stating that Jack was leaving DC! Any chance of getting a follow-up on that particular incident? Obviously Jack DIDN'T leave — and this certainly sheds new light on his treatment at DC.

The D.Bruce Berry interview was all too brief! Strange that he didn't realize Jack had passed away!

The KAMANDI OF THE CAVES sample was incredible! I can't tell you how often I've wondered about that strip... and wanted to see it! I personally think there is a market for a book that covers Jack's strip work... .or at the very least a portfolio containing his "lost strip" ideas!

All in all a superb issue! Certainly the best issue yet and that is saying A LOT! I would jump at the chance for a bi-monthly 68 page issue even if the cover price was increased. TJKC really IS becoming a "magazine"...a real testament the hard work you and your staff obviously put into it!!

Although I have each and every issue...including the TPB...will you be putting out a TPB volume II? It seems logical.

Gary Picariello

(The Kirby Estate has been more than generous with allowing us access to Jack's files, which are currently in Greg Theakston's hands. Basically, we let Greg know what we need for each issue, and hope it exists in the files — not the ideal way to put this zine together, but it's the best we can do until Greg finds time to catalog what's in the files. Since we put TJKC together very quickly each issue — and often at the last minute — Greg doesn't always have sufficient time to find exactly what we requested. And in many cases, the photocopies of Jack's pencils are too faded to be reproducible, so the good quality copies that remain are running low, especially on 1960s stuff. To keep TJKC going, we need everyone's help with tracking down art for us to print.

Speaking of Greg, a soon to be published volume of his COMPLETE KIRBY series will grant your wish for a good look at Jack's "lost strip" ideas.

Our first Trade Paperback did so well, we're considering doing a second volume — reprinting TJKC #10-15 plus more new material — for next summer. I'll keep you posted.)

#17 was so hypnotic I read it in ONE sitting! This meant I couldn't fall back to sleep on what should have been a restful Saturday morning — but what the heck.

Concerning the Golden Age Sandman; now I'm REALLY confused. Did Simon & Kirby redesign the entire feature, or was this done several issues BEFORE they got there? And if so, by whom? The way it reads here, it sounds like S&K laid out their plans, but saw some of them implemented by others BEFORE they actually started on the feature themselves.

Until this issue, D. Bruce Berry had been a total cipher to me. I thought he was some young upstart, not someone around Jack's age who was mostly on the "fringe" of comics as a profession! Gee, I keep learning more with each issue you put out!

This might go totally against the grain, but how about doing an issue that looks at how others have handled (or perhaps butchered) Kirby's works AFTER him?

Henry R. Kujawa, Camden, NJ

(The character Sandy, and Sandman's super-hero costume both first appeared in ADVENTURE COMICS #69, Dec. 1941, a few issues before Simon & Kirby took over. Both were probably the work of Paul Norris. S&K made some adjustments to the costumes when they came on board in #72, March 1942, omitting the capes and altering the masks. The costumes continued to modify up until #76, July 1942, when S&K first had Sandman's purple mask continue down to cover his shoulders—a touch that really made the costume "theirs." S&K also inaugurated the "dream" motif in #72, although it wouldn't be used to its full extent for a few issues. For the record, Sandman started wearing his super-hero costume in ALL-STAR COMICS as of #10, Apr.-May 1942, although it was drawn by Cliff Young. The shoulder-length mask showed up in ALL-STAR #13, Oct.-Nov. 1942, still drawn by Cliff Young. S&K's first ALL-STAR issue was #14, dated Dec.-Jan. 1942. Joe and Jack also did the Sandman strip in WORLD'S FINEST #6, Summer 1942, with the short mask, and #7, Fall 1942, with the shoulder-length mask.

As for spotlighting others work on Jack's characters, I've intentionally tried to keep that to a minimum. Personally, I'd rather use the relatively few pages we have each issue to show as much of Jack's stuff as possible. But if readers want to see this covered, we'll consider it.)

Yesterday, #17 arrived with my back cover on it. I must tell you how overjoyed I was with the way it was colored. Here's a colorist that really knows how to employ grays. Most colorists use intense color everywhere, giving the eye no relief. It should be correctly used on the focus spots only, which is how it was smartly used on this piece.

Re: The splash from the SOUL LOVE book — who in the devil inked this piece?

Steve Rude

(I agree that Tom Ziuko did a bang-up job on #17's covers, as usual. He doesn't get nearly enough praise for his hard work on TJKC covers. And Richard Howell says Tony DeZuniga inked the SOUL LOVE *splash!)*

TJKC #17 was another informative and insightful issue, particularly Chris Knowles' analysis of the roots of the early-'70s pop-culture horror craze that spawned THE DEMON, and Ken Penders' historical detective work on Jack's pivotal but lesser-known CHALLENGERS stories.

But, taking a leaf from Charles Hatfield's LoC in the same issue, I would caution against too autobiographical an interpretation of KAMANDI. Many commentators seem to see that series as an expression of resignation on Kirby's part. Knowles posits KAMANDI's last-human-on-earth theme as an allegory for Kirby's siege mentality toward the lesser intelligences who had stifled his earlier creative output. But since KAMANDI's was arguably the most intricate and profuse universe Kirby ever created, it's hard to imagine that the King felt overwhelmed at the time.

In a letter to TJKC #16, Richard Kyle relates KAMANDI to Kirby's inert 2001 series, maintaining that in each case, Kirby's personal defeats led him to retreat from his grander epic aspirations into "a formula story that ... never advanced." But I would submit that KAMANDI was merely an inversion of the narrative method that Kirby had used in every series to that point. Whereas his other series were clearly established narratives which tended toward ever more dynamizing variation, KAMANDI was a chaotic narrative which sought stability.

That's because, for me at least, KAMANDI's theme can be summed up in one word: Family. Kamandi is the ultimate orphan, the last of his kind. The motley assemblies of mutants, aliens, and benign anthropomorphic animals he travels among through much of the series are a surrogate family in a world that otherwise doesn't want him. Over KAMANDI's run, Americans emerged from the social turmoil of the '60s (in which the Fourth World had been conceived) and turned inward. The comeback of the human race may be Kamandi's dream, but it's not realistically his goal. The only thing within his grasp is some hours of serenity and solace with his "family."

Interestingly, the theme of guerrilla bands as a future family unit was made explicit in an issue of Marvel's simultaneous post-apocalyptic series, WAR OF THE WORLDS. Ironically, humankind's comeback was indeed that series' goal — and it wasn't necessarily a noble one: "Reclaiming the human race's right to destroy itself," writer Don MacGregor would remind us. But it was in seeking an elusive uneventfulness that Kamandi found adventure — and that Kirby unleashed some of the wildest imaginings of his career.

One other point: TJKC has always been frank and aware in pointing out racial stereotypes in Jack's earlier work. These things should be discussed rather than censored, but that doesn't rule out censure. One of the panels reprinted in #17's GREEN ARROW feature really should have borne a disclaimer about the war-time Japanese stereotypes contained therein.

Adam McGovern, Mount Tabor, NJ

(The depiction of Japanese soldiers in the Green Arrow tale was obviously a case of Jack — like many of the comics greats of years past — having drawn something that was perfectly acceptable at the time, but with hindsight isn't. Our apologies if we offended anyone.)

NEXT ISSUE: #19 is our 56-page ART THEME ISSUE ($5.95 cover price), and once you see it, we think you'll agree it's something completely different! We'll break all the rules as we take a closer look at the artistic merits of Jack's work, starting with color cover paintings by ALEX ROSS and ALEX HORLEY, based on Kirby drawings! And we're adding a BONUS 6-PAGE PORTFOLIO featuring Jack's own paintings in FULL COLOR! Then we'll feature a new interview with JOE KUBERT, in which he discusses Kirby, comics, and the Kubert School. We'll also interview KEVIN (Ninja Turtles) EASTMAN about the massive holdings of Kirby art at his Words & Pictures Museum. Plus there's a rare Kirby interview, articles exploring the subtleties and nuances of Jack's storytelling techniques, a discussion of Kirby inkers, the ins and outs of collecting Kirby original art, fan art (including the winners of our INKING CONTEST), and the usual array of unpublished Kirby art including unused pages from his books, published pages BEFORE they were inked, and more! We'll see you in mid-March! The deadline for submissions: 1/15/98.

SUBMIT SOMETHING- GET FREE ISSUES!

The Jack Kirby Collector is a not-for-profit publication, put together with submissions from Jack's fans around the world. We don't pay for submissions, but if we print art or articles you submit, we'll send you a free copy of that issue or extend your subscription by one issue.

Here's a tentative list of upcoming issues, to give you ideas of things to write about. But don't limit yourself to these – we treat these themes very loosely, so anything you write may fit somewhere. And just because we covered a topic once, don't think we won't print more about it. So get creative, get writing, and send us copies of your Kirby art!

#20 (MAY '98): KIRBY'S WOMEN

From Mother Delilah to Big Barda, the Invisible Girl to Granny Goodness, we'll explore Jack's heroines and villainesses, including a section on Simon & Kirby's romance comics. **Deadline: 3/1/98.**

#21 (JULY '98): JACK'S WHACKIEST IDEAS!

Nobody's perfect, and even Jack managed to lay a few eggs in his otherwise stellar career. So from *Red Raven* to those crazy Atlas Monsters, Arnim Zola to the Fighting Fetus, we'll have fun finding redeeming qualities in Jack's wildest, weirdest, hokiest, lamest, and most preposterous ideas, including gizmos and gadgets! **Deadline: 4/1/98.**

#22 (OCT. '98): VILLAINS

From the big guns like the Red Skull, Doctor Doom, and Darkseid to the also-rans, we'll take a closer look at what makes Jack's bad guys so darn good! If there's a Kirby villain you love to hate, write something about them! **Deadline: 7/1/98.**

SUBMISSION GUIDELINES:

Submit artwork in one of these forms:

1) Clear color or black-&-white photocopies.
2) Scanned images – 300ppi IBM or Macintosh.
3) Originals (carefully packed and insured).

Submit articles in one of these forms:

1) Typed or laser printed pages.
2) E-mail to: twomorrow@aol.com
3) An ASCII file, IBM or Macintosh format.
4) Photocopies of previously printed articles OK.

We'll pay return postage and insurance for originals – please write or call first. Please include background info whenever possible.

THE JACK KIRBY COLLECTOR #18

A TWOMORROWS ADVERTISING & DESIGN PRODUCTION IN ASSOCIATION WITH THE KIRBY ESTATE EDITOR: JOHN MORROW ASSISTANT EDITOR: PAMELA MORROW ASSOCIATE EDITOR: JON B. COOKE DESIGN & LAYOUT: TWOMORROWS ADVERTISING PROOFREADING: RICHARD HOWELL COVER COLOR: TOM ZIUKO CONTRIBUTORS: JIM AMASH STEVE BELL AL BIGLEY JERRY BOYD TOM BREVOORT SCOTT BRUNS ROBERT L. BRYANT JR. JOHN BUSCEMA LEN CALLO JON B. COOKE SHANNON DENTON PAUL DOOLITTLE KEVIN EASTMAN BRAD ELLIOT MIKE GARTLAND DREW GERACI GLEN GOLD GEARY GRAVEL DAVID HAMILTON CHRIS HARPER RC HARVEY CHARLES HATFIELD RICHARD HOWELL JIM KLEIN PETER KOCH JIM KORKIS MICHAEL KRAIGER LARRY LIEBER BRUCE LOWRY RUSS MAHERAS ALEJANDRO MARTINEZ ADAM MCGOVERN BRET MIXON WILL MURRAY MARK NAGATA MARK PACELLA NELSON PATTERSON STEVE ROBERTSON JOHN ROMITA GEORGE ROUSSOS GARY SASSAMAN BILL SCHELLY DAVID SCHWARTZ RICHARD SCOTT TOD SEISSER DANNY SERAFIN MARIE SEVERIN KEVIN SHAW JOE SINNOTT JOE STATON FLO STEINBERG JIM STERANKO THOMAS SUHLING AARON SULTAN CARL TAYLOR GREG THEAKSTON MIKE THIBODEAUX ROY THOMAS HERB TRIMPE JIM VADEBONCOUER PETER VON SHOLLY SPECIAL THANKS TO: JIM AMASH JOHN BUSCEMA JON B. COOKE KEVIN EASTMAN MARK EVANIER MIKE GARTLAND D. HAMBONE RANDY HOPPE RICHARD HOWELL MARK PACELLA JOHN ROMITA GEORGE ROUSSOS FIONA RUSSELL DAVID SCHWARTZ MARIE SEVERIN KEVIN SHAW JOE SINNOTT FLO STEINBERG CARL TAYLOR GREG THEAKSTON MIKE THIBODEAUX ROY THOMAS HERB TRIMPE TOM ZIUKO & OF COURSE ROZ KIRBY MAILING CREW: MITCH BANKS RUSS GARWOOD D. HAMBONE GLEN MUSIAL ED STELLI PATRICK VARKER AND THE OTHER KIRBY FANS IN RALEIGH, NC

JACK KIRBY
Alex Ross ASSISTS

#19 Contents:

SIDE A

SIDE B

Photocopies of Jack's uninked pencils from published comics are reproduced here courtesy of the Kirby Estate, which has our thanks for their continued support.

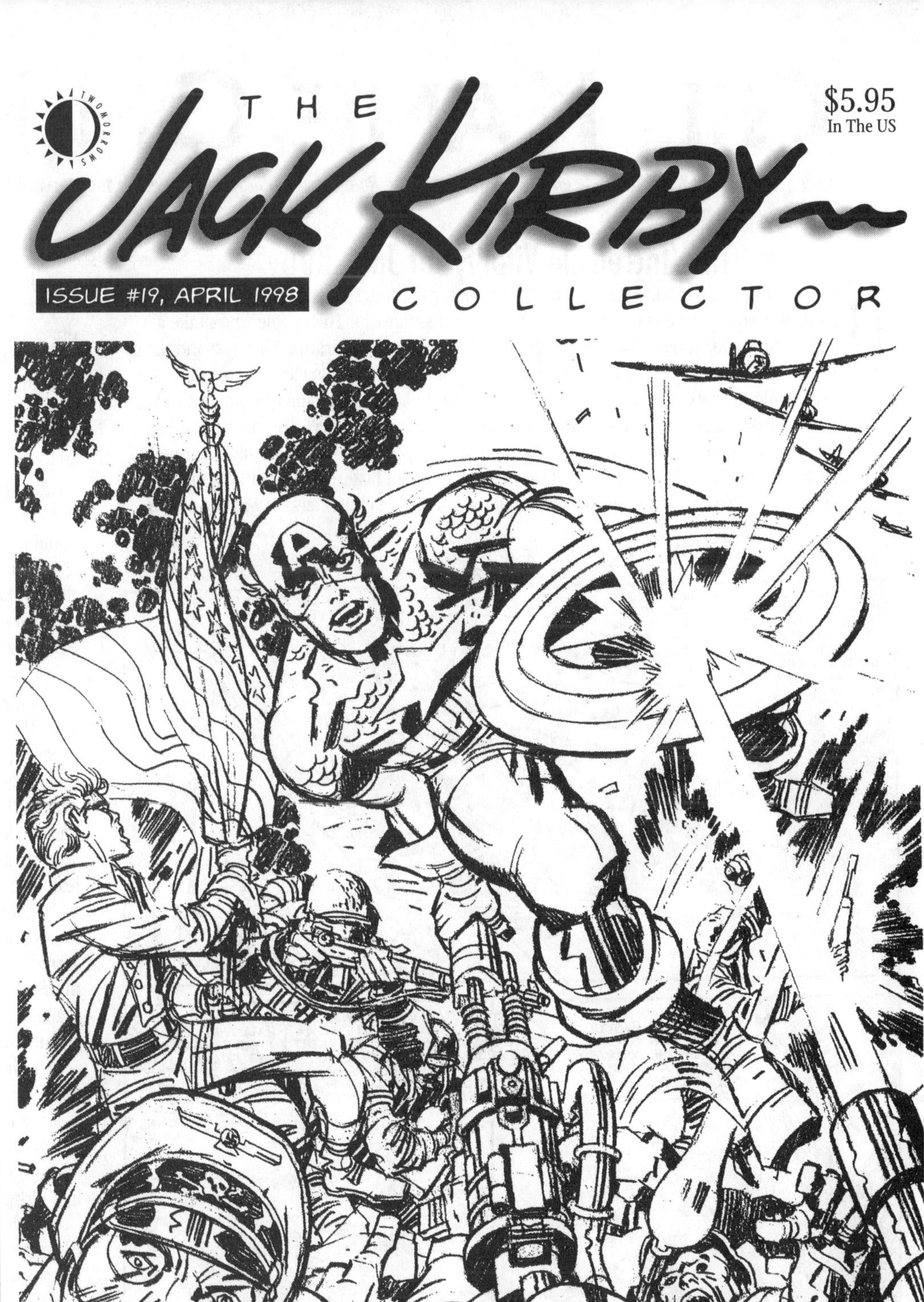

Our cover painting by Alex Ross is based on this Kirby pencil drawing, originally published in The Steranko History Of Comics, *Vol. 1. Dave Stevens also did an inked and colored version for our centerfold.*

The Jack Kirby Collector, Vol. 5, No. 19, Apr. 1998. Published bi-monthly by & © TwoMorrows Advertising & Design, 1812 Park Drive, Raleigh, NC 27605, USA. 919-833-8092. *John Morrow,* Editor. *Pamela Morrow,* Asst. Editor. *Jon B. Cooke,* Assoc. Editor. Single issues: $5.95 ($6.40 Canada, $8.40 elsewhere). Six-issue subscriptions: $24.00 US, $32.00 Canada and Mexico, $44.00 outside North America. First printing. All characters are © their respective companies. All artwork is © Jack Kirby unless otherwise noted. All editorial matter is © the respective authors. PRINTED IN CANADA.

GIL KANE ON KIRBY

(Excerpts from Gil Kane's article entitled "Bypassing the Real for the Ideal," published in the Harvard Journal of Pictorial Fiction, *Spring 1974)*

The 'Incredible Vitality' of Jack Kirby

One of the things that makes Kirby virtually the supreme comics artist is that he is hardly ever compromised by some commonplace notion of draftsmanship. The people who make a fetish of literal form have the smallest grip on the whole idea of drama. They live and die by the external, the cosmetic effect. Thus someone in the Spanish School is elevated to a kind of deity level, while their work is anti-life. It is still-born, while Kirby is absolutely raging with life.

What Kirby does is to generate incredible vitality on each page. There are four or five high points in the last decade—the first year of the *New Gods* especially—where he had so much to give that he needed someone to channel it for him. It came out faster than it could be digested. There were four different storylines at once, all those fascinating characters he was not able to follow up on.

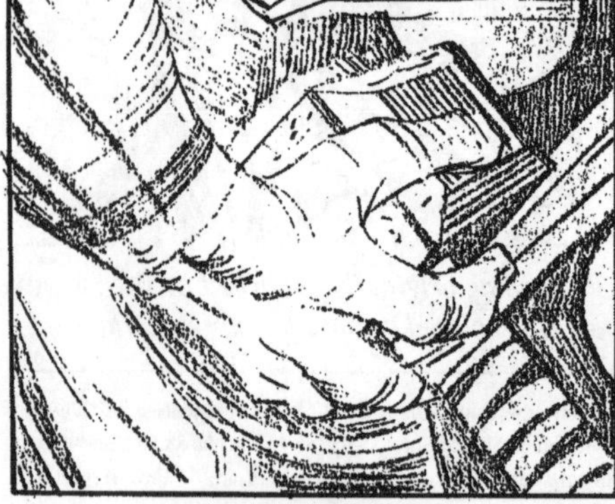

Jack does his drawing on the basis of very strong impressions he is continually registering; and what he draws communicates the impression better than a literal interpretation. His drawings don't depend on academic draftsmanship; they have a life of their own. He's the one who started this whole business of distortion, the big hands and fists — and with him, they all work, they all have a dramatic quality that makes them believable, creating enormous power in his material — and his distortion is never questioned. I do more representational figures, but the same editor will accept Jack's figures and constantly question mine. Correct is not right; what Jack does is project his qualities, and his expressionism is better than the literal drawing of almost anyone in the business.

Explosiveness & Repression

The one thing you can see in Jack's work is an angry repressed personality. First there is the extreme explosiveness of his work—not merely explosive, but I mean there is a real nuclear situation on every page. Then there is his costuming: On every one of Kirby's costumes there are belts and straps and restraints; leather buckles everywhere. There are times when he takes Odin and puts (him in a) composition of symmetry and restrained power. His women are sort of sexually neutral. I don't think Jack is very interested in drawing women, but give him a fist or a rock or a machine... if his women have any quality at all, it is a slightly maternal one.

Kirby is one of the few artists whose characters do not always have to be in a heroic posture—they can assume naturalistic attitudes. Reed Crandall and those artists 'descended' from him find it almost impossible to draw a figure that is not heroically postured. Foster, like Kirby, had naturalistic feel; Hogarth never did.

Kirby represents the artist with the most flair for the material. He is by nature a dramatist; all of his skill supports drama, not drawing. Besides everything else, Jack has an enormous facility; he can create effects that drive a person mad. He can set up a free-standing sculpture or machine with staggering weight and impact. What kind of life can he have led to have this alien sense of phenomenology? Bottled up inside of Jack Kirby is enough natural force to light New York City. And it's such a pity to see all that great stuff working without someone saying, "Easy, easy." It has just never happened—they either suppressed him entirely or forced on him ideas that were never his own. I just wish Jack were as excited now as when he first came to National. The pictures in *Kamandi* are far less vibrant than the *New Gods* material; I remember a fish-creature he did—I've never seen such force in my life!

Jack's characters are so larger-than-life that ultimately they couldn't fight the crime syndicate or even super-villains; they had to fight these cosmic figures in order to accommodate the dynamism. He is the only one that can handle that kind of story and make it believable. In order to do material about the cosmos, there has to be something monumental about the quality of the art. It is only externally that John Buscema resembles Jack; inside, he is much more like John Romita — attractive but not electric. His work doesn't have the intensity, the convolution, the distortion, it doesn't make the demands. They are constantly giving him material that he is not suited for. With *The Fantastic Four* John was not capable of that real freshness of perspective and insight that Jack managed to create with Galactus and a whole series of characters. The first 100 issues are incredible, the most unparalleled sustained effort I have ever seen in comics. He infused that material with such a sophisticated and original quality — gigantic, gorgeous machines, a real sense of cosmic power, an exploration of super space — that no one else has ever been able to approach his concepts and make them believable.

(below) Jack's pencils from this drawing were modified, then inked by Mike Royer for the original, unused cover to the Hunger Dogs *graphic novel.*

(previous page) Page 2 pencils from Thor *#156.*

The Early Marvel Magic

With big bands, when there were one or two first-rate musicians in the band, the whole band would come alive. And when the band would break up, all going different ways, the musicians would look back at that time as a kind of Olympus, when everyone was so charged by the intensity. It shows you that people can have enormous talent and never use it. It is untapped, a reserve; the potentials are never realized until a catalyst comes along. Harvey Kurtzman was a catalyst, Al Feldstein was a catalyst. Then there were artists who worked in obscurity, who had ordinary careers; by Kurtzman and Feldstein individually imposing their standards and ideas, they expanded the universes of all these artists and lifted their work to great heights.

"War may be hell! - But only when fought by a sloppy military!"

Darkseid, *Forever People* #8 (1972), p. 23

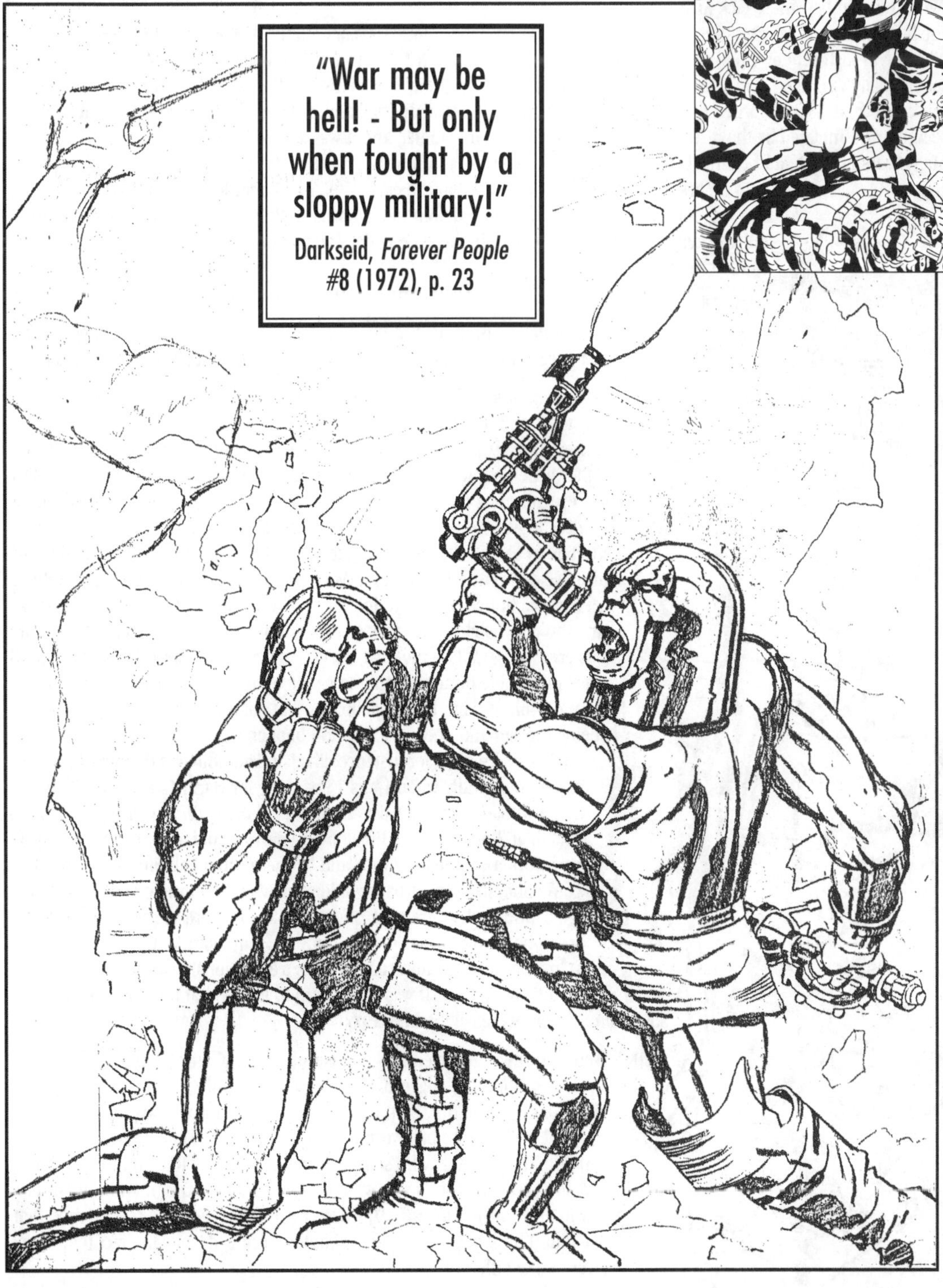

That's the way Stan Lee, with virtually a depleted comics house, was able to use Jack as a catalyst and mobilize a group of lesser artists. All of a sudden, people like Ditko came from nowhere and in a period of three years were able to build up a tremendous skill and popularity. Ditko's qualities at Marvel were second only to Jack's. I still consider one of his sequences in particular a masterpiece of pacing and suspense. Spider-Man is trapped under a huge machine, and the sequence builds up a powerful communication of 'will he, or won't he?' leading to a splash page of a super-human effort that lifts clear the machine. It is one of the most satisfying moments in comics.★

Joe Kubert Interviewed

BY JON B. COOKE

(Joe Kubert is one of the great masters of sequential art. Aside from co-creating 3-D comics and developing the fondly-recalled Tor *comic book, Joe is best remembered for his DC Comics work, including his humanistic Sgt. Rock, Enemy Ace, and the quintessential Hawkman. His adaptation of Tarzan ranks beside Hal Foster's and Burne Hogarth's. While he created in 1976 and continues to run the first comic book art school in the world — the Kubert School of Cartoon and Graphic Art — he has never stopped contributing his increasingly personal work to his public. His most recent work is* Fax from Sarajevo, *the true-life account of innocents caught in the hell that was once Yugoslavia. This lesson from comicdom's great teacher was conducted on the phone on December 19, 1997. Special thanks to the unwitting Richard Kyle for a question idea here and there.)*

"Experimenters take risks — even with humor, Mokkari!"
Simyan, *Jimmy Olsen* #146 (1972), p. 4

TJKC: When did you first meet Jack Kirby?

JOE: The first time I met Jack was very fleetingly when I was probably about 15 years old. I was still going to high school. I had started working in the business when I was 11 or 12, but when I was 14 or 15 the books were selling really well and there were not a lot of people to work on them. It was just a different time as far as the business itself was concerned. I was afforded the opportunity of inking his "Newsboy Legion"; I met Jack at that time. Being a kid, I wasn't awed or intimidated by the beautiful work that was under my hands, and it was a tremendous experience inking his stuff. Many years later I had of course gotten to know Jack real well; when he was working for DC, we knew each other pretty good. When he first started doing books for DC in the early '70s, I had a trailer and a whole bunch of kids — five children — and we took the ride out to California. Jack had invited me, saying, "Anytime you're here, Joe, drop over." He told that to everybody! And so I did with a 32-foot trailer, five children and my wife!

"Mister Invincible" eventually became "Mindmaster," the abortive movie concept we reported on in TJKC *#11.*

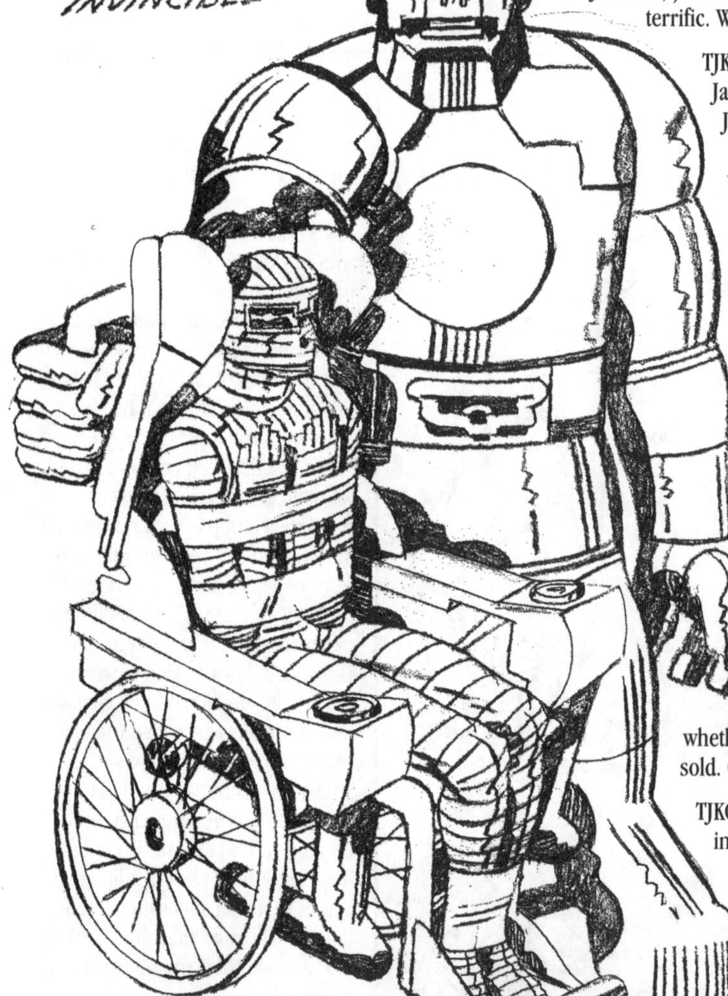

TJKC: How long did you stay?

JOE: Oh, just a couple of hours. Both he and Roz were just so warm, so nice that it was just terrific. We just barged in at that time. Afterwards we would talk about it quite often.

TJKC: When you were a kid inking "Newsboy Legion," were you aware yourself of Jack's impact on the business — was there an impact?

JOE: Every artist was very much interchangeable, but there were some guys in a higher echelon. Jack Kirby, Joe Simon, and a bunch of guys like Charlie Biro were recognized by the publishers as the guys who knew enough about the business to put together stuff that really sold. However, the publishers didn't hesitate to say, "Well, we're going to put out five Superman books and we'll hire five different artists to do it. We'll put out 'Newsboy Legion' and we'll get a whole bunch of guys to ink Jack Kirby's stuff, or if need be, we'll get a guy who pencils closely to Jack's style." We were kind of interchangeable. It was great for guys like me, just starting out because I was able to get experience in a whole bunch of stuff, in a whole variety of things that pertain to comic books — but having people at that point who were recognized as being movers and doers really didn't happen much.

There were guys, for instance, like Lou Fine who was the "Artist's Artist." I remember vividly when I was 13 working for Harry Chesler and there were a whole bunch of artists up there *[in the Quality studio]*. After high school, at 2 or 3 o'clock, I'd stop off (Harry would allow me to come up and work a couple of hours) and be there when Lou Fine's stuff would come out. All of the artists would go down to the local candy store where the comic books were sold, and we looked forward to seeing Lou's stuff. Everyone admired him — not from the standpoint of being a superstar, but just because we admired his work tremendously. We really didn't know whether his stuff sold or not. It was really hard to tell. At that time, a lot of stuff sold. Comic books were selling like crazy.

TJKC: Were you more attracted to the illustrative style of Alex Raymond, for instance, over the more suggestive style of Milton Caniff?

JOE: When I started out, even as a kid, there were three icons that all of us looked up to (and I believe you'll get this from Gil Kane, Carmine Infantino, everybody who started at that time): Alex Raymond (who did *Flash Gordon*), Milt Caniff (who did *Terry & the Pirates*), and Hal Foster (who did *Prince Valiant*). Those were the three people, a terrific mix, that we didn't have any reservations about admiring, despite the fact that their styles were quite different.

TJKC: Did you start recognizing the storytelling abilities of Caniff or Sickles over Raymond's illustrative style, which was more like magazine work?
JOE: I think probably intuitively. Y'know, I was working strictly from my gut, strictly from intuition. When Caniff did a really dramatic sequence, it would really hit me. To dedicate that to his ability to tell a story... I thought it was just the story that was doing it, not the way that he dramatized it. That only became clear to me when I started the school about 20 years ago and started analyzing all these things. Up until that time I was just drawing the way I felt! I never really analyzed what I was doing or why I was doing it, I was just doing it! It was only when I was trying to start communicating with students to explain how they should do it that I suddenly came to the realization of what I was doing! *(laughter)*

TJKC: Did that bring a revelation about other people's work?
JOE: Oh, yeah. I knew that I loved Will Eisner's stuff (I worked up in his office as a kid for a long time just erasing material, sweeping the floors, and maybe doing a half-page of artwork if Will felt that I could fill a hole there) and *The Spirit* and Will's ability to design a page and tell a story that was entertaining all the way through. We knew that he was doing something terrific but personally I didn't know why! *(laughter)* That is the way it went for us.

TJKC: When were you over at Eisner's?
JOE: Early '40s; a couple of years before Will went into the army. Maybe 1939.

TJKC: Did you want to be a comic book artist?
JOE: I always wanted to be a cartoonist. Not specifically comic books because when I started out, to become a syndicate artist was really nirvana. That was really heaven, the final destination for anybody who was a cartoonist. Comic books were just a means of getting there. As a matter of fact, a lot of the guys in the comic book business would never even say that they were doing comic books. They were absolutely ashamed of that title. The artists would say, "I'm a commercial artist" *(laughter)* — never a "comic book artist."

TJKC: Why was there this shame?
JOE: Because, at that time, it was a junk medium. The reproduction was the crudest you could imagine. Not like the books you see today, but on the cheapest kind of newsprint. The color registration was often off anywhere from a sixteenth to a quarter of an inch. The colors were absolutely flat. The Sunday newspapers got some good reproduction. Clear color; Hal Foster's stuff was done absolutely beautifully. But the comic books were looked at as junk, just for kids; one step above coloring books. I was just a kid so to me it was a thrill just doing this stuff. I always admired the work of the guys who were in the business but the guys themselves thought differently. The first opportunity they had either to get into syndication (and not many of them were able to make that jump) and advertising — anything that, first of all, paid a couple of bucks more and second of all, put them in a higher echelon, they jumped at it.

TJKC: How did you get to ink Simon & Kirby's "Newsboy Legion"?
JOE: I just happened to be there, *(laughter)* which happened more times than not in my business. A lot of times — and I tell the students here at the school the same thing — there are three things that have to be in extant in order to get work: You have to be at the right place, at the right time, with the right stuff. If any one of those things are out of place, you ain't got the job. When I was up at DC, I might have been bringing in a job and somebody might have said, "Here, this has to be done. You want to ink this job?" "Sure, fine." I took it and did it.

TJKC: Did you go home and do it, or did you do it in the office?
JOE: No, I went home. There were some people who found it more comfortable to work in the office. There were maybe a half dozen, ten guys up at DC who did their work up there. But most of the guys worked on freelance as I certainly did.

TJKC: How did you become involved with St. John Publishing?
JOE: I always felt from the start that nobody was going to take care of me but me. I always felt that in order to build some security for myself — and I felt this way even as a kid — it would

Jack drew this back-up story for Jimmy Olsen *#144 at DC in the early 1970s.*

be wise for me to work for several people rather than to put my eggs into one basket. Most of the guys would be working for two or three different publishers just to make sure that there was a steady flow of work coming through all of the time. St. John was one of those publishers with whom I was doing work. They were rather pleased with what I was doing to the extent that the publisher agreed to be the source of publishing and that I could put a complete package together and become the publisher myself for all intents and purposes. He in turn would be sort of an agent and publish the books through his auspices. That's what we did. Before I went into the Army, I was doing that for a couple of years. When I came back, I did the same thing with St. John with my buddy Norman Maurer who was my old high school friend and someone I've known all my life.

TJKC: Was there profit-sharing with St. John?
JOE: Absolutely, but it was more. We had complete and total control of the material that went into the books. If the books sold over a certain point we made more money.

TJKC: Would you say that *Tor* was your most personal work up until that time?
JOE: I would say so. It still is. I still like the character and it reflects the love I have for the Tarzan character. All he is is Tarzan in Stone Age times.

TJKC: In 1954, do you remember the "beginning of the end," with Wertham?
JOE: I've been in this business since I was 11 years old and I haven't experienced one day of unemployment in all that time. So even when the comic book business was at its worst during the Senate hearings, comics were still being put out and I was still working.

TJKC: Jumping ahead, were you aware of Jack Kirby's influence at Marvel in the '60s?
JOE: There was a time when Jack was doing some really outstanding stuff for Marvel when the edict would come down at DC from some of the editors to draw like Jack Kirby. Jack's stuff was selling so they wanted us to draw like Jack. There was an overt effort being made by a lot of artists because of the pressures from a lot of the editors to draw in Jack Kirby's style. There aren't too many artists whose work is so provocative or so pointed insofar as the sales were concerned that other artists were told to emulate one man's style, but in Jack's case that was true. For whatever reason, I never got that kind of pressure. Even at the height of Jack's popularity, I just blithely went along and did my stuff.

TJKC: Did you check out the Marvel books at all?
JOE: Somewhat. I enjoyed and loved Jack's work very much; as a matter of fact some of his early stuff is what I really loved. He did something called "The Vision" which he had inked and I thought it was absolutely fantastic — but I never felt that I wanted to emulate the work that Jack did. It was so far removed from what my interests were, like Foster, Raymond, and so on. I admired what he did. I admired it as a piece of work, but not one that I was even tempted to emulate.

TJKC: Sales from Marvel were picking up. Did you personally feel the pressure to at least check Marvel out and see what kind of appeal these books had and whether DC could come up with a counter-plan?
JOE: No. I really didn't. When I became an editor up at DC in 1968, my criteria was strictly what looked good to me. It was intuitive. I really couldn't get into the stuff that was being done up at Marvel. It just didn't interest me that much.

TJKC: How did you learn that Jack was coming over to DC?
JOE: Carmine probably told me. It was just a passing thing. It was nice to hear but it wasn't an earth-shattering thing as far as I was concerned.

TJKC: Did you feel that there was a lot of energy in the house with Kirby's arrival? There were a lot of house ads.
JOE: Yeah, I was hoping. Anything that's positive, anything that sells in a publishing company is good. My attitude has always been "Don't Kill Marvel," and my former assistant, now-Publisher Paul Levitz, has the same attitude; that is, you don't want to kill your competitor. There's more than enough room for everybody. You just want to beat him! You want to do better stuff but you don't want to put him out of business because if you do, that means that the industry can only support one company — and that's silly.

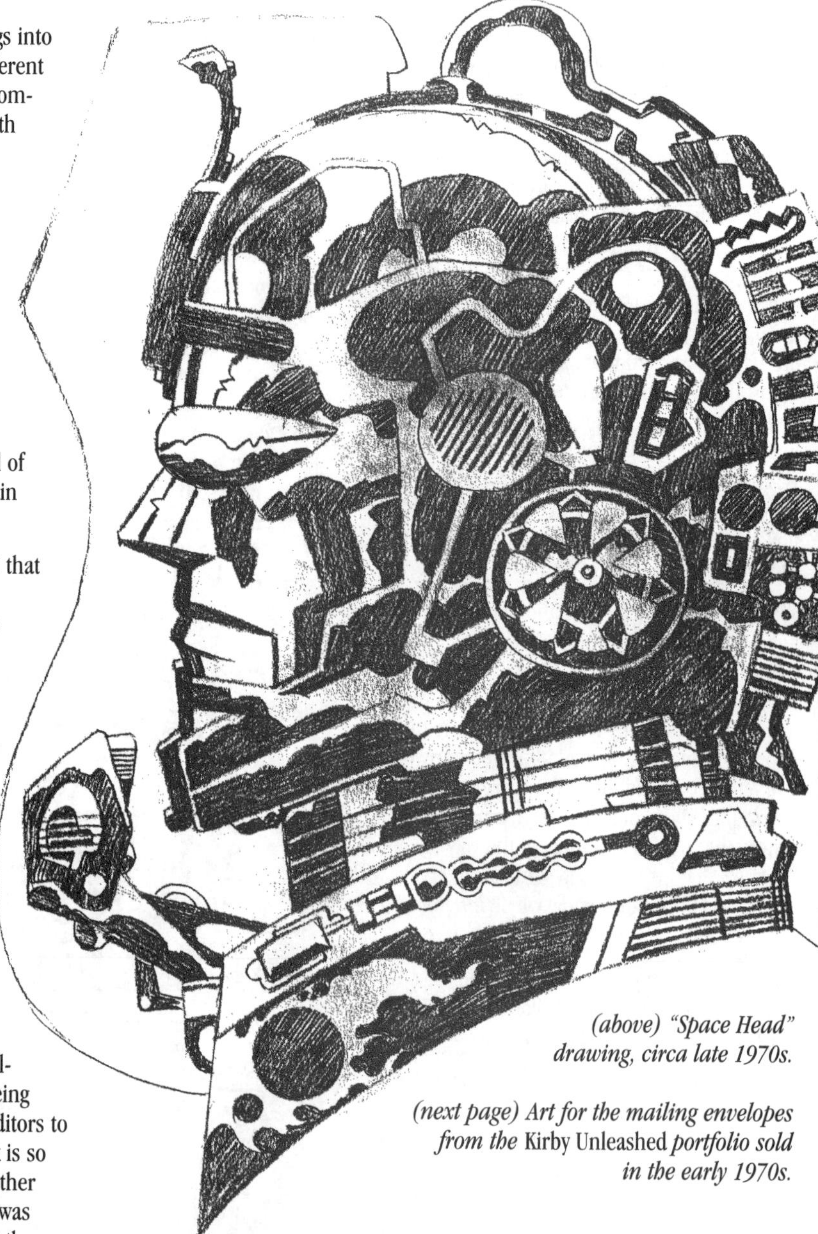

(above) "Space Head" drawing, circa late 1970s.

(next page) Art for the mailing envelopes from the Kirby Unleashed *portfolio sold in the early 1970s.*

TJKC: Did you read Jack's DC books when they came out?
JOE: To some degree because I did some of the covers: *Kamandi* and the others. In fact, with the covers to Jack's books, I tried as much as I could to get that kind of a flavor or style of drawing that reflected Jack's stuff.

TJKC: Do you know why you got the assignments to do a lot of the *Kamandi* and *Our Fighting Forces* covers?
JOE: Only because I was able to turn a lot of the stuff out. *(laughter)* I don't know how many thousands of covers I put out. I guess it showed something positive in the sales of the books and that, of course, is the final criteria — but I was also able to turn out a helluva lot of them.

TJKC: How long, on average, would it take you to turn out a cover?
JOE: It varied. Usually two to three hours. It's no big deal. It might sound like a helluva lot of work but it's really not.

TJKC: When did you start thinking about starting up an art school?
JOE: I had the thought for I-don't-know-how-many decades. The reason was because the way that I broke into the business, I had gotten all kinds of

help from a whole bunch of people in the business — but that was kind of a hit-and-miss, catch-as-catch-can situation, whenever I was able to come across somebody who I felt had something to offer, like Jack Kirby or Lou Fine or Will Eisner. "How do you do this? What kind of brush did you use here? What happens when you finish the work? How do you do a story?" All kinds of questions. That kind of information came to me hit-and-miss, sometimes a one-a-year situation. I was able to absorb — perhaps over a period of 10 or 15 years when I first started out — all the things that I felt were necessary to become a seasoned professional in the business. I always felt that, "Gee, wouldn't it be great if instead of hopping around trying to get this information (and there was no other place to get the information except in the business), people who were really committed to get into this profession had one place to come to get it all?"

One of the guys who was a tremendous help when I started the school — just in terms of information — was Jack Adler. Jack was in charge of production at DC, which is an incredibly important part of the publishing and comic book business. Jack was one of the most knowledgeable — he's now retired — guys in terms of production, reproduction, photography, color and printing that I know; just an incredibly well-versed guy. We had talked and I had asked him years before I actually started it, "What do you think are the elements that somebody just coming into this business should know?" He said, "Well, most artists have a problem in just getting down paste-ups and mechanicals." At that time, computers were unknown, of course, and to do paste-ups and mechanicals you had to have the rubber cement, the razor and all that kind of stuff. He said that most artists are not aware of how to prepare their work properly to get the best out of reproduction. Most artists didn't realize that no matter how beautiful their original artworks looked, if it was not set up for reproduction it's going to look like crap. So he said, "You've got to have a couple of these courses." So this was the beginning of setting up the ten courses that comprise the curriculum at the school.

So in talking to Jack I kept it in the back of my mind, but I wasn't prepared to give up any part of my career (which I've always loved and enjoyed) for starting a school. I felt that a school would be a good thing and living here in Dover, if I came across the physical facilities that would lend itself to this kind of thing — and as long as it was close to home so I wouldn't have to do a lot of traveling or commuting — maybe it would be worth taking a crack at it. I would set it up so maybe I would work a day or two at the school, and spend the rest of the time doing my own work. There's a big old mansion here in town that was built about a hundred years ago and it seemed to afford itself properly to the kind of school that I wanted to start. It had about 23 rooms, set out on a beautiful park-like landscape, and the price was very, very reasonable at that time. (This was 22 years ago.) So all five of my kids were out of the house, either married or big enough to be on their own, and my wife was a college graduate with a business degree, and she was at home. So I told her, "Look, this is something that I'm considering. I don't know the first thing about starting a school but it might be interesting to set this thing up, if you would handle the business end." If I had to handle the business end, I ain't gonna start anything! *(laughter)* So my wife said, "Okay, it sounds interesting. Let's take a crack at it." So we did.

TJKC: All told, do you know how many graduates the school has had?
JOE: About 500 or 600.

TJKC: Besides your artwork, you've certainly left a significant mark on comics. Joe Kubert begat Steve Bissette who begat...
JOE: *(laughter)* The most amazing part is the involvement of my two sons, who also attended and graduated the school. The fact that they were interested in doing this kind of work was just amazing to me, but having them turn out the way they did and be in the position they find themselves in today, is something that I really can't tell you how proud I am of. I'm just amazed.

TJKC: When you write, let's say *Fax from Sarajevo,* did you sit down and do thumbnails or do you actually write a full script?
JOE: I write my script in terms of thumbnails but I do it back and forth. I've told this to many guys who attempt to both write and draw: I feel that it is absolutely vital to separate the two into two distinct jobs. I take on writing in a graphic form in thumbnails with all kinds of notes all around the place. Once I block out what my story is going to be, I then dialogue the whole thing with notes. I do that script not as if it's being done for me but as if I were preparing it for another artist (because I found early on that very often if I give myself shorthand notes on what I'm doing, by the time I sit down to draw it I forget what the hell it was what I was trying to put into the script). I feel that it's two separate and distinct jobs. I think the writing has to be done as a writer regardless of what style you use to do the writing — in my case it's doing the thumbnails and graphically setting up the pages in story form, so to speak. Once I have it refined to the point where I feel that the story works in and of itself, I then divorce myself as the writer and I become the artist.

TJKC: How do you see your approach to storytelling as compared to Jack Kirby's approach?
JOE: I would say that it's purely idiosyncratic. I've never even tried to analyze it. I wouldn't even know where to begin.

TJKC: Are there any lessons to be derived from Kirby's work?
JOE: Well, the lessons are tough ones to learn. Jack's stuff was so dynamic that the drawings practically jumped off the page; plus the fact that in addition to the dynamism he was also able to achieve in great part a credibility and an emotional content with particular characters, the combination of which is really difficult to get to. He was able to do that; not all the time as in all of our cases, but the wonderful part of doing stuff for comic books is that we do so much of it and if we can get 75% really well, we're doing pretty good. When Jack was really flying — some of the Newsboy Legion stuff, even though his artwork, his style is one that is not really representational or super-realistic — he was able to achieve a credibility and believability in his characters that were just absolutely great. In his background scenes, and stuff like domestic scenes in the kitchen with a mother cooking with pots, he was still able to retain that kind of dynamism even in a simple shot, and still communicate all those feelings so that a person who either experienced or read about the stuff would be able to get something out of his drawings. He was terrific.★

Kevin Eastman Interviewed

(Kevin Eastman, half of the Eastman and Laird team that created the hugely popular Teenage Mutant Ninja Turtles, is a longtime Kirby fan. With earnings from the Turtles, Kevin founded the Words & Pictures Museum of Sequential Art in Northampton, MA, which houses one of the largest collections of Kirby original art in the world. This interview was conducted in February 1998.)

> "To laugh is to feel the beat of life!"
> Lightray, *New Gods* #1 (1971), p. 6

THE JACK KIRBY COLLECTOR: In many ways you and Peter Laird are an anomaly in the realm of comic books, because you maintained control of your ideas. Did you learn lessons from comics history, such as Siegel & Shuster's and Kirby's experiences?

KEVIN EASTMAN: Around the time Pete and I were working on the Teenage Mutant Ninja Turtles — 1983-84 — people like Gary Groth, Frank Miller, and Dave Sim were leading a big crusade for creator's rights. This was a time when Jack Kirby could not get his artwork back from Marvel, although 90% of everything that was hugely successful out of Marvel came from Jack Kirby. That's what really made us aware of protection of rights, ownership, and getting our original artwork back. Corporations made millions off Jack Kirby, much like they made millions off Siegel & Shuster. Pete and I were very much aware of what was going on with Kirby, and we share a huge debt of gratitude and inspiration and respect for the man. Our self-publishing the Turtles is due to Jack Kirby.

Jack Kirby was my inspiration to draw comic books. In a weird sort of way he brought Peter Laird and me together. When Pete and I first got together, I walked into his tiny apartment, stacked to the brim with comic books, and the first thing I saw was an unpublished "Loser's" page, penciled by Kirby. *(See* TJKC *#17)* I'd never seen a Jack Kirby original in my life, and I just about wet my pants. *(laughter)* Pete gave me that page two years later for my birthday. He's my dear, dear friend. Whenever we spent nine hours together, eight of them were spent talking about Jack Kirby.

TJKC: What do you think it was that caused you to have such success so quickly?

KEVIN: I relate it to winning the lottery. In 1983, I drew the first Turtle. I threw it on to Pete's desk to make him laugh. He laughed, he drew a version that made me laugh. I drew a version of four Turtles to top his drawing, with a title block that said "Ninja Turtles." He added "Teenage Mutant" to it. Around that time, we didn't have any distracting paying work going on, *(laughter)* so the next day we decided to tell the story of how these characters came to be, for no one other than me and Pete. We wrote and drew it, and I had $500 from an income tax refund; Pete had $200 he took from his bank account. We borrowed $1000 from my uncle, and we were able to print 3000 copies of the first issue. It was a two-color cover because it was cheap. The odd size came from walking around Dover, NH where we lived at the time. There was a free TV magazine that was a very odd size, like 9¼" x 10¾" or something like that. The front cover of the TV magazine listed the printer, so we went to the them and said, "How many copies can we get at that size with a two-color cover for this amount of money?" *(laughter)* There were no plastic bags to fit it, and we got letters from a lot of pissed-off people about it! *(laughter)* We just did it that way because it was local and affordable.

The first issue sold out, and we still had orders coming in, so we printed another 6000 which also sold out. It evolved into 60,000 copies by issue four. The peak was 135,000 copies of *Turtles* #8, but even at that point we felt unworthy because there were so many people like Jack Kirby and Frank Miller and countless others who were doing stuff that we wanted to aspire to. We didn't feel like we deserved this, but at the same time we were so grateful that our boyhood dream of drawing comics for a living had come true.

(this page and next) The still unpublished Dingbats *#2, pages 7 and 8.*

BY JON B. COOKE

We'd look at each other some days with these goofy grins on our faces. *(laughter)*

We were very lucky. When we grew up, you had to work for Marvel or DC. Around the time we created the Turtles, there was enough controversy in front of innocent little pups like us that we knew something was wrong; people like Jack that had great ideas weren't benefiting from their great creativity. We observed, and we learned.

TJKC: And you've given back; a lot of people would have taken the money and run, but Eastman and Laird gave back to the industry and the art form.

KEVIN: I blame one person: Jack Kirby. He was the greatest inspiration in my life, period. It's corny to say in one sense, but it's not corny to me at all. When I first met Jack Kirby, Pete and I were at our very first San Diego Comic Con. We heard he was in the building, and we left our table and went over to the area he was in, and we're trembling. This is pre-Turtles; we'd put out the first couple of issues, and we're just overwhelmed. There he is sitting there, with hundreds of people surrounding him, and he's the kindest, most thoughtful gentleman, talking to everyone, telling war stories. He was gallant, and he was brilliant. Every person in that crowd was staring at him like he's one of the gods he creates on his own paper. We got a chance to say "hi." He treated us with such respect; he was amazed that you approached him and were grateful for what he'd given to the community.

TJKC: When did you start collecting original art?

KEVIN: Around late 1985. We were starting to become fairly successful as self-publishers, and the revenues were starting to go beyond just paying rent, so I started buying a few pieces. But until as late as 1988, there still wasn't that much Kirby art out there that was for sale legally. You'd see stuff out there for sale, but because they weren't for sale from Jack, Pete and I refused to buy them. 99.9% of all the artwork I ended up buying was from the Kirbys. I had opportunities to buy other Kirby artwork, but it wasn't kosher, and that bothered me a lot.

At the San Diego Con, Mike Thibodeaux sold me a complete book of *Kamandi,* my number one inspiration, and sold Pete a complete issue of *Demon,* his number one inspiration. So we're going through the convention carrying our complete books of art, and there's Jack Kirby walking and talking to people. So we went up to him and he said, "Let's pose for a picture!" and we wet our pants immediately. *(laughter)* So we're standing there posing for the picture, me holding my *Kamandi* story, Pete holding his *Demon* story, and Jack Kirby's in the middle. And just as the picture's being taken, Julie Schwartz walks up and puts his fingers above Jack's head like little horns. *(laughter)* It's both the coolest and the most frustrating photo I have.

TJKC: Were you buying mostly *Kamandi* originals?

KEVIN: Around the time the Turtles were really taking off, the Kirbys made the decision to sell some of the artwork DC Comics had returned to them. *Kamandi* was my favorite comic; I thought it was brilliantly written, and very imaginative. That was my first introduction to Jack Kirby; I'd ride my bike 7½ miles to the local drug store to buy *Kamandi* because I wanted to be the Last Boy on Earth. *(laughter)* I was able to obtain a number of complete *Kamandi* stories from the Kirbys, and I was able to purchase some of his "Losers" stories. I also came across a few odd things, like *Dingbats of Danger Street.*

TJKC: When did you start conceiving of the Words & Pictures Museum?

KEVIN: Words & Pictures came around the same time, thanks to the blessings of the Turtles, when I was able to start purchasing original artwork. The original artwork world is a page of this, a page of that. One page of original artwork is not the complete work of art; comics are intended to be seen as a complete work. I thought, "How dare I keep this stuff in my closet when other people really need to see this?" I wanted to have an institution that showed the art form in the respectable light I felt it deserved, as well as in the format it was always intended to be in. If you can show a complete Jack Kirby story in its entirety, what better life is there? *(laughter)* You show the whole thing, and you can walk through and read the whole thing.

TJKC: Let's be honest; you had 10,000 pieces of artwork, and you needed a place to put them, right? *(laughter)*

KEVIN: Some people say that. I got a great tax write-off, but at the end of the day, if I can turn one person on, and inspire one person the way I was inspired, that makes it all worthwhile. If it takes 7000 square feet to show off artwork to do it, then that's what it takes. *(laughter)*

TJKC: Is it "Kevin Eastman's" museum or not?
KEVIN: In all honesty, it's both. Because of my good fortune with the Turtles, I was able to build a museum, and the museum now houses almost 20,000 pieces of my artwork. But if I want to have a personal museum where I can enjoy my artwork, I certainly don't have to open it to the public. I could have built a huge house with nothing but wall space with all this artwork around, but that's not the point; I wanted everybody else to see the same beauty that I saw in this true art form. I felt guilty that I would have artwork in a closet or a vault, and not be able to share that with the world. With the museum, you look at the different periods of comics that we love, and they reflect the times we grew up in. Our art form should be respected along with Picasso, Jackson Pollock, and N.C. Wyeth. I wanted to showcase this important art form in the setting it deserves, but I also wanted to give a bit of history here, in that the first picture and word storytellers were the cave painters, or the Mayans, or the Egyptians; through every period of mankind, you can see where this medium was important to history, and life in that period of time. Whether you'd never seen a comic in your life, or you'd been reading them all your life, I wanted you to look at it and say, "Oh my gosh, this wasn't a new discovery as of 1962." It's been here forever.

The Museum was started as a dream of mine. If anyone else can help support it, that's a benefit. If nobody else helps, that's okay too. I never thought of it as "I'll build it, and they will come," but at the same time, I hoped that they would come; not specifically the donors, but the people that would appreciate it. I'll do everything in my power to see that the Museum stays viable — but we're at a time where the Museum of Cartoon Art and the Boca Raton Museum of National Cartoon Art are having some difficulty, and so is the Words & Pictures Museum of Sequential Art.

TJKC: The Words & Pictures Museum is experiencing growing pains; up to now, it's been subsidized in great part by the success of the Ninja Turtles, but at some point, don't other creators have to support it?
KEVIN: We were blessed, and there are a lot of creators out there who were less successful than we were, and I want them to be part of the Museum. At the same time, I've always fully realized it's something that's very personal. Today, the Museum solely survives on half the profits of *Heavy Metal* magazine, half the profits I make from the Turtles, and from memberships. As long as the Turtles are kind to me, I can keep this museum going, and every person who joins with that $2 or $25 or $50 membership helps keep us open for another day, another week, another year. We're looking at tough times, where the Turtles are still out there doing well, but they aren't anything like they were in 1991-92. If in 1991 we were at 100%, in 1998 we're at 8%. It's significant; times change, kids change — but I can still support the Museum on 8%, because it's important to me, and because I have the best staff in the world. The Museum wouldn't be here without Marion Meeks and Fiona Russell. They made that Museum. They made my dreams and my fantasies come true.

Up until 1997, I'd never sold a single piece of art I'd bought for my collection, but my commitment is to see that the Museum survives. I'm talking to Christie's about letting between 5000 and 6000 pieces of my collection go in a couple of Words & Pictures Benefit Auctions. My goal at this point is to create a way to have a foundation for the Museum, so that long after I'm gone and you're gone, the Museum will still be here. I bought the building and donated it to the Museum. I put on permanent loan every piece of art in my collection for the Museum's permanent collection. I don't want to reach out to creators who have families to support and are struggling to make their own ends meet, to help support something that I built. So I really put that responsibility on myself, and I'm at the point where I can support "X" amount of dollars per year without sacrifice. Between the two auctions I'll probably let go of a third of the Museum's permanent collection, in hopes it will build a foundation that will allow the Museum to stay here forever.★

(Editor's Note: Be sure to see the donation form on the letter's page of this issue, and become a member of the Words & Pictures Museum.)

(left) OMAC *#8, page 18 (the final issue of the series). The final panel has a paste-up over it. Under it, Jack's original copy, lettered by Royer, reads: "Don't miss the climax of 'The Skuba Incident!' It's a classic!! It's THE WALKING DEAD!"*

(above) Kamandi *#36, page 4. There was heavy interference by new Editor Gerry Conway; all lettering was redone. One pasted-up caption (upper) has fallen off, showing the original Kirby dialogue (lower) underneath. Was it REALLY necessary to rephrase this?*

A Home Fit For A King

Examining the Kirby Collection at the Words & Pictures Museum, by Jon B. Cooke

In small doses and in their printed form, we all know that Jack Kirby's stories can have a totally mesmerizing effect on a reader. But imagine being exposed to dozens of his stories in one sitting, at one time, looking at the actual pages Jack drew — and you'll know what it's like to overdose with the sheer pleasure of reading unparalleled comic book storytelling. You don't have to be rich to marvel over innumerable original pages of the King's work. The Words & Pictures Museum of Northampton, Massachusetts houses well over 500 pages of Kirby's work. Comics scholar Charles Hatfield and this writer recently had the pleasure of poring over the work when we visited the museum as guests of Curator and Director of Operations Fiona Russell.

Located in the center of the state and founded in 1992 with the creative and financial input of Kevin Eastman, the museum is devoted entirely to works in the comics illustration genre. The attractive Main Street building (completely owned by the museum), situated in the down town heart of the elegant college town, has staged exhibits to a most eclectic array of subjects, from Batman to Fantagraphics, *Alien* to Paul Mavirides, and houses in its vaults nearly 18,000 pieces of original art, the vast majority on permanent loan from Eastman.

Physically the museum is small but packed; a thin, four-story building, with the ground floor housing one of the best comic book stores in the Northeast. The second floor contains the library/reading room, activity area, and administrative offices. The third floor holds the featured exhibit section which changes roughly every two months, and the top floor houses the Permanent Collection Gallery where the best of the collection hangs.

The artist best represented in the collection? "Probably Jack Kirby," Russell said, "given the number of complete stories we have by him. Up until this latest acquisition, which includes work by Kirby, we had an awful lot of Kirby's work but mostly *The Demon, OMAC,* and a lot of *Kamandi.* That's one of the things that happens when you have one philanthropist's collection. You have one gentleman whose passion happens to be Kirby and specifically those three projects, so he collected voraciously in those areas." The second and third most prominent? Richard Corben and Barry Windsor-Smith.

"It's very important to have a museum like this," said Russell. "There isn't another institution really specifically like it. There are three institutions in the country trying to do a similar type of thing — The International Museum of Cartoon Art in Boca Raton (founded by Mort Walker), the San Francisco Cartoon Art Museum, and us — and we need to work together."

"People enjoy reading comics," Russell continued, "but they don't necessarily think about the living, thinking, breathing artists and writers behind it. There needs to be an understanding that there are artists behind the comics. The artists that are working in this genre are so influential to so many other people and known to people in other areas. There definitely is a need for an institution that honors these people and presents them in a museum-style and yet with a bit of fun, zest, and a little bit of tongue-in-cheek once in awhile, much in the way that the art form looks at itself."

As with the comic book industry, the museum is going through a financial crisis that threatens its very existence. W&P cut their budget by 20 per cent last year, and have cut it again this year. "We've been subsidized for years by Kevin's generosity," Russell explained, "but as income from the *Turtles* has dropped in recent years, we're now forced to look for other means of support. To that end, we've established an endowment fund to raise $5 million and derive the day-to-day operating expenses out of the interest garnered, without ever touching the principal." But convincing other comic book pros and fans that W&P is more than Kevin Eastman's private museum has been an uphill battle. "Kevin wanted the museum to reach a certain stage so that when it was fully functioning, he could disengage and present W&P as a gift to comic book aficionados. He didn't gift an idea or concept, but gave the world a working museum. We've reached that stage and are looking for people to come on board and help."

The Endowment Campaign was started in August, 1997. The response so far? "It's been tough," Russell said. "The question from prospects has been, 'Why should I give to this? Kevin will just give and give and give and give.' So we haven't been getting the message out that this is their museum as well as Kevin's. We have to shoulder the blame, so we've hired a new Director of Finance and Development, Joe Scelsi, and he's taking the bull by the horns and doing follow-up."

Other ways of contributing? "Creators can donate works of art to the museum for two reasons," Russell said. "One, we will hold it in perpetuity in the collection, and two — which sounds sacrilegious but is enormously helpful — is to donate art that we can then auction to benefit the endowment fund. We're also working with a number of publishers to receive a percentage of ownership on some creative properties. Publishers can help us out in small but significant ways — Dark Horse and Kitchen Sink, for instance, give us two copies of every book they publish. We put one in the reading room and house the other."

Regardless of the financial challenges ahead, Russell remains firmly enthusiastic. "There's a real invigoration, a lot of positive energy, and forward momentum in the museum at this point. We just need to keep that alive so we're really aggressively going out and talking to people to make them understand that the museum really does serve an important purpose."★

Words & Pictures Museum Kirby Holdings

(Note: This list may be incomplete)

Book	Issue #	Pages
Black Panther	12	1-3, 5-7, 11, 14-15, 21, 23, 26-27, 30-31
Captain America	212	1-31
Demon	8	1-23, cover (complete)
Devil Dinosaur	9	3, 7, 21
Dingbats	2	7, 8 (unpublished)
Eternals	14	2-3, 6-7, 10-11, 14-15, 17, 22-23, 26-27
	15	1, 3-4, 10-11, 15, 17, 22-23, 27, 30-31
FF Annual	1	43 (pin-up)
Kamandi	3	1-22
	7	7-20
	8	1-20, cover (complete)
	11	1-20, cover (complete)
	12	1-20, cover (complete)
	14	1-20, cover (complete)
	15	1-20, cover (complete)
	16	1-20, cover (complete)
	17	1-18, cover
	18	1-20, cover (complete)
	19	1-20, cover (complete)
	20	1-20, cover (complete)
	21	1-20, cover (complete)
	23	1-20, cover (complete)
	26	1-17, cover
	27	1-20, cover (complete)
	28	1-6, 8-20, cover
	35	1, 12
	36	4 (other pages may also be in the collection)
	39	5, 8, 14
	40	7, 12
Machine Man	4	20 total (missing 5-7, 10, 12)
	5	1, 4, 6-7, 10-11, 13-14, 19-21
	Covers	4 covers (unsure of #s at press time)
New Gods	10	4, 6, 8-10, 12, 14-15, 17-22, cover
	11	4, 9, 10-14, cover
Our Fighting Forces	154	1-26, cover, 2-page back-up (complete)
	155	all pages and cover (complete)
	156	1-16, cover/pin-up?, 2-page back-up
	158	1-16, cover, 2-page back-up (complete)
	160	2-16
	161	1-18
	162	1-18, "Mail-Call"
	Misc.	Unused Losers page (see TJKC #17)
OMAC	8	1-18
Sgt. Fury	2	4 total pages (page 4 is one of them)
	7	1-22
Super Powers	5	2-3, 6-10, 12, 16-20, 22-23, cover
Tales To Astonish	13	"Groot" page 9
Misc:		Ninja Turtles Drawing, (2) Ninja Turtles Sketches

Secrets of the Kirby Collection

Charles Hatfield and I did uncover some interesting insights:

- *Fantastic Four Annual* #1, pg. 43. "Answers about the Fantastic Four" A rare two-up page which features remnants of Jack's distinctive handwriting which indicates he wrote the entire page, revealing overwhelming conceptual input on the FF.
- *Kamandi* #36, pg. 4. "The Hotel" Evidence of heavy editorial interference as every D. Bruce Berry-lettered caption and balloon is re-lettered and often minutely rephrased.
- *OMAC* #8, pg. 18. Last panel is a paste-up that conveniently ties up storyline but underneath we found the following Mike Royer-lettered tease which promised of a story to come: "Don't miss the climax of "The Skuba Incident!" It's a classic!! It's THE WALKING DEAD"
- *Black Panther* #12, pg. 31. Last panel is a paste-up promising new writer, new artist, new story, but beneath we found mention of a never-realized story, "Face to Face."

HOUR TWENTY-FIVE

Excerpts from the 1986 KPFK 90.7 FM Los Angeles science fiction talk radio show, where Jack Kirby, Frank Miller, Mark Evanier, Arthur Byron Cover, and Steve Gerber discussed Jack's battle with Marvel Comics over the return of his original art • Transcribed by John Morrow

> **"You can hide a platoon of assassins in a complex deal!"**
> Don Rickles, *Jimmy Olsen* #141 (1971), p. 16

HOUR 25: If you're a writer, you get to keep your manuscripts. If you're an artist, this does not necessarily obtain. Jack, what happened?

JACK KIRBY: What happened was that Marvel decided to return the pages to the artists, and they sent the releases out to the various artists that did work for them over the years. My release was quite different than the others. It was a release I couldn't sign, and that created a controversy. It mystified me; I don't know why I got this kind of a release. It was a four-page release; it was almost like a contract, whereas the average release was something I could sign. I would've signed it, and there would have been an ordinary exchange of release and pages. They created a situation in which I was stuck; it became a legal thing, and I'm sorry about the circumstance itself — but it was they who sent the release out, and it was I who can't sign it. So they kept my pages.

HOUR 25: You have done thousands and thousands of pages over the years. And I must say it's only Marvel we're talking about; with DC, there's no problem.

KIRBY: According to statistics, I've done one quarter of Marvel's entire output. There's a lot of hard work

MEANWHILE ANGEL'S DAD AND MOM ARE PREPARING TO LEAVE TO SEE ANGEL -- THEY ARE HIGH-INCOME PEOPLE -- THEY HAVE LARGE HOUSE - SPACIOUS WELL KEPT GROUNDS AND A HANDY-MAN'S PUTTING THEIR LUGGAGE IN REAR OF CAR -- MOTHER SAYS -- AREN'T WE EVER GOING TO GET STARTED? WHY COULDN'T WE FLY?
DAD SAYS -- WILL YOU STOP WITH THE HYSTERIA? ANGEL SAID HE WAS OKAY! I'M SURE WE'LL UPSET HIM MORE
ANGEL'S MOM
ANGEL'S DAD
LINCOLN CONTINENTAL OR CADDY
HANDYMAN
THEN, SECONDS LATER...
IT WON'T BE LONG NOW!

The top panel of page 19 of X-Men *#17 (bottom) was pasted over. Shown here are Jack's unused pencil layouts and margin notes that remain under the paste-up.*

behind it, and a lot of hard thinking behind it. It's something that's highly individual, highly creative, and above all, it sold very well.

ARTHUR BYRON COVER: As I understand it, when they sent you the four-page more complex form, they'd only admit to having 88 pages of artwork out of all the thousands of pages you did.

KIRBY: There's eight books involved. There's 88 pages involved. There's thousands of books I did, and all they offered was eight.

FRANK MILLER: It's very important to keep in mind that we're talking about an extraordinary situation here. Jack's work is the basic stuff that Marvel Comics has, across twenty years or so, turned into the most powerful comic book publisher in the country. The ideas that sprang from him into pictures — into a visual style they use full-time, all the time now — have not been credited to him by Marvel. Everyone in the industry, everyone anywhere near it, knows what his contribution was. Marvel is refusing to acknowledge this, and now they're withholding from him his own physical artwork which they are withholding from no one else. I read these documents they want him to sign; it's the most offensive legal creation I've ever read. It's very insulting.

STEVE GERBER: I think it's important to point out also that they never paid for the physical artwork. They don't own the physical artwork; it's there only because, apparently, possession is nine-tenths of the law at the moment.

COVER: In the latest issue of *The Comics Journal,* they had cataloged and accounted for three-quarters of the pages. For some reason since then, they've decided that there's only 88 pages, and if the situation's changed, they're not saying how or why.

HOUR 25: Did they give you a straightforward reason for this, Jack?

KIRBY: I can only guess, and I'm not going to discuss any guessing on my part. It's very hard to communicate with Marvel; they rarely answer. I leave it entirely to my lawyers. I'm trying to do it in a conventional and sensible legal manner; I try not to offend Marvel in any way, I try to be as polite as possible. I regard management as important people to work for; I always have. My job has always been to sell books. When you sell books, you benefit the publisher as well as yourself. What I do is not out of any innate disregard for management. I see it as a business; I've been a publisher myself.

HOUR 25: *The Comics Journal* reported there was a panel at Comic-Con in San Diego last July, and Jim Shooter paneled with you and Frank Miller and some others discussing this. Shooter was in the audience, and he stood up and said at one point that he thought you should have the art back. He also said that as Editor In Chief at Marvel, no decisions were made without his concurrence. That would seem to be a reasonable way to work things out, but it seems the reasonableness ended right there.

KIRBY: They'll return my art, *if* I'll sign that release — and I can't sign it.

MILLER: Beyond the amount of work Jack did and how well it sold, the fact is it's still making money. The most popular comic book in the country is the *X-Men,* which is one of Jack's. If you go down the list, probably five out of the next six down will be his. What he did for comics was enormous. The whole shape of comics in these times is based on Jack's work.

MARK EVANIER: It's not that uncommon for a new artist to apply for work at Marvel and be handed old Jack Kirby books, and told, "This is what we want."

MILLER: It was done with me.

EVANIER: There are artists to this day in the business who make their living tracing old Jack Kirby panels, rearranging them slightly, using it for their own purposes, and calling it their work.

HOUR 25: Fans come up to you with original pages of your own art; where do they get them?

KIRBY: I never ask because it embarrasses them. I tell them that the art is stolen; I have my own ideas on how it's passed around, and I've investigated it. It's not a complete picture, but I have a hazy picture of what really happens. If they're young people... I had a very young boy come up to me with a page of my artwork. I don't have the heart not to sign it. I'm not going to embarrass that child, or a female, or a very sincere fan, so I sign it. I have a high respect for the people in comics. I know the average comic fan is a heckuva guy.

EVANIER: It should be pointed out, a lot of people have made a lot of money selling Jack Kirby originals, and Jack is not one of them.

MILLER: What we're talking about here is a wealth of work, but the only thing that's in dispute here is the original physical artwork to it. This is one more way a lot of people besides Jack have made money off his genius.

HOUR 25: Jack, what are you going to do?

KIRBY: What I have to do; what any American has to do. Call it corny if you like. I'm up against a corporate giant. They've got a heckuva lot more weapons than I have. If I have one lawyer, they have ten. It's a hard battle; I do it slowly, I do it piecemeal. It's a thing that lasts a long, long time.

MILLER: Another thing that's being done is *The Comics Journal* circulated a petition among professionals, and there's been since then a protest on the part of comics professionals on Jack's behalf; writers and artists speaking out on his behalf, hoping to at least shame Marvel into behaving like humans about this.

HOUR 25: In the current issue of *The Comics Journal,* Frank Miller wrote a piece, and you begin it by saying you were at a cocktail party full of professionals, and you mentioned Kirby's name, and the silence was real thick.

MILLER: It happened many times when the subject came up. I hope that it's a temporary effect; I hope it's just a simple stroke of fear running through things. I hope that at the very least, the rest of the professionals will join in signing that petition. This is one of the very few huge issues to strike the industry. It's really up to each artist's conscience as to whether he participates in supporting Jack. Simple gratitude is what anybody working in comics owes Jack. We owe him very simply our livelihood. I would not have the career I have if not for him.

Journey Into Mystery *#117, page 16.*

EVANIER: This is not just the plight of people who worked for Marvel on Jack's characters. There would probably be no industry today if not for Jack. The fascinating thing about Jack's career is that in the 1940s, he innovated a whole kind of super-hero in Captain America, the Boy Commandos, the Newsboy Legion. If he had stopped there and never created anything else, we'd still be talking about a giant here. Then in the 1950s, he innovated romance comics, *Black Magic, Fighting American, Sky Masters, Challengers of the Unknown.* In the '60s he did it all over again, and in the '70s with the *New Gods.* It just goes on and on.

MILLER: It does show how the conditions of the industry have been very bad off and on. The 1960s turnabout that really comes from Jack's work followed a period of pretty dismal downward sales. I believe he has repeatedly built the industry up almost single-handedly. The industry has generally not invited people to do their best work, because of some legal things they insist on. Jack had always done his best, and his best has always been better than anyone else's.

HOUR 25: So what you're going to do now is keep your attorneys writing letters, and apply

Page 2 of the back-up story in Jimmy Olsen *#144. Jack got most of his '70s DC art back.*

pressure as you can in the industry, and wait?

KIRBY: Yes. I'm rather stubborn that way. I feel I've earned it, and there's no other way it can be done. I can only work according to my own resources, and that's what I'm doing. I'll do it legally, conventionally, in as friendly an atmosphere as possible.

MILLER: If I may, my personal feeling about it is it's not Jack's job. The comic book professionals, and particularly the readers, should exercise whatever voice they have in support of him. He's already given Marvel billions of dollars worth of material, he's given us years of joy, he's given us our livelihoods. I think we can come to his side on this; I don't think we should be asking him how *he's* going to pursue it.

HOUR 25: Steve Gerber, you had a dust-up with Marvel. I know you can't talk about the settlement.

EVANIER: But I can! *(laughter)*

GERBER: The disagreement was over the ownership of the Howard the Duck character. It took three years of my life and $140,000 to pursue. Some of that, thank heavens, was offset by the two dozen or so people in the industry I can still look straight in the eye, Jack among them. Jack did the artwork for the first issue of *Destroyer Duck,* which was done as a benefit comic book for the lawsuit, absolutely *gratis.* We did return his artwork, however. *(laughter)*

Some of it was offset later by a project that was initialed by Deni Sim *[Loubert]*, called the *FOOG Portfolio: The Friends Of Old Gerber Portfolio, (laughter)* done with my blessing, but totally without my knowledge. But the proceeds from both of those projects covered 20%, possibly a little more of the lawsuit. So when you talk about suing a company like Marvel, Jack is absolutely correct. You're sitting there with one, perhaps two lawyers, facing a battery of lawyers which include, in this case, an outside firm, retained locally in California to deal with the suit; Marvel's own in-house lawyers; Cadence Industries' in-house lawyers; and a firm back in New York which is under retainer to Cadence. That's what you're up against when you go into something like this. We fought it all the way to within two weeks of actually going to court. We were prepared to go into court, and at the last moment we were able to reach a settlement which I thought was fair and equitable, and in many ways less chancy than going to court with something like this. A decision against me, which was possible, would've done a great deal of harm not only to me, but to other people who might have to sue another comics publisher or the same publisher on the same basis. I didn't want to take that risk. The trial alone would've cost another $25,000, and I could've gotten stuck with some of Marvel's legal fees after that. So looking at the whole thing on balance, I had to decide that a truly equitable settlement, which I felt this was, was the way to end the dispute.

Marvel owns Howard the Duck, and Marvel has creative control over him. I'm allowed to say that because it was part of a joint press release Marvel and my attorneys and I issued at the time of the settlement.

EVANIER: One of the reasons Steve settled when he did — he's too modest to mention this — is that the comics industry at the close of the suit was not the same as at the beginning of the suit. One of the things that prompted Steve's suit in the first place was that at one point he wanted to try and work out a settlement with Marvel on parts of his contract that had been left dangling. I sent him to an agent of mine, and the agent phoned the appropriate people at Marvel, and they said, "We're not going to deal with you." They didn't recognize the rights of people to speak on behalf of artists and writers.

MILLER: We're talking about an industry that until maybe ten years ago, a contract could not be negotiated in the office of the publisher of a major comic book company, because the writer showed up with his attorney. The publisher just got up and walked out. This is a true story; I know the writer, I know the attorney, and I know the publisher. We're talking about the Dark Ages here.

EVANIER: It was 1978, I believe. *(laughter)* Largely because of Steve's lawsuit, and because of other people who said, "We're not going to take it anymore," the comic book companies grew up a little. They have yet to make proper redress on all of the old offenses, but they're now dealing in a more mature manner. They will talk to attorneys, and they will draw up legitimate contracts. They now realize they can not conduct major comic book company business like a lemonade stand. Steve's lawsuit was one of the main reasons for that.

GERBER: One of the things that the suit definitely made clear was simply that in the forty years between the creation of Superman in 1938, and my being escorted off Howard the Duck in 1978, essentially nothing had changed in the comic industry. Jerry Siegel and Joe Shuster were in precisely the same position that I was in — and Jack Kirby finds himself in that same position today; worse, in fact. Jack can not even get the physical artwork back, which Marvel never even claimed to own.

HOUR 25: That's the part that blows me away. We're not talking ownership or creation here; we're talking physical artwork pages, not the right to publish those pages.

EVANIER: There is a link here; it's the three words "work-for-hire." In 1976, the copyright laws in the country were amended to give the creator of the work a greater expanded power of copyright renewal. Prior to that time there had been some question that at the time the copyright expired, whether the copyright could be renewed by the writer of the book, or by the publisher of the book, or whoever. It was established clearly in that revision of the copyright law that the creator of the work had the right of renewal. So the comic book companies — and this happened outside comics as well — determined that they had to make themselves the creator. The phrase "work-for-hire" came into heavy usage at this point, and when you sign a work-for-hire contract with a comic book company, you are stating that the company is the creator, and has all rights of future renewal to the work, and you are an assistant. If Frank Miller writes a comic book, conceives of it, creates it, pencils it, letters it, inks it, colors it, takes it to the printer himself, if he signs that contract, he's saying the publisher did all that, and the publisher's the creator, and the publisher can not only get the right of copyright renewal, but any further legal rights that are ever granted in the future to the creator of the work.

KIRBY: You're leaving out one thing. The publisher did that arbitrarily; they printed that on the back of every check the artist ever got. If you didn't sign that check, you didn't get paid.

EVANIER: For a long time, the only way the companies attempted to qualify the rights was with the back of the check statement. That was your "contract" that you had to deposit at the bank. It was a non-negotiable contract. It was only in the late 1970s when they started selling the Hulk to television and Superman to movies that they went back and tried to retroactively clarify a lot of what they were claiming they had bought the rights to.

Jack has never signed that work-for-hire contract, and that's a key point that has to be made. Jack got this contract that nobody else ever got to get his originals back. The reason is that Jack didn't sign a work-for-hire contract.

MILLER: It's also because Jack made up a lot of stuff that's worth a whole lot. The experts I've talked to on this confirm that the physical artwork is not related to the reproduction rights to it. It is simply the artist's work, unless he sells it. Since I gather Jack hasn't been confronted with a Bill of Sale from Marvel for those originals, no matter what they may claim about the reproduction rights to the material, the physical artwork is his.

GERBER: Neal Adams brought up that Jack was living and working in New York most of the time he was doing most of those pages. He was selling them to a company which was also located in New York City. Therefore, he had to collect, and the company had to pay, sales tax on the artwork if indeed the artwork was sold. No sales tax was ever paid, no sales tax was ever collected. It's the difference between selling a service and selling a product.

HOUR 25: Jack, what are you doing now?

KIRBY: I'm working very hard. I'm creating; I'm a producer/consultant for Ruby-Spears, which does Saturday morning TV. I create concepts; I visualize them in a way in which TV people can understand them and estimate them and create shows from them. I'm essentially doing the same thing. I'm not out to be a Leonardo DiVinci, I'm not out to be William Faulkner; I'm out to sell comics, which I think is a very valid American medium. There are people who play down comics, but comics is a valid medium. It's a visual narrative; instead of words, we like the pictures, we like the balloons. If you'll go with me to the Sistine Chapel, I'll put up a couple of balloons on Michelangelo's work and we can really tell what was going on, *(laughter)* because I think they're cartoons in a way.

MILLER: I found out in researching this situation on Jack that DC to a certain extent has made efforts to reward and give credit to their major creators since 1940.

EVANIER: DC cleaned out their warehouse several years ago. Although DC is not under any legal obligation to, they've given Jack a profit participation in the usage of his *New Gods* characters in toys and shows and things like that. The people at DC are very proud of saying that they have paid Jack Kirby more money for creating Darkseid than he was paid for creating the entire Marvel Universe. So were not talking about a bunch of disgruntled writers and artists complaining that someone didn't get enough; if Marvel adopted the DC policy on this, I think everyone would be very happy.

CALLER: Jack, what exactly was the clause in your contract that kept you from signing it?

KIRBY: Specifically, I can cite one clause that didn't allow me to sue Marvel for anything at all. It violated my civil rights; as an American you should be able to sue anyone you like. But Marvel insisted that I wasn't allowed to sue Marvel, and the entire premise of the thing was humiliating to me, to my family, and being a little macho in nature, *(laughter)* I couldn't do it.

GERBER: Didn't it also say that you had to say you were not the creator of those characters?

MILLER: They said you couldn't tell your daughter.

KIRBY: It was at the point of being arrogant and abusive, and I couldn't do it. It's against my nature.

HOUR 25: I want to come back to one point, which I want to make certain does not get overlooked. We're not talking here about money, or anything except pages of original artwork.

GERBER: There's no legal concept in question; that's the other thing.

MILLER: Every few weeks, I receive a package from DC Comics, containing artwork that was drawn for them. It's a Federal Express package, and I sign indicating I received it. That's the only document DC wants me to sign, a simple receipt for the return of my property.

EVANIER: Jack is the only person in this situation. Even the people who inked his comics have gotten back some of those pages. Dick Ayers, Joe Sinnott, Chic Stone, all the people who inked those books have gotten their shares of the same stories; part of it has been returned. It's Jack's pages that are not being returned.

HOUR 25: Jack, is there anything else you would like to say?

KIRBY: I'm from the old school; I'm from a generation you fellas know nothing about. I ask nobody to do anything for me. I ask people who've been listening tonight to gain whatever knowledge they could of the field, of the personalities, and maybe to gain a little knowledge about myself; but I ask them to do nothing. If they feel like writing a letter, fine. If they don't, it's still fine with me. I'll continue my own fight. It'll go on because I want it to go on. If it stops, it'll be because I stopped it. I ask nothing of anybody. It's because of my own love for the individual that I ask nothing from it. If there are any people on my side, I thank them. It's a fulfilling sensation for me, and I thank them again.★

"Every professional must live or die by his own methods!"

Thaddeus Brown, *Mister Miracle* #1 (1971), p. 12

Gary Groth Interviewed

by Jon B. Cooke

(Gary Groth, long the enfant terrible of comics critics and bane of the comics industry, has edited the notorious and combative Comics Journal *since 1976, and has since founded Fantagraphics Books. In issue #105, the* Journal *brought Jack's battle with Marvel Comics over ownership of his original art to the attention of the entire industry. The interview was conducted via phone in February 1998 and was copy-edited by Groth.)*

> **"Fate has its own answer to the greatest of power!"**
> Etrigan, *The Demon* #5 (1973), p. 20

TJKC: Do you recall when you first heard about Jack's problems getting his art back from Marvel?

GARY GROTH: I remember Jack and Roz initially asked us to either not report it, or to soft-pedal it, because they were negotiating with Marvel, and they didn't want those negotiations compromised. I remember honoring those requests, basically sitting on it.

TJKC: What did the fight represent in the greater scheme of things? Was it simply one man against a corporate entity?

GARY: Sure it was. I think it represented, in as starkly black-&-white terms as you could possibly want, the issue of a large corporation arrayed against a single artist. This sort of thing had been going on since the beginning of comics, but they were sort of routine injustices. This represented something of a departure from that, because it wasn't just a work-for-hire issue, which had become an institutional part of comics. They had singled one man out for this treatment; he was being treated differently than other artists, and there was a reason for that: His creative contribution. The more he contributed creatively, the more severely he was singled out, and given a radically different kind of agreement to sign.

Pencils from Machine Man *#6, page 5.*

TJKC: What effect did you see in the industry of publicizing this situation?

GARY: It really mobilized the professional community. We drafted a petition, and a large number of professionals signed it. Some creators were willing to go out on a limb, which is unusual for comics. Some weren't, but certainly more creators were willing to stick their necks out at this particular time than any other time I can remember.

TJKC: It took some time, but the issue was resolved to some degree. How'd you hear about that?

GARY: Roz called me and told me. It was resolved to probably nobody's satisfaction. I think they gave him a shorter form than the original, but still a longer form than anyone else got. They deleted the more demeaning language, and gave him a percentage of whatever art was left that hadn't been ripped off or sold or given away through the years. Certainly Jack and Roz were just happy to get it behind them.

I remember Roz and Jack and I went out to dinner shortly after the thing was more or less over. I don't know if you'd call it a post mortem or a celebration; I think it was a cross between the two. It's odd; Jack was a reluctant fighter, which is not what you might expect. My impression is he really didn't want to get into this, but he felt he had no choice. I think Jack was torn too, because Marvel had been his employer. Jack had that peculiar post-war perception of American business; sort of gung-ho toward American business. My impression is it took him quite some time to get his blinders removed.

I think he shrank from conflict. In a substantial way, we — me, Frank Miller, and various other people, including many retailers and other publishers — were acting on his behalf; in a way as surrogates for him, taking the fight to the market. Temperamentally, he was unsuited to do it himself.

TJKC: When you interviewed him in *Comics Journal* #134, he sounded quite combative. He was angry; there seemed to be an obvious bitterness about the situation with Marvel. Were you surprised?

GARY: I think I was surprised at his vehemence, because he refrained from it publicly. I think he might've seen the interview as a place to be as truthful and open about that as he could've been. I don't know if I saw him combative as much as I saw a lot of pain and a lot of hurt. My most vivid recollection of that interview was when he said he had a family to support, and that he felt torn between being as independent as possible and telling corporations he worked for to go to hell, and supporting his family. He felt trapped in that position, which I think is an enormous admission for a man of Jack's generation. There was a tremendous degree of self-awareness there that he had probably not revealed. And for years I think it tore him up. But he was indoctrinated into the system, and he was taught not to complain, and not to whine; to "accept it like a man."

TJKC: Did you give Jack and Roz the opportunity to copy-edit the interview before you published it?
GARY: Usually, if the interview subject asks for it, I give it. A lot of interview subjects don't ask for it and don't care, and neither Roz nor Jack asked to see it. I didn't specifically ask them if they wanted to, partially out of pragmatic editorial concerns, because it delays the interview. I frankly thought I could copy-edit the interview as well as they could; I don't want to be uncharitable, but Jack wasn't particularly sensitive as an editor. I thought it would be a burden on both our sides if they edited it. We tried to fact-check it to some extent, and the facts still got screwed up in there. Internally I tried to edit it, because Jack's memory was not entirely accurate.

TJKC: Did you consider the effect the interview would have? For example, how Jack's comments about Stan Lee would affect their relationship?
GARY: I probably considered it momentarily, but it wasn't something I was particularly sensitive to. It's one thing to assume there will be ramifications; it's another thing to act on that. We run a lot of interviews where I think, "We're going to hurt someone's feelings, someone's going to get pissed off at this," but ultimately that's not my concern. My concern is to present the interview subject's words as accurately and truthfully as possible.

Jack's comments about Stan revealed a lot about Jack's recollection. I don't know if his recollections were literally accurate; I guess nobody knows but Jack and Stan, but it certainly reflects how Jack perceived that, and I thought that was important. There's a section where Jack said Stan didn't write anything. I don't think that's literally true; I think from Jack's point of view that's true, because Jack felt he wrote the comic by pacing it, and drawing it, and writing the descriptions in the margins; he considered that writing. And you have to accept that as Jack's perception, and you have to read between the lines. I think that also reflected a lot of bitterness on Jack's part, and that revealed the extent of his resentment. He felt betrayed. I also think there was Stan's public attitude that Jack took offense at, in the sense that Stan took too much credit. There was a feeling that Jack felt betrayed because Stan didn't stand up for him; that Jack gave all the creative energy he could to Marvel, and he got f*cked as a result.

TJKC: In spite of the *Journal* not giving much coverage to traditional super-hero comics, you

Uninked pencils from Thor *#164, page 18.*

gave great coverage to Kirby, the pre-eminent super-hero artist of all time. Why was that?
GARY: He did more than super-heroes during his career. I think one can legitimately see Kirby as an enormous creative force, notwithstanding any antipathy you have for super-heroes.

TJKC: Will Jack's "Street Code" story still be in the upcoming Fantagraphics' Jack Kirby book?
GARY: No. I sort of struck a deal with Roz, but apparently she had second thoughts about it. It's going to be all the interviews the *Journal* ran with Jack. We've got a lot of critical essays covering various aspects of Jack's career. It's got a new reminiscence by Mike Royer; it's a terrific first-person reminiscence of his period working with Jack. It'll probably be out at the end of this year.

TJKC: Was Jack a genius?
GARY: Well... (pause) probably not. I'd be hard-pressed to consider any cartoonist a genius; that's just not a word I bandy about casually. A lot of the virtues you see in comics are only because the context is comic books. So I think it's easy to bloat the virtues of any particular artist, whether it's Harvey Kurtzman or Carl Barks or Jack. I think Jack was an authentic artist, but where he was in the scale of artists, I wouldn't want to hazard a guess. But he brought a tremendous amount of creative virtue to comics and to his work.★

THE STOLEN ART

First, imagine a locked and secured storage room. It could be someone's basement, a bank vault — it might even be a warehouse somewhere. In the room is a stack of art about 4' high. Perhaps it's moldering, perhaps it's fresh as the day it was drawn, but it hasn't seen the light of day for almost 35 years, and it has a potential street value of millions of dollars. The only question is: Does this room exist at all?

To get into that room, we need to start more broadly, on the ugly topic of art theft. The following is based on interviews with a dozen collectors and industry people. It should be read as an accumulation of opinions, not necessarily hard facts.

There are few topics in the Kirby legend about which there are more bruised feelings than the ownership and distribution of his artwork. There are, as they say, heated differences of opinion. Though they might not have all the details at hand, most art collectors know that a good percentage of Jack's art was "stolen." I put quotations around that word not to be coy, but because even a small amount of research shows that the word's meaning rapidly becomes slippery.

In the Golden Age, comics were considered worthless. It's generally suspected that most of Jack's art circa World War II was thrown away or re-used for paper drives. But not all of it. For instance, two pages from *Captain America* popped up within the last year, and a cover is rumored to exist. Were these given away? Or did someone walk out of the offices with them on the sly? I've heard both versions of the story, and after fifty years, it's probably hard to prove one way or the other. If the art was given away, was it the right of the artist or the publisher to hand it over? Hard to say.

For years, DC relied on a legal decision that, for copyright protection, they needed to destroy all original art — the argument being that if an artist claimed ownership of the art, he might have a crack at owning the character. DC's policy meant that most of Jack's "Green Arrow" and *Challengers of the Unknown* artwork is lying in pieces in a landfill. However, some of the art that was supposed to be destroyed managed to survive, because staffers who were also art fans saved it. If they sold this art, was it stolen? Sure — but from whom? DC, who would have destroyed it? Or their artists, who legally had no clear rights to it at the time?

The story gets wilder when we turn to Atlas/Marvel work from the time of Jack's 1958-59 return until the end of the Silver Age. Most art before 1960 was thrown away to make room for the newer stuff, which sat in a warehouse or in the offices, until 1974 when Marvel started returning it to the pencilers and inkers. Jack, of course, went through an epic legal battle before his Silver Age art was returned in July, 1987. However, of the almost 10,000 pages he penciled through 1970, he was returned roughly 2100. So what happened to the rest of it?

The gut reaction most people have is "it was stolen!" To a large extent, this is correct. However, to better understand what happened, we need to think with the 1962 corporate mentality. They were selling products that cost 10¢, later 12¢. There was no back issue market, no organized fandom to answer to. The art, if it had any value at all, held only sentimental value. Marvel — and in the early days, Marvel was just a couple of guys in an office, not a conglomerate — gave out art for promotional pieces, or as thanks to messengers, or when kids wrote in asking for mementos.

The art that was given away was rarely Kirby. Some early collectors say that Don Heck *Iron Man* pages were the most likely things to be freebies — Kirby was different, even then. Mark Evanier says that Jack asked for his pages back in the 1960s, but couldn't get a clear response.

BY GLEN GOLD

(left) Pencils from Thor *#152, page 7.*

Since Marvel kept being acquired, it sometimes counted art as an asset, sometimes not — depending on whether it was good for their net worth. Stan Lee thought about opening a gallery, or selling it, but since no one was sure of the legal status (remember DC's vision of copyright problems), and since no one valued the art, plotting a course wasn't a high priority.

In the meantime, the art was stored, sometimes in the offices, sometimes in a warehouse. Some was lost in transit, and some was quite blatantly stolen. In 1969 and 1970, two Marvel staffers (let's call them Irving and Forbush) showed up at a Saint Louis Convention with hundreds of pages of art for sale, including Kirby *Fantastic Four* pages from 1963. These sold for about $10-15 a page. I've heard a few explanations of their actions — mostly that this was 1970, and in a counter-culture sort of way, Irving and Forbush were pissed off about the corporation — but many people I talked to simply call what they did "stealing."

Around 1971-72, the Guy who ran Marvelmania had Marvel send him a stack of original art. The idea was that he would stat it to make posters and promotional materials. However, the Guy ended up using it in lieu of salary to pay the kids who worked for him. This art included pages from *Journey into Mystery* #83, *Spider-Man* #20 and #51 (not Kirby, but hey, Ditko and Romita are nice) and various Kirby/Sinnott *Fantastic Four* books. Then he took the balance of the art and sold it to a comic book shop in Hollywood. One collector I talked to remembers seeing Kirby pre-hero monster pages gathering dust there. I myself have seen a page from *Tales of Suspense* #92 that has the "Marvelmania" stamp on the back. Marvel never pursued the return of this art, so it's unclear whether they even considered it stolen. Jack, who was much more clear on the subject — sure it was stolen — managed to recover some of it for his own use.

The Comics Journal #105 has an excellent and lengthy article about how Marvel treated their art between the early '70s and 1986. In short, it was stored haphazardly for years, but then catalogued carefully on a master list. According to the list, almost all of Jack's work — save some of the origin issues and much of his prime *FF* work — was still in Marvel's hands as of 1980. But by 1987, when Jack's art was returned, thousands of pages were gone. What happened?

The specifics are hard to determine. Generally speaking, a lot of stuff was stolen. There are a couple of factors at play — first, several people inform me that the master list was wildly inaccurate. If it said, for instance, that an envelope contained 22 pages of *X-Men* #4, it might not really have that at all. Next, the art was beginning to be recognized as valuable. As the price of comics went up, so did interest in art. Frankly, there were some flat-out unscrupulous people working in the office who helped themselves when the opportunity presented itself.

Though accusations are rampant — if you were within a hundred yards of Marvel's offices before 1986, someone somewhere swears you have *FF* #1 pages on your living room wall — no bombs will be lobbed today. Instead, I'll tell you what many people have told me. During Kirby's negotiations, his art was ordered moved from its warehouse — located at 16 West 22nd Street, according to *The Comics Journal* — and into a storage area at Marvel's offices. Several people emphasize how close this area was to the elevator, meaning a clean getaway. Shortly thereafter, art by Kirby and Ditko that was previously on Marvel's master list began showing up at New York conventions for $40-60 a page. Though Marvel was asked to step in and get the art back, they claimed that they didn't have an accurate list of their holdings, and so couldn't prove the art was in fact stolen.

For the most part, the story of art theft ends here. But there is one niggling detail that I haven't yet covered: That four-foot stack of art, the one worth so many millions.

Few Atlas/Marvel covers from before Summer 1965 have turned up. The first published covers that have appeared on the market are for *Journey into Mystery Annual* #1, *Avengers* #16, *FF* #40 and *Astonish* #67 — all from Summer '65. It's as if someone grabbed a small pile, letting the rest go to mulch. There are two schools of thought on this: First, someone has the rest of the covers; second, that they were destroyed in the printing process. To refresh your memory, we're talking about *Amazing Adventures* #1-6, *Amazing Fantasy* #15, *Avengers* #1-15, *Fantastic Four* #1-39, *Hulk* #1-6, *Journey into Mystery* #52-115, *Rawhide Kid* #17-47, *Sgt. Fury* #1-20, *Strange Tales* #68-135, *Tales of Suspense* #4-67, *Tales to Astonish* #1-66 and *X-Men* #1-12. In other words, the most valuable pages that Jack drew in his life.

Since at least 95% of the interior pages to these books have survived (the earliest I know of being a complete story from *Tales to Astonish* #1), some people think the covers must have been destroyed. The few covers widely known to have survived are either unpublished (an alternate *X-Men* #10, for instance), or statted from the splash (*Tales to Astonish* #34). Furthermore, everyone who is known to have removed artwork from the Marvel offices has, at one time or another, let some greater or lesser piece of it go, to friends, at auction, in trade, etc. I've been doing historical research, looking into fanzines from the 1960s, and though some tempting artwork shows up, no pre '65 Kirby covers — not even *Rawhide Kid* covers — are advertised.

I called Eastern Color Printing, which handled Marvel's comics, and talked to the man who, for over thirty years — the entire Golden and Silver Ages — saw every issue get printed. He told me that all the art, covers and interiors, went back from the engravers to Marvel in the same envelope. So no, the covers weren't destroyed. Also, Atlas covers that immediately predate the Kirby run exist — such as the cover to *Rawhide Kid* #16. Why would that exist and *Rawhide Kid* #17, the first Kirby issue, not survive?

Long-time collectors all have "the-one-that-got-away" stories about earlier covers that they apparently saw: *FF* #8 and *Annual* #2 are frequently cited as having once been on someone's table at some con sometime. A well-respected historian tells me he once held a pre-'65 Ditko *Spider-Man* cover. Another high-roller makes no secret of having the covers to *Journey Into Mystery* #80 and #89, from 1962 and 1963. So, there are a few covers that might exist.

This leads us back to the "they're all in someone's basement" argument. Who exactly is that? You've got me. Every time I come up with a good answer, someone has indisputable proof that it's someone else. All we can do is wait and see if they turn up eventually. I for one hope they do, not just for posterity's sake, but because I'd like to own one or two of them. There are questions, however, about ownership rights that are somewhat ambiguous.

First, there's the moral side of it — thinking about not just the pre-'65 covers, but all of Jack's art — how do you feel about buying stuff he didn't get back from the company? I have to admit that because I'm a collector, I want very badly to come up with an answer that lets me buy the art. With that in mind, remember: By this time, it's hard to tell if some pieces came from Jack or not — most dealers can't provide an extensive provenance for the art they sell. Granted, about 75% of his Silver Age art seems to have been stolen, so unless you know for sure that Jack got it back, you have a 3 in 4 chance of buying something that is, on a moral level, shady.

When it came to pursuing much of this stuff, Jack and Roz were often far too generous in many ways. What does the estate say now? Co-trustee Robert Katz says that the lawyers tell him "the trust representing the Kirbys will take whatever steps it needs to to protect the family interests." What exactly does that mean? It sounds like they're leaving their options open. Having Jack's art sell publicly for high prices can help the family's interests... or maybe not, depending on the exact situation.

In any case, the situation is currently in flux, with no definitive legal answer — it's more of a personal issue. Most of the art I own came from the Kirbys, but I'm no saint — I can't rule out buying something from the darker side of the street. But not because I'm ethically vacuous. Let's give the last words on the subject to the man himself. I met Jack Kirby only once, at the 1993 San Diego Con. I asked him what he thought of his art going for such high prices when he was unable to participate in the profits. He said, in that James-Cagney-meets-the-Thing voice, "You ever hear of a guy named Peter Paul Reubens? He drew art for a sou, and he died a pauper. Now you can't touch a Reubens for less than two million. Me, I drew art and made enough to keep my family fed. And if it's selling for so much, that's flattery. They think of it as fine art, and that's enough for me."

And it's enough for me, too.★

(above) Jack's full-color painted version of the Jupiter Plaque art (see TJKC *#5).*
(below) Another late 1960s psychedelic painting by Jack.

Two very psychedelic paintings Jack did, circa 1969.

The Kirby Squiggle & The Evolution Of His Style

by Link Yaco

How did the slam-bang illustrator of *Captain America* get to the point where his figures lacked any recognizable human muscle structure and seemed to be built almost entirely of geometric shapes (especially in the case of the Thing)?

To trace the evolution of Kirby's style, it is helpful to make some arbitrary divisions. Although Kirby's development was continuous and there were no quantum leaps in style (although his final stylistic change is abrupt), let us consider his work in designated stylistic periods.

Early Kirby (1935-39)

Kirby worked in a number of different styles but by the time he gets to *Wilton of The West,* some of the distinctive features of later Kirby are already in evidence: Curved legs, leaping figures, and recognizable Kirby faces, especially the noses. Feathered shading is far more in evidence and at times a Raymond-like influence seems apparent.

Early Simon & Kirby (1940-45)

The Early style is codified here and the distilled result is singularly Kirby, owing no debt to any influence, although a significant amount of feathering remains. It is interesting to note some of the imaginary creatures Kirby invented at the end of this period and the beginning of the next (especially for his early Harvey period, in 1945): fully-visualized killer apes, giant insects, dinosaurs, and wholly-invented monsters.

Late Simon & Kirby (1946-55)

Feathering disappears almost altogether. Kirby adopts a thick wiggly line, the precursor of the more attenuated '60s squiggle. Textures on rocks and clothing become heavier and more abstract. Rocks, in particular, become abstract designs, almost pure exercises in form.

Figures start to thicken. The skinny adolescent figure of his *Captain America* work is replaced by the more adult heftiness of his *Fighting American*. This might have been a reflection of his own physical maturity.

Post-Code (1955-1963)

After the Comics Code struck, the great homogenization of comics began. The bland, undistinctive, unthreatening, and unexciting DC house style, as epitomized by Curt Swan (no reflection on the ability of that talented artist, who actually rose above the limitations of the house style, even as he established it), set the standard of the day. When artists such as Frazetta tried to work for comics, they were told their style was "old-fashioned." John Severin was told that he didn't know how to draw war comics. It might be that Kirby lost some confidence in that period. His work for DC looks more mainstream, less dynamic, and much toned-down. Even his monster work for Marvel looks safe as milk. The monsters look like globs of modeling clay—pikers compared to the creatures he used to produce with Joe

Unpublished Stuntman *page, circa 1946, before "spotting" blacks and finished inking.*

Simon. And when he finally gets to do his own super-hero series again, *Fantastic Four,* the figures are insubstantial, weakly rendered, and the work lacks detail.

Coincidentally, as Kirby's career waned, the careers of abstract modernist painters bloomed. The New York Expressionists, notably Jackson Pollack, become the object of much media attention, and Picasso and his Cubist buddies start to get mass market acceptance. Soon nearly every respectable middle class living room in America has a Picasso print.

Perhaps while Kirby was struggling to make a living, some part of him envied these academic poseurs for making a fortune dripping squiggles of paint and reducing the human form to geometric shapes.

SUPER-HEROES (1963-65)

Within a year, Kirby seems to regain his confidence. His figures get heavier, his settings gain so much detail that his machinery becomes a hallmark of his style, and his musculature becomes robust and complicated. His machinery, like his rocks, becomes a study in abstract composition.

ARTSY (1965-ON)

And suddenly, Kirby blossomed. Maybe it was getting some recognition after the struggles of the Post-Code years. Maybe it was the *zeitgeist,* the spirit of the times.

Traditional feathering became antithetical to the Kirby style. It was always those abstract squiggles. His musculature, machinery, rocks, and just about everything became wild textural exercises. Whether he drew images of outer space, microscopic space, the Negative Zone, sci-fi cities, or futuristic machinery complexes, the result was always a controlled explosion of form and color. No wonder the long-hairs nodded knowingly and snickered.

Uninked pencils to the final page of Forever People *#11, full of Kirby squiggles and psychedelia.*

The culture of psychedelia in the mid-to-late Sixties might have been the final influence that crystallized the Kirby style. If you're old enough to remember campus life from that period, you know that Kirby's adventures into the Negative Zone and Asgard — as well as, and especially Ditko's *Dr. Strange* — were regarded as psychedelic. Both Kirby and Ditko — and later, following their lead, Steranko and Adams — utilized abstract geometric forms that gave comics a new, artsy, and sophisticated graphic identity. When Kirby introduced the Inhumans, it was the first time that super-heroes had costumes that were entirely design-oriented. Unlike Superman's "S," the Flash's lightning bolt, or the Fantastic Four's four, those design lines on Black Bolt's chest were entirely non-functional and non-representational. They were just there because they looked good!

Kirby definitely did not deliberately set out to echo the wild shapes and colors of San Francisco concert posters, and the idea of ideologically reactionary Steve Ditko doing anything to endorse the emerging "counter-culture" is absurd, but the resemblance is striking. The idea was in the air, and everyone was somehow influenced by the psychedelic style of the times. Perhaps it was the final catalyst for Kirby and freed him from the constraints of strictly representational work. Not that he had ever been terribly constrained, but his final stylistic jump took him to a design level no other mainstream comic artist has reached before... or since!★

A Monologue On Dialogue

by Robert L. Bryant Jr.

After the King left his '60s kingdom for an unhappy fiefdom at DC, the fans talked, and one of the things they said was: "Kirby can't write." What they meant was: Kirby can't write dialogue; not like Stan the Man, the babbling brook of Marvel, the writer whose "natural" dialogue for Kirby's galactic plots helped reinvent comics. In fact, Jack Kirby's dialogue was as distinctive as Stan Lee's — but like everything else, it reflects the basic schism between Marvel's top writer and its best artist.

It's a convention of comics writing that you have to underscore/emphasize in bold lettering certain parts of a sentence — maybe to help lead the reader's eye through the dialogue and captions, maybe just to set up a writer's rhythm of louder and softer words. Lee turned that convention into a formula that was simultaneously as loose as bell bottoms and as rigid as the chemistry of Coca-Cola.

Lee's "natural" dialogue emphasized nouns — it could have been anything, any component of the sentence, but Lee whipped his nouns until they bled. Lee loved words that were solid, visible, concrete, tangible — words you could pose for a picture. Look at the classic *FF* #50 (1966), the climax of the Galactus trilogy. As Reed Richards checkmates Marvel's most powerful entity and saves the trembling Earth, as Kirby's art crackles off the page with cosmic action, Lee's dialogue (admittedly some of his best) dwells on the stolid nouns and pronouns:

REED: "NO, Galactus, it is YOU who will perish... for we have found the WEAPON at last!"
GALACTUS: "The ULTIMATE NULLIFIER! ! In the hands of... a HUMAN! ...Your feeble mind cannot begin to comprehend its POWER! You hold the means to destroy a GALAXY... to lay waste to a UNIVERSE!!"
REED: "And should the UNIVERSE crumble... can GALACTUS survive??"
GALACTUS (to Watcher): "YOU did this!! Only YOU had the power... only YOU had the will! You have given a MATCH to a child who lives in a TINDERBOX!"

We know that Lee's dialogue often grated on Kirby. Words frequently didn't match what was in Kirby's mind when the scenes popped from his head onto the page. Maybe one of the reasons was a basic psychological mismatch between the two men's thinking and writing styles: When Kirby began writing his own dialogue, first at DC and then after his unhappy return to Marvel, he largely emphasized verbs. Even in Kirby's quietest scenes of the 1970s, his choice of emphasis in dialogue stresses words that run, jump, crash, explode, do things — like his images, they can't sit still. Take this reflective exchange from *Mister Miracle* #6 (1972). The art is simply head shots, but look at the way Kirby gooses the verbs until they notch up the tension level of the sentences:

SCOTT: "Earth ISN'T small! Perhaps we can LOSE ourselves in hamlets, cities — continents — !! Perhaps, in time — the forces of Apokolips will GIVE UP the hunt!!"
BARDA: "It's a DELUSION, Scott! But I'll BUY it! Only, WATCH Flashman! Megalomaniacs LOVE to make noise! ! He COULD be our Achilles' heel!"

This style isn't heresy. But to a generation breast-fed on Lee's noble nouns, Kirby's muscle verbs might have tasted weird, oddball. Many readers who griped about Kirby's "writing" were in fact hung up on his style of loud/soft emphasis in dialogue — a style 180 degrees removed from Lee's. The formula was different.

As an experiment, consider these lines from Michael Crichton's novel *Jurassic Park.* I use it here mainly because it's so Kirbyesque in scope and theme. Here's how it would have been dialogued by Lee — say in 1967, for a splash page of Reed Richards lecturing Ben Grimm about a herd of cloned allosaurs coming right at them: "The history of EVOLUTION is that LIFE escapes all BARRIERS! Life breaks FREE! Life expands to NEW TERRITORIES! Painfully, perhaps even DANGEROUSLY! But life finds a WAY!"

And here's how Kirby would have done it, say in 1971, for a scene with Mark Moonrider dissing Darkseid's plans for universal domination: "The history of evolution is that life ESCAPES all barriers! Life BREAKS free! Life EXPANDS to new territories! Painfully, perhaps even dangerously! But life FINDS a way!!!"

Hear the ring in your mind's ear? That's the Kirby flavor. Lee punched up the object being acted on; Kirby stressed the force acting on it. What a perfect psychological shorthand for two men whose names are forever linked — but who were always so far apart.★

Uninked pencils to Eternals *#4, page 8. Note how Jack emphasized mostly verbs.*

Kirby Forgeries

by Glen Gold

At the 1997 San Diego Comic Convention, an excited fan rushed to show John Morrow the excellent deal he'd just gotten: An inked Black Panther piece by Jack Kirby, about 5X7 inches, for $100. And this was an excellent price, except for one problem: It was a fake. The money was returned, the fan became wiser, and the Kirby piece? It might still be out there. If it isn't, I can tell you one thing: There are other forgeries, many of them convincing. When your pulse is racing at the thought of getting some Kirby art, take a moment, take a deep breath, and ask yourself, "Is this real?"

Here's a quick forgery primer for the art collector, with some suggestions of how not to get taken. First of all, over 99% of the Kirby artwork I've seen offered for sale is genuine, and only a very small amount is what I'd call "dubious." Even then, the motivations behind them range from the innocent to the cynical. To begin, let's consider the primary tool in producing dubious Kirby pieces: The lightbox.

To state the obvious: Kirby penciled but very rarely inked his own work. The inker's job was to go over Jack's pencils with a brush (or pen), generally by using the same sheet of paper. However, there were occasions when inkers put the penciled page on a table with a bright light as its surface, then inked on a separate page, on top of the pencils. This is called lightboxing. Greg Theakston, for instance, lightboxed the pages of the Kirby *Super Powers* books, returning Jack's pencils and retaining his own, inked versions. The only problem: When he sold the inked pages to a dealer, the dealer sold them as if they were Kirby originals.

Here's the slippery part of it — the dealer (to my understanding) neither claimed nor denied that they were Kirby originals. Instead, he set them on the table as "Kirby/Theakston" pieces, technically correct, and counted on customers not asking questions. This is probably the most common form of forged Kirby artwork. For instance, the Black Panther work mentioned at the beginning of this article was lightboxed from a sketch printed in the Kirby *Masterworks* book. Soon after, I saw another inked version of another sketch from that book, in which Jack boxes with a monster.

So, how can you protect yourself from buying a lightboxed piece? First, examine the piece closely — are there pencil marks visible beneath the inks? Some inkers (Royer, for instance) erase very vigorously, but still leave behind trace pencil marks. Other inkers (Ayers comes to mind) leave many penciled lines visible. Second, ask the dealer if the piece has Kirby pencils underneath. In my experience, even the ethically-challenged dealers don't lie — they just hope you don't ask the question, or they answer vaguely ("Pencils? I don't know, I just know it looks like Kirby to me"). Third, remember most sketches were never inked, and if they were, they were commissioned pieces that should be signed or otherwise authenticated. Just because something is signed doesn't necessarily mean it's real — Jack signed Marie Severin's version of the *Thor* #175 cover and at least one Neal Adams cover. Also, more than one person interviewed for this piece said that the only part of Kirby artwork that's easy to forge with practice is Jack's signature.

One weapon against getting taken is more of a pain than most people care for: Try to be familiar with all published examples of Kirby sketches. The *Masterworks* book, perhaps because it contains so many pencil pieces, seems to have produced the greatest number of frauds. Because it's printed on lightweight stock, it's easy to slap it on a light table and trace over the images. Back issues of the *Kirby Collector* should also provide you with many of the known sketches. I was told that someone found and almost bought a gorgeous inked Kirby street scene until they realized that it was actually the double-splash from Jack's "Street Code" story in *Argosy,* which was in fact only penciled, never inked. If you are neither obsessed nor blessed with a photographic memory, the next best way to protect yourself is to ask other people — dealers, trusted friends — what they think about the piece.

What about a lightboxed, or re-inked, version of an original page, such as an interior page? This occurs rarely, to my knowledge. Interior pages are the hardest to pass off, for several reasons: First, it takes more work to do six panels of Jack's work than one quick sketch; second, interior pages are generally worth less than covers and splashes, and thus forging them is less cost-efficient. Also, the format of the page is fairly difficult to forge properly. Take a look at the average page of original art. Not only does it have pen and ink, but it also has a number of features that require great patience to forge: Statted pages numbers, a mark at the top (either rubber stamped or hand-written)

Why would Jack do two versions of the cover to Captain America *#200? An inked version is known to exist, and the background figures here look a bit shaky, which makes us suspect this pencil version is a forgery. But the Kirby signature looks legitimate, so you be the judge.*

KIRBY PENCIL FOURTH WORLD
CHARCTER SET 11x14 $150.00

Some of the bogus Kirby art that has appeared for sale recently. Buyer beware!

indicating what book it's from; a Comics Code Authority stamp on the back; dialogue; white out; perhaps a "continued next page" printed indication; art stats; Kirby's notes in the margins (sometimes); blue pencil lines; etc. All of this takes work to reproduce. Furthermore, Jack's pages all have a secret — well, secret until now — feature that makes them if not impossible to reproduce, then at least very, very difficult.

So let me introduce you to a new thing to look for: The Kirby Seasoning. Jack drew on the same table for so many years that by the early '60s it developed a layer of pencil grit and assorted crud on it so thick that the pressure of his hand actually marked the back of the paper. The mark got darker the longer he spent on the page. This isn't a fool-proof method of authentication, but it's worth knowing about. If you're interested in a Kirby page, turn it over. Is it filthy, with a sort of graphite marbling? If so, it's probably okay. If it's clean, however, don't panic — look for Jack's pencils on the front. His stuff from the 1950s and early 1960s, before the table became "seasoned," is relatively white compared to the late '60s and '70s. In the '80s, he occasionally drew at Mike Thibodeaux's house, so his later pages sometimes are clean. Otherwise, until someone figures out how to forge it, this is a fairly good method of authenticating the work. Everything I've ever seen that was lightboxed — Theakston's *Super Powers* pages, and some *Destroyer Duck* artwork, for instance — has been spotless on back.

Because they're worth so much more, it's far more likely that covers, splashes and pin-ups are the items to be forged. The best-known example that comes to mind is a Fighting American pin-up, which was inked, but had no pencils underneath it. This piece made the rounds, fooling even some high-powered collectors until they looked carefully for the lack of pencil marks. Next is an ersatz *New Gods* #4 cover that immediately looked suspicious to the collectors who saw it last year. They had familiarized themselves with the appearance of stats and logos and paper stock of 1970s DC covers, and this piece looked weird. It was on the wrong paper and the logos were reproduced crudely. (It's very hard to describe what stats and logos should look like, and reproducing them here can't really show off the textures and glue stains that make them authentic. My suggestion is that you try to find an original art dealer at the next con you attend and look carefully at the covers; see how they're pasted up on a very specific weight of paper stock that has its own special markings.)

The death blow to that *New Gods* cover was when a potential buyer learned, through the collectors' grapevine, that another collector had owned, and still owned what was unquestionably the real version. Ultimately, it was determined that the other *New Gods* #4 piece was in fact a recreation, perhaps by Vinnie Colletta — but that didn't stop someone from trying to sell it as Kirby. This has also happened with pages from the *Heroes and Villains* book, in which dozens of inkers lightboxed over a hundred different Kirby pieces. Some of these inkers innocently sold their finished pieces as "inks-only/ no-Kirby-pencils promised," only to have them show up later advertised as Kirby originals. It would be helpful in the future if all inkers who lightbox Kirby sign their names and also indicate, somehow, "This is my work, not Jack's."

The *Captain America* #200 (see previous page) cover is somewhat of a mystery. A penciled version and an inked version are both known, but the owner of the inked version swears his has pencils underneath. Is this penciled version authentic? Did Kirby do, for some reason, two identical versions of the same cover? I asked the dealer who was representing the penciled cover if the back was clean or dirty, and I never received an answer, so I don't know what to think. But I'm glad I didn't get it — I couldn't live with the uncertainty.

A few months ago, a guy running an ad in *Comics Buyer's Guide* had sketches by Kirby, among others, advertised for insanely low prices, about a fifth to a tenth of what the market would bear. Only, they struck me as fishy. Luckily, I have about ten friends who live for this sort of thing — I faxed them copies of the sketches and, to a man, they agreed these pieces were forgeries. But I had already suspected it, because their composition felt wrong. It's hard to forge Jack's pencils — just ask the hundreds of artists who wish they drew like him. He never drew a line that looked unsure of itself, he kept perspective in his head, and he never seemed to sketch out figures as much as discover them. If a sketch looks tentative or awkward, it's probably not his work. And, as a general rule: If you think the deal is too good to be true, you're right!

So far, we have just considered pages and sketches and '70s covers. What about the higher end of the market? Because of conditions peculiar to people who can drop $15,000 at a time for a single piece, this arena is ripe for abuse. Collectors generally don't like to advertise the pricier pieces in their collections. Furthermore, huge pieces frequently trade or sell far from the public eye, with little attention or opportunity for questions to be asked. Because of the secretive nature of the high-end, I can only call this a rumor, but last year, three early Kirby covers from the Silver Age allegedly came up for sale, then were withdrawn when the buyer suspected they were forgeries. I wish I knew more to this story — what exactly tipped him off, for instance, and where they came from — but so far, it's still just a rumor.

The whereabouts of many early Kirby Marvel covers are unknown; they were either destroyed or locked away somewhere safe long, long ago. Should, say, a forged cover to *Fantastic Four* #1 appear out of nowhere, it's possible that the owner of the real cover wouldn't speak up for fear of being found out. And since the *Fantastic Four* #57 cover just sold for about $30,000, there is great incentive for a forger to start spitting out Kirby covers. On the other hand, a forger would have to feel pretty confident that either the real covers no longer exist or that the real owners wouldn't speak up. Otherwise, his crime could attract serious attention from the F.B.I. Is that an exaggeration? Nope — read on.

What inevitably trips up a forger is his greed. It makes him sloppy. In the early 1980s, an advertisement in the *Overstreet Price Guide* stated that a man who'd collected art since the 1930s had died, and his estate was handling hundreds of original strips and pages by Herriman, Foster, Hogarth, Barks, et al. This was the beginning of an audacious scam uncovered by, among others, Robert Beerbohm. Collectors told the estate "manager" what artist they were interested in, and, even more specifically, what their favorite piece of art was. Imagine the joy resulting when that very Schomberg cover or Hogarth Tarzan Sunday was available. The collectors usually had to wait a couple of months while the piece was "recovered from the warehouse" (actually, their wait was so that the printed comic book or strip could be photographed, transferred to slides and projected on a wall, where the forger penciled and inked the image, made up stats, aged the paper, and otherwise made a reasonably accurate-looking fake). I've heard varying reports about the quality of the forgeries — some people say they were good; others say that only a person blinded by his emotions could mistake them for the real thing. But, regardless of his graphic technique, he was skilled in how to forge the format: The logos, the paper, the glue stains.

His undoing was a comic convention when three proud collectors all showed off the same Lou Fine *Science* cover. Ultimately, there seemed to be at least five of them. The F.B.I. was brought in to follow up. The man died before he could be prosecuted — some of the victims apparently dragged their heels, unwilling to confess to having been conned — and most, if not all, of the forgeries were tracked down. I've asked around, and even though Kirby was one of the names on his list, no one remembers seeing any forged Kirby by this man.

He was the last of the big-time scoundrels that we know about, but every field of collecting has its forgeries, especially as the value increases. One protection we have is that with every passing year, Jack's art is increasingly well-documented. I hope this primer is a step in the right direction. If you remember just three points when buying art, you'll be better off:

1. The most-often forged pieces are light-boxed versions of sketches.
2. Look for the Kirby Seasoning on the back of regular comic book pages (or anything else he drew at home).
3. Don't be afraid to ask questions, either of the seller or other knowledgeable collectors whom you trust.

99% of the art, as I've said, is just fine, and if you're educated, you won't get bitten by that other one percent.★

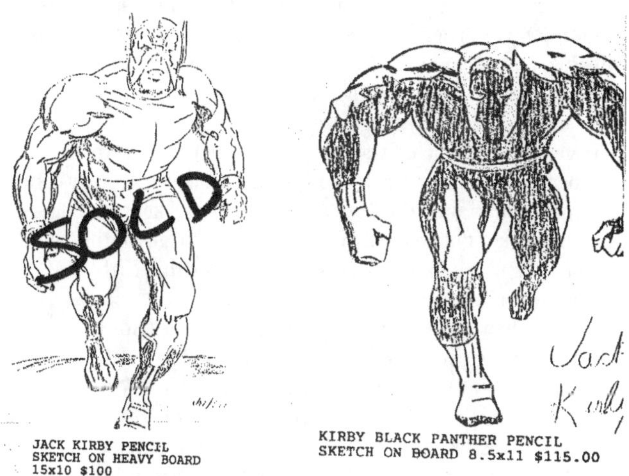

More bogus art. Note the Orion sketch is a crude, flopped version of the real drawing Jack did (as shown in TJKC *#17, page 21).*

THE ART OF COLLECTING KIRBY

by Anthony Christopher

I still remember reading my first Marvel Comic, *Fantastic Four* #8. Up to this point I had only been reading *Superman* and *Batman* comics, but the feelings which came up while reading one of Jack's books were different. These stories weren't just for children; they were exciting, powerful, and most of all, memorable. Years later (probably 1987) when I was killing time between business meetings in New York, I happened upon a comic book convention. Pete Koch had a stack of comics art for sale on a simple card table. Although he had no Kirby art, he proceeded to tell me that he owned several full books of *X-Men, Avengers,* and *Spider-Man.* A few tables later I met Mitch Itkowitz with stacks of art representing all kinds of artists, including Kirby. Then I turned a corner, and there was Jack Kirby, his wife Roz, and Mike Thibodeaux. They had five huge stacks of artwork all in manila envelopes. I couldn't believe it!

I eagerly searched though every envelope and ended up purchasing 20 pages for $300 each. I was amazed at how I could own an original page of artwork from a Marvel book for such a low price. (My company, Landmark Entertainment, hires artists regularly; I kept thinking I could not get an artist to re-create a page for the cost of a Kirby original.) I believed at that time that Kirby's artwork was undervalued.

From then on I was in a buying frenzy. Three trips to the Kirbys' brought my collection to over 1,000 pages. I began paying $1,500 for splash pages, $300 to $400 for loose pages, and $8,000 for the complete *Fantastic Four* #8 story. Price was secondary, but as I continued to purchase the art, the value began to rise. Currently, my focus is on quality and not quantity. By trading pages with other collectors and my involvement in the auctions, I am paring down my less valuable loose pages and converting them into covers, splash pages and complete stories, which are all becoming harder and harder to find.

Here are some of my comic art collecting tips:

TERMINOLOGY

It is very important when talking to other collectors and dealers that you know the lingo. Here are the basics:

"Covers": These are very hard to find and when you do, they are almost always in bad condition. This artwork was continually cut-up, pasted, statted, and white-out was used to make "corrections." In all my collecting years I have acquired only two covers. If you come across one, they are the *crème de la crème,* especially if you can find a great cover in great condition.

"Splash Pages": A splash page refers to the first page in any story or any single image interior page. Splash pages are coveted because they usually make up a full page of artwork featuring characters drawn larger than normal. These are more impressive framed than interior pages. In the early days of Marvel art, the cover and the splash would sell the book, so this was important to a young company trying to make it big. Great cover + great splash = big seller.

"Interior" or "Loose Page": In this area, collectors look for memorable pages; that is, origin pages, or images with a great villain or action. Also, if the story content was exceptional, the value increases. People buy inspirational memories from their youth. These factors will always affect the value of any interior page.

"Complete Books": Complete books are extremely difficult to get. When Marvel art was given back in 1987 and 1988, the inkers got one-third of the book and the artists, including Jack, got two-thirds of the art from the books, leaving each book broken up. Also, prior to this much of the artwork was given away or stolen. These days, it is very difficult, if not impossible, to complete a book. I have completed several, and I have books where I only lack one page. I ask myself, does this artwork even exist? If I find it, will I be able to successfully acquire it? It is like finding the Holy Grail if you do complete a book; a wonderful feeling that adds excitement to collecting. Searching for that one last page is what makes it fun. I can tell you there is no greater joy than to read a classic Marvel story from the original pages.

AUCTIONS

The auctions have been going for seven years and they are an excellent place to buy and learn from if you're willing to pay the price. If you wish to sell or buy you can get in touch with the following people:

Joe Mannarino	Jerry Weist	Philip Weiss
122 West End Ave.	411 E. 76th Street	3520 Lawson Blvd.
Ridgewood, NJ 07450	New York, NY 10021	Oceanside, NY 11572
201-652-1305	212-606-7862	516-594-0731

Unused, unfinished page from Fantastic Four *#80.*

Restoration

Because of the paper stock and the care which Marvel put into storing the art, most of the pages are in pretty good condition, with the exception of the covers. Most of the vintage material is close to forty years old and there is normal aging, glue stains, missing stats and white-out marks. It is important to deacidify these pages to keep them clean, but this is an inexpensive process. Restoration can be performed by a number of different professionals who can be contacted through the *Comics Buyer's Guide* and through various dealers.

CBG/Comic Conventions

Comics Buyer's Guide is a weekly magazine which has articles and advertisements and is the best source for a collector to sell artwork. Some collectors prefer to sell direct and great values can be found through this publication. Look for it at most comic book stores. Another good source of art is through conventions. New York, Chicago, and San Diego have the biggest conventions and all dealers or comics stores should have information on these shows.

Value

I entered the comic art world two years after Jack received his artwork back from Marvel. The page value over the years has risen from $200-300 to $2,000 - $3,000. Although the interior page market has leveled, covers and splash pages are hotter than ever. I think that it will only continue to go up. This is still a relatively young hobby and as key Marvel characters become slated for motion picture development, the popularity of the art will certainly increase. Also, when the Marvel theme park opens, I believe more people will be interested in owning original art. It only requires one furious buyer to stimulate the market.

Dealers

There are many comic art dealers in the United States. My biggest recommendation is to purchase what interests you, and you will never be disappointed. In addition, it is extremely important to obtain as much knowledge and reference material as possible in order to feel secure in your purchases. Christie's and Sotheby's auction catalogs are great reference sources to keep track of materials which have reached a level of appreciation known to treasure seekers.

Jack said to me that he believed one day this artwork would be in museums. One of my goals is to create a Jack Kirby museum and exhibit which would allow millions to see his work first-hand. Through Jack's innovative work, I have been inspired to incorporate character images into our themed entertainment creations at Landmark Entertainment. Technological advancements have allowed us to develop two-dimensional images into exciting 3-D entertainment (TERMINATOR 2 3-D, STAR TREK: THE EXPERIENCE), but the big honor was creating Super-Hero Land for MCA Universal. To take Jack's work and create an immersive environment was a real kick. I believe Jack's art will continue to influence my work as well as inspire future generations in the quest to provide thrilling and memorable entertainment for all ages.★

Jack's uninked pencils to Fantastic Four *#89, page 4.*

THE JACK KIRBY COLLECTOR #19

A TWOMORROWS ADVERTISING & DESIGN PRODUCTION IN ASSOCIATION WITH THE KIRBY ESTATE EDITOR: JOHN MORROW ASSISTANT EDITOR: PAMELA MORROW ASSOCIATE EDITOR: JON B. COOKE DESIGN & LAYOUT: TWOMORROWS ADVERTISING PROOFREADING: RICHARD HOWELL COLORIST: TOM ZIUKO CONTRIBUTORS: ORLANDO ADIAO MARK ALEXANDER JIM AMASH ROBERT L. BRYANT IAN CAIRNS TONY CHRISTOPHER JON B. COOKE STUART DEITCHER SHEL DORF KEVIN EASTMAN MARK EVANIER MIKE GARTLAND GLEN GOLD ED GREKOSKI GARY GROTH DAVID HAMILTON CHARLES HATFIELD JOHN HAUFE FRED HEMBECK RICHARD HOWELL FRANK JOHNSON GIL KANE JOE KUBERT PATRICK LAMB MIKE MCLESTER MARK MILLER BILL MILLER JIM OTTAVIANI MARK PACELLA ROY RICHARDSON MIKE ROBERTS STEVE ROBERTSON ALEX ROSS FIONA RUSSELL DAVID SCHWARTZ STEVE SHERMAN JIM STERANKO DAVE STEVENS ERNIE STINER CARL TAYLOR MIKE THIBODEAUX JOHN TRUMBULL JIM VADEBONCOEUR, JR. LINK YACO TOM ZUIKO SPECIAL THANKS TO: BILL BLACK ROBERT L. BRYANT JON B. COOKE KEVIN EASTMAN MARK EVANIER GLEN GOLD GARY GROTH D. HAMBONE RANDY HOPPE RICHARD HOWELL GIL KANE ROBERT KATZ & THE KIRBY ESTATE JOE KUBERT MARK MILLER MARK PACELLA HECTOR REYES ALEX ROSS MIKE ROYER FIONA RUSSELL & THE WORDS & PICTURES MUSEUM STEVE SHERMAN JOE SINNOTT JIM STERANKO DAVE STEVENS MIKE THIBODEAUX TOM ZIUKO AND AN EXTRA SPECIAL THANKS TO DAVID SCHWARTZ FOR KEEPING US FOCUSED ON THE IMPORTANT STUFF! MAILING CREW: MITCH BANKS RUSS GARWOOD D. HAMBONE GLEN MUSIAL ED STELLI PATRICK VARKER AND THE OTHER KIRBY FANS IN RALEIGH, NC

A Provenance Of Kirby's Art For Thor: 1/12/98

by Orlando Adiao

As with the chart that ran in *TJKC* #14, the one that follows is an informal provenance — an attempt at locating and cataloging Jack Kirby's original artwork from Marvel's *The Mighty Thor,* and where possible, its prices. I felt as if I had accomplished quite a bit with this new list, but I sat down and did the math: On this series alone, Jack drew well over 1800 published pages (covers included) — there are only about 300 on this list, and a handful of them are recreations by other artists based on Jack's work. How many of the other 1500 pages are actually missing or (Odin forbid) destroyed? My main sources of information continue to be ads placed in *Comics Buyer's Guide* and *The Jack Kirby Collector;* auction catalogs from Sotheby's, Christie's, and other houses; sightings at conventions; dealer's offerings; catalogs and websites; and other collectors. In the interests of protecting artwork from potential theft, no owners are named.

A word about some of the shorthand remarks under the "Comments" column:

• "No Thor" denotes that the main character is not depicted on that page — a factor that can strongly affect a page's value and/or desirability. For example, two separate ads that appeared in May 1997 both featured pages from *Thor* #171; the Thor-less page 8 was priced at $350, while page 12, which did portray Thor, was advertised for $650.

• "Signed by JK" means Jack Kirby's signature appears on the page — I've been told that Jack only signed pages which were returned to him by Marvel, although the absence of a signature doesn't mean a page was illicitly obtained. His signature doesn't seem to greatly influence the value or desirability of a piece.

There's a wealth of information here for collectors who follow the original art market. Prices seem to have stabilized over the past year. The issue I consider my "gold standard," *Journey Into Mystery* #112, again provides a good gauge. (I consider this issue a standard mainly because a lot of its pages have gone on the market repeatedly, providing a ready-made apples-to-apples price history. It is also sought-after among collectors as much for its many action pages involving the Hulk as for its inking by Chic Stone, as opposed to the late and rather-too-maligned Vince Colletta.) Page 7 sold for exactly the same amount at Sotheby's in June 1997 as it did at Christie's in November 1995. Other pages realized increases, but a few seemed to have hit their peaks and some prices now appear to be levelling off.

I'd like to thank everyone who volunteered information about pieces that they own or know to be in other collections. I had a lot of fun compiling this information, and your help contributed immeasurably to both my enjoyment and the list itself. I particularly enjoyed the anecdotes that a few people shared. One collector sold a complete *Journey Into Mystery* story after just a short time for more than double what he'd paid for it. Another person remembers being offered a Kirby piece that the dealer thought was used for a Marvel calendar. It turned out to be the cover for *Tales of Asgard* #1 (if the current owner is out there, contact me!).

I hope to continue revising my *Thor* list and to start on other Kirby titles, and I hope that lovers of Kirby's art will continue sharing their knowledge of other pieces and possibly the prices they were sold or acquired for. With John Morrow's permission and Randy Hoppe's technical assistance, I anticipate posting future *Thor* updates on *The Jack Kirby Collector* webpage. Please continue to send in information to my e-mail address at *Olanoid1@aol.com* or to my mailing address, Orlando Adiao, 220 West 98th St, # 7B, NY, NY 10025.★

ISSUE #	PAGE	INKER	LOCATION	DATE	PRICE	COMMENTS
JIM 112	coverA	Stone	Christie's	12/97	$1150	recreation by Stone
	1	Stone	Christie's	10/94	$2530	signed by JK
	"		ad	6/97	$4500	
	3	Stone	Sotheby's	6/95	$2070	
	6	Stone	Christie's	10/94	$1955	
	"		Exec. Invest.	6/95	$1870	reserve=$1900
	"		collector	7/97	$2500	
	"		same collector	10/97	$2000	
	7	Stone	Christie's	11/95	$2300	
	"		Sotheby's	6/97	$2300	
	8	Stone	ad	9/94	$1250	
	"		dealer catalog	2/95	$2100	
	"		ad	5/95	$1850	
	"		same ad	9/95	$1800	
	11	Stone	Christie's	11/96	$1725	
	12	Stone	Christie's	11/95	$2990	
	"		Sotheby's	6/97	$3450	
	14	Stone	Christie's	11/96	$863	
	"		dealer	6/97	$1450	
	16	Stone	Christie's	11/96	$1265	
126	9	Colletta	Christie's	10/93	$3680	splash
	11	Colletta	auction	5/96	$802	
	12	Colletta	dealer	3/95	$825	
	15	Colletta	auction ad	9/96	$400	min. bid
	? (interior pages)		dealer	5/94	$600-800	
	? (splash pages)		dealer	5/94	$3000	
127	4	Colletta	ad	8/94	$500	no Thor
	"		Toy Scouts	10/94	$325	
	5	Colletta	dealer	7/95	trade	
	7	Colletta	ad	5/95	$575	signed by JK/no Thor
	"		Christie's	11/95	no sale	offered with lot (1)
	"		ad	5/97	$450	
	"	electronic post		12/97	$550	
	13	Colletta	Sotheby's	6/94	$747	
	14	Colletta	ad	1/93	$350	
	"		different ad	8/95	$650	
		lot (1): Thor 121 p11; Thor 127 p7; Thor 141 p14 & 15; Gunsmoke 67 p10 & 12				
128	4	Colletta	ad	1/95	$1250	splash/no Thor
	"		same ad	4/95	$1000	
	8	Colletta	ad	'89?	trade	
	"		same ad	3/95	$450	
	10	Colletta	ad	'89?	trade	no Thor
	"		same ad	3/95	$450	
129	1	Colletta	Sotheby's	6/97	no sale	
	"	auction ad	10/97	100(?)*	*min. bid	
	6	Colletta	ad	'89?	trade	no Thor
	"		"	3/95	$450	
	9	Colletta	private coll.	3/95		reprinted in TJKC
	12	Colletta	ad	'89?	trade	
	"		dealer	7/94	$650	
	t.o.a. 5	Colletta	ad	'89?	trade	
	"		"	3/95	$450	
130	16	Colletta	ad	'89?	trade	
	"		collector	10/96	$575	OBO
	t.o.a. 1	Colletta	Christie's	10/94	$1725	
	2	Colletta	ad	9/95 & 2/96	$900	
	"		different ad	2/97	$885	
131	1	Colletta	ad	6/97	$3500	
	2	Colletta	Christie's	10/94	$575	
	4	Colletta	Christie's	11/96	$1725*	*sold w/lot (3)/no Thor
	9	Colletta	Sotheby's	6/94	$690	
	"		ad	10/94	$1400	
	"		same ad	5/95	$800	
	"		same ad	8 or 9/95	$500	
	"		different website	12/97	$640	
	13	Colletta	ad	'89?	$125	
				lot (3): Thor 131 p4; Thor 140 p6; Thor 175 p20		
132	5	Colletta	Sotheby's	6/96	$747	
	6	Colletta	Christie's	10/93	$690	
135	1	Colletta	collector	6/97	$2200	
136	9	Colletta	ad	3/91	$155	
137	t.o.a. 1-5	Colletta	ad	'89?	trade	complete back-up story
	"		Sotheby's	9/92	no sale	withdrawn at $1400
	"		private coll.	6/94	$3800	
140	5	Colletta	ad	5/96	$400	no Thor
	"		same dealer	2/97	$325	
	"		diff. advertiser	7/97	$350	
	6	Colletta	Christie's	11/96	$1725*	*sold with lot (3)
	13	Colletta	Christie's	10/94	$575	
	"		Sotheby's	6/96	$805	
				lot (3): Thor 131 p4; Thor 140 p6; Thor 175 p20		
141	cover 1*	Sinnott	Sotheby's	6/93	$4225	*unpublished version
	3	Colletta	ad	10/94	$450	
	5	Colletta	catalog	5/97	$300	no Thor
	"		electronic post	12/97	$400	
	6	Colletta	catalog	5/97	$475	no Thor
	"		electronic post	12/97	$575	
	10	Colletta	Sotheby's	6/94	$1380	

	"		ad	12/97	$275 (?)	
	12	Colletta	ad	8/95	$900	
	"		catalog	5/97	$875	
	"		electronic post	12/97	$975	
	13	Colletta	ad	2/95	$800	
	14	Colletta	ad	5/95	$475	no Thor
	"		Christie's	11/95	no sale	sold with lot (1)
	15	Colletta	ad	5/95	$475	no Thor
	"		Christie's	11/95	no sale	sold with lot (1)
	"		catalog	5/97	$475	
	"		electronic post	12/97	$575	
						lot (1): Thor 121 p11; Thor 127 p7; Thor 141 p14 & 15; Gunsmoke 67 p10 & 12
142	1	Colletta	Sotheby's	6/94	$2070	
	3	Colletta	dealer website	12/97	$700	
	5	Colletta	dealer	7/95	trade	no Thor
	6	Colletta	ad	4/93	$200	no Thor
	14	Colletta	private coll.	11/94	?	
	t.o.a. 3	Colletta	ad	4/94	$550	no Thor
	"		dealer website	12/97	$750	
143	10	Everett	ad	11/95	$850	no Thor
	"		Sotheby's	6/97	no sale	
	13	Everett	ad	7/94	trade	no Thor
	"		same ad	11/95	$850	
144	9	Colletta	Sotheby's	6/96	$1035	
	16	Colletta	Christie's	10/94	$518	
	"		"	11/95	no sale	
	"		catalog	5/97	$700	
	"		electronic post	12/97	$850	
146	cover	Colletta	private coll.?	2/95		
147	1	Colletta	Sotheby's	6/94	$2185	
	8	Colletta	ad	10/94	$500	no Thor
	"		same ad	7/95	$450	
	"		"	3/96	$400	
	"		"	9/96	$250	
	"		"	1/97	$350	
	"		"	4/97	$295	
	10	Colletta	ad	6/97	$450	
	"		dealer	10/97	?	
	11	Colletta	ad	2/96	$450	
	12	Colletta	ad	1/93	$325	
148	1	Colletta	ad	'93	$1100	
	"		diff. advertiser	11/94	$1500	
	6	Colletta	private coll.	'91	$100	
	16	Colletta	private coll.	'91	$100	
149	5	Colletta	P Weiss auction	4/95	$833*	*no Thor/sold w/ pgs. 6 & 15
	6	Colletta	P Weiss auction	4/95	$833*	*no Thor / signed / sold w/ pgs. 5 & 15
	"		ad	7/97	$325*	*or $600 with pg. 15
	8	Colletta	ad	4/94	$550	
	9	Colletta	ad	4/94	$465	
	11	Colletta	ad	4/94	$435	
	14	Colletta	ad	4/94	$550	
	15	Colletta	P Weiss auction	4/95	$833*	*no Thor/sold w/ pgs. 5 & 6
	"		ad	7/97	$325*	*or $600 with pg. 6
						lot (4): Thor 149 pp 5, 6, 15
150	1	Colletta	dealer offer	12/90	?	
	"		private coll.	11/94	$975	
152	cover	Colletta	?	'92		rptd. in Art of Jack Kirby
	1	Colletta	private coll.?	2/95		
	2	Colletta	ad	12/97	$525	
	3	Colletta	ad	2/96	$575	or $1000 with pg. 4
	"		website	12/97	$825	
	4	Colletta	ad	2/96	$575	or $1000 with pg. 3
	"		website	12/97	$825	
	8	Colletta	private coll.	1/93	$250	
	9	Colletta	Christie's	10/93	$748*	*sold as a lot with Thor 153 pg. 2
	13	Colletta	dealer	3/97	$325?	no Thor; JK self-portrait?
153	1	Colletta	ad	5/97	$2500	
	2	Colletta	ad	'89?	$125	
	"		Christie's	10/93	$748*	*sold as a lot with Thor 152 p9
	3	Colletta	ad	2/96	$350	no Thor
	"		"	5/96	$250	
	8	Colletta	Christie's	10/94	$552	
	19	Colletta	ad	12/97	$2800	Odin splash/no Thor
159	4	Colletta	ad	4/94	$475	
	5	Colletta	private coll.	'92	$125	
160	1	Colletta	private coll.	7/94	$1500	
	4	Colletta	ad	'89?	$100	no Thor
	20	Colletta	ad	10/94	$375	
161	cover	Colletta	Sotheby's	6/96	$2300	
	2 - 3	Colletta	?	2/97		double-page photo collage; art drawn by JK,
	5	Colletta	ad	10/97	$850	splash/no Thor
	6	Colletta	private coll.	1970	$28	fundraising auction/no Thor
	15	Colletta	ad	8/94	$675	
	"		Toy Scouts	10/94	$575	
	17	Colletta	dealer's catalog	12/93	$400	
	"		ad	6/95	$400	
163	12	Colletta	Sotheby's	6/95	no sale	passed at $550
	"		ad	9/96	$600	
	18	Colletta	?	'92		rptd. in Art of Jack Kirby
164	1	Colletta	ad	2/96; 5/96	$950	
	6	Colletta	catalog	1974	$20	
	15	Colletta	catalog	1974	$20	no Thor
	19	Colletta	catalog	1974	$20	
	20	Colletta	catalog	1974	$20	
165	4	Colletta	Christie's	10/93	$460	no Thor
	18	Colletta	Christie's	10/93	$483	
	"		P Weiss auction	3/96	$500-700	
167	cover 1*	Colletta	private coll.	12/90	$700	*unpublished cover
	8	Colletta	catalog	1974	$20	no Thor
	9	Colletta	catalog	1974	$20	no Thor
	10	Colletta	catalog	1974	$20	
	11	Colletta	catalog	1974	$20	
	12	Colletta	catalog	1974	$20	
	19	Colletta	ad	5/97	$350	no Thor
169	12	Klein	ad	8/94	$300	no Thor
	"		collector	11/94	?	
	14	Klein	Exec. Invest.	3/96	$300?	
	16	Klein	private coll.	3/95		rptd. in TJKC
	17	Klein	Exec. Coll.	3/96	$500?	
	"		ad	8/96	$495	
170	cover 1*	?	ad	12/97	$4250	*unpublished version
	5	Everett	private coll.	12/90	$100	
	7	Everett	private coll.	3/95		reprinted in TJKC
	8	Everett	ad	3/95	$400	
	9	Everett	catalog	9/96	$500	
	"		website	12/97	$825	
	11	Everett	catalog	1993	$375	
	12	Everett	website	1/98	$500	
	13	Everett	ad	3/95	$400	no Thor
	18	Everett	website	12/97	$825	
171	1	Everett	private coll.	12/97	$1000	
	4	Everett	ad	8/96; 12/96	$200	no Thor
	"		"	5/97	"	
	6	Everett	ad	8/96	$350	no Thor
	"		coll. website	1/98		
	7	Everett	ad	8/96	$350	no Thor
	8	Everett	ad	8/96; 5/97	$350	no Thor
	9	Everett	ad	8/96; 12/96	$350	no Thor
	10	Everett				no Thor
	12	Everett	ad	5/97	$650	
172	cover	Everett	collector	1/95	$4400	
	"		private coll.	12/97	$4000	
	4	Everett	ad	7/97	$350	no Thor
	5	Everett	dealer	1/91	$150	no Thor
173	11	Everett	ad	2/95	$500	
	"		same dealer's auction	5 & 11/95	$300	min. bid
	"		same dealer's ad	8/96	$450	
	12	Everett	private coll.	1991	$70	
174	14	Everett	ad	5/94	$1000*	*with pg. 16
	"		2nd advertiser	9/96	$525	
	16	Everett	ad	5/94	$1000*	*with pg. 14
	"		2nd advertiser	10/94	$550	
	"		2nd advertiser	7/95	$525	
	18	Everett	catalog	10/92	$200	
175	1	Everett	dealer	6/94	$2200	
	"		"	7/95	$2500 or trade	
	"		Sotheby's	6/97	$2300	
	19	Everett	dealer website	1/98	$500	
	20	Everett	Christie's	11/96	$1725*	*sold with lot (3)
						lot (3): Thor 131 p4; Thor 140 p6; Thor 175 p20
176	cover	Everett	private coll.	11/97	$4000	
	1	Colletta	private coll.	3/89		
	2	Colletta	ad	1992?	$300?	
	"		private coll.	9/96	$400	
	6	Colletta	ad	10/95	$350	no Thor
	9	Colletta	private coll.	1/97	$230	no Thor
	13	Colletta	ad	1991	$50	half page/no Thor
179	7	Colletta	ad	9/96	$325	no Thor
	"		"	2/97	$250	
	9	Colletta	ad	6/95	$550	
	12	Colletta	ad	8/94	$275	half-page; no Thor
253	cover	Verp./Romita	collector	11/94	$2200	
	"		"	12/96	$2100	
	"		2nd coll. ad	5/97	$2200	
Tales of Asgard						
	1 cover	?	collector	1988	$120	
	"		dealer	1989	$250	
Thor Annual						
	1 cover	?	?	'92	?	rptd. in Original Comic Art
	1	Colletta	ad	4/97	$4800	

N.B.: Art denoted "coverA" is a recreation based on a Kirby cover, but not executed by him.

ART HISTORY KIRBY-STYLE

Thanks to Jim Vadeboncoeur, Jr. for tracking down the original article

On May 3, 1969, the California tabloid magazine *Peninsula Living* featured an article on those costume designs Jack did for the University of California–Santa Cruz's production of *Julius Caesar,* which ran May 15-25, 1969. The director of the play, Sheldon Feldner, was looking for a way to set his production apart from previous versions, and being a big comics fan in 1969, he thought of Marvel. Sheldon sent a letter to Marvel to request help in designing the costumes, only to find out that both Stan Lee and Jack Kirby were big Shakespeare buffs. Stan asked his artists if anyone was interested in designing the costumes, and Jack — who had recently moved to California — volunteered.

Sheldon said, "An assistant and I drove down, and stayed at Jack's overnight. We watched *Spartacus* on TV and talked about Roman armor, but mostly, we listened to Jack talk about *Julius Caesar.* Talking about *Thor,* Jack said he doesn't draw authentic Norse armor, but tries to get the essence of it. I said that was what we wanted to get at, too: Something that could be both ancient and modern."

Here are Jack's costumes for Julius Caesar, Portia (the wife of Brutus), and a Soothsayer. These drawings are black-&-white adaptations by Robert Page of the UCSC art department, working from Jack's full-color renderings which, alas, are nowhere to be found. Does anybody have any idea what happened to Jack's originals?

The article went on to mention that Jack talked a great deal about the importance of using color creatively, and the director used many of Jack's suggestions. After assassinating Caesar, the conspirators threw their robes open to reveal a blood-red lining, which was Jack's idea. Also, Jack modeled the cut of their robes after the silhouette of a vulture; and while it's traditional for Caesar to first appear onstage in civilian clothes, at Jack's suggestion they had him appear initially in military garb, so people would find it more believable when the character eventually installed himself as dictator.

The task of converting Jack's fantastic designs into actual costumes apparently caused some difficulty, but they managed to improvise with materials such as old army blankets, longjohns, sponges, and lots of vinyl and plastic. Jack visited the campus once during pre-production, and was to return for the opening night performance.

As for being paid for his efforts, Sheldon said Jack told him, "Not to worry about it — we couldn't afford him. He felt that because it was for college students, that it was a contribution he wanted to make."★

KIRBY GILBERTON COMPANY ART

From The Complete Guide To *Classics Illustrated* Vol. 1
Submitted by John Haufe, Asst. Editor of Classics Collector *Magazine*

Classics Illustrated #35: "The Last Days Of Pompeii." March 1961.

Classics Illustrated #162A Special Issue: "War Between The States." June 1961. Pgs. 1-7, 24-29, 55-59, 77-84.

Classics Illustrated #165A Special Issue: "To The Stars!" Dec. 1961. Pgs. 29-31.

World Around Us #30: "Undersea Adventures." Feb. 1961. Pgs. 1 & 64.

World Around Us #31: "Hunting." March 1961. Pgs. 1, 6-11, 25-29.

World Around Us #32: "For Gold And Glory." April 1961. Pgs. 15-23.

World Around Us #35: "Spies." August 1961. Pgs. 37-39, 46-47, others?

World Around Us #36: "Fight For Life." Oct. 1961. Pgs. 33-43, 47-48.

Classics Illustrated #160: "The Food Of The Gods." Jan. 1961. "Coming Next" ad only, on inside front cover.

(left) Jack's unused cover for a Cleopatra story, which was only shown in a "next issue" ad in Classics Illustrated *#160 (January 1961). In* Comics Journal *#134, Jack had this to say about* Classics Illustrated:

"...they didn't like the way I folded Cleopatra's skirt. It was run by perfectionists, and I was not the guy to work for perfectionists, so I left soon after. I couldn't be that fussy or that perfect with my figures or my costumes. I felt that the story was very, very important, and all of it had to mesh to make any sales."

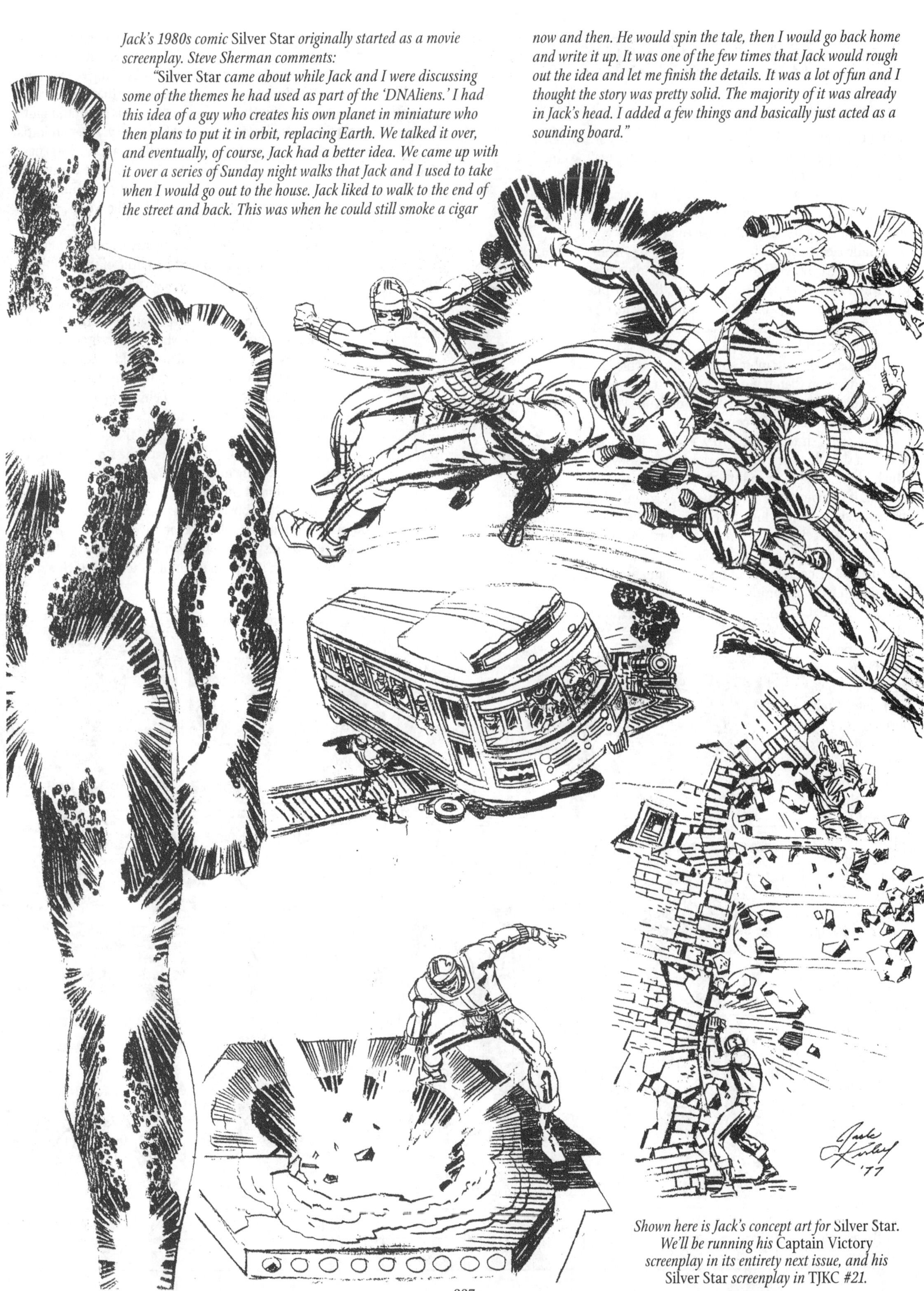

Jack's 1980s comic Silver Star *originally started as a movie screenplay. Steve Sherman comments:*

"Silver Star *came about while Jack and I were discussing some of the themes he had used as part of the 'DNAliens.' I had this idea of a guy who creates his own planet in miniature who then plans to put it in orbit, replacing Earth. We talked it over, and eventually, of course, Jack had a better idea. We came up with it over a series of Sunday night walks that Jack and I used to take when I would go out to the house. Jack liked to walk to the end of the street and back. This was when he could still smoke a cigar now and then. He would spin the tale, then I would go back home and write it up. It was one of the few times that Jack would rough out the idea and let me finish the details. It was a lot of fun and I thought the story was pretty solid. The majority of it was already in Jack's head. I added a few things and basically just acted as a sounding board."*

Shown here is Jack's concept art for Silver Star. *We'll be running his* Captain Victory *screenplay in its entirety next issue, and his* Silver Star *screenplay in* TJKC *#21.*

The Kirby Flow

by Ian Cairns

(Originally published in a European magazine called The Panelhouse.*)*

I hope in the following piece to offer a means by which one of the central aspects of Jack Kirby's work—his storytelling abilities—may be further appreciated.

By analyzing a piece from a period when his approach seemed to be stripped to its bare essentials and mapping out its visual flow, we can isolate a "Dramatic Heartbeat" at its core. This is not a "Draw Comics The Kirby Way" formula; a slavish adherence to it will no more create a "Kirby comic" than the plagiarists who trace his work or mimic his style do. Kirby had various ways of thinking which he chose depending on the particular needs of each story; this is one which lends itself to graphic simplification, which I hope readers can then build on to develop their own abstract diagrams and explore the underlying structures in their own favorite comics.

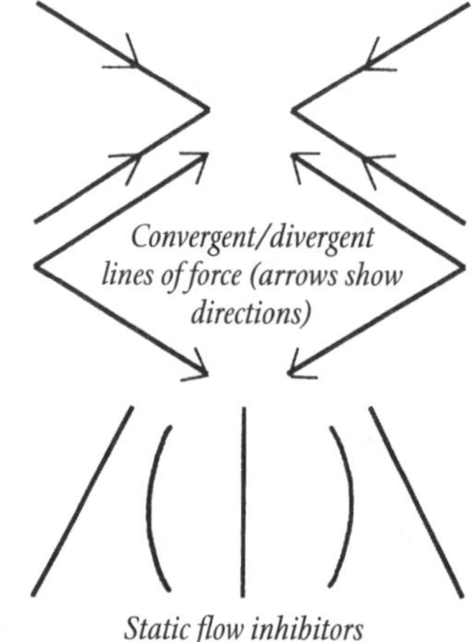

Convergent/divergent lines of force (arrows show directions)

Static flow inhibitors

The pages shown from *X-Men* #10 are designed around a straightforward left-to-right linear flow, which I have broken down into the components shown at right. If we ignore the overall page design and place the panels in a straight line, with a median horizontal superimposed on them, we get the graphic map of its structure shown below.

It can be seen that Kirby designed each panel not in purely three-dimensional visual terms, but on a two-dimensional framework intended to facilitate or inhibit the momentum of the story he was telling. Plagiarists who steal his style or lift his figures out of context miss the point of his work completely; nothing exists of itself, but always in relation to what he wants to communicate. I think this device also helps explain the stories I've read of his ability to draw a comics page as though he were literally just tracing a projection from his mind's eye; in a way he was. He intellectually conceptualized the dramatic needs of the story, "saw" the simplified two-dimensional figure on the page, then drew the three-dimensional contents of the panel to fit within that design.

By referring to the finished comics page while keeping in mind the dramatic map of it, we can see he used a variety of drawing techniques to reinforce it. Perspective, light and shade, mass or form and the folding or hanging of clothing around it, all abstracted into a coherent graphic shorthand.

The choice of shot or focal depth of each panel is again thought through and related to the dramatic needs of the story. After an initial kick between the opening vertical and the story flow proper, the general pattern is one of a gentle flow into and across the page. He controls the tension as a musician controls dynamics; the flatter the image, the more the content is to be carried in the words. He uses crescendos and diminuendos of depth to surround key visual moments in the narrative. Look at how he builds to the explosion in the middle of the second page and then controls our return to the story flow. Let's look at this explosion more closely (second page, panel three): Contrary to expectations, it doesn't leap off the page, but instead pushes back against the story flow. If anything the main action could be seen as going back into the picture; Ka-Zar's struggle takes place behind Zabu, who is in turn behind the discarded rifle and the leg of the partially described figure fleeing the scene. Looking at it again, the greatest jump in depth perception is actually with the story flow. Kirby wants to keep the momentum going and overcome the attraction of this high point in the action.

While the above structure can only be applied to a limited period in his working life, I hope that it will serve as a basis with which to appreciate the visual coherence of his thinking. A good story in itself is not enough; it's the manner of its telling which makes it come alive.★

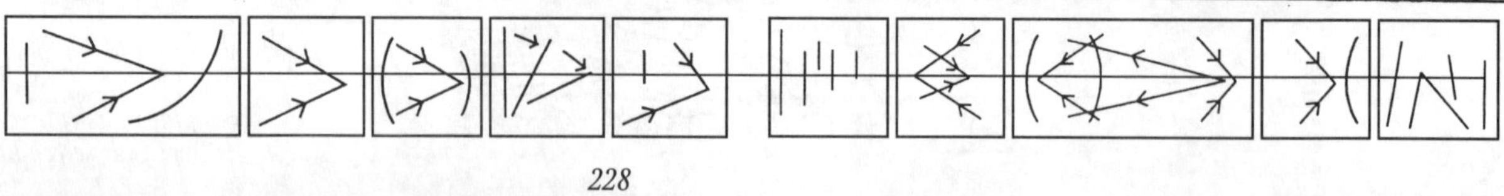

MASTER OF STORYTELLING TECHNIQUE

An examination of a single panel, by Mark Alexander

When it came to visual storytelling Kirby knew every trick in the book. Although he's usually regarded as an artist who would put everything in a panel but the kitchen sink, here's an example where he consciously used minimalism to advance characterization.

On page five of *Sgt. Fury* #4, Fury returns to the Howlers' barracks after being separated from his men during an air-raid. Upon his arrival, the guys bombard him (no pun intended) with commentary. The composition of the panel is based around a semi-circle formed by the Howlers heads. Beginning with "Reb" Ralston, the drawing moves your eye from left to right, following the arc to "Dum-Dum" Dugan. At this point one's gaze is drawn left and center, to Fury's right eye where it abruptly stops. There's no way it will ever land anywhere else.

The dialogue balloons correspond accordingly. In a subtle (almost sneaky) fashion, the name of each Howler is mentioned, and by purposely omitting everything from the panel except the heads, the reader is subconsciously manipulated to connect the name and face of each character. There's nothing else to focus on. Once this is done, and the reader knows who the players are (remember this was a fairly new series), the story moves on. The most impressive aspect of this sleight-of-hand trick is its subtlety. I was completely unaware of what had transpired until the second reading, which proves how effective it was.★

THE DRAWING LESSON

by Carl Taylor

At the 1972 San Diego Comic Convention, I first met Jack and saw many color pictures he had done — some of characters that wouldn't appear in comics until 20 years later. Jack was doing free sketches, and just as it was my turn to get one, his son Neal found Jack and whisked him away, telling him, "You've got to stop doing these!" I think Jack could see how disappointed I was, but I understood at the time why his son stopped him. Back in those days Jack would do free sketches if he thought you were a true fan of his work, but greedy opportunists ended up stopping many pros from that occasional kindness, because the artist would often find the same sketch on sale less than an hour later.

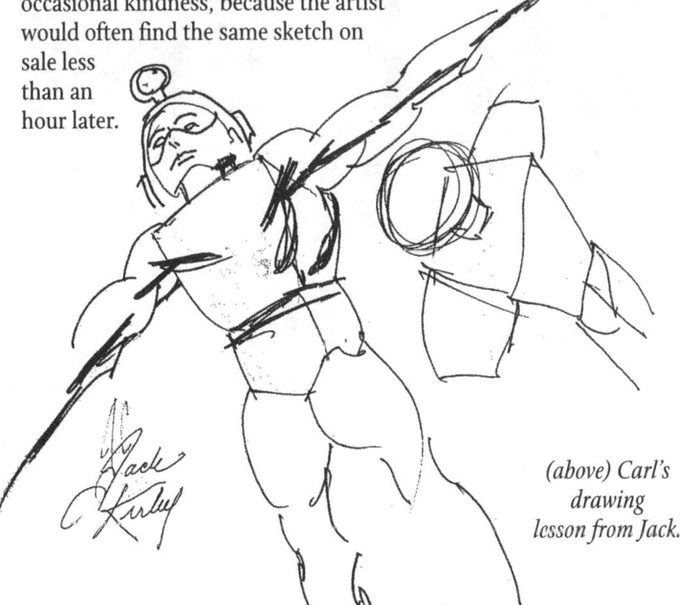

(above) Carl's drawing lesson from Jack.

The next year at the 1973 convention, I got my second chance to meet Kirby and show him some of my work. As he looked at my drawings he could see I was heavily influenced by his style, but my figures lacked fullness; I didn't understand how to draw figures in perspective. Whenever I attempted to draw a panel from a more complex angle, my figures would look flat. Jack pointed this out to me and asked me for a piece of paper, so he could show me just what he meant. I remembered what his son said the year before, and gave him a manila envelope to draw it on instead, so he wouldn't think I was going to try and sell it. There were many fans standing around, so it became a dramatic moment to watch him draw from so close. He continued to explain as he drew, and after he finished I thanked him, and worried that he might not have understood why I gave him the envelope to draw on when he could see I had a drawing pad.

Jack's original 1960s painting of Captain Victory (he was renamed Captain Glory and used over 20 years later at Topps Comics).

Throughout the next year I analyzed my work and tried to apply what he explained to me. At the 1974 con, Jack looked over my work, suggested art supplies, and gave me even more advice. He asked me, "Have you ever drawn anything four or five feet high?" He also told me if I couldn't sell the art he was urging me to produce, to contact him and "I'll see what I can do."

I was too intimidated to draw what he suggested! But I did buy the art supplies, and showed up at the 1976 con with lots of huge color pictures and colorful handmade portfolios for the art show. I won best artist in the Super-Hero Category. Jack Kirby, Theodore Sturgeon, and Jack Katz were the judges. Jack told me later, "I pushed for that."

On the last day of that '74 convention, I'd gotten Kirby to sign that '73 drawing lesson — not so much for his signature, but so that he could see that even though I gave him a manila envelope to draw it on, I really did appreciate and treasure that art lesson.★

DON'T ASK, JUST CITE IT: TOWARDS A TOTAL TAXONOMY

by Jim Ottaviani

Critical discussion of Jack Kirby's art and the elements he employed to create his seminal visual style is inexplicably absent from the literature of academe[1]. Though work has proceeded on other fronts in comics scholarship, unfortunately the pioneering semantic efforts of Mort Walker[2] have yet to be expanded upon in an in-depth fashion. With the appearance of august journals like *The Jack Kirby Collector*, the need has become pressing. Scholars of sequential art[3] (or as moderns would say, "juxtaposed pictorial and other images in deliberate sequence"[4]) have too long suffered from a paucity of impenetrable jargon. To date they have no way to describe pages of Kirby's work without having to rely on tedious everyday language or expensive and bulky photoduplication methods.

In an attempt to begin addressing this shortcoming the following terms, along with examples, are offered to *TJKC* readers:

some very sinnotty kirby krackle

royerist jacknees

KIRBY KRACKLE

Clumps of bulbous energy dots found surrounding intergalactic heralds, characters with newly-acquired cosmic power, and just about any outer space scene drawn in modern comics.

KIRBYTECH

Organic, apparently functional, and everywhere[5].

JACKNEES

Thick, square, and large, these are the sort of patellae you'd need if you wanted to hold yourself up while lifting 374 tons of scrap iron over your head.

KINGFINGERS

Thick, square and large (and often all of roughly the same length), these are the kinds of fingers you'd need if you wanted to hold onto 374 tons of scrap iron. You rarely see a Jack Kirby character play a guitar. Kingfingers are why.

KING'S EYE VIEW

A daring inversion of the classic Eisnerhead angle[6], this tight focus perspective begins at the chin and proceeds dramatically upward.

THE GROUP YELL

Often accompanying a cominatcha (see below), this is the preferred mode of expression in any and all Overpowering, Dramatic, and Action-Packed scenes, as well as most sensitive, quiet, and touching ones.

kingfingers

king's eye view

group yell (royerist variety)

[1] A thorough search through *Dissertation Abstracts International* (© 1997, University Microfilms International) reveals a shocking result: Exactly zero (0) doctoral dissertations even mention Jack Kirby in their title or abstract. Given that the database covers over one million theses from universities worldwide, this startling lack of coverage makes the following question nigh unto rhetorical: Is it any wonder that our ivy-covered halls of higher learning are commonly seen as failing us in terms of addressing relevant modern problems?

[2] Mort Walker, "Lets get down to grawlixes," reprinted in *Backstage at the Strips*, NY: Mason/Charter, 1975.

[3] Will Eisner, *Comics and Sequential Art*, Tamarac, FL: Poorhouse Press, 1985.

[4] Scott McCloud, *Understanding Comics*, Northampton, MA: Tundra Publishing, 1993.

[5] See also Frank Miller's *Ronin* (New York: DC Comics, 1986-87) for a modern updating.

[6] See virtually any installment of *The Spirit* — many classic examples appear in *The Spirit Casebook* (Princeton, WI: Kitchen Sink Press, 1990).

early sinnotty cominatcha

kirby chips

COMINATCHA

Kirby characters don't merely break the fourth wall[7]. They Lunge and Leap and Dive and Plummet and Crash through it. Even when they don't.

ROYERIST

An adjective used to describe the hot, stylized, and angular line Mike Royer added to the already stylized and angular kingfingers and jacknees. A perennial favorite. Contrast with sinnotty.

SINNOTTY

An adjective used to describe the cool, naturalistic, and silky smooth line Joe Sinnott added to even the squarest of kingfingers and largest of jacknees. A perennial favorite. Contrast with royerist.

KIRBY CHIPS

Named after the little flecks of matter that Jack Kirby scattered behind every moving object to show it was so massive that it ruined the pavement[8]. Not to be confused with Marvel Chipping[9].

The above, of course, does not represent a comprehensive list. Indeed, the descriptors are drawn almost exclusively from art Jack Kirby produced from the Silver Age onward. Thus, while it pertains to the majority of his oeuvre in terms of sheer output, it doesn't address all of the genres he worked in. For example, both westerns and romance comics had their own distinct idioms, and Kirby made pioneering contributions to both; nor does it even begin to cover related forms that his contemporaneous artists brought to the medium[10].

Building upon these basic terms, though, scholars can give discourse upon and connoisseurs can deconstruct pages or even whole issues according to representativeness and desirability. Students of the form can describe Kirby devices in much the same way heraldic scholars deal with coats of arms. Eventually, enjoyment of the King's work may be supplemented, or even replaced, by analysis. We can only hope to reach this point — a pinnacle of respect that few fields ever attain — by creating a vocabulary so arcane that scholars can use it to obscure rather than enlighten. So fellow Kirby scholars are implored to augment this list. Though an exhaustive taxonomic study would require the stamina, creativity, and productivity of a... well, a Jack Kirby... this is all the more reason to start now. A journey of twenty-one thousand pages[11] begins with a single panel[12].★

royerist

sinnotty (note kirbytech at bottom of panel)

7 Not to be confused with the Fourth World.

8 See "Drama" in *Understanding Minicomics Interactive,* Matt Feazell, 1995.

9 From the grading section of any of Robert Overstreet's *The Overstreet Comic Book Price Guide,* as in page A-19 in the 25h edition, New York: Avon, 1995.

10 Ditkohands and Steve's Slouch from the famous *Spider-Man* artist come immediately to mind.

11 The estimated output of Jack Kirby, over the course of his career, as reported in Ray Wyman's *The Art of Jack Kirby,* Orange, CA: Blue Rose Press, 1992.

12 See Lao-tse's *The Way and Its Power.*

Jack Kirby's ~~Inkers~~ Collaborators

by Mike Gartland

Writing an article about the people who've inked Kirby's pencils could, in itself, reach magazine-size proportions. The list reads like a who's who of professionals who were all experienced and competent artists in their own right; and as any professional inker will tell you, you have to know the ins and outs of drawing before you can ink properly. Inkers generally help contribute to the mood and expression of the pencils and overall story; and even though many have attested that Kirby produced some of the tightest penciled pages (tightest meaning complete, with shading, blacks, line weight, and texture already in place), there can be no doubt that many were able to add a little of themselves to the finished work. I, therefore, would like to refer to these gentlemen as collaborators rather than inkers.

From his earliest days in the industry, Kirby rarely inked his own pencils. Generally a comic book artist would pencil and ink his own work, and sometimes do the lettering as well; this was before guys would settle into regular "full-time" inking or lettering jobs. Freelancers were expected to be able to do it all if the need arose; but Kirby wasn't a lone worker. From his beginnings he worked in a "shop" environment; this pretty much continued when he joined up with Simon. Simon knew that Kirby was more valuable to the team as a penciller and in an industry where deadlines meant money, why have your best penciler take up valuable time inking when you could get someone else to ink, thereby getting a few more penciled pages out of your artist?

This isn't saying that Kirby didn't or couldn't ink his own work from time to time; many fine examples, from the '40s on up, show that his inks were just fine. Perhaps inking wasn't to his liking or, probably more so, he just didn't have the time; Kirby was after all, first and foremost, a producer, and many professionals have stated their amazement at the output of pages Kirby could produce in a given time frame. This amount would definitely have been reduced if he had to go back and ink the pencils. It might be considered a blessing in disguise that he didn't ink his own work all that much; it enabled him to create that much more art for us to enjoy. Also, when he hit his stride at Marvel, he was pumping out creations and ideas so fast that in many instances his inventions and characters would change from page to page; thanks to his collaborators, many of these inconsistencies were caught and corrected.

There isn't enough space here to cover all of the talented people I'd like to, so I've broken this down by decade, giving my personal opinions along the way.

The '40s

Prominent Collaborators: Syd Shores, Al Avison, Al Gabrielle, Reed Crandall (artist of the '40s *Blackhawk* & *Uncle Sam*), Dick Briefer (famous for work on *Frankenstein*).

Most Prominent & Personal Favorite: Joe Simon. Far and away no one collaborated with Kirby as purely as Simon. It's not true Kirby art, it's a "look"; each man added to the other. The Simon & Kirby "look" could not surface when they worked separately; a true collaboration.

(above) Frank Giacoia's inks from the cover of Fantasy Masterpieces #5.

The '50s

Prominent Collaborators: Joe Simon, Mort Meskin (one of Jack's personal favorite artists), Marvin Stein, John Severin, Christopher Rule, Steve Ditko.

Most Prominent: Wallace Wood. The Kirby/Wood artwork on *Sky Masters* and *Challengers of the Unknown* is indeed beautiful to behold, but in my opinion, it's an example of not only two powerful artists coming together, but of two distinctly divergent styles failing to mesh. Wood's inks tend to overshadow Kirby's pencils rather than blend with them. When the inker ends up having the work look more like his than the artist's, I feel the inker fails.

Personal Favorite: Dick Ayers. It was Ayers who helped make those great Kirby monsters as grotesque as they were, and if you don't think this is true, just look at the Kirby/Ayers *Hulk* of the early '60s; the definitive *Hulk* as far as I'm concerned. Ayers' prior expertise with westerns further enhanced Kirby's western stories; he added an historic authenticity to the backgrounds, horses, guns, etc. Kirby's pencils, under Ayers, became not sleek and polished like Wood's, but definitely stylized and handsomely blended.

(right) Bill Everett's Thor *inks were a radical departure from the Colletta inks that preceded them.*

Vince Colletta's inks on Thor*; he excelled at mood and beautiful women.*

The '60s

Prominent Collaborators: Dick Ayers, Steve Ditko, Don Heck, Wally Wood, Vince Colletta, Bill Everett, Frank Giacoia, George Roussos, Paul Reinman, Sol Brodsky, John Romita, John Verpoorten, Syd Shores, Mike Esposito, George Klein.

Most Prominent: Joe Sinnott. The favorite of many, Sinnott inked Kirby during one of the most innovative and creative periods in comics: Kirby's "cosmic" period. No one could do a better job on Kirby's intricate and complex machines and he, with Kirby, gave the "look" to the only true version of the Silver Surfer in my book.

Personal Favorite: Chic Stone. Stone's clean thick lines gave the artwork an almost three-dimensional look and he was, in my opinion, the first artist to allow the power of Kirby's pencils to show through. When Marvel became a media item in the mid-'60s, it was Kirby/Stone art that was invariably used to show off the Marvel "look" and "style."

Honorable Mentions: Ditko and Heck. Fine examples of distinctive styles working with Kirby's pencils without overpowering them; they left an unmistakable look to the art. It's almost like: What would Ditko and Heck's art look like if they drew like Jack Kirby?

Wood's Sky Masters *inks: Beautiful or overpowering?*

Bum Rap: Vince Colletta. In the beginning of his working with Kirby, the artwork actually looked very nice, especially if you ever got to see the originals. It's later on when Colletta rushed even faster to finish, and when he used assistants, that the artwork became a mess. The main problem was that Colletta's fine ink lines never translated well to the smaller printed page; so, a bum rap? It's still debated.

Unpublished Captain Victory *page with Thibodeaux inks.*

The '70s

Prominent Collaborators: Mike Royer, Vince Colletta, Joe Sinnott, Frank Giacoia, Neal Adams, D. Bruce Berry, John Verpoorten, Al Milgrom.

Most Prominent & Personal Favorite: Mike Royer. By this time Kirby had more control over how his art would appear in print, and he wanted someone who could show his distinctive style through inking without embellishment, so Royer might truly be considered a Kirby *inker.* Still, Kirby's work with Royer in the '70s is as memorable and distinctive a "look" as was his work with Simon 30 years before.

The '80s

During the '80s Kirby's work finally began to diminish in output, so I would have to say that of the few new collaborators who worked with him during this time, Mike Thibodeaux would be the most outstanding. Alfredo Alcala would be the most interesting, Greg Theakston turned in some serviceable work, and Mike Royer turned up occasionally to add some finesse to Jack's later work.

In closing, I guess this article wasn't so much an informational tool for anyone, as much as it was a big "thank you" to all of these guys who've worked so hard over the years, helping to give Jack's pencils life and beauty. If anything is to be learned from this, I think it should be that inking a story can be just as difficult as drawing one, and it's obvious to me that the Sinnotts and Ayers and Stones all put a part of themselves and their unique talents into the pencils of Jack Kirby. If you disagree, that's fine — but someday sit yourself down and make yourself a nice pencil drawing, preferably on bristol board; then get yourself a bottle of black ink and a brush (may I recommend a Windsor-Newton #3?). Now ink that drawing and see what you get. Then imagine doing 20 pages (or more) a month of that inking; it's not as easy as it looks, is it?! And don't forget to get a big bottle of white ink for corrections; you're gonna need it!

Now thank these guys!!★

Inking Contest Winners

We had a total of 74 entries in our inking contest, making for some stiff competition! After allowing a few extra days for the stragglers to get their entries in, we sent 8½" x 11" photocopies of each entry to judges Mike Royer (who judged the amateurs) and Joe Sinnott (who judged the professionals). To keep things fair, we blacked out all the signatures, and assigned each entry a number. Mike and Joe carefully examined each entry, and were free to base their decisions on any criteria they chose. We welcomed them to include their comments on the entries, which we've displayed here. Congratulations to Ernie Stiner (pro) and John Trumbull (amateur) on being chosen, and to everyone who entered; you're all winners, and you should be proud of your efforts in this very competitive contest! Special thanks to Mike and Joe for taking the heat, and agreeing to judge the contest for us!

#1 VERY ASSURED BRUSH LINE THAT SHOWS MUCH CONFIDENCE AND EXPERTISE. VERY FAITHFUL TO JACK'S ORIGINAL. WEIGHT OF BEAUTIFUL OUTLINE, ESPECIALLY ON ORION IS WHAT IMPRESSED ME MOST.

FIRST PLACE (PRO): Ernie Stiner of Uniontown, PA
(see his "Thing" piece on the cover of this issue!)

(here and next page) Joe Sinnott's comments on the Professional entries

WOW—! DECISIONS ··· DECISIONS!

FIRST, LET ME SAY I WAS VERY IMPRESSED BY THE NUMBER OF FINE ENTRIES IN THE AMATEUR INKING CONTEST.

SECOND, LET ME TAKE ISSUE WITH THE TERM "CONTEST." I'VE BEEN LOOKING AT A LOT OF INTERESTING AND IMPRESSIVE WORKS AND I FEEL IT'S UNFAIR TO LIST MY CHOICES AS "WINNERS" IN A CONTEST. EVERY ENTRANT SHOULD BE COMPLIMENTED FOR ACCEPTING THE CHALLENGE OF KIRBY'S PENCILS AND "GOING FOR IT!"

AFTER ALL, ALL ART IS SUBJECTIVE. IN THE LATE 1950s, AL "JAZZBO" COLLINS STATED: "ALL IS COOL, AND COOL IS EVERYTHING."

SO··· HERE ARE THE PICKS I FEEL WERE THE "COOLEST".

'TIL LATER
COMFILY— MIKE R.

FIRST PLACE (AMATEUR): John Trumbull of Dover, NJ
(see his "Orion" piece on the inside front cover of this issue!)

(above) Mike Royer's comments on the Amateur entries

SECOND PLACE (PRO):
Roy Richardson,
White Plains, NY

SECOND PLACE (AMATEUR):
Mike Roberts,
Bixby, OK

#2 HARD NOT TO PICK THIS #1. INKER HAS PUT JUST A FRACTION OF HIS ARTISTIC PERSONALITY INTO HIS EFFORT AND YET RETAINS THE INTENT OF KIRBY'S ART. WOULD LIKE TO HAVE SEEN THE INKER'S WORK ON THE THING.

THIRD PLACE (PRO):
Mike McLester,
London, England

THIRD PLACE (AMATEUR):
Patrick Lamb,
Dover, NJ

MOST ORIGINAL
(as chosen by editor John Morrow):
Fred Hembeck

#3 EXCELLENT BRUSH CONTROL AND FAITHFULNESS TO KIRBY'S PENCILS. HARD TO CHOOSE BETWEEN 1. 2. OR 3.

COLLECTOR COMMENTS

Send letters to: The Jack Kirby Collector
c/o TwoMorrows • 1812 Park Drive
Raleigh, NC 27605 or E-mail to: twomorrow@aol.com

(I hope you liked our "split-issue" this time out. Since it's the Art Theme Issue, I used the flip-book format to have some fun with the layouts on half of the issue, while keeping the familiar look for the other half. But before you write asking, I think we'll stick with the old format from here on; it takes so much time to redesign every article that our publishing schedule would undoubtedly suffer otherwise.

Now, a couple of corrections. A number of readers disagreed with Will Murray's assertion that the Captain America figure in Larry Lieber's drawing (shown in TJKC #18, page 8) was by Joe Simon. Also, the pencil drawing we showed on page 50 was from SILVER STAR, not MACHINE MAN. Okay, on to your letters:)

I don't look forward to the day when TJKC is back to 16-36 pages because of dwindling fan contributions, but I know I echo Kirbydom when I say, "Better that than no zine at all!" Morrow, Cooke, and regular contributors Charles Hatfield, R.J. Vitone, and Mark Evanier are always interesting, well-informed, and on top of the different aspects of the subject matter.

On the matter of filling pages until (hopefully) more xeroxed art and articles come in, don't be shy in using pages and covers already printed. Kirby did hundreds of covers that have not been reprinted in GERBER'S (or Marvel's) PHOTO-JOURNALS, the OVERSTREET PRICE GUIDE, or checklists/magazines devoted to comics. We all know what the FF / THOR / CAP / X-MEN covers look like, so it'd be good to concentrate on the '50s/'60s westerns, golden-age, romance, and even the '70s Marvel covers Jack did. How about a cover gallery in each issue in conjunction with that issue's theme? And while I enjoy the articles and the overall work thoroughly, why not print the art you have in a larger format? Analysis and commentary are fine, but it can be overdone. Let the art speak for itself.

Whatever you do to continue publication will be fine! This is the finest fanzine I've ever seen and it sets a new standard of excellence.

Jerry Boyd, Mountain View, CA

While I enjoy the histories and anecdotes, as a frustrated comic book artist I am primarily interested in the visible artwork. I would prefer that more space be allotted to the artwork; by this I MEAN BIGGER! Not so much the convention sketches and knock-off pieces, but the uninked pencils and stats. I would like to be able to see the details with particularity, the stray lines and missteps or preliminary layouts which are still visible. A 1-1, or even greater reproduction size would be great and you wouldn't need as much artwork for continuing issues. Those of us who are interested in Jack Kirby's art will spend at least as much time on these detailed copies as we would on the personal opinions of a fellow fanboy.

Clifton F. Marley, Robbins, NC

(We've received a number of letters similar to these two over the last few years, so let me explain our approach to art reproduction in TJKC. Most of the photocopies of Jack's pencils that we show in TJKC are of very poor quality, due to the out-of-date copying technology that was used in Jack's 1970s copier, and due to them fading over time. In many cases, we spend hours cleaning them up after scanning, and that still doesn't get an image that approaches Jack's original pencils. Showing them at reduced size cleans them up even more. If you take a page from TJKC and blow it up 200% on a good copier, the enlarged image you get will be very close in quality and size to the "originals" we're working from. However, in instances like this issue's SILVER STAR art, where we're working from a modern, good-quality copy of the original, I'm more inclined to reproduce the work at larger size. And while I try to get a piece of Kirby art on nearly every page, this magazine's not just about the art; it's about Jack Kirby the person, his collaborators, and his career in general, so I don't want to slight the text. But for all you Kirby fans clamoring for larger art repros, be sure to check out our next Trade Paperback, THE COLLECTED JACK KIRBY COLLECTOR, VOLUME TWO, shipping in July. It'll feature more than a few full-page repros of Jack's pencil pages.)

Stan Lee has never grasped that his SILVER SURFER book failed because the real appeal was the character Jack had created—who was visible to the reader in Jack's drawings, even if Stan's words were not quite the right words. No wonder sales declined from the beginning—Stan betrayed him right from the start.

It's also interesting that it never seemed to have occurred to Lee that since—by his lights—the Surfer's appeal was to adults, then the smart thing would be to put out a magazine-size comic in full color for adults, not a dinky newsprint comic book. Not a black-&-white magazine; a color magazine with comics stories. People like Kirby and Jim Steranko (who also "suffered" from being of interest to adults) would have been perfect for such a magazine, if it had come into being during their tenure at Marvel. But I have never heard that such a magazine was ever planned or contemplated.

When he talks about credits in his interview, Roy makes a significant observation. Since there was no big money involved, he says, credits were of little importance. In other words, credit was unimportant because comics were unimportant—and they were unimportant because there was no money in comics. The three guys at Marvel who saw that comics were important regardless of the money were Jack—he talks about it in his interview in this issue, and in practically every interview I've ever seen with him—and Jim Steranko, who was very interested in the theory as well as practice of comics, and the intellectually adventurous Steve Ditko. Nobody else got it. The others did not see that there was an order of magnitude between what they were doing, and what Jack was capable of and what Steranko was striving for and what Ditko was trying to say—money or not.

Roy talks of telling Jack that he would give Jack "credit" for plots by Roy, thinking that what Jack wanted was "credit"—that is, a credit-line, which Roy himself was relatively indifferent to. This is evidently what Stan wanted—

credit-lines—so Roy evidently thought this was what Jack wanted, too. But what Jack clearly wanted was recognition for his accomplishments. Not a credit line as such, accurate or not, but recognition. Jack knew he was doing something of worth and he wanted his name on it. Stan Lee missed this about Jack, which I believe is the real reason for the break-up. As Stan evidently saw it, Jack was a machine—gifted, unique, admirable, but a machine—to draw situations that Stan could then bring to life. Consequently, what difference could it make to Jack (or Steve Ditko) if he rewrote his work—after all, there was a Jack Kirby (or Steve Ditko) credit-line for the drawings.

(Regarding the NEW YORK HERALD-TRIBUNE piece that—according to Roy—Stan feels may have been the source of ill-feeling between himself and Jack: Had Stan wanted, he could have written a letter to the paper saying how valuable and gifted Jack was. As far as we know—or Jack knew, evidently—Stan didn't. 'Nuff said.)

With Jack, Stan was too superficial to see that those stories and situations and characters were inventions of a high order by someone more fundamentally creative than he. And, with Ditko, that a gifted creative intelligence, in important ways as gifted as his own, was at work.

With Kirby and Steranko—and Ditko—you could experience the thrill of the new. With Stan, the thrill was often there as well, in a different way. But Stan sacrificed—unknowingly, I think—too much that was far better than his own creations. In the short run, it gave Stan fame. In the long haul, it is taking it away.

A lot of thought went into those Marvel comics, but not into the larger aspects of packaging, demographic exploitation, and market penetration. There was no vision, no long-range plan; not just for comic books but for mature comics magazines and for book publications—where the real money was.

From all this, we can see that the problem with Marvel and the comic book field is that it never had a strategist—an architect—somebody to bring structure and organization to the medium. Stan was an exceptional comics writer and a good line editor. However, he did not have the skill to be an executive editor or a publisher, and should never have held this power. A lot has been written about Jack needing an editor; some of it is true. All creative people need an editor—an advisor—and so did Stan, far more than Jack.

Richard Kyle, Long Beach, CA

(Richard, as usual, has some strong, thought-provoking opinions, and we're glad to hear them. Let me take this opportunity to remind readers that Roy Thomas has signed on as Contributing Editor on our new TJKC-style publication, COMIC BOOK ARTIST! Roy will be resurrecting his legendary 1960s fanzine ALTER EGO in CBA's pages, contributing a special 16-page AE section in each issue. Considering Roy's depth of comics knowledge and jam-packed files, you can be sure it'll be a treat for long-time comics fans. The first issue of COMIC BOOK ARTIST is on sale in April; look for the ad elsewhere in this issue.)

Charles Hatfield's comments in TJKC #18 on the ETERNALS series were well taken. His view of the series as Kirby's greatest (and perhaps only great) one after the Fourth World is a theme that can't be sounded too often. In particular, it was the King's furthest development of a concept he pioneered with NEW GODS: That of the ensemble (rather than solo or team) super-hero cast. Concentrated in one title rather than wound through three, the ETERNALS' dispersed narrative made quite sophisticated use of this ensemble approach, even more daringly than NEW GODS — whose own, more modest level of cast rotation has nonetheless been painted by some as being excessive and confusing (ironic in light of the labyrinthian continuity demanded by today's fans).

P.S. In answer to a rhetorical question Hatfield poses, shortly before THE ETERNALS' debut I heard Stan Lee tell a comic-con audience that Marvel dropped the RETURN OF THE GODS title to avoid a copyright dispute with DC over their execrable contemporaneous RETURN OF THE NEW GODS series.

Adam McGovern, Parsippany, NJ

The reason for this letter is to give you further details about the public domain law referred to in TJKC #17. Most of TJKC's readers must have wondered why characters like Superman or Batman, which are older than 56 years, are not yet public domain. From January 1, 1978- on, the second 28-year period after the renewing was changed to 47 years. So the total amounts to 75 years after the creation. Here is a list of the years in which a few of Jack's characters will become public domain:

Captain America: 2016
Fantastic Four: 2036
The Incredible Hulk: 2037
New Gods: 2046

It seems that, unfortunately, Jack's creations are far from out of Marvel's and DC's clutches.

Jerome Wicky, FRANCE

(Let's see: I'll be 84 years old when NEW GODS is public domain. Everybody's invited to my house for a big party when it happens!)

I believe Issue 18 was the best Comics-Oriented Magazine I've ever read. I don't want to depress you, but I certainly don't know how you're going to top it. The cover is as brilliant a piece as Kirby ever did. Its color, its perspective, its general all-around-feel embodies what was the magic of Kirby and Marvel in the late '60s, early '70s.

The real gems of the issue, though, had to be the interviews with the Bullpen of the day. I'm sure I'll never read as diverse a collection of interviews as those, nor do I imagine I'll witness such intimate glimpses into the workaday lives of the people from that era. Everybody came across as warm, vulnerable human beings. Their stories were honest and bittersweet, filled with the joys of having been involved in something special, yet also acknowledging the unfulfilled aspects of their careers. It truly hurt to read that the great John Romita felt inferior and that Herb Trimpe couldn't appreciate his tremendous work. Their artwork seemed so inspired — how could they not have known! And to read how John Buscema shamelessly copied Kirby's compositions — incredible! For the first time I was able to see these giants as people and I honestly came away humbled by it. Jon Cooke, Jim Amash, and the others are to be commended for bringing such revelations out of our heroes.

Lyle S. Tucker, Roswell, NM

(Let me again thank all the Bullpenners who agreed to be interviewed for #18. They were all very candid with their responses to the questions asked, and it made for a really memorable issue. And thanks again to Joe Sinnott for inking the cover for us.)

I don't mind that R.C. Harvey in your January issue disagrees with my conclusion about the Lee-Kirby authorship controversy, but I must protest his statement that I overlooked the possibility that an artist can grow. Judas Priest! Of course I understand that an artist can grow. Nothing in my essay stated or suggested otherwise (see THE COMICS JOURNAL #181). The point I made was that, to believe Jack Kirby was the author of the 1960s Marvel stories and the antithetical NEW GODS stories, one must believe that a mature artist, producing self-expressive work, completely changed his mind over a relatively short period of time about something important to him, mocked his previous views, and then never said or wrote anything about his abrupt and radical change of mind. The difficulty I had believing that was one of the factors that led me to conclude in my essay that "Jack Kirby was not the author of Marvel. The work at Marvel was a collaboration, with enormous creative contributions made by Kirby, Lee, and Ditko. But... if only one man can be the author of Marvel, [Stan Lee] has a greater claim to that title than anyone else" (p. 77).

I think many Kirby supporters feel it diminishes his stature if he is not given sole credit for his work at Marvel. I disagree. I think Kirby's collaborations with Joe Simon and Stan Lee, combined with his solo work, especially on the NEW GODS stories, amounts to a fabulous body of work, and I would have to think long and hard before I would say that anyone else in comic books has equalled, let alone surpassed, the quality and significance of that body of work. It is not necessary to eclipse Stan Lee for Jack Kirby to shine brilliantly.

Earl Wells, Johnsonville, NY

(The aim of this magazine isn't to eclipse Stan's — or Joe Simon's for that matter — contributions to the books Jack work on. But Stan Lee's name is on the first page of every Marvel comic published, whereas Jack's is nowhere to be found in most cases. So if Kirby fans have a knee-jerk reaction when it comes to crediting Jack, I think it's understandable; Stan's gotten sole credit for their collaboration for years, so why shouldn't Jack? Hopefully, due to moves Marvel has recently made toward crediting Jack on the new SILVER SURFER animated series — and possibly on their comics in the near future — all of the "who-did-what" hoopla will die down soon, and we can all feel good about crediting both men for their accomplishments.)

I have to say this much-ballyhooed NEW GODS collection is a HUGE disappointment. Bad paper, printing, and your pal Jim Amash's greytones were too dark and wildly overdone, hiding Jack's art and obscuring Royer's wonderful inking. Clearly Jim didn't know that what looks good on computer prints darker! Lessons in value and simple restraint are desperately needed as well. Next time, how about putting the money for greytones into better paper and print what was expected: PURE B&W KIRBY (no tones)! I know you had no control of this DC project; just thought it's pure hypocrisy if you continue to praise this mistake. Jack would have hated it.

Bill Wray, Sierra Madre, CA

(Sorry, Bill, but you're way off-base here. I got to see some of Jim Amash's hand-colored guides — he didn't do the computer work on it, just the guides — and the folks who put the actual grays in didn't follow his guides very faithfully. In my opinion, Jim's stuff looked lots better than what was printed, as he exhibited exactly the kind of restraint you mentioned, taking great care not to overpower Jack's art. And while Jim and I both would've preferred to see the book done without graytones, I don't think it turned out bad at all. Since it sold well enough for DC to start working on other Kirby volumes for future release, somebody else out there must have felt the same way. And since this was an opportunity for young fans to get exposed to Jack's epic, and for Roz and his kids to make a few bucks, I'd kinda think Jack would've been very pleased with it.)

NEXT ISSUE: It's GIRLS, GIRLS, GIRLS in our special issue spotlighting KIRBY'S WOMEN! #20 (52-pages, $4.95) features new color covers inked by KEN STEACY and RICHARD HOWELL, and a centerfold inked by MIKE ROYER! Included is a RARE KIRBY INTERVIEW, plus a new interview with DAVE (Rocketeer) STEVENS, discussing Kirby and the fairer sex! We'll also interview Jack's daughter LISA KIRBY, and explore Jack's female characters, from MOTHER DELILAH, MEDUSA, and the INVISIBLE GIRL to GRANNY GOODNESS, BIG BARDA, GALAXY GREEN, and many more! There's also a lengthy section on Simon & Kirby's ROMANCE comics, plus an amazing array of unpublished Kirby art including unused pages and published pages BEFORE they were inked from MR. MIRACLE, IN THE DAYS OF THE MOB, GALAXY GREEN, THE ETERNALS, and more! Accept no substitutes: THE JACK KIRBY COLLECTOR is the #1 KIRBY 'zine, and the only one AUTHORIZED BY THE KIRBY ESTATE! We'll see you in mid-June! The deadline for submissions: 5/1/98.

IN MEMORIUM: ROSALIN

Steve Sherman writes:

Here is a photo taken of Roz at her 75th birthday party on September 27th. Little did I know that it would be the last one. Roz was laid to rest next to Jack on Friday, December 26th at 12 p.m. It was a small crowd, mostly family and close friends, including Stan Lee, Sergio Aragonés, Mike Royer, and Mike Thibodeux. At Roz's service, Mike Thibodeux, Steve and Robert Katz (Roz's nephews), Tracy Kirby, Mark Evanier, Mark Miller, and Neal Kirby spoke about Roz and what she meant to all of us. It truly is the end of an era, not only in terms of the history of comics, but for the extended Kirby family. Roz was a remarkable lady; not only a gracious hostess to the multitude of fans who trekked to the Kirby home over the decades, but a very funny woman whose sense of humor never faded, even in the face of Jack's passing and her own illnesses.

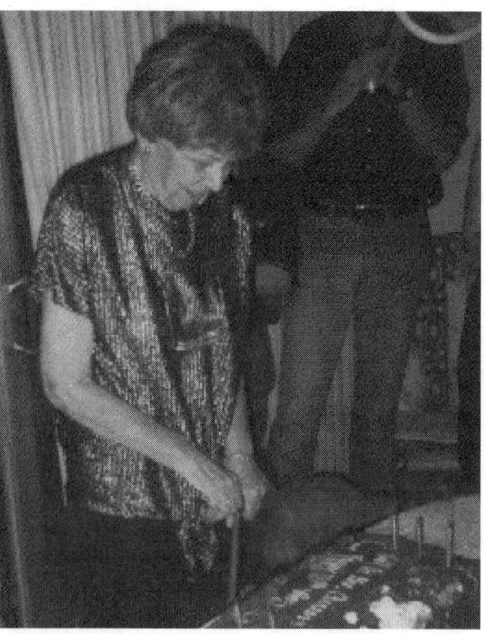

For close to 30 years, Jack and Rosalind Kirby were the "unofficial" Uncle and Aunt, Mom and Dad, to Southern California comics fans. Their home was always open, their hospitality legendary. No one left without feeling that they had experienced something special. It was with profound sadness that those of us who gathered at the Kirby home realized that this would be the last time. After countless Fourth of July parties, weddings, birthdays, and celebrations, the time has come to close the book. The artwork will be removed from the walls of the studio where Jack created a multitude of heroes, the kitchen where we gathered to laugh and tell stories; all will be packed up and moved. And we will be left with memories of two people who touched a generation of fans around the world. Hopefully, Jack and Roz are together again, somewhere, somehow, because that's the way it should be.

Mark Evanier's Eulogy For Roz Kirby:

One Tuesday in July of 1969, I drove down to Irvine, California to meet my favorite comic book artist. I thought I'd meet him and maybe get an autograph and an interview for my fanzine but it didn't work out that way. When I left, I had no autograph and no interview, but I did have two new people in my life... two people who would come to be important to me in ways I cannot fully articulate, even now, even to myself.

I was not alone in this experience. Millions of us loved the comic books that came out of the Kirby house. Most of us who were privileged to visit there instantly came to love the man who made them happen, and the woman who made them possible.

We loved Jack because of his brilliant imagination and his outstanding decency and sense of humanity. And we loved Roz because... well, first of all, because she loved Jack. She dressed him and fed him and drove him and cared for him. And often, just this side of dawn, she'd go into his studio and tell him to, for God's sake, put down the pencil and come to bed.

You rarely see two people who so totally and truly belonged together, each putting themselves second so the other could be first. Every time we went to a restaurant, Jack would look at the menu and announce what he was going to order. And then Roz would tell him what he should eat and he would change his order... because he knew (a) that she was always right and (b) that she had only his best interests at heart.

You couldn't help but appreciate the synchronicity: Jack sitting there 'til all hours, cobbling up tales of great champions, protecting the world from total annihilation... and Roz sitting there in the next room, protecting Jack. Compared to her, the super-heroes had it easy — because Jack, God love him, needed a lot of protecting.

We never saw her go off-duty, never saw her flinch. One time at a convention in the '80s, a stooge for one of the comics companies started yelling at Jack, denouncing him for a stand which struck all of us as a simple matter of independence and integrity. Before any of us could rush to Jack's defense... before Jack himself could even raise his voice, there was Roz, telling off the corporate goon better than any of us could. The guy is still probably trembling... because nothing scared her when her life partner was threatened, and Jack was the same way about her.

When I think of her today, I think of her courage and I think of her compassion. I think of how proud she was of her family: Susan, Barbara, Lisa, and Neal, and all the grandchildren and in-laws and nieces and nephews and everyone.

And then there was that extended family: All of us writers and artists and comics fans who thought of Jack and Roz as surrogate Aunt and Uncle. There's no way to estimate the number of talented folks who received valuable encouragement and inspiration from them both. Since word spread that we had lost her, they've been calling to commiserate. One author was practically kicking himself that he hadn't yet sent her his new book. It may well be a huge hit but something will always be missing for him: He didn't get to show it to Roz and get her approval.

It was never dull around them. I remember Jack telling the story of sitting there in his studio one day when Roz was coming home from the store. Her foot slipped on the brake and she plowed through the back of the garage, right into Jack's workspace. No one was hurt and Jack, in a strange way, enjoyed the shock of it all. He said to me, "I'm sitting there drawing and I hear a noise... and suddenly, here's Roz comin' right through the wall." Then he paused and added, "You know, we've been married half a century and she's still finding ways to surprise me."

In an equally strange way, I think Jack would have liked the fact that she survived him a few years. Not that anyone wished that loss on her, but she did deserve that brief time in the spotlight. The day before Jack's funeral, she told me she was worried that all the people who called and came to the house would drift away... because really, they only cared about Jack.

That never happened. They called and they came, to the point where she sometimes announced, tongue-in-cheek, she was sick of all the attention. At the San Diego Comic Convention, they stood and cheered her, because they knew that Jack Kirby was a two-person operation.

Today, we're all sad to lose her. But we're glad he's got her back.

Dr. Mark Miller's Eulogy for Rosalind Kirby:

My name is Mark Miller, and I believe that I am one of hundreds, if not thousands of non-kin Kirby family members. Like so many others in this huge extended family, I treasured my moments with Rosalind and Jack. Like so many others I considered it a thrill and an honor to drive up Sapra Street to the home of the King and his Queen. My first trip to the Kirby household occurred about 15 years ago. As many of you have experienced, Rosalind welcomed me as if I were another family

KIRBY, 1922-1997

member she had yet to meet. I had not planned to stay long, only wanting to explain just how great an impact Jack's work had on my life. Instead, in that magical household, minutes became hours and hours became dinnertime. How many meals must Rosalind have served to those of us she had welcomed into her home?

Because of my training, I was able to discuss medical issues with Rosalind and at times I helped to "translate" into simple English what the doctors had told her about herself or Jack. I recall Rosalind being characteristically flippant when I informed her that the lung disease she had was usually associated with a mold found on farms. "Farms," she said. "What do I know from farms? I live in the city."

Over the years, I — like so many of you — experienced Roz being ill or even being hospitalized, only to bounce back again. "Don't worry," she'd tell me. "What's everyone worried about?" Although some three years may have passed since the event, I vividly recall Lisa phoning to inform me that Rosalind had just had a pacemaker placed after medics had resuscitated her. As soon as I was allowed to speak with Roz, she began reassuring me and again told me "not to worry." That event — seeing Roz so fragile yet so optimistic — moved me to write Terry Stewart, then-President of Marvel Comics. With Roz's permission, I wrote down my concerns about her fragile condition and emphasized the fact that she was the link to that Jack Universe now known as Marvel Comics. I also shared with him that Rosalind lived humbly and in fact at times had to sell one of Jack's pieces of artwork simply to make ends meet. To my surprise Terry called me shortly after he had received my letter. We spoke at length and he said he would review Rosalind's situation with his team of lawyers and then get back to me. He and I spoke again on a few occasions until the day that he called me to say that I could have the privilege of informing Rosalind that Marvel Comics had deemed it appropriate and fair to begin a monthly pension in honor of Jack and Roz's contributions to the company.

Calling Roz with the news was one of the proudest moments of my life. I must say that she did not really believe me for the first several minutes of our conversation. Perhaps this was because she had endured so many years of silence on Marvel's part. But if the industry has failed to give Jack his due, there was always the extended family of Kirby fans, the countless letters, phone calls and visits through which Jack and Roz had daily testimony to just how many lives they had touched.

I was not lucky enough to have been born a son or a nephew or even a distant cousin of Rosalind's, yet she treated me with a motherly kindness that I will always treasure. I thank you Roz, for allowing me into your home and into your life. Wherever I go, I will take you with me.

To the family of Rosalind Kirby, from Shel Dorf:

Please excuse the lateness of this, but I just learned of the death of your Mother. Needless to say my heart goes out to you for the loss.

We all made history together and I'm proud of being of service to the Kirby career all those years. We built a tower and his light was always at the top of it shining for the world to see. So now Jack is together with his favorite inker once again.

On my next visit to Temple I will say a special prayer for her. I leave it to the wordsmiths of our field to write about Roz. As for me I just want to thank you for sharing your folks with us. They labored in a brutal business and there were many heartaches to be endured. I am proud that the San Diego Comic-Con I created did nothing but give them pleasure and happiness and surrounded them with love all those years.

An open letter from the Kirby Family:

The Kirby Family would like to thank all of the fans who have sent their kind words of support and sympathy. Over the years many people have shown great kindness to Roz and Jack. The Kirby Family would like to thank Mike Thibodeaux for all his help, especially to Roz after Jack's death. We would like to express our appreciation to Mark Miller, for orchestrating the campaign to get Roz a pension from Marvel. We would also like to thank Terry Stewart for giving Roz the pension, and Joe Calamari for giving Jack credit (finally) where credit is due. We are grateful to Mark Evanier for many things. Finally, we would like to thank John Morrow for keeping the genius of Jack Kirby alive for all of us.

With great love to all — thank you.

A very special Thing drawing, which adorned the walls at the Kirbys' house for years.

JACK
KIRBY-D.S.